Duquesne Studies
Philosophical Series

EDITORS
Henry J. Koren and
Andre' Schuwer

BEING AND LOGOS

THE WAY OF PLATONIC DIALOGUE

SALLIS, John. Being and Logos; the way of Platonic dialogue. Duquesne University (dist. by Humanities), 1975. 544p (Duquesne studies. Philosophical series, v.33) 74-10964. 20.00. ISBN 0-391-00353-4. C.I.P.

CHOICE JULY/AUG. '75

Philosophy

B 395
S16

That v.32 in this series, *Phenomenology and the return to beginnings* (CHOICE, Jul.-Aug. 1974) was also by Sallis (Duquesne) explains why this book, for better or worse, will have a limited readership, largely constituted by philosophers who identify with the phenomenological movement, which is presently outside the mainstream among English speakers. The present volume is devoted to the interpretation of six Platonic dialogues: *Apology, Phaedrus, Meno, Republic, Cratylus,* and *Sophist.* This interpretation or "careful reading" is focused on three questions: "What is philosophy?," "What is *logos?*," and "What is being?" About this project, Sallis says that "what is called for is that we undertake to free the dialogues to themselves, to let them recommence, to become participants in them, even if from a distance." *Being and Logos* will be of interest to graduate and advanced undergraduates who appreciate such writers on ancient philosophy as Martin Heidegger and Leo Strauss. No bibliography. Index of proper names and topics.

Philosophical Series
Volume Thirty-Three

BEING AND LOGOS

THE WAY OF
PLATONIC DIALOGUE

John Sallis

Distributed by Humanities Press, Atlantic Highlands
for
DUQUESNE UNIVERSITY PRESS, PITTSBURGH

First printing

Printed in the United States of America

Library of Congress Cataloging in Publication Data

Sallis, John, 1938-
  Being and Logos

  (Duquesne studies. Philosophical series, v. 33)
  Includes bibliographical references.
  1. Plato Dialogues. 2. Socrates. I. Title.
II. Series.
B395.S23   184   74-10964
ISBN 0-391-00353-4

for Jerry

CONTENTS

ix

xiv

οὐκ ἐμοῦ ἀλλὰ τοῦ λόγου ἀκούσαντας ὁμολογεῖν σοφόν ἐστιν
ἕν πάντα εἶναι

Heraclitus
Fragment 50

PREFACE

This attempt to engage in an originary reading of certain Platonic dialogues has its provocation. The form which such provocation takes may be—in some respects, must be—alien to Greek thought; as, correspondingly, a provocative saying delivered through the Pythian priestess is alien to the circle of our thought, i.e., is incapable, as provocative, of breaking immediately into that circle. The form of the provocation testifies to our distance from the beginnings that precede the philosophical tradition.

But, if it were otherwise, if there were no provocation operative, an *originary* reading would be unthinkable.

What is called for is that, granting the provocation as such, we hold out against it in order to move away from it onto the way of Platonic dialogue. What is called for is that we undertake to free the dialogues to themselves, to let them recommence, to become participants in them, even if from a distance. The question is whether we are also destined to remain at a distance from the matters fundamentally at issue in the dialogues. Can we from our distance rejoin the movement of those matters, the movement which constitutes the way of Platonic dialogue?

Considerable portions of this study were presented in more preliminary form in a series of graduate courses on the Platonic dialogues given at Duquesne University during the period 1970-73. For help at various stages in the preparation of the work I am grateful to Edward Ballard, André Schuwer, James Daniel, John Vielkind, Frank Capuzzi, Ann Vielkind, Steven Wyatt, and my wife Jerry.

INTRODUCTION

Section 1. On Reading Plato

This work is devoted to the interpretation of certain Platonic dialogues. At the most immediate level, it is simply an attempt to *read* thoughtfully certain of the dialogues; that is, it is simply an exercise in careful reading. Such an exercise is to be contrasted with treatises of the kind that would purport to present straightforwardly something called "the philosophy of Plato." And such an exercise is, in the first instance, the offspring of the suspicion that is cast on every such treatise as soon as one reflects, even momentarily, on the well-known fact that Plato himself wrote no treatises expounding "his philosophy": to propose to write a treatise on the philosophy of one who wrote no treatises is, to say the least, questionable—especially since, on the basis of what he did write, it appears that he avoided such kind of writing for quite important reasons. Furthermore, it is equally questionable to propose to present, in whatever form, something called "the philosophy of Plato." Why? Because it is highly questionable whether there is any such thing as the philosophy of Plato—that is, whether philosophy as presented in the Platonic writings is such as can ever be appropriately spoken of in such a phrase—that is, whether philosophy can ever be the philosophy *of* someone or whether, on the contrary, such a phrase does not already betray a falling away from the demand placed on philosophical thought, a falling away in the direction of opinions, which indeed are the possessions of particular men and particular cities.

To propose a treatise on "the philosophy of Plato" is questionable in the sense that the questions which such a proposal provokes are such as to generate suspicion regarding the proposal. And so, we propose to practice simply reading the dialogues thoughtfully and carefully. But to read carefully includes also taking care to ask about the reading itself and not just plunging precipitously into what is to be read, losing ourselves, as it were, in it as though it were obvious what is required on the part of a reading in order for it to be adequate to the dialogues. The reflective question must not be suppressed, least of all at the beginning. Thus, even to begin reading carefully includes being prepared to learn, in the wake of such questioning, that simply reading the dialogues is no simple affair at all.

To ask about the reading itself, to inquire as to what is demanded of it, requires, in the first instance, that we address ourselves to the peculiar difficulties that are attendant upon such reading merely by virtue of its being a reading of Platonic writings. One such difficulty results from the peculiar form taken by nearly all the Platonic writings. These writings are dialogues, and, most significantly, the author does not appear as a speaker in any of the dialogues. There are only two references to Plato in the dialogues: one is little more than a simple reference to his presence along with other companions of Socrates at the master's trial (*Apol.* 34 a); the other is a simple reference to his absence (on account of illness) from the scene of Socrates' death (*Phaedo* 59 b). Thus, Plato never speaks in his own name—except perhaps in the letters. But, aside from their dubiousness on purely philological grounds, there is the astounding fact that in the most important letter, where we would expect to hear Plato speaking in his own name about the most important matters, what we actually hear is that philosophy cannot be put into a written work and that Plato himself has certainly composed no work containing his really serious thoughts (*Letter* VII. 341 c). We can hardly help reflecting that this letter is itself something written; the result is that the self-reference of what is said in the letter denies it the status of a simple straightforward document.

But, regardless of how one deals with the letters, the fact remains that in the dialogues *Plato never says anything.* This means that when we preface a statement from a dialogue with the words "Plato says," we usually are proceeding on the basis of certain unquestioned assumptions regarding the character of the dialogues; and nearly always we are saying more than we are justified in saying. It is we, not Plato, who say "Plato says," and, accordingly, it is incumbent upon us to give testimony for what we say. Such testimony is not to be given simply by noting and labeling as Plato's own a certain set of opinions put forth by one whom we take simply as spokesman for Plato; nor, on the other hand, is it to be given by seeking some non-apparent set of opinions behind those that are presented in the dialogues through the mouth of Socrates and the other major speakers. It is not a matter of seeking Plato's opinions at all, for philosophy is what is fundamentally at issue in the dialogues, and philosophy is never a matter of someone's opinions; it is rather that decisive transcending of opinion through which man is subordinated to a higher measure in such a way that, thereby, it is established that man is not the measure of what is. Thus, a reading of the dialogues can be thoughtful, philosophical, only if it lays aside the common opinion about the relation between philosophy and opinion. To read a dialogue thoughtfully and carefully does not mean to ferret out the opinions of which the dialogue would be the expression but rather to make explicit what the dialogue makes manifest regarding the matters which it puts at issue. We practice reading a dialogue not by recording and labeling—much less by "independently testing"—the opinions of which common opinion takes a dialogue to consist but rather by so comporting ourselves to the dialogue as to let that manifestation of which the dialogue consists come to fruition. Simply to read the dialogues is no simple matter at all; on the contrary, it is a task that makes great demands upon us.

Another difficulty, obvious to everyone, lies in the remoteness of the Platonic writings from contemporary thought and language. This remoteness, especially of the language, is a problem with which any attempt to read the dialogues carefully must continually contend; and we can contend with this problem only by making ample use of the relevant philological scholarship. In doing so we have, indeed, to be continually on guard against taking over inadvertently the extra-philological presuppositions that all too often accompany items of philological scholarship. Nevertheless, it is necessary to insist most stringently that the project of a philosophical interpretation not become an excuse for philological irresponsibility.

The Platonic dialogues are also remote in another, more profound sense: they are separated from us by a tradition that has interpreted them and that has worked-over in fundamental ways the matter for thought that was established in the dialogues. If we are to avoid the hopeless confusion involved in interpreting the foundation of the tradition in terms of the tradition that is founded, it is necessary that we seek to get behind this tradition. We must attempt to set out of action that sedimented understanding of the dialogues that one has mostly in mind in using that dubious phrase "the philosophy of Plato"; or, in more appropriately Platonic terms, we must cease being so captivated by the usual (i.e., traditional) opinions about the matters at issue in the dialogues—we must cease being so captivated that we forget to ask those questions capable of exposing the partiality of these opinions and of initiating a movement of questioning beyond the level of such opinions. What is required is that we undertake the *task* of gaining access to the Platonic writings in their originary character.[1] This is a task for which we today perhaps have an exceptional endowment inasmuch as we are, in a unique way, wrested

---

[1] The need to take seriously the task of getting behind the hardened tradition of Platonic interpretation prescribes several of the formal features of the procedure adopted in this study. Thus, we shall proceed throughout by way of "commentary" on specific dialogues and shall abstain almost entirely from more detached, "free-floating" considerations, since it is precisely when we forego remaining in direct contact with the Platonic texts that we are most easily seduced into inadvertently covering over the matter of Platonic questioning with the apparent obviousness of what has been decided by the tradition of interpretation. Before we could undertake such more detached considerations with appropriate assurance of their originary character, it would be necessary for us already to have read the dialogues thoughtfully and carefully—to have read them with a degree of patience and concentration for which we still lack even the measure. By contrast, the present work seeks only to begin reading the dialogues thoughtfully and carefully. Not only does it deliberately stop far short of the level of a detached consideration but furthermore it can give no more than a first intimation of the difficulties with which such a consideration would need to contend.

In our reading we shall also attempt to attend to the dialogues in the way that befits their character as wholes. This attempt has nothing to do with claiming to offer "exhaustive accounts"—such a claim would betray nothing less than the grossest misunderstanding and degrading of the dialogues—but rather is an attempt to practice that reticence by which whatever is taken up in a dialogue is allowed to reflect and be reflected by the character of the dialogue as a whole. The practice of such reticence requires that in dealing with passages from different dialogues we attend to their embedment in different conversations; and, though it cannot be laid out explicitly in every case, the extent of correspondence of context should prescribe the limits within which passages from different conversations may be brought together in interpretation.

out of the tradition and thrown against it.[2] But however this may be, to gain access to the dialogues in their originary character can only mean to gain access in our questioning to the originary manifestation of the matter for thought that takes place in the dialogues. Such access is not to be gained prior to a thoughtful and careful reading of the dialogues but only in and through the movement of questioning that belongs to such reading. Already we can anticipate that the task of reading the dialogues in a way that is genuinely appropriate to them is a *radical and philosophical undertaking.*

Thus, to read the dialogues thoughtfully and carefully is identical with gaining access to the dialogues in their originary character; and the latter, in turn, is equivalent to our engaging ourselves with the dialogues in such a way as to let that manifestation of which the dialogues consist come to fulfillment. This engagement involves two requirements: it is required, first, that we pose questions to the dialogue and, second, that we comport ourselves to the dialogue in such a way as to *free* it to respond to the questions posed. Thus, two kinds of preliminary considerations are in order. First, we need to set out briefly the principal questions to be posed in our interpretation and to indicate in a preliminary way

---

Finally, in view of the task *vis-à-vis* the tradition, we shall—especially in connection with certain exceptionally delicate passages—avoid translating some of the very important Greek words, most notably in those cases where it appears that the usual translations would tend to transpose the considerations into an all-too-familiar traditional mold. For the sake of convenience, these words will be transliterated into Latin script. In dealing with questions of translation our primary concern will be negative, namely, to avoid letting what is said in the Platonic text fall so easily into traditional terms as to halt or utterly divert the movement of the questioning. It is perhaps not too much of an exaggeration to say that the "real translations" are to be found in the interpretations and that the translations given of the actual Greek texts are intended primarily to "hold open" the "space" for the interpretation, that is, to prevent closing off of the questioning. In some cases we shall adopt (with only minor changes) the renderings given in certain English translations of the Platonic dialogues, though in many cases our methodological procedures will preclude simply taking over the existing translations. In addition to the translations given in the Loeb Classical Library edition of Plato's works, some use has been made of Guthrie's translation of the *Meno* (in *The Collected Dialogues of Plato,* ed. Edith Hamilton and Huntington Cairns [New York: Random House], of Hackforth's translation of the *Phaedrus* (Indianapolis: Bobbs-Merrill, 1952), and especially of Bloom's translation of the *Republic* (New York: Basic Books Inc., 1968).

[2] Cf. Gerhard Krüger, *Einsicht und Leidenschaft* (Frankfurt a. M.: Vittorio Klostermann, 1963), pp. x-xviii.

the appropriateness of these questions. Then, since it is possible to free the dialogues only by comporting ourselves to them in a way that accords with their character as dialogues, we need to provide, on the basis of clues taken from the dialogues, a preliminary determination of the character of Platonic dialogue as such. This determination will, in turn, serve to make evident the way in which the activity of interpretation belongs integrally to the dialogues themselves.

All of these considerations are preliminary—the formulations of the questions, the indications of their appropriateness, and the determination of the character of Platonic dialogue. Their confirmation and their deepening can come only through the interpretation itself.

Section 2. The Questions: Philosophy, *Logos,* Being

We need to lay out in preliminary fashion the principal questions to be taken up in our interpretation, then, to indicate the relations between these questions, and, finally, to show how the structure of our work as a whole is generated by these questions and the relations between them.

Three principal questions are to be taken up. The first of these questions is: What is philosophy? It is hardly necessary to justify the appropriateness of posing this question to the dialogues. It is a question which is constantly and evidently at issue in the dialogues, especially in the sense that the dialogues constitute a concrete presentation of philosophical activity. The dialogues present philosophy as deed—that is, they respond immediately to the question, not so much in its initial form ("What is philosophy?"), but primarily in that form in which it is transposed into a question concerning the deeds, the practices, that define a certain exceptional kind of man. The dialogues respond more immediately to the question, "Who is the philosopher?"; and on those few occasions (perhaps most notably in the *Phaedrus* and in the *Republic*) when a dialogue responds to this question not only in deed but also by way of explicit discussion, it becomes evident that within the context of the dialogues the two questions, "What is philosophy?" and "Who is the philosopher?" are one and the same question. In the dialogues philosophical activity is concretely presented, it is presented in an individual mode. In other words, what in the most immediate sense is presented is not philosophical activity as such, disembodied from those who engage in it, but rather the concrete practice of particular men. In most of the dialogues philosophical activity is presented in the person of Socrates; and in most, if not all, of the dialogues in which this is not obviously the case the activity and speakers are, nonetheless, to be understood in relation to Socrates, as, for example, in the long final section of the *Parmenides* where the gymnastics, in which Socrates does not speak, are, nevertheless, practiced for the sake of his education as a philosopher (*Parm.* 135 c − 136 c). Either directly or indirectly the presentation of philosophical activity accomplished by the dialogues is mostly, if not entirely, a presentation of Socrates' practice. This is to say that in its most immediate form our first question is: Who is Socrates? (cf. *Letter* II. 314 c).

The second question is: What is *logos*? This question is less immediately appropriate. In posing it we have in mind the double meaning of the verbal form *"legein,"* which means both to say, to speak, *and* to lay in the sense of bringing things to lie together, collecting them, gathering them together; and we have in mind the question posed by this double meaning, namely, the question as to how it is that saying (and, in general, everything that we include under the title "language") could have presented itself to the Greeks as a laying, a gathering together. We have in mind a primordial."experience" of language as "gathering lay," an "experience" in which the early Greek thinkers were caught up and from out of which their speaking proceeded.[3] And we also have in mind the very serious question as to whether this "experience," however much achieved in early Greek thought, still resounds at all in the Platonic writings or whether, on the contrary, in these writings the decisive steps have already been taken towards the reduction of

---

[3] Cf. Martin Heidegger, "Logos (Heraklit, Fragment 50)," *Vorträge und Aufsätze* (Pfullingen: Verlag Günther Neske, 1954), pp. 207-229.

logos to language in a sense which lacks any essential connection with letting things lie together. Thus, the more specific question which we pose for our reading is: To what extent and in what forms (if any) does the original sense of *logos* remain in force in the Platonic writings? The determination of this extent has important consequences for determining the degree of solidarity between the Platonic dialogues and the writings of the so-called "pre-Socratic" philosophers: to the extent that the "pre-Socratic" "experience" of *logos* shows itself in the Platonic writings—thus proving to be not "pre-Socratic" at all—to that degree the relevant solidarity is strengthened. And to the degree that this solidarity is strengthened, we are able to call into question the pre-dominant interpretation of Greek thought as having undergone its most drastic turn through the impact of Socrates and Plato. Furthermore, the question of *logos* is integrally attached to a host of other fundamental issues in the dialogues; in particular, the development of this question opens up the possibility for radically re-thinking that entire complex of issues that is usually designated, very inappropriately, as "the theory of ideas." Finally, it should be remarked that in posing the question "What is *logos*?" we have also in mind the reference which this question (which is to be posed to the dialogues) has to the character of the dialogues themselves as peculiar presentations of *logoi*. We note that this back-reference extends even to the question itself, and we anticipate that by attending sufficiently to the issue indicated by the question we might eventually be forced even to drop our initial formulation of the question.

The third question to be posed in our interpretation is the least immediately appropriate. The question is: What is being? It is, indeed, the most questionable of the three questions, especially in this straightforward formulation, and it can easily be made to collapse if we address ourselves to it immediately rather than letting it be addressed by our interpretation of the dialogues. In the question "What is being?" we ask about being by asking what it *is*, i.e., by using a form of the word "being," so that the answer to the question is presupposed as the very condition for understanding the question in the first place. In the question we ask also about a "what." Presumably, this means in Plato's Greek to ask about an *eidos* (or *idea*). So, in the question we ask for the *eidos* of being. But what are we to make of such a question in view of the fact that the very determination of the sense of *eidos* belongs integrally to the Platonic way of determining the sense of being? Prior to the work of interpretation it is perhaps best that we not try to make anything of the question: we just let the question stand.

With our three questions now in view we need next to trace out, in an appropriately preliminary way, the connections between these questions. If we begin with the first question in its most immediate form—as the question "Who is Socrates?"—the relevant connections almost immediately establish themselves. For we note that the presentation of Socrates in the dialogues—their "answering" of the question "Who is Socrates?" and, thereby, of the question "What is philosophy?"—is primarily a presentation of Socrates' speeches, of his *logoi,* and only secondarily of other things. Most of what we learn about Socrates we learn from what he says or from what others say about him. It is primarily through the presentation of Socratic *logoi* and of the other *logoi* connected with and provoked by Socratic *logoi* that philosophy itself is presented in the dialogues.

By their way of taking up these questions the dialogues thus point to a peculiar intimacy between philosophy and *logos.* In a sense the relation between philosophy and *logos,* as presented in the dialogues, can even be said to be one of identity. Socrates, the philosopher, is one who occupies himself almost entirely in speaking with others; he says that this occupation keeps him so busy that he lacks the time to attend to the affairs of the city or even to his own affairs (*Apol.* 23 b).[4] Philosophizing takes place, as it were, as *logos.* But the identity requires the full sense of *logos.* Man is the living being endowed with speech (ζῷον λόγον ἔχον), and every man comes to speak unless prevented from doing so by some exceptional infirmity; but not every man comes to practice

---

[4] While in this respect Socrates' engagement with *logos* places him outside the affairs of the city, in another respect it is a mark of his solidarity with his city if considered in view of the Athenian's statement in the *Laws* (641 e): "our city, Athens, is, in the general opinion of the Greeks, both fond of speech (φιλόλογος) and full of speech (πολύλογος)."

philosophy. The prisoners gazing at the shadows on the wall of the cave speak incessantly, but they do not ascend out of the cave unless something exceptional impels them, even forces them, to do so. Philosophy is not identical with just any speaking but only with a speaking in which the highest possibilities, the genuine ends, of speaking are brought into play. To bring these into play involves establishing speech in its proper connection to the speaker, to the listener, and, most of all, to the things spoken of. Along with speech in the restricted sense, these accordant connections and whatever is necessary for them belong also to philosophy; we begin to see how complex that identity that joins philosophy and *logos* really is.

It is precisely through the question of the accordant connection between *logos* and the things spoken of that the connection between our second and third questions becomes evident. In its simplest formulation, the question is whether the relevant accord is an accord between two items one of which is strictly subordinate to the other in the straightforward sense of being once and for all placed under the demand to conform to the other. More precisely, does the relevant accord consist only in a simple conforming of *logos* to something which has already become manifest and which in its way of becoming manifest sustains no prior connection with *logos*? Or, does *logos* belong somehow to the very process in which beings become manifest, in which they come to stand in their truth (ἀλήθεια)? Does *logos* belong to that process of gathering together in which beings are brought forth into manifestness? To the extent that this question—whether *logos* belongs to the gathering of beings—can be answered affirmatively, the general question of *logos* coalesces with our third question, the question of being.

Our posing of these three questions—regarding Socrates (philosophy), *logos,* and being—as the principal questions to which we shall attempt to let some of the dialogues respond determines to a large degree which of the dialogues should receive primary attention in our interpretation. Also, our preliminary sketch of these questions and of their interrelation allows us, by way of anticipation, to delineate the general structure of the interpretation as a whole. The full significance and vindication of this structure are to be found, of course, only in the interpretation itself.

The interpretation will be divided into two principal parts. This division corresponds to the need for an interpretive mediation between the first and the second question and between the second and the third question. Thus, Part I will have to do with mediating between the question "Who is Socrates?" (with which, as the most immediate of the questions, it will begin) and the question "What is *logos*?" onto which the first question will be allowed to open. This part will, therefore, be entitled "Socratic *Logos*." In it we shall attempt to work out—always in closest attendance to the dialogue being read—the complex of issues in which the first and the second question meet and through which their development can be secured. More specifically, we shall begin with a reading of the *Apology* (Chapter I), for in this dialogue Socrates' practice as a whole is presented in that form which is most immediately accessible (in that form which is most nearly accessible to the men of Athens at large). A fundamental ambivalence will quickly become evident in Socrates' practice, an ambivalence with regard to the city, an ambivalence by which Socrates both belongs to the city in a radical sense and yet transcends the city in a sense no less radical. The one side of Socrates' ambivalent practice, that side by which he belongs to the city, will be considered through a reading of the *Meno* (Chapter II), in which Socrates appears concretely engaged in that exposing of ignorance that constitutes his service to the city. The other side of his practice will be considered through a reading of the *Phaedrus* (Chapter III), in which we shall find Socrates making a sojourn outside the city in order to discuss those matters which most decisively transcend the city and which require of the philosopher that he transcend the city. Throughout Part I we shall be directed towards the question of *logos,* which in the interpretation of the *Phaedrus* will finally become the dominant question.

Part II will be, in a sense, coordinate with Part I: in it we shall undertake to mediate between the second and the third of our principal questions. That is, we shall attempt—attending constantly to the dialogues being read—to let the question of *logos* open up onto the question of being. We shall begin with a reading of the *Cratylus* (Chapter IV), in which the question of *logos* is developed in a form in which it is, in a sense, most remote from the question of being, i.e., as the question of names. Yet this remoteness is precisely what is illuminating, for it allows the *Cratylus,* in its peculiar comic way, to make manifest the connection between *logos* and being in all its questionableness. A reading of the *Republic* (Chapter V) will then provide a sustained development of the question of being and a preliminary development of the relation between *logos* and being. Here, in particular, we shall need to set about trying to re-think from the ground up the problem of the *eide* and its involvement in the problems of being and of *logos.* Finally, we shall turn to the *Sophist* (Chapter VI) and seek to attend most carefully to this most profound and most demanding of all the Platonic writings on being and *logos.*

In another sense, Part II will not be merely coordinate with Part I. This is indicated by the fact that its title "Being and *Logos*" is also the principal title of our work as a whole. What is important in this regard is that Part II, while mediating between the questions of *logos* and of being, also will take up into this mediation the mediation that will already have been accomplished under the title "Socratic Logos" in Part I. Specifically, through our reading of the *Republic* the ambivalence of the philosopher's practice will again be brought into prominence, so that the *Republic* will prove, in a certain sense, to incorporate a "repetition" of the *Apology;* but this "repetition" will be for the sake of gathering up the question of the philosopher into the questions of being and of *logos.* Finally, it will prove to be of utmost significance that the most fundamental Platonic reflection on the problem of being and *logos* takes place (as a "digression") in the course of an attempt to determine the identity of the one who is most difficult to distinguish from the philosopher, namely, the sophist; in the *Sophist* all three questions will prove to be gathered up into their most fundamental unity.

Section 3. The Way of Platonic Dialogue: Preliminary Reflections

In order for the posing of our questions to the dialogues to issue in a fruitful development of these questions, it is necessary that we comport ourselves to the dialogues in such a way as to *free* them to respond to the questions. For such comportment what is required is an accord with the character of the dialogues as such. Therefore, in our reading of the dialogues we need to proceed on the basis of an understanding of the nature of Platonic dialogue, an understanding to be concretely reflected then in our activity of interpretation. More precisely, since really to interpret a dialogue means to gain access to the manifestation of the matter at issue that takes place in the dialogue, what we require is an understanding of the manifold *way* in which a Platonic dialogue, by virtue of its character *as* a dialogue, lets whatever is at issue in it become manifest. We need in advance an understanding of *the way of Platonic dialogue.* However, we have no such understanding in advance but can come to have it only by a thoughtful and careful reading of the dialogues, not only because such reading is what first really exposes us to the exemplification of this way but also because this way as such embodies what the dialogues themselves make manifest with regard to the connection between *logos* and the process of becoming manifest. The circularity is evident: we need already to have read the dialogues in order to know how really to read them. This circularity is no objection to be eliminated at the outset as the condition for even beginning but rather is simply the circularity necessarily intrinsic to any interpretation in which one avoids taking for granted, in advance and independently of what is to be interpreted, that one knows what is demanded of the interpretation. What the circularity prescribes, if properly regarded, is that we must begin with a preliminary understanding of the way of Platonic dialogue—that is, that we must begin by laying out in preliminary fashion what we need in order to begin to take up the way. Although even such "pre-understanding" must be based on clues taken from the dialogues, it can receive its vindication and its proper depth only in the course of the interpretation itself.

Our initial task is, therefore, to formulate such a preliminary determination of the way of Platonic dialogue. For purposes of this determination we shall take our principal clues from the *Phaedrus,* for of all the dialogues the *Phaedrus* is the one which is most openly addressed to the consideration of the nature of written works as such. The determination involves three principal features of the dialogues.

The first feature is the peculiar *dramatic character* of the dialogues. This dramatic character can be thematized in terms of what we shall call the dimensionality of the dialogues. A dialogue is a whole in which there are certain dimensions appropriate to one another and to the dialogue as a whole. This dimensionality is perhaps most readily apparent in the distinction between what is said in a dialogue as a whole and the context in which it is said. However, we need a more precise formulation. Some clues for our formulation can be taken from what Socrates himself says regarding *logoi* in the *Phaedrus*. The relevant statement occurs in the course of his criticism of the written *logos* of Lysias, which Phaedrus has read to him earlier:

> Well, there is one point at least which I think you will admit, namely that any *logos* ought to be constructed like a living being, with its own body, as it were; it must not lack either head or feet; it must have a middle and extremities so composed as to suit each other and the whole work (264 c).

If we take Socrates' statement as alluding to the dimensions proper to a dialogue, then what are these dimensions?

In the first place, a dialogue has a dimension of *logos*. In the loosest sense this is the dimension of the speeches presented in the dialogues. The more specific sense we tend to construe in terms of the post-Platonic understanding of *logos* as something like "rational" or "theoretic" discourse; and then we are tempted to regard this dimension as the truly "rational," "demonstrative" part of the dialogues; if we go still further and come to regard this dimension alone as the really philosophical part of the dialogues, then it can even appear feasible to set about abstracting this dimension from the total context of the dialogues so as, eventually, to be able to formulate, independently of what are presumed to be mere "artistic trappings," something called "the philosophy of Plato." But the curious redundancy "rational discourse" catches only the shadow of the original duality that sounded in the word *"logos,"* and it is of utmost importance, especially in a study in which the Platonic determination of *logos* is a principal issue, that we resist the tendency to interpret such post-Platonic determinations back into the work of Plato. When we regard it as self-evidently correct to allow *logos* to be taken as *ratio,* hence, as reason, we reaffirm, without even really considering the matter, one of the most overwhelmingly decisive transitions in that movement away from the Greeks that constituted the course of Western thought. To assume, in advance, a specific, well-defined determination of *logos* in this direction—to take for granted in an interpretation of Platonic writings subsequent notions of "rationality" and "demonstrative argument"—is to be misled by the tradition, made possible by Plato's work, into ignoring the *original struggle* with the problem of determining *logos* which takes place in the Platonic writings and which is of the greatest decisiveness for the entire tradition. To interpret, in this manner, the beginning of the tradition in terms of the tradition to which this beginning gave rise is to risk covering over decisively the depth of the questioning in which the Platonic writings are engaged; it is to risk obscuring the genuine richness of the Platonic problematic. In the dialogues themselves what we find initially is not one formally well-defined type of *logos* to be designated as "rational" or "theoretic" but rather a variety of types with only more or less vague affinities. For example, we find that type of *logos* which consists primarily in criticism, in the purging of opinions, as in Book I of the *Republic.* We find another type that is little more than sheer eristic tempered with irony, as in several of Socrates' speeches in the *Euthydemus.* Sometimes we find Socrates speaking in the way appropriate to mathematics, either in more or less straightforward fashion (*Meno*) or in such fashion as to transcend the domain of mathematics (*Rep.* VI — VII). We find *logoi* permeated by imagery, as in the sun analogy, and we find *logos* which is about *logos,* which may, as in the *Cratylus,* take the form of etymology. The unity running through these diverse types, that is, the determination of *logos* in that specific form which we vaguely indicate (but also decisively conceal) when we speak of "rational discourse," is not something that is clear in advance but rather is initially a *problem.* At the outset the unity of this dimension is evident as a unity perhaps primarily by contrast with the other dimensions of Platonic dialogue.

The second dimension of Platonic dialogue is that of *mythos.* It is presumably through its mythical dimension that a dialogue has something corresponding to the feet of a living being, that it has within itself a link to the earth, a bond to something intrinsically opaque, a bond to an element of darkness in contrast to that which is capable of being taken up into the light of *logos.* However, the contrast must not, in advance, be too rigidly drawn: a *mythos* is itself something spoken, and the contrast is, to that degree, a contrast within *logos* itself, or, perhaps more fundamentally, a contrast which is to be understood as determined from out of a prior domain in which *logos* and *mythos* are the same.[5] Whatever the final character of the contrast may be, what is of utmost importance initially is that *mythos* not be taken, in advance, as merely an inferior kind of *logos,* as a meagre substitute for something else intrinsically more desireable, as a mere compromise between knowledge and the *logos* appropriate to it, on the one hand, and sheer ignorance and its inevitable silence, on the other hand. The contrast between *logos* and *mythos* is not a contrast between a perfected and an imperfect discourse.[6]

A dialogue has both a middle as well as extremities or members. It has, on the one hand, its central speeches and, on the other hand, the dramatic details, variously alluded to, regarding the setting of these speeches and the characters who deliver them; these details, no less than the speeches, are fitting with respect to one another and with respect to the whole. As obvious examples, we might mention that in the *Gorgias* Socrates discusses rhetoric with the famous teacher of rhetoric and some of his pupils; that in the *Laches* Socrates discusses courage with two distinguished generals, Laches and Nicias; and that in the *Symposium* speeches are given in honor of love at a banquet animated by festivity and erotic play. As somewhat more provocative examples, we might mention that in the *Cratylus* Socrates discusses a thesis about speech held by Cratylus who throughout the greater part of the dialogue maintains utter silence; and that in the *Theaetetus*

---

[5] See Martin Heidegger, *Was Heisst Denken?* (Tübingen: Max Niemeyer Verlag, 1954), pp. 6-7.

[6] See especially the way in which the question of the place of myth in the dialogues has been thematized and developed (in special reference to the problem of self-knowledge) by Edward G. Ballard, *Socratic Ignorance: An Essay on Platonic Self-Knowledge* (The Hague: Martinus Nijhoff, 1965), pp. 159-168.

Socrates discusses perception ("sense-experience") with the type of man who is almost least reliant upon perception, the mathematician. And then there is the example of examples: in the *Phaedo* the question of immortality is discussed while Socrates awaits his impending death. Yet, not just such broad features but every detail of this kind has its proper importance. To put it in still stronger terms, nothing is accidental in a Platonic dialogue. In the interpretation of a dialogue not only is it inappropriate merely to extract from the speeches those which measure up to some external, or at least later, standard of what constitutes "philosophic discourse"; it is equally inappropriate to abstract the speeches themselves from the dramatic features to which they are joined in the dialogues.[7]

A dialogue is like a living being, and presumably as in the case of a living being, it not only speaks but also does something,

---

[7] This directive may be regarded as, among other things, an insistence that one take with utmost seriousness the ancient reports about the stories that were current about how Plato took great care to "comb and curl" his dialogues (cf. *The Republic of Plato,* ed. James Adam [Cambridge: Cambridge University Press, 1965], Vol. I, p. 1). In modern times the recognition of the significance of the dramatic character of the dialogues goes back to Schleiermacher, who in his Introduction to his translation of the dialogues wrote regarding Plato's work that "in that, if in anything, form and subject are inseparable, and no proposition is to be rightly understood except in its own place and with the combinations and limitations which Plato has assigned to it" (Reprinted in *Great Thinkers on Plato,* ed. Barry Gross [New York: Capricorn Books, 1969], p. 71). A number of recent commentators have especially pursued the direction indicated by Schleiermacher. Leo Strauss writes that "One cannot separate the understanding of Plato's teaching from the understanding of the form in which it is presented." Again, he writes: "In a word, one cannot take seriously enough the law of logographic necessity. Nothing is accidental in a Platonic dialogue; everything is necessary at the place where it occurs. Everything which would be accidental outside of the dialogue becomes meaningful within the dialogue. In all actual conversations chance plays a considerable role: all Platonic dialogues are radically fictitious" (*The City and Man* [Chicago: Rand McNally and Co., 1964], pp. 52, 60). Allan Bloom, following Strauss, writes in the "Preface" to his translation of the *Republic* that "the dialogues are so constructed that each part is integrally connected with every other part; there are no meaningless accidents." Bloom adds: "Every word has its place and its meaning, and when one cannot with assurance explain any detail, he can know that his understanding is incomplete. When something seems boring or has to be explained away as a convention, it means that the interpreter has given up and has taken his place among the ranks of those Plato intended to exclude from the center of his thought" (*The Republic of Plato,* tr. Allan Bloom [New York: Basic Books, 1968], p. xviii). See also Paul Friedländer, *Plato,* tr. Hans Meyerhoff (Princeton: Princeton University Press, 1958-1969), esp. Vol. III, p. 191; also Jacob Klein (who cites much of the relevant literature), *A Commentary on Plato's Meno* (Chapel Hill: The University of North Carolina Press, 1965), esp. pp. 3-10.

accomplishes something in deed; presumably a dialogue has among its members something corresponding to the hands with which man, that living being endowed with speech, accomplishes so many of his deeds. We take the third principal dimension of dialogue to be that of *ergon,* of doing, of deed. By incorporating this dimension the dialogues mediate that opposition, common to the Greeks, between *logos* and *ergon;* for in the dialogues the deed is not just something spoken about but is a dimension belonging to the dialogue itself. In other words, a dialogue is a discourse in and through which something is done, a discourse in and through which certain deeds are accomplished by certain of the speakers with respect to other participants in the dialogue. One very frequent type of *ergon,* especially evident in the *Meno,* is that in which a character is dramatically unveiled, in which something about him is concretely exhibited in and through what is said. Another type is present in the *Lysis* in which the various participants, discussing friendship without being able to reach any defensible conclusion, nevertheless become better friends through the discussion. In the Platonic dialogues the dimension of *ergon,* no less than that of *mythos,* belongs together with the dimension of *logos.* [8]

The reference in Socrates' statement to the need for a *logos* to have an appropriate middle can be taken, in dynamic terms, as alluding to the mediation which a dialogue accomplishes between its various dimensions. A dialogue is a whole in which the dimensions are appropriate to one another and to the whole, and there is incorporated into a dialogue a movement of mediation between the principal dimensions, a mirror-play between these dimensions. Furthermore, there is an analogous mirror-play within each dimension of a dialogue. *The totality of this mirror-play constitutes the dramatic character of a dialogue.* By virtue of its dramatic character, that is, through the mirroring interplay between and within the dimensions of a dialogue, a dialogue always makes manifest more than is explicitly said, and what is explicitly said takes on its

---

[8] Strauss writes in this connection: "In the same way we must understand the 'speeches' of all Platonic characters in the light of the 'deeds' " (*City and Man,* p. 59). See also Klein, *Commentary,* esp. pp. 17-18.

full sense only as a moment within the whole of the mirror-play. It is imperative that in seeking to interpret the dialogues we regard them in their character as dramas—that is, that we attend to their multiple dimensions and to the mirror-play which unfolds between and within these dimensions.[9]

The second feature of the dialogues to which attention needs to be drawn by way of preliminary determination is suggested by a curious omission in Socrates' comparison, cited above, between a *logos* and a living being. Specifically, Socrates compares *logos only to the body* of a living thing and fails to indicate what, if anything, corresponds on the side of *logos* to the soul of a living being. This omission is especially striking in view of the fact that Socrates' own exemplary *logos* earlier in the *Phaedrus* took the form of a myth of the *soul*. What, then, is the soul of a *logos*? What, specifically, is the soul of a written *logos,* of a dialogue?

This issue is elaborated somewhat later in the *Phaedrus* in the passage where Socrates discusses written *logos* (274 b − 278 b). He observes that when written *logoi* are questioned they refuse to answer; just as a painting, when questioned, simply continues to maintain its "solemn silence," so it is with written *logoi,* which, when questioned, simply continue forever to say the same thing. Written works lack an appropriateness to the one to whom they are addressed; they do not know how to address the right people and not address the wrong ones. Written *logoi* do not easily yield dialogue, and in this respect they are inferior to spoken *logoi.* Presumably, the Platonic written works, by being cast in the form of dialogues, are intended to minimize this defect of the written *logos.*

The essential contrast, however, is not that between written *logoi* and spoken *logoi;* spoken *logoi* also, though intrinsically

---

[9] It should be noted that the nature of that imitating or imaging proper to *logos* is a principal theme of inquiry in several dialogues, perhaps most openly in the *Cratylus*. A more adequate understanding of the "mirroring" structure of the dialogues would need to take into account such inquiry, which shows, among other things, that the kind of imitating appropriate to *logos* (hence to a Platonic *logos,* a dialogue) is distinct from the kind of imitative relation that obtains between a portrait of a man and that man himself (cf. below, Chapter IV, Section 5). Here the reflexivity of the interpretive problem is evident: in order to elicit Plato's teaching regarding logos we must interpret the Platonic dialogues; but, since the dialogues themselves exemplify this teaching, we need already to understand this teaching in order to interpret the dialogues properly.

more capable of allowing dialogue, by no means guarantee it. [10]
The question which must be asked in both cases is whether the
logos accomplishes its end, and both the written and the spoken
logos are to be judged in these terms.[11]   But what is the relevant
end? It is, in the first instance, the accomplishment of dialogue;
but this end is, in turn, subordinated to another, namely, that
what is spoken of in the *logos* be "written in the soul" of the one
who hears. A *logos* can be of really serious import only if there
attaches to it an *ergon,* not the kind of *ergon* which can be
incorporated, as in a Platonic dialogue, into the *logos,* but an
ergon in the soul of the one who hears the *logos.* If a *logos*
succeeds in accomplishing the appropriate deed in the soul of the
hearer, it makes no difference whether it is spoken or written. The
written *logoi* of Plato imitate the spoken *logos* only because the
latter is intrinsically more fit to accomplish this deed.

What is the deed to be accomplished by *logos*? Socrates says of
written *logoi* that they serve only to remind those who already
know that about which they are written. Yet, such reminding,
such provoking of recollection, is precisely the end which
Socrates, sometimes even explicitly, declares himself to be pursuing by means of his spoken *logoi,* as, for instance, in his
discussion with the slave boy in the *Meno. Logos,* whether spoken
or written, serves only to provoke recollection in the soul of the
one who hears. Mere *logos,* whether written or spoken, lacks a soul
as long as it does not accomplish the deed of provoking recollection in the soul of the one who hears or reads it. The soul of *logos,*
that by virtue of which it is not just a body but a living being, is
nothing other than the human soul on which it is written. Granting that in this respect the dialogues are an imitation of Socratic
activity, that it is for the sake of the appropriate deed that the
Platonic *logoi* have the form they do—what is, then, called for on

---

[10] It should be noted in this connection how Socrates often criticizes spoken *logoi*
when their length, for example, prohibits the possibility of dialogue (cf., for example,
Prot. 334 c — 336 d). Even when he is compelled to speak at length, as in the
Symposium, he mitigates the compulsion by introducing an imaginary character and
transforming his speech into a recounting of a dialogue.

[11] See Philip Merlan, "Form and Content in Plato's Philosophy," *Journal of the
History of Ideas,* 8 (1947), p. 426.

the part of one who undertakes to read and to interpret the dialogues is that he dialogue with them in such a way as to let them exercise their deed of provocation. And this means that to interpret the dialogues of Plato is not merely to re-present a certain particular philosophical position; it is to seek to gain access to philosophy as such, to seek to begin philosophizing, through a response to the provocation which the dialogues are capable of exercising.[12]

The final feature of the dialogues to which we need to attend is their *playfulness*. Socrates speaks openly of this playfulness in the *Phaedrus*: he tells Phaedrus that in written *logos* there is necessarily much that is playful (277 e). A further clue regarding the character of the relevant playfulness is to be found in Book VII of the *Republic*. In that discussion in which Socrates, educating Glaucon, discusses with him the way in which the philosopher is to be educated, Socrates remarks that the education of children, of beginners, ought to be accomplished not by force but rather by means of play (536 e − 537 a). This prescription is not to be passed over as pertaining only to children in the literal sense, for just prior to this remark Socrates has observed that, in fact, he and Glaucon have been playing and has suggested even that because they forgot that they were playing they were led astray into an inappropriate display of spiritedness (536 c). Whatever else may pertain to it and to its beginning, philosophy is begun in play. It is in play that one begins to philosophize, and, at least to the extent that it is this beginning which the dialogues aim to provoke, their playfulness is appropriate and calls for a responsive play on the part of one who seeks to interpret them. The playfulness of the dialogues takes various concrete forms, but it is perhaps most apparent in those dialogues which, like the *Cratylus,* most transparently exhibit the form of comedy.

---

[12] In this connection Klein writes: "Paul Friedländer's remark 'The dialogue is the only form of book that seems to suspend the book form itself' could perhaps be elaborated on as follows: a (Platonic) dialogue has not taken place if we, the listeners or readers, did not actively participate in it; lacking such participation, all that is before us is indeed nothing but a book" (*Commentary*, p. 6). Bloom writes that "The Platonic dialogues do not present a doctrine; they prepare the way for philosophizing" ("Preface" to *The Republic*, p. xvii). See also Hermann L. Sinaiko, *Love, Knowledge, and Discourse in Plato* (Chicago: University of Chicago Press, 1965), p. 12.

But not just any kind of play is appropriate to the beginning of philosophy; it must, says Socrates, be a play which is *lawful* (*Rep.* 424 e — 425 a), lawful even in the sense of being bound by something beyond itself.[13] In Book I of the *Laws* the Athenian describes man as "a puppet made by gods, possibly as a plaything, or possibly with some more serious purpose" (644 d); and then in Book VII, affirming more definitely that the best part of man is contrived to be a plaything of god, he insists that men ought to pass their lives playing at the most beautiful play—sacrificing, singing, and dancing—so as to be able to win the favor of the divine and to repel their foes (803 c — e). Playing man is simultaneously something like a plaything of the gods, yet to the extent that philosophy begins in play man comes to some awareness of this condition only through play. That play in which philosophy begins is precisely such as to bring to light through the play itself that by which the play is already bound from its inception. It is in this connection that we are to understand what is at issue in the *Sophist* when the Stranger asks Theaetetus whether there is "any more artful and more graceful kind of play than the imitative kind," to which Theaetetus answers, "Certainly not" (234 b). More playfully, the origin of such play can be said to lie in the tendency of every living being to leap (*Laws* 673 c).

Thus, a dialogue, in its manifold dimensions and their mirror-play, is directed to a deed; a dialogue is be-souled only in the provoking of recollection; and a dialogue, in its playfulness, calls for a lawful play of interpretation. It is required that the play of interpretation be conjoined to the play of the dialogue, as, for instance, in the *Euthydemus* the discussion between Socrates and Crito is conjoined to the discussion which Socrates is recalling for Crito. This is to say that the interpreter must become—though in a different way—one of the interlocutors of the dialogue.

---

[13] Thus, in Book VII of the *Republic* Socrates can say that great precautions must be taken to insure that the young do not misuse *logoi* "as though it were play, always using them to contradict" (539 b); his reference is to a kind of play which, in contrast to that exemplified in the philosophical exchange between Socrates and Glaucon, is not lawful, not bound by anything beyond itself. Much the same holds of that mere play of which the Athenian speaks at one point in Book II of the *Laws* (667 e).

PART ONE.

SOCRATIC *LOGOS*

CHAPTER I

PROVOCATIONS OF SOCRATIC *LOGOS:*
APOLOGY OF SOCRATES

"The lord whose oracle is in Delphi neither speaks out nor conceals but gives a sign."[1] This saying of Heraclitus itself gives a sign. This saying is a sign which, if we attend properly to it, makes manifest what is initially at issue in the problem of Socratic *logos.* It poses *"legein"*—hence *"logos"*—over against "concealing," and it puts both in opposition to "giving a sign." The latter is named as the activity proper to Apollo, who signifies through the oracle at Delphi and who is "lord" over man—that is, who exercises command over man in that signifying through the oracle. Apollo, speaking through the oracle, gives a sign of such a kind that what is signified is neither totally illuminated ("spoken out") nor totally obscured ("concealed"); nor is it just partly illuminated and partly left obscure. Rather, the sign is given to be *interpreted,* and its signifying commences only with the commencement of the interpretation. Philosophy as presented in the activity of Socrates originates through such interpretation. And even beyond its point of origin philosophy remains engaged in a perpetual interpreting of those most familiar Delphic signs "Know thyself" and "Nothing in excess." For taking up the question "What is philosophy?" in the form of the question "Who is Socrates?"—for taking up, specifically, the question of Socratic *logos*—it is appropriate to begin with that Socratic *logos* which most explicitly brings to light the bond joining Socratic *logos* as such to that divine saying, that sign-giving, in which man's subordination to Apollo is put at issue.

The *Apology of Socrates* ('Απολογία Σωκρατοῦς) is the only

---

[1] ὁ ἄναξ οὗ τὸ μαντεῖόν ἐστι τὸ ἐν Δελφοῖς οὔτε λέγει οὔτε κρύπτει ἀλλὰ σημαίνει. Heraclitus, Fr. 93. The translation given is that of Kirk and Raven, *The Presocratic Philosophers* (Cambridge, 1962), p. 211.

Platonic dialogue which includes the name of Socrates in its title. This corresponds to the fact that the *Apology* is the dialogue which most explicitly has to do with the question "Who is Socrates?" Furthermore, the *Apology* is unique in its *way* of dealing with this question. For, in the first place, it deals with this question within a context in which it is the most pressing of all questions, in which the answer to this question is literally a matter of life or death—hence the exclusiveness with which the *Apology* is dedicated to this question. And, secondly, by virtue of this context, the answer which Socrates presents is addressed explicitly to "the many," to the men of Athens, to men in the city—which is to say that in the *Apology* Socrates carries out that way of answering the question "Who is Socrates?" which demands the least on the part of those to whom it is addressed. The *Apology* is peculiarly appropriate to the beginner.

In all three of its dimensions the *Apology* poses an answer to the question "Who is Socrates?" First of all, Socrates simply says—in several regards—who he is. He says this especially in the testing of the various counter-images that are presented in the form of the accusations against him. What is especially remarkable in this connection is that this way of affirming who he is constitutes, not only a refutation of the counter-images and an assertion over against them of a truthful image, but also a *concrete exhibition* of that very practice which defines who Socrates is. The very way in which Socrates constructs his image—in the course of confronting, testing, and refuting the opinions embodied in the accusations—exemplifies the image constructed. Consequently, the question "Who is Socrates?" is answered in the *Apology* not only by *what* Socrates says but also by his *way* of saying it, by what he does; Socrates' speech is a testimony not only in speech but also in deed (cf. 32 a)—not only in *logos* but also in *ergon*.[2]

---

[2] In this connection we should take note of a story that is related twice by Xenophon (*Memorabilia* IV.viii. 4 − 5; *Apology* 2 − 4). Xenophon tells that he was told by Hermogenes that after Meletus had filed his indictment Socrates was heard discussing everything except his trial. Hermogenes then took it upon himself to tell Socrates that he ought to be thinking about his defence. Socrates answered: "Don't you think that I have spent my life practicing this?" He then explained "that he had never done anything else but to examine what things were just and unjust, and to do justice and avoid

Neither the description of his practice as one of questioning men in the city nor the exemplification of such questioning in deed permits, however, an adequate unfolding of the depth that belongs to Socrates' practice. This depth is primarily unfolded, rather, in the mythic dimension of the *Apology*. Socrates explicitly presents his practice as originating in a response to a sign given through the Delphic oracle. At the simplest level, this means that the already established mythical tradition supplies a context for Socrates' presentation of his peculiar practice and its motivation. But it also means something more fundamental. Socrates, as one who is engaged in unlimited questioning, is compelled to carry this questioning so far that finally he must question the questioning itself, must ask "What about the what?" "Why the why?" And even if he should resist this radicalization of his questioning, it is forced upon him when the men of Athens bring him to trial precisely because of what his incessant questioning has provoked. What is crucial is that Socrates "answers" the second-order question, the question about questioning, by setting his practice back upon a *mythos*. He confronts this most dangerous question—the question which amounts to a calling of questioning, of his practice, into question—by explicitly attaching his practice to a *mythos,* that is, to a basis that is not immediately dissolved by the reiterated recoil of questioning upon itself.

Section 1. The Prologue to the *Apology* (17 a – 19 a)

The *Apology* is composed primarily of three speeches: first, the long defence speech (19 a – 35 d), second, the speech in which

---

injustice—which he thought was the finest possible practice for his defence." The remark indicates not only that Socrates' life was a "defence in deed" in contrast to his "defence in speech" presented in the trial (cf. Leo Strauss, *Xenophon's Socrates* [Ithaca: Cornell University Press, 1972], p. 129), but also it indicates the basic continuity by which what he does in the trial (the deed of speaking) is precisely a continuation of what he has been doing. Xenophon goes on to tell that Socrates told Hermogenes that when he tried to consider his defence his daimon opposed it. Thus, the continuity—which Socrates himself stresses (not without irony) at the beginning of his speech in Plato's *Apology*—is enforced even by Socrates' daimon.

Socrates discusses and proposes alternative penalties (35 e – 38 b), and, finally, the speech delivered by Socrates after the sentence has been imposed (38 c – 42 a). The first speech is preceded by a prologue which consists of two parts: a preface (προοίμιον) in which Socrates speaks about speech and a setting forth (πρόθεσις) of the charges. We must attend to the opening with special care.

(a) The Preface (17 a – 18 a)

Socrates begins:

> How you, men of Athens, have been affected by my accusers I do not know; but, however that may be, I almost forgot who I was, so persuasively did they speak; and yet there is hardly a word of truth in what they have said (17 a).

In this opening statement and the elaboration of it that comprises the rest of the preface there are three principal issues to be noted.

First, Socrates refers to the persuasiveness of his accusers' speeches and mentions that he has been so affected by them that he almost forgot who he was. Thus, the *Apology* begins with the identity of Socrates (who he is) being thrown into question. This is what his being brought to trial amounts to—a placing of the question "Who is Socrates?" in the arena of contention. Indeed, Socrates suggests that his accusers contend so persuasively that he almost forgets the answer which he presumably brought with him to the trial. But he does not quite forget; and, in fact, his answer to his accusers—that is, the body of the *Apology*—is Socrates' manifold assertion of who he is. As such it is the measure of the irony involved in Socrates' opening his defence with the suggestion that he has barely escaped being plunged into self-forgetfulness by the persuasive speeches of his accusers.[3]

Second, it should be observed that Socrates addresses the members of the court as "men of Athens" (ὦ ἄνδρες ʾΑθηναῖοι)

---

[3] See the more elaborate and more obviously ironic praise of rhetoric at the beginning of the *Menexenus* (234 c – 235 c); Socrates speaks of those who are so eloquent and persuasive that, when he has heard them, "it is scarcely on the fourth or fifth day that I recover myself and remember that I really am here on earth, whereas till then I almost imagined myself to be living in the Islands of the Blessed—so expert are our orators."

rather than using the more customary expression "judges" (ὦ ἄνδρες δικασταί). In contrast to Meletus, who does not hesitate to call them "judges" (24 e), Socrates studiously avoids so addressing them throughout his entire defence speech. Only in the last part of his final speech, in which he addresses himself only to those members of the court who voted for his acquittal and in which he draws the contrast between those who claim to be judges and those true judges who sit in judgment in Hades (41 a)—only there does he finally use the other form of address (ὦ ἄνδρες δικασταί). Only those who have voted for his acquittal are addressed as judges, and they are so addressed only after they have proved themselves by their vote.[4] Socrates says that in calling them judges he is speaking correctly (40 a). The point is that inasmuch as Socrates takes it upon himself to decide to which of the "men of Athens" the name "judge" belongs, he is himself assuming the stance of a judge.[5] In the *Apology* we are presented not only with the judgment passed by the would-be judges on Socrates but also with Socrates' passing of judgment on those who claim to judge him. Socrates judges the would-be judges. This is presumably why he remarks at the very beginning that he does not know how they have been affected by the speeches of his accusers: he does not know whether they are sufficiently in possession of the proper virtue of a judge (cf. 18 a) to have withstood the persuasion of his accusers, and he will come to know this only by himself passing judgment on them in the course of the trial.

---

[4] Meyer relates this feature to the peculiar temporal structure of the *Apology*. In general, this temporal structure arises from the fact that the verdict, decided between the first and the second speeches, and the sentencing, which occurs between the second and the third speeches, are events which utterly transform Socrates' situation, thus requiring of him a drastic reorientation in moving from one speech to the next. In the specific case of the form of address, it is noted that Socrates uses the expression ὦ ἄνδρες δικασταί only after everything has been decided. This would not be the case in a typical defence speech, in which, on the contrary, the reservation with regard to addressing the members of the court as "judges" would be made to serve for the intimidation of the judges. By contrast, the change of the situation, the peculiar temporal progression, is exploited by Socrates in such a way as to allow him to use this reservation for the purpose of marking his judgment of the judges—that is, to divert this devise of speech from the kind of use typical in defence speeches to a more properly Socratic use. See Thomas Meyer, *Platons Apologie* (Stuttgart: W. Kohlhammer Verlag, 1962), pp. 41-42.

[5] Cf. George Anastaplo, "Human Being and Citizen: A Beginning to the Study of Plato's *Apology of Socrates*," in *Ancients and Moderns*, ed. Joseph Cropsey (New York: Basic Books, 1964), pp. 16-17.

Socrates brings the would-be judges to trial, and in trying these "men of Athens" he places Athens itself on trial.

Socrates insists, finally, that there is hardly any truth in what has been said by his accusers. Specifically, he adduces as the most evident of those lies that they have clothed in persuasive speech their contention that he is a clever speaker. It is significant that Socrates seizes upon this particular issue. For it is, as he notes, a contention which his subsequent speaking will refute, not only in speech but also in deed; his defence speech will not be a clever speech in the sense suggested by Socrates' accusers.[6] Yet, still more important, Socrates' focusing upon this issue, which he then elaborates in the remainder of the preface, has the effect of making his prefatory speech of defence, which anticipates the defence as a whole, into a description of his relation to speech. From the very outset Socrates' relation to *logos* is posed at the center of the considerations, and Socrates' defence is prefaced by a speech about speech, about the speech of Socrates in contrast to that of his accusers. Socrates informs the "men of Athens" that from him they will not hear fine speech embellished with choice phrases, that, instead, he will speak in the same way that he is accustomed to speaking in the market place and elsewhere; in other words, he indicates that in his defence speech he will continue precisely that kind of speech which defines his practice, which is to say that his defence speech will itself constitute an exemplification of that very practice against which the accusations have been brought. To the extent that such practice, such Socratic

---

[6] Xenophon calls special attention to Socrates' avoidance of the standard tricks used in court and to the import of this: "Other men in trials customarily appeal to the jurors for favors, flatter them, and plead illegally, and through such behavior many frequently are freed by the jurors; yet when he was indicted by Meletus, Socrates was not willing to play any of the usual illegal tricks in court. He would have been acquitted easily by the jurors had he followed these practices just a little" (*Memorabilia*, IV. iv. 4).

But Meyer has shown that in the Platonic *Apology* Socrates does not simply avoid the peculiar clever turns of court speech, as though he were completely unfamiliar with them, but rather employs them for a different end. Thus, the *Apology* presents Socrates as capable of speaking in the clever way of the court speakers, as capable, therefore, of defending himself by this means, but as prevented from doing so by his peculiar relation to *logos*. See Meyer, *Platons Apologie,* esp. pp. 65, 119 – 124; also the remarks by Burnet in his annotated edition of the *Euthyphro, Apology,* and *Crito* (Oxford, 1924), p. 67. On this basis it may be said that Socrates' speeches in the *Apology* constitute an answer in *ergon* to the charge that he practices eristic.

logos, transcends the city, to the extent that it is intrinsically at odds with the city, Socrates is, as he says (17 d), a foreigner—not, however, just because he is in court for the first time and not because he is ignorant of the speeches of the courts. The gulf which separates Socratic *logos* from the speech of the courts and makes it seem almost like a foreign tongue is anything but a mere lack of familiarity. On the contrary, what, most comprehensively, constitutes this gulf is the dedication of Socratic *logos* to truth (ἀλήθεια): "Now they, as I say, have said little or nothing true; but you shall hear from me the whole truth" (17 b). But what does this mean—that Socrates will speak the truth in contrast to those who deliver the finely embellished speeches of the courts? What does it mean to speak the truth, and what must be the character of Socratic *logos* if its distinctiveness lies in its dedication to truth?

At this point what is important for our inquiry is not that we have an ample supply of answers to this question but rather that we let there be something genuinely questionable in this question, that we take the utmost pains to avoid letting the question be dissolved by the all-too-available semblance of obviousness. A first step in this direction is provided if we take note of a connection which Socrates later makes between presenting the truth and speaking in such a way as not to hide anything from those who are addressed (24 a). In speaking the truth Socrates speaks in such a way as to avoid letting what he speaks about be hidden. But what he speaks about primarily is himself, and in speaking the truth with regard to himself he is speaking in such a way as to make manifest who he is. What must be the nature of truth and of *logos* and what must be their connection if true *logos* is that which is dedicated to taking a stand against letting things remain hidden?

(b) The Setting Forth of the Accusations (18 a – 19 a)

Socrates turns to the accusations brought against him by his accusers. Yet, he turns to them in a curious way: he introduces an additional set of accusations brought against him by a large group of mostly unidentifiable accusers. In other words, rather than immediately setting out in his speech to try to remove the accusations actually brought against him, Socrates does precisely the opposite, adding accusations and multiplying the number of accusers. So, it appears that Socrates begins his defence by doing just the opposite of what he really needs to do in order to defend himself effectively. To this extent Socrates indeed proves from the outset what he said he would prove in deed, namely, that he is not a clever speaker. By the criteria of clever court speech, Socrates begins with a sheer blunder. But these criteria do not provide the measure of Socratic *logos,* and the cleverness of the beginning of Socrates' speech is of a different order.

Alongside the accusations actually being brought against him by Meletus, Anytus, and Lycon, Socrates introduces what he calls the "first false accusations" and the "first accusers," those who for many years have been speaking against him (18 a − b). These accusers are so pervasive that they are elusive, and it is not even possible to name them, except for the one who is a writer of comedies. The result is that they are especially difficult to cope with, for, as Socrates notes, they cannot be called up in court and interrogated. Nevertheless, the accusations which they have authored are most decisively present in the court, present in the form of prejudices ingrained over a long period of time in such "men of Athens" as those who would be judges over Socrates. It is thus that Socrates confesses his awareness of the great difficulty to be expected in trying to remove the accusations by a single speech.

Socrates says that his "first accusers" are the more dangerous because, as he tells the "men of Athens," "they got hold of most of you in childhood and accused me without any truth, saying, 'there is a certain Socrates, a wise man, a ponderer of the things in the air and one who has investigated the things under the earth and who makes the weaker *logos* the stronger'" (18 b). [7]

---

[7] It should be noted that the expression "σοφὸς ἀνήρ" ("wise man") is hardly a compliment. Also "φροντιστής" ("ponderer") was a kind of nickname for Socrates; in the *Clouds* Aristophanes called Socrates' school the φροντιστήριον ("thought-factory," "think-tank"). The "things in the air" (τὰ μετέωρα) include both heavenly bodies and "meteorological" phenomena in the more restricted sense; but note that when the accusations are repeated at 19 b "τὰ μετέωρα" is replaced by "τὰ οὐράνια." Cf. Burnet, pp. 75-77. Regarding the second accusation, making the weaker *logos* the stronger, see Aristophanes, *Clouds,* 112.

When Socrates begins his answer to the accusations, he adds that he is also held to teach others those same things in which he is accused of engaging. Thus, the "first false accusations" are: (1) that he ponders things in the heavens and beneath the earth; (2) that he makes the weaker *logos* the stronger; and (3) that he teaches these same things to others.

Socrates does not yet name the "later accusations," those being explicitly brought against him. What is important, however, is that, without mentioning explicitly the two "later accusations" (impiety and corrupting the youth), he connects them in significant ways with the "first false accusations." Specifically, he observes that those who hear that he has to do with what is in heaven and beneath the earth easily conclude that he does not acknowledge (respect, hold in esteem, give recognition to) the gods (οὐδὲ θεοὺς νομίζειν).[8] Since, furthermore, he obviously is thought to corrupt the youth primarily by teaching his objectionable practices to them, it follows that the "first false accusations" provide the basis for the "later accusations," that they constitute the already established prejudice on which Socrates' later accusers are primarily depending in pressing their charges, and that, consequently, the "later accusations" can be effectively resisted only if these underlying accusations, these "first false accusations" are exposed and countered. This is why Socrates begins his defence by introducing additional accusations.

Socrates says to the "men of Athens" that his first accusers spoke to them at that age at which they were most likely to believe what they heard, to some of them in their youth, to others in childhood (18 c). In other words, Socrates is contending that he is not the one who is guilty of corrupting the youth—that, on the contrary, those first accusers, the effects of whose accusations

---

[8] There has been considerable discussion regarding the precise meaning of the expression "θεοὺς νομίζειν." Cf. Burnet, p. 78 and R. Hackforth, *The Composition of Plato's Apology* (Cambridge, 1933), p. 60; also Bruno Snell, *The Discovery of the Mind*, tr. T. G. Rosenmeyer (Cambridge: Harvard University Press, 1953), pp. 26-27. What is perhaps most essential in understanding the expression and avoiding the difficulties involved in the opposed positions of Burnet and Hackforth is that we avoid presupposing that at the pre-philosophical level there is already established a rigid distinction between a "theoretical" recognition of the gods ("believing in their existence") and the recognition which is accorded to them in the performance of rituals and the observance of customs linked to the gods.

against Socrates provide the condition under which he is being brought to trial, have engaged in a corruption of the opinions of the youth regarding Socrates—that, to this extent, these first accusers are more nearly guilty of having practiced corruption of the youth.

Section 2. The Way of Socrates

(a) Aristophanes and Anaxagoras (19 a − d)

Socrates begins his actual defence by indicating that Meletus, in bringing him to trial, is relying on the old prejudices to secure his case. Thus, these old prejudices, i.e., the "first false accusations," must be answered first; once they are removed, the "later accusations" explicitly being brought against Socrates will presumably collapse almost of their own accord. We must be prepared to see what is revealed about Socrates through the collapse of the accusations.

Socrates does what his accusers would have done had they been open about the accusation: he states the three "first false accusations" in the legal form of a sworn statement. His first explicit movement of defence is then to identify the main identifiable disseminator of those opinions about himself that have provoked these accusations: he reminds the "men of Athens" that they have themselves seen these opinions portrayed in the comedy of Aristophanes in which Socrates is presented as "swinging round" on high and proclaiming that he is treading on air in addition to uttering a vast amount of other nonsense.[9] In fact, this reference to the portrait of Socrates given in Aristophanes' *Clouds* links the

---

[9] We leave open the question whether or not the comic poets and Aristophanes in particular are to be distinguished, in the final analysis, from the anonymous advocates of the "first false accusations." Cf. Burnet, p. 79. This issue, hence the question of the fundamental intent of Aristophanes in the *Clouds,* hence the question of Aristophanes' real relation to Socrates is elaborately developed by Leo Strauss, *Socrates and Aristophanes* (New York: Basic Books, 1966). Suffice it to say that according to Strauss' analysis Aristophanes is by no means to be regarded as an enemy of Socrates (cf. p. 5), even though the contention between them is considerable (cf. esp. p. 311).

comedy explicitly only with the first accusation (specifically, with the charge that he ponders things in the heavens). But, in effect, the opinions behind all of the "first false accusations" that Socrates has just stated are readily evident in the Aristophanean Socrates. In Aristophanes' comedy Socrates is portrayed not only as searching out heavenly matters up in the air aloof from other men and the city but also as master of the "think-tank" in which pupils can learn the "unjust *logos*," learn to make the weaker *logos* the stronger (cf. esp. *Clouds*, 112). Furthermore, the Aristophanean Socrates' inquiries into the air are quite explicitly linked with an assault carried on in *logos* against the gods, even against Zeus himself; that is, these inquiries are linked, with an undue self-elevation above mere mortals, or, as Strepsiades puts it in his final and perhaps most telling indictment, with a committing of *hubris* against the gods. The incipient corruption is hardly less at the level of the city: the power of the Socratic *logos* over Strepsiades reaches its breaking point and the final and most basic turn of the comedy is reached only when that *logos* becomes the advocate even of mother-beating and, by implication, of incest— that is, only when that *logos* has brought Strepsiades and Pheidippides within sight of the most monstrous crime with its power of undermining the family and thereby the city.[10] Whatever the comic poet's specific intent may have been, the fact remains that in the *Clouds* the "first false accusations" are already linked up with the accusations of impiety and corrupting the youth, and beneath this complex of accusations there is the unmistakeable appearance of *hubris* against the gods accompanied by an undermining of beliefs essential to the well-being of the city.

For Socrates fully to refute the accusations that are, in effect, presented in Aristophanes' comedy would thus amount to his refuting all the accusations, old and new, brought against him. Thus, the *Apology* as a whole—at least the long defence speech— represents Socrates' answer to Aristophanes, to the extent that such could be presented to the men of the city.

At the simplest level Socrates refutes the images of himself presented in the "first false accusations" by assigning these images

---

[10] Strauss, *Socrates and Aristophanes*, pp. 43-44.

to those to whom they properly belong, thereby indicating the inappropriateness of the images to himself. The first such image, the one which Socrates explicitly links to Aristophanes' comedy, that is, the image of Socrates as one who inquires about things in the heavens—this image he assigns to Anaxagoras. The actual assigning comes somewhat later in the defence speech, namely, in the course of Socrates' confrontation with Meletus and, specifically, in connection with the explicit accusation of impiety, the later accusation that is derived from the image of Socrates pondering things in the heavens (26 d − e). Meletus accuses Socrates of saying that the sun is a stone and that the moon is earth. Socrates replies: "Do you think you are accusing Anaxagoras, my dear Meletus?" Socrates rejects the image by re-assigning it to the one of whom it really is an image, in this case to Anaxagoras. The re-assignment serves, in effect, to enhance the force of Socrates' denial that he has to do with such things.

Socrates' distinguishing of himself from Anaxagoras and his denial that he has to do with the kind of inquiries typical of Anaxagoras have always been decisive for the question "Who is Socrates?" That is, the distance which Socrates puts between himself and the earlier inquirers about nature (φύσις) has always been crucial for the interpretation of the sense of the Socratic-Platonic determination of philosophy. Already among the ancients (e.g., Cicero) Socrates was seen as the one who brought philosophy down from the heavens and into the cities of men, that is, as one who brought a basic shift away from "natural" and especially "cosmological" inquiry towards a concern with the human things, with the questions of good and evil, justice and injustice, with all those things that pertain especially to man in the city. Especially in the accounts of Socrates' practices found in Xenophon this interpretation seems to be borne out. For example, near the beginning of the *Memorabilia* (in a context involving explicit reference to the accusations brought against Socrates at his trial) Xenophon observes that Socrates did not hold discussions on the nature of the cosmos, that, furthermore, he declared people who concerned themselves with such things to be foolish, and that, in contrast, he was always engaged in discussing human things; Socrates' questions were, according to Xenophon, questions such

as "What is beautiful?" "What is just?" "What is moderation?"
"What is madness?" "What is a city?" "What is a statesman?"[11]
Near the end of the *Memorabilia* Xenophon again takes up this
issue, adding a further important element to it: he says that
Socrates turned his back on those who inquire as to how the god
contrives the heavenly things, because he believed that men could
not discover this and that the gods were displeased with any man
who asked about what they did not want to disclose, so much so
that one who concerned himself with such matters ran the risk of
losing his sanity altogether, as did Anaxagoras.[12] In effect, then,
the Xenophontic Socrates is presented as maintaining that to
inquire about the heavenly things is to overstep the properly
human bounds, to trespass the limits prescribed to man. Thus,
from Xenophon's perspective Socrates' turn from "cosmological"
to human concerns represents a restraining of oneself within the
limits proper to man.

But the Xenophontic Socrates is not the Platonic Socrates.
Rather, with respect to Socrates' turn away from the concerns of
earlier inquirers, the image presented by Xenophon shows no more
than the one side of Socrates' practice that can with some appropriateness be turned towards the "men of Athens." In fact, if we
consider the Platonic Socrates, we find that it is *only* when he
speaks to the "men of Athens" that he is content simply to set
himself over against Anaxagoras and those others who inquire
about things in the heavens and beneath the earth. By contrast,
when his more intimate trial commences on the day of his death,
when he is required to vindicate his practice to his closest friends
(*Phaedo* 63 b, e; 95 c), he does not merely oppose himself to
Anaxagoras. Neither does he suggest that the initiation of his
peculiar practice involved a shift away from inquiry regarding the
things in the heavens and beneath the earth. On the contrary,
Socrates' final speech in the *Phaedo* is a myth about the earth in
which he speaks of the regions beneath the earth and of the purer
regions above the air, far beyond the misty hollows where men
dwell. Socrates' very last speech before his death is, most remark-

---

[11] Xenophon, *Memorabilia,* I. i. 11 – 12, 16.
[12] *Ibid.,* IV. vii. 6.

ably, a speech about the things in the air and beneath the earth, i.e., a speech about precisely those things about which Socrates was, according to the old prejudices, suspected of inquiring. This does not mean that Socrates merely says one thing to the men of the city and then does and says the opposite when he is with his friends. It does not mean that he merely lies to the "men of Athens"—after having initially characterized his speech in terms of its adherence to truth. What it means is, rather, that what can be presented, made manifest, to the men of the city *only* as a simple unqualified shift away from inquiry about a particular matter can be made manifest to Socrates' closest friends as something more subtle, as a shift from one *way* of inquiry to another. Socrates can truthfully distinguish his practice from the inquiries of Anaxagoras and those others who have inquired about the things in the air and beneath the earth, not because he eschews inquiry about such things but rather because, whatever the matter at issue, Socrates asks about it in a way that is radically different from the way of Anaxagoras and his kin. The difference lies in the peculiar relation of Socratic questioning to *logos*. What distinguishes the way of Socrates is that it is explicitly a way of *logos*.[13]

(b) In Search of Causes (*Phaedo* 95 e − 102 a)

In order to get even a preview of the Socratic way in its character as a way of *logos,* it is necessary that we go beyond the limits of the speeches of the *Apology,* addressed, as they are, to the "men of Athens," who already suspect that Socrates is guilty

---

[13] This is not to deny that Socrates grants a *relative* priority to those matters that especially concern man in the city. However, the priority of these questions is not to be understood as involving a sheer exclusion of questions about the cosmos (cf. esp. *Tim.* 26 c − d: Timaeus' speech about the cosmos is introduced as a fitting sequel to Socrates' speech of the previous day about the city, and the two speeches are even thematically linked when Critias proposes that feast of *logos* to which Socrates is to be treated). Furthermore, the priority of questions about the city derives, not from the intrinsic order of significance of political things, but rather from the fact that the one who begins to philosophize is always already caught up in a city and that even when he has begun he retains a peculiar relation to the city. Nevertheless, the movement into philosophy is also a transcending of the city, and it is this transcendence which serves to relativize the priority of the political things. This issue will be developed in the final section of this chapter and especially in the interpretation of the *Republic* given in Chapter V.

of engaging in a kind of violence by means of *logos*. Specifically, it is necessary that we attend to that speech of Socrates' last day in which he recalls for his friends how he came to his way of inquiry.

Confronted with the problem of the immortality of the soul, specifically, with the objection which, at an advanced point in the discussion, Cebes has raised against their earlier efforts with this problem, Socrates advises his friends that a thorough investigation of coming-to-be (γένεσις) and passing-away (φθορά) must be undertaken. He so advises them, however, only after he has paused for some time to meditate. It is as though, confronted by his own death, Socrates looks into himself, back into his own past: he proceeds to supply the basis for the necessary investigation of coming-to-be and passing-away by recalling how his own way of investigating came to be. First of all, he tells how as a young man he was enthusiastic about the kind of wisdom that is called "investigation of nature" (περὶ φύσεως ἱστορία); he tells how he questioned regarding the causes (αἰτίαι) by which things come-to-be and pass-away, asking, for example, whether heat and cold, by a sort of fermentation, bring about the organization of living things.[14] He tells how he inquired about the heavens and the earth until finally he came to an awareness of his inadequacy for such inquiry. As testimony of this inadequacy he offers the fact that he was so blinded by these inquiries that eventually he no longer knew things which previously he had been confident of knowing. For example, formerly he had believed that he knew quite well— that, in fact, it was plain to everyone—what causes a man to grow. But, as a result of his inquiries he was thrown into doubt even about such seemingly obvious matters as this. Socrates' own growth consisted in his coming to see that the common opinions regarding growth are questionable. It is significant that, according to Socrates' account, what primarily provoked that condition of doubt in which his inquiries about nature resulted were problems having to do with number and pre-eminently with "ones": with the fact that, though each is one, they can become two when they

---

[14] For historical details related to this passage, see R. Hackforth, *Plato's Phaedo* (Indianapolis: Bobbs-Merrill, 1955), p. 123 and John Burnet, *Plato's Phaedo* (Oxford, 1911), pp. 100 ff.

approach each other, though Socrates was unable to say whether it is one or the other unit or both that became two; also with the consequent fact that, because the two arose by bringing ones together, it cannot be the case that the opposite procedure, namely division of a one, could cause it to become two, which is to say that every "one" is intrinsically indivisible (96 a — 97 b). At this point we are not yet in a position to thematize the real significance of these problems regarding number; but it is important that we avoid simply dismissing them as empty puzzles to be easily resolved once a more refined kind of thinking about numbers is brought into play, as though we could so easily brand Greek mathematical thought as something still "undeveloped" and unclear to itself. And, letting these problems stand as problems, what is then important is that we observe how unequivocally Socrates declares that it was on just such problems that his first method (μέθοδος) ran aground.

Socrates continues his account by relating that one day he heard someone reading from a book by Anaxagoras in which it was maintained that *nous* arranges all things in order and causes all things. Socrates thought to himself that, if this is so, then *nous*, in arranging things, would certainly arrange each thing as it is best for it to be. The result was that Socrates recast his inquiry regarding causes, no longer looking to elements or opposites as causes but rather examining only what is *best* with respect to the thing being considered. Having thus seen that to examine the cause of something is to examine the highest good of that thing, Socrates turned eagerly, so he relates, to the work of Anaxagoras only to be totally disappointed, since the causes actually assigned to things by Anaxagoras turned out to be of precisely the same order as those which Socrates had already abandoned (97 b — 99 c).

Consequently, Socrates tells Cebes, he set out on a "second voyage [δεύτερος πλοῦς]¹⁵ in search of causes":

> After this, then, when I had failed in investigating beings [τὰ ὄντα], I decided that I must be careful not to suffer the

---

¹⁵ The proverbial phrase "δεύτερος πλοῦς" has the sense of "next best way," i.e., it carries the implication of inferiority to a πρῶτος πλοῦς. The phrase is said to have originated in the practice of taking to the oars in the absence of a wind. Cf. Hackforth, *Plato's Phaedo*, pp. 127, 137.

misfortune which happens to people who look at and study the sun during an eclipse. For some of them ruin their eyesight unless they look at its image [εἰκών] in water or something of the sort. I thought of that danger, and I was afraid my soul would be blinded if I looked at things [τὰ πράγματα] with my eyes and tried to grasp them with any of my senses. So I thought I must have recourse to *logoi* and examine in them the truth of beings [τῶν ὄντων τὴν ἀλήθειαν] (99 d – e).

It is especially striking how Socrates stresses that his second voyage in search of causes set out from an awareness of a danger and of the need for protection against it. The danger is that he might follow a course that would finally result in blindness in his soul. But where are such courses to be found and, hence, avoided? One such course is only hinted at through the analogy Socrates uses, namely, that course on which one would so elevate his vision as to seek to look directly at the sun, that is, at what makes it possible for things to be visible, or, more fundamentally, at what lets things be manifest as such. In this connection it is not insignificant that Socrates speaks of those who look at the *eclipsed* sun: the very condition under which one can undertake to observe the sun and can remain more or less oblivious to the danger is precisely that in which the sun is "covered over," so that, as always, it is primarily the light and not its source that is available to one's view. The blindness that would result from looking at the sun cannot even claim the compensation of a preceding vision of the source of all visibility.

The primary reference of Socrates' statement is, however, not to a course on which one would gaze at the sun but to a course on which one would remain completely attached to the visible things and would attempt to grasp them by the senses alone, oblivious to that source and even that illumination that lets them be manifest. Here too the final result is blindness. That is, if one seeks to grasp beings directly and in that way that is most immediate, if one seeks a grasp on things as they are most immediately manifest to all men, then, to the extent that one remains within such a comportment, one's soul grows blind to beings. If, in the autobiographical cast of the account, looking at the sun corresponds to

Socrates' quest for the good (under the inspiration of Anaxa-goras), then the attempt to grasp things directly by the senses corresponds to that preceding stage of inquiry that was brought to its aporetic end by the problems concerning number.

Both kinds of seeing end in failure and blindness—*unless*, as in the case of Socrates, the pursuit of such seeing somehow issues in the awareness of the danger. In other words, the pursuit of such seeing can open up the possibility of another alternative only if it leads into a more acute awareness of ignorance—so that, as Socrates said (96 c), one no longer knows what he previously knew, or, rather, what he previously *thought* he knew. More precisely, what is required is an awakening to an ignorance intrin-sic to oneself—an ignorance which is not an ignorance with regard to this or that but which, rather, is a constituent in man's com-portment to everything, an ignorance which, as a result, holds man at a distance from total and immediate revelation of beings, a distance which he can ignore only at great peril.

The awakening to one's ignorance is the pre-condition for the Socratic alternative, for what he calls a "second voyage" in con-trast to the other two taken together. This second voyage, Socrates says, is analogous to the way of those who look at the image of the sun in water. On this way it is *logos* which serves as the medium in which the images of beings can be safely studied. It is by having recourse to *logos* that the danger which attends the other two ways can be avoided: this is to say that the way of *logos* is such as to "mediate" the difference between the things that can be manifest and that which lets them be manifest, i.e., that it is such as to let man maintain himself within the dispersion of this difference; it is to say also that the way of *logos* is such as to institute the appropriate restraint against seeking a grasp on things as they are immediately manifest, i.e., that it is such as to open up that distance in which things can become more truly manifest, that is, manifest in their proper being.

Even this cursory indication of the character of the way of *logos* already suffices to suggest the inadequacy of the analogy that Socrates has drawn between seeing an image of the sun in water and studying beings in *logoi;* in fact, Socrates himself, having introduced the analogy, goes on almost immediately to withdraw what is misleading in it. Specifically, he denies that "he who studies beings [τὰ ὄντα] in *logoi* is looking at them in images any more than he who studies them in deeds [ἐν τοῖς ἔργοις]" (100 a). This means that *logoi* do not simply provide us with images of beings in the sense of copies to be gazed upon in the absence of the beings themselves. The *logoi* do not provide some kind of substitutes, as it were, for the beings themselves, but rather they serve to open up a way of access to beings that is appropriate to a being like man whose comportment to beings is intrinsically linked to ignorance. They let something become manifest in something like the way that a deed, itself unfolding before our eyes, makes manifest something about the soul of the man responsible for the deed. The *logoi* serve as images *only* in the sense of that in and through which the beings themselves, the originals, are made manifest. The *logoi* serve to bring to manifestness the beings themselves; and because the beings are not immediately manifest to man, because they are not to be gotten in grasp through the senses, it becomes necessary for Socrates to undertake his second voyage in search of causes by having recourse to *logoi*. In its very beginning, this having recourse to *logoi* takes place as a posing of a "hypothesis" (ὑπόθεσις), that is, as a peculiar "placing under" or "laying down," which, carried out from a *logos*, issues in the posing of such things as beauty itself and good itself.[16]

The way of Socrates, the way which he is able to take and is required to take once he has awakened to ignorance, the way of Socrates' second voyage, is a way of *logos*. And the way of *logos* is a way, the appropriate way, for man to gain access to beings. Man begins on this way by a posing which, linked to *logos*, results in a setting-up of what in the Platonic dialogues are often called *eide*. We see, in an appropriately preliminary way, how the problem of Socratic *logos* leads finally into the problem of being and *logos*; and we see how the latter problem is, at the beginning, focused in the problem of the "hypothetical" *eide*.

---

[16] It is, of course, necessary to avoid letting the word "ὑπόθεσις" fall into the mold of modern conceptions; we must take special care to hold it at a distance from the sense which "hypothesis" has in modern science. Also we should avoid assuming that the "method" of hypotheses is to be regarded as a method of "arguing" from one proposition to another and that, correlatively, the "hypotheses" are propositions in some later sense. Cf. R. S. Bluck, *Plato's Phaedo* (Indianapolis: Bobbs-Merrill, 1955), pp. 160-164.

Section 3. Service to Apollo (19 d — 24 b)

By attending to part of what Socrates tells his closest friends on
the day of his death, we have gained a sketch of the Socratic way
in its character as a way of *logos*. But this sketch is only provi-
sional, only an anticipatory sketch, for, in fact, at this stage of our
investigation we are by no means yet prepared to hear in its full
resonance a discussion as demanding as those which Socrates holds
with those closest to him. If we are properly to prepare ourselves
we need now to step back from the level of the *Phaedo* in order to
go about collecting the complex of issues by which we will
eventually be able to take up in its full depth the problem which
we have only glimpsed in our anticipatory sketch, the problem of
being and *logos*. Thus, we return now to that order of speech
appropriate to one who has yet really to begin: we resume our
consideration of Socrates' defence speech in the *Apology*.

(a) Images of Sophistry (19 d — 21 a)

The second and third of those old prejudices to which Socrates
himself has called attention accuse him of making the weaker
logos the stronger and of teaching others those same questionable
things in which he engages. Socrates answers these accusations
with an abrupt denial, and, as previously, he proceeds to give force
to his denial by re-assigning the image represented in these prejudices to those to whom it properly belongs. Socrates mentions the
names of Gorgias, Prodicus, and Hippias, and launches into his
characteristically ironic praise of the wisdom of the sophists,
distinguishing himself from these possessors of a more than human
wisdom, who, if they really possess such wisdom, would indeed be
able teachers.

Along with the image which Socrates transfers from himself to
the sophists, two other images pertaining to sophistry are evoked.
The first portrays the sophists as not only teaching but also
making money by their teaching; but if they take money for their
instruction, then in good commercial fashion they must offer
some "ware" in exchange for the fee they receive, i.e., some

positive information or skill. We will soon learn that, by contrast, Socrates takes away something from those with whom he converses, namely, the presumption that they know. At this point, however, Socrates is content to recall a conversation which he had with Callias regarding the selection of a teacher for the latter's two sons; thus, Socrates introduces dialogue into his speech and in this way shows in deed a principal respect in which his practice differs from that of the sophists.

The other image which Socrates evokes pictures the sophists as wandering from city to city, acquiring influence over the youth in each city to which they come. In this image Socrates captures the chief source of Athenian prejudice against the sophists, that they were foreigners who unduly influenced the youth of other people's cities.[17] Very soon we will learn that Socrates also has been engaged in a kind of wandering but that his wandering, carried on solely within the city, has been undertaken not as a result of a claim to possess knowledge and to be capable of teaching it to others but rather as a result of a peculiar awareness of ignorance.[18] But in order to show what provokes his own journey, that journey which constitutes his practice in that form that is most evident to the men of the city, Socrates has first to tell of a journey which Chaerephon once made from Athens to Delphi. Socrates' real answer to the accusation of sophistry consists in his setting his practice back upon a *mythos.*

Socrates' account of his practice in terms of its relation to the Delphic oracle, which is the most important such account in the *Apology,* is prefaced by two remarks which serve to indicate something of the character of the account. First, Socrates puts into the mouth of a hypothetical listener the question as to how the prejudices against Socrates arose in the first place. Since they certainly would not have arisen and become so widespread had Socrates not been doing something other than what most people do, it is incumbent upon him, in face of those prejudices which he himself began by invoking, to explain how they were originally provoked. Socrates responds to this demand with an acknowledg-

---

[17] Cf. Burnet, p. 85.
[18] Cf. Meyer, *Platons Apologie,* pp. 133-135.

ment that he has indeed gotten his reputation because of a kind of wisdom. But, he insists that his is a "human wisdom" ($\dot{a}\nu\theta\rho\omega\pi\acute{\iota}\nu\eta$ $\sigma o\phi\acute{\iota}\alpha$), to be contrasted with the greater than human wisdom claimed by the sophists. This contrast is of utmost importance for the account that is about to commence; it is, in effect, a contrast between a wisdom which would remain within properly human limits and a wisdom which would pass beyond those limits. It is a contrast between a wisdom which would knowingly incorporate ignorance and a wisdom the very claim to which would amount to a display of ignorance regarding one's ignorance.

Secondly, Socrates proceeds, amidst clamor from the "men of Athens," to insist that what he says is not his own statement. Specifically, he refers what he says to the god of Delphi. Thus, in what he now proceeds to say Socrates will serve as the spokesman for Apollo. This is especially significant in view of the fact that what he is about to say is, in effect, how he came to be one who speaks for Apollo. Speaking for the god of Delphi, Socrates tells the story of how he came to serve as spokesman for this god. In this peculiar way of setting his practice back upon a *mythos,* we see the unity and mirror-play of the dimensions of the *Apology:* the *logos* unfolds into a *mythos* the very telling of which exemplifies in *ergon*—and is, in effect, *said* to exemplify in *ergon*—just that practice the origination of which is being related.

(b) The Saying of the Oracle (21 a – 24 b)

The story begins: Socrates' companion Chaerephon once went to Delphi and asked the oracle if there was anyone wiser than Socrates; the Pythian priestess answered that there was no one wiser. This saying of the oracle proved to be of utmost decisiveness for the initiation of Socrates' practice. In fact, the remainder of the story consists of a description of Socrates' response to this pronouncement of Apollo delivered through the oracle. It was precisely in the unfolding of this response that Socrates' practice originated.

Socrates' first response was one of puzzlement:

For when I heard this, I thought to myself: "What is the god saying, and what riddle is he propounding? For I am aware that I am not wise either much or little. What then is he saying by declaring that I am the wisest? He certainly cannot be lying, for that is not lawful for him" (21 b).

Here it is clear why Socrates was puzzled, why he was not able immediately to accept what was said: it was because of his awareness of his lack of wisdom, because of his awareness of his ignorance. But, though unable straightforwardly to accept the pronouncement of the god, Socrates was, on the other hand, almost equally incapable of rejecting the saying, since it was the saying of a god. The tension involved in being unable either to accept or to reject the saying given through the oracle is what provoked Socrates' initial state of puzzlement.

Eventually, however, the god's saying provoked Socrates to do more than merely puzzle:

And for a long time I was at a loss as to what he meant; then with great reluctance I proceeded to investigate him somewhat as follows (21 b).

It is evident why Socrates proceeded to the investigation "with great reluctance": it is because to investigate is opposed to that belief and acceptance that would usually be accorded a divine pronouncement, considerably more opposed than merely remaining in a more or less indecisive state of puzzlement. To investigate regarding what the god said is to entertain seriously the possibility that the pronouncement of the god might be false, that it might be a lie. The tension of the situation is only heightened by the assurance that the god could not possibly have lied (cf. Rep. 382 e).

This issue becomes still more explicit in the next sentence:

I went to one of those who had a reputation for wisdom, thinking that there, if anywhere, I should refute the utterance and should show the oracle "This man is wiser than I, but you said I was wisest" (21 b − c).

Thus, Socrates set out to refute the pronouncement. He set out to prove that what Apollo had said through the oracle was false—to prove, in other words, that the god had lied, either in the sense of presenting to Chaerephon something false in the guise of truth or else in the sense of that lying to oneself which is identical with ignorance (cf. Rep. 382 a − b). Socrates set out questioning other men *as* a way of calling the god himself into question.

Hence, Socrates' practice, his ceaseless questioning of others, began as a response to the pronouncement of Apollo. Socratic *logos,* at least that aspect of it which is most manifest to the men of the city, originated as a response to a *logos* given by Apollo through the oracle. It originated as a *questioning* response: Socrates responded to the saying of the oracle by questioning it, by calling it into question, by trying even to refute it. What is perhaps most important is that Socrates responded in this way because of his profound awareness of his ignorance.

We can now see the ambivalence of that situation in which Socrates' practice began. On the one hand, Socrates is aware of his ignorance; he is aware that his is, at most, a merely human wisdom that falls far short of the wisdom of the god. But, on the other hand, precisely because of this awareness, Socrates has to call into question that saying of the god that imputes to him an exalted wisdom, at least compared with other men, and which in so exalting him with respect to his wisdom gives apparently no weight to that ignorance of which Socrates is so keenly aware. In behalf of his ignorance, on the strength of his awareness of his ignorance, Socrates has to undertake to refute what the god has said, to show that it is false; and this would amount to showing either that the god practices deception in what he says or else that the god made his pronouncement on the basis of ignorance, in which case Socrates would prove to know more even than the god. Precisely because of his acute sense of that ignorance which makes him subordinate especially to the god himself in matters of wisdom, Socrates, confronted with the saying of the god, has to challenge the god in a way which, at least from a distance, appears inappropriate for man. In other words, confronted with the saying, Socrates could maintain himself within those limits disclosed by his awareness of his ignorance, only by taking issue with the god in a way which seemingly negates that very subordination to the god that is at issue. The delivery of the god's pronouncement to Socrates placed him in the position of being able to restrain himself within the properly human limits *only* by means of an activity which, at least from the sort of distance that separates the "men of Athens" from Socrates, appears to trespass beyond those limits.

Something of this peculiar tension inherent in the Socratic mission was seen by Nietzsche, who said of Socrates:

> The genuine religious task which he set himself—to put the god to the test in a hundred ways to determine whether he had spoken the truth—betrays a bold and frank bearing with which here the missionary walks by the side of his god. This putting of the god to the test is one of the finest compromises between piety and freedom of spirit that has been invented.[19]

What Nietzsche did not see—or, at least, did not say—is that to take up the question "Who is Socrates?" in its proper dimension requires that one attempt to grasp this practice, not as a mere compromise between two different directions, but rather in its fundamental unity, i.e., in the way that it unfolds into a unity.

The story continues. Socrates tells how he questioned the politicians, the poets, and the artisans in his attempt to find someone wiser than himself so as to refute the Delphic saying. But in each case, so he relates, his efforts failed, for again and again he found those whom he questioned less aware of their ignorance than was he and, to that extent, less wise. In reference specifically to the politicians Socrates gives an important description of the intent of his questioning; he says of a politician whom he questioned:

> This man seemed to me to seem to be wise to many other people and especially to himself, but not to be so; and then I tried to show him that he thought he was wise but was not (21 c).

---

[19] *Menschliches, Allzumenschliches,* Zweiter Band, Zweite Abteilung: "Der Wanderer und Sein Schatten," ¶ 72.

Here the structure relevant to the questioning is evident. The questioning begins in a situation in which something (the politician) *seems* to be one thing but *is* something else. More precisely, he *is not* what he *seems* to be to "the many"—that is, there is a drastic difference between what *seems* and what *is*. This difference between seeming and being is, in turn, something which *seems* to Socrates, something which shows itself to him in such a way that he has an opinion about it at the beginning of his questioning. Socrates' questioning is then aimed at verifying what *seems* to him, i.e., at making manifest in the politician the divergence between what he seems to be and what he is, i.e., at distinguishing between seeming and being in the sense that through the deed of questioning they are set apart and each disclosed as itself. And this amounts to Socrates' confirming the identity of what *is* with what initially *seemed* to him.

As he tells the story, Socrates repeatedly indicates that he was aware that his questioning was provoking hatred. He indicates, furthermore, how his practice of questioning led to the accusation that he is guilty of corrupting the youth: finding pleasure in hearing him examine people, many young men came to accompany him and eventually to imitate him (23 c – d). Socrates adds the observation that, when it was asked what he taught the young men so as to corrupt them, those who accuse him had nothing to say and so have resorted to the stock charges against philosophers. It is at this point that Socrates mentions the names of all three of his accusers, Meletus, Anytus, and Lycon (23 e): what he has accomplished is an exposure (though only in *logos* thus far) of what lies behind the accusations they are bringing against him, an exposure which makes it manifest that it is not piety and love of the city (as it *seems*) but ignorance and resentment against one who makes it his practice to expose ignorance. Again we see how Socrates' defence of his practice is, at the same time, an engagement in the very practice being defended.

Socrates insists that, despite his awareness of the hatred being provoked by his questioning, it was necessary, nevertheless, for him to continue his practice because of its relation to the god. Thus, he presents his practice as no merely human affair but rather as something decisively stamped by its having originated as a response to the saying of Apollo. Later he indicates, even, that his practice, rather than dispensing with its relation to the god, extends this relation in the sense of his coming to have other means of receiving the divine saying, now understood as a command:

> I have been commanded to do this by the god through oracles and dreams and in every way in which any man was ever commanded by divine dispensation [θεία μοῖρα] to do anything whatsoever (33 c).

This extension points to a more fundamental transformation of Socrates' practice.

The situation in which Socrates' practice originated was one of virtually unmitigated tension. However, Socrates' way of pursuing his concrete practice was such that it served eventually to transform the very situation of the practice. We need to see how this transformation was brought about and what the new situation was that resulted from it.

Socrates undertook his questioning of the men of the city, of the politicians, poets, and artisans, as a way of questioning the god's saying that had been delivered through the oracle. And, though Socrates, unable to accept straightforwardly what was spoken out through the oracle, set out to refute the saying, what eventually results from his questioning is neither acceptance nor refutation but rather an *interpretation* of the saying. It is this interpretation that brings about the relevant transformation. The situation to which Socrates' practice is linked, hence the meaning which that practice has for Socrates, undergoes a fundamental transformation when Socrates comes to realize concretely that, in the words of Heraclitus, "The lord whose oracle is in Delphi neither speaks out nor conceals but gives a sign"—a sign to be interpreted.

The concrete basis for the interpretation is provided by Socrates' questioning of other men, by what this questioning brings to light:

> I thought to myself, "I am wiser than this man; for neither of us really knows anything beautiful and good, but this man

> thinks he knows something when he does not, whereas I, as I
> do not know anything, do not think I do either. I seem, then,
> in just this one little thing to be wiser than this man at any
> rate, that what I do not know I do not think I know either
> (21 d).

The interpretation results when this insight into his own peculiar
wisdom is connected to the Delphic saying:

> It is likely that the god is really wise and by his oracle means
> this: "Human wisdom is of little or no worth" (23 a).

Socrates adds that in the saying the god uses him only as a
"paradigm." It is as if the god were to say that the wisest man is
the one who, like Socrates, recognizes how meager his wisdom is.
Thus, the saying of the oracle is finally interpreted as a pronouncement regarding the properly human condition. It is interpreted in
such a way that what it says comes to correspond with that
awareness which Socrates has of his ignorance, that very awareness
in defence of which Socrates initially opposed the god. The interpretation resolves that tension that belonged to the beginning of
Socrates' practice. It brings the terms of that tension into unity.

The interpretation brings a new situation. What is most obvious
about this new situation is that Socrates' practice ceases to be a
calling of Apollo's saying into question; his questioning of others
ceases to be a means by which to call the god himself into
question. However, this does not at all mean that through the
interpretation Socrates' practice loses its connection with Apollo
and his saying. On the contrary, it is only after Socrates has
accomplished the interpretation that the genuine connection
which his practice sustains with the god can become evident.
Whereas previously his practice was undertaken as a way of calling
the god's saying into question, this initial phase eventually proves
to have been, in fact, the way to the interpretation of the saying;
in light of this interpretation, Socrates can now himself say what
the oracle said; he can become the *spokesman* for the oracle, since
what it says is, granted the interpretation, identical with what
Socrates "knows." After the interpretation has been accomplished, Socrates' practice of questioning becomes explicitly what

it simultaneously proves to have been from the beginning: service to Apollo.[20]

To whom does this spokesman for the god speak? To whom does he address the interpreted saying? He addresses it, first of all, *to himself.* Having questioned the politicians, poets, and artisans, he says in reference to the latter:

> I asked myself in behalf of the oracle whether I should prefer to be as I am, neither wise in their wisdom nor ignorant in their ignorance, or to be in both respects as they are. I replied then to myself and to the oracle that it was better for me to be as I am (22 d – e).

Serving as the god's spokesman, Socrates delivers the oracle's question to himself, and he replies to himself and thus to the oracle for which he speaks. This is to say that Socratic *logos,* insofar as Socrates directs it to himself, is dedicated to the renewal of his awareness of ignorance and the correlative sense of proper limit—to the renewal of that on the basis of which Socrates was originally willing to oppose even the god himself, that which, however, turned out to be brought to light still more forcefully and significantly through the interpretation of the god's saying. As spokesman for the god, Socrates addresses himself in such a way as to re-enact the interpretation of the saying.

But Socrates is also Apollo's spokesman to other men, and his questioning of them, having ceased to be a way of calling the god into question, becomes something done in obedience to the god, in service to Apollo. What does Socrates say to men in the city? He says the same thing that Apollo said to him in that saying which he had to interpret, namely, that human wisdom has its

---

[20] The character of Socrates' practice as service to Apollo is even more explicit in Socrates' discussion with his friends in the *Phaedo:* speaking of the prophetic power which swans receive on the day of their death, he characterizes them as "Apollo's birds" and then describes himself as their fellow-servant devoted to the same god (84 e – 85 b). In this same connection it should be noted that when Socrates' friends arrive on the day of his death Socrates tells them that, among other things, he has been composing a prelude to Apollo (60 d). Furthermore, we learn at the very beginning of the *Phaedo* that Socrates' execution has been postponed because of the mission to Delos, which the Athenians send because of a vow once made to Apollo (58 a – b): even the date of Socrates' death is linked to Apollo, determined by service to Apollo.

proper limits and is meager in comparison with divine wisdom. However, for the most part, he does not "speak this out" but rather *shows* it through what he speaks out, i.e., by speaking with others in such a way that the meagerness of their wisdom is exhibited, made manifest. Socrates delivers the saying of the oracle to others by distinguishing in deed between seeming and being, by showing that what *seems* to be a more than human wisdom *is not* such. In this way Socrates' practice is an advocating, both to himself and to others, of the famous Delphic commandments, "Know thyself" and "Nothing in excess."

Socrates says:

> Therefore I am still even now going about and searching and investigating at the god's command anyone, whether citizen or foreigner, who I think is wise; and when he does not seem so to me, I give aid to the god and show that he is not wise. And by reason of this occupation I have no leisure to attend to any of the affairs of the city worth mentioning, or of my own, but am in vast poverty on account of my service to the god (23 b − c).

Socrates' practice is service to Apollo. One result of this practice is that it draws Socrates away from the affairs of the city, almost immediately making him suspect in the eyes of the men of the city. Another result is that this service, which consists in proclaiming both in *logos* and in *ergon* the poverty that is proper to man, has reduced Socrates to poverty. But that is just the question: what about the poverty of one who is dedicated to proclaiming the poverty of all men? What about Socratic poverty? What about the poverty of the philosopher?

Section 4. Socrates and the City (24 b − 42 a)

We have disengaged several senses pertaining to the determination of Socratic *logos*. First of all, Socratic *logos* was described as a *logos* which is distinctive by virtue of its dedication to truth; such dedication, in turn, appeared in the guise of a taking of a stand against letting things remain hidden. This preview was then elaborated in terms of the relation of *logos* to what Socrates describes as his second voyage in search of causes. Socrates tells how, having escaped the threat of blindness attendant upon the first voyage, that is, having awakened to that ignorance that permeates man's comportment with all things, he undertook a second voyage by having recourse to *logoi,* that is, took that way on which *logos* serves as way of access to beings. Finally, Socratic *logos* was thematized in terms of the way in which it was provoked by the saying of the Delphic oracle. As so provoked, Socratic *logos* was initiated as a way of questioning, of calling into question, the pronouncement sent from Apollo through the oracle. But eventually the very practice into which Socrates was provoked came to supply the basis for an interpretation of the god's pronouncement—an interpretation through which Socratic *logos* was then determined as pertaining to the service of Apollo.

Especially in the last of these determinations it is already evident that, regarded in its most immediate aspect, Socratic *logos* is pre-eminently something carried on *with other men in the city,* specifically as a questioning aimed primarily at making manifest the ignorance of the men of the city. In a sense this side of Socratic *logos* is almost the exclusive issue of the *Apology,* inasmuch as Socrates' peculiar way of questioning other men in the city is the root of those accusations now finally brought publicly against him. But Socrates defends himself by first telling the story of how that questioning which has provoked the accusations was itself provoked by the saying given through the oracle. Nevertheless, the story of the original provocation constitutes only the first of the three parts of Socrates' defence speech (which is itself the first of the three speeches comprising the *Apology* as a whole). By contrast, the second part of the defence speech (24 b — 28 a) involves a shift away from the "first false accusations" to the accusations actually being brought against Socrates in the trial and, correlatively, a shift away from the discussion of the provocative origin of Socrates' practice to its concrete, public character as a questioning of other men in the city. In the final main part of the defence speech (28 a — 34 b) Socrates then combines the perspectives of the first two parts; thereby he is able decisively to confront the accusations by presenting his practice as mediation between the god and the city.

(a) The Philosopher's Stand with respect to the City

Socrates has already succeeded in exposing in *logos* the ignorance and hatred behind the accusations actually being brought
against him in the trial. Now he turns to confront these accusations head-on. He begins by citing them explicitly: the charge is
that Socrates is guilty (ἀδικεῖν) of corrupting the youth and of not
acknowledging (οὐ νομίζοντα) the gods acknowledged by the city
but other strange daimons (ἕτερα δὲ δαιμόνια καινά).[21] Socrates
proceeds then to confront these accusations by confronting his accuser Meletus, by drawing Meletus into a dialogue
through which the ignorance and hatred behind the accusations
get exhibited not only in *logos* but also in *ergon.*

Socrates' questioning of Meletus is no less an exemplification of
the distinctively Socratic practice than was Socrates' response to
the "first false accusations." But, whereas in the previous section
Socrates' practice was exemplified primarily with respect to
Socrates' serving as spokesman for Apollo, his cross-examining of
Meletus exemplifies his practice primarily in its character as a
delivering of the oracle's saying to other men. This means that
Socrates' questioning of Meletus is directed especially towards
revealing the disparity between Meletus' claim to wisdom (implicit
in his making the accusations against Socrates) and his actual
condition. By involving Meletus in self-contradiction, by leading
him to admit more or less patent absurdities, and by repeatedly
forcing him into a position where he has no alternative but to take

---

[21] Regarding the meaning of "νομίζειν" in this context cf. above n. 8. Of the other
problems raised by this formulation, the most important has to do with the accusers' use of
"δαιμόνια." Hackforth suggests that they use here the plural of "δαιμόνιον," which was
never a substantive in classical Greek, because they wanted an unusual word which
would suggest both that the gods that Socrates believed in were no true gods and that τὸ
δαιμόνιον which Socrates was always talking about was the chief of them (*Composition
of Plato's Apology,* pp. 67-68). Cf. Burnet, pp. 102-106.

Xenophon discusses in some detail the more immediate, specific provocation behind
these accusations. Behind the accusation that Socrates corrupts the youth there were the
specific cases of Alcibiades and Critias, "companions of Socrates" who had "wrought the
greatest harm to the city" (*Memorabilia,* I. ii. 12). Also, according to Xenophon, what
led directly to the charge of impiety was Socrates' well-known claim to receive signs
from his daimon (*ibid.,* I. i. 2 − 3). This means that what is immediately at issue in the
charge is the daimon, and this is presumably why Socrates bases his refutation of the
accusation on his belief in the daimonic thing.

refuge in silence—by these means Socrates makes manifest the ignorance of Meletus that is behind the accusations. Perhaps most of all what Socrates exposes is Meletus' ignorance of his own ignorance, his ignorance of himself. Nevertheless, Socrates does not merely expose the ignorance but rather, in doing so, conducts a uniquely vehement attack on his respondent. In other words, Socrates brings his accusation against his accuser Meletus—the accusation that Meletus is hubristic (ὑβριστής) and unrestrained (ἀκόλαστος)—and gives force to that accusation by what he exposes with respect to Meletus.

Socrates' way of beginning his defence, his invoking of the old prejudices, already indicated that the accusations being brought against Socrates by Meletus are nothing more than explicit forms of the city's accusations against the philosopher. Having taken his stand against Meletus, it is then incumbent upon Socrates to open up the confrontation into one in which he takes his stand with respect to the city. The way in which he is to take this stand is indicated by a curious shift which Socrates introduces at the very end of his discussion with Meletus. In order to confront Meletus' charge of impiety, Socrates has been speaking at length about gods and daimons. But then, when in the last sentence he draws his explicit conclusion, he abruptly adds a third term: heroes (27 e – 28 a). When he then proceeds to a further defence against the old prejudices, what he, in effect, does is to pose an image of himself as a hero.

For example, he takes up the hypothetical question as to whether he is not ashamed for having followed a pursuit that now puts him in danger of death. To this question he answers that one should consider not the danger of death but only whether what one does is just or unjust. To the hypothetical poser of the question he says: "For according to what you say all the demigods would be fools who died at Troy, including the son of Thetis" (28 b - c). Having thus drawn Achilles, the paradigmatic hero, into his consideration, Socrates then proceeds to draw out explicitly the analogy between himself and such a hero as Achilles: a hero will never desert his station in battle (cf. *Laches* 28 d – e); and, just as Socrates would have done wrong had he not remained steadfastly at his station in battle at Potidaea, at Amphipolis, and at Delium, so likewise should he now desert, for fear of death, the station assigned to him by the god (28 d − 29 a). Given his stand by the god, Socrates is bound to take and to maintain that stand in relation to the city—whatever the consequences.

Socrates' stand with respect to the city is characterized by a fundamental ambivalence. On the one hand, Socrates belongs to the city: he was born, nurtured, and educated in the city, and more than any other Athenian he has remained in the city, thereby ratifying to the utmost his implicit agreement to abide by the laws of the city (cf. *Crito* 50 d − 52 d; *Meno* 80 b); and only in his own city can he really engage in his distinctive practice (*Apol.* 37 c − d). More importantly, Socrates is, according to the account which he gives to the "men of Athens," *Apollo's gift to the city* (30 d − e), who as gift of the god takes no pay from his pupils and is reduced to poverty. Socrates is the one who speaks *to* the city *for* Apollo, who delivers the god's sign to the city in such a way as to perform for the city that service described in the famous analogy which Socrates draws between himself and a gadfly.

But Socrates is not simply given over to the city; rather, as gift to the city, he retains his connection to the one who gives, i.e., to the god himself. In other words, precisely because of his peculiar way of belonging to the city, he is in a sense always also outside the city. Though he rarely travels beyond the walls of Athens (in a literal sense), he is, nevertheless, always beyond the city by virtue of the fact that his very relation to the city is prescribed primarily by something which transcends the city. Socrates' way of being in the city (as gadfly), his specific mode of comportment to the men in the city (questioning), is not determined by the city nor by Socrates' "genetic" bond to the city; it is determined, rather, by something which transcends the walls of Athens and of every particular city. Socrates' speaking to the city is determined by Apollo's speaking to Socrates.

At a more concrete level, Socrates' exclusion, his aloofness, from the city is portrayed in the fact that he has never engaged in public affairs beyond what was mandatory for a citizen. In explaining to the "men of Athens" this public reticence, which contrasts so thoroughly with his private loquacity, Socrates refers to two things that have restrained him from entering public life. The first is that very daimon—that "voice" (φωνή) as he now calls it— which was ridiculed in the charge brought by Meletus but then, as it were, turned against Meletus in Socrates' questioning of him. This voice, Socrates now insists, has always held him back from entering public life (31 c – d). In light of Socrates' stress (in his earlier discussion with Meletus) on the connection between gods and daimons, we are presumably to understand that what speaks to Socrates through this restraining voice is just the god himself (cf. 33 c), so that it would be Apollo himself, Socrates' master beyond the city, who holds Socrates aloof from the city. Second- ly, Socrates tells the "men of Athens" quite frankly that, if he had engaged in politics, he would have been put to death long ago and would have done no good to anyone: "A man who really fights for what is just, if he is to preserve his life for even a little while, must be a private citizen, not a public man" (32 a). Socrates cites as proof in deed the case of the ten generals in the handling of which he opposed the illegal procedure of trying them all together, despite the fact that he was barraged with shouts and threatened with arrest and imprisonment.[22] Also he refers to the incident in which the Thirty ordered him and four others to bring Leon the Salaminian from Salamis to be put to death; the other four went to Salamis and arrested Leon, but Socrates simply went home and would perhaps himself have been put to death had the government not been quickly put down (32 a – e). What these incidents indicate is the intrinsic tension between philosophy and politics. This tension, the measure of which is taken in the *Republic,* is, in the *Apology,* gone through in deed in the confrontation between Socrates and his accusers and would-be judges.

But there is tension and discord not only between philosophy and politics but also, more generally, between philosophy and the city as such—to such an extent, in fact, that the city, not just the politicians, brings Socrates to trial. In this connection the *Apology* presents a situation which curiously mirrors just that conflict with which, according to his story, Socrates' practice began: Socrates, the gift of Apollo to the city, has been called into question by the

---

[22] Cf. Xenophon, *Memorabilia,* I. i. 18; and Burnet's historical notes, pp. 133 ff.

city and accusations brought against him, just as the gift which Chaerephon brought from Apollo (the saying) was called into question by Socrates and charged with being false. And just as there had to be an interpretation of the saying for Socrates, so there is now need of an interpretation of Socrates' practice for the men of the city. But in both cases it is Socrates himself who has to serve as interpreter. The fact that he succeeds in interpreting for himself the god's pronouncement, thereby resolving the initial tension, serves, however, to make still more obtrusive his failure in the other case—or, rather, the failure of the "men of Athens" to appropriate the interpretation. Because of the way the philosopher appears to the city, because this way could not be brought to coincidence with Socrates' interpretation of himself as gift of Apollo, Socrates was condemned.

(b) How the Philosopher Appears to the City

Provoked by Apollo, Socrates' practice, in turn, provokes the "men of Athens" to send Socrates to his death. The latter provocation rests upon the way the philosopher appears to the men of the city. This way of appearing, the composite image, is composed both from the old prejudices already operative before the trial and from the way that Socrates' bearing during the trial (the bearing which he insists is prescribed by his practice) appears to his would-be judges.

We have seen that early in his defence speech Socrates indicates how his practice of questioning the men of the city has provoked those same men to stir up prejudices and eventually to bring accusations against him. Taking it upon himself to serve as Apollo's spokesman, Socrates destroys men's claims to wisdom, exposes their ignorance. But only to the extent that these same men, by being made to encounter their ignorance, come to the insight that ignorance and especially awareness of ignorance pertain essentially to an appropriately human wisdom—only to this extent can they see in that practice, which Socrates claims is service to the god, anything other than a sheerly destructive intent by one who would make himself appear superior at their expense.

And to those men of the city who have gained no insight into the relation of ignorance to human wisdom, Socrates' own profession of ignorance can appear only as a technique, especially as a kind of dissimulation used for drawing other men out in order then to be able easily to refute them.

By his own testimony, Socrates is dedicated to incessant questioning. To those "men of Athens" who fall short of a genuine awakening to their own ignorance and to the place of ignorance in human wisdom, the force of that questioning with which Socrates confronts them can appear only as an expression of arrogance and of contempt for others. This is the case not only for those relatively private conversations which Socrates has held over the years with the men in the city and which have provoked the old prejudices against him; it holds perhaps even more for the defence speech itself in which Socrates is forced to accommodate his speech to an inappropriate public form. Presuming to judge the would-be judges— and, at least to that extent, Athens itself [23] — Socrates comports himself in a way which, though prescribed by his very dedication to his practice, can hardly fail to appear to men of the city as arrogant.[24] The occurrences of such an appearance are especially marked by the way in which Socrates' defence speech is punctuated by noisy disturbances in the court. The points at which these outbursts occur are indicative of those elements in Socrates' speech which most provoke the "men of Athens." There is such a disturbance, for example, where Socrates first draws the distinction between human wisdom and greater than human wisdom and insists that anyone who attributes to him the latter is lying (20 e); but the accusations constitute precisely such a kind of attribution, and Socrates is, in effect, charging his accusers with perjury. Again, there is a disturbance at just that point at which Socrates is about to report the question which Chaerephon put to the Delphic oracle and the response which he was given (21 a): to the majority of the "men of Athens" Socrates

---

[23] Ballard develops the issue in this direction by showing how Socrates' actions in his trial and afterwards serve to make manifest in the most effective way possible a disparity in the city analogous to that which Socrates had previously been dedicated to uncovering in individual men. *Socratic Ignorance*, pp. 15 ff.

[24] Cf. Meyer, *Platons Apologie*, p. 17.

appears as one who proclaims that he was proclaimed by the god to be the wisest of men. Finally, there is an outburst just after Socrates has told the "men of Athens" that "no greater good ever came to pass in the city than my service to the god" (30 a − c).

Again, Socrates' peculiar comportment, dangerous to himself, arrogant in the eyes of the many, is evident in the short epilogue to his defence speech (34 b − 36 d). Having indicated that he has finished his defence (i.e., that what follows does not belong to his defence), Socrates then goes on to say that he will not bring his children and relatives into court so as to beg for acquittal from the "men of Athens." He openly expresses his reason for foregoing this customary kind of appeal: it is not the duty of a judge to grant favors but rather to give judgment; Socrates adds that, should he follow this customary practice, hence, in effect, attempting to persuade the "men of Athens" to break their oaths, then he would, in fact, be proving himself guilty of that accusation of impiety against which he has attempted to defend himself. But how does this Socratic abstinence appear to the "men of Athens"? Not only does Socrates refuse to humble himself to the extent of begging for acquittal but also, at this extremely crucial juncture in the trial, he takes it upon himself to tell those who are claiming to judge him what their duty is as judges. Likewise, in his final speech Socrates explicitly passes judgment on the judges—i.e., he judges which of them are really judges (40 a)—and, speaking to those who voted against him, he says of his accusers: "And now I shall go away convicted by you and sentenced to death, and they go convicted by truth of villainy and wrong-doing" (39 b). But the one who has in deed carried through this conviction of the accusers, the one who has judged them in the name of truth, the one who from the very outset characterized his speech by its dedication to truth, is Socrates himself.

In the last part of his last speech in the *Apology* Socrates again takes up, without explicitly noting the fact, the analogy posed earlier between himself and the hero of heroes, Achilles. But now Socrates, having maintained his heroic stance, calls into question the word of the Homeric hero, specifically, his word about Hades. Speaking of those in Hades, Socrates says: "If what we are told is true, they are immortal for all future time, besides being happier in other respects than men are here" (41 c). By whom are we told this? Perhaps by Socrates? Certainly not by Achilles. For when Odysseus goes to Hades what he hears from the soul of Achilles is the following:

> Nay, seek not to speak soothingly to me of death, glorious Odysseus. I would rather be on the soil, a serf to another, to a man without lot whose means of life are not great, than rule over all the dead who have perished.[25]

To the majority of the "men of Athens," to those lacking the proper virtue of the judge, to those for whom the way of Socratic *logos* remains inaccessible, Socrates appears in such a negatively provocative guise that, denied other effective alternatives by Socrates himself, they sentence him to death. It is appropriate that the *Apology* concludes with a final testimony to Socratic ignorance and to divine wisdom:

> But now the time has come to go away. I go to die, and you to live; but which of us goes to the better lot, is known to none but the god (42 a).

---

[25] *Odyssey*, XI. 488 – 491.

CHAPTER II

IGNORANCE AND RECOLLECTION:

MENO

The *Meno* is a concrete presentation of that side of Socrates' practice by which he is attached to the city. Socrates, the gift of Apollo to the city, performs his distinctive service to the city primarily through his involvement with ignorance. In its most obvious form this involvement with ignorance amounts to an *exposing* of men's ignorance and pre-eminently of their ignorance of their ignorance. Correspondingly, the *Meno* is a presentation of an exposing of Meno's ignorance carried out by Socrates in speech and in deed. Inasmuch as precisely this aspect of his practice, his function as gadfly, is what most of all was to provoke his eventual condemnation, it is highly appropriate that in the *Meno* not only is Socrates accused of stinging those with whom he comes into contact (though, significantly, as a "sting ray" rather than a "gadfly") but also near the end of the dialogue one of those who was later to accuse him publicly (Anytus) appears on the scene and openly warns Socrates of the danger to which he is exposing himself by his practice (94 e). Yet, Socrates' practice in the city, his involvement with ignorance, is an exposing of the ignorance of others not for the sake of exalting himself but rather for the sake of making concretely manifest how ignorance and especially awareness of that ignorance belong essentially to appropriately human wisdom. Socrates' practice in the city is a testimony to the intrinsic relation of ignorance to human wisdom. One way—a mythical way—of speaking about this relation is by regarding human wisdom as bound to recollection. This is the way taken in the *Meno.*

In its most fundamental and unitary form the matter that is at

64

issue in the *Meno* is the *relation between whole and parts;* indeed a considerable part of our interpretive effort will be devoted to considering how this unitary matter gathers up into itself the many themes taken up in the course of the dialogue. With regard to this matter the *Meno* especially brings to light the appropriate comportment of man as one of mediating between part and whole; it exhibits such mediating as that which enables man to be what he properly is. Since that which allows man to be what he properly is constitutes nothing less than human virtue itself (ἀρετή: cf. *Rep.* 353 b — e), what the dialogue brings to light is virtue. The *Meno* is in a fundamental yet manifold sense a dialogue on virtue.

In order to accord with our preliminary determination of the way of Platonic dialogue as such (cf. Introduction, Sect. 3), it is imperative that our interpretive attempt be attuned from the outset to the manifold dimensions of the *Meno* and to the interplay which unfolds in the dialogue as a whole. We need especially to see how the question of whole and parts is fundamental in each of the dimensions of the dialogue—how it is taken up in *logos* and posed in such fashion as to gather into unity the various themes explicitly discussed, how it is the most fundamental issue in that myth which Socrates relates at the center of the dialogue, and, finally, how it is taken up in the dimension of *ergon* by being reflected in what is exhibited about the characters of the dialogue.

Section 1. Meno (70 a — 79 e)

(a) Who Is Meno? (70 a — 71 d)

The problem of whole and parts as a problem of human mediation is posed abruptly in the discussion with which the *Meno* commences. Meno asks how virtue is acquired, whether by teaching, by practice, by nature, or by some other means. Socrates ironically praises Meno's countrymen, contrasting the situation in Thessaly with the dearth of wisdom in Athens, and then responds to Meno's question *by calling it into question.* Socrates' response is cast in terms of the problem of whole and parts, specifically, in terms of the relation between a property and that to which it pertains:

> I share the poverty of my fellow countrymen in this respect and confess to my shame that I have no knowledge about virtue at all. And how can I know a property of something when I do not even know what it is? [ὁ δὲ μὴ οἶδα τί ἐστι, πῶς ἂν ὁποῖόν γέ τι εἰδείην;] Do you suppose that somebody entirely ignorant who Meno is could say whether he is handsome and rich and wellborn or the reverse? Is that possible, do you think? (71 b).

Meno's answer is an unqualified negative, which serves to exhibit how meager Meno's grasp of the question really is.[1] Clearly, this answer, suggested already in Socrates' way of posing the question, is by no means so self-evident as Meno takes it to be, for one could, in some sense, know—for instance, by way of a report—that there is a Thessalian named Meno who is handsome, rich, and wellborn without knowing who Meno is either in the sense of being able to recognize this man Meno by his appearance or in the sense of knowing some basic feature definitive of who he is.[2] In fact, the entire dialogue constitutes a testimony *against* the apparent self-evidence of Meno's answer by showing that Meno himself, though, indeed, all too aware of being handsome, rich, and wellborn, does not know who he is. This is the question especially of the first half of the dialogue in the dimension of *ergon,* and we see how at the very beginning this question, "Who is Meno?," not only is posed but also is more or less explicitly linked to the problem of whole and parts in such a way as to suggest that Meno is one who is oblivious to this issue.

This suggestion is intensified and specified in two additional terms of the dialogue introduced in the opening exchange. When

---

[1] This same priority of the question "What is virtue?" over the question "How is virtue acquired?" is stated, though more tentatively, by Socrates in the *Protagoras* (361 a – c). This statement occurs, however, not at the beginning (as in the *Meno*) but only at the very end of the dialogue where it serves to thematize something brought to light by the actual course of the dialogue itself culminating in the curious exchange of positions by Socrates and Protagoras.

[2] Cf. Walter Bröcker, *Platos Gespräche* (Frankfort a.M.: Vittorio Klostermann, 1967), pp. 110-111.

Meno expresses surprise over Socrates' admission that he does not know what virtue is, Socrates insists that he has, to the best of his belief, "never yet met anyone who did know" (71 c) and hints that Meno, in particular, does not know. With this remark Socrates anticipates the answer which the dialogue will give to the question as to who Meno is: What basically characterizes Meno is ignorance and, most of all, an ignorance of his ignorance.[3] Meno, as one who is ignorant, does not know who Meno is—though, indeed, he knows that he is handsome, rich, and wellborn. Meno, as one who is ignorant of self, who is ignorant of his ignorance, does not even know what question is to be posed.

The second additional term is introduced when Meno, expressing his surprise at Socrates' admission of ignorance regarding what virtue is, asks him whether he did not have occasion to meet Gorgias when the latter paid his visit to Athens and whether he did not think that Gorgias knew what virtue is. Socrates replies:

> I have not a good memory, Meno, and I cannot say just now what I thought at the time. Probably he did know, and I expect you know what he used to say about it. So remind me what it was, or tell me yourself if you will. No doubt you agree with him (71 c – d).

What is significant in this answer is the contrast which Socrates draws between his own memory and that of Meno. Meno is one who remembers what is said, what Gorgias said; he is one who remembers words, and his opinion is a function of this remembering. Socrates, on the other hand, is prone to forget the words he has heard.[4] The distinction between Socrates and Meno (the

---

[3] That what is distinctive about Meno's ignorance lies in the fact that it incorporates an ignorance of his ignorance is suggested by a comment which Socrates addresses to Meno: Gorgias, Socrates says, "got you into the habit of answering any question you might be asked with the confidence and dignity appropriate to those who know the answers" (70 c). In the *Sophist* (229 c) the Stranger refers to such ignorance as "supposing [δοκεῖν] that one knows a thing when one does not know it"; he adds: "Through this, I believe, all the errors of thought are caused in all of us." Cf. *Laws* 863 c, 731 e – 732 b.

[4] See Socrates' remark in the *Protagoras* (334 c – d) about his being forgetful; also Alcibiades' comment at 336 d. It must be noted, however, that the relation between Socrates and Protagoras is by no means one involving such sheer opposition as we find in the *Meno*. This is especially apparent at the end of the *Protagoras* (361 a – b).

ignorant one) is, thus, posed as a radical difference between their memories, and it is suggested that Meno's ignorance is somehow linked to his peculiar kind of memory. The irony inherent in Socrates' posing the difference in a form which makes Meno appear superior is readily evident, for that forgetting of words, which is characteristic of Socrates, is by no means necessarily negative but is, on the contrary, equally capable of being a forgetting exercised precisely in the interest of a recalling of what is spoken about in the words.[5] Compared to the latter, Meno's memory, a memory which clings to words, appears as constituting a defect and a source of ignorance.[6]

Thus, in the opening exchange three terms are introduced that bear upon the question as to who Meno is. These terms are: ignorance (self-ignorance), memory (of words), and the problem of whole and parts (as a problem of mediation). It remains to be seen how the dialogue collects these terms into a whole.

(b) Whole and Parts (71 e – 74 b)

Meno offers three successive answers to the question "What is virtue?" In examining these it is imperative that we avoid assuming in advance that we know in general what constitutes an appropriate answer to this kind of question. If such answers are to be designated as "definitions," we must take care that this translation does not cover over the issue of the questioning and substitute for it the presumptive self-evidence of a traditional word. Such care is necessary inasmuch as the search for an answer to the question "What is virtue?" is at the same time a determination regarding what kind of speaking ($\lambda\acute{\epsilon}\gamma\epsilon\iota\nu$: cf. 76 a, b, 77 b, 78 b; $\epsilon\acute{\iota}\pi\epsilon\hat{\iota}\nu$: cf.

---

[5] Cf. esp. *Crat.* 439 a – b. Almost all of Part Two bears on this issue.

[6] Klein has pointed out (*Commentary,* pp. 43-46) the appropriateness of the name "Meno," which means literally "stay as before" or "stay put." In the course of the dialogue Meno proves to be one who does just this, who stays put in his ignorance, who is incapable of learning. Klein discusses also the significance of Socrates' statement, "I have not a good memory, Meno, . . . [Οὐ πάνυ εἰμὶ μνήμων, ὦ Μένων, . . .]," pointing to the fact that the words "μνήμων, ὦ Μένων" form a kind of jingle which highlights the fact that Meno's name (Μένων) is a deranged form of the word "remembering" (μνήμων), which stems from the word "memory" (μνήμη). This is taken to suggest a derangement of Meno's memory.

76 d) is constitutive of an appropriate response to such questioning.

According to Meno's first answer, the virtue of a man consists in managing the city's affairs capably, while the virtue of a woman consists in properly conducting her household. Meno adds, without specifying them, that there is another virtue for a child, another for an old man, another for a slave, etc. (71 e − 72 a). Socrates immediately poses his objection: Meno has presented him with a swarm of virtues whereas he asked only for one; and Meno has failed to present precisely that one virtue for which Socrates asked—he has failed to present the one in which all members of the swarm are the same, the being (οὐσία), the *eidos,* which makes all of them to be virtues. Meno has presented the many rather than the one in which they belong together; he has presented only the parts of virtue, not the whole. And, Socrates observes, it is the one, the whole, which "ought to be kept in view by anyone who answers the question 'What is virtue?'" (72 c − d). An appropriate answering must somehow proceed in relation to a condition in which the whole is held in view.

There follows a protracted explanation (72 a − 73 c) by Socrates of his seemingly straightforward objection and of what is sought in answer to the question, "What is virtue?"—an explanation which, if regarded only in terms of such intent, appears almost tedious and out of keeping with Plato's usual dramatic economy, even if it is granted that the need which Socrates presumably sees for such explanation serves to underscore Meno's ignorance, to stress that he not only has no answer but fails entirely to understand what is asked for in the question. In its full intent, however, the explanation is not a mere repetition of Socrates' objection to Meno's answer but, on the contrary, a development of that objection—that is, a development of the problem of whole and parts. What Socrates, in effect, shows is that, in spite of this objection that Meno provided only a swarm of virtues, there is, in fact, readily evident in this swarm a certain unity. Socrates proceeds to collect the swarm into its unity: in the only two cases which Meno explained, the virtue of a man and that of a woman, virtue was presented as a matter of properly directing or governing whatever it is appropriate for the person to direct in view of his particular station. In more general terms it is a matter of the proper practice of one's art (τέχνη)—though Socrates is quick to add that such practice requires moderation and justice, that it requires certain virtues. The obvious difficulty here, the same difficulty which Socrates turns against Meno in the latter's next definition—namely that virtue is being defined in terms of virtues—does not, however, entirely veil the definition which Socrates is suggesting: that virtue has to do with the pre-condition for the proper practice of any art.[7] But Meno was oblivious to the question and to the whole for which it asked; he saw only the parts, and only now that the whole has been brought into view by Socrates can he venture the attempt to define virtue as a whole. Yet, in bringing this whole into view Socrates has been reticent to a degree sufficient to allow him to remain with the task of evoking from Meno a sense for the question and sufficient to permit Meno the illusion that the subsequent definition is his own.

Indeed, in a sense it is his own. Virtue, he now says, is "simply the capacity to govern men" (73 c). Again Socrates objects—again in essentially the same terms. He asks whether virtue, so defined, applies to a child or to a slave; the point is, of course, that virtue pertains to the practice of any art, not just to the art of the ruler as Meno has implicitly assumed. Meno's second answer, though formulated as a definition of the whole, captures at best only a part; in place of that whole which Socrates brought into view it substitutes a part. For Meno the whole is still not in view in the appropriate way even though in a sense his answer is, by means of Socrates' prelude to it, directed towards the whole. It is in one sense, however, even inferior to the first definition which, though it too delivered only parts, did not in its way of formulation lay claim to grasping the whole and which, therefore, at least escaped that blatant disparity between what is claimed and what is actually accomplished that characterizes Meno's second answer.

Socrates proceeds immediately to bring another objection to bear on Meno's definition of virtue as the capacity to govern men: he insists that one must add to this statement the qualification "justly but not otherwise"—that, in other words, the activity of

---

[7] On the relation of virtue to art see especially Ballard, *Socratic Ignorance*, Ch. III.

governing men is virtuous only if it is itself governed (cf. *Gorgias* 491 d). Meno agrees to this qualification on the ground that "justice is virtue" (73 d), to which Socrates retorts that justice is not virtue but rather a virtue alongside others such as wisdom, courage, and moderation. The outcome is, therefore, that the discussion has led to the same problem encountered in the case of Meno's first answer; it has led to the discovery of several virtues rather than virtue itself, of parts rather than the whole.[8]

Just prior to Meno's third answer to the question "What is virtue?" Socrates urges Meno to "stop making many out of one, as the humorists say when somebody breaks a plate." He adds, "Just leave virtue whole and sound and tell me what it is . . . " (77 a). Here Socrates makes it explicit that it is the problem of whole and parts which is the source of the difficulty involved in both of the answers which Meno has given. In both cases Meno has delivered only parts of virtue, not the whole for which Socrates asked, although, indeed, as Socrates suggests without elaborating, there is a difference between the kind of parts yielded by the two attempts to answer the question (74 a). Whereas the first answer presented virtue strictly in reference to those individuals whose virtue it would, in each case, be (largely, but not exclusively, in function of the art practiced by each)—the second answer (as made evident in Socrates' second objection to it) yielded parts of virtue not in this sense but in the sense of the various virtues (such as justice, moderation, courage); in the latter case the partition of virtue is not a partition with respect to individual men or groups of men.

(c) *Logos* and the Whole (74 b – 77 b)

In the interim between Meno's second and his final answer to the question "What is virtue?" Socrates gives, at Meno's insistence, a definition of shape (σχῆμα) purportedly to illustrate to Meno what is required in the case of the question regarding virtue.

---

[8] It should be observed that in the *Protagoras* (329 d – e) the problem of the relation of the virtues to virtue itself is explicitly posed as a problem of the relation of part to whole.

Shape, he says, is "the only thing which always accompanies color" (75 b). Meno, however, immediately objects that this is a simple-minded answer, since it presupposes that one know already what color is. Socrates, not without irony, abandons his statement and proceeds to establish Meno's explicit agreement with some new terms which are then incorporated into a definition of shape as "that in which solid terminates." To this statement—that shape is "the limit of solid"—Meno makes no objection but, instead, insists that Socrates now state what color is; such a statement is, according to Meno's objection, required for the completion of Socrates' earlier statement that shape is that which always accompanies color. Socrates responds by sketching a curious image of Meno as a tyrant,[9] and then, alluding to Empedocles' theory of effluences, he proceeds to define color as "an effluence from shapes commensurate with sight and perceptible by it" (76 d).

In this exchange there are two principal points that bear upon the problem of whole and parts and upon the question regarding what is appropriate to any response to the kind of questions being posed in the dialogue. First, it is to be noted that Meno enthusiastically endorses Socrates' statement about color: "That seems to me an excellent answer"; and that Socrates responds to this endorsement with the words, "No doubt it is the sort you are used to." What Socrates is suggesting is that Meno gives the definition his approval not because he understands it but rather only because it sounds familiar to him, only because he hears in it the echo of something already imprinted on his memory. Socrates observes, further, that Meno could probably make use of the pattern provided by the definition for the purpose of defining many other things such as sound and smell—that, in other words, Meno is one

---

[9] Socrates says (76 b): "Anyone talking to you could tell blindfold that you are a handsome man and still have your admirers." Meno asks: "Why so?" Socrates answers: "Because you are forever laying down the law as spoiled boys do, who act the tyrant as long as their youth lasts."

Meno is thus characterized by the image of the tyrant. Yet, a tyrant is precisely the worst kind of ruler, the one least capable of governing men. Hence, the image expresses the incongruity between Meno and his definition of virtue; Meno is not virtuous even by his own definition. Furthermore, the only capacity which Meno has for governing is derived from his youthful good looks, from what is proverbially transitory in contrast to knowledge which Socrates later describes (98 a) as "tied down" so that it does not sneak away.

who answers all questions by indiscriminantly applying a pattern committed to memory. Meno is one who uncritically transfers what is appropriate for one part to any other part and thereby betrays that he is blind to the whole within which each part has its distinctive locus, which, in turn, prescribes its relation to the other relevant parts. It is significant that Socrates, in contrast to Meno's enthusiasm for the definition of color, expresses his own conviction that the first definition of shape (as the only thing which always accompanies color) is, in fact, the best of his three statements. Not only is Socrates suggesting that this statement, by correlating shape and color, hints at an answer concerning virtue, i.e., that it is correlated with knowledge[10] —not only is he pointing to an instance in which the application of a pattern would be highly appropriate; he is also hinting that the first definition operated within a more appropriate purview of the whole.

The involvement of the problem of whole and parts in the question of definition is especially brought to light in connection with one of the terms, or cluster of terms, to which Socrates gets Meno to agree prior to the second definition of shape. Socrates says:

> Tell me, therefore, whether you recognize the term "end" [τελευτή]; I mean limit [πέρας] or boundary [ἔσχατον] —all these words I use in the same sense. Prodicus might perhaps quarrel with us, but I assume you speak of something being bound or coming to an end. That is all I mean, nothing subtle (75 d − e).

Of course, Socrates is being subtle and in his irony even being subtle about his sublety. It is, indeed, not a matter of subtle distinctions such as might be drawn between the three terms introduced. On the contrary, the sublety lies in the fact that these words are not simply terms which Socrates requires for the subsequently formulated definition of shape; more importantly, they are words which, in what they all more or less express, bear decisively upon the character of genuine definition. In contrast to the conception which Meno betrays in his objection to the defini-

---

[10] Klein, *Commentary*, p. 70.

tion of shape in terms of color and in his insistence, even later, that color be defined, Socrates is pointing to the fact that genuine definition does not consist in a regress, in principle unlimited, to ever new words which, in turn, would have always to be defined; rather, in definition there is a limit, a bound, a coming to an end. That *logos* which is called for by such a question as "What is virtue?" does not simply terminate in *logos*—which would be tantamount to saying that it never terminates except arbitrarily. But then the problem is: What is that in which such *logos* comes to its end? What is it that limits a definition? The complexity of the problem—sufficient to forestall any all-too-easy answers—is evident in the fact that this very question is an instance of that kind of question the appropriate kind of response to which is at issue in the question itself. Nevertheless, the course of the *Meno* thus far has clearly served to refer this problem to that of the whole and to suggest that the limit of such *logos* is the whole. This remains almost entirely unthematized; but it serves to let the myth of recollection appear on the horizon.

The same point can be seen in the relation between Socrates' definitions. Socrates defines shape in terms of color, and, once Meno objects that this definition presupposes that one know what color is, Socrates abandons the definition for the sake of one more congenial to Meno. Yet, when Meno still insists upon hearing the definition of color, Socrates obliges with the statement, "color is an effluence from shapes commensurate with sight and perceptible by it"—that is, Socrates defines color *in terms of shape.* Socrates, in other words, completes the circle thereby testifying again that definition is not properly a regress to ever new words. But Socrates remains mostly silent about the issue behind this whole apparent digression, for the circle which he has traced out can be instructive only because it retraces what is already traced out in the relevant whole with a view to which definition needs to proceed. One like Meno who is oblivious to the whole is not only unable to provide an adequate definition but is also incapable even of seeing that defining is as such problematic; much less is he able to come to grips with that problematic. Meno is blind to the questionableness that accrues to all questioning, and this is why Socrates' response to Meno's very first question—namely to question it—was so highly appropriate. Meno remains ignorant of questioning as such and testifies that he is bound—perhaps hopelessly—to an ignorance of ignorance.

(d) Memory and the Whole (77 b — 79 e)

Meno's final definition is drawn from his memory. He quotes an unnamed poet and then states his own definition as a paraphrase of what was said by the poet: Virtue is "desiring fine things and being able to acquire them" (77 b). This definition reaffirms dramatically what was already suggested at the beginning of the dialogue—that what distinguishes Meno is his memory; and the course of Socrates' refutation of this definition is such as to bring Meno's memory into connection with the problem of whole and parts. Socrates easily dismisses the first conjunct of the definition (desire of fine things): he simply points out that, in fact, this conjunct distinguishes nothing since all men desire fine, i.e., good, things—that, consequently, the pursuit of evil is always the result of ignorance as to what is good (77 b — 78 b). To this conjunct, which says nothing, Socrates, thus, replies by pointing to what does need to be said about virtue: that and how it is linked to knowledge. With respect to the second conjunct (being able to acquire fine things) Socrates, on the other hand, grants that Meno "may well be right" (78 c), but, when Meno removes all doubt as to what he means by fine or good things by identifying them with wealth and high office in the city, Socrates renews the objection used against the second definition: in order to be virtuous such acquisition must be accompanied by justice, moderation, piety, or some other part of virtue. The discussion is, thus, brought back again to the same point as before: "The point I want to make is that whereas I asked you to give me an account of virtue as a whole, far from telling me what it is itself you say that every action is virtue which exhibits a part of virtue . . ." (79 b). Hence, Socrates again poses the question: "Does anyone know what a part of virtue is without knowing the whole?" (79 c). The outcome is that Meno's definition has again been led back to the problem of whole and parts; and in this case it has been done in such fashion as to suggest, more specifically, that the kind of memory which distinguishes Meno is insufficient for bringing the whole into view. One suspects that even in the earlier definitions, which Meno put forth in his own name, Meno's obliviousness to the whole was tied to an exercise of his peculiar kind of memory—that, in fact, as the opening exchange suggested, Meno is only repeating what he has heard Gorgias say.

Socrates adds an exhortation to Meno to avoid answering the question about the whole in terms of the parts of the unknown whole, since, as he says, "I believe we rejected the type of answer that employs terms which are still in question and not yet agreed upon" (79 d). However, Socrates has *not rejected* this type of answer but only shown in each case that it is this type of answer that Meno is proposing and posed the *question* of its appropriateness. It is rather Meno who rejects this kind of answer; and, when he attacks Socrates for giving such a type of answer (Socrates' first definition of shape), Socrates' subsequent procedure, namely his completion of the circle as well as his expression of his preference for the definition which is guilty of what Meno charges, indicates beyond doubt that it is *only* Meno and not Socrates who rejects this kind of answer. Socrates' ironic exhortation to Meno serves, not to express a conclusion or an abiding principle, but rather to exhibit the difference which is about to be brought explicitly to light in the conflict between the paradox posed by Meno and the story about recollection told by Socrates.

Section 2.   Meno and Socrates (79 e — 86 d)

(a) Meno's Paradox (79 e — 81 a)

Meno is utterly perplexed, but his response is to draw an image of Socrates rather than of himself: Socrates, he says, is like the flat sting ray which numbs whoever comes into contact with it (80 a). Socrates' answer, that if he paralizes others it is because he is himself paralyzed, is prefaced by his observation that Meno has drawn this image of him in order to incite him to paint a pretty picture of Meno in return. Socrates insists, however, that he will not oblige Meno in this respect (80 c); and, indeed, it is entirely unnecessary for Socrates to draw an image of Meno, for Socrates' questioning has served already to elicit from Meno himself just such an image. Meno is one who is characterized by ignorance, an ignorance which is linked to his peculiar kind of memory and which is manifest in two respects, as ignorance of self (specifically, of his own ignorance) and as ignorance of wholes. This image is now to be thrown into bold relief in the paradox which Meno proceeds to pose. There is no need for Socrates to draw the image.

Meno says:

> But how will you look for something when you do not in the least know what it is? How on earth are you going to set up something you do not know as the object of your search? To put it another way, even if you come right up against it, how will you know that what you have found is the thing you did not know? (80 d).

Socrates restates the paradox expanding it into an explicit denial of the possibility of inquiring or learning: one cannot learn what he already knows nor, if Meno is right, what he does not know.

It is significant that Socrates introduces this restatement by two comments: he says, first, "I know what you mean" and then he asks, "Do you realize that what you are bringing up is the eristic argument . . . " (80 e). He suggests thereby that the paradox is a standard sophistical puzzle merely stored up in Meno's memory and that Meno completely fails to realize what an immense issue he is raising. That the paradox has its source in that complex of ignorance and memory that constitutes Meno is highlighted by his very statement of the paradox, which amounts to a claim to have learned, on the basis of what has been stated, that learning is impossible.[11]   After all, he claimed at the beginning of the dialogue to have learned from Gorgias what virtue is, and, hence, he granted the possibility of learning; if he now knows that learning is impossible he must have learned this since the beginning of the

---

[11] Cf. Jerome Eckstein, *The Platonic Method: An Interpretation of the Dramatic-Philosophic Aspects of the Meno* (New York: Greenwood Publishing Corp., 1968), p. 30.

dialogue. But Meno is oblivious to this conflict between what he says and his saying of it. He is ignorant of the ignorance which is prescribed by the paradox and which renders the discovery, if not the statement, of the paradox impossible. The question of the coherence of what is said with the saying of it and the one who says it entirely escapes Meno.

The paradox is related to Meno's immediately preceding comparison of Socrates with a sting ray. Whatever Socrates' effect may be on those whom he questions, this paradox would definitely produce paralysis in anyone who accepted it.[12] It would not, as does Socrates' questioning, lead to an awareness of ignorance (as evidenced in Meno's very statement of the conflict) but would rather constitute an excuse for ignorance; it would not lead through the awareness of ignorance to genuine inquiry but would rather put an end to all inquiry so that one would, as the name "Meno" says and the character Meno does, stay as before. So, Meno is, in fact, the sting ray, and Meno is just the one who stays as before. His incapacity throughout the dialogue thus far to engage in inquiry is in perfect agreement with the consequence of his paradox. The paradox presents in the order of *logos* what has been portrayed in the exhibition accomplished in the dialogue.

Meno's paradox is based on a definite pre-conception regarding knowledge and, though it is not made fully explicit, it is, nevertheless, to this pre-conception that Socrates' resolution of the paradox is primarily directed. The paradox is based upon a conception of knowledge which takes no account whatsoever of the way in which something is normally recognized as unknown, namely as a gap or discontinuity in a field of things otherwise known.[13] Meno's conception ignores the fact that something is ordinarily recognized as being unknown—and, hence, is able to serve as a theme for inquiry—by the way in which it is related to what is known. Meno, on the contrary, assumes in the paradox that the domain of knowledge is totally discontinuous, that it consists of discrete, individual items none of which are linked in any way to any others. It is, in other words, assumed that the domain of

---

[12] Cf. Klein, *Commentary,* p. 91.
[13] Cf. *ibid.,* p. 92.

knowledge is a mere collection of discrete parts which are in no way linked together into a whole, which are in no way subordinate to a whole in the light of which it would be possible to recognize them as unknown. Thus, it is again Meno's ignorance of the whole which is at the root of what he says. The conception of knowledge presupposed by the paradox is the same conception that underlies Meno's opinion that one must avoid any "answer that employs terms which are still in question and not yet agreed upon." It is the same conception as that which, because it takes no account of the whole, can regard definition only as an endless regress to ever new terms.

(b) Recollection and the Paradox (81 a – e)

Socrates undertakes to explain how Meno's contention that learning is impossible fails by relating something which he has "heard from men and women who are wise regarding divine things . . ." (81 a). He pauses as though to look within himself for the story to be recalled and then proceeds to tell that the soul of man is immortal (i.e., subject to repeated rebirth) and that for this reason "a man must live all his days as righteously as possible"; he adds a quotation from Pindar describing how Persephone sends those who have paid for their crimes back to earth to become heroes. It is remarkable that none of this bears directly on the problem at hand; indeed, the statement that the soul is immortal proves in the light of what Socrates subsequently relates to have such a bearing, but the other two items, the statement about living righteously and the quotation from Pindar, remain discontinuous with the rest of the account.[14] There is no immediately evident reason to suppose any connection between learning and the soul's ascent from the realm of Hades and Persephone to the sun above. The discontinuity, especially that of the statement about living righteously, serves only to indicate the bearing of the entire account on the question of virtue, and its incoherence with respect to the rest of the account aptly portrays the state of the question

---

[14] Cf. *ibid.,* pp. 92-95.

regarding the relation of knowledge to virtue at this point in the dialogue. The remainder of Socrates' account, by contrast, speaks directly to the issue which Meno has raised:

> Since the soul is immortal and has been born many times and has seen all things both here and in Hades, there is nothing that it has not learned. So it is no wonder that it can recollect what it already knew before about virtue and other things. For all nature is akin [ἄτε γὰρ τῆς φύσεως ἀπάσης συγγενοῦς οὔσης], and the soul has learned everything, so that if a man has recollected one single thing—learned it as we say—he is capable of finding out all the others, provided he has courage and does not grow weary of searching. For seeking and learning are wholly recollection [τὸ γὰρ ζητεῖν ἄρα καὶ τὸ μανθάνειν ἀνάμνησις ὅλον ἐστίν] (81 c – d).

In what way and to what extent does this story, this myth of recollection, resolve the paradox posed by Meno? To what extent is there, as Socrates suggests (81 a), a "true *logos*" enveloped in the myth? Why is it so enveloped and why is it presented in the guise of something received from people who know of divine things?

Meno's paradox poses two alternatives: with regard to anything one either knows it (in which case to learn it is superfluous and even, in a strict sense, impossible) or does not know it (in which case it is, as Meno's argument shows, quite simply impossible to learn it). The story with which Socrates would resolve the paradox does not challenge either of these alternatives; what it does challenge is their exclusiveness. Between sheer ignorance and perfect knowledge Socrates inserts a third alternative: the condition of having once learned but now forgotten. This condition is different from ignorance precisely by the fact that, though one may have no knowledge of the matter immediately available, with some effort one is able to recollect to some degree what was once known and later forgotten. The condition posed as a third alternative is also distinct from the state of knowing as posed in the paradox: in the former knowledge is a task to be undertaken whereas in the latter it is something simply present. It is in view of this contrast that Socrates says immediately after his relating of the story that the paradox cited by Meno would have the effect of making us lazy whereas what he has put forth would produce energetic seekers of knowledge. Thus, we may say that the third alternative which Socrates poses between the two immovable poles of the paradox consists not just of another, intermediate pole but rather of a movement between ignorance and knowledge. The condition of man is posed as a mixture of ignorance and knowledge; in order that knowledge might predominate in that mixture it would be necessary to undertake the work of recollection which that mixed condition makes possible; and this work would require, as Socrates says, that we have courage and not grow weary of searching.

Thus, Socrates' story resolves Meno's paradox to the extent that it establishes that man's condition coincides with that third alternative, that movement-founding mixture of ignorance and knowledge. The two additional elements in the story serve to indicate this coincidence. The first of these elements is Socrates' statement that "all nature is akin." Things which are akin belong together, are fitted to one another, by virtue of what they are; and they can be gathered together without violence being done to them, gathered together even in such fashion that what they are is made manifest in and through the gathering. The reference to the issue of whole and parts is evident, and the suggestion is that the movement which Socrates has introduced between ignorance and knowledge is a movement of gathering up into unity, of gathering the parts which are akin into that whole to which they belong in virtue of their kinship. Furthermore, Socrates' statement that all nature is akin bears directly on that pre-conception of knowledge which, as we pointed out, is operative in Meno's paradox. Specifically, to say that all nature is akin is to invoke that whole which is lacking in Meno's pre-conception of knowledge, that whole by virtue of which "pieces of knowledge" are so linked together as to render possible the transition from something known to something unknown. To pose the kinship of all nature is to pose the possibility of movement from ignorance to knowledge in the immediate sense correlative to the possibility of coming to know something (previously unknown) by means of its kinship with something else (already known). But it does not yet quite secure this possibility, for the latter requires also that one somehow have in view that by which the terms of the movement are already joined together in their kinship. One must, in this precise sense, already know all things. Hence, we come to the final element in the story: the soul has learned everything. What is not presently known in the explicit sense is at least sufficiently manifest—for instance, through its connection with something else—that we are able to recollect it.

In order to show that the condition of man coincides with that condition which Socrates has posed as resolving Meno's paradox, it would thus be necessary to show that the human soul has learned all things—or, more precisely, that that in and by which things belong together (i.e., those wholes to which they belong in their kinship) is always already sufficiently manifest as to permit recollection. For showing this it hardly suffices to appeal to the immortality (repeated rebirths) of the soul and to the consequence that the soul would have had many previous lives in which to acquire this knowledge. Aside from the immense questionableness that permeates the entire issue of immortality, such an account would, in effect, simply transfer the problem from this life to previous lives, and there is no reason to suppose that Meno's objection would apply any less to such former lives than to the soul's present life. Nor is much accomplished by saying that the acquisition of knowledge occurs when the disembodied soul resides in Hades. For even in Hades the philosopher would be obliged to continue his questioning (cf. *Apol.* 41 b)—at least to the extent that residence in Hades is regarded straightforwardly as a counterpart to life on earth—and so the question would remain: How is the acquisition of knowledge possible? How can the soul—in this life or in former lives, in this world or in the other world—come to know what it does not already know?

It is clear that the questioning could continue, that what Socrates says in the little story in a sense only postpones the question. How is it that the soul has learned everything if, on the one hand, learning is impossible except as recollection while, on the other hand, this learning is already presupposed by all recollection and hence not an instance of it? The questioning could continue, but it does not. Apparently, the fact that it does not is linked, most immediately, to the fact that Socrates' respondent is Meno, who never knows what question is to be asked, who is largely oblivious to what is demanded in order really to question, who clearly is not capable of discerning the questions that remain behind the story which Socrates reports having heard from certain authorities. The story suffices for depriving Meno of his excuse for his ignorance and thereby for bringing him again under the demand for inquiring.

The myth of recollection is Socrates' answer to Meno, not only to the paradox posed by Meno but to all that has become manifest regarding Meno since the beginning of the dialogue and which is given unified expression in the paradox. It answers the question with which Socrates has repeatedly confronted Meno and by which Socrates has brought explicitly to light Meno's obliviousness to the whole, the question as to whether one can inquire about a part when he does not know the whole. The recollection myth answers this question by opening up a distinction between two ways of knowing a whole: on the one hand, a knowing mixed with ignorance, a knowing which is always already granted and without which no inquiry would be possible; on the other hand, an immovable knowing, unmixed with ignorance, a knowing without which one can, indeed, still inquire about the parts.

It is not, however, only to what Meno has said that the myth is addressed but also to what has been exhibited about Meno through what he has said; the answer, in other words, is addressed to Meno not only with respect to what he says but also with respect to who he is. In effect, the recollection myth, by its way of mediating between the extremes of sheer ignorance and perfect knowledge posed in Meno's paradox, makes evident Meno's ignorance of that condition in which knowledge and ignorance are mixed, that condition posed by Socrates as the condition of man. The myth shows, in other words, that Meno is ignorant of the involvement of ignorance in human knowledge; this is the deeper sense in which, as was already indicated from the outset, Meno's ignorance is pre-eminently an ignorance of ignorance. In turn, it is precisely as correlative to this mixture of knowledge and ignorance that the wholes (in which things belong together in their kinship) are manifest as such to man; hence, it is evident why Meno's ignorance of ignorance appears (e.g., in his definitions of virtue) as an ignorance of wholes. Finally, the myth addresses itself to the fact that Meno's ignorance is tied to his peculiar kind of memory by the way in which it links knowledge and inquiry to another, radically different kind of memory, namely recollection. After Socrates has related the story about recollection—in which he has spoken not only about recollection but also about virtue, the kinship of things, and the immortality of the soul—Meno singles out the thesis that learning is recollection, and it is only to this that his comments are directed. Meno hears in this thesis an echo of his own experience, his own dependence on his memory. Indeed, for him too all learning is recollection, not, however, a recollecting tied to self-knowledge but rather a recollecting of what Gorgias and others have said.

(c) Recollection and Imaging (*Phaedo* 72 e — 75 d)

However much Socrates' story about recollection may suffice as an answer to Meno, it does not, if considered more strictly in reference to the question at issue, suffice for terminating the questioning that is provoked by the paradox. If we set out of play the aura with which Socrates surrounds the story for the sake of Meno, if we penetrate beneath the level of the story in that form in which Socrates told it to Meno, then we can see how very inaccessible the deeper level of the questioning is to Meno and thus can understand the appropriateness of Socrates' adopting a way of presentation which effectively closes off this deeper level for Meno. The relevant depth consists in the fact that what is contested in the confrontation between Socrates' story and Meno's paradox is *questioning itself.* The paradox would put an end to all questioning, since if its alternatives were really exclusive nothing could be posed as not yet fully known, i.e., as *questionable.* By contrast, Socrates, violating the paradox already by his very calling of it into question, poses as correlative to the mixture of knowledge and ignorance those wholes which are indeed manifest yet questionable—hence, capable of sustaining a questioning. In the question of recollection the very possibility of questioning is at issue. Here questioning comes up against the question of its very possibility. It is little wonder that Socrates effectively closes off the level of such questioning from Meno, who has throughout the discussion up to this point proved remarkably ignorant both of his ignorance and of what is really required for genuine questioning.

But Socrates does not always converse with one from whom, as with Meno and with the "men of Athens," it is appropriate to close off the deeper level of the questioning. He converses also with his closest friends, especially with the various young men with whom he is erotically involved, and on two such occasions he explicitly takes up the question of recollection. The topics of these two conversations correspond roughly to the two principal directions of questioning that are left untouched, as it were, beneath what Socrates says in the *Meno*. We have indicated already what remains to be shown: that those wholes in which things are gathered in their kinship are always already sufficiently manifest as to permit recollection. Here there are two principal questions. First, it needs to be asked how it is that the wholes are always already manifest to us. The *Meno* already indicates (but in a way that fails to show the genuine dimension of the question) that the appropriate response to this question would be a recollection of that past time in which the soul was exposed to an immediate manifestation of the wholes. But this recollection for the sake of establishing that learning is recollection, this recollection which would serve to establish man's condition as a mixture of ignorance and knowledge, can be in accord with that very establishment of man in his proper ignorance only insofar as it lets what is recollected remain also enshrouded in its proper obscurity. The recollection must be such as to grant to what is recollected its intrinsic concealment; a Platonic way of granting this is to let the recollection fall into the form of a myth. Such a recollection of the mythical past is undertaken by Socrates in his second speech in the *Phaedrus* (see Ch. III, Sect. 2 c, iii).

The second direction of questioning that remains untouched in the *Meno* has to do with exhibiting the character and structure of the activity of recollecting. Such an exhibition is undertaken in the other conversation about recollection which Socrates has with those close to him, the conversation in the *Phaedo*. We need to attend carefully to this conversation in order to see how the issues involved in recollection take shape in that questioning beneath the level of the *Meno.*

In accord with the context of the dialogue as a whole, both thematically and dramatically, Cebes introduces the issue of recollection as providing a means of proving the immortality of the soul (*Phaedo* 72 e — 73 a). We note immediately the contrast with the story about recollection in the *Meno* in which the thesis that learning is recollection is derived from the immortality of the soul rather than conversely. This contrast indicates how thoroughly questionable the connection is between recollection and the immortality of the soul; we suspect that neither the story told in the *Meno* nor the specific conversation we are considering in the *Phaedo* is situated at the level at which a genuine questioning of this connection could be initiated.

Simmias, Cebes' companion, asks about the "demonstration" (i.e., "showing forth"—$\dot{\alpha}\pi o\delta\epsilon\iota\xi\iota\varsigma$) of the thesis about recollection. We note that Simmias is perceptive enough to take account in his request of the relevant reflexivity; he refers to the fact that he does not presently recollect (that learning is recollection), and, shortly after the discussion of recollection gets under way, he announces that he has begun to recollect. Cebes responds to Simmias' request by invoking precisely the kind of "demonstration" of recollection that we shall find exemplified in the *Meno* in the upcoming episode with the slave boy: when people are questioned properly they are able to answer correctly of their own accord, which they could not do unless they had already within themselves knowledge which they merely recollect in answering the questions. He refers also to the role that diagrams can play in such recollection; again, this is a feature that is especially prominent in the exhibition of recollection in the *Meno.* Hence, Cebes' presentation regarding recollection follows essentially the same direction as that in the *Meno.* It is as though the inquiry about recollection needs to begin with a recollection of one direction as a way of preparing to set out in another direction, in a direction which leads to a deeper level of questioning. Openly contrasting this other direction with the way laid out by Cebes, Socrates explicitly introduces it as a way of offering further instruction to

Simmias, that is, as a way of helping him to recollect that learning is recollection (73 a — b).

If we momentarily overlook Cebes' reference to diagrams, then it may be said that, according to his presentation, recollection amounts to little more than simply retrieving something that is stored away intact inside the person recollecting, retrieving it in the sense of bringing it forth to the outside in the form of an answer. The only determinate thing that would appear to be involved in evoking it is the question posed to the person. By Cebes' account, it seems almost as though what is decisive in recollection is the mere transfer of something from inside to outside, its "expression" in the literal sense. It appears almost as though the relevant movement would be an externalizing of a "piece of knowledge" rather than a movement of the soul from ignorance to knowledge. However, when Socrates takes up the issue, he turns the entire discussion in a different direction, a direction only vaguely hinted at in Cebes' reference to diagrams. Socrates shifts the entire discussion in the direction of a consideration of how some things announce themselves, become manifest, through other things. This is the deeper level at which the discussion of recollection is now situated: the level at which the relevant movement is a movement of manifestation, on the side of things, and a movement from ignorance to knowledge, on the side of the person recollecting.

Socrates begins by establishing the general connection between recollection and this new level: When through the perception of one thing a man comes to know some other thing distinct from it, then this second thing can be said to have been recollected (73 c — d). Thus, in quite formal terms, recollection involves the movement from one thing which is perceived to another thing which is made manifest through the perception of the first thing but which is distinct from the first thing. It is evident that the consideration of recollection, once it is brought to this new level, must center on the character of and relation between these two things.

From Socrates' initial statement it is clear that the two things between which the relevant movement takes place must be sufficiently connected for the perception of the first to make the

second manifest. On the other hand, Socrates' statement emphasizes that these two things must also be distinct—sufficiently
distinct for movement between them to be possible. What must be
considered is the connection and distinction, more generally, the
sameness and difference, by which these two things are related.

Socrates offers a series of examples designed to clarify this
relation (73 d — 74 a). These examples fall into three groups. The
first group consists of two examples. First, Socrates notes that
when a lover sees a lyre or a cloak or anything else belonging to his
beloved he is reminded of, recollects, his beloved. The principal
significance of this example, taken alone, is that it introduces an
erotic element into the discussion; more specifically, this example
indicates that it is *eros* that joins the person recollecting to that
which is recollected, i.e., to that (the beloved) which becomes
manifest through the perception of something else (lyre, cloak).
However, with this example almost nothing is indicated about the
relation between the two things between which the movement
pertaining to recollection is sustained, i.e., the thing perceived and
the other thing which is made manifest thereby. The other example in the first group—that when one sees Simmias, one often
recollects Cebes—to the extent that it is a particularization of the
erotic relation posed in the previous example, hints that *eros* may
also have something to do with the relation between the terms of
the movement pertaining to recollection.[15]

The second group, which also consists of two examples, is
separated from the first by an important addition: Socrates
focuses the entire discussion on those cases where the thing
recollected is something which has been forgotten through time
and inattention. The emphasis is thus to be placed on cases in
which what is made manifest through the perception of something
else is not a thing that happens not to be manifest but that
could just as easily be so; the emphasis is to be placed on what is
necessarily (e.g., with the kind of necessity belonging to time)
withdrawn from immediate manifestness to us. However, having
made this addition, the enforcing of the emphasis is temporarily

---

[15] The connection between *eros* and recollection, playfully alluded to here, is
developed extensively in the *Phaedrus*. See Ch. III, esp. Sect. 2 c, iv.

postponed for the sake of another development that takes place in the transition from the first to the second group of examples. This development consists in the explicit introduction of the theme of *imaging* and *images*. In place of the lyre or cloak by the perception of which the boy would be recollected, Socrates now poses the case in which a *picture* of a horse or of a lyre leads one to recollect the man who owns them. The second example involves a similar transformation of the corresponding example in the first group: in place of one's being led by the sight of Simmias to recollect Cebes, he poses the case in which one would be led by the sight of a *picture* of Simmias to recollect Cebes. The specific changes in the transition from the first example of the first group to that of the second group are also noteworthy: not only does the boy mature into a man but also the cloak, which could cover and conceal the boy, is replaced (when the theme of imaging is introduced) by a horse, which could serve for the man's movement; in the transition the one thing that is retained is the lyre, and we wonder just what kind of harmony is required. However these matters may be, what is decisively important in the transition to the second group of examples is that the first of the two things between which the relevant movement occurs, i.e., the thing which is perceived and through the perception of which the other thing is made manifest—this thing has the character of an image. The relation between the two things is an imaging.

This character of the relation becomes evident in the final example, which in a sense is the simplest of all: by seeing a picture of Simmias one can be led to recollect Simmias. Yet, this example requires two qualifications; these qualifications are necessary in order to keep the entire consideration from collapsing into an all-too-easy manipulation of the image-original schema. The first qualification corresponds to the shift of emphasis, noted above, towards those cases in which the original is such as to be necessarily withdrawn from immediate manifestness. This means that the image, in letting the original become manifest, does not simply perform a more or less dispensible function; it is not as though the original could become manifest also without the image, but rather, in the kind of cases towards which the emphasis is shifted, the original *needs* the image in order to become manifest. In such cases the relation of imaging is not simply a relation between two things equally capable of being immediately manifest (cf. Ch. IV, Sect. 5). The second qualification is almost explicit in what Socrates says: one can be led to recollect both by like (ὅμοιον) things and by unlike things. This means: to be an image, i.e., to be a thing through the perception of which something else is made manifest, is not identical with being a likeness. To image and to resemble are not the same.

The remainder of the consideration of recollection (74 a − 75 d) has chiefly to do with another example, which, however, is of an entirely different order from those mentioned previously. The example is: the equal itself (αὐτὸ τὸ ἴσον). What most obviously distinguishes this example from the entire preceding series is the fact that the emphasis, previously alluded to in what was said, is now put in force: the equal itself is necessarily (by virtue of what it is) withdrawn from immediate manifestness. In other words, it becomes manifest only through something else; and this is why, having posed the equal itself, Socrates then begins his considera-tion of it by insisting that we have come to know the equal itself by seeing images of it, by seeing things like equal sticks and equal stones. Distinguishing between these images and the withdrawn original which they serve to make manifest, Socrates identifies recollection as presence to such manifestation. But then, finally, he decisively reverses the initial order of the terms: Although indeed we can come to know the equal itself only through seeing things like equal sticks and stones, we can, on the other hand, apprehend the latter as approaching but falling short of the equal itself only if we already in some sense know the equal itself. That is, we can recognize the images *as* images of the original, hence, as making that original manifest, only if the original, the equal itself, is somehow manifest in advance.

Socrates extends the result: it holds not only for the equal itself but also for the beautiful itself, the good itself, the just itself, the holy itself and all such things. Just as the equal itself, as the whole in which equal sticks, stones, etc. are gathered up, must be somehow manifest in advance, so likewise with all other such wholes. Yet, they cannot be immediately manifest; their manifest-ness must involve also a concealment.

Recollection is the movement of the soul correlative to that movement of manifestation in which a whole becomes manifest through an image. In this fundamental sense, recollection is a mediation between whole and parts. As such, recollection is founded upon the capacity of man, with his peculiar mixture of knowledge and ignorance, to apprehend an image *as* an image, that is, to apprehend the original that shows through it. Recollection is founded on the non-immediate manifestness of the original wholes to the human soul.

If one were to seek a still deeper level of questioning regarding recollection, it would be necessary to take up this primordial relation between the soul and the original wholes. In the subsequent conversation in the *Phaedo,* which is appropriately introduced as a natural sequel to the discussion of recollection,[16] it is precisely this relation which is taken up and described as a matter of kinship. But we are not yet prepared for that level of questioning. We return to the *Meno.*

(d) Exhibition (81 e — 85 c)

From the outset of the further discussion Meno proves to be oblivious to the reflexivity which, by contrast, Simmias took into account in asking about recollection. In response to the thesis that learning is recollection, Meno asks: "Can you teach me that it is so?" (81 e). Socrates points to the contradiction inherent in Meno's question: Meno wants to learn that one does not learn but only recollects; and, though Socrates ironically gives Meno credit for having been aware of this contradiction, it is apparent that Meno was merely repeating a formula—that, as he acknowledges, "It was just habit." On the other hand, there is clearly a sense in Meno's question which is not subject to this contradiction, since the myth does not, as does Meno's paradox, deny that learning occurs but only interprets learning as recollection. Meno's request,

---

[16] After the short "digression" that follows the discussion of recollection Socrates says: "But let us return to the point where we left off, if you have no objection" (78 a — b). He proceeds immediately to introduce the question of the kinship between the soul and the original wholes.

properly understood, is that Socrates help him to recollect recollection. The problem now becomes that of whether Meno is
capable of really carrying through such recollection. His initial
blunder strongly suggests that he is not likely to succeed in that
recollection of recollection to which Socrates now invites him.

Socrates proposes to give an exhibition or display (ἐπίδειξις) of
the recollection myth by questioning a slave boy about geometry.
He proceeds, in other words, to make recollection manifest by
presenting a case of actual recollecting, to let the myth be reflected in concrete activity, in deed. He questions the slave boy
regarding the length of the sides of a square of area eight, proceeding by question and answer in reference to diagrams drawn in the
sand.[17] The problem itself is appropriate to the fundamental
issue: it is posed as a problem of discovering a side (yielding a
square of area eight) of which a given side (yielding a square of
area four) is a part; but the relation of part to whole proves to be
different from what the boy quite naturally expects; and the
solution turns out to involve the construction of the desired whole
within a yet larger whole.

In its dramatic dimension, on the other hand, the entire episode
with the slave boy serves to provide a reverse image of the stages
through which Meno has passed in being questioned by Socrates.
On the one hand, the slave boy, initially ignorant and ignorant of
his ignorance, is through Socrates' questioning brought to awareness of his ignorance and, subsequently, to an insight into the
solution to the problem Socrates has posed to him; on the other
hand, Meno, beginning in the same condition and displaying the
utmost confidence that he knows what he soon proves not to
know, fails, even after Socrates' questioning has revealed his ignorance, to acknowledge that ignorance, instead blaming Socrates
(the "sting ray") for his own inability to answer. Meno remains
established in an ignorance of ignorance; he "stays put" in it. This

---

[17] It should be noted that in the problem which Socrates poses the given side and the
side sought are incommensurable and that, consequently, an answer in terms of the
length of the given side cannot (in Greek mathematics) be given; the side sought can only
be drawn or shown. Hence, Socrates instructs the boy: "If you do not want to count it
up, just show us on the diagram" (84 a). The geometrical problem mirrors the more general
character of the entire discussion: it is a matter of showing, of exhibiting the myth of
recollection. Cf. Klein, *Commentary*, p. 99.

curious inverse imaging is made especially evident in the aside comments which Socrates makes to Meno in the course of his questioning of the slave boy.[18]

But what does the episode with the slave boy offer as regards the myth of recollection? Obviously, it is not in any usual sense a proof of the contents of the myth; Meno's blunder in posing his question made it evident that proving, for example, in the sense of convincing someone by "arguments" that something of which he was previously ignorant is true, makes no sense here. On the contrary, if the story about recollection is true, one can learn that this is so only by recollecting it. Hence, the only appropriate kind of proof in this context is one which is an exhibition, that is, one in which the myth is transposed into the dimension of concrete activity in such a way that action can embody its content, in such a way that the action of learning can convey its truth. In other words, the answer to the question about the possibility of learning is, in a sense, a successful effort to learn, since it is just this which is able, if anything is, to provoke the recollection of recollection.

(e) Who Meno Is (85 c — 86 d)

The first half of the dialogue concludes with a brief exchange between Socrates and Meno.[19] Socrates restates the myth of recollection and the thesis that learning is recollection, and Meno

---

[18] The first stage of the discussion in which the boy is confident that he knows the answer corresponds to Meno's display of confidence at the beginning of the dialogue; Socrates comments to Meno that the boy thinks he knows the answer (82 e). The second stage of the discussion in which Socrates refutes the boy's answers and leads him to an awareness of his ignorance corresponds (as a reverse image) to Meno's response after Socrates had successfully attacked his answers to the question about virtue; unlike the slave boy, Meno (the tyrant) did not become aware of his ignorance but rather blamed Socrates for his own failure. Socrates explicitly points to the fact that the slave boy has come to acknowledge his ignorance and then subtly draws the contrast with Meno: "So in perplexing him [the slave boy] and numbing him like the sting ray, have we done him any harm? . . . Up to now, he thought he could speak well and fluently, on many occasions and before large audiences . . . " (84 b). This, of course, is what Meno, not the slave boy, claimed (80 b). In the final stage of the discussion the slave boy is led to recollect the answer to the problem; this corresponds to the presently underway attempt by Socrates to lead Meno to recollect. Cf. Klein, *Commentary*, pp. 99-101.

[19] Cf. esp. the consideration of this section given by Klein, *Commentary*, pp. 180-189.

expresses his agreement. It is then proposed by Socrates that they return to the question, "What is virtue?"; Meno, however, insists that, instead, they take up the question which he originally posed, the question as to how virtue is acquired.

By retelling the myth and then proposing the resumption of the inquiry into virtue, Socrates, in effect, invites Meno to serve now as an exhibition of the myth through his own effort to learn. It might even be said that, regarded dramatically, the purpose of the myth and the episode with the slave boy is to entice Meno to undertake the effort of learning, i.e., of recollection. The question, of course, is: Has Meno understood what has gone on in the exhibition with the slave boy? Has he recollected the truth of recollection to a degree sufficient to allow him to set aside his habitual repetition of what others have said and follow the lead of Socrates' questioning? In fact, it becomes almost immediately evident that Meno has not understood, and this fact is intensified by his continual assent to what Socrates has said. He simply returns to the question which he posed at the very beginning of the dialogue thereby betraying that he has learned nothing in the course of the dialogue and that his assent to what Socrates has said has been totally empty, for, if he had understood the recollection myth, he would realize that this initial question to which he now wants to return has been seriously called into question. The myth suggests, contrary to what Meno assumes, that teaching and learning are not necessarily opposed to being given by nature or acquired by practice; the episode with the slave boy, in fact, exhibits the unity of these.

Socrates' restatement of the myth not only serves to invite Meno to undertake the effort of learning but also gives Meno the opportunity to hear the echoes of words heard previously (when Socrates originally told the myth) and now imprinted on his memory. It serves, in other words, to show that Meno's assent involves no more than an assent to what is imprinted on his memory. This is made especially evident by the fact that Meno entirely fails to notice that when Socrates restates the myth he reverses the terms of the inference. Whereas previously (81 c) he inferred that because the soul is immortal it possesses knowledge, in the restatement he says: "If the truth about beings [τῶν ὄντων] is always in our soul, then the soul is immortal" (86 b). The two statements sound alike and easily deceive one who is nothing more than a collection of memories.

It is now clear why Meno's ignorance is linked to his memory. Meno's memory consists only of traces left by what others have said. Each such opinion may, indeed, contain some morsel of truth, but these opinions—drawn uncritically from disparate sources, that is, not assembled in the light of a unifying whole— involve inconsistencies if taken together; they cannot be brought together into a coherent whole. Meno's memory thus mirrors perfectly the domain of knowledge as he assumed it to be consti- tuted when he stated the paradox of inquiry. What Meno *is* with regard to whole and parts is identical to what he *says* in this regard.

Section 3. Meno and Anytus (86 d — 96 d)

We have now reached the point which divides the *Meno* into its two principal parts, and we need, by way of anticipation, to indicate how these two parts are related. The first part of the dialogue incorporates the three more or less unsuccessful attempts by Meno to define virtue, Socrates' relating of the story about recollection, and the episode involving the slave boy. The unity of this part lies in the fact that it constitutes in the dimension of deed primarily an unveiling of the character Meno, an answering of the question "Who is Meno?" It exhibits Meno in his ignorance, and, coupled with the image of the historical Meno as a deceitful, unscrupulous, treacherous character who subordinated everything to his desire for enormous wealth, as a man who represented an extreme of non-virtue,[20] it yields as its concrete result an implicit yet unmistakable linking of non-virtue to ignorance. This link is precisely the other side of that linking of virtue to knowledge the explicit discussion of which is to constitute the second half of the dialogue. The two parts are, consequently, parts which belong

---

[20] Xenophon, *Anabasis*, II, vi, 21 — 29.

together in the whole by virtue of their own inherent connection. They are connected not simply by the fact that both involve discussion of virtue but, more fundamentally, by the fact that both say the same thing though in different dimensions—or, perhaps better, by the fact that the first part exhibits dramatically what the second part discusses explicitly.

(a) Virtue and Knowledge

Socrates, again drawing an image of Meno the tyrant,[21] nevertheless complies with Meno's proposal to return to the question as to how virtue is acquired. He attaches to his compliance, however, the condition that the question be considered on the basis of the hypothesis that virtue is knowledge; yet, as soon as the hypothesis is granted, Meno's question is presumed answered: virtue is acquired by teaching. Hence, the next step is to investigate the hypothesis, that is, to test a particular answer to Socrates' question regarding what virtue is. By introducing the method of hypothesis—illustrated with an example from mathematical procedure which Meno would hardly reject whether he understood it or not—Socrates simply circumvents Meno's question and returns to the question: What is virtue? Socrates proceeds immediately to advocate the identity of virtue and knowledge in the following way: virtue, as something good, is advantageous; yet for anything to be advantageous it must be rightly used, that is, used with knowledge, and, therefore, virtue is knowledge either in whole or in part (87 d — 89 a).

---

[21] Socrates says: "If I were your master as well as my own, Meno, we should not have inquired whether or not virtue can be taught until we had first asked the main question—what it is. But not only do you make no attempt to govern your own actions—you prize your freedom, I suppose—but you attempt to govern mine. And you succeed too . . . " (86 d). Thus, Meno is one who attempts to govern others without governing himself, while Socrates is one who is his own master, who governs himself. This image of Meno is simply a transcription of Meno's definition of virtue as the capacity to govern men; correspondingly, the image of Socrates is a transcription of his attack on that definition, which took the form of insisting that governing others presupposes governing of oneself. The same point is made explicitly in this section when Socrates says that "the goodness of non—spiritual assets depends on our spiritual character . . . " (88 e). It is, again, established dramatically by the fact that Socrates, who governs himself, ends up governing Meno; by introducing a mathematical analogy he forces Meno back to the question, "What is virtue?"

Thus, the dialogue arrives at that conclusion which has been implicit from the beginning: the identity of virtue and knowledge. The dialogue is, it seems, at its end; yet, the conclusion retains one explicit qualification, a qualification in terms of the problem of whole and parts, and the dialogue continues. Socrates, expressing his uncertainty about the conclusion that virtue is knowledge, notes that if the conclusion holds and if, therefore, virtue is taught, then there must be teachers. A new character, Anytus, now joins in a search for these teachers, who turn out to be neither the sophists, nor just any decent Athenian citizen, nor the honored men of Athens' past. It is concluded that there are no teachers and that, consequently, virtue can apparently not be taught.

These developments in the dialogue raise two especially pertinent questions. First, it needs to be asked why the dialogue continues beyond that point at which the identity of virtue and knowledge is established. What are the sources of those doubts that prompt Socrates to renew the discussion? With regard to the dramatic side of the dialogue what is crucial is Meno's agreement (89 a) to Socrates' thesis that virtue is knowledge, an agreement which presumably means that Meno has himself come to know that virtue is knowledge. Yet this result conflicts with the entire picture which the dialogue has given of Meno as a paradigm of ignorance. Could Meno, who has consistently proved incapable of learning anything, have conceivably gained, i.e., recollected, such a fundamental truth? Furthermore, if virtue is knowledge and if Meno has knowledge (i.e., that virtue is knowledge), then it must be concluded (on this purely formal level) that Meno is virtuous; but Meno is not virtuous, as is made explicit in Socrates' portrait of him as a tyrant at the beginning of this section; thus, Meno does not have knowledge. How, then, is his semblance of knowledge to be accounted for?

There is another reason why the dialogue must continue, and it is hinted at in the qualification which Socrates attaches to his conclusion: Virtue is knowledge either in whole or in part. The qualification, in fact, pertains not only to virtue but also to knowledge. Is it the whole of knowledge that is to be identified with virtue (or with a part of virtue)? Is the knowledge of the shoemaker and, in general, the kind of knowledge required for the practice of a particular art (τέχνη)—a kind of knowledge one, indeed, learns from a teacher—to be included? Does not the discussion with Anytus serve to indicate that, on the contrary, virtue, if it is knowledge, is a distinctive kind of knowledge? [22] Does it not, at least, give evidence that this knowledge is not identical with that involved directly in some particular art?

(b) Anytus and the Whole

The second general question to which we must attend concerns the character Anytus. He enters abruptly and quite late in the dialogue. Why is the dialogue encumbered with this additional character? Why could not Meno say what Anytus says? Why is it Anytus who joins Socrates in the search for teachers of virtue? Certainly a contrast between Meno and Anytus is apparent; whereas Meno pays allegiance to the sophists, Anytus honors the city and its heroes and gives testimony of his loyalty by warning Socrates against criticizing the heroes of the city. [23] Obviously, the dismissal of the sophists as teachers of virtue could not be performed by Meno; for this purpose Anytus is presumably required.

However, the role of Anytus in the dialogue is considerably more significant than would be the case if he served only for dismissing the claims of the sophists. What is most important about this character is the way in which he stands in contrast to

---

[22] The *Protagoras* is especially relevant to this issue. Early in the dialogue (319 b – 320 b) Socrates contends, counter to Protagoras, that virtue cannot be taught, appealing as in the *Meno* to the example of the statesmen who have been unable to pass their virtue along to their sons. Later (334 a – c) Protagoras speaks of the good in such a way that he, in effect, makes it a matter of knowledge in that narrow sense associated with τέχνη. Then, when the discussion returns to the question at the end of the dialogue, Socrates finds himself maintaining, quite contrary to what he said initially, that virtue can be taught (361 a – b). It should especially be noted that Socrates makes a point of saying that the question as to what kind of knowledge is to be identified with virtue is being left open (357 b).

In this connection note also the reference in the *Euthydemus* (289 b) to a kind of knowledge which, unlike "technical" knowledge, combines both how to make something and how to use what is made.

[23] Regarding Anytus' role as one of Socrates' accusers, see *Apol.* 29 c, 36 a. There is considerable ancient testimony regarding this character; see especially Xenophon, *Apologia Socratis,* 29, where Anytus' responsibility for giving his son a poor upbringing is mentioned. For further discussion and extensive bibliography see Klein, *Commentary,* pp. 223-225.

Meno, for it is by way of this contrast that the problem of whole and parts is finally exhibited in its full scope as a problem of mediation. The key to the basic feature that distinguishes Anytus in contrast to Meno is found in the discussion with Socrates in which Anytus vehemently denies that the sophists are those teachers of virtue for whom he and Socrates are searching:

Socrates: Has one of the sophists done you a personal injury, or why are you so hard on them?

Anytus: Heavens, no! I have never in my life had anything to do with a single one of them, nor would I hear of any of my family doing so.

Socrates: So you have had no experience of them at all?

Anytus: And do not want any either.

Socrates: Then, my fine fellow [ὦ δαιμόνιε], how can you know what is good or bad in something when you have no experience of it?

Anytus: Quite easily. At any rate, I know their kind [τούτους γοῦν οἶδα οἴ εἰσιν] whether I have had experience or not.

Socrates: You must be a seer [μάντις], Anytus, for how else you know about them, judging from what you tell me yourself, I cannot imagine (92 b − c).

This passage indicates the character of Anytus' opinions. They are opinions about the whole which remain oblivious to the parts and which, hence, lead Anytus to claim to know about the sophists "as a whole" despite his having had nothing to do with any particular sophist. Socrates' response to such opinions is highly appropriate and serves to highlight their character: most of his discussion with Anytus deals with individual examples—that is, it is an invocation of parts. By contrast, Meno is one who clings always to parts, who remains oblivious to the relevant wholes, and Socrates' objections to his opinions have repeatedly taken the form of a demand for the whole. Anytus embodies the whole without the parts, Meno the parts without the whole. Neither is capable of mediating between parts and whole.

This contrast corresponds to the conclusions which are associated with Meno and Anytus respectively with regard to the question whether there are teachers of virtue. To Meno, who adheres to parts but remains oblivious to the whole, it seems obvious that there are teachers of virtue, and he is surprised that Socrates entertains doubts about this matter (89 e). Indeed, Meno is correct provided one takes only parts into account and does not ask about the whole which, as the myth of recollection suggested, must already be implicitly known in order for knowledge of parts to be gained. On the other hand, Anytus, who holds opinions about the whole while remaining oblivious to the parts, serves as the respondent in the discussion leading to the conclusion that there are no teachers of virtue, and in this discussion he offers virtually no resistence to Socrates. He is intent only on attacking the sophists and on maintaining that there are good men in Athens, without in the least insisting on the question of teachers of virtue. Indeed, this conclusion too is correct if, in conformity with what Anytus embodies, account is taken only of the whole; it must already be implicitly known and cannot in the usual sense be learned from a teacher.

Thus, both conclusions are, in a sense, true—at least as long as the simple identification of knowledge with virtue remains un-clarified. This is what Socrates proceeds to suggest when, after the search for the teachers, he resumes the discussion with Meno. Meno indicates that his countrymen disagree on the question whether virtue can be taught and that he himself wavers on this issue (95 b — c). What Meno, thus, betrays is that he can see in this issue only a conflict of opinions, that he is unable to see the unity of these two views, to grasp them as aspects of one whole, namely the whole view of knowledge presented in the myth of recollec-tion. Socrates quotes Theognis' expression of both views and with utmost irony asks Meno: "Do you see how he contradicts him-self?" (96 a).

Section 4. Meno, Socrates, Anytus (96 d — 100 c)

(a) Opinion

We need to focus on two conclusions drawn in the final section of the dialogue. The first is Socrates' formulation of the distinc-tion between knowledge (ἐπιστήμη) and true opinion (δόξα ἀληθής). This distinction provides the means (essential from a dramatic point of view) for accounting for Meno's semblance of knowledge. More importantly, the introduction of opinion into the considerations serves to name that mixed condition, that mixture of ignorance and knowledge, which was found to underlie recollection. Opinion is thus correlative to that manifestness of the wholes which is always already granted and which is permeated simultaneously with concealment. In other words, men opine in accordance with the way that things seem to them, i.e., in accordance with the partial manifestness of the original wholes. [24] Insofar as things in their seeming both reveal and conceal themselves, both truth and falsity belong to all opinions: hence the difficulty of formulating a distinction between true opinions and false opinions, hence also the difficulty, made explicit here by Socrates (98 c), involved in preventing true opinion, once it is posed, from simply coalescing with knowledge. [25]

Nevertheless, Socrates does insist on this distinction: Knowledge, he tells Meno, results when true opinions are tethered so that they will not "run away from a man's soul" (98 a; cf. *Euthyphro* 11 b − d), when they are tied to causes in one's "reckoning" (αἰτίας λογισμῷ). What are these causes to which knowledge, unlike true opinion, is tied? Socrates openly declares that the process of tethering is identical with recollection. But we have seen that recollection is presence to the movement of manifestation of those original wholes in which things are gathered up in their kinship. To tether opinions to causes, so as to transform them into knowledge, means to let these opinions be measured by the manifestation of the wholes.

(b) Divine Dispensation

The *Meno* ends with the curious conclusion that virtue is acquired by "divine dispensation" (θεία μοίρα—100 b). In this

---

[24] This entire complex of issues and especially the question of opinion will be developed at length in Ch. V in the course of the interpretation of the middle books of the *Republic*.

[25] These difficulties, merely touched on here in the *Meno*, are developed extensively in the second part of the *Theaetetus* (187 a − 201 c). From that discussion they are taken over into the *Sophist* in connection with which we shall consider them in Ch. VI.

connection it should be noted that in the corresponding discussion in the *Protagoras* (320 c − 328 d) in which Protagoras includes alongside one another all the alternatives mentioned by Meno as well as this conclusion, the acquisition of virtue by divine dispensation forms the content of the story (μῦθος) related by Protagoras. In the *Meno* too the statement that virtue is acquired by divine dispensation has to do with myth; this conclusion is, in effect, nothing less than an image of what the myth of recollection has brought to light regarding man's condition. Man is, so the myth teaches, able to learn, to acquire knowledge, only because he already possesses an implicit knowledge of the original wholes— i.e., only because the manifestation of the wholes is always already granted, dispensed to man in a way that cannot, however, be made immediately manifest. But if virtue is knowledge, and if knowledge depends on this dispensation, then the acquisition of virtue depends on the dispensation of this gift. As the highest gift, as that by which man is given his highest possibilities, this gift must be a gift of the gods, divine dispensation.

But "divine dispensation" is only an image, and, having introduced it, Socrates immediately expresses reservations. However, it is an image which is peculiarly appropriate to the context of the *Meno*. This dialogue has portrayed the character Meno as one who is oblivious to wholes and has, subsequently, led to the invocation of wholes by means of the character Anytus. But the wholes of Anytus' opinions prove to be hardly more satisfactory than the parts with which Meno's memory is filled; the relation to wholes which is exhibited in Anytus is not the appropriate relation that is pointed to in the myth of recollection but only a parody of it in the guise of divine dispensation to Anytus the seer.

Meno embodies parts without the whole, Anytus the whole without the parts. What the contrast brings to light is the issue of mediation. It is a contrast between two men who are equally incapable, though for opposite reasons, of that mediation between whole and part which is at the source of knowledge and virtue. In this contrast along with that mediation with which it, in turn, stands in contrast—that mediation exemplified in Socrates—in these terms the dialogue as a whole is gathered up. If virtue is linked to the mediation between whole and parts, then there is a teacher of virtue found in the *Meno*, namely Socrates himself; yet, because of what this teaching requires on the part of the one to be taught, Socrates does not succeed in teaching virtue to Meno and Anytus, and in deed there appears to be no teaching of virtue in the *Meno*.

Socrates' final request is that a discussion between Meno and Anytus, between the separate poles of the mediation, be initiated. But Socrates, the genuine mediator, is preparing to leave as he makes this final ironic request.

CHAPTER III

BEYOND THE CITY:

PHAEDRUS

In the *Phaedrus* Socrates, whom even the threat of death could not drive from the city, playfully admits to being lured outside the walls by the prospect of hearing a worthy speech. One of the speeches which Socrates himself delivers while outside the city is a speech about the perfection of speech; and in this speech, which takes the form of dialogue with Phaedrus, he insists that the toil required for such perfection is one "which a wise man ought not to undergo for the sake of speaking [λέγειν] and acting [πράττειν] before men, but that he may be able to speak and to do everything, so far as possible, in a manner pleasing to the gods" (273 e — 274 a). But in the *Phaedrus* the god who has the principal role is no longer Apollo, who gives Socrates to the city, but rather Zeus, who leads whoever can follow up to that height most distant from the cities of men.

In what sense is it possible for man to engage in such movement beyond the city? What is the character of that surpassing of the city which Socrates and Phaedrus playfully enact in their walk outside the walls? How does *logos* belong to that gift through which man is granted the power of engaging in such movement beyond the city?

Section 1. The Setting (227 a — 230 e)

In the opening conversation, which takes place as Socrates and Phaedrus are walking into the country, Phaedrus relates in some

104

detail the events preceding his meeting with Socrates, and both he and Socrates speak of the various features of the countryside through which they are walking. This conversation is no mere series of embellishments to be passed by quickly on our way into the dialogue. Here there is no mere description of nature—neither "for its own sake" nor for our "aesthetic enjoyment." Here there is no mere painting of a scene in the sense of a concrete context essentially unrelated to the issues later developed in the speeches about love and the conversation about rhetoric. On the contrary, one of the most fundamental features of every Platonic dialogue consists in its exclusion of all such merely external connections; what is put at issue in the discussion that takes place in a dialogue and the concrete context in which the discussion is presented as taking place are never extrinsic to one another but rather belong essentially together through the mirroring of each in the other, that is, belong together in the mirror-play. In the case of the *Phaedrus* there runs throughout the opening conversation an exceptionally rich play of images through which the matters which the dialogue as a whole puts at issue are collected and made manifest in an appropriately preliminary way. The way in which the matter is initially posed, the way in which it is set for consideration—the setting, as it were, of the matter—thereby exemplifies precisely that attachment to images for which Socrates speaks in the dialogue.

(a) The Opening Question (227 a – b)

In order to enter appropriately into this setting of the matter at issue, we need to attend with special care to the question with which the *Phaedrus* opens. Socrates asks: "My friend Phaedrus, where are you going and where do you come from?"[1] We need to see how this opening question opens onto the dialogue as a whole.

It should be considered, first of all, that Socrates' question is directly addressed to Phaedrus. Who is Phaedrus? We learn something about him from the other two Platonic dialogues in which he

---

[1] Ὦ φίλε Φαῖδρε, ποῖ δὴ καὶ πόθεν;

appears. In the *Protagoras* (315 c) he is briefly mentioned as in company with the physician Eryximachus at the gathering of sophists in the house of Callias; he, his companion, and some others are reported to be asking the famous sophist Hippias some questions about nature and astronomy. In the *Symposium* Phaedrus is again paired with Eryximachus, who presents him as "the father of the speeches," as the one who is responsible for the proposal that there be a series of speeches honoring love (177 a – b). Phaedrus' own speech, the first in the series, is a celebration of love as the cause of our greatest good; what is most striking about Phaedrus' speech and most important for the dramatic movement of the *Symposium* as a whole is the close link which the speech maintains with the traditional *mythos.*

It appears, then, that Phaedrus is one who associates with physicians and sophists, who has some interest in investigations of nature, and who draws heavily upon mythical things. These characteristics are confirmed in the *Phaedrus.* When the dialogue begins, Phaedrus is following the advice of the physician Acumenus (father of Eryximachus); and later Phaedrus reveals that he is conversant with the teachings of Hippocrates regarding the nature of the human body (270 c). He has just come from listening to Lysias, and later he betrays some familiarity with the rhetorical techniques taught by the leading sophists of the day (266 c ff.). And he asks Socrates about the mythical things, thereby providing the occasion for the posing of the question whether such things are really mythical or whether they are rather matters of nature (229 c). In all these characteristics there are allusions—but only allusions—to who Phaedrus is in the *Phaedrus.*

In the opening question Socrates calls Phaedrus by name. His name (Φαῖδρος) means "bright," "beaming," "radiant." So, in terms of his name, Phaedrus is one who is radiant, one who shines. And, indeed, in the dialogue itself a principal task will be to attend to a way of radiance, of shining—specifically, to the way in which, through such shining as that embodied by Phaedrus, something else shines in such a way as to announce itself. For this something that so announces itself Socrates uses the name "being" (οὐσία). The *Phaedrus* has especially to do with being in its way of shining forth—that is, with "the beautiful" (τὸ καλόν).

In the opening question Socrates does not simply call Phaedrus by name but uses a particular form of address: He calls him "my friend Phaedrus" (ʾΩ φίλε Φαῖδρε), using the vocative of "φίλος," related to "φιλία" (love, friendship). In this phrase Socrates not only indicates that *philia* and what is akin to it will be a principal theme of the *Phaedrus* but also suggests *how* it will be made a problem in the dialogue. He uses a form of *philia,* rather than of *eros,* though the latter is what is specifically at issue in the *Phaedrus.* What is the difference, then, between *philia* and *eros*? One way of regarding this difference is expressed by the Athenian in the *Laws* (VIII, 837 a): speaking of *philia* he says that when this feeling "becomes intense [σφοδρός], we call it *eros.*" The *Phaedrus* makes a problem of *philia* by taking up as an issue the kind of intensity that distinguishes *philia* from *eros.* Such intensity is understood as madness.

In the opening question Socrates asks Phaedrus where he is going and where he comes from. This question can be understood at three distinct levels. First of all, it can be taken in its most literal sense, and, indeed, it is to an understanding of the question at this level that Phaedrus' answer is most immediately relevant: he comes from listening to Lysias in the house of Epicrates and is going for a walk outside the wall. Also, however, the question can be understood as concerning Phaedrus not just *qua* individual but rather *qua* man. This constitutes the second level of the question. At this level Phaedrus' answer says: men are formed in the city— this is where they come from—and they are formed especially by the speeches they hear in the city. In fact, it will turn out that Phaedrus is literally carrying such a speech with him when he leaves the city. This fact, in turn, throws suspicion on his answer to the other part of the question. Do men go outside the city? Do they really succeed in getting beyond the walls? Or, rather, do not most men remain merely "men of Athens" in the sense which that phrase receives in the *Apology*? Yet, the *Apology* is the self-presentation of one man who does go beyond the city in the most decisive way: Socrates is beyond the city precisely by virtue of his way of being in the city. And it is because Socrates is aloof from the city in this profound sense that he is tried and convicted by the "men of Athens."

There is a third and highest level at which the question Socrates asks of Phaedrus can be understood. It can be understood as a question about the ultimate whither and whence of the human soul, that is, as a question about the origin and the end that define the destiny (μοῖρα) of the human soul and thereby give to the soul its proper limits. To the "men of Athens" Socrates appears as one who hubristically places himself beyond certain of these limits—for example, in his comportment with respect to Apollo as he describes it in the trial, not to mention his appearance of arrogance in his questioning of others.[2] Yet, against the men of Athens Socrates maintains that his relation to the god and to his own ignorance constitutes precisely his way of maintaining himself within his proper limits. Obviously the issue can be decided, i.e., there can be a true judgment regarding Socrates, only if these limits constitutive of man's *moira* and the appropriate means for man's maintaining himself within this *moira* are somehow determined. Such determination is, however, intrinsically inaccessible to the "men of Athens"; for its sake one needs to leave the city. This determination is the most comprehensive matter at issue in Socrates' principal speech in the *Phaedrus.*

To the opening question Phaedrus answers in some detail. Where is he going? He is going for a walk outside the wall. Why?

---

[2] In the *Apology* Socrates' appearance of *hubris* is correlative to his actual leveling of the charge of *hubris* against Meletus (*Apol.* 26 e; cf. above, Ch. I, Sect. 4 a). This appearance becomes more explicit in the *Symposium,* presumably because it is more evident to the symposiasts than to the "men of Athens" at large. Specifically, when Socrates finally arrives at the banquet at Agathon's house and is invited by Agathon to sit next to him so that he might share the wisdom that has come to Socrates on his way to the banquet, Socrates, with apparent irony, draws a contrast between his own meagre and dream-like wisdom and the wisdom of Agathon which has shone forth on the previous day in his tragedy performed before the multitude; Agathon then replies: "You are hubristic, Socrates, and a little later on you and I shall go to court on this matter of your wisdom, and Dionysus shall be our judge" (175 c – e). In the last part of the *Symposium* Socrates is openly put on trial for *hubris* by the drunken Alcibiades (219 c, cf. 215 b).

It should be noted that in Athenian legal proceedings "ὕβρις" simply meant "an aggravated personal assault" in contrast to the slighter kind which was called "αἰκία." The significance of the fact that Socrates gives the appearance of *hubris* and the import of his being explicitly tried for *hubris* in the *Symposium* can be seen only if the word is grasped in its fundamental sense as an attempt to transgress one's proper limits. The most explicit formulation of this sense is given in Book IV of the *Laws* (715 e – 716 b). Cf. also Richard Lewis Nettleship, *Lectures on the Republic of Plato* (London: Macmillan, 1964), pp. 97-98.

Because he has been sitting all morning listening to speeches and is in need of a refreshing walk. He is going outside the wall on the advice of the physician Acumenus, who says that this is more invigorating. So, Phaedrus is going outside the city in order to relieve his fatigue, to purge himself of the effects of sitting in the city listening to speeches. This is his expressed intention, which should, however, be contrasted with the suspicion which Socrates later expresses that actually Phaedrus is going outside the city in order to practice the speech he has learned or brought with him from the city.

Where, specifically, does Phaedrus come from? He has been listening to Lysias, son of Cephalus. Socrates asks if Lysias is in the city. Phaedrus replies: Yes, at the house of Epicrates, which previously belonged to Morychus,[3] near the Olympieum. The playful allusiveness of these details can be seen if we consider why Socrates asks if Lysias is in the city. The reason is that Lysias is the son of Cephalus, who, as we learn from the *Republic,* lives in the Piraeus. In this connection it can be said that, just as the *Republic* begins with Socrates' going down from Athens to the Piraeus, so the *Phaedrus* begins by relating that Lysias has come up from the Piraeus. To what place in Athens has he ascended? He has come up to a house near the Olympieum, the temple of Zeus. Lysias has ascended almost to the abode which Zeus has in the city. But just such an abode (freed of its link to the city) and just such an ascent are what will be spoken of in the great myth of the soul which Socrates tells while he and Phaedrus are outside the city. The movement of such ascent will prove to be something extraordinarily demanding, and we wonder how Lysias fares in the ascent. We wonder whether his ascent is not perhaps something like a comic version of the genuine ascent spoken of in the myth. But, at least, Lysias does not ascend all the way to the temple of Zeus—or, if he does, he does not remain there. He stops at the house of Epicrates and *delivers speeches.* What do speeches have to do with his journey? What does *logos* have to do with the ascent towards the abode of Zeus?

---

[3] Regarding these two characters see G. J. De Vries, *A Commentary on the Phaedrus of Plato* (Amsterdam: A. M. Hakkert, 1969), pp. 34-35.

(b) Love of Speeches (227 b − 230 e)

Phaedrus' answer to the opening question has served to focus attention on the events that preceded the meeting between Socrates and Phaedrus. The event that is to constitute the dialogue itself is first projected as a recounting and then, shortly thereafter, as a repetition of those preceding events.

Phaedrus offers to tell Socrates about Lysias' speech if he will come along on the walk. Socrates agrees, and Phaedrus proceeds to tell him that the speech was about love but that it involved a very clever twist: it argued that favors (in the erotic sense) should be granted to the non-lover in preference to the lover. Socrates immediately responds by saying that he would indeed be pleased if it should also argue that favors should be granted to the poor, the old, and so on for all the various qualities which Socrates himself shares with the majority of men; in this case, he adds, the speech would present an attractive democratic view. This first burst of irony that Socrates directs at the speech of Lysias serves not only to place the non-lover on the side of the many but also to point to the kind of intention which Socrates discerns behind the composing of such speeches. This intention, i.e., the end which such speeches are meant to serve, is political in a broad and, at the same time, pernicious sense: such speeches belong to that arsenal of means by which men attempt to persuade others in such a way as to serve their own advantage.

Socrates is so determined to hear of the speech that he is willing to extend the walk as far as necessary. When Phaedrus insists that he could never recite from memory such a speech, composed, as it was, by one of the cleverest writers of the day, Socrates accuses him of indulging in pretense: he knows Phaedrus well enough to realize that Phaedrus heard the speech not just once but several times and that finally he borrowed the book and read the speech; then, Socrates continues, when Phaedrus grew tired, he went for a walk, probably with the speech memorized; as he was going outside the walls to practice it, he was happy to meet a lover of speeches with whom to share the speech he had learned; and so he might just as well drop his pretense of hesitating to deliver the speech, since he has (Socrates is quite sure) already decided to deliver it whether anyone requests it or not. When Phaedrus still insists that he does not know the speech by memory and is about to proceed repeating only the general drift of it, Socrates spies the written speech under Phaedrus' cloak. He demands that Phaedrus read it to him (227 b — 228 e).

In this exchange regarding the speech of Lysias and Phaedrus' relation to it we need to note what is brought to light about Socrates. Especially we need to consider how Phaedrus remarks to him that the topic of the speech is one which is appropriate for Socrates' ears. The reason for the appropriateness, Phaedrus explains, is that the speech was about love (ἐρωτικός) (227 c). Why is it that an erotic speech is especially appropriate to the ears of Socrates? Presumably, it is so because of Socrates' own expertise in erotic matters, because Socrates is one who, to an exceptional degree, knows about love matters. Indeed, Socrates' skill in such things is confirmed in the other two Platonic dialogues that deal extendedly with love. In the *Lysis* (204 b — c) Socrates, confessing his incapacity in most matters, insists, by contrast, that by some means or other he has received from the gods the gift of being able to recognize quickly a lover or a beloved. In the *Symposium* (177 d — e, cf. 198 d) he is still more emphatic: he says that he claims to understand nothing but erotic matters (τὰ ἐρωτικά). And certainly the events and the speech with which the *Symposium* ends, certainly the portrait which Alcibiades there gives of Socrates' curious engagement in love affairs, in which he proves so skillful as to be able to pose as beloved rather than lover with such young men as Charmides, Euthydemus, and Alcibiades himself (222 b)—certainly these make it evident that Socrates' knowledge of erotic matters is not something aloof from the erotic pursuit itself, however radically Socrates may transform the character of such pursuit. Socrates' expertise in erotic matters is an engagement, and, though he indeed transforms these matters, he does not do so in the guise of a disinterested, unerotic spectator of erotic affairs (cf. *Sym.* 213 c — d, 214 c — d, 216 d; also, e.g., *Char.* 154 b, 155d, *Lovers* 133 a).

Socrates is a lover. What does he love? This is indicated by Socrates himself in the course of his recounting of what he thinks happened prior to the meeting between himself and Phaedrus. The relevant point is that, according to Socrates, Phaedrus was pleased to meet a "lover of speeches" (τῶν λόγων ἐραστής) as he was heading outside the wall, for such a meeting promised him the opportunity of having someone on whom to practice the speech of Lysias. Thus, by Socrates' own description of himself, he is a lover of *logoi.*

But speeches are not the only things that Socrates loves. He is also engaged erotically with some of those who, like Phaedrus, offer him speeches. In the first casting Phaedrus is to practice delivering to Socrates a speech in which a non-lover addresses a beloved in such a way as to win out (to gain erotic favors) over the lover. In other words, what is initially posed is an "acting out" by Phaedrus and Socrates of the relation between the non-lover and the beloved. So, initially Phaedrus is cast in the role of the non-lover who is seeking gratification of his sexual desires, and Socrates is cast in the role of the beloved to whom the non-lover delivers the speech. But then it is discovered that "Lysias is present" (228 e), that is, that Phaedrus is in possession of the written speech of Lysias, so that Phaedrus' bond with the role of the self-seeking non-lover is, as it were, loosened. When the non-lover of Lysias' speech is later unmasked as a lover in disguise, [4] the play between Socrates and Phaedrus thereby becomes transparently that of lover and beloved, though as in those cases cited by Alcibiades in the *Symposium* there is a curious reversal with respect to who is lover and who is beloved. But the reversal is in the reverse direction from that about which Alcibiades remarks: in the *Phaedrus* Socrates ends up playing lover and Phaedrus beloved—or better, what begins as erotic play between Socrates and Phaedrus unfolds into an actual practice of Socrates' love for Phaedrus, a practice which exemplifies that teaching regarding love for which Socrates speaks in the dialogue. Indeed, this erotic engagement between Socrates and Phaedrus is indicated near the beginning of the erotic play, specifically, in Socrates' curious remark: "O Phaedrus, if I don't know Phaedrus, I have forgotten myself. But neither of these things is the case" (228 a). The reference is to the connection between the erotic engagement with

---

[4] At the beginning of Socrates' first speech (237 b). See below, Section 2 b.

another and knowledge of oneself, a connection that will finally be thematized when at the end of his second speech Socrates says that one "sees himself in his lover as in a mirror" (255 d).

Thus, Socrates is a lover of Phaedrus—or, in dramatic terms, will emerge as such through the love play of the dialogue. Socrates is a lover of *logoi* and of Phaedrus, and thus we come upon the problem regarding how these belong together, these two loves of Socrates. This same problem is posed dramatically when it turns out that Phaedrus has been hiding the speech of Lysias under his cloak.

Socrates and Phaedrus turn aside and go along the Ilissus looking for a place where they can sit and read.[5] Both are barefooted, and they go along the river with their feet in the water. Nothing is yet said about crossing the river; but later, in the heat of the speech-making, the question of crossing the river will become crucial, and Socrates will actually threaten to set off across the river (242 a). In this connection we note that in the *Republic* there is also an important image of a river, the river of Lethe, and that, in fact, the *Republic* concludes with the task of making "a good crossing of the river" (621 c) and that it thereby gathers up in this image much of what the *Republic* has made manifest about the matter at issue. In its most immediate meaning, the crossing of the river of Lethe constitutes that *ascent* by which the soul returns from Hades to another life on earth. Though, indeed, there is no simple correspondence between the imagery of the *Republic* and that of the *Phaedrus*—we must even guard against that formalism which would all too easily assume such a correspondence—nevertheless, the indications that an ascent is also at issue in the various dimensions of the *Phaedrus* are significant with regard to the role which the image of the river plays in this dialogue. The question is: What is required for a "good crossing" of the shallow river Ilissus?

Phaedrus points to a tall plane tree, noting that there is shade under it and a good breeze and grass on which they can sit or lie (229 a – b). We wonder whether there might be some exceptional

---

[5] For discussion of the exact route taken (including map) see Léon Robin, "Notice" in *Oeuvres Complètes,* Tome IV, 3ᵉ Partie, "Phèdre" (Paris, 1966), pp. x-xii.

need for protection from exposure to the sun. As Socrates and Phaedrus walk towards the tall plane tree they engage in a discussion of mythical things. The discussion is provoked by a question which Phaedrus asks regarding the place along the river where they are walking: he asks whether it is not the place where Boreas is said to have carried off Oreithyia. Socrates answers that the spot to which Phaedrus is referring is two or three stades farther down. We wonder at Socrates' acquaintance with the countryside, especially if we bear in mind (cf. *Crito* 52 b) that Socrates was almost notorious for never leaving the city and, even more, if we anticipate the thematic discussion of this Socratic practice which is to come (230 c – e) just after the discussion of mythical things. However little Socrates is acquainted with the country outside the walls, he does seem rather well-informed about those features that have some connection with the kind of things told of in myths.

In the name of the god, Phaedrus asks Socrates about the truth of such stories about gods: "By Zeus, Socrates, do you believe this mythic tale [μυθολόγημα] to be true?" Socrates answers:

> If I disbelieved, as the wise men [οἱ σοφοί] do, I would not be out of place; then I might contrive [σοφιζόμενος] and say that while the maiden was at play with Pharmaceia a blast of Boreas pushed her off the neighboring rocks and that when she had died in this manner she was said to have been carried off by Boreas (229 c – d).

The crucial word in this reply (σοφίζομαι) has a double meaning: it means "devise," "contrive," in the sense, for example, of skillfully composing an explanation, but it also means "deceive," "play subtle tricks." The word is derived from the same root as "οἱ σοφοί" ("wise men"), so presumably the double meaning is also to resound in the latter.[6] The point is that by playing on this double sense Socrates is being thoroughly ironic about those "accounts," those "contrivances," by which the "wise men" perform their subtle trick of changing mythical things into natural things. In

---

[6] See the note concerning the function of the criticism of οἱ σοφοί in W. J. Verdenius, "Notes on Plato's *Phaedrus*," *Mnemosyne* IV 8 (1955), p. 268. See also the more general interpretation by Hermann Gundert, "Enthusiasmos und Logos bei Platon," *Lexis*, 2, 1 (1949), pp. 25-46.

fact, he goes on immediately to say that such men are not entirely enviable, for, having "explained" the Boreas myth in this way, they must then proceed "to explain" Centaurs, Chimaera, Gorgons, and all sorts of strange creatures. There would seem to be no end to the appearance of such creatures which threaten to overpower man's puny means not only to defend himself but also to contrive accounts.

The "wise men" of whom Socrates speaks not only contrive but also in their contriving they deceive, that is, conceal things in such a way as to deceive others about them. This side of their practice is especially evident in reference to the specific myth spoken of here, that of Boreas and Oreithyia. According to the story, Oreithyia was a lovely Athenian maiden with whom Boreas, the north wind, fell in love; her father, Erechtheus, refused, however, to give her to Boreas. Then one day when she was playing on the bank of the river, Boreas swept down in a great gust and swept her away. Later she bore him two sons. What is the effect of the "contrivance" wrought by the "wise men" in the case of this story? Whereas the myth presents the fate of Oreithyia (who was playing with Pharmaceia, i.e., sorcery) in terms of love, as brought by the love of a god for her, the "contrivance" makes no mention of love; it conceals, as it were, whatever love may have had to do with her fate. It might be said that the only result which the "wise men" can see in Oreithyia's being loved by a god and playing with things like sorcery (which is not unrelated to madness) is a descent into death; they suppress the alternative of which the myth speaks, that the outcome might be an ascent into the company of the gods.

Socrates proceeds to describe his own attitude regarding myth by telling, first of all, how he abstains from those kind of "contrivances" which he has just attributed to the "wise men":

> But I have no leisure for them at all; and the reason, my friend, is this: I am not yet able, in accord with the Delphic inscription, to know myself; so it seems to me ridiculous, when I do not yet know that, to investigate alien things. And so I renounce such and, accepting the current belief about these things, as I was saying just now, I investigate not these

things but myself, to discover whether I am a monster more complicated and more furious than Typhon or a gentler and simpler animal to whom a divine and modest fate [μοῖρα] is given by nature (230 a).

Thus, Socrates does not busy himself with contriving "explanations" for the things told of in the myths, he does not occupy himself with dissolving mythical things into natural things, because he is too much occupied with the task of knowing himself. This does not mean, however, that Socrates simply ignores the myths, nor does it mean that, having, as he says, accepted the current belief about them, he is then indifferent to them in every respect except the most extrinsic. That Socrates sustains a more essential relation to the myths is evident in the very way he describes that task of self-knowing on account of which he has "no leisure" for the "contrivances" of the "wise men": he describes his task precisely in reference to, in terms of, the *mythical* creature Typhon, and he describes it also as linked to the Delphic inscription, which means, recalling the elaboration of Socrates' relation to the oracle given in the *Apology* (cf. Ch. I, Sect. 3 b), that he indicates its link to mythical things. The very task of self-knowledge and Socrates' way of being led into that task are ultimately linked to mythical things, and, rather than contriving "explanations" which would dissolve the mythical cast of these things, Socrates lets such things be directive and illuminating for his task of self-knowing. The way in which the mythical things belong together with the task of self-knowing is portrayed in its most nearly public, i.e., most easily accessible, form in the *Apology*. We shall see that a more essential form of this connection is presented in the great myth of the *Phaedrus*. At this point, however, it suffices merely to note that it is Typhon to whom Socrates refers in giving the mythic cast to his task of self-knowing—Typhon, the most frightful offspring of the earth, a monster with a hundred heads who rose up against the gods, who was, as a result, killed by Zeus' thunderbolt, and whose defeat marked the securing of the reign of Zeus. Socrates seeks to know whether he is of a "Typhonic" or "un-Typhonic" nature—that is, to place himself with respect to his proper subordination to the god of bounds, Zeus himself (cf. *Laws* 842 e).

The entire opening section of the *Phaedrus* concludes with an explicit reference to the fact that the situation of the speech-making now about to commence is a very unusual one for Socrates. When Socrates exclaims that Phaedrus has been the stranger's perfect guide in bringing him to such a charming place, Phaedrus answers:

> Whereas you, my wonderful friend, strike me as the oddest of men. Anyone would take you, as you say, for a stranger being shown the country by a guide instead of a native: never leaving town to cross the frontier nor even, I believe, so much as setting foot outside the walls (230 c − d).

Socrates responds:

> I am a friend of learning [φιλομαθής]. The country and the trees are not willing to teach me anything, but the men in the city are. Yet you seem to have discovered the charm for getting me out (230 d).

What is the charm with which Phaedrus is able to charm Socrates into leaving the city? What does he use in order to lure Socrates out of the city, in order to accomplish what even the threat of death could not do? Socrates himself identifies it: It is with *logoi,* in this case a written *logos,* that Phaedrus draws him out into the country. Indeed, we suspect that it is on account of this same thing that Socrates normally does *not* leave the city: men in the city speak, trees and countryside do not, and Socrates is a lover of speeches. It seems that in the *Phaedrus* Socrates leaves the city for the same reason that usually prevents his leaving the city, for the sake of *logoi.* It seems that Socrates' attachment to *logoi* is stronger even than his bond to the city.

Section 2.   The Three Speeches (230 e − 257 b)

(a) Lysias' Speech (230 e − 237 a)

Phaedrus reads Lysias' speech. This speech, written in first person, is addressed to a boy by a man who claims not to be his lover. The theme of the speech is that it is better for the boy to grant his favors to a non-lover than to a lover. The speech consists mostly of a disorderly and repetitive listing of various advantages to be gained by the boy if he consorts with a non-lover. Much is made of the fact that the lover is lacking in self-control and moderation, that he acts from passion, and that his passion is anything but dependable; by contrast, the non-lover is presented as one who does not act out of compulsion but rather according to his view of his own best interest.

In fact, the entire speech is addressed to the self-interest of the beloved (cf. esp. 233 e) and is designed to show how his self-interest is furthered by the same arrangement that furthers the self-interest of the non-lover. The underlying assumption of the speech as a whole is that the lover, the non-lover, and the beloved are completely selfish, that they are concerned with and need be concerned with nothing but their own private advantage. Their only motivation appears to be *desire* of one sort or another, the difference between lover and non-lover consisting only in the fact that, whereas the lover is completely given over to lust for sexual pleasure, the non-lover also desires other things. In effect, there is in Lysias' speech an "implicit cynicism" regarding human motivation.[7] This is especially evident in the form of address adopted in the speech: It is put in the mouth of a non-lover whose own interest would be served if the boy to whom he speaks accepted the thesis of the speech.

As soon as Phaedrus finishes reading Lysias' speech, he asks Socrates' opinion about it. Socrates exclaims that he has indeed been overcome by it, not, however, because of the merit of the speech but rather because he watched Phaedrus and saw how delighted Phaedrus was by the speech while reading it. Phaedrus immediately accuses Socrates of playing, of making fun of (παίζειν) the speech, and, invoking the name of Zeus, he implores Socrates to give his honest judgment of the speech. Socrates ironically denies having even noticed whether the author of the speech has said what he ought to say; this irony with respect to the content of the speech serves to leave open this question in

---

[7] Sinaiko, *Love, Knowledge, and Discourse,* pp. 26-28.

order that it might later be dealt with in a much more effective way than would be possible here, namely, in the transition from Socrates' first speech to his second speech. By contrast, the present transition focuses exclusively on the failings which the speech exhibits on its formal side, i.e., regarded simply in its rhetorical manner.

Even in this respect Socrates refers only to the most general defect of the speech, namely, that it says the same thing two or three times. When Phaedrus then takes issue with this criticism, insisting that the very merit of the speech lies in its having omitted none of the points that pertain to the topic, Socrates openly states his disagreement and alludes to having heard better speeches on the same matters. When Phaedrus inquires where Socrates has heard them, he answers that at the moment he cannot say but insists, nevertheless, that he is certain of having heard something better—from Sappho or Anacreon, or perhaps from some prose writer. Why is he so insistent? He explains:

> Good sir [ὦ δαιμόνιε], there is something welling up within my breast, which makes me feel that I could find something different and something better, to say. I am of course well aware that it can't be anything originating in me, for I know my own ignorance; so I suppose it can only be that it has been poured into me, through my ears, as into a vessel, from some external source; though in my stupid fashion I have actually forgotten how, and from whom, I heard it (235 c – d).

Socrates is filled with inspiration, something has been poured into him. Nevertheless, his is an inspiration to which irony is not alien. His very statement of his condition is framed by indications of his ironic forgetting of the source from which he has been filled. Phaedrus clearly recognizes that Socrates is being ironic on this point. But what is important is to see what the irony accomplishes, that is, to see that Socrates' ironic forgetting serves to bind the condition of inspiration and the awareness of that condition *to* the awareness of ignorance in a peculiarly radical way: The awareness of ignorance requires that a source of one's wisdom be posed beyond oneself; this same awareness, if sufficiently radical, requires, furthermore, that one confess his ignorance of the very nature of the source. One way of confessing that ignorance is to tell of the source in a mode of telling which openly grants the concealment of the source from man.

Phaedrus now insists on hearing from Socrates this speech that is different from and better than the written speech of Lysias. In exchange Phaedrus extends to Socrates a curious promise: "Then I promise, like the nine archons, to set up at Delphi a golden life-size statue, not only of myself but of you also" (235 d – e). In mentioning the nine archons and the setting up of a statue, Phaedrus is referring to a practice instituted by Solon by which the nine archons took an oath that if they transgressed any one of the laws they would dedicate a golden statue of a man.[8]

So, if Socrates delivers a speech that is better than Lysias' speech, then Phaedrus will set up golden statues, following the practice of the nine archons. But the archons are under oath to set up such statues only in case they transgress a law. Hence, if Socrates delivers a better speech, then Phaedrus must by that very fact have been convicted of breaking a law. But in such a case, what law would Phaedrus have broken? His reference to Delphi as the place where he would set up the statues (this reference is lacking in Aristotle's account of the practice) and the fact that Phaedrus' promise comes immediately after Socrates' most radical statement yet about his ignorance (previously linked explicitly with the Delphic injunction—229 e) strongly suggest that the law which Phaedrus would prove to have broken would be the Delphic command "Know thyself." But how would Phaedrus prove to have trespassed this "law"? More precisely, in case Socrates should prove to deliver a better speech, how would Phaedrus then prove to have broken this command? Presumably, it would be on account of his having proved not really to know Socrates very well, in the sense of not knowing that Socrates can give (or, at least,

---

[8] "And he [Solon] established a constitution and made other laws, and they ceased to observe the ordinances of Draco, except those relating to homicide. They wrote up the laws on the Boards and set them in the Royal Colonnade, and all swore to observe them; and the Nine Archons used to make affirmation on oath at the Stone that if they transgressed any one of the laws they would dedicate a golden statue of a man; owing to which they are even now still sworn in with this oath." Aristotle, *Athenian Constitution*, VII, 1.

recall) a better speech then Lysias'. But how would Phaedrus' failure to know Socrates constitute a violation of the Delphic command, which enjoins Phaedrus to know himself, not Socrates? This could be the case only if the two tasks, knowing himself and knowing Socrates, were not independent, only if there were an essential connection between them. And, in fact, an essential connection between self-knowledge and knowledge of a person with whom one is erotically engaged has already been alluded to (cf. 228 a), and already, in relation to that allusion, we have made reference to the explicit establishment of this connection that finally occurs near the end of Socrates' second speech (255d; cf. above, Sect. 1 b). Presumably it is in view of this connection that Phaedrus proposes to set up statues both of himself and of Socrates. This amounts to a proposal to set up images through which to see himself and his beloved, and by coming to see his beloved he comes that much more to see himself; thus, the penalty which Phaedrus will pay for violating the Delphic command will be of precisely such a character as to serve to re-establish him in an obedience to the command, in the task of self-knowing. Finally, it should be noted that the connection between self-knowing and knowing one's lover/beloved is introduced very shortly after the present passage in almost the same form in which it was previously introduced. More precisely, a reciprocal form of the previous formula is introduced, cast in terms of Phaedrus' self-knowledge rather than Socrates'. Phaedrus is urging Socrates to go ahead and deliver his speech so as not to force him to repeat what Socrates had said to him earlier. But then in threatening to repeat the formula Phaedrus does repeat it: "O Socrates, if I don't know Socrates, I have forgotten myself" (236 c).

Socrates responds to Phaedrus' curious promise by playfully suggesting that, if Phaedrus thinks it is his opinion that Lysias' speech fails in every respect and that he can compose another speech on the same theme totally different from Lysias' speech, then Phaedrus is like those statues he would erect ("golden")—that is, unknowing to the most drastic extent. As a result, Phaedrus makes a concession: he will allow Socrates to make use of the point that the lover is less in control of himself than the non-lover and will require of Socrates only that he speak better on the other points without saying the same thing as Lysias. Having made this concession, which allows Socrates to remain somewhat closer to Lysias in his speech, Phaedrus then revises his earlier promise: If Socrates can do what Phaedrus now asks, then, in Phaedrus' words, "up with your statue in wrought gold beside the offering of the Cypselids at Olympia" (236 b). Noting that the city of Olympia served as the main sanctuary of Zeus, it is evident that what Phaedrus is doing is transferring the statue of Socrates from Delphi (where Apollo has his oracle) to Olympia (the sanctuary of Zeus). The suggestion is that, if Socrates should succeed in bettering Lysias, he would then have succeeded in that ascent to the abode of Zeus which Lysias enacted prior to the beginning of the dialogue. On the other hand, however, we are left wondering whether Socrates really would succeed, for the statue, though it would be in Olympia, would be beside the offering of the Cypselids, which was in the temple dedicated not to Zeus but to Hera.

With playful irony Socrates suggests that he was only jesting when he said he could give a better speech than that of Lysias, that he was attacking Phaedrus' beloved Lysias only in order to tease Phaedrus. It is at this point that Phaedrus threatens to repeat that formula which Socrates used on him earlier when he hesitated to speak—and in threatening to repeat it actually does so. Then, he goes on to strengthen his threat: he threatens to compel Socrates by force, warning Socrates that they are alone in a solitary spot and that he is stronger and younger than Socrates. His words suggest physical force, but we immediately learn that the reference is to a different kind of compulsion: Phaedrus threatens never again to recite or report any more speeches to him. As Socrates prepares to deliver his speech, he remarks that Phaedrus has indeed found the appropriate means of compulsion to exercise on one who, like himself, is a lover of *logoi* (236 b − e).

(b) Socrates' First Speech (237 a − 243 e)

In taking the oath which consists of the threat never again to present any speeches to Socrates, Phaedrus wonders by what god he ought to swear—whether perhaps by the plane tree. We recall that previously (229 c, 234 e) he has sworn mostly in the name of Zeus. It is to be expected that the speech which Phaedrus now forces Socrates to deliver by this oath will have some peculiar bearing on man's need of protection from undue exposure to the sun and perhaps to other gods as well.

Yielding to the compulsion exercised by Phaedrus, Socrates prepares to deliver his speech. His preparation consists of three steps. First, he informs Phaedrus that he will keep his head covered during the speech so as to be able to rush through it "without looking at you and breaking down for shame" [αἰσχύνη] (237 a). To Phaedrus this remark very likely suggests that Socrates is apprehensive lest his speech prove inferior to the written speech of Lysias. For Socrates, however, the shame will be due to the unworthy portrait of love that will be presented in the speech.[9] Socrates' covering his head during the speech amounts to his adopting a kind of mock anonymity by which to dissociate himself from the speech. It is also important that, having covered his head, he does not see Phaedrus throughout the entire speech; the speech is delivered in the marked absence of any vision of his beloved.

Socrates' second step in preparation for his speech is his invocation of the Muses: "Come then [᾽Αγετε δή], clear-voiced Muses, . . . aid in the tale [μῦθος]." Socrates adds in his invocation that the tale is being told under compulsion and that its aim is that he, whom Phaedrus already considers wise, may seem even wiser to his friend (237 a — b). It should be noted that the Muses, whom Socrates here invokes for inspiration, preside over music (μουσική). Presumably, then, we are to understand what follows as music (in the Greek sense). In fact, the very phrase with which Socrates begins his invocation (᾽Αγετε δή) is the typical introductory formula of a dithyramb, a hymn to Dionysus.[10] In this connection, it should also be observed that the word which Socrates uses to describe what he is about to present is *"mythos."*

---

[9] R. Hackforth, *Plato's Phaedrus* (Indianapolis: Bobbs-Merrill, 1952), p. 35, n. 4; also De Vries, *Commentary,* p. 82.

[10] De Vries, *Commentary,* p. 82. De Vries notes that Socrates' speeches also show many other dithyrambic traits.

Socrates' final preparatory step is in a sense already part of the speech. But it is set apart from the rest of the speech and, in a very important way, distinguishes Socrates' speech from the speech of Lysias. Whereas Lysias' speech is presented directly in first person, so that all we know about the speaker is what he chooses to reveal to the boy (namely that he is a non-lover), Socrates prefaces his speech with an account of the situation of the speaker. According to this prefatory account, the speaker is a lover who is pretending to be a non-lover and who is trying to persuade the beloved that it is better to accept a non-lover; in that way he hopes to win the beloved for himself (237 b). Thus, by virtue of this preface the entire speech is presented from its very outset as a peculiar kind of "lie."[11]   As Socrates intimated earlier with regard to Lysias' speech (227 c – d; cf. above, Sect. 1 b), so here it is explicit that the intention behind the speech, i.e., the end to which it is dedicated, has nothing to do with truth but only with persuading others in whatever way is advantageous to oneself. What is even more striking, however, is that in the present case the speech is an attack on the lover which is being used precisely to further the interest of the lover; the disguised lover is making use of an attack on love precisely in order to win out in the erotic contest for the beloved. What he says in the speech (the castigation of love) conflicts with his very involvement in that pursuit for the sake of which he makes the speech. Clearly it is suggested that the disguised non-lover regards what he says about love in the speech, not as the truth, but as a useful lie. Thus, the first "improvement" which Socrates makes in Lysias' speech is to preface it with an indication that it is a lie. Indeed, after the preface Socrates goes on, in the manner of Lysias' speech, to present the speech in first person; but the disclosure of the situation, i.e., the preface which is *not* put into the mouth of the disguised lover but which, on the contrary, betrays the trickery he is using, serves to dissociate Socrates himself from what is said in the speech. Presumably, it is only with such dissociation as he acquires by covering his head and by unmasking the disguised lover that Socrates can present a speech incorporating the absurd thesis of Lysias' speech. Under

---

[11] Cf. Sinaiko, *Love, Knowledge, and Discourse*, pp. 31-32.

compulsion from Phaedrus, Socrates can bring himself to give the speech only by presenting what he says as a report on what someone else (the disguised lover) said in a situation where the intention was not to speak the truth but to deceive in such a way as to further the interest of the speaker. Maintaining his distance from it, Socrates presents the improved version of the speech of Lysias in order thereby to make evident the basic failings of Lysias' speech with regard both to form and to content.

Socrates, speaking for the disguised lover, begins by insisting on the importance of agreeing on what love is, in order then to be able to keep the "definition" in view in considering the further question as to whether the lover or the non-lover is to be preferred. The first of the two main parts of the speech is thus devoted to determining what love is and what "power" ($\delta\dot{\nu}\nu\alpha\mu\iota\varsigma$) it possesses. This determination involves four steps. Socrates begins by noting that it is manifest to everyone that love is a kind of desire [$\dot{\epsilon}\pi\iota\theta\nu\mu\dot{\iota}\alpha$ $\tau\iota\varsigma$ $\dot{o}$ $\ddot{\epsilon}\rho\omega\varsigma$]. The difficulty is that non-lovers also have desires—in fact, desires for that same thing to which the desires of lovers are directed, the beautiful ($\kappa\alpha\lambda\dot{o}\nu$). Hence, the description of love as a kind of desire does not suffice to distinguish the lover from the non-lover; both desire the beautiful. So, as the second step, Socrates proceeds to lay the basis for another account of what love is. He does so by observing that in man there are two ruling and leading things ($\iota\delta\dot{\epsilon}\alpha$)[12] : on the one hand, the innate desire for pleasure and, on the other hand, acquired opinion ($\delta\dot{o}\xi\alpha$) that aims at what is best. Thirdly, Socrates notes that these two things sometimes agree but sometimes are in strife and that sometimes one and sometimes the other has the greater strength. Thus, there are two basic conditions depending upon which of the two things leads. To one of these conditions Socrates gives the name "moderation" ($\sigma\omega\phi\rho\sigma\dot{\nu}\nu\eta$): "When opinion [$\delta\dot{o}\xi\alpha$] guides us by *logos* towards what is best and is stronger, that strength is called moderation." But, on the other hand, "when desire [$\dot{\epsilon}\pi\iota\theta\nu\mu\dot{\iota}\alpha$] drags us without *logos* [$\dot{\alpha}\lambda\dot{o}\gamma\omega\varsigma$] towards pleasure and has come to rule within us, the name given to that rule is *hubris*" (237 d – 238 a). Finally, Socrates proceeds to speak of *hubris* as

---

[12] See the note regarding this usage in De Vries, *Commentary*, p. 84.

thus determined. He observes that there are many forms of *hubris,* including gluttony and drunkenness, and that love is one such form:

> When desire, pursuing the pleasure of the beautiful, has gained strength over the opinion of *logos* that strives towards the right and has acquired from other desires akin to it fresh strength to strain towards bodily beauty, that very strength [ῥώμη] provides it with its name: it is called love [ἔρως] (238 b — c).

After this determination of what love is, there is a brief interruption during which Socrates and Phaedrus remark about how inspired Socrates is (238 c — d). The second part of the speech (238 c — 241 d), which commences after this brief interruption, amounts then to an application of the determination of love arrived at in the first part to the question, inherited from Lysias, as to why it is not in the best interest of a boy to accept a lover. In this application Socrates proceeds in an exceptionally orderly fashion. He states the various disadvantages which the acceptance of the lover would have for the intellect, for the body, and for the possessions of the boy. To this enumeration he then couples a list of ways in which the lover would fail even to give pleasure to the boy both while the love lasts and when it has ceased. The orderliness of the account serves by contrast to make evident how lacking the speech of Lysias was with regard to its formal structure.

Several issues need to be developed with regard to this speech as a whole. First, it should be noted that Socrates' first statement regarding what love is (that it is desire) is just the view that was implicitly assumed in Lysias' speech, so that Socrates' abandoning of this answer amounts to a rejection of Lysias' speech. Lysias assumes that love is sheer desire for sexual pleasure, but, as Socrates' speech makes evident, the non-lover (e.g., the one making the speech) also desires sexual pleasure (that is why he is making the speech). The result is, then, that there is no real difference between lovers and non-lovers but, at most, only the difference between more and less intense desire. But if the difference between lovers and non-lovers collapses, then irreparable damage is done to the thesis of Lysias' speech, namely, that the non-lover is to be preferred over the lover. In a sense, it may, then, be said that Socrates "prevents" the complete breakdown of Lysias' thesis by posing another "leading thing" in man besides desire. At the same time, this allows him to make more explicit the basic attitude towards love that underlies Lysias' speech.

Next, it needs to be stressed that according to Socrates' speech (in contrast to Lysias') love is not just desire of a certain kind, not just desire of the beautiful; rather it is the condition of *hubris* that results when a certain kind of desire becomes the dominant leading thing in man. So, love is a kind of *hubris*. As such, it is explicitly opposed to moderation ($\sigma\omega\phi\rho\sigma\sigma\acute{\nu}\nu\eta$) and also to *logos*. Near the end of the speech (241 a) this opposition is extended so as to become the opposition between *nous* and moderation, on the one side, and love and madness ($\mu\alpha\nu\acute{\iota}\alpha$), on the other. The same basic opposition is again at issue when, speaking of the disadvantages with respect to the intellect that would be gotten by accepting the lover, Socrates observes that the lover would be jealous and would prohibit the boy not only from consorting with others but also from "consorting with that which would most increase his wisdom, by which I mean divine philosophy [$\dot{\eta}$ $\theta\epsilon\acute{\iota}\alpha$ $\phi\iota\lambda\sigma\sigma\phi\acute{\iota}\alpha$]" (239 b). Thus, the opposition is also an *opposition between love and philosophy*. Yet clearly there is something problematic here: Philosophy, by the very word, is a kind of love—at least, a kind of *philia* if not of *eros*.

Finally, it needs to be seen how beneath these oppositions that are set out within the speech there is a fundamental conflict, running throughout the speech, between the circumstances under which Socrates makes the speech and what he actually says in the speech. In other words, there is a conflict between what Socrates *says* and the circumstances that surround the *deed* of saying it, and, in the final analysis, what primarily refutes the *logos* is the corresponding *ergon*. This basic conflict has two sides with respect to which it can be thematized. On the one side, it is expressed in the fact that Socrates, the lover of speeches who gives speeches on love, establishes in the speech a basic opposition between love and speech. What is a unity in the person of Socrates (*logos* and *eros*) is radically separated in the speech he makes. This conflict is

especially remarkable in view of the fact that it is through Socrates' character as a lover of speeches that Phaedrus compels him
to give this speech.

The other side of the conflict can be seen if we attend to
Socrates' repeated reference to his state of inspiration. Even before he began the speech, he spoke of something welling up within
him and suggested that the speech he knew had been poured into
him. At the beginning of the speech he invoked the assistance of
the Muses, and at the very end of his speech he finally broke out
into verse. Especially in the little dialogue that intervenes between
the two main parts of the speech (thus "disrupting" the unity of
the speech) Socrates proclaims himself divinely inspired: "For
truly there seems to be a divine presence in this spot, so that you
must not be surprised if, as my speech proceeds, I become as one
possessed; already my style is not far from dithyrambic" (238 c –
d). These descriptions by Socrates of his own condition while
giving the speech leave no question as to which side of the basic
opposition (set out in the speech) Socrates belongs on in his
presentation of the speech. His speaking is, by his own testimony,
a matter of being possessed, of speaking in dithyrambs; his condition is one which is much more like madness than it is like
moderation. In his making of the speech it is not a matter of
following acquired opinions, of soberly setting out something
which he already securely possesses, but rather a matter of receiving something into the space engendered by his awareness of
his ignorance; it is a matter of having something delivered over.
The circumstances under which Socrates presents the speech place
him on the side of love, *hubris,* and madness rather than that of
opinion, *nous,* and moderation. Socrates, disguising himself as a
non-lover through what he says in the speech, betrays the fact of
the disguise and proves to be a lover in the presentation of the
speech. This is the conflict: the speech is an attack on love
presented by one who in that very presentation reveals himself as
standing on the side of love. It is little wonder that Socrates
refuses, from shame, to look at Phaedrus during the speech: in the
conflict between what he says and the circumstances under which
he says it, he imitates that trickery which in the speech the
disguised lover perpetrates on his beloved.

Having enumerated the evils that result from consorting with a
lover, Socrates abruptly ends his speech. Phaedrus is surprised, for,
as he immediately remarks, he had thought that Socrates was only
in the middle of the speech and that he would go on to say as
much about the non-lover as he had said about the lover. Socrates
replies that one need only say that for each evil for which the
lover has been blamed there is a corresponding good belonging to
the non-lover. Socrates thus reminds us of the extent to which the
entire second part of the speech as delivered was little more than a
straightforward application of the "definition" of love reached in
the first part of the speech. What is most important, however, in
Socrates' refusal to deliver the other half that Phaedrus expected
are the further indications which it provides of that basic conflict
which could already be seen in the speech itself. This conflict
arose because of the tension between what was said in the speech
and the fact that the circumstances of Socrates' delivery of the
speech placed him on the side of all those things that were
castigated in the speech. Now this tension is brought almost fully
to light: Socrates describes himself as possessed by the nymphs
and as speaking not in mere dithyrambs but in heroic verse (241
e); he calls himself a seer (μάντις), and he speaks of how prophetic
(μαντικός) the soul is. Erotic, prophetic, "mad" Socrates cannot
bring himself to praise the calculative soberness of the Lysias-style
non-lover.

Socrates is so intent on avoiding having to give that half of the
speech that would praise the non-lover that he announces that he
will cross the river so as to get away before Phaedrus exercises
further compulsion on him. Shamed by the duplicity which he has
enacted in imitation of that of the disguised lover in the speech,
Socrates proposes just to go off across the river without Phaedrus,
that is, simply to abandon his beloved and the compulsion which
only a beloved can exercise. To cross the river so as to abandon his
beloved would amount, however, to enacting a stance opposite to
that maintained in delivering the speech; such an abandoning of
love and of the compulsion under which one can be placed by love
would amount to an enactment of an attempt to bring Socrates'
stance into accord with what he said in his speech, that is, to
eliminate the basic conflict that ran throughout the speech. The

question is whether Socrates could make "a good crossing of the river" by abandoning his beloved.

Socrates is restrained from crossing the river. Though he identifies his *daimon* as the restraining force, it is clear that Phaedrus is hardly irrelevant to Socrates' being held back from the crossing. He warns Socrates that it is almost noon and urges him to wait until it is cooler; and he adds: "Let us wait and discuss what we've heard; when it has got cool perhaps *we* will go" (242 a). Socrates is held back with his beloved, presumably because of the danger to which he would be exposed should he venture to abandon his beloved and cross the river in the noonday sun. The question is how the tie with the beloved can, for the crossing of the river, provide that protection from the sun which otherwise might be supplied by something like a plane tree.

Socrates responds to Phaedrus' proposal by exclaiming that with respect to *logoi* Phaedrus is godlike (θεῖος) and really wonderful (ἀτεχνῶς θαυμάσιος). He speaks of how many speeches Phaedrus has produced (more than anyone except Simmias) either by speaking them himself or by compelling others to do so, and he reveals, finally, that Phaedrus has become the cause of still another speech which Socrates is now about to deliver. The suggestion is that the beloved serves, as it were, for making a good crossing of the river by the way in which he is able to call forth *logoi*. And indeed that speech which Phaedrus now calls forth from Socrates will be a speech in which Socrates will make manifest how *logos* and *eros* belong together as pertaining to the means given to man for making a good crossing of the river.

Socrates says that, when he was about to cross the river, his *daimon,* which always acts as a restraining force, came to him and forbade him to leave the spot before making atonement for some offence against the divine. Now Socrates openly condemns the speech he gave under compulsion by Phaedrus. The need for atonement he casts in a mythic mold: Love, the son of Aphrodite, is a god and so cannot be anything evil, whereas both Socrates' speech as well as Lysias' speech have contended that love is evil; thus they have committed an offence against love, and, consequently, a purification is now necessary. In terms of the conflict involved in Socrates' first speech, what is now required—now that

Socrates has been held back from abandoning his beloved—is that the speech be brought into accord with the stance of the speaker, that is, that a new speech be given which, in what it says about love, madness, and philosophy, is in accord with the erotic, "mad" philosopher.

Socrates specifies the kind of purification which he is to undergo. He takes his directive from Stesichorus:

> And so, my friend, I must purify myself; now for such as offend with regard to mythology [μυθολογία] there is an ancient mode of purification, unknown to Homer, but known to Stesichorus. When Stesichorus lost the sight of his eyes because of his defamation of Helen, he was not, like Homer, at a loss to know why, but as a true poet [μουσικός] he understood the reason and promptly wrote the lines:
>> False, false the tale:
>> Thou never didst sail in the well-decked ships
>> Nor come to the towers of Troy (243 a).

Here we should especially note that Stesichorus' offence consisted in his defamation of Helen, the paradigm of a beautiful human being. Likewise, Socrates, in what he said about love in his speech, did offence not only against love "in general" but against his beloved Phaedrus. It will be recalled that throughout his delivery of the speech Socrates kept his head covered so as to avoid looking at Phaedrus. He cut himself off completely from the vision of someone beautiful; the example of Stesichorus suggests that such a withdrawing assault on the beautiful beloved carries with it the danger of becoming blind to such beautiful ones if not to the beautiful as such.

Stesichorus, having committed an offence in *logos* against Helen, carried out his atonement in *logos*, that is, he atoned for his offence by writing another poem recanting his defamation. Likewise, Socrates will atone by making another speech, the only difference being that he will do this before suffering any punishment. From its very outset there is one very significant difference in this new speech: Socrates now uncovers his head. Now he sees Phaedrus there before him in his radiance and now he addresses himself to Phaedrus. He asks:

Where is that boy I was talking to? He must listen to me once more and not rush off to yield to his non-lover before he hears what I have to say (243 e).

Phaedrus answers: "Here he is, quite close beside you, whenever you want him." Socrates no longer reports a speech made by a disguised lover but in his second speech speaks as lover to his beloved.[13]

(c) Socrates' Second Speech (243 e – 257 b)

Socrates' second speech is delivered as a means of purification from the offence against *eros* committed in the previous speech. The second speech will do honor to love both in what is said and in the way it is said. In other words, Socrates will praise love, and that very praising will be an exemplification of love as so praised. This character of the speech is hinted at in the very beginning. Attributing his previous speech to Phaedrus, who compelled him to deliver it, Socrates says that the speech which he is now to deliver will be by Stesichorus, son of Euphemus, of Himera. The speech will be a speech of passion (ἵμερος), of a lover, and will be, in what it says, an auspicious (εὔφημος) speech.[14]

(i) Madness (243 e – 245 c)

Socrates rejects outright the thesis shared by the two previous speeches, namely, that the non-lover should be favored because he is sane (σωφρονεῖ) while the lover is mad (μαίνεται). In opposition to this thesis Socrates now asserts that the greatest goods (τὰ μέγιστα τῶν ἀγαθῶν) come to us by means of madness (μανία), *when* that madness is sent by the gods. He thus introduces, in effect, a division of madness into two kinds, ordinary human

---

[13] Sinaiko speaks of the love between Socrates and Phaedrus "as a dramatic exemplification of the conception of love developed within the myth" which is related in the second speech and thus says that "Phaedrus, the lover of discourse, is at the moment of the second speech the incarnation of beauty itself to his lover Socrates" (*Love, Knowledge, and Discourse*, pp. 298, n. 28; 109). Cf. Friedländer, *Plato*, III, p. 227.

[14] Cf. De Vries, *Commentary*, pp. 113-114; also Hackforth, *Plato's Phaedrus*, p. 56, n. 1.

madness and divine or god-sent madness. From this division Socrates then proceeds to make a further division of divine madness
into three kinds, that involved in prophesy, that which deals in
purifications and sacred rites, and that exemplified in the poet.
Socrates speaks briefly of the goods received by man as the fruit
of such kinds of madness. Then he concludes this first part of his
speech by proposing a fourth kind of divine madness: love.

There are three matters which we need especially to note in this
consideration of madness. First, it is evident that this first part of
the speech exemplifies what Socrates will describe much later in
the dialogue as the method of collection (συναγωγή) and division
(διαίρεσις). Although there is here no explicit process of collecting,[15] the speech begins with the collected result ("madness") and
then proceeds explicitly by way of division of the term of collection into its kinds. This procedure contrasts somewhat with that
of Socrates' first speech in which there was no single encompassing
term arrived at as the unity then to be divided. Once "desire" had
been shown to be inadequate, Socrates simply posed two directive
things (desire and opinion) and derived from them the conditions
(*hubris* and moderation) then to be divided; neither the two
directive things nor the correlative conditions were developed
from out of an encompassing unity. There is also another, more
important difference between the general structure of the two
speeches. In the first speech the procedure of division yields a
definition of love which is then taken as the unquestionable basis
for all the further assertions made in the speech; the answer to the
question as to what love is, is simply applied to the treatment of
the further question of whether the lover or the non-lover ought
to be preferred. By contrast, the procedure of division at the
beginning of the second speech yields *only* a supposition which is
still to be tested and for which all the remainder of the speech is
needed by way of confirmation and interpretation.[16] The divi-

---

[15] It can perhaps be said that the collection which yields the unity divided at the
beginning of this speech (i.e., madness) is carried out, mostly unthematically, in the
previous two speeches and especially in the reflections on them. See especially 235 e —
236 a.

[16] Cf. Sinaiko, *Love, Knowledge, and Discourse,* pp. 42-44. This important aspect of
the structure of the second speech as a whole is thematized in Sinaiko's detailed outline
(pp. 40-41).

sion, having arrived at "love," offers, not a definitive answer to the question as to what love is, but only a starting-point from which to be able really to pursue the question. Socrates makes this explicit when he poses the result of the collection and division as what has still to be shown: "What we have to prove is . . . that this sort of madness is a gift of the gods, fraught with the highest bliss" (245 b − c).

Second, we should note that in speaking of the first kind of divine madness, prophecy ($\mu\alpha\nu\tau\iota\kappa\acute{\eta}$), Socrates makes mention of the Delphic oracle: "It was when they were mad that the prophetess at Delphi and the priestess at Dodona achieved so much for which both states and individuals in Greece are thankful; when sane they did little or nothing" (244 a − b). One of the greatest things that the Delphic oracle did, its means of delivering its greatest gift to Athens, was to convey Apollo's saying about Socrates, which, in turn, first provoked Socrates into that practice of questioning through which he came to serve as the gift of the god to the city (cf. Ch. 1, Sect. 3). Thus, it may be said that madness was somehow involved at the very point of origin of Socrates' practice—that Socrates, the philosopher, has some special relation to madness, not only when he roams the enchanted countryside with Phaedrus but from the very beginning of his practice.

Finally, we should note how the context and the theme of Socrates' second speech serves to indicate that Socrates, the philosopher, is related not just to one of the four kinds of divine madness but to all four of them, so that the presentation of the speech is, as it were, a collecting *in deed* of the terms reached by division at the beginning of the speech. Already we have seen that Socrates' speech-making about love is to exemplify the love spoken about, that it is to constitute Socrates' way of making love to Phaedrus; this, along with the connection to be explicitly made in the speech between love and philosophy, indicates how Socrates, in making the second speech, embodies the fourth kind of divine madness. As regards the third kind, that of the poet, we recall that somewhat earlier (237 a) Socrates invoked the Muses, and we note that, in fact, it is only now, in the second speech, that he will go about telling a *mythos*. Furthermore, the entire speech has been undertaken by Socrates for the expressed purpose of purifying himself from the offence committed against love in the previous speech; it thus embodies the second kind of divine madness, that having to do with purification rites. But how, finally, is Socrates' speech linked to prophecy? In what way is the speech prophetic and thus especially appropriate to one who is servant to Apollo?[17]   It is not prophetic in the sense of foretelling this or that event but rather in the sense that it tells the destiny of the soul as such. More precisely, it foretells the destiny of the human soul by, first of all, recollecting the beginning of man's present condition.

(ii) The Question of the Soul (245 c − 246 a)

In order to show that love is a kind of madness sent by the gods for man's greatest benefit, it is necessary, according to Socrates, to learn the truth about the nature of the soul, both divine and human, observing the deeds ($\check{\epsilon}\rho\gamma\alpha$) and the "passions" ($\pi\acute{\alpha}\theta\eta$) of the soul. Marking explicitly the beginning of the "proof" ($\grave{\alpha}\rho\chi\grave{\eta}\ \delta\grave{\epsilon}$ $\grave{\alpha}\pi o\delta\epsilon\acute{\iota}\xi\epsilon\omega\varsigma\ \check{\eta}\delta\epsilon$), Socrates then proceeds to speak of the immortality of the soul.

In what sense is what now follows in Socrates' second speech a proof? How, for example, can Socrates call the forthcoming myth of the charioteer a proof or even part of a proof?[18]   He can do so only because what he understands by *"apodeixis"* is not simply interchangeable with what we understand by "proof." Especially through the influence of modern symbolic mathematics, the relevant sense has become so attenuated that the word "proof" has almost entirely lost the root sense of *"apodeixis"* and has to some extent even taken on a contrary and decisively non-Greek sense. *"Apodeixis"* means a showing forth, an exhibiting of something

---

[17] In the reflection on the speeches that is carried out in the second half of the dialogue Socrates relates each of the four kinds of divine madness to certain gods: prophecy to Apollo, purification to Dionysus, the madness of the poet to the Muses, and the madness of the lover to Aphrodite and Eros (265 b).

[18] The word *"apodeixis"* in Socrates' statement applies not just to the immediately following section but to the entire remainder of the second speech. Cf. De Vries, *Commentary*, p. 120.

about something, a making manifest of something so that it might be seen in its manifestness. Thus, for the Greeks a proof was anything but a mere technique of the sort that could be employed in almost total detachment from content and that could serve as an appropriate substitute for insight into the matter itself in its manifestness.

In fact, the only part of Socrates' second speech that gives the appearance of being a proof in the later sense that we tend to take for granted is the short section which immediately follows Socrates' announcement of the "beginning of the proof." This section has almost invariably been taken as a "proof of the immortality of the soul." However, if it is closely examined and if its position within the second speech as a whole is taken into account, then it can be seen to be not so much a proof (not even in the sense of *"apodeixis"*) as rather a peculiar way of laying out what is to be proved (i.e., shown forth, exhibited) in the second speech as such.

The section in question consists of three parts, and we need to consider each in some detail. The first part has the form of a regress from what is to be shown back to the conditions from which it follows. The first step of this regress goes from the assertion that all soul is immortal[19] back to the assertion that the ever-moving is immortal, which is taken as self-evident. We note that what, granted this regress, would need still to be proved is that the soul is ever-moving. However, rather than going immediately to a proof of this unexpressed premise, Socrates, instead, introduces a further regress: he says that only what is self-moving is ever-moving. This identification he justifies on the ground that what is self-moving (i.e., what by its very nature moves itself) could cease to move only by abandoning its very nature, which is impossible. It should be noted that Socrates does not refer, as yet, to the new unexpressed premise that would now need to be established in order to render the regress effective, namely, that soul is self-moving by its very nature.

The regress as a whole can be represented schematically as follows:

---

[19] Ψυχὴ πᾶσα ἀθάνατος. Here "πᾶσα" is ambiguous: it may have either a collective sense ("all soul") or a distributive sense ("every soul"). Cf. De Vries, *Commentary,* p. 121.

(1) All soul is immortal.

↑

(2) The ever-moving is immortal. (Unexpressed premise: Soul is ever-moving.)

↑

(3) The self-moving is ever-moving. (Unexpressed premise: Soul is self-moving.)

From this schema it is clear that the effect of the regress is to introduce between the terms with which it begins, namely "soul" and "immortal," mediate terms having to do with movement. This effect can be represented thus:

(1) soul–immortal
(2) soul–ever-moving–immortal
(3) soul–self-moving–ever-moving–immortal

The structure of the regress thus suggests that it is a matter of letting the question of the soul's immortality be mediated by the question of the soul's movement. We need to see specifically what this mediation involves.

Whereas the first part establishes mediately that what is by its very nature self-moving is immortal, the second part of the section in question develops this assertion directly by identifying that which moves itself (in the strict sense) as the origin (ἀρχή) of movement for all other things that are moved. As such, the self-mover cannot come into being, for it is that from which, as origin, everything that comes into being does so; if it should itself come into being, then it would cease to be origin. Neither can the self-mover be destroyed, for then there would be nothing from which anything could come into being. Thus, as origin, that which is self-moving can neither come into being nor be destroyed, since otherwise the whole of that which comes to be would collapse into utter immobility. The conclusion is that what by its very nature moves itself is immortal.

In different ways each of the first two parts shows that if the soul is self-moving (in the strictest sense), then it is immortal. In effect, this means that Socrates, proceeding from something like the common opinion that when a man dies his soul persists and is carried away to Hades, has shown that this question of the continued persistence of the soul, the question of immortality, is conditioned by the prior question as to whether and how the soul moves itself. The "popular" question is, as it were, carried back to the question of the movement of the soul. By focusing on this regression, we begin to see how this entire section is related to the great myth that follows in the second speech, how it is a beginning of the *apodeixis* in the sense of laying out in its thematic connection what is to be shown forth: What Socrates tells of in the myth, indeed, in the entire speech from this point on, are the essential *movements of the soul.*

If the soul is by its very nature self-moving, then it is immortal. But is the soul self-moving in this sense? The third part of the section we are considering is addressed to this question. Socrates says: "And now that we have seen that that which is moved by itself is immortal, we shall feel no scruple in affirming that precisely that is the being and *logos* of soul [Ψυχῆς οὐσίαν τε καὶ λόγον], to wit self-movement" (245 e). If this affirmation is assured, then the whole matter is settled. If the soul is in its very being a self-mover, then, since whatever is a self-mover in this strict sense has been shown to be immortal, it follows quite straightforwardly that the soul is immortal. But there is more than slight occasion in the developments thus far to wonder whether the matter is really so straightforward as this. One can hardly help being provoked to wonder by the fact that the self-mover which Socrates describes as origin of the movement of all other things that are moved would seem to have little in common with a soul which, like that of Socrates, can have need of purification for having committed an offence against something higher than itself. Would it be at all possible to identify the originary self-mover with a soul that is called on to be concerned with its ignorance, with a soul which can be, as Socrates is now, inspired, that is, moved to speak by something beyond itself?

We need, therefore, to consider with utmost care the "justification" which Socrates offers for his assertion that the being and *logos* of the soul is self-movement. What he appeals to is the fact that a body which derives its movement from a source within itself is besouled, whereas a body with only external sources of movement is soulless. So, what he is, in effect, saying is that from the fact that a body which has the source of its movement in itself is thereby besouled—that from this fact it follows that the being and *logos* of the soul is self-movement. But this is indeed a curious conclusion. For the movement to which Socrates appeals, seemingly as a case of that self-movement definitive of the soul, is not, in fact, a movement of the soul at all but rather a movement which the soul causes in the body. In other words, what is moved in the case to which Socrates refers is not the soul but the body, and this case is quite simply not a case of self-movement in the strict sense. Thus, the case hardly suffices for showing straightforwardly that the being and *logos* of the soul consist in its being self-moving; on the contrary, it hints that the question of the soul's movement is perhaps not at all a simple matter when the soul is embodied.

The result is that the character of the soul as self-moving is left in question by the present section. Even if it is asserted in general, as it is here as well as in the *Laws*, [20] that the being and *logos* of the soul consists in its moving itself, it does not necessarily follow

---

[20] The context of the corresponding discussion of the soul in Book X of the *Laws* is drastically different from that of the discussion in the *Phaedrus,* first, because of the immense difference between the *Laws* as a whole (which is dedicated so relentlessly to the affairs of the city and from which Socrates is entirely absent) and the *Phaedrus* (in which Socrates, outside the city, speaks largely of what is beyond the city) and, second, because in the *Laws* the soul is discussed in the course of a discussion, not of love, but of the gods (specifically, in order to allow the Athenian to refute those who maintain that the gods exist by art rather than by nature). These drastic differences of context should warn us against simply transferring what is said in the *Laws* to the *Phaedrus* as presumed explication of the latter. Nevertheless, it should be noted that the Athenian identifies self-movement as the *logos* of the soul and speaks of the soul, thus defined, as the ἀρχή of motion and the oldest of all things; it is especially emphasized that soul is prior to body (896 a – c). And, in a manner not unlike that in the *Phaedrus,* the soul is described as controlling all things, even the things in the heavens: "Soul drives all things in heaven and earth and sea by its own motions" (896 e). It should be noted, however, that immediately before this description the Athenian inserts a remark that throws darkness on the entire matter: "One soul, is it, or several? I will answer for you—'several.' Anyhow, let us assume not less than two—the beneficient soul and that which is capable of effecting results of the opposite kind." Also it should be noted that when the Athenian proceeds to name the kinds of motion proper to the soul he does not speak of the movement of bodies but rather of "wish, reflection, foresight, counsel, opinion, true or false, pleasure, pain, hope, fear, hate, love" (897 a). Clearly, in such cases there is some question whether the soul simply moves itself or whether it is not also in some sense moved by something else (e.g., when something is loved or hated).

that its self-moving must have that radically originary character that would exclude all dependence on anything beyond itself. In fact, if we recall the purpose of the entire consideration of which the present section is the beginning, namely, to show that love is a gift sent by the gods to man for his greatest benefit, then there is good reason to suppose that the self-moving that is proper at least to the human soul is not at all identical with that totally originary self-moving which Socrates has described: for such a self-mover would hardly be in need of any gifts and, even if it were, it could never in any way be moved by the reception of them.

Thus, the movement proper to the soul—and especially to the human soul—remains in question in the present section. In fact, of the two kinds of movement that Socrates actually mentions—the movement of the whole heaven (of the whole of that which comes to be) and the movement of besouled bodies—neither is a movement of the soul.[21] Despite all that the present section says in general about the movement of the soul, it does not mention a single instance of such movement. It leaves us entirely in the dark as to what kind of movement the soul can execute. But by alerting us to the overwhelming significance of the question of the soul's movement, it prepares us for that showing forth of such movement that is about to commence in the great myth. To this extent it is an appropriate beginning to the *apodeixis.*

(iii) The Movement of the Soul (246 a – 249 d)

It is a matter of telling what the nature of the soul is by telling of the movements proper to the soul. Yet, such telling is too demanding for man: to tell that long tale about what the soul is would be more befitting to a god. For man it is more appropriate to tell what the soul resembles. Accordingly, Socrates will speak in this way (246 a).

So, Socrates will tell about the soul by means of an image; he will employ a mode of telling in which what is shown forth in the telling is shown forth through an image. We should note the contrast with the mode of speaking used in Socrates' first speech,

---

[21] Cf. Sinaiko, *Love, Knowledge, and Discourse,* p. 48.

from which he is in the present speech seeking to purify himself. In the first speech the telling did not maintain that distance from the matter told of that is now to be sustained by the mediation of the image but, on the contrary, proceeded almost immediately to say with presumed definitiveness what the matter itself (i.e., love) was, in order then to be able simply to apply the "definition" to the question at issue. Also we should note how Socrates' proposal to use a mode of telling animated by images and at least to that extent akin to myth exemplifies what Socrates said near the beginning of the dialogue about self-knowledge and myth (229 e – 230 a; cf. above, Sect. 1 b). The soul (of the inquirer) is to come to know the soul—that is, he is to come to know himself—through a telling linked to images, through the telling of a myth. This amounts to something like an incorporation of myth into the task of self-knowledge.

The image which Socrates introduces is appropriate. Since what is in question is the movement of the soul, he uses the image of a vehicle of movement, a chariot—or, more precisely, of the moving powers pertaining to a chariot. He says: "Let it be likened to the union of powers in a team of winged steeds and their charioteer" (246 a).[22]

With this image in view Socrates proceeds to draw two basic distinctions. First, he distinguishes between the souls of gods and those of men. In the case of the gods all the steeds and all the charioteers are good and of good stock (ἀγαθοὶ καὶ ἐξ ἀγαθῶν), but in the case of other beings this is not entirely so. In the case of the human soul there are two steeds to be controlled by the

---

[22] There are several ambiguities that have been noted in the presentation of the image. First of all, the word "ζεῦγος" ("team of horses") does not necessarily mean "pair of horses"; although it will be definitely said that in the case of *human* souls there are two horses, this is not definitely asserted of all souls (cf. Hackforth, *Plato's Phaedrus*, p. 69, n. 3). Secondly, in the phrase "ὑποπτέρου ζεύγους τε καὶ ἡνιόχου" it is not clear whether "ὑποπτέρου" ("winged") applies both to the horses and the charioteer or only to the former. The principal clarification that is provided regarding this matter comes at 251 b where the soul is described as feathered all over (cf. Friedländer, *Plato*, Vol. I, p. 193; De Vries, *Commentary*, p. 126).

In the introduction of the image Socrates does not explicitly mention the chariot itself. It is not evident whether this omission is dictated by the function given the image here, i.e., whether the chariot itself is irrelevant to this function. Certainly, it is clear, almost from the beginning, that the chariot cannot be identified with the body.

charioteer, one of them beautiful (καλός) and good and of good stock, the other having the opposite character. On account of the latter steed the work of the charioteer of the human soul is difficult. Yet, even granting this difficulty and the difference from which it derives, we should, nevertheless, observe to what extent the differentiation of human from divine souls serves to bring out simultaneously their similarity: two of the powers of the human soul seem to correspond quite precisely to their counterparts in the divine soul.

The second of the distinctions drawn by Socrates at this point is the distinction between mortal and immortal living beings. The importance of this distinction for the wider issue of the second speech lies in the fact that Socrates draws it by giving a first sketch of an originary movement of certain souls. He says that when the soul sheds its wings it "sinks down until it can fasten on something solid, and settling there it takes to itself an earthly body" (246 c). The resulting composite is a mortal living being, in contrast to the gods whom we fancy as having soul and body united for all time (immortal living beings).[23] So, what makes a being mortal is its having originated from that peculiar movement of the soul that Socrates here sketches, the movement down to earth, the movement of embodiment, that ensues when the soul loses its wings. Whereas the soul that is capable of remaining fully winged traverses the heavens and cares for (i.e., moves) all that is soulless, presumably in the manner portrayed in Socrates' description of the self-mover in the previous section, by contrast the soul which loses its wings becomes the origin (ἀρχή) of movement for a single living being.[24] It becomes such a restricted origin of movement by virtue of the originary movement which it undergoes. This movement of embodiment is the first of several originary movements of the soul that are to be told of in the second speech.

Socrates' sketch of the movement of embodiment raises a further question: Why do certain souls lose their wings? How does

---

[23] In the statement the stress is presumably to fall on our *fancying* the gods to be such a composite (by mere contrast with that imperfect composite which we are), not on their actually being such, for in the sequel it appears that the souls of the gods are engaged in kinds of movement which are prior to the movement of embodiment.

[24] Sinaiko, *Love, Knowledge, and Discourse,* p. 59.

it happen that those souls that come eventually to be attached to an earthly body undergo that loss as a result of which they are cast into the movement of embodiment? In order to take up this question, Socrates tells of a second kind of movement of souls, a processional movement that is even more originary than the movement of embodiment. He tells, first, of the procession of the souls of the gods and only afterwards of the corresponding movement of other souls.

Socrates describes the grand procession of the gods and daimons as they move through the heavens caring for all things. The abruptness with which he begins his description accords well with his curious way of presenting the description, a way which tends to suggest an abrupt "flashing-up" of a vision of the procession being described:

> And behold, there in the heaven Zeus, mighty leader, drives his winged team: first of the host of gods and daimons he proceeds, ordering all things and caring therefor: and the host follows after him, marshalled in eleven companies. For Hestia abides alone in the gods' dwelling-place; but for the rest, all such as are ranked in the number of the twelve as ruler gods lead their several companies, each according to his rank (246 e – 247 a).

Next, Socrates distinguishes certain special occasions from this usual procession of the originary movers. These special occasions he describes with the names "feast" (δαίς) and "banquet" (θοίνη). The third kind of movement of the soul—at least of the souls of gods—is the *movement up to the divine banquet*. When they go to their feasts and banquets, the gods make the steep ascent up to "the summit of the arch that supports the heavens." And once they have made this ascent, easy for the chariots of the gods but difficult for the others on account of the wicked steed, then they "come forth and stand upon the back[25] of the heavens and straightaway the revolving heaven carries them round and they look upon what is outside the heavens [τὰ ἔξω τοῦ οὐρανοῦ]"

---

[25] νώτῳ: on the back, in the sense of the back of an animal, hence, upper surface (cf. De Vries, *Commentary*, p. 135).

(247 c). This movement as a whole, the movement pertaining to the divine banquet, is the most significant movement of all.[26]

What do the souls feast upon at the divine banquet? In other words, what do they see in the place outside the heavens? Socrates proposes to do what no poet has done or will do: to speak the truth about this place. He says:

> This place [τόπος] has the colorless, shapeless, intangible being [οὐσία ὄντως οὖσα][27] with which all true knowledge [ἐπιστήμη] is concerned and which is visible only to *nous*, the pilot of the soul (247 c – d).

The souls in attendance at the divine banquet are carried around by the revolution of the heavens and are brought back finally to the place from which they began. While being carried around, they receive their proper nourishment by gazing upon being. Socrates adds: In the revolution the soul "beholds justice itself [αὐτὴν δικαιοσύνην], moderation [σωφροσύνη] and knowledge [ἐπιστήμη], not the knowledge that is neighbor to becoming [γένεσις] and varies with the various things to which we ascribe being, but the knowledge of being which is [ἀλλὰ τὴν ἐν τῷ ὅ ἐστιν ὂν ὄντως ἐπιστήμην οὖσαν]" (247 d – e). He tells, finally, how, when the soul has feasted on all the other beings, it then descends and how, when it has returned home, the charioteer tends the

---

[26] The image of the divine banquet is the most important point from which to understand how the *Phaedrus* is related to the *Symposium*, which presents a human banquet corresponding to the divine banquet of the *Phaedrus*. Also we shall find (in Ch. V) that it is very significant that the *Republic* takes the place of a banquet; this feature, if considered in its full bearing, probably gives the best indication of the relation of the *Republic* to the *Symposium* and to the *Phaedrus*.

[27] It is virtually impossible to translate the phrase "οὐσία ὄντως οὖσα" with any suitability from the point of view of philosophical interpretation. The difficulty stems from the fact that all three words are derivatives of the same word (εἰμί: I am), so that, most literally (and awkwardly) the phrase says something like: (the) beingly being being. To avoid this obviously intolerable awkwardness by substituting what for "common sense" are synonymous forms, e.g., forms of such words as "real" and "actual," amounts to a prejudicing of the interpretation along the lines of post-Greek thought that are sedimented in such Latin derivatives. To use some form of the word "true" to alleviate the apparent redundancy of the Greek is simply to introduce arbitrarily an element entirely lacking at this point in the text. To use some form of the word "exist" is, to say the least, to risk taking for granted the *later* distinction between essence and existence. In an interpretation such as the present one, aimed precisely at retrieving the problem of being in Platonic thought and at freeing it from the weight of "Platonic" tradition, none of these expedients can be allowed.

steeds, giving them ambrosia to eat and nectar to drink. Apparently it is only the charioteer who gazes on the beings and who is nourished thereby. Once the steeds have pulled the chariot up to the top of the arch of heaven (whatever their precise role may be in this ascent) their work is apparently done. They are not responsible for carrying the chariot around in that revolution in which the charioteer gazes on the beings; nor, it seems, do they feast their eyes on being and receive thereby their proper nourishment. The latter is indicated by the fact that they need to be fed by the charioteer after the return home. We are not told anything further about the ambrosia and the nectar.

The obvious question is: What is the being ($o\dot{v}\sigma\acute{\iota}\alpha$ $\ddot{o}v\tau\omega\varsigma$ $o\dot{v}\sigma\alpha$) of which Socrates speaks here? But, in fact, this is not in the least an obvious question but, on the contrary, the least obvious of all questions. Its lack of obviousness is initially apparent in the fact that the question, as formulated, already presupposes its answer, presupposes that we know what the "is" means as the very condition of the possibility of even understanding the question. But are such complications really in order? Doesn't Socrates go on to tell us that by such beings he means things like justice itself, moderation itself, and knowledge itself? And, even if there does seem to be here some confusing of knowledge with its "objects," is it not as clear as can be that what Socrates is talking about here is in the so-called "world of forms"? Is the present passage not, in fact, one of the principal expressions of what is called Plato's "theory of forms"? Certainly this is indisputable. But it is indisputable precisely because it says nothing essential. And we say nothing pertinent to the matter at issue as long as we merely substitute the word "form" ("$\epsilon\hat{\iota}\delta o\varsigma$") for the word "being" ("$o\dot{v}\sigma\acute{\iota}\alpha$") and fail to think through what *eidos* means for Plato. There is absolutely nothing in the dialogues that is less obvious than the meaning of *eidos,* unless it be the meaning of being. Indeed, it is questionable—or, at least, should finally be made questionable— whether Plato, or even Socrates, can be said to have held any "theories," much less a "theory of forms," which, despite all its currency, is little more than a formula designed to "protect" us against really getting engaged in the fundamental level of questioning in the Platonic dialogues. Should we not at least *wonder* at the fact that this presumably fundamental "theory" is presented here in the *Phaedrus* in the context of a myth poured out by an inspired Socrates in an elaborate purification rite undergone because of an offence committed against love?

Having spoken of the gods, Socrates proceeds to tell of the processional movement of the other souls. These other souls try, in particular, to imitate that third kind of movement previously described, the movement upward to the divine banquet. They try to follow the gods up to that height from which they might feast their eyes on being itself, but the ascent is difficult for them because of the unruly steed that is a constituent of all such souls:

> As for the rest, though all are eager to reach the heights and seek to follow, they are not able: sucked down as they travel, they trample and tread upon one another, this one striving to outstrip that. Thus confusion ensues, and conflict and grievous sweat: whereupon, with their charioteers powerless [κα-κία], many are lamed, and many have their wings all broken; and for all their toiling they are baulked, every one, of the full vision of being, and departing therefrom, they feed upon the food of opinion (248 a – b).

Here it should be noted that these souls lose the power of their wings because they strive to ascend higher than they are really capable of ascending, because they strive to outstrip one another, with the result that they end up being cast down to earth. However, it is important to observe that this striving is not mere rivalry, not a mere unfounded desire to outdo others. Socrates says:

> Now the reason wherefore the souls are fain and eager to behold the plain of truth, and discover it, lies herein: to wit, that the pasturage that is proper to their noblest part comes from that meadow, and the plumage by which they are borne aloft is nourished thereby (248 b – c).

This says that the sight of truth is what nourishes those very wings by which the soul is enabled to ascend to the sight of truth. In other words, in order to ascend to the sight of truth, the soul needs that very nourishment which it can get only by ascending to the sight of truth. This is the *circle* in which the other souls, and, in particular, the souls of men, are ensnared. It is the condition expressed in this circle that is at the root of the striving.

The constraint of this circle is articulated in the order of lives which Socrates now lays out in the name of necessity (Ἀδράσ-τεια).[28] In its first birth, its first embodiment, the soul cannot become a beast but takes on one of the nine kinds of human lives. To the one who has seen the most in the ascent up towards the scene of the divine banquet, there is allotted that kind of life which, in turn, allows one the highest possibility given to mortal living beings for cultivating what is needed for the ascent. Socrates says that "the soul that has seen the most will enter into the birth of a man who will grow into a lover of wisdom [φιλόσοφος] or a lover of beauty [φιλόκαλος] or one who is musical or who is a lover [ἐρωτικός]" (248 d); and we are to understand that what is described here is a single kind,[29] the unity of which it is our task to grasp if we are truly to understand who the philosopher is. For all other souls necessity assigns an order of life corresponding to the extent of the soul's vision of the plain of truth prior to embodiment. These orders of lives indicate, in effect, the greater and lesser degrees in which men are bound into the circle constitutive of man's fundamental condition. The tyrant is the one who is most rigidly and hopelessly bound into this circle; the philosopher is the one whose bond allows him the greatest freedom.

Up to this point Socrates has considered three kinds of movement of the soul, embodiment, procession, and the movement pertaining to the divine banquet. These three kinds of movement are progressively more originary, and, as such, they all pertain pre-eminently to a mythic past in which the soul first came to be subject to embodiment and opinion. Now, on the other hand, Socrates proceeds to project those other limits that belong to the delimitation of the *moira* of the embodied soul, namely, the mythic future in which the soul will return to its primal condition. The total course of the soul's sojourn requires, with one very

---

[28] Cf. De Vries, *Commentary*, p. 142.

[29] Cf. Hackforth, *Plato's Phaedo*, p. 83; also Sinaiko, *Love, Knowledge, and Discourse*, p. 80. ˙

important exception, ten thousand years for its completion. After this time the soul regains its wings and returns to the place from which it came, presumably, re-engaging itself then in those more originary movements of procession and of divine banqueting. [30] This total course is divided into ten periods. During each of these periods the soul lives a life on earth, after which it is judged and then carried away to one of two places where it then passes the remainder of the thousand-year period; some go under the earth for punishment, others who are appropriately prepared by the life they had led go upward to a region of the heavens. When the thousand-year period is completed, then the souls—whose *first* embodiment was determined by the law of necessity in view of their accomplishment in the divine banqueting—come forth and draw lots and choose their next life. The total course is of the same duration (ten such thousand-year periods) for all souls *except* that of the philosopher: if a soul chooses the life of the philosopher for three successive thousand-year periods, then he returns to the original place after three thousand years rather than requiring the ten thousand years needed by all other souls (248 e − 249 b).

This passage is such that not only do specific matters mentioned in it remain questionable—for example, the curious intertwining of *moira* with individual decision and choice—but also the very sense of the passage as a whole is left in the dark to such an extent that we find it difficult even to carry through our wonder in any very determinate form, for instance, really to wonder in a productive fashion at the fact that Socrates' delimiting of the soul's whither and whence is cast in the form of myth. From all these issues we single out one which we take as most immediately broached as a question by the passage and as most directly taken up in the

---

[30] Bluck shows that there is no reason to assume, on the basis of the Platonic text, that once a soul has completed the ten-thousand-year cycle it would then be immune from another "fall." Thus, a soul which had not sufficiently cultivated what makes it akin to the divine might again (i.e., after having completed the ten-thousand-year cycle) have difficulty ascending to the site of the divine banquet and, as a result, might again undergo the movement of embodiment, being thus set upon another ten-thousand-year cycle. This entails that the "fall" described in Socrates' speech need not be taken as a kind of "original fall." R. S. Bluck, "The *Phaedrus* and Reincarnation," *American Journal of Philology,* 79 (1958), pp. 156-164.

sequel. The question is: What is it about the philosopher that makes him capable of being so distinguished from all other souls? What is it about the philosopher that makes it possible for him to escape re-embodiment after a mere three thousand years, in contrast to the ten thousand years required by all other souls? What must be the character of the philosopher in order for him to have this capacity? This is the same question as the one under the direction of which we have proceeded all along: Who is the philosopher?

Socrates' answer to this question involves two stages: before showing what distinguishes the philosopher he, first, lays an appropriate basis by indicating what it is that distinguishes all souls that are capable of taking on human form. What distinguishes them is that they have *seen the truth.* In mythic terms, this means that all such souls must have attended the divine banquet, or, more exactly, must have come close enough to the banqueting to have been able at least to catch a glimpse of the beings beyond the heavens. Why must they have beheld the beings? Why must they have seen them in their manifestness, in their truth? Because otherwise they would not be capable of what the human soul is capable of. Socrates' description of this capacity is one of the most crucial passages of the entire dialogue:

> For a human being must understand according to *eidos* what is said [ξυνιέναι κατ᾽ εἶδος λεγόμενον], going from many perceptions to a one gathered together by reckoning [λο-γισμῷ] This is a recollection [ἀνάμνησις] of those things which our soul beheld when it journeyed with god and, looking down upon the things which now we suppose to be, gazed up to being as such [τὸ ὂν ὄντως] (249 b – c).

This statement resumes at a more fundamental level the consideration of recollection in the *Meno* (cf. Ch. II, Sect. 2 b); at this fundamental level it proceeds in the direction of a recovery of the mythic past and a focusing on the issue of *logos,* in contrast to the corresponding considerations in the *Phaedo* (cf. Ch. II, Sect. 2 c). The statement requires considerable commentary.

It should especially be noted that in this statement human understanding is described as a *gathering,* as a *collecting of many into one.* The many that are gathered up in such gathering are explicitly identified as perceptions (αἴσθησις), presumably in the sense of something made present to the senses (αἴσθημα). In gathering up any such many into a one, it is necessary that the one into which the many are to be gathered be itself directive in the gathering. In other words, it is necessary to gather *according to* the one of the gathering. Socrates' statement gives a name to such gathering into one according to the one. It is named: understanding according to *eidos.* This means that an *eidos* is, in the first instance, the one of a gathering, a one into which and according to which many things made present to the senses are gathered. This connection between *eidos* and the gathering of many into one is of utmost importance as point of departure for thinking through the sense of *eidos* in the Platonic dialogues.

Next, it needs to be observed that, in order to carry through a gathering of a many into a one and, certainly, in order to do so in accordance with that one, the one which is directive for the gathering must somehow be available to the gathering prior to the carrying through of that gathering. The one of the gathering must somehow be manifest in advance. Thus, the problem of human understanding, as understanding according to *eidos,* is concentrated in the question as to how, amidst the many "perceptions" with their apparent immediacy and exclusiveness, there is manifest a genuine one, that is, a one which can never in itself be also many and which, consequently, is capable of serving for the collecting of many into one. Amidst the radical multiplicity of what is presented in sense experience how does it happen that "ones" are manifest?

In Socrates' statement the decisive indication with regard to this matter is found in his use, at two points in the statement, of words that are derivatives of *"logos."* In the first place, he says that man "must understand according to *eidos* what is *said* [λεγόμενον]." Obviously, this does not mean that the consideration has only to do with the understanding of what we hear said, with the understanding of the speech of other men, for Socrates goes on to speak of perception at large (αἴσθησις) as well as of recollection of those things which man once *saw* at the divine banqueting. Nor does Socrates' reference to "what is said" mean that only the understanding of what we hear said is specifically an understanding according to *eidos*. In fact, Socrates' reference to "what is said" is not in the least intended to identify the content that is subject, as it were, to being understood according to *eidos*, but, on the contrary, this reference is a compressed explanation of how it is possible for man to understand everything according to *eidos*. This intention is confirmed by Socrates' second use of a derivative of "*logos*," the slightly more remote derivative "λογισμός." In order to avoid traditional pre-conceptions, we translate this word by the relatively neutral word "reckoning"; but this translation does not secure what is most important for the present problematic, namely, that we hear the word "*logos*" resounding in this word. By Socrates' statement, the gathering together is accomplished by a "reckoning" that is intrinsically linked to *logos*.

Man can understand everything according to *eidos*, because everything can become something said and because as capable of becoming something said everything is already implicitly gathered into a one. As soon as we speak we already are engaged in collecting manys into ones, in carrying through with a certain degree of explicitness that collecting that is already pre-delineated in the speech which we take up in our speaking—pre-delineated, for example, by the way in which a name (ὄνομα) can be, in an initially simple sense, the name of many things and, hence, the one into which those many things are gathered up. By being gifted with speech, by being already caught up in *logos*, man always already has available an already accomplished, anonymous collecting of manys into ones, a collecting which he resumes in his speaking. This is why Socrates says that the gathering takes place by a "reckoning" that is intrinsically linked to *logos*: it is *logos* which makes available, makes manifest, the ones of the collecting.

However, if such a collecting is to be truthful, there is clearly a further requirement to be met. If, more precisely, the collecting is to be such that it makes the things themselves manifest as they themselves are, if it is to be a collecting of the things as they are themselves collected, then the collecting cannot be dictated simply and with finality by the already accomplished collecting intrinsic to *logos*. To formulate the further requirement in a merely preliminary way, there must be something seen, something made manifest in the order of things themselves, that is capable of vindicating that way of collecting in which we are always already engaged through our engagement in *logos*. This further element is specifically brought out by Socrates' use of the word *"eidos"*: this word is derived from a verb (*"εἴδω"*) the most straightforward meaning of which is "see." Thus, the root meaning of *"eidos"* is: that which is seen, the seen, that which presents itself to a seeing, that which shows itself so as to be manifest to a seeing. This root meaning is of utmost importance for thinking through the originary sense of *eidos* in the Platonic dialogues.

So, the ones must somehow be made available to a seeing and not merely taken over as already pre-delineated in *logos*. However—and this is of most decisive significance—the ones, the *eide*, can *not* be directly seen by men: in terms of the myth, the *eide* lie beyond the heavens and can be seen, gazed upon directly, only by one who is in attendance at the divine banquet. Consequently, since man must see them for the sake of truthful understanding yet cannot see them directly, he must see them indirectly. But what does it mean to see them indirectly? Granted that it cannot be solely a "seeing" in *logos* (such as Socrates describes in his considerations in the *Phaedo*—cf. above, Ch. I, Sect. 2 b), what, then, must be the character of such indirect seeing? Socrates does not say—or, rather, he does say but only in a way that is respectful of the recoil of the issue interrogated upon the interrogation itself. Socrates calls the relevant "indirect seeing" by the name "recollection" (*ἀνάμνησις*), and, by so calling it, he removes it from the sphere of direct and exhaustive apprehension and attaches it to the remoteness of the mythical past. It is a matter of recollecting what we once beheld when we were in attendance at the divine banquet. "Recollection" is, in effect, the name for a properly human re-enactment of the divine banquet.

Socrates can now speak directly to the question as to what distinguishes the philosopher and makes him capable of escaping the cycle of rebirth so much sooner than can others:

> Therefore it is just that the thought [*διάνοια*] of the philosopher alone recovers its wings; for it is always, so far as

possible, near in memory to those things a god's nearness to which makes him truly god (249 c).

The philosopher is the human being who partakes to the greatest degree of the nourishment proper to the gods. He does not merely continue to "feed on opinion" but struggles to feast his eyes on the beings themselves, even though in that very struggle he must take account of the fact that he can never, in his present condition, feast directly on them but must have recourse to indirection, to the way of "memory." Why is the philosopher capable of returning to the company of the gods sooner than other souls? Because, all along, the philosopher is closer to the gods and to what makes them gods and because his practice consists precisely in the proper cultivation of this proximity.

(iv) The Beautiful (249 d – 257 b)

Noting that all of his speech so far bears on the fourth kind of madness (i.e., love), Socrates asserts this to be the best of all forms of inspiration (ἐνθ ουσίασις). He proceeds to describe the course of erotic madness:

> And when he that loves the beautiful is touched by such madness he is called a lover. Such a one, as soon as he beholds the beautiful of this region, is reminded of the truly beautiful, and his wings begin to grow (249 d – e).

What is especially to be noted here is Socrates' reference to *the beautiful.* Whereas previously he spoke simply of remembering the beings themselves once seen at the divine banquet, now he speaks exclusively of remembering the beautiful. This restriction is of utmost importance, and it is the theme of the considerations that now commence.

Socrates begins these considerations by stressing the difficulty of recollection. Although every human soul has beheld the beings, it is not easy to be reminded of those things by the things that are immediately ("perceptually") presented to the soul in its embodied condition; for many souls behold the beings only for a very short time, while others have suffered such abysmal forgetfulness in their embodiment as to make recollection exceedingly difficult. Thus, there are only a few who are capable of remembering much; and even these few, when they are confronted with images of those beings beyond the heavens, are amazed and are unable to understand what has come upon them. This means, more precisely, that even those few who are struck, as it were, by what shows itself through the images immediately manifest to embodied souls are not, as a rule, able to recollect explicitly what they are struck by in the image; even these few are, in other words, incapable, for the most part, of really distinguishing image from original in such a way as to recognize each as itself.

Socrates elaborates the reason for the difficulty. In "earthly" images of justice, moderation, and other such things there is, he says, no brilliance, splendor, lustre ($\phi\acute{\epsilon}\gamma\gamma o\varsigma$), so that only a few— and they only implicitly and with great difficulty—are able to discern, by the dull organs with which these images are approached, that which is imaged through these images. In other words, justice, moderation, and other such things do not shine brightly through their images; they do not shine through their images with sufficient splendor, lustre, brilliance, to allow the embodied soul to distinguish the "original" that is imaged from its image. The obvious question is: Is there anything that does shine with sufficient brilliance? And, if there is such, what is the appropriate way for it to be declared such by the erotic, inspired Socrates?

Socrates says:

> The beautiful it was ours to see in all its brightness in those days when, amidst that happy company, we beheld with our eyes that blessed vision, ourselves in the train of Zeus, others following some other god; then were we all initiated into that mystery which is rightly accounted blessed beyond all others (250 b).

In this declaration it should especially be noted that Socrates does not speak of the beautiful as though he had immediate access to it; he does not just straightforwardly declare the beautiful to be in itself exceptional among those beings beyond the heavens, as though he were himself attending the divine banquet and gazing upon the beings from that vantage point that could allow such a declaration. On the contrary, Socrates speaks of the beautiful in a way that befits the delimitation of the human condition that is being presented in the myth as a whole: he recollects the beautiful, recollects it explicitly as what they saw when they once traveled in company with the gods at the divine banquet. This character of his declaration is especially clear in the statement with which he marks the conclusion of the explicit recollection: "There let it rest then, our tribute to a memory that has stirred us to linger awhile on those former joys for which we yearn" (250 c).

What is Socrates saying about the beautiful in this recollection? He says that in that former time the beautiful was seen in all its brightness. So, what he stresses is the brightness, the splendor, the lustre with which the beautiful then shone; within the recollection the suggestion is that the beautiful is distinguished by the brilliance of its shining. Yet, again, it must be stressed that Socrates is only recollecting; and this means that, since such recollecting is provoked by "earthly" images of the beautiful, it must be asked: What is the "earthly" image of the beautiful that is here provocative of Socrates' own recollection? Presumably, it is Phaedrus, so that Socrates' entire recollection of the beautiful is directly linked to his love for Phaedrus. It is, in effect, Socrates' erotic relation with Phaedrus which lets the recollecting *logos* about the beautiful originate.

Socrates says that in that former time they (i.e., himself and Phaedrus) traveled in the train of Zeus, whereas others followed other gods. Later Socrates says that a lover imitates his god and seeks a beloved who resembles his god (252 d – e). This means, then, that Socrates and Phaedrus, in their erotic involvement with one another, "imitate" Zeus, that they are "Zeus-like," which means, by Socrates' own testimony, that they are "of a philosophical and commanding nature" (252 e). But what kind of commanding or leading is at issue in this conversation that takes place beyond the city? It is a leading which, in imitation of that of Zeus, transcends the cherished opinions on which men of the city feed, transcends them for the sake of the beings themselves in their truth. Just as Zeus leads the way to the divine banquet, serving thereby as the "mighty leader" (μέγας ἡγεμών–246 e), so

Socrates is capable of leading (ἡγεμονικός), is actually engaged in leading, the way to the properly human banquet, to the feast of recollection at which men partake indirectly of that nourishment which the gods receive directly.

Having carried out his recollection, Socrates proceeds then to speak of the present human situation with regard to the beautiful:

> Now the beautiful, as we said, shone bright amidst these visions, and in this world below we apprehend it through the clearest of our senses, clear and resplendent. For sight is the keenest mode of perception vouchsafed us through the body; wisdom [φρόνησις], indeed, we cannot see thereby—how passionate had been our desire for her, if she had granted us so clear an image of herself to gaze upon—nor yet any other of those beloved things, except the beautiful; for the beautiful alone this has been ordained, to be most manifest to sense [ἐκφανέστατον] and most lovely of them all (250 d – e).

With this statement Socrates makes it clear that what, from the human standpoint, distinguishes the beautiful from all the other beings that lie beyond the heavens is not simply that in itself the beautiful shines more brilliantly for those in attendance at the divine banquet. It is not simply a matter of its shining more or less brilliantly but rather a matter of its shining in a radically different way. To men the beautiful itself shines, not simply by itself, not immediately, but only through beautiful things, only through its "earthly" images. What distinguishes the beautiful is that it shines in the region of the visible, the "earthly," and thus renders being accessible to man in his condition of being bound to the visible through his body.[31] In the first instance, the beautiful is that *eidos* which is most manifest to man in his embodied condition, that *eidos* which shows itself as such, which shines forth, in the midst of the visible. The beautiful is that "original" which shines amidst images in such a way as to open up and make manifest for man the difference separating image from "original." Still more fundamentally regarded, "the beautiful" names the way in which being itself shines forth in the midst of the visible. An openness to

---

[31] Cf. Martin Heidegger, *Nietzsche* (Pfullingen: Verlag Günther Neske, 1961), Vol. I, pp. 218-231.

this shining forth belongs among the most basic conditions pertaining to the beginning of philosophy.

Socrates has now revealed that possible outcome of the erotic engagement by virtue of which love can be said to offer man the greatest blessings: when the lover gazes upon the beauty of his beloved, the beautiful itself shines through the latter in such a way that the lover can be led to recollect what he once saw in that remote past when he traveled in company with his god. What the erotic engagement offers the lover, most fundamentally, is a way of re-enacting the divine banquet, of partaking mediately, through "memory," of that nourishment which is not available to him in the form of an immediate contemplation of being.[32] By opening man onto the shining of the beautiful itself in and through the beautiful beloved, love provides man with the means for mitigating, in an appropriately human way, his otherwise radical separation from being.

Now that this fundamental possibility offered by love has been brought to light, all that remains is for Socrates to describe the course which the development of love follows and then, finally, to bring the entire speech explicitly to bear on the question inherited from the speech of Lysias. Socrates begins the description by telling about what happens when a lover with a sufficiently capable memory beholds his beloved. When such a lover gazes upon a godlike face or a bodily form that amply images the beautiful, there comes over him a shuddering and then a reverence for the beautiful one as if he were a god. Then sweating and fever seize him, "for by reason of the stream of beauty entering in through his eyes there comes a warmth, by which his soul's plumage is fostered"; and thus "does the soul of him who is beginning to grow his wings feel a ferment and painful irritation." The soul, so afflicted, throbs and palpitates, oscillating between the extremes of joy in the presence of the beloved and pain in his absence. Because of the mingling of these alternating sensations, such a soul is greatly troubled by its strange condition—which condition is called "love," at least in the speech of men (251 a — 252 b).

So, in terms of the chariot image, the outcome of the erotic

---

[32] Cf. Sinaiko, *Love, Knowledge, and Discourse,* pp. 78, 85, 96.

engagement for a lover who is sufficiently capable of recollecting is that his wings, the loss of which marked the origination of his embodiment, again begin to grow. In other words, the lover begins to receive that nourishment that is necessary in order to ascend towards the sight of truth. In this connection we should recall how, according to Socrates' earlier account, that striving of the soul which results in the loss of its wings and ultimately in its embodiment is the result of a peculiar circle in which the human soul is ensnared: the circularity consists in the fact that the sight of truth is precisely that which nourishes the wings by which the soul can ascend to the sight of truth, so that the soul's sighting of the truth would appear to presuppose itself. The point is that Socrates' present description of the course of love presents love as a way of surpassing this circularity, a way which, granted that the circle is no mere makeshift, could come to man only as a gift from something higher than himself.

Socrates proceeds to tell how not only the lover but also the beloved is offered this fundamental possibility by the erotic engagement; indeed, this extension is required by the very point of departure of the speech, namely, Socrates' intention of showing, contrary to Lysias' speech, that the lover is of greater benefit to the beloved than is the non-lover. Socrates says that as the beloved

> continues in this converse and society, and comes close to his lover in the gymnasium and elsewhere, that flowing stream which Zeus, as the lover of Ganymede, called the "flood of passion," pours in upon the lover; and part of it is absorbed within him, but when he can contain no more the rest flows away outside him; and as a breath of wind or an echo, rebounding from a smooth hard surface, goes back to its place of origin, even so the stream of beauty turns back and re-enters the eyes of the beautiful one; and so by the natural channel it reaches his soul and gives it fresh vigor, watering the roots of the wings and quickening them to growth, whereby the soul of the beloved, in its turn, is filled with love. . . . His lover is, as it were, a mirror in which he beholds himself (255 b − d).

Thus, there is a peculiar reciprocity between lover and beloved. The beauty of the beloved is reflected back to him by his lover in such a way that he too is provoked by the sight of something beautiful into recollection of the beautiful itself. And, as the original beautiful one in the erotic engagement, the beloved, in being provoked into recollecting the beautiful, is involved in a recollection which bears upon his own knowledge of himself. The erotic engagement is capable of serving for the Socratic task of self-knowledge. And *in deed* Socrates has related to his beloved Phaedrus a myth which serves to make manifest to them some things of utmost importance about their own souls.

Thus, Socrates concludes his speech, which has been a palinode for his earlier offence against love, by praying to love that he might retain the blessings of love: "Take not from me the lover's art with which thou hast blest me" (257 a). The basis for the prayer is provided by what Socrates' second speech as a whole has brought to light regarding love and its blessings. Love is that madness which, as gift of the gods, comes over man in such a way as to open him to the beautiful. It is that divinely bestowed condition in which man is exposed to the provocation of the beautiful, that is, to the shining forth of being in the midst of the visible to which embodied man is tied. Open to this provocation and, to the same extent, capable of speech, gifted with exposure to the shining forth of being and, equally, with an engagement in *logos*, endowed with *eros* and *logos*, man is capable of recollection—that is, of re-enacting the divine banquet in a properly human way.

Socrates has now spoken in a way appropriate to love, and the follower of Zeus ends his speech appropriately by praying to love that his beloved Phaedrus may direct himself towards love and philosophical *logos*.

Section 3. The Perfection of Speech (257 b — 279 c)

The structure of the second of the two major parts of the *Phaedrus* is generated by the four principal topics taken up in this part and by the relations between these topics. The topics are: (1) the merits of written speeches, in contrast to the spoken word; (2) the connection between speech and knowledge; (3) dialectic, in contrast to current rhetoric; and (4) the relation between speech and the soul. These topics are not, however, merely taken up sequentially in the course of this part of the *Phaedrus,* for the matters themselves are related in a way that is not merely sequential. Something of that relation can be seen in the following outline of this part of the dialogue:

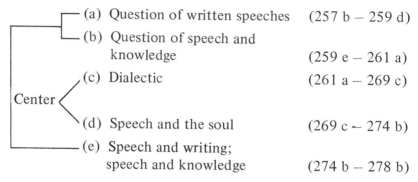

	(a) Question of written speeches	(257 b – 259 d)
	(b) Question of speech and knowledge	(259 e – 261 a)
	(c) Dialectic	(261 a – 269 c)
Center	(d) Speech and the soul	(269 c – 274 b)
	(e) Speech and writing; speech and knowledge	(274 b – 278 b)

On the surface it appears that the single issue which unifies all that is taken up in the second part of the *Phaedrus* is that of rhetoric. Certainly it is the case that rhetoric is at issue throughout this part, but, precisely by the way in which it is put at issue, the entire discussion decisively transcends the consideration of rhetoric regarded as a mere technique of speech-making. The fundamental issue of this part of the dialogue is speaking as such, that is, *logos,* and in relation to this issue rhetoric in the narrow sense of a technique for constructing persuasive speeches appears only as a meagre contrast to what is really demanded of one who would speak in the way which befits the fundamental possibilities granted by the power of *logos.* In terms of the structure sketched above, what this part does primarily is interrogate *logos,* first, in terms of the relation of speech to that which is spoken about in the speech (which amounts to an investigation of dialectic) and, second, in terms of the relation of speech to the speaker and the listener (that is, its relation to the soul). Thus, the considerations of dialectic and of the relation of speech to the soul form the center, and it is by passing through this center that the other two questions can be decided.

The second part of the *Phaedrus* has not only its peculiar

structure but also a definite relation to the first part of the dialogue. This relation is essential to the significance of the second part and, retrospectively, even to that of the first part. The general character of the relation can be indicated by distinguishing between three levels that are operative in the *Phaedrus:*

(1) Speech about speech (about love)   (Part II)

(2) Speech about love   (Part I)

(3) Love (Socrates–Phaedrus)   *(Ergon)*

The crucial point is that, as the first part of the dialogue (the speeches about love) constitutes, in effect, a commentary on the underlying deed, on the development of the concrete erotic engagement between Socrates and Phaedrus, so the second part of the dialogue, as a speaking about speech, is a reflection—at some points, even explicitly—on what was done in the speech-making of the first part. But what, most comprehensively, was accomplished in the course of the delivery of the three speeches in the first part? There was accomplished a clearly discernible *perfecting of speech* leading up to the second speech of Socrates. Thus, what the second part of the *Phaedrus* reflects upon, more fundamentally, is the perfection of speech. Its question is: What is required of speech in order that it assume its most perfect form? What is good speech?

(a) Written Speeches (257 b – 259 d)

The discussion with which the second part of the dialogue begins is·dedicated to posing the question of the perfection of speech. It is important to note the precise terms in which this question is posed.

Since this discussion immediately follows the conclusion of Socrates' second speech and since the entire second part of the dialogue is a reflection on the activity practiced in the first part, it is appropriate that Phaedrus begins by drawing a brief comparison between the speeches of the first part. Specifically, he draws out the contrast between the second speech of Socrates, the beauty of which has provoked his wonder, and the speech of Lysias; he remarks even that the latter would inevitably make a poor showing should he try to compete with Socrates by giving another speech. Phaedrus proceeds then to specify the contrast in a definite direction by focusing on the most obvious difference between the speeches of Socrates and the speech of Lysias, namely, the fact that the latter was a written speech. The question Phaedrus now poses is whether there is something intrinsically inferior about written speeches, whether there is something blameworthy about being a speech-writer. He suggests an affirmative answer by mentioning that he has lately heard a politician reproaching Lysias for being a speech-writer; and he refers, furthermore, to the fact that the men of greatest influence in the cities have been reluctant to write speeches for fear of being labeled as sophists by posterity.

Socrates counters Phaedrus' suggested answer by insisting that the politicians who so vocally denounce speech-writing do not really mean what they say. He points out, with a comic touch, that these men too are speech-writers, the only difference being that their speech-writing takes a slightly more subtle form: they are so enamored of whatever praise is bestowed on their written speeches that they add at the beginning of each speech the names of those who praise it, writing, for example, "It was voted by the people that. . . ." In fact, it is precisely by speech-writing of this variety that they achieve their greatness. Whatever they may say about speech-writing, *in deed* they admire it.

Thus, the suggestion is that Lysias is not to be reproached merely on the ground of being a speech-writer, that, in other words, there is nothing intrinsically shameful about this practice. Socrates reinforces his suggestion by referring to orators and kings who succeed in acquiring the power of a Lycurgus, a Solon, or a Darius by means of their written speeches and who in this way win immortality in their cities as speech-writers. The point is that, far from being something shameful, speech-writing is, on the contrary, a source of power and a means for great achievements in the city. To those in the city who are capable of properly taking it up, speech grants such power that they are able even to overcome mortality in a decisive, if properly human, way. What is the character of the power of speech if it can be measured only against the power of death? Whatever else it may be, it is a power by which men can be overpowered, not only the men to whom the speech is addressed but also the very one who seeks to appropriate for himself the power that belongs to speech. How is such a man overpowered? He can be overpowered inasmuch as the very power of speech can serve to deceive him about himself so as to make it possible for him to come to "deem himself a peer of the gods while still living" (258 c).

Because the power of speech is such as also to deceive, there is need to perfect speech. Noting how Socrates has initially linked this issue to the city, we anticipate that the discussion of the perfection of speech will progress beyond the city, thus re-enacting both what Socrates and Phaedrus carried out in deed when they went outside the walls at the beginning of the dialogue and what Socrates accomplished in the great myth by presenting the ultimate whither and whence of the human soul.

Socrates proceeds to pose explicitly the question of the perfection of speech. He asserts outright that there is nothing shameful (αἰσχρόν) in writing speeches but that the shame consists, rather, in writing not beautifully (μὴ καλῶς) but shamefully and badly (αἰσχρῶς τε καὶ κακῶς). Therefore, he concludes, the problem is to determine what constitutes a writing done beautifully and what constitutes its opposite. It is important to note here the precise terms of the problem, for they serve to indicate in advance the direction in which a perfected speech will be sought: for the most part, Socrates uses, on the positive side, the word "καλῶς" ("beautifully") and, on the negative side, its opposite, "αἰσχρῶς" ("shamefully"). So, it is a matter of writing or speaking *beautifully*. The question of the perfection of speech, the question of good speech, is specified in the question: What is beautiful speech? Presumably, a speech which is written or spoken beautifully is a speech that is in accord with the beautiful itself. This means that it is a speech which is properly linked to the beautiful as the way in which being shines forth in the midst of the visible to which man is attached in his embodied condition. On the negative side, this means that beautiful speech must be such as would exclude any claim to being based on immediate access to being; on the contrary, it must be a speech which is appropriate to the condition of man, which consists in his having access to being only through the shining of the beautiful and the recollection which that shining is capable of provoking. Beautiful speech must be a speech which contributes to letting the shining forth of the beautiful provoke a genuinely human re-enactment of the divine banquet.

To the introduction and initial specification of the question of the perfection of speech there is appended the little myth of the cicadas. The connection of the myth to what has preceded it lies in the fact that in telling it Socrates is alluding in playful fashion to the *need* which man has of such beautiful speech as has just been put at issue. This is especially evident in the "conclusion" which Socrates draws immediately after having related the myth: "Thus there is every reason for us not to yield to slumber in the noontide but to pursue our talk" (259 d). What is this reason for their pursuing their talk? What need is it that dictates that they should continue speaking?

Socrates suggests that, in pursuing their talk, they would be imitating the cicadas overhead, who, as he says, are "singing after their wont in the hot sun and conversing with one another" (258 e). According to the little myth itself these cicadas, in turn, only imitate the race of men from whom they sprang. The story Socrates tells begins with these men:

> The story is that once upon a time these creatures were men—men of an age before there were any Muses; and that when the latter came into the world and music made its appearance, some of the people of those days were so thrilled with pleasure that they went on singing, and quite forgot to eat and drink until they actually died without noticing it. From them in due course sprang the race of cicadas (259 b – c).

Now, by continuing their talk Socrates and Phaedrus would be imitating (mediately) these men, so that what Socrates and Phaedrus are to accomplish by means of speech will be an image of what these ancestors of the cicadas accomplished—or, rather, conversely, the accomplishment portrayed in the myth will serve as an image of what Socrates and Phaedrus are to accomplish in deed by means of speech. But what did those men from whom the cicadas sprang really accomplish? By their enthusiastic engagement in singing they gained a certain independence from the demands of the body; that is, they achieved a certain disengagement from the needs that are linked to the condition of embodiment, which, in turn, holds man at a distance from the divine banquet. Their becoming so engaged in singing that they forgot to eat and drink serves to image the movement in which one would come nearer to the sight of the beings themselves in their truth as they are beheld by those in attendance at the divine banquet. Indeed, for embodied man such a movement must inevitably shatter against the fact of embodiment and of that distance of which embodiment is the guarantee: these men, forgetting to eat and drink, finally died as a result. But they died without even noticing it. The power of their song can be measured only against the power of death.

Speech is needed in order for man to be drawn towards being (cf. esp. *Phaedo* 99 d — e; and Ch. 1, Sect. 2 b). This need is further indicated by the peculiar function which Socrates attributes to the cicadas: they go and report to the Muses regarding how the Muses are honored by men. The cicadas and song and speech are intermediaries between men and divine, specifically between the philosopher and those Muses (Calliope and Urania, concerned with *logos* and the heavens) whose music the philosopher practices. Yet, as intermediary, the cicadas, singing in the hot sun, and the speech of the philosopher, dedicated to the philosophical Muses, also involve a usually concealed danger: Socrates speaks explicitly of the need that he and Phaedrus steer clear of "the bewitching siren song" of the cicadas (259 a — b). This danger is, in turn, correlative to another need which is alluded to by the fact that the myth refers to music and singing rather than just to speech. The point is that the kind of speech at issue, the kind of speech capable of providing for that need indicated in the myth, must involve a certain harmony, a certain accord. The failure of this accord in any one of the several respects in which it is required is what actualizes the danger. It is to the unfolding of the various senses of this accord that the remainder of the dialogue is largely devoted.

(b) Speech and Knowledge (259 e – 261 a)

Socrates now poses the first specific question regarding what is required for beautiful speech: "Then does not a beautiful speech presuppose that the speaker see in thought [διάνοια] the truth about the matters of which he is to speak?" (259 e). Phaedrus answers with the common objection to the positive answer which he assumes Socrates would give to this question: An orator speaking in court does not need to know what is really just but only what would seem just to the men who are to pass judgment. An orator, i.e., one who presumably is a practitioner of beautiful speech, needs to know *only* what *seems* just to those who are judging. Likewise, Phaedrus insists, with respect to the good and the beautiful itself such a man needs to know, for the sake of his speaking, only what *seems,* not what *is.*

Socrates makes a curious response to Phaedrus' contention: " 'Not to be lightly rejected,' Phaedrus, is any word of the wise, but we must see if they are right; so we must not dismiss what you just said" (260 a). In fact, however, Socrates does go on to reject the kind of exception on which Phaedrus' answer has drawn. Indeed, he goes on to reject, in appropriately comic fashion, any orators who are so unknowing that they might (as in the example Socrates gives) try to persuade Phaedrus to buy a horse for military-political purposes while not themselves knowing what a horse is but knowing only that Phaedrus is of the opinion that a horse is one of those tame animals which has the longest ears. Indeed, Socrates rejects outright the whole prospect of a rhetoric which could claim to be an art (τέχνη) while, on the other hand, requiring no knowledge of that which is to be spoken of in the speeches which such rhetoric would teach one to make. In other words, Socrates unconditionally expels from the sphere of art all rhetoric of the sort that would remain aloof from inquiry into that about which it speaks, i.e., all rhetoric of the sort that would simply amount to sheer technique.[33] But if rhetoric of this sort is no art, then it cannot be the means for the perfection of speech. It

---

[33] This issue is especially prominent in the *Gorgias,* although the basic dramatic character of that dialogue—which begins with the words "πόλεμος καὶ μάχη" ("warfare and battle") and which is shaped by the progressively more violent verbal warfare

is not to the example of such orators as those Phaedrus refers to that one must look in search of the means for the perfection of speech.

The question is whether Socrates' deflating of the current opinion about rhetoric as sheer technique is to be taken as indicating that Socrates' original question as to whether beautiful speech presupposes "knowledge" was only an assertion disguised as a question for purposes of drawing out and refuting Phaedrus' opinion on the matter. Was Socrates' response to Phaedrus' contention that one need know only what seems and not what is—his citation of the words of Nestor (who was pre-eminent in speech above all the Achaeans): "Not to be lightly rejected"[34] —was this mere politeness in the face of his beloved's parroted opinions or perhaps even veiled sarcasm regarding these opinions? To put the question in terms of the matter at issue: Is beautiful speech such as is preceded by and based upon a seeing of the spoken-about things in their truth? Does one first see (in $\delta\iota\acute{\alpha}\nu\text{οι}\alpha$) the things in their manifestness as what they are and then in speech only transpose into communicable form (i.e., express) what has already been seen?

(c) Dialectic (261 a – 269 c)

Socrates steers the discussion towards the theme of dialectic by pursuing further the question already raised regarding rhetoric,

---

between Socrates and his interlocutors—is so drastically alien to that of the *Phaedrus* as to preclude anything other than the most general kind of comparisons. Nevertheless, we should note that in Socrates' discussion with Gorgias there is a precise formulation of the relevant difference between a way of speaking which incorporates knowledge of what is spoken of and a way of speaking which is a mere technique of persuasion (459 b – c). Also, in his discussion with Polus, Socrates openly declares that rhetoric (of the Gorgian sort, sheer technique) is in no sense an art ($\tau\acute{\epsilon}\chi\nu\eta$) but rather a routine ($\grave{\epsilon}\mu\pi\epsilon\iota\rho\acute{\iota}\alpha$) (462 b); Socrates then goes on to draw the proportion: rhetoric is to justice as cooking is to medicine (465 c). The most decisive condemnation comes when rhetoric, which Gorgias himself defined as knowledge ($\grave{\epsilon}\pi\iota\sigma\tau\acute{\eta}\mu\eta$) about *logoi* (449 e), is branded by Socrates as $\acute{\alpha}\lambda\text{ογ}o\nu$ (465 a).

It should be noted that, even in our relatively loose usage of it, the word "technique" in its *modern* sense betrays a radical opposition to the Greek "$\tau\acute{\epsilon}\chi\nu\eta$." Suffice it to say, in the context of the present study, that this opposition is anything but a mere indifferent change of word-meanings.

[34] *Iliad*, II. 361; regarding Nestor's pre-eminence see II, 368.

that is, by seeking to justify further his insistence that rhetoric, conceived as a mere technique of speech-making, cannot bring about the genuine perfection of speech. He proceeds by securing Phaedrus' agreement that rhetoric has to do with "a kind of leading of the soul by means of *logoi*" (261 a). Socrates proposes to add that such "leading" may take place in private places as well as in courts of law, but Phaedrus insists that rhetoric be kept within its narrow political context. One effect of Phaedrus' insistence is to exclude all the speech-making that took place in the first part of the dialogue from the sphere of rhetoric and, thereby, to pose for Socrates the task of so developing the discussion of rhetoric as to be able eventually to exhibit at least his second speech as an instance of perfected speech.

Initially, however, Socrates proceeds on the terms on which Phaedrus insists: they consider rhetoric in the form of public oratory. On this basis Socrates proceeds to show how what is effective about rhetoric, even in the form of public oratory, is, in fact, a characteristic quite independent of whether or not the form of public oratory is involved. Specifically, he points out that rhetoric, as Phaedrus construes it, would need to be capable of making anything look like anything else, in order that the orator might have the power of making whatever he speaks about appear in the way that is most advantageous for the interested party. Rhetoric, as the "art" of speaking persuasively in court, would need to be, as Socrates says, a means "which enables people to make out everything to be like everything else, within the limits of possible experience" (261 e). In other words, rhetoric would need to be an art of eliminating—that is, concealing—all differences, all distinctions between things. Appealing to the example of Zeno, thereby alluding to an eliminating of differences which would be carried out for philosophical purposes,[35] Socrates insists that this power of eliminating differences is what is decisive irregardless of

---

[35] Such an eliminating of differences could take the form of collection in the sense to be explained by Socrates below. It could also serve—in a way more in accord with Zeno—as a means of developing or defending the Eleatic teaching regarding the one (see *Parm.* 128 c – d). It might also serve—in a way related to both of these alternatives—for provoking the posing of the "Platonic" ones, that is, for "motivating" the opening up of the distinction between visible and intelligible (see *Parm.* 128 e – 130 a).

whether one is considering court speeches or some other kind. In the discussion which follows, the irrelevance of Phaedrus' restriction of rhetoric to a narrow political context becomes progressively more apparent; in dramatic terms the entire discussion of rhetoric, as a discussion of the perfection of speech, has now begun its passage beyond the city.

Even an effective court rhetoric must be capable of concealing differences between things, especially in the sense of being able, by proceeding by sufficiently small steps, to make a transition from anything to its opposite without being detected. But in order for a speaker to be able to do this effectively, he needs to know what he is concealing; he can shift undetected from one thing to its opposite through intermediate steps only if he is aware of the relevant sameness and difference involved at each of these steps. Yet, presumably, in order to know how a thing is like and unlike other things one must know that thing itself in its truth. Thus, it appears that there can be no effective rhetoric independently of the knowledge of things. The perfection of speech—ironically, even the perfecting of that deceptive power on which the standard court speech depends—requires that the things be manifest in their distinct being. The perfection of speech must be understood in reference to the manifestness of what the speech is about.

However, it is of utmost importance to observe that this does not mean that beautiful speech is mere expression of something already achieved in a prior seeing of things in their distinct being. Socrates indicates this—though, at this point, only in preliminary fashion—by calling attention to the fact that at least in the case of some names men do not agree regarding what is named by them, hence, obviously, are not in possession of some prior vision of what is named:

> *Socrates:* When someone utters the name "iron" or "silver," we all think the same thing, do we not?
> *Phaedrus:* Certainly.
> *Socrates:* But what about the names "just" and "good"? Don't we diverge and dispute not only with one another but with our own selves?
> *Phaedrus:* Yes indeed (263 a).

At least in such cases as these we clearly do not enjoy, prior to speaking, an exhaustive vision of what is named by the names in our speech; it is not as though whenever we speak we have just come fresh from a round of divine banqueting. What is spoken about is not simply manifest once and for all prior to our speaking, and, in fact, it is significant that we compensate for our lack of sight not just by looking more intensely but by speaking and disputing with ourselves and with one another. This means that speaking is an essential means by which we are able to come closer to the things themselves in their truth, that it belongs to the means by which man is able to make the things themselves manifest (cf. Sect. 2 c, iii). *Logos* is no mere expression of what is already manifest but has to do with the original unfolding of the things into manifestness.

In accord with the importance which differentiation has now assumed—by the fact that beautiful speech has been shown to be directed to things in their distinctness from other things—Socrates adds to the previous account of human understanding as gathering or collection a second procedure which he names "division" ("διαίρεσις"). This procedure consists in "dividing things according to *eide*, where the natural joints are, and not trying to hack off parts like a clumsy butcher" (265 e). As examples of this procedure Socrates offers his own two speeches from the first part of the dialogue; and, in turn, by presenting them as exemplifying the procedure of division he clarifies what was left largely unclarified when the speeches were delivered, namely, the relation between them. He explains that the two speeches both began from the same thing, namely, madness,[36] and then proceeded by division, the first speech dividing to the left until it finally reached a kind of sinister love which it justly reviled, the second speech dividing to the right until it reached a divine love which it appropriately praised as the source of our greatest blessings. By bringing the two speeches into relation with a common term of collection in such a way as to offer them as exemplifications of division, Socrates, in effect, carries through a collecting of the two speeches themselves.

---

[36] It should be noted that Socrates, quite curiously, uses for this single *unifying* term three different, though more or less synonymous, words: ἄφρον, παράνοια, and μανία.

This curious interplay between collection and division is not without significance. Whereas collection is the procedure by which many are gathered into a one in which they belong together, division serves to exhibit the one of a collection in terms of the distinct many which it gathers. The important point is that a proper precedure of determination involves an interplay of collection and division—an interplay which is possible only because division is not just a simple opposite of collection that would merely undo what is accomplished by collection but rather is correlative to collection in such a way that both procedures converge on the same goal, the exhibition of determinateness.[37]

Once the necessity of the reference to what is spoken about is thought through, it becomes evident that perfected speech takes the form of collection and division, that is, of dialectic. This is the kind of *logos* which Socrates, the lover of *logoi,* loves pre-eminently:

> Believe me, Phaedrus, I am myself a lover of these divisions and collections, that I may gain the power to speak and to think; and whenever I deem another man able to discern a natural one and many, I follow "in his footsteps where he leadeth as a god" (266 b).

Socrates would follow the dialectician, just as, in that former time, he followed in the train of Zeus up to the summit of the arch that supports the heavens. The point is that collection and division—as constituting a way of laying out, exhibiting, things in their determinateness, in their proper and distinct being—pertain in a fundamental way to the means given to man for re-enacting the divine banquet.

Socrates concludes the discussion of dialectic with a humorous recitation of the stock techniques of current rhetoric, the principal point being the implied contrast with Socrates' immediately preceding description of the perfection of speech in terms of dialectic. In fact, however, the contrast is explicitly drawn, not between

---

[37] The very brief discussion of collection and division in the *Phaedrus* hardly provides a sufficient basis for a thorough consideration, which, instead, must take its bearings primarily from the *Sophist* and the *Statesman*. We shall attempt such a consideration below in Ch. VI.

rhetoric and dialectic, but between rhetoric and three arts which, as it were, substitute for dialectic. What is especially important, then, is the implied relation between dialectic and these other three arts, medicine, tragic poetry, and music. Dialectic heals the soul from the wounds suffered in the mishap that occurred while the soul was striving upward towards the scene of the divine banquet, the wounds peculiarly related to the body.[38] Also, dialectic draws the soul upward towards the gods, exalts the soul as in the case of a tragic hero. But, finally, dialectic avoids the nemesis that befalls the tragic hero or, at least, radically transforms that nemesis, inasmuch as it incorporates a harmony, an accord, not only with the things spoken of in such beautiful speech but also with the fundamental condition of man the speaker.

(d) Speech and the Soul (269 c — 279 c)

For the sake of the perfection of speech it is required that speech be in accord not only with the things spoken of and with the speaker but also with the soul of the one spoken to. Clearly, such an accord is necessary if speech is to be "written in the soul" of the one who hears; and we have seen (cf. Introduction, Sect. 3) that such an inscription is required in order that speech be besouled and thus really like a living being (264 c, 276 a, 278 a)—that is, it is required for the perfection of speech. In order for one to speak in a way that is in accord with the soul of the hearer,

---

[38] In this connection it is appropriate to refer to that part of Aristophanes' story in the *Symposium* (190 e — 191 a) according to which Zeus, having split men in half, instructed Apollo to turn the face and the half-neck to the side where the cut had been made, in order that man might be made more orderly by sight of the knife's work. Having done this, Apollo *healed* the wounds of men, but he left a few wrinkles around the naval to remind men of what they had suffered. Apollo's service to man thus consisted in healing him, not by restoring him to his original wholeness, but rather in a way appropriate to his present condition; and in healing man Apollo gave him a bodily sign to warn him against the danger of acting in a way not in accord with his subordination to the gods. The suggestion is that it belongs to the task of the philosopher, as in service to Apollo, to dedicate himself to re-enacting Apollo's healing deed, i.e., to the establishing of a wholeness appropriate to man's condition and to the interpreting of the bodily signs capable of securing man in that condition.

In this connection we note also in passing that in the *Charmides* Socrates masquerades as a physician (155 b — e).

it is presumably necessary that one know both about souls and about what kind of accord is appropriate. It appears, then, that the perfection of speech requires knowledge of the nature of the soul, of how it acts and "suffers," and, beyond that, the establishing of correspondence between souls and speeches—that is, a classification of souls, a classification of speeches, and a relating of the two classifications in such a way that it would then be pre-determined what kind of speech is in accord with what kind of soul (271 a – b).

However, the problem is that in attempting such a collection and division of souls and speeches, we encounter the same complication, the same peculiar circularity, that was found in considering the connection between speech and the things spoken about. Just as one does not have, prior to speaking, an exhaustive vision of the things, which would then only get "expressed" in speech, so, likewise, a knowledge of the soul and of the soul's relation to speech does not simply precede speech. On the contrary, speech belongs to the way by which we come to have such knowledge. This is most evident in the case of the soul: we learn about the soul of another, not so much by seeing (in whatever form) but by speaking with him. The peculiar involvement of this issue is indicated by the fact that, whereas, on the one hand, the perfection of speech would appear straightforwardly to require a collection and division exercised on souls and speeches, on the other hand, the very practice of collection and division by which the perfection of speech would be accomplished is itself an affair of speech, even a perfected speech, a beautiful speech. The involvement is still more evident if we extend the reflection upon the speaking practiced in the first part of the dialogue and observe that Socrates' second speech, the perfected speech *in deed*, rather than presupposing knowledge of soul, is what first raises the question and what makes manifest in an appropriate way the "whither" and "whence" of the human soul.[39]

---

[39] In connection with this general issue it should be noted that the seemingly very straightforward summary statement at 277 b – c ("A man must know the truth about all the particular things of which he speaks or writes. . . ."), which might seem to affirm a simple order of dependence, is quite conspicuously "framed" by two passages dealing with the question of the written word and indicating that written words are more playful

Speaking of what is required for one to practice perfected speech, Socrates says that one

> will assuredly never acquire such competence without considerable diligence, which a wise man ought not to undergo for the sake of speaking and acting before men, but that he may be able to speak and do everything, so far as possible, in a manner pleasing to the gods (273 e — 274 a).

This means, not that the appropriateness of speech to the one spoken to (whether oneself or another) is unimportant, but only that it is subordinated to a higher measure, a final measure that most fundamentally determines the perfection of speech. What is required in order that man speak what is pleasing to the gods? The case of Socrates' response to the Delphic pronouncement indicates to what extent the accord of human speech with the gods is a problem for the philosopher; it indicates to what extent the very origination of philosophy is linked to a peculiar discord in this regard.

How is one to dare an answer to the question as to what is pleasing to the god—especially in view of such disasterous examples as that of Euthyphro? Socrates' second speech indicates how an answer is to be ventured. It does so by actually venturing an answer—an answer, not in terms of any of the usual human actions performed in service to the gods, such as worship and sacrifice, but in terms of man's subordinating himself in an appropriate way to that to which the gods are themselves subordinated as the very condition of their being gods (cf. 249 c; *Euthyphro* 10 a — d). What is pleasing to the gods is that which they themselves enjoy when they ascend to the summit of the arch of heaven so as to join in the divine banqueting. What is pleasing to the gods is the *manifestness of the beings,* that is, *truth.*

What the perfection of speech requires, that is, what is required in order that one speak what is pleasing to the gods, is that one properly subordinate himself to the truth. What is required is that

---

than serious and that the point is to sow the words in the soul of the hearer (274 b — 277 a; 277 d — 278 b). The self-reference is evident: the point is that if these words are sown in one's soul, if one undertakes what these written words (about knowledge, speech, etc.) prescribe, one can then be led into the relevant "circularity."

one be directed to the manifestness of the beings, that is, engaged in re-enacting the divine banquet, and that, at the same time, one be so directed in a way that befits man's condition of being separated from immediate access to the beings, on which, by contrast, the gods are able to feast their eyes. What is required is something like that harmony between inner and outer for which Socrates prays at the very end of the *Phaedrus*. What is required is that man knowingly establish himself within his *moira,* which includes establishing himself knowingly in his ignorance. One name for such establishing is moderation (σωφροσύνη).

The conclusion of the *Phaedrus* indicates the level which the erotic engagement between Socrates and Phaedrus has reached: each sets out with a message for a beloved, Phaedrus going to speak to Lysias, Socrates to Isocrates (cf. *Sym.* 210 a − b, 211 c). And just as Socrates concluded the first part of the dialogue with a prayer to love, so now—before taking his message to his beloved Isocrates, who is linked to him not only in *eros* but also literally in *logos,* in name—Socrates concludes with a prayer to Pan. We should observe that Pan is "displaced" like man, being half animal and half god, that he is a musician, and that, according to what the inspired Socrates of the *Cratylus* says, he is either *logos* or the brother of *logos* (Crat. 408 d; cf. Ch. IV, Sect. 4 d). Socrates' prayer to Pan is an invocation addressed to *logos* in its capacity to unfold into music, into the proper accord, so that—together with that opening onto the shining forth of being, that is, together with the love that belongs to divine madness—*logos* might give man the means for *placing* himself.

We are left wondering whether Socrates and Phaedrus cross the river Illisus on their way back to the city.

POSTSCRIPT TO PART ONE
THE WAY OF PLATONIC DIALOGUE:
FURTHER REFLECTIONS

In coming to consider the last part of the *Phaedrus* we have returned full circle to the point from which we began—that is, to those passages from which we took our initial clues regarding the character of the dialogues and, hence, our preliminary directives for reading the dialogues. We have made our return to this point by way of an attempt at a thoughtful and careful reading of three dialogues. In turn, this reading of the *Apology,* the *Meno,* and the *Phaedrus* has served to clarify who Socrates is, hence, who the philosopher is, hence, what philosophy is; and through the reading the question about philosophy has been allowed to unfold especially in the direction of the question of *logos,* so that the question became that of Socratic *logos,* of philosophical *logos,* of that *logos* that is so perfected as to be fit for the accomplishment of its true end. In our reading of the last part of the *Phaedrus* this theme—the perfection of *logos*—finally became explicit.

Thus, by proceeding from a preliminary understanding of the character of the Platonic dialogues, which are themselves a distinctive kind of *logos,* we have in our reading come upon the thematic development of the question of *logos* in certain dialogues. It is appropriate that we now let the peculiar reflexivity which the dialogues involve in this regard assert itself explicitly—that reflexivity consisting in the fact that the dialogues, as *logoi,* take up thematically the question of *logos,* so that in bringing something to light about their theme they also bring to light something about themselves. In the first place, this requires that we indicate how those three features of Platonic dialogue, which in our preliminary reflections could only be posed in response to certain clues, are, in fact, grounded on certain aspects of what the dialogues bring to light regarding *logos.* In other words, we need to see how the features of the dialogues, as themselves *logoi,* are ways of fulfilling the very requirements for perfected *logos* that the dialogues lay down.

These requirements are laid down by means of a situating of *logos* within the context of the relevant total accomplishment. This total accomplishment coincides with what is called recollection in the *Meno*. It amounts to what was called, in terms of the *Phaedrus* myth, an appropriately human re-enactment of the divine banquet. It amounts to a mediation of that radical separation from being which, according to the retrieve of the mythic past, opened up with the movement of embodiment. It is the accomplishment of that movement of the soul from ignorance to knowledge which is correlative to the movement in which the original gathering wholes become manifest.

How is *logos* situated within the context of this total accomplishment? What is *logos* specifically charged with accomplishing? As that already accomplished anonymous gathering of parts into wholes (i.e., of manys into ones), as that gathering which man always resumes in his speaking, *logos* is what makes original wholes initially available, especially in their character as wholes of a gathering. Though, indeed, *logos* alone does not suffice for making the wholes manifest *as* original wholes, it is essential as what primarily grants the point from which the appropriate movement of the soul can begin. *Logos,* pertaining to the total accomplishment, pertains in an especially crucial way to the beginning of philosophy.

How are the three features of Platonic dialogue that were thematized in our preliminary reflection grounded on the determination of *logos* with respect to its charge within the total accomplishment of philosophy itself? We recall the second of the three features—the feature comprised by the fact that a dialogue is directed towards provoking recollection in the soul of the one who hears. For one who, like Meno, is oblivious to the movement from ignorance to knowledge and oblivious to what such movement demands, this feature can involve nothing more than the simple capacity of the written word to refresh one's memory in the most mundane sense, to restore memories such as those with which Meno is stuffed. But, regarded for what it is, this directedness towards the provocation of recollection is nothing less than a directedness towards that total accomplishment within which *logos* is situated. It is a directedness towards provoking the hearer into a re-enactment of the divine banquet, that is, into a mediation of man's separation from being. Such mediation is, in the terms of the *Meno,* a mediating between whole and parts, which mediating is identical with human virtue. In this sense—but *only* in this sense—the dialogues can be said to be directed towards provoking virtue.

The first of the three features of Platonic dialogue is their dramatic character. This dramatic character, as determined in our preliminary reflections, consists in the dimensionality of the dialogues—i.e., their incorporating multiple dimensions of which we named, specifically, the dimensions of *logos, mythos,* and *ergon*—and the mirror-play within and between the dimensions of a dialogue. With regard to its grounding, this feature can be understood through reference to the fundamental directedness of the dialogues towards provoking virtue. Thus, whatever else it might accomplish, the multiform dimension of *logos* serves to gather the wholes as already available in *logos* and to render them determinate in a way which makes them fit for serving to establish the point of initiation of the appropriate movement of the soul. Just as this collecting and rendering determinate is bound up with an accomplishment, specifically, with the initiation of the movement of the soul from ignorance to knowledge, so, correspondingly, the dimension of *logos* is accompanied by a dimension of *ergon* and linked up with it through a mirror-play. And, finally, corresponding to the need to project, in advance of the soul's proper movement, the space of the movement, which can be made determinately manifest only (if at all) through the execution of the movement—corresponding to this there is conjoined with the other dimensions of Platonic dialogue a dimension of *mythos.* In this connection the *mythos* thus serves as a way of openly granting a concealment, hence, as a way of knowingly bearing testimony to human ignorance—to the involvement of a concealment and an ignorance at least in the beginning of philosophy if not in its fulfillment.

The way of Platonic dialogue is, fundamentally considered, the way in which the dialogues let the matter at issue become manifest. But the matter that is pre-eminently at issue is being itself, which, at the level of our reading thus far, means: the original gathering wholes. How are the original gathering wholes allowed to become manifest? How do the dialogues let them become manifest? The dialogues let them become manifest in the way that is proper to them. That is, the original gathering wholes can be brought to manifestness only by a way that accords with the structure of their own mode of manifestation. Already we have seen ample indication that this structure is that of imaging, though we have hardly even begun yet to clarify the precise character of such imaging. Because the structure of the manifestation of being is one of imaging, the dialogues—dedicated to this movement of manifestation and the corresponding movement of the soul—engage in a complex imaging within and between their dimensions. To their dramatic character there belongs a complex mirror-play.

And, more generally, the dialogues have, as the third feature in our preliminary determination, the character of play. For philosophical *logos* has to do with what is not immediately manifest, with what has, rather, to be allowed to come to manifestness. Its matter is not immediately available in such a way that one could simply and seriously involve oneself with it. The matter has, rather, to be invoked, called to put in an appearance. Play is such a way of calling to what is concealed.

The reflexivity of the dialogues with respect to the issue of *logos* prescribes not only that the initially posed features of the dialogues be set back upon the ground provided them by the determination of *logos* achieved in the thematic considerations within the dialogues but also that this grounding initiate, in turn, a further determination of the way of Platonic dialogue, a determination more engaged in the matters themselves than our preliminary determinations could possibly have been. But, in deed, the two oppositely-directed tasks prescribed by the reflexivity have begun to coalesce, and the further determination has already been initiated in the development of the grounding. It has become evident that to respond to a Platonic dialogue is not so much a matter of taking certain features into account—although such features may continue to serve as important directives—but rather a matter of letting ourselves into the movement which the dialogues are directed towards provoking, of letting ourselves into philosophy, of beginning (playfully) to philosophize.

PART TWO

BEING AND *LOGOS*

CHAPTER IV

LOGOS AND ITS PARTS:

CRATYLUS

The *Cratylus* is a *logos* about *logos*. Yet, it is such in a different way from the second part of the *Phaedrus,* not only because it lacks direct contact with a perfecting of *logos* in deed of the kind on which the second part of the *Phaedrus* directly reflects, but also because of the peculiar way in which it thematizes *logos.* The *Cratylus* is, most immediately, addressed to the question of the nature of name (ὄνομα)[1]; names constitute the matter which the dialogue most directly puts at issue. Yet, more fundamentally, the questioning undertaken in this dialogue makes an issue of names precisely in their function as parts of *logos.* Thus, it puts *logos* at issue with respect to its parts.

How does the *Cratylus* put *logos* and its parts at issue? In what

---

[1] It should be noted that the Greek "ὄνομα" is not strictly identical with the English "name," primarily because it does not signify proper name as exclusively as does "name." Nevertheless, the central meaning of "ὄνομα" is proper name, and it is evident in the *Cratylus* that it has as its primary sense—even though at various places in the dialogues "ὄνομα" is used to designate almost all the more important kinds of words, including pronouns, adjectives, nouns, verbs, and sometimes seems to be very close to the English "word." Yet, in the *Cratylus* the primary reference to proper name is important, since it already suggests a link between an ὄνομα and things, which is just what is taken for granted in the dialogue and then interrogated as regards its character (e.g., whether it is natural or conventional). Within the context of the *Cratylus* "name" is clearly a more suitable translation than "word" if for no other reason than that a name is the name of something, whereas "word" does not carry this reference to something. Certainly, "ὄνομα" should not be rendered as "language," "statement," or "discourse," not only because of the philological objections but also because the relation of ὄνομα to *logos* is a principal problem for Plato both in the *Cratylus* and elsewhere. On the meaning of "ὄνομα" see R. Robinson, "The Theory of Names in Plato's *Cratylus,*" *Revue Internationale de Philosophie,* 9 (1955), pp. 221-223; and Klaus Oehler, *Die Lehre vom Noetischen und Dianoetischen Denken bei Platon und Aristoteles* (München: C. H. Beck'sche Verlagsbuchhandlung, 1962), pp. 56-59.

connection does it let them be problematic? It does so in connection with their relation to things. Thus, the *Cratylus* is from the
outset animated by that problem that was posed both by the
Meno and by the reflection in the second part of the *Phaedrus:* the
problem of the referral of *logos* to the things taken up in *logos,* or,
more generally, the problem of the limit of *logos.* What the
Cratylus brings into questioning in such a way as to make manifest
has to do with the limits of *logos,* with the way by which that
which limits *logos* can be made available for such a limiting, and
with the way in which *logos* can be limited by its appropriate
limit, with the way in which the limiting is accomplished. Inasmuch as this limiting is what makes it possible for *logos* to achieve
its proper end, what is made manifest by the *Cratylus* has to do
with the virtue (ἀρετή) of *logos.*

Despite its dedication to the issue of the referral of *logos*
beyond itself—or, rather, precisely because of its way of carrying
through this dedication—the *Cratylus* is, of all the dialogues, the
one which is most exclusively confined to *logos,* the one which is
most exclusively a *logos* about *logos.* This unique degree of exclusiveness should serve to warn us in advance against taking what
transpires in this *logos* about *logos* too lightly or too straightforwardly. The very project of a *logos* about *logos* involves from
the outset a curious reflexive complication: it is an inquiry regarding *logos* which itself takes the form of a *logos* and thus already
takes for granted that which is to be investigated. A *logos* about
logos is such that any radical separation between the investigation
itself and what is being investigated is precluded; the investigation
itself is always already involved in, must make use of, just that
which it is to investigate. The situation of a *logos* about *logos* is in
this respect similar to that involved in the project in which one
seeks to answer the question "What is knowledge?"—in which one
seeks knowledge of knowledge (cf. *Theaet.* 196 d – 197 a). But
there is one decisive difference: knowledge, if it really is such, is
true, but *logos,* like opinion, is capable of being false (cf. *Gorg.*
454 d).

Especially because of the peculiar intertwining of the investigation with what is to be investigated by means of it, a *logos* about
logos is of such a character that it persistently tends towards

assuming the character of a comedy. It tends towards comedy not only in the sense in which perhaps every dialogue stands near, and at certain points becomes, comedy by virtue of the fact that each abstracts its specific matter from the whole on which this matter, nevertheless, depends, hence omitting something which, strictly speaking, cannot be omitted.[2] Though, indeed, the repeated attempt in the course of the *Cratylus* to restrict the discussion to names, to a consideration of the parts of *logos* which would take no account of the whole, invites comedy in this sense, what is still more important is that a *logos* about *logos* tends towards comedy in a way already suggested in the *Meno,* specifically in the character Meno where what is omitted is just the awareness of ignorance and, hence, the awareness of what is demanded of and appropriate to man in his ignorance. In the case of a *logos* about *logos* the threat of such self-forgetfulness is perhaps greatest of all, for the utmost effort and reflectiveness is required in order to avoid losing sight of the reflection back upon itself that attends an investigation of *logos* which itself takes place in *logos.* If in undertaking a *logos* about *logos* one is oblivious to the peculiar involvement of the investigation itself in *logos,* then one inevitably mistakes the project actually undertaken for something else, and there is a fundamental incongruity between what one takes himself to be accomplishing and what one, in fact, does accomplish, an incongruity which is pre-eminently comical inasmuch as its source lies in a forgetting of the situation which underlies the project.

The *Cratylus* is a comedy. But it is such not just in the sense that an incongruity of this sort is involved in what is undertaken in the dialogue. Rather, more significantly, such an incongruity is instituted by Socrates precisely in order that, by letting the incongruity unfold to the point at which it becomes manifest as what it is, the fundamental bond which binds man to *logos* might be brought to light. It is not simply that there is a comic element in the configuration of the project undertaken in the *Cratylus;* rather, the comedy is enacted by Socrates in such a way that in the course of the comedy something decisive comes to light. In the *Cratylus* Socrates acts out the comedy. This is to say that there is

---

[2] Cf. Strauss, *City and Man,* pp. 61-62.

a continual interplay of speech and deed in the dialogue and that the incongruity that is played out between what is said to be the deed undertaken and what, in fact, is the deed accomplished is central to the dramatic character of the dialogue as a whole. Furthermore, it is precisely at the point where this incongruity is first instituted in its full structure that Socrates, in his etymological endeavors, draws into the *logos* about *logos* almost the full range of those things told of in the myths; and it is in relation to the fundamental incongruity, that is, in terms of the character of the *Cratylus* as a comedy, that Socrates' invocation of *mythoi* must be understood.

We have said that what the *Cratylus* brings into questioning so as to make manifest is the relation between names and things. Yet, this relation as it is brought to light through the unfolding of the comedy proves to be such that names both serve to make things manifest and, on the other hand, are in need of being limited by what they themselves first make manifest. There is a need for things already to be manifest in order for names to be properly limited and, on the other hand, a need for names already to be properly limited in order for things to be made manifest. What is thus called for is an appropriate mediation between names and things capable somehow of establishing harmony between the need which each has for the other. No less than in the *Meno,* Socrates here assumes the role of mediator, and the entire dialogue consists of a complex of mediating accomplishments on the part of Socrates. At the very outset of the dialogue he is explicitly called upon to mediate between the opposed positions maintained by the other two characters of the dialogue—between, on the one hand, the position of Cratylus, according to which there is a natural bond between names and things, and, on the other hand, the position of Hermogenes, which is an explicit denial of any such natural connection between names and things.[3] At its most

---

[3] The principal source regarding the historical person Cratylus is Aristotle's *Metaphysics:* (a) Aristotle writes with reference to Plato: "For, having in his youth first become familiar with Cratylus and with the Heraclitean doctrines (that all sensible things are ever in a state of flux and there is no knowledge about them), these views he held even in later years" (Bk. I, 987 a 31 − b 1); (b) he writes with reference to various earlier thinkers: "And again, because they saw that all this world of nature is in movement, and

explicit level the dialogue consists of Socrates' effecting a mediation between these two characters in a way which stands in marked contrast to the course taken by the *Meno* in which Socrates' attempt at mediation provoked little more than abuse and threats and in which the two respondents, in the end, "stayed put" at their original positions. In the *Cratylus,* on the other hand, each respondent is led by Socrates to affirm the opposite position, with the result that there is a curious dramatic interchange between these two characters in stark contrast to the fact that there is almost no verbal interchange between them throughout the entire course of the dialogue; each of them talks almost exclusively with Socrates, for they have already given up talking to one

---

that about that which changes no true statement can be made, they said that of course, regarding that which everywhere in every respect is changing, nothing could truly be affirmed. It was this belief that blossomed into the most extreme of the views above mentioned, that of the professed Heracliteans, such as was held by Cratylus, who finally did not think it right to say anything but only moved his finger, and criticized Heraclitus for saying that it is impossible to step twice into the same river; for *he* thought one could not do it even once" (Bk. IV, 1010 a 6 – 14).

There has been considerable debate as to whether *in the dialogue* Plato depicts Cratylus as a convinced Heraclitean. However this issue is resolved (and it depends heavily on how one reads the next to the last statement by Cratylus – 440 d – e), the fact remains that it is primarily his theory of names which characterizes the Cratylus of the dialogue; that it is, in fact, Socrates who introduces the Heraclitean view, indeed, long before Cratylus even enters the discussion; and that the dialogue persistently suggests that Cratylus accepts the Heraclitean position only because he has been led to think that it follows from the application of his theory of names and in a sense bears it out. The problem which thus arises is how the depiction of Cratylus in the dialogue is to be reconciled with the description (quoted above) which Aristotle gives of the historical person Cratylus as the most extreme Heraclitean. On this issue see especially G. S. Kirk, "The Problem of Cratylus," *American Journal of Philology,* 72 (1951), pp. 225-253; also the criticism and counter-proposal by D. J. Allan, "The Problem of Cratylus," *American Journal of Philology,* 75 (1954), pp. 271-287.

The other respondent, Hermogenes, is referred to several times by Xenophon as a close associate of Socrates (*Memorabilia,* I. ii. 48; II. x. 3-6; IV. viii. 4-6; *Apologia Socratis,* 2 ff., etc.). Plato includes him among those who were present at Socrates' death (*Phaedo* 59 b). Also he is reported by Diogenes Laertius (III, 6) to have been a follower of Parmenides, though there is considerable suspicion that this presumed Eleaticism was derived from the contrast drawn in Plato's dialogue (see the references in Friedländer, *Plato,* II, pp. 340-341). Nevertheless, as Friedländer points out (II, p. 198), fragment 8 of Parmenides suggests a basis for a legitimate identification of Hermogenes' position regarding names with the position of Parmenides. But here, of course, one is speaking, not of the historical figure, but of the Hermogenes of the dialogue. In view of the uncertainty regarding both of these characters (considered historically) and the suspicion that the reports regarding them may be dependent on Plato's dialogue, we shall abstain from making any extensive use of the reports regarding the historical persons in the attempt to understand the Hermogenes and Cratylus of Plato's dialogue.

another before the dialogue commences. Yet, the mediating activity in which Socrates compels Cratylus and Hermogenes to exchange positions is only the surface of the comedy. Beneath this surface Socrates brings to light the fact that with respect to the fundamental problem Cratylus and Hermogenes "stay put" hardly less than do Meno and Anytus and that each of them even "stays put" at essentially the same place as the other. But all of this comes to light only within the compass of another mediating activity, a curious attempt to mediate between names and the originals from which they derive, a mediation which becomes, in fact, a comic attempt to retrieve the originals by which an immediate measuring of names could be effected. It is in and through the unfolding of this comic undertaking that the way of a genuine mediation between names and things is lighted up. What is important in the *Cratylus* is not just the various forms of mediation undertaken but, even more, the interplay between these.

Section 1. The Problem of Names (383 a — 384 c)

(a) Cratylus (383 a — 384 a)

The opening sentence of the *Cratylus* alludes to the issue of the dialogue as a whole: Hermogenes asks whether Socrates ought not be made a partner in the *logos*. We are told immediately that the *logos* in which Hermogenes and Cratylus have been engaged concerns *logos;* specifically, it concerns the nature of name, of a part of *logos*. It is Hermogenes who tells Socrates of the point of contention in the discussion that has transpired and of the curious course which the discussion has followed. Except for a noncommittal response to Hermogenes' suggestion that Socrates join the discussion, Cratylus remains silent.

According to Hermogenes' report Cratylus has been maintaining that there is an intrinsic correctness or fitness (ὀρθότης) in names, which is the same for both Greeks and barbarians. This fitness of names is a fitness with respect to the things of which they are names, and each thing has a right name of its own by nature (φύσει). A name belongs by nature to that of which it is the name. For a sound (φωνή)[4] simply to be posited, in whatever way, as the name of a thing does not suffice to guarantee that it is truly the name of that thing.

It is essential that we thematize the precise character of Cratylus' position to the extent that this is possible on the basis of Hermogenes' report. From the outset it needs to be observed that Cratylus' position does not, strictly speaking, exclude the possibility that for certain purposes it may be necessary for a name to be posited as the name of the thing; it does not exclude the possibility that a positing may be necessary in order for a particular sound to be a name in the sense of an instrument actually used by men in speaking about things. His position does not commit him to regarding names as fully ready-made by nature, simply at man's disposal without any positing on his part. Thus, Cratylus is not maintaining that names exist in the full sense by nature—though, indeed, he does not deny this. The opposition between Cratylus and Hermogenes—the opposition which Socrates is called upon to mediate—is not simply the opposition between the thesis that names exist by nature and the thesis that they exist by convention; indeed, the very possibility of the mediation is tied to the fact that it is not this more straightforward opposition that is at issue. In this regard it is correct to say that the problem of the *Cratylus* is not primarily that of the origin of names, for it is not with respect to this issue that Hermogenes and Cratylus are at the outset fundamentally at odds.[5] Although indeed the question of the origin of names is taken up in curious fashion later in the dialogue, it is not primarily in relation to this question that Socrates initially undertakes his mediating activity.

What Cratylus is maintaining is that, whatever else may be necessary in order for a sound to be a name in the full sense—and regarding this nothing is said nor is it positively suggested at this point that anything else is necessary—there is a natural fitness which makes certain sounds the right names of certain things. This

---

[4] On the meaning of "φωνή" in this context, see G. J. De Vries, "Notes on Some Passages of the *Cratylus*," *Mnemosyne,* IV 8 (1955), p. 290.

[5] Cf. Robinson, "Theory of Names in Plato's *Cratylus*," esp. pp. 224, 230-234; also Friedländer, *Plato,* II, pp. 196, 201, 340 (n.2).

natural fitness is prior to any positing of names by man, and such a positing, if it is to posit the right names of things, must be in accord with this natural fitness. Thus, for a thing simply to be called by a certain name by certain men does *not* suffice, according to Cratylus, to guarantee that it is the name of that thing. Even if all mankind should call Hermogenes by the name "Hermogenes," this would afford no guarantee that "Hermogenes" is his name; if, as Cratylus insists, his name is not naturally fit with respect to the man Hermogenes, then it is not his name at all.

Cratylus' curious claim of being in a position to deprive Hermogenes of the rightful possession of his own name serves at the very outset to mark Cratylus' position as one which incorporates, implicitly or explicitly, certain peculiar claims and which needs to be examined as regards its right to what is claimed. It serves also to anticipate the comic character which will be found to adhere to the claims in which Cratylus' position involves him. That Cratylus embodies a certain comic incongruity is already indicated by Hermogenes' account of the peculiar course taken by the discussion prior to the time at which Hermogenes invited Socrates to join it. When asked by Hermogenes to explain what he meant, Cratylus has suggested that he possesses a special knowledge of names which settles the entire matter once and for all; but he has refused to divulge and explain the wisdom to which he lays claim and, instead, has spoken only in the manner of an oracle. On the one hand, Cratylus claims superior wisdom regarding names, a wisdom which enables him to determine which are the natural names of things and, hence, presumably, to use the correct names in explaining his position to Hermogenes; but, on the other hand, he refuses to speak in anything other than oracular pronouncements, for which an interpreter, in the form of Socrates, must be called in. Cratylus in his presumed wisdom regarding the parts of *logos* breaks off the *logos* with Hermogenes, either because he is unable to explain his wisdom or because he regards it as more fitting to speak in the manner appropriate to divine pronouncements. Furthermore, once the interpreter arrives, Cratylus withdraws into utter silence; he says nothing whatsoever while Hermogenes is telling Socrates of the previous discussion and of the impasse to which it came. In fact, Cratylus remains completely silent throughout the discussion, already begun between Socrates and Hermogenes, which occupies the greater part of the dialogue.

(b) The Initial Appeals (384 a – 384 c)

It is appropriate that Hermogenes appeals to Socrates and asks that he either interpret the oracular pronouncements of Cratylus or else present his own view regarding the fitness of names. It is appropriate especially because of Socrates' own peculiar relation to that other oracle the service to which determines his practice, a relation which embodies a duality analogous to that expressed in Hermogenes' request. Socrates' response to the request involves three somewhat distinct parts which together set the stage for the ensuing discussion. He begins by appealing to an ancient saying (παροιμία) to the effect that knowledge of beautiful things (τὰ καλά) is hard to gain; to this he adds that knowledge of names is no small matter. Thus, Socrates addresses himself to the question about names by making an appeal to names—to an ancient saying. In so doing he anticipates precisely that structure which will be exhibited in the long investigation of names which forms the center of the dialogue: the judging of the fitness of names by means of an appeal to the ancient, the original names. At the same time, Socrates' initial response, as an appeal to names, portrays that situation which is to be determinative for the investigation of names and which is at the root of its comic character: namely, that the investigation of names will itself take place by the use of names or, more generally, that the investigation of *logos* will take the form of a *logos* about *logos*.

Socrates proceeds, secondly, to refer to the instruction regarding names offered by Prodicus, confessing that, since he has heard only the one-drachma course and not the complete education in names which the sophist offers, he does not, in fact, know the truth about this matter but is willing to inquire about it. Thus, Socrates points to the general relation of the problem of names and *logos* to the problem of sophistry[6] and the specific relation of

---

[6] What is perhaps most telling in this connection is that the task (set in the *Euthydemus* 288 b – c) of mastering the Protean sophist and forcing him to reveal his true shape is accomplished in the *Sophist* primarily through a reflection on *logos*. Cf. Ch. VI.

the position represented by Hermogenes to that of the sophists. At the same time, Socrates places at the beginning of the discussion an acknowledgement of his ignorance, specifically, of his ignorance regarding names; yet, by proposing to inquire he points, not only to his possession of that partial and implicit acquaintance with names demanded with respect to the *theme* of inquiry by the recollection story of the *Meno,* but also to the fact that he knows sufficiently about names as the *means* of inquiry, that he knows something regarding which names, which mode of *logos,* is appropriate for inquiring about names.

The third part of Socrates' response is a reference to Cratylus' previous claim to deprive Hermogenes of the right to his own name. Socrates alludes to the comic beginning when he observes that Cratylus was probably making fun of Hermogenes; and he lets the comedy unfold by explaining what Cratylus had not explained: Hermogenes is no true "descendent of Hermes," the god of commerce and the market, because he persistently fails in his attempts at making money.[7] Cratylus provides the conditions for the comedy; Socrates sets the comedy in motion.

Section 2. The Art of Naming (384 c – 390 e)

(a) Hermogenes (384 c – 385 b)

Hermogenes now states explicitly his own position in opposition to Cratylus. Names, he says, do not belong to things by nature. The right name of a thing is simply the name given to it by agreement and convention (συνθήκη καὶ ὁμολογία). He cites the example of changing the names of slaves and observes that in such cases the later name is no less right than the earlier one. Names, he contends, belong to things, not by nature, but only by law (νόμος) and custom (ἔθος) (384 c – e).

In Hermogenes' statement of his position there is a significant

---

[7] See Xenophon, *Memorabilia,* II. x.

ambiguity, and, as in the case of Cratylus, the ambiguity is decisive for the subsequent mediating performed by Socrates. Indeed, Hermogenes' position is definite enough in that respect by which it is opposed to the view of Cratylus: for Hermogenes it is not only the case that a positing is required in order for a sound to become a name; it is also the case that such positing is all that is required. Thus, it is clear that according to him the positing is the sufficient condition for the existence of a name in the full sense. However, with respect to the positing itself Hermogenes' statement is ambiguous, especially as regards the proper agent of such positing.[8] In this connection he suggests, in effect, at least three alternatives, which, though they seem to be taken by him as identical, are, in fact not so at all. In the first place, the example of changing the name of a slave suggests that a positing which is no more than a mere *fiat* by an individual man—though presumably one in a certain position of power—suffices to make a particular sound the name of a particular thing. But, secondly, Hermogenes also speaks of the fitness of a name, i.e., its being the name of a particular thing, as deriving from agreement and convention, that is, from a more complex positing which would not, in general, be reducible to a *fiat* of an individual man. Finally, he speaks also of law and custom as determining names; in this case the positing would no longer be correlative either to an individual nor to just any random association of individuals but would have, in the broad sense, a political character. It is noteworthy that as one proceeds through these three alternatives the positing itself as an actual event recedes into a certain indistinctness. The actual positing act by an individual man who changes the name of his slave is determinate enough; but in the case of custom it becomes in most cases exceedingly difficult to indicate the relevant positing activity, situated, as it is, somewhere in the indistinct past. What is significant here is that from the beginning a certain elusiveness of the positing activity and, thus, of the one who posits names is suggested. In the course of the dialogue the original giver of names will, indeed, prove to be elusive—to such a degree that in chasing

---

[8] Cf. Robinson, "Theory of Names in Plato's *Cratylus*," p. 228; also De Vries, "Notes on Some Passages of the *Cratylus*," p. 291.

after him Socrates, Hermogenes, and Cratylus will repeatedly mistake someone else for him.

Hermogenes' statement raises the question not only of the agent but also of the character of the positing by which something becomes a name. The example of the slave whose master deprives him of his earlier name—just as Cratylus would rob Hermogenes of his name—is especially important in this regard. What is distinctive about this example is that the naming takes place in a situation in which that activity and the one who carries it out are in no way bound by that which is named. But is it, in fact, the case that the relation of namer to named is the same as that of master to slave, so that the activity of naming can with right be carried out with complete disregard, in total independence, of that which is named? More precisely, is it the case that, when naming is carried out in the way exemplified in Hermogenes' example, such naming succeeds in accomplishing the function definitive of naming, i.e., in serving the end proper to naming as such? Clearly this issue can be decided only if the function of naming as well as the character which allows it to perform this function are brought to light. It can be determined whether, in general, a name merely imposed by a naming defined by the relation of master to slave is a fit name only if the end and the virtue of naming are properly understood.

Socrates' immediate response to Hermogenes' statement serves to force the expressed position into its most extreme form by making explicit that alternative which was suggested by Hermogenes' example of the slave. He secures Hermogenes' agreement to three points: first, that the positing is sufficient to make a sound the name of something (whatever name is given to something is its name); second, that this holds regardless of the agent of the positing (whether it be a private person or a city); and, third, that this also holds regardless of what thing it happens to be that is being named (whether it be a man or a horse) (385 a — b). Consequently, Hermogenes' position assumes the form of the assertion that a name is right regardless of the character of that positing or naming in which it is bestowed. Anything which is posited as a name, which is named "the name of some thing," is the name of that thing. Within the domain of names that which is (a name) is merely relative to a positing, which, in turn, is, in the extreme case now explicitly acknowledged by Hermogenes, relative to the individual man. Protagoras is on the horizon.

(b) Truth and Measure (385 b – 386 d)

With Hermogenes' position driven to its extreme, the purging is ready to begin. The way in which Socrates begins it is decisive for the entire course of the dialogue. Whereas up to this point the discussion has, almost without exception, been devoted to names and their fitness, Socrates now initiates quite abruptly a consideration of *logos* and its truth (ἀλήθεια). He proposes that that *logos* "which says things as they are is true, and that which says them as they are not is false"[9]; Hermogenes concurs, oblivious to the disastrous consequences which his concurrence will have. The entire section which follows (385 c –386 d) is devoted primarily to drawing out the results of this proposal. In order to purge Hermogenes' position—that is, to mediate in discussion with Hermogenes between his position and that of Cratylus—it is, as we saw, necessary to interrogate naming with respect to its end and its virtue. It is of utmost significance that Socrates prefaces this interrogation with a *logos* on true *logos*—that, in other words, he invokes the whole of which names are parts.

The working out of Socrates' proposal regarding true *logos* proceeds in two stages. In the first stage he brings the proposal to bear upon the problem of names by explicitly linking names to *logos* in terms of the relation of parts to whole: if there are such things as true and false *logos* and if names are parts of *logos,* then names may be true or false.[10] This result is then juxtaposed to

---

[9] Ἆρ' οὖν οὗτος ὃς ἂν τὰ ὄντα λέγῃ ὡς ἔστιν, ἀληθής · ὃς δ 'ἂν ὡς οὐκ ἔστιν, ψευδής; (385 b).

[10] It should be noted that there has been much debate regarding this passage, which some have taken to be an instance of the simple fallacy of division, of the indiscriminate inference from the character of the whole to that of the parts—an inference the untenability of which is shown by the distinction formulated in the *Sophist* (261 d – 262 e) between names and *logos.* Certainly the transition from the truth of *logos* to that of names is not explained or justified in this passage; but viewed in its context it is appropriate that it is not explained, since this entire section serves for posing the *question* of names in its full scope, as a question bearing upon τὰ ὄντα, in order to provide the basis for the subsequent interrogation of naming through which the connection between name and *logos* might be brought to light. One suspects even that there is

Hermogenes' position: "Then whatever each particular person says is the name of something, that is its name for that person" (385 d). This juxtaposition reveals, but leaves unsaid, the crucial point: if there is a truth and falsity of names and if names are strictly relative to an individual positing, then, at least in the sphere of names, truth is relative to the individual. Yet, if the truth of names is linked to the truth of *logos,* then, to the degree that the latter is determined by the former, the truth of *logos* becomes relative to an individual position. Since, furthermore, the truth of *logos* consists in its saying the things which are (τὰ ὄντα) as they are, Hermogenes' position, in regarding names as relative to an individual positing, in effect makes that which is, and the way in which it is, relative to the individual. Socrates has forced Hermogenes' position to reveal that affinity at which Socrates only hinted earlier: his position is identical with that of Protagoras, according to which "man is the measure of all things, both of the things which are, as they are, and of the things which are not, as they are not."[11] Indeed, Hermogenes fails to see this identity; he simply continues to affirm his original position.[12] Socrates, however, proceeds to name the unrecognized kinsman of Hermogenes.

The second stage of Socrates' working out of his proposal regarding true *logos* is a direct confrontation with the position of Protagoras; his criticism reproduces on a smaller scale the most decisive point of the criticism of Protagoras contained in the long first section of the *Theaetetus.* However, unlike the radical criticism in the *Theaetetus,* which exhibits Protagoras' view as caught

---

irony in the fact that Socrates, the one who mediates between whole and parts, does not here mediate at all but moves directly from whole to part and that the irony is that which is required for the full posing of the question. As regards the related passage in the *Sophist* it is sufficient at this point to note that the Stranger speaks of names as indicating or showing being, even though his principal concern is to distinguish the function of naming from that of *logos* (261 e).

Regarding this issue see Victor Goldschmidt, *Essai sur le "Cratyle"* (Paris, 1940), pp. 51-52; R. Robinson, "A Criticism of Plato's *Cratylus,*" *Philosophical Review,* 65 (1956), pp. 324-341; K. Lorey and J. Mittelstrass, "On Rational Philosophy of Language: The Programme in Plato's *Cratylus* Reconsidered," *Mind,* 76 (1967), pp. 1-20; and especially J. V. Luce, "Plato on Truth and Falsity in Names," *Classical Quarterly,* 63 (1969), pp. 222-233.

[11] πάντων χρημάτων μέτρον ἄνθρωπον εἶναι, τῶν μὲν ὄντων, ὡς ἔστι, τῶν δὲ μὴ ὄντων, ὡς οὐκ ἔστιν (*Theaet.* 152 a).

[12] Cf. *Prot.* 322 a, where Protagoras explicitly links sound (φωνή) and names (ὀνόματα) to art (τέχνη).

in the fundamental contradiction of denying, in what it puts forth, the very possibility of its being put forth as true (170 a − 172 c), the criticism leveled against Protagoras at this point in the *Cratylus* remains, in its explicit formulation, on the level of a counterposing of opinions. Socrates secures Hermogenes' agreement that there are bad men and that there are good men; relying then upon an identity (which is not elaborated) of the good (χρηστός) with the wise (φρόνιμος), Socrates concludes to the fact that some men are wise and some foolish—a fact which contradicts Protagoras' "truth" that all things *are* to each individual as they *seem* to him. If there is a real distinction between wisdom and ignorance, then the measure (μέτρον) of what is (as it is) must be something other than what appears to or is opined by just any individual man.

Several observations are in order regarding this criticism of Protagoras. In the first place, it should be noted that it is especially appropriate that Socrates makes use of the distinction between wisdom and ignorance in order to deprive man of the position of μέτρον which Protagoras would grant to him, for, according to the image presented in the *Apology,* the wisdom of Socrates consists pre-eminently in his capacity to make this distinction—to such an extent even that he opposes a god on the ground of and for the sake of this distinction (cf. Ch. I, Sect. 3). That he does not, however, direct Hermogenes' attention first of all to this distinction but to the distinction between good and bad is perhaps no less appropriate inasmuch as it points up the peculiar condition of Hermogenes at this stage in the dialogue. Hermogenes in one breath affirms his original position regarding names and in the next breath denies the Protagorean position to which it leads; and, though, indeed, he confesses his perplexity, he has within the context of the dialogue still to experience that profound perplexity to which his contradiction could bring him and by which he could be initiated into that wisdom of ignorance that is correlative to the Socratic capacity to distinguish between wisdom and ignorance. One suspects that Hermogenes has not experienced his own ignorance to the same degree that he has experienced the wickedness of other men.[13]

---

[13] In this connection it should be noted also that in the *Theaetetus* the discussion regarding knowledge of the good (ἀγαθόν − 166 d), the just (δίκαιον − 172 a, 177 c), and

Secondly, it should be observed that the confrontation with Protagoras serves to introduce into the discussion an entire dimension previously only hinted at. To say, contrary to Protagoras, that it is not the case that what appears (φαίνεται) to each man *is* for him, i.e., to say that the individual man is not the measure of what is (as it is) and of what is not (as it is not)—this is to say that what appears to each man is in need of a measure (μέτρον) by the application of which what is would be determined. The consequent problem of discovering that measure, to which what appears to the individual would be subjected in the determination of what is, is the fundamental problem of the *Theaetetus*. A brief detour through this dialogue will serve to bring into view the proper dimension and import of this problem.

Several features of the *Theaetetus* point quite directly to this problem. Thus, the actual conversation represented in the dialogue begins with Theodorus, the accomplished mathematician who is a "gift of god," being set up as the judge who is to provide the measure of the likeness between Socrates and Theaetetus (144 d – 145 b); and the dialogue ends with a reference to those other judges who claim the capacity to measure the extent of Socrates' crimes against the city (210 d). But in the conversation itself, though indeed Theodorus is called in to witness the most decisive measuring of Protagoras' position (169 a), it is, in fact, Socrates who is the embodiment of the measure—who, more precisely, is not the measure when he serves as spokesman for Protagoras, who is not the measure as the individual man Socrates, but who *is* the embodiment of the measure inasmuch as his peculiar wisdom allows him to practice the art of the midwife.[14] The high point of this practice lies in the testing, the measuring, by which it is determined whether the offspring is a false image (εἴδωλον) or the fruit of a true birth (150 b – c)[15] —in other words, the measuring

---

the advantageous (ὠφέλιμον –177 d – 178 a) plays a crucial role in sustaining against Protagoras that form of the distinction between wisdom and ignorance that is capable of making his position destroy itself.

[14] "Then we may quite reasonably put it to your master that he must admit that one man is wiser than another and that the wiser man is the measure, whereas an ignorant person like myself is not in any way bound to be a measure, as our defense of Protagoras tried to make me, whether I liked it or not" (179 a – b).

[15] Cornford points out that structurally Socrates' description of his art of midwifery at this point in the *Theaetetus* corresponds quite precisely to his introduction of

of it with respect to its being what it is brought forth as being. In the course of the discussion—and in the very progression of the discussion from perception, to opinion, to *logos*—it is repeatedly made evident that *logos* has a most important bearing upon that measure for which the search is being conducted. For instance, in his very first movement beyond the mere statement of Protagoras' position, Socrates links this position to that of the Heracliteans, to the "secret doctrine" according to which nothing is one thing just by itself. If, as has been agreed at this point, appearance means nothing more than perception ($\alpha\check{\iota}\sigma\theta\eta\sigma\iota\varsigma$—151 e) and if, as Socrates insists, what is perceived is never *one* thing, then it is not the case that what appears *is*; and Protagoras is, in effect, refuted almost from the outset. The crucial point lies in the way in which Socrates casts his contention regarding what is perceived: he says that it cannot be called by any right name; if it is called ($\pi\rho\sigma\sigma\alpha\gamma\sigma\rho\epsilon\acute{\upsilon}\omega$) "large," then it also appears small—and likewise with whatever it is addressed as (152 d). As Socrates formulates it in the corresponding discussion in the *Republic,* it no more is what one asserts it to be than it is not what one asserts it to be (479 b).[16] When what appears (in the sense of being perceived) is addressed as *being* (heavy, large, etc.), it shows itself, within the compass of the addressing, as also *not being* that as which it is addressed. *In response* to a calling of it by name, *in response* to a *logos* which addresses it as being some one thing, that which appears (in the sense of being perceived) shows itself both as being and as not being that as which it is addressed. It is *logos* which initiates the measuring by letting what appears show itself as in need of measure with respect to being. This is reflected in the very structure of that inquiry that occupies the long first part of the *Theaetetus:* whether perception *is* knowledge is to be discovered not by perception but by *logos* (i.e., by speaking with one another about the matter), and the high point of the testing is reached

recollection in the *Meno*. See *Plato's Theory of Knowledge* (New York: Liberal Arts Press, 1957), pp. 27-28. In most general terms this correspondence indicates that the measure which is here at issue is linked to memory, which is to say, in terms of our interpretation of the *Meno*, linked to the whole. In this connection see the discussion of the relation of perceptions to memory imprints in the *Theaetetus*, esp. 194 a – b.

[16] It should especially be noted how this mixing of the "is" and the "is not" bears upon the instituting of the distinction between visible and intelligible. Cf. *Republic,* 524 a – d, together with Ch. V, Sect. 3 c and 5 c, ii.

when, through the questioning, it is made manifest that perception no more *is* knowledge than it *is not* knowledge (182 e).

To say, however, that *logos* initiates the measuring is by no means to say that *logos* is quite simply the μέτρον by which what is, is determined as such. Thus, in the *Theaetetus* Socrates' application of *logos* to appearance, which lets it be manifest as both being and not-being, is followed by a curious insistence that *logos,* in turn, be measured by things: we must not make use of the name "being" (εἶναι) or of any other names which bring things to a standstill but must rather speak in accordance with nature (157 a − c). As he later puts it with greater irony, the advocates of the Heraclitean position will need to institute some new dialect (φωνή). Yet Socrates' irony here does not simply consist in the assertion, without affirmation, of what he knows to be false. He has already, even within his account of the Heraclitean position, indicated that we measure ourselves against something (154 b), and he is ironic with respect to the Heraclitean measuring of *logos* by appearance only because appearance has, in advance, been narrowed down to what is perceived. It is significant that, when the *logos* of the *Theaetetus* finally becomes, in the last part, a *logos* about *logos,* this still does not suffice for answering the question about knowledge.

Most fundamentally the *Theaetetus* is, as we have here briefly indicated, a dialogue in search of the μέτρον, which Protagoras mistakenly identified with the individual man. As such, this dialogue can take on its explicit cast—as an inquiry in response to the question "What is knowledge?"—only because knowledge (ἐπιστήμη) is (as with "truth" in the *Cratylus*) in advance understood in correlation with what is (as it is) and, hence, as possible only through a determination effected by the appropriate μέτρον.[17] To

---

[17] That the entire search for an answer to the question "What is knowledge?" proceeds in the light of a prior understanding is, of course, already required by what is shown in the *Meno.* What is distinctive about the case of knowledge is that the pre-understanding concerns not only the *theme* of the inquiry but the inquiry itself as an attempt to gain knowledge. Socrates says to Theaetetus: "Then, doesn't it strike you as shameless to explain what knowing is like, when we don't know what knowledge is? The truth is, Theaetetus, that for some time past there has been a vicious taint in our discussion. Times out of number we have said, 'we know,' 'we do not know,' 'we have knowledge,' 'we have no knowledge,' as if we could understand each other while we still know nothing about knowledge. At this very moment, if you please, we have once more

an equal degree this same problem is at issue in the *Cratylus,* and this is the basis of the profound affinity between these two discussions the dramatic dates of which, as we shall see, coincide (cf. Sect. 3 d).

Returning now to the discussion of Protagoras in the *Cratylus,* we note that Socrates here draws out in a more straightforward manner the consequence of his criticism of Protagoras' dictum that what appears (to a man) is identical with what is (for him). The consequence is that the things which are (and the way in which they are) are not simply relative to the individual man. On the contrary, the things which are have a being (οὐσία) of their own independently of those perpetually varying ways in which they appear to various individual men.

However, just before he explicitly draws this conclusion, Socrates quite abruptly introduces, alongside the position of Protagoras, another position which he associates with Euthydemus; this position Socrates characterizes by the thesis that all things belong equally to all men simultaneously and perpetually. What is especially curious is that he then conjoins the denial of this position with his denial of Protagoras' position and *on this basis* proceeds to ascribe to things a being of their own, despite the fact that the denial of Protagoras' position alone would seem to suffice for this ascription (386 d — e).

This position associated with Euthydemus suggests, in the first place, an extension corresponding to the ambiguity in Hermogenes' statement regarding the agent of the positing of names. Just as for the latter the positing was, in one breath, assigned to just any individual man (who, for example, might change the name of his slave) and, in the next breath, extended beyond the individual man by the introduction of convention and custom, so the position of Euthydemus suggests a replacement of the Protagorean individual by all men. Socrates does not elaborate the precise character which such an extension might take, and, indeed, there is no great need for him to do so, for his overriding intention at this point is to deny that what is (as it is) is relative to man, either

---

used the words 'know nothing' and 'understand,' as if we had a right to use them while we are still destitute of knowledge" (196 d — e). The situation regarding knowledge is in this respect quite analogous to the attempt in the *Cratylus* at a *logos* about *logos.*

singly or collectively, and thus, through this denial, to ascribe to it a being of its own.

But there is a second, more important issue involved in Socrates' introduction of the position of Euthydemus at this point in the dialogue. This second issue can be made evident if we take our clue from that dialogue which carries as its title the name of the man with whom Socrates associates this position. In the *Euthydemus* we need in this connection to note especially the response which Socrates makes near the end of the dialogue to the eristic which Dionysodorus and Euthydemus have been practicing with regard to the beautiful and the gods. Socrates, in effect, makes the eristic recoil upon itself by arguing that, when Dionysodorus says that nothing is beautiful or, more generally, that there are no differences at all, he not only sews up the mouths of others—that is, refutes them, as he professes to do—but also seems to do others the favor of sewing up his own mouth (303 d — e). The suggestion is that what Dionysodorus says undercuts the very possibility of his being able to say it. If there are no differences, then everything can with equal right be said of everything, which is to say that nothing can be said with any claim to be more truthful than anything else that is said. This statement *(logos)* is obviously self-referential; the statement that there are no differences, that, hence, everything can with equal right be said of everything, cannot claim to be any more truthful than its own denial. Every statement will be true—even the statement that not every statement is true.[18] Yet, in another sense, every statement will be false: since what is named in a statement (cf. *Soph.* 262 d — e) is—as Socrates will soon state explicitly—distinguished, discriminated *as* different from certain others, it follows that every statement, by virtue of the fact that it differentiates where there are no differences, fails to say what is as it is and falls short of truth. In distinguishing what is not distinguished by nature, it says what is not as it is not: it is false.[19]

---

[18] This incapacity to sustain itself is a principal point of affinity between Euthydemus' position and the position of Protagoras, with which it is here conjoined by Socrates. Cf. especially *Theaetetus,* 170 a — 171 c.

[19] The same point is evident in the corresponding discussion in the *Theaetetus* (183 a — b). Socrates says: "Now it seems that what has in fact come to light is that, if all

The thesis of Euthydemus that there are no differences would elevate man to the condition proper to the gods, the condition in which he would be wholly free of lies, in which he would, of necessity, be altogether true in his *logos* (cf. *Rep.* 382 e). Yet, in the *Euthydemus* Socrates' statement of and response to Dionysodorus' eristic conclusion comes immediately after an argument which, incorporating a discussion of the proper names of gods, concludes with a comic identification of the gods with animals—with, in other words, a denial of the differences which distinguish the gods. Correspondingly, the comic thesis of Euthydemus, elevating man to the position of a god with regard to *logos* by declaring all his *logos* to be true, ends up, by its denial of all differences, making all *logos* false; man's position among the gods turns out to be no different from a position among inarticulate animals. The comic character of man's claim to speak the speech of the gods—a central comic element of the *Cratylus*—is here indicated.

What is most significantly at issue in the thesis of Euthydemus is the denial of all differences and the disasterous import which this has for *logos*. Socrates' denial of this thesis is for the sake of an affirmation of differences; this affirmation of differences amounts to the contention that in the domain of the things which are, in distinction from the Heraclitean domain portrayed in the *Theaetetus,* it is not the case that, if something is called "large," it also appears small. By attaching to his denial of Protagoras' position a denial of the position of Euthydemus, Socrates affirms not only that things have a being of their own but also that this being involves a distinctness with respect to one another. And Socrates, in stating the position of Euthydemus, explicitly reminds Hermogenes of one difference which they have already established, the difference between good and bad. In this reminder Socrates intro-

---

things are in change, any answer that can be given to any question is equally right; you may say it is so and it is not so—or 'becomes,' if you prefer to avoid any term that would bring these people to a standstill." Theodorus answers appropriately: "You speak correctly (ὀρθῶς λέγεις)." Socrates adds: "Except, Theodorus, that I used the words 'so' and 'not so,' whereas we have no right to use this word 'so'—." It is here that Socrates then speaks of the need on the part of the Heracliteans for a new dialect. The truth ascribed to all statements, on the grounds provided by the Heracliteans or by Euthydemus, deteriorates into universal falsity.

duces the word virtue (ἀρετή), thereby setting the stage for the positive inquiry that now commences.

(c) The Virtue of Naming (386 d — 388 a)

The problem of naming (ὀνομάζειν) has now emerged as the theme to which the interrogation needs to be directed. Furthermore, the responses which Socrates has, up to this point, made to Hermogenes' statement of his position in opposition to Cratylus have served to bring to light the structure of the problem. Over against Hermogenes' position it needs to be asked whether the ambiguity which Hermogenes allowed with respect to the agent of naming can be sustained, whether a naming is, as this ambiguity suggests, equally sufficient for establishing the name of something regardless of who the agent might happen to be. But in order to be able to take up this question it is necessary, first of all, to interrogate naming itself, that is, to inquire about the proper end and the proper virtue of naming. Socrates' further elaboration of the problem has indicated the direction which this inquiry must take. He has linked names to *logos* by means of an otherwise unexplained part-whole relation; then he as explicitly linked *logos* to the things which are, through his proposal that true *logos* is that which says things as they are. One is thus led to suspect that a true name is, analogously, one which *names* things as they are; and, presumably, the true name of something would be the right or fit name of that thing. Yet, the suspicion is tempered by the fact that the part-whole relation, which might justify the simple analogy between *logos* and naming, remains unclarified.

Socrates directs the questioning, first, to the determination of the proper virtue of naming (386 e — 388 a). Taking as his point of departure the immediately preceding ascription to things of a being (οὐσία) of their own, he extends this result to the domain of doing or action (πρᾶξις). The suggestion is not only that actions, as themselves a kind of things which are (εἶδος τῶν ὄντων), have, as do all things, their proper being; but also that actions, as exercised upon things which are, have a proper nature (φύσις) in accord with the proper being of that on which they are exercised.

This second sense becomes explicit in the discussion which commences at this point. Socrates proceeds towards the identification of the virtue of naming by posing an analogy between art (τέχνη) and *logos,* based on the fact that both are actions. He observes that, when we undertake to cut or to burn something, we ought not proceed according to just any opinions about cutting and burning and with just any kind of instruments; on the contrary, if such action is to be done rightly (ὀρθῶς), it must be done in accord with the nature of what is to be cut or burned and with the instruments which are proper for the action. It should be noted that Socrates' examples, cutting and burning, are themselves appropriate to what he is speaking about: whether one's end, in speaking, is to separate (to distinguish) or to eliminate the distinctness of the thing (to abolish differences, as does Euthydemus), in either case one is obliged to proceed in the way appropriate to the things and with the appropriate instruments; but in the latter case this would be impossible, for, as we have seen, a speaking which would seek to abolish differences would intrinsically lack appropriateness to things. The linguistic analogue of burning is no proper end of *logos,* and Euthydemus succeeds only in burning himself.

Socrates explicitly extends the pattern discernible in art to the case of speaking (λέγειν): speaking is an action, and, consequently, speaking can be done rightly (ὀρθῶς) only if one speaks with the appropriate instruments and in the way appropriate to the things about which one speaks, i.e., in the way in which it is natural for things to be spoken. Socrates' statement hints also that there must be an appropriateness to the one who speaks; but, when he proceeds, by means of the part-whole relation between names and *logos,* to apply the result to naming, he appears to forget about the requirement that speech be appropriate to the speaker. This forgetfulness, only hinted at here, will become progressively more evident and will determine the basic structure of the comedy which is now being prepared.

Socrates concludes that naming cannot simply be done arbitrarily but must be done in accord with things and by means of the proper instruments. This conclusion poses two sets of questions. First, if naming is to proceed in accord with the way in which things by their nature ought to be named, then the namer must, in advance, know the nature of the things, the way in which they ought to be named, if he is to name them rightly. How is it, then, that he has or gains such knowledge? And is every man capable of this knowledge, so that—even though, contrary to Hermogenes, not every namer names rightly to the extent that he names at all—every man is at least capable of being the agent of a rightful naming? Again the question of the agent of naming emerges.

The second set of questions raised by Socrates' description of the virtue of naming concerns the instruments of naming. Socrates now draws a direct analogy between art and naming, whereas previously *logos* served as the mediating link in the relation; and by means of the analogy he easily identifies names as the instruments of naming. Again, the examples to which he refers are appropriate to the issue. As previously, he mentions the action of cutting, but now, fittingly enough, the example of burning is omitted. In naming, the proper end is not to abolish distinctness but to establish it. In place of burning Socrates now mentions weaving and boring (or penetrating); but when he proceeds to identify the respective instruments of the actions, he omits cutting also, and, mentioning only boring (done with a borer) and weaving (done with a shuttle), he concludes, by the analogy, that naming is done with a name. The proper end of naming, it is suggested, is not simply to establish differences irregardless of whether or not there already were such differences prior to the establishing; on the contrary, the proper end is to penetrate to the things themselves so as to bring to light the differences that adhere to things by nature—things which, however, we need explicitly to distinguish in their differences, just as in weaving we separate the warp from the woof. On the other hand, the naming in which Socrates himself is here involved—the naming by which the instrument of boring (τρυπᾶν) is named "borer" (τρύπανον), by which that of weaving (κερκίζειν) is named "shuttle" (κερκίς), and by which that of naming (ὀνομάζειν) is named "name" (ὄνομα)—playfully exemplifies that pattern of naming which, in contrast to the demand to attend to the things being named, attends, in fact, only to the connections between names. This contrast between attending to the affinities and differences of things and attending to

those of names is fundamental in the comic incongruity that is
being prepared.

It is evident that questions are raised by the identification of
names as the instruments of naming. How is the namer provided
with these instruments? Where does he get them? And how does
he know that the names which he uses as instruments in his
naming are fully proper for that naming? How is he to be assured
that the instruments he uses are fit for boring and weaving rather
than cutting and burning?

(d) The End of Naming (388 a – c)

Before confronting directly the questions implicitly raised by
his description of the virtue of naming—the questions of the agent
of naming, of the origin of names, and of the testing of their
fitness—Socrates proceeds to extend the analogy between naming
and art in such a way as to make explicit the proper function, the
end, to be accomplished by naming. Drawing specifically upon the
example of weaving, Socrates proposes that in naming we accomplish two things: we teach (διδάσκειν) and we distinguish (δια-
κρίνειν) things according to their natures. Thus, he says, "A name
is, then, an instrument of teaching and of distinguishing beings, as a
shuttle is of distinguishing the web."[20] Despite the fact that it is
not teaching but rather distinguishing which has it analogue in the
art of weaving, Socrates draws the conclusion that, just as the
weaver is the one who will use the shuttle well, so the teacher is
the one who will use a name well, who will be able to use it in
such a way that the proper end is accomplished. However, in terms
of the analogy which Socrates has so carefully developed, his
conclusion *ought* to be that, just as the weaver (i.e., the one who
can separate in the proper way the warp from the woof) is the one
who will use the shuttle well, so *the one who can distinguish
according to nature* is the one who will use a name well. Presumably, we are to understand that one is able to be a teacher
precisely to the degree that he can distinguish beings, that, in

---

[20] Ὄνομα ἄρα διδασκαλικόν τί ἐστιν ὄργανον καὶ διακριτικὸν τῆς οὐσίας, ὥσπερ
κερκὶς ὑφάσματος (388 b – c).

other words, the one function of naming—to teach one another—is dependent upon the other function—to distinguish beings. The apparent subordination of teaching one another, which involves communication, serves to strengthen Socrates' implicit *denial that the proper end of naming is communication.* The primary function of naming is to distinguish beings, not to communicate with one another.[21]

If Socrates' statements regarding the virtue and the end of naming are now brought together, the general structure of the problem that is taking shape becomes evident. According to his description of the virtue of naming, things must be named in accord with their proper being if that naming is to achieve its end. Yet, according to his account of the end of naming, it is precisely through naming that we distinguish beings, that we distinguish things according to their nature and, thus, come to have before us the things in that natural distinctness which belongs to them but which is not manifest in the way they appear to us in perception. The problem is evident: How is it possible for naming to be done in an accord with what is and with the way it is if naming is itself required in order to make manifest what is as it is? It appears that naming, in order to be done rightly, presupposes itself.

(e)   The Origin of Names (388 c — 389 a)

Socrates now confronts directly the problems of the agent of naming and of the origin of names. Still extending the analogy between naming and the arts of weaving and boring, he observes that when the weaver uses the shuttle he uses the work of the carpenter, who is in possession of the relevant art; and he asks, following the analogy, whose work it is that the teacher uses when he uses names. When Hermogenes is unable to identify the analogue of the carpenter, Socrates abruptly breaks with the analogy and proposes that it is the law (νόμος) that provides names. Then he proceeds to repair the analogy by concluding that when the

---

[21] Cf. Raphael Demos, "Plato's Philosophy of Language," *The Journal of Philosophy,* 61 (1964), p. 597.

teacher uses names he uses the work of a lawgiver (νομοθέτης), who, by analogy with the carpenter, must likewise possess the relevant art. The consequence is that not every man is able to give names but only the lawgiver who possesses the appropriate art and who by virtue of his art is properly a name-maker (ὀνοματουργός) (388 c — 389 a).

It should be observed that with this development the discussion decisively abandons the thesis suggested by Hermogenes' example of changing the name of a slave and made explicit in Socrates' subsequent response. Not every man is capable of naming but only he who possesses the relevant art, who is capable of an activity of naming which exhibits the relevant virtue and which, consequently, accomplishes the proper end of such activity. For a name to be given to something by just any individual does not suffice to guarantee that it is the name of that thing. Indeed, in a sense Hermogenes' extreme alternative was already undercut when Socrates criticized Protagoras and especially when Socrates ascribed to naming a proper virtue and end, since whatever can be done well or badly requires an appropriate art to guarantee that it be done well. But with the explicit naming of that art and of the artisan who practices it, the position of μέτρον with respect to the names of things is explicitly withheld from just any individual *qua* individual, and it becomes evident that, in his discussion with Hermogenes, Socrates is mediating between Hermogenes and Cratylus.

It is important that we attend to the precise structure of the mediation which is being effected by Socrates. On the side of Cratylus he has granted that indeed there is a natural fitness of names. However, he has subordinated this fitness of names to the activity of naming: the fitness of a name consists in its being fit to serve as an instrument in an activity of naming which accomplishes its end, i.e., an activity by which we succeed in teaching one another and in distinguishing beings. Furthermore, by linking the fitness of names to the activity of naming, Socrates resolves in a curious way the question, left open in the statement of Cratylus' position, regarding the necessity of a positing of names. For Cratylus a positing, if it were necessary at all, would be secondary in the sense of being totally determined in content by that natural connection between sound and thing by virtue of which a certain sound is the naturally fit name for a certain thing; the positing would do no more than simply affirm a connection already established by nature. For Socrates, however, not only is a positing necessary but also the fitness of a name is determined in relation to the positing. Thus, by bringing the positing into the central position Socrates has granted, with Hermogenes, that the positing plays a determining role with regard to the fitness of names; yet, at the same time, he has insisted that there must be a fitness in the positing itself. Thereby, Socrates rejects the Protagorean extreme, exemplified in the example of changing the name of a slave, while, on the other hand, affirming the third of those alternatives originally suggested by Hermogenes: it is the law which provides the names which we use. Yet, Socrates grants this alternative only at the cost of abandoning the analogy between naming and the arts of weaving and boring, in such a way that when, subsequently, he repairs the analogy by positing the lawgiver, who posits the law and thereby also posits names, both the positing and its agent have been withdrawn from the sphere of what is readily determinable. Whereas one could readily identify the carpenter who provides a particular weaver with his shuttle, the name-maker is separated from the names and from the ones who use them—separated by the law and, presumably, also by custom ($\check{\epsilon}\theta o\varsigma$) which was originally mentioned together with it. Who is the lawgiver, the name-maker, that provides those names which Socrates and Hermogenes are using in their discussion? Socrates says that he seems to be "of all the artisans among men the rarest" (389 a). Socrates has drawn the entire problematic together in the problem of naming only to transpose this positing of names into the remote sphere of a primal lawgiver. The problem of mediating between Cratylus and Hermogenes has been recast into the task of mediating between the primal giver of names and the user of names.

This basic recasting of the problematic is in accord with, is even demanded by, the paradox which emerged from Socrates' accounts of the virtue and the end of naming. On the one hand, naming must be carried out in accord with the nature of the things named if it is to fulfill its end; on the other hand, this end is precisely the distinguishing of the natures of things, so that it is naming which makes manifest just that which is required as its prior directive. Naming presupposes itself, and, consequently, it becomes necessary to recast the problematic by distinguishing between the naming which is presupposed and the naming which presupposes it. On the one hand, there is the naming which proceeds in accord with the natures of things and which, therefore, requires a prior knowledge of the proper and distinct being of things. This naming is an original positing of the names of things, and it accomplishes a distinguishing of things (i.e., the end of naming) precisely because it is from its outset carried out in view of the distinctness of things. This *naming as positing* is reserved by Socrates for that rare lawgiver. On the other hand, there is the naming which uses as instruments the available names in order to accomplish, by means of the activity of naming, a distinguishing of things in their proper and distinct being. This naming is not an original positing of the names of things; it is a naming of which all men are to some degree capable but which is done well, i.e., in such a way that the end is accomplished, only by the teacher. It is a using of names, a *naming as using.* In this case what is determining is that which Socrates previously described as the end of naming in its undifferentiated sense; in the case of naming as positing what is determining is that which he previously described as the virtue of naming. His distinguishing between the two types of naming serves now to dissociate the virtue from the end, so that, in particular, the question is raised regarding the proper virtue of naming as using. What is that by virtue of which the teacher is able to accomplish the end of naming as using, i.e., the distinguishing of things in their proper and distinct being? The proper virtue of that kind of naming in which Socrates and Hermogenes are themselves engaged has become questionable; in fact, this questionableness was already foreshadowed by the way in which Socrates' description of the end and the virtue of naming proceeded contrary to the natural order: from virtue to end rather than from end to virtue (cf. *Rep.* 353 b − e). Socrates' own naming of the end and the virtue of naming did not proceed according to the nature of the things, and, consequently, it has now to be revoked in view of the things. But the thing in view of which it is revoked is primarily man himself who, in most, if not all, of his naming activity, does not posit, in an originary sense, the names of things in function of a prior understanding of the proper and distinct being of things but who, for the most part, makes use of names already at his disposal. By distinguishing between naming as positing and naming as using, Socrates has, in effect, recalled the previously forgotten appropriateness which naming must have *to the namer himself.* It remains to be seen whether this distinguishing between the name-maker and the name-user, this *naming* of the lawgiver and the teacher, is a naming which is in accord with the nature of things and is appropriate to the namer himself.

(f) The Making and Testing of Names (389 a − 390 e)

Socrates describes briefly the activity by which the lawgiver posits the names of things. Again, his procedure is determined by the analogy between naming and the arts. Just as the carpenter makes a shuttle by looking to the shuttle itself, the *eidos,* and embodying it in a certain material, so the maker of names looks to the name itself, the *eidos* of the name, and embodies it in sounds and syllables. More precisely, just as the carpenter looks to the shuttle which is fitted by nature for a particular kind of weaving and embodies that form in the wood, so the lawgiver looks to the name which is fitted by nature for each thing and puts it into sounds and syllables.[22] Only if he posits names with a view to the

---

[22] It has been noted that, compared with the corresponding discussion in Book X of the *Republic,* there is a curious complication involved in this description—namely, that what the carpenter looks to and embodies in a material is referred to both as the shuttle as such and as the specific shuttle (coordinate with others) which is fitting for a specific kind of weaving. The same complication is transferred to the case of names. Cf. J. V. Luce, "The Theory of Ideas in the *Cratylus," Phronesis,* 10 (1965), pp. 23-24. However, this complication need not be regarded as simply a confused version of what is later put forth clearly in the *Republic,* for its context is drastically different from that of the discussion in the *Republic.* In terms of the peculiar problematic of the *Cratylus* it is perhaps most appropriate to regard this complication as exhibiting the complication into which Socrates is led by his adherence to the analogy between naming and the arts—namely, the complication engendered by his speaking of the natural names as *eide.* His giving of the name *"eidos"* to names fails to take account of the fundamental difference between names and those *eide* which can be regarded as kinds and for which the method of collection and division is appropriate: a name cannot be a species of another name, as one kind of shuttle is a species of shuttle as such—though, of course, what is named by a given name may be a species of what is named by another name. Names are not even species (or instances) of the name "name" but rather of what is named by this name.

natural names themselves does he perform his art with excellence; on the other hand, however, different lawgivers may indeed use different sounds and syllables, just as different carperters use different materials. What is essential is that it be the proper *eidos* that is embodied (389 a − 390 a).

Socrates broaches the question of the testing of the fitness of names by means of a final extension of the basic analogy. Specifically, he asks who it is that is best able to direct the work of the lawgiver and to judge the fitness of the names made by him, to judge whether he has embodied the proper form in the sounds and syllables. He draws on the analogy: just as the weaver, who uses the shuttle, is best able to know whether it has been well made, so the user of names is most capable of knowing whether the names made by the lawgiver are well made. Yet, Socrates makes it clear that it is not just any user, not just anyone who might happen to utter certain sounds, that has this capacity but only he who uses names in the way befitting them. The user who is capable of judging the work of the lawgiver is he who knows how to ask questions and make replies; such a man Socrates identifies as the dialectician. Just as the weaver is the one who uses the shuttle well, so the dialectician is the one who uses names well; and to use them well means to make use of them in an appropriate questioning and answering. If names are to be well made, the work of the name-maker must be directed by the dialectician; and if the fitness of those names which he has made is to be properly judged, this judgment must be rendered by the dialectician (390 b − d).

Socrates concludes that the positing, the giving, of names is not a trifling matter of which just anyone is capable. On the contrary, he now says, Cratylus is right in insisting that names belong to things by·nature and that the only proper artisan of names is he who is capable of embodying in letters and syllables the name which belongs by nature to each thing. Socrates takes the side of Cratylus; yet, in just that statement in which he sides with Cratylus he addresses Hermogenes by the name of which Cratylus would deprive him (390 d − e).

In fact, Socrates' conclusion says considerably more than was, according to Hermogenes' report, maintained by Cratylus. Indeed, Socrates grants that things have names by nature, thus concurring with Cratylus' position; but for Socrates these natural names are not the same as any of those names of which men make use; they are not even names of which men could make use in the ordinary sense, and, consequently, the fact that Hermogenes' name is not one of these natural names does not sufficiently justify depriving him of it. Socrates' vindication of Cratylus' position is, in effect, a mediation between Cratylus and Hermogenes: the natural names are granted but in such a way that a positing is required in order to transform them into those names used by men, a positing which, in turn, is subordinated to the peculiar use made of names by those who use them well. Socrates has succeeded in mediating between Cratylus and Hermogenes only at the cost of opening a gulf between the natural names and the properly human names of which Socrates and Hermogenes are themselves making use. Cratylus, on the other hand, continues to maintain utter silence, thus aptly portraying that side of the gulf corresponding to his position—the side of those natural names which are inherently unsounded and which must be put into sounds by an artisan of names.

But what are these natural names which, like the *logos* in the world-soul (*Tim.* 37 b), are prior to any sounding and which only subsequently are put into sounds and syllables by the artisan of names? And what is the status of this name-maker within the *logos* of the *Cratylus*? Furthermore, how is the subordination of the art of the lawgiver to that of the dialectician to be understood apart from the obviously questionable analogy with certain manual arts? It would appear that the one most capable of directing and judging the work of the name-maker would be he who is most capable of looking to those *eide* which the name-maker seeks to put into sounds and syllables. Yet, the dialectician, who is declared to be the proper director and judge, is not characterized in terms of his vision but rather in terms of his capacity to ask questions and give answers. How is it that questioning and answering serve for the directing and judging of the work of the name-maker? And, bringing this result together with the earlier statement that it is the teacher who uses names well and the suggestion that, in turn, teaching is dependent upon the distinguishing of the proper being of things, how is it that such distinguishing takes place in the activity of questioning and answering? What is the proper nature of questioning itself and of making reply to questions?

Socrates' mediating *logos* with Hermogenes has exhibited something of the proper nature of questioning. What is to follow will exhibit the response to the questioning. What is of utmost importance here is that we let the exhibition unfold instead of invoking those answers which we all too easily gather up from post-Platonic thought and with which we almost inevitably cover up what is genuinely questionable in the questions which Socrates has posed.

Section 3. Human Names and Divine Names (390 e – 397 a)

(a) Natural Names (390 e – 392 b)

Socrates and Hermogenes have discussed the art of naming. In the etymologizing that forms the long middle section of the dialogue they will engage in a curious practicing of this art. The section of the dialogue that immediately precedes this practice serves to sketch the problems at issue in the etymologizing and the situation which underlies it, thus providing a bridge from the discussion of naming to the practice of naming.

Hermogenes finds it difficult to yield immediately to the mediation which Socrates has attempted. He asks, therefore, that Socrates show or display (δεικνύναι) to him the natural fitness of names. But Socrates hestitates; he refers to the result achieved thus far, speaks of the need for inquiring (ζητεῖν) into this fitness itself, and then proposes that they investigate (σκοπεῖν) it (390 e – 391 b).

Socrates' response serves to bring Hermogenes' request into accord with what has preceded. In his request Hermogenes fails to distinguish between those names to which the name-maker looks and those names which he makes. In fact, however, it is only to the former, to the *eide* which the artisan of names looks to and which he puts into sounds and syllables, that Socrates ascribes a necessary natural fitness. The names which are naturally fit, of necessity and in the full sense, are those unsounded names which are viewed rather than spoken; they are not the properly human names which Socrates and Hermogenes have at their disposal and of which they are making use in the discussion itself. What it would mean to display these naturally fit names in their natural fitness remains highly indefinite: how could they be displayed in *logos* without being put into sounds and syllables and thereby ceasing to be natural names in the full sense? On the other hand, Socrates has not proclaimed as naturally fit the human names which he and Hermogenes have at hand and for which something like a showing could be immediately undertaken. On the contrary, the fitness of these names depends entirely upon whether the name-maker responsible for them has practiced his art with excellence. In other words, in the case of human names there is no guarantee that they are well made and, hence, fit; consequently, what is appropriate with respect to these names is not simply a showing but rather a testing, a measuring, of their fitness.

How is the fitness of human names to be tested? Two ways suggest themselves. The first of these ways would consist in determining whether the name-maker has done his work well, that is, in determining whether he really has succeeded in putting the natural names into sounds and syllables so that the natural name and thus the fitness with respect to that which is named are fully preserved in the human name. This way would amount to measuring the human name by the natural name; it would find in the unsoundable natural names that measure (μέτρον) by which to determine the fitness of human names. In dramatic terms, the silence of Cratylus would become the measure of the *logos* of Socrates and Hermogenes.

In response to Hermogenes' question as to how one is to investigate the fitness of names, as Socrates has proposed, Socrates instructs Hermogenes to seek the help of those who know. Among those whose assistance is to be sought Socrates mentions Homer (391 b — d). He proceeds to a discussion of what is said by Homer regarding names. This discussion contains Socrates' commentary on the first of the two ways in which the fitness of human names might be measured.

Socrates refers to the fact that Homer often distinguishes between the different names which gods and men give to the same thing. He observes, furthermore, that in such cases Homer indeed gives us a wonderful (θαυμάσιον) *logos*—that to be able, as Homer claims, to declare the natural names of things to mankind is indeed something grand (σεμνόν) (391 d — 392 a). Homer's *logos* is provocative of wonder, it is something grand in a sense suggestive both of majesty and of a possible excess, because it constitutes a claim, on the one hand, to be able to declare in speech the natural names as they are prior to every sounding and, on the other hand, to know and to be able to speak the speech of the gods, at least that part of it which consists of names. Socrates has thus identified the natural names with the divine names; the result is that the claim to be able to test the fitness of names by the first of the two ways, i.e., by applying to them, as measure, the natural names, amounts to claiming that one knows and is able to speak the speech of the gods. Socrates remarks that perhaps such matters are, however, too great for men like himself and Hermogenes to understand and proposes, therefore, that they confine themselves to an inquiry into the different names which are given to the same thing by different men (392 b). What is suggested is that the claim involved in Homer's *logos* is an excessive claim, that this claim which must underlie the attempt to measure the fitness of names by an invocation of divine names is excessive and, hence, itself in need of measure. The *logos* which would measure *logos* in this manner is itself in need of measure. The gulf previously opened up between, on the one hand, the natural names, to which the name-maker looks and which he puts into sounds and syllables, and, on the other hand, the human names of which men make use, has become a gulf between the human and the divine. The name-maker, the lawgiver, who translates the speech of the gods, a speech unspeakable for men, into the *logos* of men, begins to resemble a mediator between the human and the divine. But who is this mediator, and how is he related to that other mediator between gods and men, namely Socrates?

(b) Prelude to the Comedy (392 b — 396 d)

Socrates proposes the second way of testing the fitness of human names: he proposes to test them without the Homeric appeal to divine names, to confine the testing to the domain of human names. This is the way which has already been deemed most appropriate in the preceding discussion in which Socrates insisted, on the basis of the analogy with the arts, that the user is the one who can best determine whether the work of the artisan of names is well done. If the appeal to divine names is prohibited, then the fitness of human names is to be regarded as their fitness for serving as instruments in a naming which accomplishes its end. Thus, the testing of the fitness of names in this second way will amount to using the names in an activity of naming so as to determine whether they serve to allow this activity to accomplish its proper end, that of teaching others and distinguishing things in their proper being. The fitness of names is to be determined in and through a naming in which they are used as instruments.

The first function to be performed by naming is the teaching of one another. Thus, a name will, in this respect, be fit if it can serve as an instrument in a naming by which something is taught and, hence, is learned. But in order that something be learned by means of a naming, that which is to be learned must be made manifest by the naming. Consequently, a teaching of one another can be accomplished through a naming only if that naming achieves its other proper end, the distinguishing of things in such a way as to make them manifest in their proper being. Fundamentally, the fitness of a name consists in its fitness to serve as an instrument in a naming which distinguishes what is as it is.

How, then, is the fitness of names, so regarded, to be determined? Presumably one must engage in a naming, using as an instrument the name to be tested, and must attend to the distinguishing that is accomplished by it. The difficulty, however, is that here we encounter essentially the same circularity that was involved in Socrates' earlier discussion of the virtue and the end of naming. In order to determine that a naming has accomplished a distinguishing of things in their proper being, it does not suffice merely to attend to the distinguishing accomplished by the naming, for not just any distinguishing is a distinguishing according to nature. It must also somehow be ascertained that the distinguishing accomplished by the naming is appropriate to things as they are themselves distinguished in their proper being. In order to determine whether the distinguishing accomplished by a naming is such that that naming genuinely accomplishes its end, the distinctness instituted by the naming must be measured against the distinctness which belongs to the proper being of things. But how is it that we have access to this distinctness in such fashion as to be able to take it as the measure of what is accomplished in naming? Is this measure any more accessible to man than are those divine names that would serve as measure for the first way of testing the fitness of human names?

It is to this aporia involved in the measuring of the fitness of names that Socrates implicitly addresses himself in the discussion which now ensues. To distinguish things according to nature by means of a naming, to make them manifest in their proper being through a naming, requires not only that what is by nature distinct be set apart but also, correlatively, that what by nature belongs together, what by nature is akin, be brought together through the naming. Thus naming, if it is to accomplish its end, must take place as a delineating of parts and, simultaneously, as an assembling of each part as a whole; it must take place as a division into parts and a collection of each such part.

Socrates addresses himself to this unitary activity—setting apart what is not akin while assembling what is akin—by seizing immediately upon the most obvious sense of kinship, the kinship sustained between parent and offspring. Still referring to Homer's *logos* but only where it deals exclusively with human names, Socrates proposes that there is a fitness in calling the son of Hector by the name Astyanax (king of the city), king of that which his father Hector defended. Admitting, however, that the fitness is not made entirely clear by this account, Socrates proceeds to add another: the name "king" (ἄναξ) and the name "holder" (ἕκτωρ) are virtually the same, for a man is the holder of that of which he is king (392 d – 393 b). The names of Hector and his son, though they sound different, are nearly the same; the difference lies primarily in the sounds and not in what is put into the sounds. Thus regarded, the names serve to bind together the father and the son, to bind together what is akin. Socrates insists that in such cases it makes no difference that sounds are transposed or that one set of syllables is used rather than another so long as the being of the thing is made manifest in the name (393 d, 394 a – c). He observes, further, that the same kind of assembling, as with Hector and his son, is involved in the names of animals: the offspring of a horse is called a horse and thus bound together, by the name, with the parent to which it is akin. However, Socrates takes care to note that what is being said applies only to natural births and would not apply if a horse, contrary to nature, should produce a calf (393 b − c). This reservation is crucial: the point is that affinity by nature is neither identical with nor unfailingly determined by affinity based on birth; on the contrary, an affinity by birth has always to be tested in order to determine whether it corresponds to an affinity by nature or whether there has been an unnatural birth. Merely to attend to such apparent orders of kinship as that of birth does not suffice to make manifest that natural kinship with which the outcome of naming ought to accord. Socrates even warns Hermogenes that he should keep watch and not let himself be tricked, for, if one simply followed this pattern in dealing with names, one could insist that the son of a king be called a king (393 c)—which obviously would often be unfitting, as Socrates himself later indicates (394 d − e). Indeed, just such an inappropriateness already vitiated Socrates' first example: Astyanax never became king of the city defended by his father, for Troy was destroyed and the young Astynax was hurled from the towering wall of Troy to his death.

This problem of accord between the distinctness made manifest by naming and the distinctness belonging to things by nature is at issue in the little comedy which unfolds in the preliminary set of etymologies (394 e − 396 c). Socrates traces out the genealogy reaching from Orestes back to Uranus and seeks in each case to show by etymological analyses the fitness of the name. Yet, the very order of his speech is determined by kinship in the order of birth, which has just been shown to be inadequate for measuring the fitness of names; there is a ironic appropriateness in the fact that he proceeds in the order opposite that of natural birth, from son to father rather than from father to son.

The first two etymologies, of Orestes and Agamemnon, are relatively straightforward. But with the third etymology, that of Atreus, something quite curious happens: it turns out that his name makes manifest, not one, but three things, his stubbornness (ἀτειρές), his fearlessness (ἄτρεστον), and his ruinous act (ἀτηρόν). Indeed, there is reason to say that these three things, brought together by the name, coalesce in Atreus; however, the question which is provoked is whether this is a natural affinity, since Atreus' infamous act (serving to Thyestes the flesh of the latter's own children) was so counter to nature that it caused the sun to turn back on its course.[23] It would seem that the bringing together of the three things in the person of Atreus produced something contrary to nature and that, correspondingly, the three things brought together by his name do not belong together by nature.

The next two etymologies provide a commentary on what is transpiring. Pelops sees only what is near just as in the etymologies what is being seen is only what is distinguished by this curious sort of naming, not the distinctness which belongs to things themselves in their proper being; and it is hinted that what is developing is weighted down by misfortune, as was Tantalus. What the etymologies are beginning to make manifest is, not the things named, but rather the situation of the naming itself.

In the case of Zeus the name is said to be like a *logos*. It is divided into two parts, and some use one part, calling him Zena (Ζῆνα), others the other part, calling him Dia (Δία). Neither part alone makes his nature manifest, but the two together reveal him as the god through whom all living things have the gift of life (δι' ὅν ζῆν ἀεὶ πᾶσι τοῖς ζῷσιν ὑπάρχει). The etymologizing has diverged into an assembling of names rather than an assembling by names of things as they are by nature already assembled. In turn, Zeus' father Cronus, on the basis of a seemingly arbitrary choice of the root word and the fact that he was the father of Zeus (kinship by birth), is declared to be, of all things, a great intellect! The naming being carried on in the form of etymologizing is utterly oblivious to the proper being of the things being named. The climax is reached when Uranus makes his appearance as one who looks upward to the things above and, consequently, as the astronomers say, has come to have a pure mind. But what is above is sky, and when Uranus (sky) looks to what is above he looks to himself. The comedy ends with a reflection upon itself, with a purification which brings to light the need to look to the things beyond, to the things in their proper being. The structure of this

---

[23] There are several variants of this story (cf. *Oxford Classical Dictionary*, p. 144). In the *Statesman* (268 e − 269 a) the Stranger refers to the quarrel between Atreus and Thyestes and to the sun's being turned around in its course.

little comedy coincides almost entirely with the structure of the remainder of the *Cratylus.*

At the end of the preliminary etymologies Socrates observes that if he could remember the genealogy of Hesiod he would go on to examine the names of the earlier ancestors of the gods so as to determine whether his wisdom regarding names would hold good to the end (396 c − d). But if he should proceed just one step further back he would, according to Hesiod's genealogy, descend from sky (Uranus) to earth (Gaea).[24] Yet this first little comedy is only the anticipatory beginning of the great comedy that is about to commence—the comedy in which this descent will be fully enacted.

Another sense of Socrates' remark about seeking the more remote ancestors of the gods is evident if the genealogy is transposed from the order of birth to that of names. In this case the search would be directed to the origins, the originals, of which the names just discussed are copies made by the lawgiver. If these originals could be brought to light, then, indeed, it could be determined whether Socrates' wisdom concerning the fitness of the names he has tried to explain holds good to the end. In this case the second way of measuring the fitness of names would be brought to completion by a reversion to the first way. But Socrates does not make this turn back to the first way, and he explicitly mentions his memory as that which prevents him from doing so. It is thus suggested that memory is instrumental in that return to origins which in one sense or another is required for testing the fitness of names—instrumental both in the sense of decisively limiting such a return and in the sense of providing for its possibility, since Socrates does remember a portion of Hesiod's genealogy and initiates, in comic fashion, such a return by following the genealogy.

(c) The Appeal to Divine Names

The questions which have emerged come together in the question of the accord between the distinctness made manifest by

---

[24] *Theogony,* 126-128.

naming and the distinctness which properly belongs to the being of things. If a name is to be measured with regard to its fitness, then the distinguishing accomplished by a naming in which that name is used as an instrument must be measured against the distinctness belonging to things themselves. Such a measuring is possible only if one somehow has access to what is to serve as the measure. The result is that the fitness of a name, the accord between the proper being of things and what is made manifest in the naming for which the name in question serves as an instrument, cannot be determined solely within the compass of the naming itself. On the contrary, an *appeal* beyond the naming and what it makes manifest is required. This is why the second way of testing the fitness of names can so easily revert, in the end, to the first way. But the first way is not only equally questionable but also is suggestive, as Socrates has hinted, of a hubristic excess.

The question of the appeal beyond naming is implicitly posed in Socrates' discussion of the names of the letters of the alphabet (393 d — e). Ostensibly, this discussion is introduced in order to illustrate Socrates' point that, as with the names of Hector and his son, it makes no difference if letters are transposed, added, and subtracted so long as the name serves to make the thing named properly manifest. Thus, in the case of most of the letters of the alphabet other letters are added to the letter being named in order to form the name itself; for example, η, τ, and α are added to β in order to form the name of this letter. All that is required for the name to be fit is, according to Socrates, that the letter being named be included and its force made plain. Yet, Socrates does not explicitly mention what is most decisive about this example— namely, that the name contains that which it names. In such a case what is being named is already accessible precisely in the name itself and, consequently, no appeal beyond the naming is required. But this very special case serves to call attention to the fact that in all other cases what is named is *not* contained, hence accessible, in the name itself and that in all such cases the measuring of the fitness of names requires an appeal beyond the name to the named. At the same time, this example presents that pattern of proceeding from the name to what is contained in it which will be taken over in the attempt to determine the fitness of names by means of etymology; and it serves, therefore, to exhibit the presupposition under which the etymologies are forced to labor to the extent that they exclude an appeal beyond the compass of naming.

This same issue, that of the appeal beyond naming, was, in fact, already indicated in an ironic way when, in response to Hermogenes' request to be shown the fitness of names, Socrates immediately made an *appeal* beyond the *logos* being carried on by himself and Hermogenes. On the one hand, he appealed to Homer, to the *logos* of Homer; on the other hand, he appealed to the sophists, to the *logos* of the sophists regarding names; more precisely, by instructing Hermogenes to get his brother to tell him what he had learned from Protagoras, Socrates appealed to a *logos* about the *logos* of Protagoras (391 b − d). The irony of the appeal lies in the fact that Socrates, in making an appeal beyond the *logos* in which he and Hermogenes are engaged, *appeals only to some further logos,* despite the fact that the measure of the fitness of names requires an appeal beyond naming, beyond *logos,* to the things named. The irony is even compounded in the appeal to Protagoras whose *logos* is nothing less than an explicit denial of just that proper and distinct being to which the appeal must be made.

It is especially appropriate that it is in the course of invoking the *logos* of Homer regarding names that Socrates touches upon the question of knowing and declaring the natural names and makes the identification of these natural names with divine names, with a part of the speech of the gods (391 d − e). If, in seeking to measure the fitness of names, an appeal is made only to a further naming (as is the case here), then, in order for the appeal to be capable of making possible such a measuring, this appeal must be ultimately an appeal to divine names, to the naming carried on by the gods, to that naming which, employing the natural names of things, necessarily distinguishes things in their proper being. In order for an appeal to some further naming to provide the basis for a measuring of human names, that naming to which the appeal is made must be such that it distinguishes things as they are distinguished by nature and thus makes manifest that natural distinctness of things which is required as measure for determining the fitness of human names. The appeal, if it is to be effective, must constitute a claim to know the speech of the gods, at least the part of it which consists of names, for only in this case would the measure capable of measuring the fitness of human names be made available. More generally, as long as one simply engages in naming or appeals to some further naming, the presumption that one is thereby able to measure the fitness of names amounts to a claim to be able, at least in part, to speak the speech of the gods, and one is no less guilty of hubristic excess than was Homer himself.

(d) Inspiration (396 d – 397 a)

Indeed, this entire section of the dialogue, from Hermogenes' request to be shown the fitness of names up through the preliminary series of etymologies, is repleat with indications that in the measuring of the fitness of names here being initiated by Socrates something extremely curious is taking place. Thus, at the end of Socrates' very first attempt, his discussion of the *logos* of Homer regarding the fitness of names, Socrates asks Hermogenes whether there is perhaps nothing in what he has been saying, whether he is perhaps wrong in supposing that he has understood Homer's opinions about the fitness of names (393 b). Again, after he breaks off the preliminary etymologies that were guided by Hesiod's genealogy, he observes that the wisdom operative in his etymologizing is a wisdom which has come suddenly to him from a source which he cannot identify (396 c – d). The brief discussion which then follows (and which forms the conclusion of this section of the dialogue) intensifies and interprets this observation.

Hermogenes remarks that Socrates appears to be suddenly inspired and to be uttering oracles (χρησμῳδεῖν). The remark could hardly be more appropriate, for that measuring of the fitness of names which Socrates has just initiated intrinsically involves the claim of being capable of speaking the speech of the gods. Socrates' way of measuring names must, if it is to be effective, involve a speaking of the divine names, an uttering of what is said by the gods, an uttering of oracles. Furthermore, since the divine names, by virtue of their identification with the natural names, are essentially unspoken, even unspeakable for man to the extent that his speech is a sounding, the claim by man to be able to speak the speech of the gods is a claim to silence. It is thus fitting that Socrates, now described as an inspired utterer of oracles, is thereby brought together with Cratylus, who likewise has been charged by Hermogenes with uttering oracles[25] and who, in fact, has maintained utter silence except for a single brief and noncommittal response at the very beginning of the dialogue.

Yet Socrates, in curious contrast to Cratylus, does not retreat into silence but rather directs his speech to the situation of the preceding discussion. What he says is even more inspired than that speech on account of which Hermogenes characterized him as an inspired utterer of oracles, for, contrary to his earlier admission of ignorance regarding the source of his wisdom, he now identifies that source. His statement is one of the most crucial in the entire dialogue:

> Yes, Hermogenes, and I am convinced that the inspiration came to me from Euthyphro the Prospaltian. For I was with him and listening to him a long time early this morning. So he must have been inspired, and he not only filled my ears but took possession of my soul with his superhuman wisdom. So I think this is our duty: we ought today to make use of this wisdom and finish the investigation of names, but tomorrow, if the rest of you agree, we will conjure it away and purify ourselves, when we have found some one, whether priest or sophist, who is skilled in that kind of purifying (396 d − 397 a).

Socrates traces that inspiration which now possesses him back to the inspiration of Euthyphro which he caught during a conversation with the latter that took place earlier on the same day as the present conversation. We are, of course, not told explicitly that this conversation is the same as the one presented in the dialogue

---

[25] That in the case of Cratylus, Hermogenes uses the word "μαντεία" while in the case of Socrates using the word "χρησμῳδεῖν" must, in terms of the problematic of the *Cratylus* itself *at this point,* be regarded as making no difference, since Socrates has just insisted at some length (393 d, 394 a − c) that it is of no importance whether one set of syllables or another is used so long as the same thing is made manifest by the name.

Euthyphro—we could be directly told this only by Plato himself, who always remains silent in this and every dialogue. But if we attend to the *Euthyphro* and to the basic connection of its problematic to that of the *Cratylus,* there can be no question but that it is to the conversation presented in the *Euthyphro* that Socrates is referring at this point in the *Cratylus.* In the dialogue which carries his name as title Euthyphro is explicitly referred to as a seer (μάντις — 3 e). Furthermore, he presents himself as one who has knowledge specifically about Zeus, Cronus, and Uranus (5 e — 6 a), precisely the three figures with which Socrates' preliminary series of etymologies in the *Cratylus* has just concluded.[26]

The connection becomes still more evident and more significant if the portrait of Euthyphro provided by the discussion itself is recalled. In the course of the discussion presented in the *Euthyphro* four definitions of the holy (τὸ ὅσιον) are put forth by Euthyphro in response to Socrates' questioning. All of these definitions come together in the second definition according to which the holy is what is pleasing to the gods (6 e — 7 a). The first definition, that the holy is what Euthyphro is now doing, namely prosecuting his father for a wrong doing (5 d), requires the second as its basis; Euthyphro is doing what the gods (namely Zeus) did, what is, thus, pleasing to them, what is, therefore, holy. The third definition simply qualifies the second, restricting the holy to what is loved by, is pleasing to, *all* the gods (9 d); and the final definition, according to which the holy is that part of justice having to do with service to the gods, turns out upon examination to be identical with the second definition (12 d, 15 b). Thus, the dialogue as a whole presents Euthyphro as one who claims not only to know and do what is holy but also to know what the holy is, namely that it is what is pleasing to the gods.

But what do these claims involve? As Socrates indicates when he questions Euthyphro as to how he can be certain that all the gods are pleased by what he is presently doing (9 a), Euthyphro's claims suggest a certain hubristic excess—an excess not unlike that suggested by Socrates' own undertaking in the *Cratylus.* Further-

---

[26] Cf. D. J. Allan, "The Problem of Cratylus," *American Journal of Philology,* 75 (1954), pp. 271-287, esp. p. 273.

more, if Euthyphro's claims are seen in their basic presuppositions, then his situation can be regarded as virtually the same as that of Socrates in the *Cratylus*. Whether something is pleasing to the gods is determined by that thing itself, not by the god's love for it: it is not because they love it that it is holy; rather they love it because it is holy (10 d). Thus, to claim to know what is pleasing to the gods is to claim to know things as they present themselves, as they appear, to the gods. Yet, for the gods, who name things by their natural names (*Crat.* 391 d − e), whose speech is necessarily true (*Rep.* 382 e), who have no lack of wisdom (cf. *Rep.* 382 d, *Sym.* 204 a), there can be no separation between appearance and being, between the way in which things appear to them and the way in which things *are* in their proper being. But this identity does not hold for man. What immediately appears to man are not, as especially the *Theaetetus* shows, the things in their proper and distinct being, and man requires names in order to distinguish things in their proper being. Yet the only names which, at this stage of the problematic of the *Cratylus,* can with complete assurance be regarded as distinguishing things properly are the natural names, the divine names. Euthyphro's claim to know what is pleasing to the gods, if viewed within the context of the present portion of the *Cratylus,* amounts to the same claim being made by Socrates, the claim to be able to speak the speech of the gods. Furthermore, to the extent that the discussion in the *Euthyphro* is determined by Euthyphro's reliance, in his first presentation of his case to Socrates, upon the stories told by Homer (5 e − 6 c), his situation is, as with Socrates, determined by an appeal only to some further *logos* and the contexts of the two dialogues corre-spond. It is no accident that at the heart of the *Euthyphro* Socrates refers to an unnamed poet who commands that Zeus is not to be named by men and then explicitly states his opposition to what the poet commands in this command which itself does call Zeus by name (12 a − b).

Both Socrates and Euthyphro, equally inspired, claim implicitly the capacity to speak the speech of the gods. Yet, the way in which they unfold this claim and the situation it involves could hardly be more different: Euthyphro breaks off the questioning and hurries away to attend to his questionable prosecution of his father, while Socrates in the *Cratylus* proposes to continue the questioning, the investigation of names, into which his inspiration has led him; he even regards this continuation of the questioning as what is appropriate to the situation, as what he ought to do. Socrates' response to whatever appears to issue from the gods, whether through Euthyphro, Ion, or the Delphic Oracle, is to question in such a way as, ultimately, to call what has so appeared into question. Such a response is, however, utterly removed from vulgar agnosticism; it is Socrates' peculiar way of comporting himself to the gods, a comportment which lies at the basis of his peculiar practice.

Socrates points to the excessiveness of the claim involved in his present wisdom regarding names when he mentions the need for a purification to follow the completion of the investigation of names. He says that tomorrow they will need to purify themselves and that they will need to find someone, a priest or a sophist, who is skilled in such purifications. This purification, which Socrates places, in anticipation, at the end of the investigation of names, will prove to be prepared, to be in a sense already underway, in the *Cratylus* itself, in the investigation of names. This investigation will, at the very least, serve to indicate the relevant purification. Nevertheless, Socrates here states explicitly that the purification will take place tomorrow. He and his respondents will presumably perform the purification, and at least a part of that purification will involve finding a priest or sophist who is skilled in such purifications. This is precisely what is found in the *Sophist:* in the last of the preliminary definitions the sophist appears as one who is skilled in purifying the soul of excessive claims to wisdom, an office so exalted that the speakers hesitate to assign it to the sophists (*Sòph.* 230 b — 231 a).[27] Furthermore, this finding of the purifying sophist occurs just prior to the initiation of the inquiry that occupies the greater part of the *Sophist,* the inquiry regarding the truth and falsity of *logos.* The purification which Socrates anticipates in the *Cratylus,* though it is already prepared in this dialogue, is decisively carried through in the *Sophist.*

---

[27] It should be observed also that in the process of division used in the *Sophist* the art of purification is obtained by division of the art of distinguishing (226 c — d).

The day of Socrates' trial begins with the conversation with Euthyphro that is presented in the dialogue so named; the conversation takes place while Socrates is awaiting his trial (2 a), and the dialogue concludes by ironically linking that knowledge of divine things which Euthyphro claims with the charge to be brought against Socrates regarding his relation to the gods (15 e — 16 a). The conversation presented in the *Cratylus* occurs later the same day, and still later that day occurs the trial itself as presented in the *Apology*. The conversation presented in the *Sophist* occurs on the following day. In turn, the conversation in the *Sophist* is designated as a continuation of the conversation of the day before—presented in the *Theaetetus*—which Socrates had with Theaetetus "shortly before his own death" (*Theaet.* 142 c) and which concludes with Socrates going to meet the indictment drawn up against him by Meletus while, at the same time, promising Theodorus that they will continue the conversation on the following day (210 d). Thus, the conversations presented in the *Euthyphro,* the *Cratylus,* and the *Theaetutus,* as well as the trial itself as presented in the *Apology,* all have as their dramatic date the day of Socrates' trial. It is appropriate that Socrates prepares for his trial by discussing gods, names, and the measure of things, for Socrates' practice, on account of which the charges are brought against him, is precisely an engagement in a peculiar form of *logos* which is provoked by Apollo but which simultaneously, in calling that provocation into question, is itself questionable, is suggestive of *hubris* and of the consequent need for an appropriate measure of Socrates and his *logos.* When, on the following day, the purification is performed, it is not Socrates but rather a "higher power," a stranger from Elea, who performs it (*Soph.* 216 b); and it is not Hermogenes and Cratylus who serve as respondents, but rather an image of Socrates himself, the young Theaetetus. And what this purification uncovers is the measure of *logos.*

(e) Dialectic and Etymology

In the earlier discussion in which the distinction was drawn between the maker of names and the user of names Socrates stated explicitly that it is the man who uses names well that is capable of

testing the fitness of names, of determining whether the work of
the name-maker has been done well. This man he identified, first,
as the teacher and, later, as the dialectician. He indicated, further,
that the dialectician is one who knows how to ask questions and
make replies. Thus, the activity of questioning and answering
constitutes that form of naming in which names are used well, in
which the proper end of naming is accomplished, in which, therefore, things are distinguished in their proper being. Yet, at the
same time, this activity of questioning and answering is such that
within it the fitness of names can be measured; it is an activity
which is of such a character that in instituting a distinctness it
simultaneously can certify that this distinctness corresponds to
that of things as they are and that, consequently, the naming
genuinely lets things be manifest as they are.

By indicating that the questioning and answering characteristic
of the dialectician are directed by a certain knowledge—he is the
one who *knows* how to ask questions and give answers—Socrates
suggests that not just any questioning and answering, of the sort of
which all men are capable, is properly named dialectic.[28] What,
then, is the specific form taken by that activity of questioning and
answering distinctive of the dialectician? What is that form of
questioning and answering which can serve for testing the fitness
of names? To what is such questioning directed, and what is it that
is made manifest through the questioning so as to make an
answering possible? What Socrates has said serves only to raise
these questions, not to answer them; indeed, the remainder of the
dialogue constitutes a search for the answers and thus itself exemplifies, specifically in the form of comedy, precisely that which it
seeks.

But already in the preliminary etymologies Socrates has construed this questioning and answering in a specific way, and he will
do so more explicitly in what is about to commence. It has taken
(and will continue to take, throughout the long central part of the
Cratylus) the form of an activity carried on solely within the
compass of names. The questioning is directed to names, and the
answering is made possible by means of the manifestation in these

---

[28] See the corresponding discussion of *logos* in the *Theaetetus,* 206 d – e.

names of other names hidden in them. In other words, Socrates has construed the activity of questioning and answering in a way which follows quite precisely the pattern exemplified in the case of the names of the letters of the alphabet. But in all other cases what is named is not, as with the names of the letters, contained in the name. Thus, the making manifest of something contained in the names being questioned can succeed in measuring the fitness of those names only if what is made manifest in the names are the natural names, the divine names; the etymologies constitute a search for the divine names hidden away in human names. The comedy consists in the fact that this character of the search is not recognized as such. What Socrates and Hermogenes undertake involves a claim which is not explicitly recognized and which prohibits them from accomplishing what they, nevertheless, take themselves to be accomplishing. While they undertake something which, in order to be accomplished, would require that divine names be discovered in human names, what they, in fact, discover in human names are only other human names. The forgetfulness which underlies the comedy is a forgetfulness of the situation of the questioning itself—that it proceeds solely within the domain of names, that the only names which Socrates and Hermogenes have at their disposal, the only names they can speak, are human names, and that the names to be discovered in the names they speak are no less human than those in which they are discovered. The comedy is based on a forgetfulness of the question of the appropriateness of naming to the namer—an appropriateness which Socrates has only hinted at. The comedy is based on a self-forgetfulness.

Section 4. The Etymological Comedy (397 a – 421 c)

(a) Ways of Interpretation

There are various ways in which the etymological investigations that occupy the central part of the *Cratylus* can with some right be made the object of interpretation. In the first place, these investigations may be regarded primarily with respect to their character as etymologies in the narrow sense, as attempts to discover the origins, or, more precisely, the relatively original names, from which other names are derived. In such a case interpretation would take the form of a scientific philological inquiry which, measuring the etymologies by the canons of modern linguistic science, would seek to determine the range of validity of the etymological connections proposed by Socrates. Such an inquiry could, however, be definitive only if it were, in advance, made evident that the goal of modern scientific etymology coincides with that of the etymologies undertaken in the *Cratylus*; in other words, the import and the appropriateness of such an inquiry could be determined only in the light of an interpretation of the dialogue as a whole capable of making evident the function of the etymologies within this whole. In fact, virtually everything which our interpretation has thus far brought to light dictates against letting the goal of the Platonic etymologies simply coalesce with that of scientific philology.[29] The attempt to recover the more original names is not undertaken for its own sake but rather in the interest of the problem of the fitness of names; once this is recognized, then it is evident that no etymology in the usual sense, regardless of whether it measures up to the modern scientific standards, could suffice to accomplish that which Socrates and Hermogenes are attempting. Once the comic incongruity that is at the heart of the etymological investigations is recognized, the question of the scientific validity of the etymologies put forth becomes secondary if not irrelevant; its principal service would then be to call attention to those etymologies which are, by scientific standards, especially fanciful and which perhaps need, for just this reason, to be especially attended to in the interpretation of the comedy. In this same connection, it needs to be stressed that, except in an ironic or a comic sense, there is no trace

---

[29] Cf. Joseph Derbolav, *Der Dialog "Kratylos" im Rahmen der Platonischen Sprach- und Erkenntnisphilosophie* (Saarbrücken: West-Ost-Verlag, 1953), p. 29; also Friedländer, *Plato,* II, p. 206 f.; also Bröcker, *Platos Gespäche,* p. 336.

of an attempt in the *Cratylus* to bolster some philosophical theory by means of a science of etymology; the etymologies turn out to support what is commonly presumed the Platonic "position" to no greater extent than they support the opposite position associated with Heraclitus.

A second way of interpretation reverses the perspective of the first. Rather than regarding the etymological investigations of the *Cratylus* as serious scientific investigations of the origins of names, they may, on the contrary, be regarded as caricatures meant to ridicule certain of Plato's contemporaries (such as Antisthenes) who apparently engaged in etymologies with the intention of establishing positive philosophical results.[30] However, such an approach presumes that the etymological investigations in some sense constitute a comedy and thus points back to the prior task of making this comic character evident. Regardless of whose teachings are incorporated into the comedy, what is of primary importance is that the issues of the comedy be regarded as they are taken up in the comedy itself in such a way that the peculiar seriousness of the comedy can become manifest. If the function of the dialogue is not merely polemical, then the historical inquiry regarding the identity of those against whom the comedy is directed is, at best, of secondary importance.

The following interpretation of the etymological investigations of the *Cratylus* represents a third way. Reverting to the task of making evident the character of the comedy as such, it involves attending to the multiple levels of sense inherent in the etymological accounts in order to thematize what they bring to light beneath, yet along with, what is explicitly said. Such an interpretation seeks to clarify what it is that the etymological investigations genuinely bring to light in connection with that which they are, in comic fashion, put forth *as* bringing to light. Such measure and directives can be taken only from the dialogue itself if their

---

[30] See Derbolav, *Der Dialog "Kratylos,"* pp. 24-26; also Goldschmidt, who regards the etymological section as an assemblage of what earlier thinkers had put forth in favor of the doctrine of flux and as indicating by its peculiar character Plato's break with his teacher Cratylus (*Essai sur le "Cratyle,"* esp. pp. 90-96); also the discussion by Ronald B. Levinson, "Language and the *Cratylus*: Four Questions," *Review of Metaphysics*, 11 (1957-58), esp. pp. 31-32.

appropriateness is to be assured; and, consequently, the interpretation must take its bearings from the total philosophical-dramatic context in which the etymologies are put forth. For such an interpretation the central question is: What does the etymological comedy as a whole bring to light with regard to the fitness of names, and how does it bring this to light in the course of the various series of etymologies? This question will, in turn, prove to be inseparably connected to a second question: What does the etymological comedy bring to light with regard to itself?

(b) Structure of the Etymologies (397 a − c)

Socrates observes that a plan of investigation has now been outlined. The preceding section has served to sketch the lines of the project now to be undertaken, and the preliminary series of etymologies have exemplified the kind of investigation of names which will occupy the long central section of the dialogue. Socrates succinctly indicates the form which the investigation is to take: what is to be determined is whether names, of themselves, bear witness to their fitness. In other words, the fitness of names is to be determined solely in terms of what can be made manifest in the names themselves (397 a). These opening remarks by Socrates invite us to attend, in advance, to the structure of the investigation that is to follow.

What will be utterly decisive in the structure of the etymological investigations will be the discovery of another name, hidden, as it were, in the name being investigated—the discovery of a name presumed to be the original of which the name being investigated is derivative. Guided by the original name thus discovered, the etymologist will then proceed to describe the naming, the positing, in which this original name was assigned to that of which it is the name, indicating, in particular, the nature distinguished by this name. Its distinguishing of this nature will then be put forth as demonstrating the fitness of the original name and, hence, also the fitness of the derived name in which the original is contained though hidden. Thus, the etymological investigation will consist of a discovery of the original name that is concealed in the name being investigated, a re-enactment of the naming in which the original name was bestowed, and, in many cases, an account of how the original name happened to get disguised.

It is assumed that such an investigation suffices to demonstrate the fitness of the name in question. However, in terms of the earlier discussions there are only two conditions under which this assumption would be justified; and, thus, in the project here being initiated there is an unthematized, presumably unrecognized, claim which must be tacitly made in order for the project to be regarded as sufficient for demonstrating the fitness of names. In order for a name to be fit it is necessary that it serve to distinguish things as they themselves are already distinguished in their proper being. Thus, in the first place, its fitness could be demonstrated if that original naming could, in the re-enactment of it by the etymologist, be exhibited as proceeding from the things themselves, as taking place in a situation in which the things themselves are manifest in their proper being. Hence, it is also essential to the structure of the etymological investigations that they exhibit the naming not only with respect to what is named but also with respect to the namer himself and the situation in which the naming takes place; Socrates' identifications and descriptions of the original namers will, however, tend to exhibit their situation as anything but one in which things are manifest in their proper being and, consequently, will serve to betray the comic character of the entire undertaking. Furthermore, in order for the etymologist to be able to exhibit the original naming as one which proceeds in view of the things themselves in their proper being, it would be necessary that he himself proceed in view of the things themselves, that the things themselves be manifest to him in their proper being. But the possibility of this is excluded from the very beginning, since the investigation of names is to be directed solely to what can be made manifest in the names themselves. It is from the outset cast as an investigation which remains essentially confined to the domain of *logos,* and, as a result, the first of those conditions capable of serving to justify what is claimed in the project is excluded by the very character of the project.

There is a second condition under which the etymological

investigation could accomplish that which it is assumed capable of accomplishing; this condition is, in fact, the only possibility that remains once the restriction of the investigation to the domain of *logos* is put into effect—as it is from the very beginning. This condition is that the original name, discovered in the name being investigated, be a natural name, that is, a divine name. Its divine character would suffice to demonstrate its fitness, since the gods call things by their fit names (391 d − e); but only in this case could it be determined solely within the domain of *logos* that the name being investigated serves to distinguish things as they are already distinguished in their proper being. Since, within the limitation imposed on the etymological investigations, a name could be recognized as divine, as belonging to the speech of the gods, only by one who knew the divine names, who to that degree was capable of speaking the speech of the gods, the investigations thus involve the implicit claim on the part of the inspired Socrates to be able to speak the speech of the gods. This claim is comically betrayed in the course of the etymologies by the manner in which Socrates often reverses the explicit order of investigation so as to make it appear as though his re-enactment of the naming were a re-enactment of a naming to which, as presumably with the gods, things are in advance manifest in their proper being; and the comedy is accentuated by the contrast between Socrates' divine pose and the identity of those whom he names as the original namers. Finally, the comic character of the entire undertaking is perhaps most evident in the fact that, while tacitly claiming in his inspired state to discover in the names being investigated the divine names which are their originals, the inherently unsoundable *eide* put into sounds and syllables by the elusive name-giver, the presumably original names which Socrates actually discovers are no less sounded than are the names being investigated; indeed, the very discovery of the original names is based solely on the similarity of their sounds and syllables to those of the derivative names.

The comic situation is hinted at in Socrates' choice of the point from which to begin the etymological investigations. He observes that the names of heroes and men might prove deceptive, since such names are often given for reasons other than the fitness of the name to the thing named. In particular, he notes two reasons which often dictate the giving of these kinds of names: Heroes and men are often named after their ancestors; also many such names are given as the expression of a prayer, as, for example, the name "Theophilus" ("beloved of god") (397 b). In the former case the name would be given in accord with the order of birth, which as Socrates has previously indicated, does not necessarily coincide with the natural order in accord with which things must be named if their names are to be correct; in the latter case the name precedes the unfolding of the nature of the thing named and constitutes a peculiar effort to determine the nature by means of the name; in neither case is the name given in accord with the proper being of the thing named. Over against these cases Socrates proposes that they will be more likely to find correct names in the case of eternal beings. He says nothing to explain what these eternal beings are, except that they are not the names of individual heroes or men; but he does conclude, though without further explanation, that it is, therefore, appropriate that they begin with the name "gods." It is clear that by considering what is eternal the difficulties involved in the cases of heroes and men will be avoided: what is eternal will not have been named either in terms of that from which it came into being or in such a way as to attempt to determine what subsequently comes into being. Yet, Socrates makes also a positive proposal regarding the names of such things: in the case of eternal things the names ought to have been given with the greatest care; he even suggests that perhaps some of these things were given their names by a power *more divine* than is that of men (397 b — c). The positive reason for considering the names of eternal things is Socrates' suspicion that the names given to such things were given by a more divine power—that, in other words, in such cases the names are more likely to be divine names. It is a matter of beginning not only with the name "gods" but also with the names given by the gods. And, indeed, as we have see, if the investigation is to succeed, these names not only must be (or at least contain) divine names but also must be recognized as such. Socrates must know the speech of the gods.

(c) Descent (397 c – 400 c)

We are prepared for a re-enactment of the god's bestowal of the name "gods" upon themselves. Indeed, Socrates begins with the re-enactment of the relevant naming, and only in the course of it does he explicitly extract the original from the derived name. But what is re-enacted turns out to be anything but a naming activity carried out by gods; it is rather a naming carried out by the earliest men of Greece, men who were ignorant of all gods except sun, moon, earth, stars, and sky, but who, seeing that these were eternally moving or running, called them gods (θεούς) from this running (θεῖν) nature, and who, when they later learned of the other gods, simply extended this name to them. The name "gods," rather than being given by some more divine power to whom the things named would be properly manifest, is, on the contrary, exhibited as having been given by the near-barbarians of the remote past on the basis of what they most immediately saw and in sheer ignorance of most of the things to which the name was later extended without any regard for the appropriateness of the extension. Socrates' re-enactment exhibits the relevant naming as virtually the opposite of one which would be carried out by the gods and in view of the things in that proper being which is not manifest in immediate appearance. Furthermore, the eternality of the gods, on account of which, presumably, Socrates began with this name, turns out to consist in the fact that the gods known to the original namers are eternally running. The eternality of the gods is an eternality of movement. The giving of the name "gods" is a naming in which what is named is in perpetual movement, and this naming is such that the name itself is determined by this character of being perpetually in motion. Yet, both the *Theaetetus* (e.g., 183 b – c) and the later part of the *Cratylus* itself (439 d) drive home the point that that which is perpetually moving cannot be named correctly. That naming, with the re-enactment of which Socrates initiates the etymological comedy, is not only a naming whose agents are decisively less than divine and which, therefore, offers no guarantee of the fitness of the name given; it is a naming in which the name given is necessarily unfit.

The etymology of the name "gods" initiates the first of several series of etymologies; it is followed by etymologies of the names "daimon," "hero," "man," "soul," and "body." In the course of this series of etymologies Socrates and Hermogenes repeatedly call attention to the order in which the particular etymologies are taken up, though it is never indicated what determines this order. What is most apparent regarding the order is that the etymologies proceed in a direction opposite to that of the preliminary series of etymologies given earlier: whereas previously Socrates began with certain heroes and proceeded to gods and finally to the ancestors of the gods, now he begins with the gods and descends through daimons and heroes to man and finally to the body. Whereas Socrates proposed to consider the names of eternal things and, presumably on this account, began with the gods, he ends up at the conclusion of this first series by giving an etymology of what is proverbially non-eternal, the body. Although, indeed, in this series he remains free of the order of birth by virtue of the fact that he considers no names of individuals, nevertheless, it is as though some curious compulsion draws the investigation from heaven to earth.

If we attend more carefully to this curious descent, it becomes evident that what is brought to light by the first series of etymologies is precisely the situation of human questioning and speaking. In other words, what is illuminated by these etymologies is just that which was overlooked in undertaking the etymologies—that which must be overlooked in order for Socrates implicitly to claim the knowledge, either of things themselves or of the divine speech, which would render him capable of measuring the fitness of names in the manner proposed. Thus, the first part of the etymological comedy is a thinly veiled commentary on itself, on what is comic about the comedy.

More specifically, these etymologies focus on the position of the philosopher, that position, intermediate between human and divine, which is exemplified in the character of Socrates' practice as service to Apollo, as mediation between the god and the city (cf. Ch I, Sect. 3 – 4). In the *Symposium* a daimon ($\delta\alpha\dot{\iota}\mu\omega\nu$) is identified by Diotima as an intermediate capable of wielding the divine and the human into a unity (202 e – 203 a); and it is to this name that Socrates now turns. Referring to the daimons as the first race of men, Socrates proposes that it was because they were wise and knowing (δαήμονες) that Hesiod called them daimons (δαίμονες); he proceeds then, independently of Hesiod, to extend the name to all men, living or dead, who are wise and good (397 e – 398 c). The etymology serves as Socrates' means, not of justifying the fitness of the name "daimon," but of extending the name in such a way as to suggest that the philosopher, like a daimon, occupies a position intermediate between the divine and the human.

This indication of the demonic posture of the philosopher is made explicit and at the same time called into question by the etymology which immediately follows, that of "hero." According to Socrates' account the name "hero" (ἥρως) derives from "love" (ἔρως) and indicates that a hero is one who is born of love, specifically, of love either of a god for a mortal woman or of mortal man for a goddess. Either this, he says, is the reason for the name, or it is because the heroes were dialecticians, able to ask questions (ἐρωτᾶν) (398 c – e). Thus, the hero turns out to be a different kind of intermediate from the daimon; he is born of contact between human and divine rather than being an original instituter of such contact. The hero is intermediate not by virtue of being wise, as is a daimon, but by virtue of love and *logos,* as a lover of *logos,* and this corresponds to the fact that the philosopher is not one who is wise but who rather is in search of wisdom, who is intermediate between ignorance and wisdom (cf. *Phaedr.* 278 d; *Sym.* 203 e – 204 a). Socrates, the hero of the drama presently underway, is not a daimon but rather a lover of *logos* who is subject to a daimon; and Socrates' daimon serves to restrain him within the limits appropriate to a man who seeks to mediate between god and man (cf. *Phaedr.* 242 b – c; *Apol.* 31 d).

Socrates briefly interrupts the etymologizing in order to refer again to the inspiration which he has received from Euthyphro and which is at work in his present undertaking. The interruption is comically appropriate following, as it does, an indication of the character of Socrates' own position—a position which is precisely such as to render him incapable of that testing of the correctness of names which he is claiming to accomplish, inasmuch as that position denies to him both the speech and the vision of the gods. Joined to this is the fact that what the etymologies are actually accomplishing is not a measuring of the fitness of names but of the fitness of man to undertake such measuring.

The etymologies continue, focusing more distinctly on the condition of the one who undertakes them. The etymology of "man" removes man still further from the daimons; man is one who, if he mediates between human and divine, does so in the way appropriate to one who is human; according to the etymological account, man (ἄνθρωπος) is set back among the animals and distinguished from them solely by the fact that he not only sees things but also looks up at (ἀναθρεῖ) what he sees, that is, examines it (ἐπισκοπεῖ), takes it up into an account (λογίζεται), takes it up into *logos* (399 c); man is the animal possessing *logos*. Socrates, implicitly claiming—by virtue of undertaking to test the fitness of names—to possess a vision by which names could be tested or a divine speech that would match such vision, is, in fact, gaining access to the nature of the things named only through the names themselves. What he is, in fact, doing is in perfect accord with the earlier conclusion that it is through names that we distinguish things in their proper being but is utterly out of accord with what he claims to be doing, namely testing the fitness of names. What is striking about the comic incongruity is that, while claiming to re-enact an original naming so as to test the fitness of the names given, Socrates is, in fact, engaging in a naming which succeeds in distinguishing something in its proper being, namely man himself.

The next two etymologies are introduced by drawing the distinction between soul and body. The first of the etymologies given for "soul" (ψυχή) appears straightforward: the soul is so called because those who named it thought that when it is present in the body it is the cause of its living, giving it the power to breathe and reviving it (ἀναψῦχον). Socrates does not say whether in this way the soul was named correctly; rather, he immediately has a vision of something else, which, as he says, would be more convincing to Euthyphro and his followers. He proceeds to explain soul as that which carries, orders, and holds (ἔχει) not only the body but all nature (φύσις), for which reason it would fittingly be named φυσέχη, which is refined into ψυχή (399 d – 400 b). Indeed, this etymology, in which Socrates explicitly claims to have established the fitness of the name, would be more congenial to Euthyphro, for, in effect, it totally subordinates the body to the soul and, in subordinating even the nature of things to the holding capacity of the soul, it suggests an elevation of man perhaps even beyond the position of the gods, who themselves, according to the great myth in the *Phaedrus,* only behold being. It is appropriate that Socrates concludes the etymology by remarking to Hermogenes that there is something laughable (γελοῖον) about this name having been given with such truth. The comedy lies in the fact that the naming is appropriate, not to what is named, but to the comic posture of those who endorse it. In the etymology itself there is an ironic reference to the comedy: indeed the soul is what is ordering things here in the etymological naming, despite the pretense to a vision capable of testing names. Its vision is only of a distinctness instituted by its own naming activity, not of the distinctness of things themselves, and all that the namer succeeds in bringing to light is himself.

To the comic elevation of the soul there is counterposed in the etymology of "body" the entombment of the soul: the body (σῶμα) is the tomb (σῆμα) of the soul. The soul, imprisoned in the body, can hardly, as Euthyphro would have it, carry and hold the body—much less can it, as Anaxagoras would say, order and hold all nature. Nevertheless, the etymologizing itself is such that in it the soul does order things; it orders them, not in the sense of bestowing upon them that distinctness which belongs to their being as such, but rather in the sense of instituting with respect to them an order of distinctness by means of the naming itself. Thus, Socrates presents another etymology of "body" as that by which the soul gives any signs which it gives, so that "body" (σῶμα) is just a variant of "sign" (σῆμα). The human soul's establishing of order, which may or may not correspond to that of things themselves, is accomplished by *logos,* by a giving of signs. This *logos* is inseparably linked to the body; it is through the body that signs are given, which is to say that the *logos* to which man is bound is no divine language of silence but a speech in which the constituent names are sounded. The body is, Socrates adds by way of a third etymology, the safe (σῶμα) for the soul. It is the bodily sign which is man's protection against the hubristic excess of Euthyphro—both in the sense of the sign which the soul gives through the body (*logos*) and in the sense of the body as itself a sign, which, according to the speech of the comic poet in the *Symposium,* was so arranged by Apollo as to remind man of his primal fall (190 e — 191 a).

In this first major series of etymologies Socrates set out to test the fitness of the names discussed. In terms of the structure yielded by the dialogue up to that point such a testing could succeed only by means of an appeal either to a vision of things as they are by nature distinguished in their being or to divine names which would match and even guarantee such a vision. In fact, no such testing as this has been executed, nor, presumably, could it be executed. However, what is significant is that, regardless of what he proposed to do, Socrates has, indeed, succeeded in distinguishing something by means of the naming in which his etymologizing has involved him. What he has brought to light in the naming is just the condition of man from out of which the naming itself proceeds—what the naming succeeds in distinguishing is just the namer himself. And what is of utmost importance here is the accord that is exhibited between the distinctness instituted by the naming and the distinctness which by nature belongs to that to which the naming is addressed. In other words, what results here is not just a distinguishing whose appropriateness to the nature of things themselves must remain utterly questionable as long as man is denied an immediate vision of the "place beyond the heavens"; it is rather a distinguishing which is such that the appropriateness of that distinctness which it institutes by means of the activity of naming is confirmed by that very activity itself. This is portrayed dramatically by the fact that the series of etymologies takes the form of a descent. Having set out to test the fitness of names, Socrates is compelled, instead, into an activity of naming, of making distinctions and procuring a vision only through naming. Over against what he set out to accomplish, what he actually does serves to exhibit precisely that bond to *logos,* to spoken signs and the body, which the naming itself brings to light.

The reflexivity of the naming is such that the names are confirmed in their appropriateness to what is named. This is to say that Socrates has, in fact, succeeded in showing the fitness of the names considered; but he has done this in a way utterly different from that provided by the earlier discussion of naming. He has succeeded in testing the names within an activity of naming; yet his success has been totally dependent on the fact that the naming, the questioning and answering, was directed at himself.

(d) Measure (400 d – 408 d)

Hermogenes now asks that Socrates consider, not the names pertaining to man, but rather the names of the gods. The way in which the first series of etymologies has brought to light the situation of the namer requires that Socrates introduce this next series with a distinction between two kinds of correctness of names. The first kind is exemplified by the names which the gods call themselves, and now Socrates states without qualification that of the gods and the names by which they name themselves we know nothing. In fact, since the names by which they call themselves are correct, are the natural names which distinguish them as they are by nature distinguished, to know these names would be tantamount to having knowledge of the gods. Socrates refers, therefore, to a second kind of correctness with respect to the names of the gods—namely the kind exemplified when, as in prayers, we call them by the names which are pleasing to them. He proposes, thus, that they announce to the gods that they do not intend to. investigate about them, that they do not claim to be capable of such, and that, instead, they inquire regarding what opinions men had in giving the gods those names by which they call them. He adds that in such an inquiry there can be no offense (ἀνεμέσητον) (400 d – 401 a).

The question obviously raised by Socrates' proposal, especially if the example of Euthyphro is recalled, is how it is that man knows what names are pleasing to the gods. Presumably, he could know this only to the degree to which those prayers in which he used the names in question succeeded or failed to succeed in genuinely invoking the gods. Names, it appears, are now to be regarded as invocations, and their demonstrated capacity to invoke is what determines this second kind of correctness, the only correctness of which human names are, it seems, capable.

The etymologies of the names of the gods are governed by the directive which Socrates expressed earlier (391 b) when Hermogenes first asked to be shown the natural fitness of names. What Socrates explicitly proposed in response to Hermogenes' request was that they inquire regarding what kind of correctness belongs to names. In effect, the first series of etymologies has served to show that any correctness that might belong to the names used by men must be something different from that kind of correctness that would belong to the speech of the gods. The second series of etymologies constitutes, then, not so much a testing of the names which men give to the gods, as rather an interrogation of that kind of correctness that could be had by human names.

Human names are no longer to be regarded as imperfect copies of divine names, such that the latter would provide the measure of the fitness of the former. Human naming—at least, man's naming of the gods—is no longer to be regarded as an imitation of a naming which the gods would execute but rather as an invocation of the gods. On the other hand, the naming which man performs has persistently been characterized in terms of its end, namely to distinguish things according to their proper being. The etymology with which the second major series commences brings these two issues together. Socrates begins with the name "Hestia" (Ἑστία) and refers to this beginning as being according to custom. One custom was that every meal began with a sacrifice to Hestia, which suggests that a banquet is now commencing; yet in the *Phaedrus* myth Hestia is the only one of the twelve Olympians who remained at home on the occasion of that journey to the top of the arch of heaven culminating in the divine banquet. Referring to the extraordinary men who originally gave the goddess her name, Socrates links "οὐσία" to "ἐσσία" and, thereby, to "Ἑστία," so that the name "Hestia" proves to be only a variant of the name "being" (οὐσία). The invocation of Hestia is nothing less than the invocation of being itself. The distinguishing of the proper being of things has now assumed the form of an invocation of being. However, it should be noted that Socrates concludes his discussion of "Hestia" by observing that in place of "ἐσσία," the name which mediates between being and the goddess, some men use the name "ὠσία," which he connects with "ὠθοῦν" (pushing power) in such a way as to argue that, rather than invoking the goddess, what they invoke is the flux of Heraclitus.

Socrates has proposed to investigate man's naming of the gods. The etymology of "Hestia" has served to identify this naming with the invocative naming of the being of things. The subsequent etymologies of the gods serve to characterize such a naming.

The invocation of the gods, as an invocation of being in its proper distinctness, is itself a distinguishing by means of names, and the question is in every case whether the invocation is effective, that is, whether the distinctness thereby instituted calls forth being as it is. But, in any case, as an establishing of distinctness, such a naming institutes an order which is distinct from the total indistinctness which is characteristic of the Heraclitean flux and which is approximated by perceptual appearances,[31] though to establish the order is not, of course, to guarantee that it is an order which corresponds with that of being itself. Nevertheless, naming is, with this crucial reservation, an overcoming of the domain of Heraclitean flux; the invocation of the gods is an overcoming of the flux characteristic of the streams and springs (and associated with such by virtue of the famous saying of Heraclitus—402 a) which Socrates finds named in the names of the ancestors of the gods (Cronus, Rhea, Oceanus, Tethys—402 a – d)—just as the advent of the gods involved, according to the myths, an overthrow of the Titans.

Yet it is not only a matter of posing an order over against the flux; it is not only a matter of addressing an invocation to the gods, to being. Rather, it is also required that the invocation be effective—that it prove "pleasing to the gods" in such wise as to

---

[31] In this connection one should note the curious way in which Socrates (in the *Theaetetus,* beginning at 152 c) introduces and then executes an identification of the thesis of Protagoras with the flux doctrine of the Heracliteans. In fact, the identification is dependent on the fact that throughout the first part of the *Theaetetus* an abstraction from δόξα and from *logos* is operative.

evoke a response and, thereby, prove itself as a genuine invocation. In other words, it is necessary that the naming be limited by that which is named, that it call forth what is named in such fashion as to have present before it that which can properly measure and limit that delimitation accomplished by the naming. Such limiting is alluded to, in the appropriate mythical guise, in Socrates' etymology of the name "Poseidon" (Ποσειδῶν), the bond (δεσμός) of the feet (ποδῶν), so called because the one who gave the name was restrained while walking by the power of the sea (402 d – e). The same issue is mythically presented in more positive form in the etymology of the name of Hades, who has the power to speak so beautifully that he binds all who come to him, who is, thereby, the great benefactor. And though he refuses to consort with men as long as they remain in their embodied condition, Socrates observes that, nevertheless, the god bestows great blessings upon those who are on earth (403 a – 404 b)— presumably by the way in which he consorts with Persephone (404 d), who, dividing her time between the two worlds, is according to Socrates' etymology, wise in being able to grasp, touch, and follow what is in motion (404 c – d).

If that naming in which man engages is to bring to light the natural distinctness proper to things themselves, it must succeed in making present that which can testify to its invocative power. Yet, unless it is assumed in advance that the distinctness instituted by naming is identical to that which properly belongs to things, unless, in effect, the process is superfluous by which what is named is made manifest as testimony capable of limiting, measuring, the naming, there is required the possibility of a measuring being effected. There is required not only an invocation and an announcement by itself of what is invoked but also a mediation between the naming and that which, evoked by it, provides, nevertheless, the measure of it. There is required the philosopher, the servant of Apollo, who mediates between men and the gods— the philosopher, who is himself called forth, provoked into his practice by Apollo.

Socrates proceeds to develop the etymology of the name of the god Apollo, discovering in the name "Apollo" names indicating the four functions which Socrates attributes to his god: music, prophesy, medicine, and archery. He stresses that Apollo not only has music as one of his functions but also that he is musical in the sense that his name and his nature are in harmony (404 d – 406 a). Apollo, the doubly musical god, is the one who provokes Socrates into the practice of music (μουσική), which in the next etymology is explained as deriving its name from "searching" (μῶσθαι) and "philosophy" (406 a), and the end to which that practice is directed is a harmony of name and nature as exemplified by Apollo, a harmony between the naming invocation and that which is invoked, which announces itself as the proper measure of naming. Indeed, a name may, as in the cases of "Leto" and "Artemis" be given on the basis of various opinions (406 a – b). What is essential, in these and every instance, is that the appropriate mediation be exercised between the name and that which is called forth by the name as its measure.

The philosopher, the mediator, is a lover; love is, according to the *Phaedrus* myth, that gift of the gods to man by virtue of which he is able to mediate, that is, to partake mediately of that divine nourishment to which he is denied immediate access (cf. Ch. III, Sect. 2 c, iii). Socrates proceeds to give etymologies of the name of the goddess of love, Aphrodite, and of the god who presides over tragedy, Dionysus (cf. esp. *Sym.* 175 e), the only god who, like the philosophical hero and even love itself according to Diotima's account (*Sym.* 202 c – 203 e), was the offspring of both mortal and immortal. Socrates notes, however, that there is both a serious (σπουδαίως) and a playful (παιδικῶς) account of these names; others, he says, will have to be asked about the serious one, but he agrees to give the playful account on the ground that even the gods have a sense of humor. The playful account of the name "Dionysus"—the "comic" account of the god of tradegy—changes the god's name to "Didoinysus," since he is the giver (διδούς) of wine (οἶνος), and Socrates adds that wine (the name of which he also changes) makes most drinkers think they have an intellect (νοῦς) when they have not (406 b – c). But Socrates, according to the testimony of his lover-beloved Alcibiades and of the finally Dionysian events of the *Symposium* itself, is one who remains unaffected no matter how much wine he consumes (*Sym.* 214 a). Socrates is one who thinks he does not have an intellect while, in fact, he does—that is, he is one who is aware of his ignorance and who is in that way wise, even if he presents to the "men of Athens" the appearance of laying claim to possessing that "divine intelligence" meant by the name "Athena" and of being that "noble master of light" meant by the name "Hephaestus."

Having undertaken an enterprise which, in effect, would require a collapse of the distance separating man from the gods, which, specifically, would require that man share the vision or speech of the gods, Socrates has through that very undertaking, through the etymologies, let the ultimately comic character of the enterprise come to light, yet in such a way that, simultaneously, he has indicated the character of that mediation between name and named that is appropriate to one who must, as man must, give signs by means of the body. It is fitting that Socrates attempts to break off the etymologies of the names of the gods with the remark: "For gods' sake, let us leave the gods, as I am afraid to talk about them; but ask me about any others you please, 'that you may see what' Euthyphro's 'horses are' " (407 d).

But Hermogenes insists on hearing the account of one more god, namely Hermes, since Cratylus has denied to Hermogenes his own name on the ground that he is no descendent of Hermes. Socrates complies and explains that "Hermes" (Ἑρμῆς) has to do with *logos:* the god in an interpreter (ἑρμηνεύς), a messenger (ἄγγελος), he is thievish and is deceitful in speech and is a bargainer. Socrates emphasizes that all this has to do with the power (δύναμις) of *logos.* He refers to his earlier contention (398 d) that "εἴρειν" means to speak (λέγειν) and to Homer's use of the name "ἐμήσατο," which means "contrive" (μηχανήσασθαι); then he says: "From these two names, then, the lawgiver imposes upon us the name of this god who contrived speaking [λέγειν] and *logos*" (408 a – b).

There are several points to note regarding this etymology, which is perhaps the most important in this entire series and which, except for the etymologies of "Iris" and "Pan," which simply elaborate that of "Hermes," brings the discussion of the names of the gods to its conclusion. First, it should be noted that Socrates explicitly refers to something said in a previous etymology, namely that "εἴρειν" means "to speak" (λέγειν). The earlier etymology in which this identification was made is that of "hero." It is highly appropriate that Socrates connects the discussion of the hero with that of Hermes, since not only do both serve as messengers, mediators, between men and gods but also both have a definite connection with *logos*. In particular, the hero is one whose mediating activity is an activity of *logos*, in contrast to one who would mediate, or claim to do so, by virtue of possession of wisdom. By linking the discussion of Hermes with that of the hero, Socrates indicates that what is at issue in the etymology of the name of this god is the account of that mediation which is serious in contrast to the comic mediation portrayed in the etymology of "Dionysus," where Socrates referred to, but refused to give, the serious account. Presumably, the refusal was necessary on the ground that the serious account requires a consideration of *logos*, hence, in the present context has its proper locus in the discussion of the god who not only mediates between human and divine but also delivers messages from the gods to men.

It should be noted, secondly, that the etymology of "Hermes" is followed by a single sentence concerning Iris, whose name is also linked to "εἴρειν" and explained by the fact that she is a messenger. This is significant in light of Socrates' comment in the *Theaetetus*, in connection with the description of wonder (θαυμάζειν) as the origin (ἀρχή) of philosophy, that "he who said that Iris was the child of Thaumas made a good genealogy" (*Theaet.* 155 d). In relation to the *Cratylus* this says: wonder is the origin of *logos* and as such the origin of philosophy itself. How it is that wonder originates *logos* remains, for the time being, unexplained.

Thirdly, it should be especially observed how Hermes, connected by his name to *logos*, is characterized: he is one who not only delivers the messages of the gods but also is a deceiver, even a thief—presumably, in his capacity of delivering and interpreting messages. Socrates remarks explicitly that all this has to do with the power of *logos*. The power of *logos* is a power both to enlighten and to deceive, both to reveal and to conceal. This entails that *logos* carries no guarantee of its truthfulness, that within *logos* itself there is no certification that the distinctness instituted by *logos* coincides with that which is proper to being itself, that, consequently, there is a need for a measuring of *logos,* that is, for a mediation between *logos* and that which is capable of providing its measure and appropriately limiting it. The character of *logos* as empowered both to reveal and to deceive is further elaborated in the etymology of "Pan," who, Socrates says, because he is the son of Hermes, is either *logos* or the brother of *logos.* In the course of this etymology Socrates explicitly states that with respect to all things ($\pi \hat{\alpha} \nu$) *logos* is both true and false ($\lambda \acute{o} \gamma o \varsigma \ldots$ $\dot{\alpha} \lambda \eta \theta \acute{\eta} \varsigma \ \tau \epsilon \ \kappa \alpha \grave{\iota} \ \psi \epsilon \upsilon \delta \acute{\eta} \varsigma$). The true part, he continues, "is smooth and divine and dwells aloft among the gods, but falsehood dwells below among common men, is rough and like the tragic goat; for tales ($\mu \hat{\upsilon} \theta o \iota$) and falsehoods are most at home there, in the tragic life" (408 c). It should be recalled in this connection that Socrates explicitly made a point of giving only the comic account of the name of Dionysus, the god of tragedy.

Fourthly, it should be noted in what way the conclusion that *logos* is both truthful and deceptive is reached by Socrates. It is reached by means of an etymology of the name "Hermes," by taking the name as indicative of the nature of the thing named by it. Yet, if this is so, then the result recoils upon the very means by which it was reached: if *logos* has the power both of revealing and of deceiving, then what guarantee is there that that part of *logos* used to establish this result, i.e., the name "Hermes," is not itself deceptive so as to vitiate the result? Would it, in other words, be possible that in examining the name "Hermes" we are being deceived about the deceptive power of *logos*? Clearly not, for then we would be in the impossible situation of being deceived by *logos* into thinking that deception on the part of *logos* is possible. We could not be deceived about deception if deception were impossible, and either it is true that *logos* can deceive us or we are being deceived by *logos* into thinking that *logos* can deceive; but in the latter case too *logos* proves capable of deception, the fact establishes the possibility, and the result—that *logos* has the power of deception—remains. What is significant about this peculiar self-referential establishment is that it exemplifies precisely that which it denies, namely that *logos* can guarantee its own truthfulness without a mediation being exercised between the *logos* and an appropriate measure. This is significant in a way quite analogous to Socrates' earlier example of the names of the letters of the alphabet (393 d — e; cf. Sect. 3 c), for just as in this earlier example what was named was contained in the name itself, so here too what is spoken about is nothing beyond *logos* itself. Again, as in the earlier example, this serves to highlight the fact that in virtually every other case such self-containment is lacking, and an appeal beyond naming and *logos* is necessary.

Finally, we should note Socrates' statement that from the two names "εἴρειν" and "ἐμήσατο," which he has identified with "*logos*" and "contrive," "the lawgiver imposes upon us the name of this god who contrived speaking and *logos*" (408 a). This is in accord with the fact that *logos* has the power of deception, that, in terms of the earlier discussion of the making of names, the lawgiver did not in all cases adequately embody the natural names of things in sounds and syllables. Socrates' present statement identifies Hermes as the one who contrived *logos*; this means, presumably, that Hermes either invented the speech of the gods or was the original lawgiver of human speech. But the mention of contrivance excludes the first possibility, since the speech of the gods is such as to be wholly truthful. It appears, then, that Hermes, with his propensity to theft and deceit, is mythically identified with the original lawgiver who instituted human speech and whose work was presumably made use of by subsequent lawgivers—such as those we shall meet later in the dialogue.

Just before the final etymology of this series (i.e., that of "Pan") Hermogenes grants that Cratylus was right in saying that "Hermogenes" is not his name, since, indeed, he is no good contriver of speeches, as would be appropriate to a descendent of Hermes (408 b). On the contrary, it is Socrates who has proved to be the genuine descendent of Hermes, who has contrived the etymological *logos*, which, often arbitrary to the point of absurdity, does not at all accomplish that which it was and presumably still is put forth as accomplishing, but which, on the other hand, does bring something decisively to light, namely the deceptive power of *logos* and the need for a mediating measuring of *logos*. This is to say that Socrates' own contriving of *logos* exemplifies just that duality of truth and falsehood which is brought to light as inhering in *logos*. Hermogenes' relinquishing of his name not only serves to point to Socrates as the genuine descendent of Hermes—as, hence, related to Pan, who is half tragic—but also serves to set the stage for the swarm of etymologies that follow.

(e) Movement (408 d – 421 c)

Socrates repeats his request that they deal no more with the gods. Hermogenes agrees as regards such gods as they have been dealing with but insists on hearing about another kind of gods, such as sun, moon, stars, etc. Three points are especially to be noted regarding the etymologies which Socrates proceeds to give in compliance with Hermogenes' request.

The first point has to do with what transpires in connection with the etymologies of "fire" ($\pi\hat{\upsilon}\rho$) and of "water" ($\ddot{\upsilon}\delta\omega\rho$). When asked by Hermogenes to explain these names, Socrates says that they are too much for him and then quite explicitly calls Hermogenes' attention to the fact that in such cases he makes use of a contrivance, namely he declares such names to be of foreign origin (409 d – 410 a). Socrates imitates the contriving lawgiver Hermes; inasmuch as Hermes' contriving is linked to the power of deception which accrues to *logos,* Socrates announces, among other things, that it is the capacity which *logos* has for falsehood that is now to be brought under scrutiny.

The second point concerns Socrates' etymology of the two names of the year, "$\dot{\epsilon}\nu\iota\alpha\upsilon\tau\acute{o}\varsigma$" and "$\ddot{\epsilon}\tau o\varsigma$." He explains that the two names are really one and, referring to his earlier discussion of the name "Zeus," explains the two names by referring them back to a whole ($\ddot{o}\lambda o\varsigma$) *logos.* The statement is: "that which examines within itself" ($\tau\grave{o}\ \dot{\epsilon}\nu\ \alpha\grave{\upsilon}\tau\hat{\omega}\ \epsilon\tau\acute{\alpha}\zeta o\nu$); it is, he says, by a division of this *logos* that the two names are formed (410 c – e). The significance of this example lies in the fact that the individual names are secured in their fitness by being incorporated in a whole and, specifically, in a *logos.* The establishing of the fitness of a name— that is, in its genuine form, the measuring of a name—is linked to the part-whole relation sustained between name and *logos.* But just as this relation previously was left almost totally unclarified (at 385 b – c; cf. Sect 2 b, esp. n. 10), so here its link to the measuring of names is passed over without further explanation.

Yet, it should be observed that in the present etymology Socrates explains that both names for year refer to the fact that it brings things to light and examines them and also that in the immediately preceding etymology of "seasons" what is decisive is "division" (410 c – d).

Thirdly, it needs to be observed that several of those names which Hermogenes asks Socrates to explain have, in a sense, already been dealt with at the very beginning of the first major series of etymologies. In the etymological account which Socrates gave of the name "gods" he referred explicitly to the fact that this name was given by men who knew of only a certain kind of gods, namely sun, moon, earth, stars, and sky. Thus, several of those names about which Hermogenes asks, in fact, almost all the ones for which Socrates proceeds to provide relatively straightforward etymologies,[32] are the names of things whose naming has already been described, at least that naming in which the name which they have in common was given to them. What should be noted is that in the earlier description of this naming Socrates explained that that in reference to which the name "gods" was given to them was their running nature, their character of being in perpetual movement (397 c – d; cf. Sect. 4 c). But, as we observed, it is precisely in reference to perpetual movement, which would amount to a total lack of any distinctness, that any correct naming is impossible, so that the naming of the gods, which Socrates has re-enacted, is necessarily a giving of incorrect names. Hermogenes' proposal that they return to such naming serves both to announce the character of the etymologies that occupy the remainder of the discussion and to raise the question whether Hermogenes has at all grasped what Socrates has brought to light through the first two series of etymologies.

Before he launches on the investigation next proposed by Hermogenes, the investigation of the noble names that relate to virtue, Socrates provides a commentary on that relating of names to movement which Hermogenes' previous request referred back to and which will largely occupy the remainder of the etymological

---

[32] That is, those that remain once one has excluded "fire" and "water," which are declared to be of foreign origin, the names for the year, which involve a detour through a *logos*, and "air," for which Socrates gives a ridiculously long list of alternatives.

comedy. Socrates' commentary takes the form of a story about the ancient inventors of names:

> The very ancient men who invented names were quite like most of the present philosophers who always get dizzy as they turn round and round in their search for the nature of things, and then the things seem to them to turn round and round and be in motion. They think the cause of this belief is not an affection within themselves, but that the nature of things really is such that nothing is at rest or stable, but everything is flowing and moving and always full of constant motion and generation (411 b – c).

The reference is, first of all, to the general question that dominates virtually the entire *Cratylus,* the question whether what is instituted by naming, in this case by the ancient lawgivers, corresponds with the proper being of things themselves—whether what is instituted by naming is prescribed by the things themselves or by the confused opinions on the part of the namer. But what is perhaps most important in the story is that the instituting to which reference is made, the instituting of perpetual change, is no instituting at all, but rather the negation of that proper being assigned to things by Socrates in the earlier criticism of Protagoras and Euthydemus. Socrates suggests that in such a case the suspicion ought to be that the confusion lies not in the things named but in the namer himself—that one ought to ask whether it is the things or the namer that is in movement. This duality, the movement of things over against the movement of the soul, is fundamental in what follows.

The string of etymologies which now commences proceeds almost without interruption to the end of the entire etymological undertaking. Socrates begins with the names of wisdom ($\phi\rho\acute{o}\nu\eta\sigma\iota\varsigma$) and related things, proceeding then to other virtues (e.g., justice, courage) and to the name "virtue" itself. There is no very clear demarcation into distinct series, not even at the end when he turns to the etymologies of such names as "being," "truth," and even "name" itself. Along with the lack of that distinctness that was so clearly evident in the earlier series of etymologies, there is also a very marked quickening of pace;

Socrates races along, as he himself explicitly notes (414 b), from one etymology to the next at an increasingly more rapid pace. These dramatic features are in perfect accord with what is at issue throughout these etymologies: the relation between names and movement.

At that point where Socrates explicitly calls attention to his pace, he has just been engaged in an etymologizing which curiously deviates from the usual pattern. He is investigating the names of the virtues and explains the name "ἀνδρεία" (courage) by removing the delta from it so as to form the name "ἀυρεία," signifying an opposing current or flow. But then, rather than proceeding to discuss another virtue, he notes that the names "ἄρρεν" (male) and "ἀνήρ" (man) also refer, like "ἀνδρεία," to the upward (ἄνω) current or flow. The digression is excusable; also the further digression to "γυνή" (woman), derived from "γονή" (birth), and to "θῆλυ" (female), derived from "θηλή" (teat). But then, when he proceeds from "θηλή" to "θάλλειν" (flourish) (413 e — 414 a), it begins to become evident to what degree the entire enterprise is bound up in names, explaining names by other names, which themselves would always require to be explained by still other names, and so on without limit. Just as in the *Meno,* where Meno demanded of Socrates a definition of the name "color" which Socrates had just used in order to define the name "solid"—the demand which Socrates ironically satisfied by defining color in terms of solid (cf. above, Ch. II, Sect. 2 c)—so here too the question is that of the appropriate limitation of *logos* which would absolve one from the demand for the never completed reiteration within *logos*; one wonders how long Socrates would continue with the etymological regress he has begun before he would finally resort to his contrivance and declare some name to be of foreign origin.

In another sense, however, the long string of etymologies, beginning with the discussion of "wisdom" and running to the end, do not move solely within the medium of *logos,* and to this degree they serve to clarify the question of the limit of *logos.* Specifically, these etymologies are characterized by the fact that nearly every name considered is found to designate some aspect of movement—for the most part, explicitly the movement of things.

In fact, there is one instance in which Socrates introduces in striking fashion a discussion of the nature of things in order to determine the fitness of the name—though, of course, the determination is ultimately comic, since the name gets explained eventually by another name. In reference to the name "just" (δίκαιον) he relates that those who suppose all things to be in movement say that there is a penetrating power which passes through all of nature, which is the instrument of creation, and which is the swiftest and subtlest element; this element which pierces (διαϊόν) they identify as the just (δίκαιον). But, Socrates continues, having heard this, he still persists in asking the question "What is the just?"; and those whom he asks think that he asks tiresome questions and try to satisfy him by saying all sorts of different things, so that, as Socrates says after a reference to Anaxagoras' teaching regarding *nous,* he ends up being "more perplexed" than before he undertook to learn about the nature of the just (412 c — 413 d). What Socrates relates here is a compressed version of the story he tells in the *Phaedo* regarding how he passed from inquiries regarding nature, through an eventually disappointing discovery of Anaxagoras' thesis regarding *nous,* to his definitive practice (*Phaedo* 96 a — 100 a; cf. above, Ch. I, Sect. 2 b). What is lacking, however, in the story as told in the *Cratylus* is an account of that second voyage which he undertook after his perplexing encounter with the investigators of nature, that voyage which was initiated by his having recourse to *logos.* In the *Cratylus* Socrates does not mention this voyage, for the dialogue as a whole is a re-enactment of its initiation.

What is called for is not that one remain within an unlimited *logos* of the sort that could be limited only by the contrivance of declaring some name to be of foreign origin. On the other hand, what is called for is not an abandonment of *logos* for the sake of an inquiry into nature, which either would lead to blindness in the soul, as Socrates indicates in the *Phaedo,* or else would resolve into the comic predicament of inadvertently proceeding by way of *logos* while disclaiming (in *logos*) this way. What is called for is not an abandonment either of names or of things but rather an appropriate mediation between them.

Immediately after Socrates calls attention to the pace at which he is proceeding—this, in turn, following immediately after the curious diversion noted above—he gives an etymology of the name "τέχνη." This name, he says, denotes possession of mind (ἕξιν νοῦ); he justifies this by removing the letter tau from the name "τέχνη" and then inserting omicron between the chi and the nu and between the nu and the eta, thus obtaining "ἐχονόν." Hermogenes, by contrast with his usual enthusiasm regarding Socrates' explanations of names, charges that this is a poorly done explanation (414 b – c)—that, in other words, Socrates' explanation of "τέχνη" is not itself a proper practice of τέχνη. Shortly thereafter, Socrates says: "For now that τέχνη is disposed of, I am nearing the loftiest height of my subject, when once we have investigated contrivance [μηχανή]"—which he proceeds to explain as meaning "much accomplishment" (415 a). That τέχνη is disposed of in favor of contrivance and that with the latter Socrates nears the loftiest heights indicates, most straightforwardly, the increasing arbitrariness of the etymologies Socrates is giving; it indicates, as was suggested earlier, that he is imitating that contriving lawgiver Hermes and exploiting the power which *logos* has of deceiving. On the other hand, however, it should be recalled that the specific contrivance to which Socrates refers is that which involves declaring a name to be of foreign origin. By declaring a name to be of foreign origin, however, what Socrates, in effect, does is to cut off the indefinite regress which threatens every one of the etymologies; this is made especially evident in the immediately following etymologies in which several names are explained by derivation from "κακόν" (bad), which, when asked about by Hermogenes, is dealt with by the contrivance of declaring it to be of foreign origin (416 a). To declare that a name, arrived at in the explanation of other names, is of foreign origin is to terminate the unlimited regress within *logos* itself. It is to enact within *logos* the limitation of *logos* by something which is really foreign to it and which is capable of measuring it. It is to enact within the domain of names the mediation between name and named.

When charged by Hermogenes with putting in a poor performance in the case of the name "τέχνη," Socrates offers as his excuse the fact that the original names have been completely buried by those who, caring nothing about truth, have inserted and changed letters for the sake of euphony. He cites the example of the name "κάτοπτρον" (mirror) and suggests that it is absurd that the letter rho was inserted in it. The absurdity is, then, that "visible" (κάτοπτον) is replaced by "mirror" (κάτοπτρον). With respect to the general problem, Socrates is suggesting by his reference to these names that names do not mirror what is named in the way that would allow one to remain totally on the way of *logos*; rather, names have a certain capacity for making what is named visible, manifest, for invoking it as their own measure. Indeed, Socrates already hinted at this in the *Phaedo* where, in describing that second voyage which begins with a recourse to *logos*, he denied explicitly that to proceed by way of *logos* is the same as proceeding by means of images (*Phaedo* 99 e − 100 a).

The first major series of etymologies, which descended from "gods" down to "body," constituted an exceptional kind of naming in which, by virtue of its self-reference, the naming itself provided the measure of the *logos* put forth. In every case except the first—the etymological re-naming of the gods, which proved to be intrinsically incorrect—the *logos* was such as to be sustained as truthful by what it invoked. In the second series of etymologies, those of the names given by men to the gods, such invocation, as it is involved outside the sphere of self-reference, was brought to light. Now, in the last set of etymologies, beginning with the names of the virtues, almost every name is found to be indicative of some aspect of movement; yet, as will be make wholly explicit later (439 d), as, in fact, is already entailed by the earlier criticism of Protagoras and especially of Euthydemus, and as is comically exemplified at the very outset of the etymologies when Socrates explains how the gods were so named, perpetual movement, the flux of Heraclitus, is precisely such that it cannot be correctly named; even to refer to it as such, as we have just done, would require, in order to be correct, that—as Socrates says with utmost irony in the *Theaetetus* (157 a − b, 183 b)—a new dialect be invented in which there would not be such names as "being" (εἶναι). In this long third section the etymological comedy reaches, as Socrates so tellingly remarks, its "loftiest height": all of the name-giving in which the aspects of movement are named, the name-giving re-enacted in the etymological accounts at an increasingly more rapid pace, is a giving of names to what cannot be rightly named. In total contrast to the first series of etymologies, the name-giving re-enacted in the final set is such that what is invoked by the naming fails in the most radical way to sustain that naming.

Towards the end of the final set of etymologies a curious change becomes evident. This change is initiated in the account of the name of love (ἔρως), which, Socrates explains, is so named "because it flows in [ἐσρεῖ] from without, and this flowing is not inherent in him who has it, but is introduced through the eyes" (420 a − b). The relation of this to what is said regarding love and the beautiful in the *Phaedrus* is evident (cf. Ch. III, Sect. 2 c, iv); but what is here of utmost significance is that when love enters the discussion there is a transfer of the relevant movement from things to the soul. The next etymology is that of "opinion" (δόξα), which is taken to be derived either from "the pursuit [δίωξις] which the soul carries on as it pursues the knowledge of the nature of things, or from the shooting of the bow [τόξον]." Socrates comments that the latter is more likely, but then he explains the shooting of the bow by analogy with the movement of the soul towards the being of each thing (420 b − c). The movement now at issue is not that of things but that of the soul. The comic transfer of movement from the soul to things, which Socrates described in the story of the dizzy name-makers, is now reversed and given a completely new sense. That such movement of the soul supervenes after the wealth of etymologies in which names were found to designate the movement of things could hardly be more appropriate. That naming which makes manifest nothing but flux is a naming which, measured by what it invokes, exhibits nothing less than the greatest discord with what is named. But, presumably, what is required in order to overcome the aporia in which such a measuring results is that movement of the soul itself which, in the terms of the *Phaedrus* myth, would bring it closer in memory to being. What is required is a human enactment of the divine banquet, and, indeed, it is love which the *Phaedrus* portrays as capable of initiating such an enactment. Shortly later, when

Socrates gives his account of the name "truth" (ἀλήθεια), saying that truth is so called because it is divine wandering (θεία ἄλη), it is to the divine banquet, for which the gods ascend to the top of the vault of heaven, that he refers. It is evident why in his earlier invocation of the goddess Hestia as being itself Socrates signaled the beginning of a banquet. It is by having recourse to names and *logos* that man sets out on the second voyage described by Socrates in the *Phaedo,* and it is thus that he initiates the appropriately human enactment of the divine banquet. And when Socrates comes to give his account of the name "name" (ὄνομα), he takes it to mean being of which the search is (ὃν οὗ μάσμα ἐστίν), resorting for his explanation of "name" to a *logos* of which he takes it to be a compressed form.

The etymologies conclude with an explanation of "being" (ὄν) and "not being" (οὐκ ὄν). "Being" is said to mean "going" (ἰόν); and at this point where the search would properly end, we are left wondering whether this "going," hence "being," is a movement of things or of the soul. And we are left wondering whether at this terminal point of the divine wandering man again assumes the form of the dizzy name-makers and brings the comedy to its conclusion.

Section 5. Imitation (421 c — 427 e)

(a) The Primary Names (421 c — 422 b)

Through the etymological comedy a fundamental disclosure of *logos* and its parts is accomplished, and to that degree the inspiration possessed by Socrates proves to be something utterly different from that of Euthyphro. Nevertheless, the disclosure accomplished through the etymologies is immersed in the dramatic unfolding and is principally an illuminating by way of allusion and implication. Socrates' comic attempt to measure the fitness of names gets transformed into an illumination of the way in which names are genuinely to be measured, but the peculiar structure of the comedy precludes any thematic focusing on this measuring.

The remainder of the *Cratylus* has as a primary task to thematize the teaching which has emerged in the comedy. Yet, even in this thematization the comedy will, though in a different way, be continued.

The issue which has especially emerged through the etymologies, at least to the degree permitted by the dramatic context, is that of the limitation of *logos* and, specifically, of names. Within the scope of the comic restriction of the investigation to the domain of names, this issue takes the form of the question regarding how the limitless regress that threatens the etymologies is to be terminated. Immediately following the completion of Socrates' final etymology, Hermogenes poses a question which makes this matter explicit: how, he asks, would Socrates answer if someone should ask about the fitness of those names to which Socrates has traced back the names being explained (421 c). Hermogenes' question lights up decisively the fundamental comic situation that has determined the entire etymological undertaking: the fitness of names has been explained only in terms of other names, only by taking the fitness of other names for granted. The fitness of the name "being" (ὄν) has been explained only by assuming that the name "going" (ἰόν) is correct with respect to that to which it is applied, an especially curious assumption in light of the way in which Socrates' final etymology leaves us wondering whether the movement so named is the movement of things or of the soul and whether, in the latter case, it is the movement characteristic of the dizzy name-makers or of those who re-enact the divine wandering up to the top of the vault of heaven. What about the name that is put forth in the etymology as the original? How is one to respond to the demand for a further etymology capable of uncovering a still more original name and to the unlimited repetition of this demand?

Socrates addresses himself to Hermogenes' question by referring to that kind of response of which he has already made use in the course of the etymologies, the contrivance of saying that the names asked about are of foreign origin. He refers also to the possibility that because of the lapse of time separating them from the really original names, these names have become so distorted that the ancient speech (παλαιὰ φωνή) would appear foreign to them (421 c – d). The question is how those names which are original in the sense of being capable of terminating the otherwise limitless regress within *logos* are to be discovered and recognized, certified, as such. Presumably, this certification would be possible only if that capacity required of such names, the capacity for limiting the regress, were itself understood. In this respect there would be no difficulty if the original names were identified with those natural names which belong to the speech of the gods; such names, by nature adequate to the things named, would be such as to require no further regress. The difficulty is, however, that the divine names cannot be found in the first place. As with the ancient speech to which Socrates refers, these names would appear utterly foreign to us, not, however, because the original sounds have been distorted but because these original names are by nature unsounded. Man cannot speak the speech of the gods, for the human soul is so bound that it can give signs only through the means provided by the body.

If the divine names are not to be found, how, then, is the etymological regress to be limited? How are human names to be exhibited as capable of terminating the regress non-arbitrarily? Socrates stresses that unless such a limit can be established the only alternative is simply to abandon the question, to terminate the questioning arbitrarily: "But let us bear in mind that if a person asks about the phrases [ῥήματα] by means of which names are formed, and again about those by means of which those phrases were formed, and keeps on doing this indefinitely, he who answers his questions will at last give up" (421 d – e).[33] A limit must, therefore, be secured.

---

[33] Socrates' conspicuous introduction here of ῥῆμα alongside ὄνομα should be especially noted, even though this word has already been used previously in the dialogue. In an earlier passage (399 a – b) it serves to denote a collection of names in contrast to a single name, denoted by "ὄνομα" (cf. also 385 c). More precisely, "ῥῆμα" is generally used to refer to a complex of names which, though not a complete statement (λόγος), still is no mere collection but rather has a certain unitary sense. The word "ῥῆμα" is also used in a more specific sense to denote a predicate, presumably because such a complex serves pre-eminently for that determination of a name by which a *logos* is formed (cf. esp. *Soph.* 262 b – c); there is a still more specific sense according to which "ῥῆμα" signifies a verb. For further discussion and references see Oehler, *Die Lehre vom Noetischen und Dianoetischen Denken,* pp. 56 ff. Within the context of the *Cratylus,* where names are at issue as parts of *logos,* where, consequently, the articulation within

Socrates proposes that this terminal point should consist of those names which are the elements of the other names and *logoi* but which are not themselves composed of other names. The divine names in reference to which he has previously sought to measure the correctness of human names are thus replaced by a special set of human names. The decisive difference is that the primary names now proposed fall immediately under the demand that their correctness be shown. The correctness of all names composed from them could then be genuinely measured by the etymological regress back to the primary names. In all cases except that of the primary names the measuring of the correctness of names by means of etymologies would be justified; the consequence, however, is that some completely different means of measuring the fitness of the primary names must be found (422 a – b).

(b) Naming as Imitation (422 b – 424 a)

If the correctness of the primary names cannot be measured by any further regress within *logos,* then, presumably, it can be measured only by that which is named. Thus, Socrates now recalls what was established prior to the etymologies regarding the correctness of names: for a name to be correct means that it is capable of showing, of making manifest, the being of the things named. Socrates notes that, in fact, this holds both of the primary names and of those names which are derived from them but that in the case of the latter kind of names the capacity of making manifest derives from the fact that they are composed of the primary names (422 d). Only the primary names need to be tested with respect to their capacity for making manifest the being of the

---

logos itself is at issue, it is adviseable that the more specific senses of "ῥῆμα" not be presupposed; thus, we use as translation the word "phrase." In the present context what is significant about Socrates' introduction of ῥῆμα alongside ὄνομα is that it indicates explicitly something that was, in fact, already evident in the etymologies, namely that the regress is not simply from one name to another but also requires, at the very least, the use of certain phrases by which to explain these names. What is, more generally, suggested is that the regress is a movement not just within the order of names but within *logos* as such.

things named; once this is accomplished, the correctness of all other names could be guaranteed by means of etymologies.

There is a significant ambiguity introduced here in Socrates' recall of what was earlier established regarding the correctness of names. In fact, in the earlier discussion between Socrates and Hermogenes what was agreed to constitute the fitness of a name was not that the name itself be capable of making manifest the being of the thing named but rather, in terms of the analogy with art that was sustained throughout almost the entire analysis, that the name be a fit instrument for a certain kind of naming. Specifically, what was proposed in the earlier discussion was that the correctness of a name consists in its being fit to serve as an instrument in a naming by which the end to which all naming is directed is accomplished, namely to distinguish things in their proper being (388 b – c; cf. Sect. 2). What makes manifest the being of things is not simply the name *per se* but rather the naming in which the name serves as an instrument; and Socrates has, though without further explanation, proposed that the kind of naming in which the relevant end, to make things manifest in their proper being, is accomplished takes place as a questioning and answering.

This ambiguity, which permits the capacity for making manifest to be easily ascribed just to the name itself in such a way that the naming and the namer are forgotten, will be decisive as the discussion proceeds and will, in effect, allow a resumption of the comedy already unfolded in the etymologies. Initially, however, Socrates does not propose the investigation of the primary names in a way which would ignore the relevant naming but, rather, precisely in reference to the naming. He asks how, if we had no voice, we would go about making things manifest to one another. He answers to himself that we would do so by making signs with our hands and head and body generally (422 e). This beginning is appropriate: not only does it hold in view the naming activity but also, in contrast to a beginning made by laying claim to the speech or vision of the gods, it reiterates that bond which Socrates brought to light in the first series of etymologies, that by which man is bound to make signs through the means provided by the body.

Socrates proceeds to develop his explanation by introducing the notion of imitation (μίμημα). If we wished, for example, to make manifest what is above and light, we would raise our hands towards heaven in imitation of the nature of the thing in question; likewise, in all other such cases the thing being considered would be made manifest by means of a bodily imitation of it (423 a − b). Socrates extends the account to the cases involving the voice: when we make something manifest to one another by means of the voice, we do so by means of an imitation of the thing; hence, a name is a vocal imitation of the thing named, and the activity of naming is an activity of imitating, by means of the voice, that which is named. However, in spite of Hermogenes' endorsement of this explanation, Socrates insists that a further refinement is necessary, on the ground that, according to the explanation as developed thus far, one would be obliged to agree that when someone uses his voice to imitate an animal he is naming that animal (423 b − c). Whereas the previously attempted account of names involved in a decisive way the supposition that the gods name themselves by the correct names, the present explanation, if left as it is, would bring us ridiculously close to the absurd contention that even animals, by the sounds which they utter and which men imitate with their own voices, name themselves correctly.

Socrates explains the further refinement that is required. He refers to the fact that things (πράγματα) have sound (φωνή) and shape (σχῆμα) and that many have color (χρῶμα) and insists that the art of naming does not consist in the imitation of these "qualities" belonging to things; to name a thing does not mean to imitate the sound of the thing by means of the sound of the voice.[34] Abruptly, Socrates recalls what was established earlier in the criticism of Protagoras and states, though in the form of a question, that a being (οὐσία) belongs to each thing, just as does a color and the other "qualities" just mentioned. He adds that a being, in fact, belongs even to color, sound, and other such things.

---

[34] Within the eristic context of the *Euthydemus* the question is raised by Dionysodorus whether it is possible to say things as they are. To say things as they are is identified by Ctesippus as speaking the truth. Euthydemus asks then whether one who speaks the truth speaks bigly of the big and hotly of the hot (284 d − e).

He concludes that if one could imitate the being of something by means of letters and syllables, he would make manifest what that thing really is (423 e); he would then have named the thing in such a way as to accomplish the end to which naming is directed and, thereby, would have certified the fitness of the name used in the naming.

It is of utmost importance to observe what has happened through Socrates' seemingly straightforward refinement of the account of naming as imitation. It should be noted, first of all, that from the beginning of the present account there is something which distinguishes it from the discussions of the virtue and end of naming that occurred prior to the etymologies. Specifically, it should be noted that Socrates introduces the entire discussion of imitation by considering a situation in which one person engages in making manifest to another something which, in fact, is already manifest to the person who engages in the imitative activity, if not to the one whom he addresses. What the imitator engages in is not an originary act of making manifest, not a making manifest to himself; and, indeed, only because what is to be made explicitly manifest to another by the imitative activity is already manifest to the imitator, is he able to imitate it in an appropriate way. The point is, then, that the end proper to naming is now taken, in contrast to the earlier discussion, to be nothing more than that of communication—of communicating something from one person, to whom what is to be communicated is already manifest, to another person, to whom also, presumably, what is communicated would need to be to some considerable degree already manifest in order for him to identify the imitative communication as such.

In light of this assignment of naming to an end different from the one previously assigned, the full import of that refinement which Socrates introduces into the account becomes evident. If naming, as the communication of something already manifest to the communicator, were only an imitation of the sound, shape, or color of things, there would be no great difficulty, for it can be presumed that the sound, shape, and color of things are always manifest to any man who attends to those things, provided his organs of sense are properly functioning. But can this be presumed when it is a case—as Socrates insists it always is—of communicating the being of the thing or of its sound, shape, or color? Does not especially the criticism of Protagoras indicate that the proper being of the thing is just that which is not immediately manifest but rather is in need of being made manifest? And is it not to be made manifest precisely by means of the art of naming? It appears that that naming, described by Socrates in terms of imitation, already presupposes naming and that the account of naming as imitation can stand only as long as the ignorance of the namer is overlooked, the ignorance constituted by the fact that being is not immediately manifest to him but has, rather, by way of mediation to be made manifest. A resumption of the comedy is being prepared.

(c) Imitation and the Making of *Logos* (424 a – 426 b)

Socrates asks Hermogenes about the identity of the man who could imitate the being of things by means of sounds and syllables, and Hermogenes identifies him as that name-maker (ὀνομαστικός) for whom they have been searching (424 a). The identification is appropriate, especially since that maker of names in search of whom they originally set out was characterized as one capable of looking to the natural names and putting them into sounds and syllables. Almost the same capacity appears to be required on the part of the imitative maker of names.

Referring to the names left still in need of testing at the end of the etymologies, Socrates proceeds to seek the basis for such testing by re-enacting that original imitative activity by which the name-maker made the primary names. What follows is, thus, in effect, just another etymological account, analogous to those that occupied the preceding part of the dialogue except for the fact that Socrates postpones the specifically etymological task of establishing the link between the names in question and the original, primary names from which they derive. Socrates recounts in first person the making of the primary names. Since names are composed of letters, the first step in the making of names consists in the separation of the vowels and of the other sorts of letters into their various respective kinds (κατὰ εἴδη). The second step consists in giving names to things in such a way as to see what they themselves are and whether there are any kinds among them as there are among the letters. Having secured this dual classification—of letters, on the one hand, and of things, on the other—we could then proceed to apply the letters to the things in the fitting way, using one letter for one thing when this is what is appropriate or many letters if that is required. Thus, we could proceed to combine letters into syllables, then from syllables to form names (ὀνόματα) and phrases (ῥήματα),[35] and then, finally, by this art of naming we could make *logos* itself (424 b − 425 a).

In this account there are several features which need to be noted. Already in Socrates' description of the first step by which the name-maker sets about making the primary names there is something curious, namely that the kinds into which the letters are separated not only must already be manifest but also are kinds which already have their names; Socrates refers explicitly to the separation from the other letters of the consonants or mutes as they are called by certain men. One suspects that some naming, even some logos, must already have transpired before this original naming could have begun.[36] Socrates' account of the second step in the work of the primal name-maker is still more curious. What is required in this second step is that names be given to things in order that the name-maker might see what the things really are and, thereby, determine whether in the case of things too, as with the letters, there are kinds according to which things could be properly separated. Socrates' description of this second step, thus, not only serves to indicate that there is need of naming

---

[35] On the meaning of "ῥῆμα," see above, note 33.

[6] In the *Philebus* (18 b − d) Socrates tells a story meant to illustrate his contention that "reaching the one must be the last step of all." According to this story the unlimited variety of sound was once discerned by some god or perhaps some godlike man. Referring specifically to Theuth (cf. *Phaedr.* 274 c − 275 b), Socrates tells how this god (or godlike man), after distinguishing the kinds of sounds, "divided up the noiseless ones or mutes until he got each one by itself, and did the same thing with the vowels and the intermediate sounds; in the end he found a number of the things, and affixed to the whole collection, as to each single member of it, the name 'letter.' It was because he realized that none of us could ever get to know one of the collection all by itself, in isolation from all the rest, that he conceived of 'letter' as a kind of bond of unity, uniting as it were all these sounds into one." The name-maker of the *Cratylus* has the sounds already bound into the unity of the name "letter."

in order that the proper being of things be made manifest and an appropriate collection and division of them into their distinct kinds effected but also indicates in the most pointed fashion that the imitative activity, as it has been described, could not coincide with that activity by which names were first made but, on the contrary, presupposes for its very possibility that names are already available to the imitator. This is to say that the primary names for which Socrates and Hermogenes are searching could not be primary names at all and that the search, therefore, is hardly less comic in character than was the earlier search for divine names. In complete incongruity with what he proposes to re-enact, namely the making of the primary names, what Socrates, in fact, re-enacts is a great circle, leading, first, from *logos* to names, then to the letters and the classification of letters and things on the basis of what names and *logos* make manifest, then to the formation (by combination of the letters) of names, phrases, and finally *logos* itself.

It is significant that Socrates' description of the making of the primary names by the original name-maker is narrated in first person as though this making were something which he and Hermogenes were themselves doing or, at least, preparing to do; for that making of names, presumed to be original, proves to be no less bound to already established names and *logos* than is Socrates' descriptive re-enactment of it. Immediately after the completion of his description of the name-making activity, Socrates abruptly corrects himself for having narrated the account in first person: arriving at that point at which he says, "so now we shall make *logos* by the art of naming," he suddenly notes, "No, not we; I said that too hastily." He proceeds to tell Hermogenes that actually this composite character was given to *logos* by the ancients and that the task which is incumbent upon himself and Hermogenes, if they are to examine such matters in the appropriate way, is to take to pieces what was put together by the ancients, in such a way as to determine whether it was properly put together (425 a — b). The irony of Socrates' proposal is that this analysis, presumed capable of leading back to a point prior to names and *logos* from which the correctness of such could be tested, is, in effect, just a reversal of the direction in which the circle is traversed, and, if, beginning with the established *logos,* presumably wrought by the ancients out of the raw material of letters, one should take apart what was once put together, what one would eventually arrive at would be, not some point prior to *logos,* but just more *logos.* The consequence is that the regress to the origination of the primary names, the regress by which Socrates has proposed to limit the regress which threatens the etymologies, proves itself to be without limit.

Socrates' comment that he does not believe he could succeed in taking names to pieces in the way proposed is a highly ironic understatement. Remarking at how laughable (γελοῖα) these notions about the earliest names must seem, he proceeds to review the other possibilities available for dealing with the question of the correctness of names. One could, as do the tragic poets, simply insist that the gods gave the earliest names and that, consequently, they must be correct—that is, one could identify the earliest names with the divine names, as Socrates did when he assumed the role, not of a tragedian, but of a comedian. Or, he continues, one could say that the earliest names are of foreign origin—as Socrates did on several occasions in the course of the etymologies. Or, thirdly, one could insist that it is impossible to investigate the earliest names because of their antiquity—as Socrates did in response to Hermogenes' criticism of his etymology of "τέχνη." Yet all of these alternatives, Socrates observes, "are merely very clever evasions on the part of those who refuse to offer any account (λόγον διδόναι) of the correctness of the earliest names" (425 d – 426 a). Socrates, passing entirely over the fact that he has himself persistently made use of just these kinds of evasions since well before the beginning of the etymological comedy, proposes that, however difficult it may be, they ought to initiate that analysis of names which would take *logos* apart as it was originally put together by the maker of names. The comedy resumes.

(d) The Comic Regress (426 b – 427 e)

Socrates repeats his opinion that his notions about the earliest names are laughable (γελοῖα). Now he adds, however, that these opinions are also hubristic (ὑβριστικά). Indeed they are, for the analysis which Socrates has proposed is, in effect, an attempt to break the bond which binds man to a mediation by way of *logos.* The regress to the origination of the earliest names is no less comic than the ascent to divine names.

Socrates begins the analysis by proposing that the letter rho seems to be an instrument expressing motion (κίνησις), explaining later that the tongue is least at rest and most agitated in pronouncing this letter (426 c, e). This beginning indicates already what is comic about the regress, namely that, while proposing to return to the point of origination of *logos,* it remains wholly within *logos;* for what Socrates establishes is not a relation between a letter and things but between a letter and a name—in fact, since the retrieve itself is executed in *logos,* a relation between the name of a letter and the name of a thing. Having assigned the letter rho to movement—which recalls the entire issue involved in naming movement as it was raised in the etymologies—Socrates proceeds then to explain the name "movement," presumably in order to make manifest what is named by the name, what, hence, has the letter rho assigned to it. But when he proceeds to explain it, his explanation takes the form of an etymology, which he is able to patch together only by changing and inserting letters and appealing to nothing less than his contrivance of declaring certain names to be of foreign origin (426 c − e). Throughout his elaborate etymology of the name "κίνησις" he passes over the most striking incongruity: that although the letter rho is supposed to be expressive of κίνησις, this letter does not occur in the name "κίνησις." Yet, in comic terms, this is appropriate, since the name "κίνησις"here exemplifies those names which are already presupposed when the name-maker, mistaking himself for an originator, sets out making names by assigning the letter rho to things having to do with movement, to things already collected in the unity of the name.

Socrates does not prolong his account beyond a few examples. It should be noted, however, that in these examples he does not, in fact, perform the analysis which he had ironically proposed as appropriate for men like himself and Hermogenes, the analysis which would take *logos* apart in order eventually to reach those elements from which it was first put together. On the contrary, he simply re-enacts the beginning of the putting together of *logos,* just as in describing earlier how *logos* is put together he inadvertently lapsed into a first person narrative. But the difference between the two directions is only the difference between the two directions in which a circle may be traversed; it is ultimately no difference at all, for in both cases one begins with already established *logos* and remains bound to it throughout.

Having completed his brief re-enactment of the making of names, Socrates says: "This, Hermogenes, appears to me to be the account of the correctness of names, unless, indeed, Cratylus has some other view." Hermogenes refers again to the difficulty, spoken of at the beginning of the dialogue, which he has with Cratylus, who, maintaining that there is a correctness of names, does not say clearly what it is. Yet now Socrates' clarity has replaced Cratylus' obscurity, and Socrates has in the discussion with Hermogenes provided a comic restoration of that position which Cratylus puts forth with the seriousness and obscurity of an oracle. Hermogenes asks Cratylus, who has maintained total silence throughout the entire discussion between Socrates and Hermogenes, to join the conversation and declare whether he agrees with what Socrates says about names.

Section 6. Cratylus (427 e – 437 d)

(a) Falsehood (427 e – 429 e)

Cratylus' first remark suggests an accord with what Hermogenes has reported about him: in response to Hermogenes' suggestion to him that he might learn from Socrates or else instruct him, Cratylus says, "But, Hermogenes, do you think it is an easy matter to learn or teach any subject so quickly, especially so important a one as this, which appears to me to be one of the most important?" Hermogenes insists that Cratylus ought, nevertheless, to join the discussion for whatever small progress might be made, since Cratylus owes it both to Socrates and to him. Socrates adds his plea that Cratylus enter the discussion, expressing his uncertainty about the opinions he has expressed and with characteristic irony offering to be put down as a pupil of Cratylus if the latter proves to have a better account of the correctness of names. Cratylus again responds, affirming, as Socrates had suggested, that he has attended to this question of names and indicating that perhaps he might make Socrates his pupil. The only difficulty, he notes, is that he agrees with Socrates' "oracular utterances," whether Socrates is "inspired by Euthyphro or some other Muse" (427 e – 428 c).

It is important to note Hermogenes' reference to a debt owed by Cratylus both to him and to Socrates. In the case of Hermogenes, the debt presumably stems from Cratylus' having robbed Hermogenes of his name, as was reported at the very beginning of the dialogue. This act was, in a sense, justified in connection with Socrates' etymology of the name of Hermes (himself a thief), and immediately after this etymology Hermogenes granted explicitly that, since he was not good at contriving *logos,* Cratylus must have been right in declaring him to be no true "descendent of Hermes" (408 b). Yet, what is now the status of Cratylus' deed against Hermogenes in light of the dissolution of the etymological undertaking into the attempt, just completed by Socrates, at an analysis capable of retrieving the earliest names? Or, to construe the deed in different terms, what is required on the part of Cratylus in order to justify his deed and in this sense pay the debt owed to Hermogenes? Presumably, what is required is that he give an account of names in terms of which Hermogenes' name could be shown not to be his name at all.

Just such an account has been given by Socrates, and this, apparently, is why Cratylus is in debt to him. Yet, Socrates' account both in the etymologies and in the subsequent re-enactment of the imitative origination of names has been given in the mode of comedy, and it is precisely this feature which, in the end, distinguishes Socrates from one who, inspired by Euthyphro, would issue oracular pronouncements. Cratylus' explicit references to the latter suggest that he is oblivious to the fact that the Socratic restoration of his position regarding the correctness of names has been a comic restoration. The question is: what will happen when Cratylus, oblivious to the comedy, attempts to repay what he owes to Socrates by engaging in the discussion?

Socrates responds to Cratylus' endorsement of what he has said by expressing more pointedly his own doubts about it and proposing that what he has said be re-examined. He adds that the worst sort of deception is self-deception, since in this case the deceiver is always present and never stirs from the spot (428 d). With this remark he alludes to the comic character of the previous undertakings, for what the comedy brought to light was a kind of self-deception which, in general, consists in taking oneself to be accomplishing one thing while, in fact, one is doing something quite different and, in particular, consists in presuming to gain access to divine names or to the originary naming while, in fact, remaining completely bound to already established human names. Presumably, however, since he appears to be oblivious to the comic character of these undertakings, it is Cratylus rather than Socrates who is threatened by such self-deception.

Socrates recalls that the correctness of a name consists in the capacity to show what the things are; he adds then the second of those ends to which naming was assigned in the discussion prior to the etymologies: names, he says, are given with a view to teaching. It should be noted that he passes over entirely the difficulties which became evident when after the etymologies the second of these ends, restricted to mere communication, became dominant. This fact is important, because he proceeds to develop the discussion with Cratylus by taking this end, teaching, as his point of departure. He secures Cratylus' agreement that teaching is an art and has its artisans, but, when he asks about the identity of these artisans, Cratylus identifies them as the lawgivers, referring to the fact that they were so identified by Socrates in the beginning (428 e − 429 a). But Cratylus is wrong: those whom Socrates identified as practitioners of the art of naming, and, specifically, for the purpose of teaching, were the teachers and, later, the dialecticians, capable of questioning and answering. The lawgiver was introduced by Socrates only in relation to the further question regarding who it is that provides those names which are used by the teachers, and, in a sense, the lawgiver in his curious elusiveness has been a subject of comedy almost ever since he appeared on the scene. It is of utmost significance that for Cratylus the genuine artisan of names is taken to be the lawgiver, who would originate human names by having recourse either to divine names or to an unaccountable vision of the being of things; this places him in stark contrast to Socrates for whom, both in his discussion of naming and in his naming in deed, the genuine artisan of names is the teacher or dialectician who makes use of already established *logos* and who, as Socrates insisted, is alone capable of directing and judging the work of the lawgiver.

Socrates recalls the analogy with art which was so instrumental in the earlier discussion, in such a way as to suggest that some lawgivers produce better and others worse work. But then he notes that, contrary to the analogy, Cratylus does not believe that one name is better and another worse. The conclusion is that all names are correct—at least, as Cratylus adds, "all that are really names." Socrates raises the question of Hermogenes' name and asks whether we are to suppose that "Hermogenes" is not his name at all or that it is his name but is not correct. When Cratylus insists that it is not his name at all but rather the name of someone else whose nature would make it fit, Socrates extends the conclusion from part to whole, from name to *logos:* if one says that he is Hermogenes, one is not even speaking falsely. Socrates asks Cratylus whether he means to say that it is impossible to speak falsely ($\psi\epsilon\upsilon\delta\hat{\eta}$ $\lambda\acute{\epsilon}\gamma\epsilon\iota\nu$) at all, and Cratylus confirms that this is his position, on the ground that to speak falsely involves the absurdity of saying what is not. When Socrates ironically inquires whether Cratylus, in maintaining this position, has some unexpressed subtlety in mind, Cratylus states bluntly—in reference to Socrates' hypothetical case in which a man would address Cratylus by the name "Hermogenes"—that such a man would be just uttering senseless sounds (429 a – e).

It is remarkable that Cratylus entered the discussion with a comment about how difficult it is to learn or teach any subject—a comment which, regarded in terms of what Socrates says (with which Cratylus has expressed his agreement), is a confession of how difficult it is *to speak well* on any subject—and that now, after such a brief exchange, he denies the very possibility of speaking badly, that is, falsely. One either speaks well or else does not speak at all but only utters sounds. Was Cratylus, then, only uttering senseless sounds when he made his initial comment?

(b) Images (429 e − 433 b)

In the example which Socrates cited for Cratylus it is a matter, not of someone assigning to Hermogenes that name which Cratylus insists is not his name, but rather of someone who, addressing hospitable greetings to Cratylus, mistakenly calls him by the name "Hermogenes." Cratylus' proclamation that such a man would simply be uttering senseless sounds, that is, Cratylus' insistence that he is not a decendent of Hermes, not only serves to dissociate him from the theft with which he has been charged but also suggests that he is oblivious to that deceptive power of *logos* which came to light in connection with the etymology of "Hermes"; the latter is fully born out in his subsequent denial of the possibility of false *logos*. The example serves also another purpose, which is hinted at in the question that Socrates puts to Cratylus in reference to the hypothetical situation: he asks him whether such a person, in greeting him by the name "Hermogenes," would be speaking to or addressing him or someone else or no one at all. It is clear that in such a situation, where the man grasps Cratylus' hand and speaks hospitably, he is addressing Cratylus regardless of what he might mistakenly call him. But this is clear only in light of the total situation of the speaking; if, on the contrary, one focuses, as does Cratylus, solely on the name which the man utters, it is then questionable whom he is addressing. The example and Cratylus' response to it tend to bring into effect that forgetting of the naming for the sake of a concentration solely on the name, as was already hinted at in the discussion immediately following the etymologies. Almost the entire remaining discussion with Cratylus will proceed under the power of this curious self-deception.

Cratylus' denial that a name can be poorly assigned and still be a name and his consequent denial of the possibility of false *logos* constitutes, in effect, a collapsing of the space between names and things. Socrates proceeds to re-establish this space, distinguishing explicitly the name over against the thing named and describing the name as an imitation (μίμημα). He draws the analogy with paintings, which are imitations of things, though, as Socrates observes, in a different way (430 a — b). The difference is to be understood in terms of the earlier account which Socrates gave Hermogenes: a painting imitates colors and shapes, i.e., what is immediately manifest by means of perception, whereas names imitate the being (ούσία) of things, which is not immediately manifest. This difference, referred to but not elaborated here, needs to be kept constantly in view in the following discussion.[37]

Socrates develops the admittedly imperfect analogy between names and paintings. In a way parallel to the discussion of false opinion in the *Theaetetus* (191 c — 195 d), he refers specifically to the assigning of the imitation to that which is imitated. One can assign the image of a man to the man and the image of a woman to the woman, in which cases the assignments are correct; on the other hand, one can assign the image of the man to the woman and that of the woman to the man, in which cases the assignments are not correct. Thus, a correct assignment is one in which the thing is assigned that which belongs to it and is like it. Socrates, applying the analogy to the case of names, states his position: in the case both of painting and of names, that kind of assignment in which the thing is assigned the imitation which is like it is to be called correct and, in the case of names, not only correct but also true; the other kind of assignment in which the unlike imitation is assigned is to be called incorrect and, in the case of names, false. This statement of his position Socrates claims to put forth in order that he and Cratylus might not wage battle in *logos* (430 c — d). The remark is ironically to the point inasmuch as Socrates' statement of his position is, in effect, a proposal that they wage battle, not just *in logos,* but *regarding logos.* For that to which Socrates assigns the name "correct" is not, in fact, the imitative name but

---

[37] In this connection the Stranger says in the *Statesman* (277 c), "And yet it is more fitting to portray any living being by speech [λέξις] and *logos* than by painting or any handicraft whatsoever to persons who are able to follow it; but to others it is better to do it by means of works of craftsmanship."

rather the assignment itself, that is, the *logos* in which the name is assigned to the thing. In connection with Socrates' specific statement that in the case of names such correctness is also to be called "truth," it should be remembered that it was precisely at the point, near the beginning of the dialogue, where Socrates explicitly linked names to *logos* (as part to whole) that the question of correctness gave way to that of truth (385 b − c; cf. above, Sect. 2 b).

Since Socrates' statement has, in effect, shifted the entire discussion from the correctness of names to the truth of the *logos* in which names are employed, it is not surprising that Cratylus is dissatisfied. Yet, it is questionable whether he has at all grasped what is at the root of his dissatisfaction, for, rather than speaking of this shift, he instead appeals to the admitted imperfection of the analogy between naming and painting, suggesting that, whatever may be the case with painting, in the case of names such an incorrect assignment is impossible. Socrates, ironically restoring the analogy, invites Cratylus to indicate that difference between painting and naming which renders the analogy imperfect. He asks:

> What difference is there between the two? Can I not step up to a man and say to him, "This is your portrait," and show him perhaps his own likeness or, perhaps, that of a woman? And by "show" [δεῖξαι] I mean bring before the sense of sight. . . . Well, then, can I not step up to the same man again and say, "This is your name"? A name is an imitation, just as a picture is. Very well; can I not say to him, "This is your name," and then bring before his sense of hearing perhaps the imitation of himself, saying that it is a man, or perhaps the imitation of the female of the human species, saying that it is a woman? Do you not believe that this is possible and sometimes happens (430 e − 431 a)?

Of course, there is a difference, a decisive difference, between the two instances to which Socrates refers; it is not the case that a name is an imitation *just as* a picture is. It is not the case that a name is something brought before the sense of hearing in the same way that a picture is brought before the sense of sight. In fact, there are two fundamental differences. The first of these stems from the fact, elaborated when names were first characterized as imitations (423 e), that what is imitated by a name is the being (οὐσία) of the thing named. Thus whereas what is imitated by the picture is something immediately manifest to perception, what is imitated by the name is not immediately manifest. In the first case, consequently, both the imitation and what is imitated are immediately manifest to perception, and the recognition of the picture as an imitation of the man would presuppose nothing beyond what is immediately manifest to perception. But in the case of a name that which is imitated is not immediately manifest in perception but rather is in need of being made manifest, and only on the basis of such a making manifest could the name be recognized as an imitation of the man (cf. *Theaet.* 163 b – c). Since in the instance described the man is being shown his own name, what would be required is that his own being be manifest to him; what would be required is self-knowledge.

The second difference is connected with the first. In the case of a picture both the imitation and what it imitates are immediately manifest, and the assignment of the picture to the man requires no more than a showing, as Socrates says, in the sense of bringing before the sense of sight. But in the case of a name its character as imitating the man is not apparent, and the name must be explicitly assigned to him: one must, as Socrates indicates, not only say to the man "This is your name," but also must say of the imitation that it is of a man or, in the case of an incorrect assignment, that it is an imitation of a part of the human species (γένος). In other words, in the case of the name of the man, the name must be assigned by means of *logos*—a *logos* which does not simply serve to call attention to the relation of likeness between two already manifest terms, as when one says to the man, "This is your portrait," but which serves to make manifest what is imitated to the degree necessary to allow the name to be recognized as an imitation. In the case of the picture it is only a matter of correctness; in the case of the name it is a matter of truth.

Cratylus grants the ostensible point of Socrates' example, utterly oblivious to the fact that this, no less than Socrates' previous statement, shifts the entire discussion from the consideration of the correctness of names to that of the truth of *logos* and, correlatively, from names to naming. Socrates proceeds ironically to establish that, if names can be incorrectly assigned, then phrases likewise may be incorrectly assigned and that, if this is so, then *logoi* too can be so assigned—that, consequently, false *logos* is possible (431 a – c). Yet the putting together of *logos* which Socrates here effects moves in a circle, no less than did that of the primal maker of names that Socrates described earlier, and is bound already to *logos* from the beginning.

Though invited by Socrates to do so, Cratylus has failed to distinguish between—that is, to name properly—the case of pictures, which imitate the color and shape of the thing imitated, and the case of names, which imitate the being of the thing imitated. Consequently, Socrates lets the distinction collapse entirely, presumably because Cratylus is, at least at this point of the discussion, oblivious to it. Socrates refers again to the earliest names, those which were regarded in the preceding discussion with Hermogenes as made by the original name-maker, and says that it is possible in such names, as in pictures, to render all the appropriate colors and shapes or not to render all of them, or to render some of them imperfectly; in the case of painting the first alternative yields a good picture, the other two alternatives a bad one. When Socrates proceeds to apply the analogy, he implicitly calls attention to the fallacy that underlies it by mentioning that names imitate the being of things, but then he passes over the fallacy and concludes that names may be made well or badly in the same way as may pictures. It is fitting that at precisely this point Socrates again refers explicitly to Cratylus' mistaken identification of the artisan of names as the lawgiver (431 c – e). What Socrates has, in effect, done, after Cratylus' failure to take up Socrates' invitation, is to restore in all its basic features the position of Cratylus: the difference between the two kinds of imitation (exemplified by names, on the one hand, and pictures, on the other) has been obliterated, the shift from name to *logos* has been reversed, and, correlatively, the abstraction of names from the naming in which they serve as instruments has been put into effect. All three of these features are exemplified in the lawgiver, who is presumed to look to the natural names or the being of things as though there were no problem in making them accessible to his vision, who is presumed to practice an originary making of names independently of any already established *logos,* and who is presumed, therefore, to make the instruments of naming rather than using them as instruments in naming. Cratylus and the lawgiver, whom he quite appropriately identifies as the genuine artisan of names, stand in marked contrast to Socrates, for whom the genuine artisan is the dialectician. The question is whether Socrates' restoration of Cratylus' position is, as with his posing of the lawgiver, ultimately comic. The answer is already evident in the incongruity between Cratylus' position as restored by Socrates and Cratylus' contention that all names are correct.

Cratylus attempts to resolve the incongruity. He objects that, if one changes or transposes the letters of a name, then it is not the case that the name is written though written incorrectly; on the contrary, he insists, it is not written at all but has become a different name entirely. Socrates, ironically suggesting that perhaps they are not considering the matter rightly, proceeds to grant that what Cratylus says may be true in the case of those things which, as he says, "must necessarily consist of a certain number or else not be" (432 a); he observes, that, for example, the number ten or any number, if added to or subtracted from, immediately becomes another number. But, he insists, this does not hold of images in general. An image need not render everything that pertains to the thing imitated; in fact, it cannot render everything without ceasing to be an image, as Socrates illustrates with the comical example of an image of Cratylus which would imitate not only his color and shape but also his flexibility, warmth, motion, life, and intellect and which, consequently, would be, not an image of Cratylus, but rather another Cratylus (431 e − 432 c). Socrates' example indicates what is required of Cratylus: it is the same thing which Socrates previously invited him to do, namely to distinguish between the two kinds of imitation. A number is not something which has shape or color nor any of those things that are immediately manifest in perception. This is emphasized in the corresponding passage in the *Theaetetus* (195 e − 196 c) where the entire effort to account for false opinion in terms of the assignment of perceptions to thoughts—as the *Cratylus* is attempting to account for false *logos* in terms of the assignment of names to things—runs aground precisely in the case of numbers. To imitate a number is not to imitate colors and shapes but, as Socrates has insisted in the case of names, to imitate something which is not immediately manifest. Indeed, in these cases it might very well be that there are no imperfect images in the only sense in which Cratylus can understand such but that the distinction between good and bad images must be determined in an entirely different way—for example, in terms of the capacity to serve in a naming which makes what is named become manifest. But Cratylus remains oblivious to these matters; he recognizes only that kind of image which is exemplified in the imitation of colors and shapes, and it is fitting that Socrates drives home his point regarding such images by speaking of an image of Cratylus which turns out to be identical with Cratylus.

Socrates concludes that one must allow for the possibility of imperfect imitations, bad images, which, nevertheless, are images; one must allow for the possibility of incorrect names which are, nonetheless, still names. It must be granted that a name may contain an inappropriate letter; but, then, this cannot be restricted to names but may be extended up to the level of *logoi,* which, consequently, also may contain inappropriate parts. Again Socrates has re-enacted the building up of *logos*—this time with the comic Cratylus clearly in view. Socrates affirms that either this conclusion must be accepted or else they must search for some other type of correctness in names (432 d — 433 b).

(c) Cratylus and Hermogenes (433 b — 435 d)

Socrates has pointed out that, unless Cratylus finds some other type of correctness of names, he must grant the possibility of poorly made images which, nevertheless, are images; he must allow that a name can be the name of a thing even though it is a poor imitation of the thing; otherwise, Socrates observes, Cratylus cannot avoid contradicting himself. Cratylus accepts this conclusion (433 a — b); and, thus, he appears to have been brought into accord with himself—in the sense that there is now an accord between Cratylus' position as exemplified in the figure of the lawgiver and his opinion regarding the possibility of poorly made names. Specifically, the latter has been drawn by Socrates into accord with the former; yet, when we recall that the lawgiver has persistently proved to be comical, we suspect that the incongruities embodied in Cratylus' position have not all as yet been resolved. Furthermore, it is evident in the contrast between the lawgiver and the dialectician that there is anything but an accord between Cratylus and Socrates. The remainder of the dialogue consists in Socrates' effort to dissolve this discord. But, first, the degree of accord between Cratylus and Hermogenes needs to be measured.

Socrates restates the conclusion they have reached. The residual discord is betrayed in Cratylus' response: he struggles to free himself from the conclusion that something can be a name and not be well given. When he agrees with Socrates that a name is a showing (δήλωμα) of the thing, a making it manifest, Socrates asks whether he can suggest any better way of making names this than by making them as much as possible like the things which they are to make manifest. Specifically, Socrates asks him whether he would prefer the account put forth by Hermogenes and others, the account according to which "names are conventional and show something to those who have agreed about them and knew the things beforehand," so that convention (συνθήκη) is the only kind of correctness of names. Confronted with this alternative, Cratylus states emphatically that showing the things by means of likeness is superior to showing by means of chance signs (433 b − 434 a).

Is this alternative which Socrates offers Cratylus really the position of Hermogenes? And who are those unnamed others who also put it forth? Socrates' reference to the thesis that all names are conventional establishes that the position described is that which Hermogenes put forth at the beginning of the dialogue and which he had tried to maintain in the ill-fated discussions with Cratylus prior to the beginning of the dialogue. However, the further thesis which Socrates presents as belonging to this position was not so explicitly put forth in Hermogenes' statement at the beginning of the dialogue. Furthermore, the thesis that names are conventional, which Socrates says is put forth by Hermogenes, is, in fact, not any longer put forth by Hermogenes. Almost at the outset of his discussion with Socrates he relinquished this thesis in favor of the position that there is a natural correctness of names, a natural correctness which he asked Socrates to show him—thereby initiating the etymologies—and which he took to be definitively accounted for in the discussion of the primary names immediately following the etymologies. What about the other thesis, that names show something to those who have agreed about them and knew the things beforehand? We have seen that the condition under which it must be maintained that a name shows a thing only to those who knew it beforehand is that in which naming is regarded only with respect to the second of those ends assigned to it by Socrates and in which this end (teaching) is narrowed down to mere communication; if naming is only communication—and not that by which we distinguish things in their proper being—then the names involved can do no more than show what is already known beforehand, that is, for the most part, draw attention to something whose manifestness is already guaranteed by perception. But this is precisely the condition which was put into effect in Socrates' discussion with Hermogenes following the etymologies and under which the entire discussion of naming as imitation has proceeded. This part of the thesis is, consequently, still put forth by Hermogenes even though he has abandoned his initial thesis that names are merely conventional. Even if there is, as he now has affirmed, a natural likeness between names and things, the things must be manifest in order for their names to direct us to them and, hence, in that sense, show them. Yet it is not only Hermogenes who affirms this part of the thesis but also Cratylus; on this point, that things must be known beforehand in order for their names to show them, Hermogenes and Cratylus are in perfect agreement.

The other part of the thesis refers to the agreement, the convention, as something established. Yet, Hermogenes has abandoned the opinion that the correctness of names is based on the establishing of a convention and, on the contrary, has been led by Socrates to agree that the relevant establishing is an establishing by the lawgiver of a natural connection between names and things. Yet, when

Socrates re-enacted this primal instituting of the connection between names and things, what came to light—though without being thematized—was that this instituting already presupposes names and *logos*. What actually was accomplished when Socrates re-enacted the name-making activity was only an assignment of names to things which already had names. And even the claim of this new assignment to be natural was comically undermined by the fact that it proved to be names, rather than things—or, at best, things as collected in the unity of the already established names—to which the lawgiver ended up assigning names and the parts of names. Consequently, the activity of the lawgiver is not fundamentally different from the case, cited by Hermogenes at the beginning of the dialogue, in which one changes the name of a slave. The establishing which the lawgiver effects is nothing but the establishing of a convention. Contrary to what he thinks, Hermogenes is still, in fact, maintaining just the same position that he stated at the very beginning of the dialogue. In his case the appearance of movement from one position to the opposite position is nothing more than appearance.

But still, who are the others who also put forth this position? One of them is Cratylus; for he has stated explicitly his agreement with the accounts of naming as imitation and of the name-making activity of the lawgiver and is, in fact, now engaged in the discussion designed to elaborate these accounts. Another of those who puts forth this position is Socrates. In fact, he is the only one who has been able to put it forth in the sense of developing and articulating it. All three characters of the *Cratylus* put forth the same position, the position which Socrates has just described. But they do not all put it forth in the same way; already in his identification of the artisan of names as the teacher and dialectician rather than the lawgiver it is evident that Socrates puts forth this position in a different way. Most of all, what we have seen throughout is that he put it forth as comedy. Socrates' activity of teaching Hermogenes and Cratylus, of mediating between their respective positions, does not, as at first appeared, consist simply in leading them to exchange positions; his mediating activity consists rather in performing the comedy by which their positions are shown to be identical.

But the accord between Cratylus and Hermogenes has, within the comedy, still to be made fully manifest; it has still to be shown that, in fact, Cratylus' position is that names are conventional. Socrates appeals to the conclusion that, if names are to be like things, then the letters must be, by their very nature, like the things. He returns then to that assignment of letters to things that was described earlier in the discussion with Hermogenes and recalls that the letter rho signifies movement, speed, and hardness and that the letter lambda is like smoothness and softness. He calls attention then to the fact that what they call σκληρότης (hardness) is called by the Eretrians σκληρότηρ. He asks Cratylus whether the final rho means to the Eretrians the same thing that the final sigma means to Cratylus and himself. Cratylus has no alternative but to answer that they mean the same and do so insofar as they are alike; actually in the assignments previously given by Socrates in discussion with Hermogenes sigma was explicitly assigned to something different, to things which resemble blowing (427 a), but neither Socrates nor Cratylus here recalls that assignment. Socrates asks Cratylus whether rho and sigma are alike, and Cratylus answers that they are alike at least for the purpose of expressing motion. The conflict is evident, and Socrates drops the point in order to ask Cratylus about the lambda in "σκληρότης": how is it that the name "hardness" has in it a letter which signifies softness? When Cratylus answers that perhaps it ought not be there, referring to the cases in which Socrates removed and inserted letters, Socrates retorts that, nevertheless, they themselves understand one another when they use the name in its present form. So how is it that the name shows the right thing even though it contains not only a letter which imitates that thing but also a letter which imitates its very opposite. Cratylus resolves the contradiction in the name by transferring it to himself: that we understand the name to indicate hardness is, he says, a matter of custom (ἔθος). Securing his agreement that custom is the same as convention (συνθήκη), Socrates makes the conclusion explicit: things can be shown by both like and unlike letters by virtue of the effect of custom and convention, and so, as Socrates says, Cratylus has made a convention with himself (434 a – 435 a). Yet, ironically, this convention is not just arbitrary but rather makes explicit the identity of Cratylus' position with that of Hermogenes.

Observing that Cratylus has again withdrawn into silence, Socrates suggests that *logos* would probably be most excellent if it were based on likeness. He concludes that we are, however, forced to make use of the expedient of convention in order to establish the correctness of names (435 b − d).

(d) Cratylus and Socrates (435 d − 437 d)

The accord between Cratylus and Hermogenes has been made explicit. The dramatic issue now becomes the discord between Cratylus and Socrates.

At the beginning of the dialogue Hermogenes complained to Socrates about Cratylus' unwillingness or inability to communicate the reasons for his thesis regarding the correctness of names. Now we have seen that it is precisely in connection with the question of communication that Cratylus has proved unable to maintain even the appearance of difference between his position and that of Hermogenes, and it is appropriate that Cratylus again tries to withdraw into silence. But, unlike Hermogenes, Socrates proves capable of compelling him to continue the discussion.

The question of communication, which drives Cratylus again to seek recourse to silence, reflects the entire structure of the discord which the dialogue as a whole has brought to light and which is exemplified dramatically in the discord between Cratylus and Socrates. To regard *logos* only under the aspect of communication, in the way which underlies the entire discussion of imitation, is to regard naming only with respect to its capacity to indicate what is already manifest in advance of the naming. Naming thus gets understood in terms of the kind of imitating exemplified by painting in which what is to be imitated is manifestly present to the imitator, with the result that the relevant question becomes that of whether what the imitator makes is a faithful image of what he sees. What becomes important when the issue is regarded in this manner is not the naming activity but rather the name itself, and the former tends to be ignored for the sake of the latter;

in turn, this amounts, in effect, to a shift from the question of *logos* to that of names, from truth to correctness.

Thus, the question whether communication is the proper end to which naming is assigned lies at the very heart of the issue, at the source of the discord between Socrates and Cratylus. It is with this question that Socrates forces Cratylus out of his silence. He asks him abruptly: of what do names make us capable, and what is the good (καλόν) accomplished by them? Cratylus answers that their function is to teach (διδάσκειν) (435 d). With this answer he restores the second of those ends which Socrates assigned to naming and takes the first step in removing that restriction of naming to communication under which the entire discussion since the etymologies has labored. Yet, the first end, that of distinguishing things according to their proper being, remains yet to be restored. And the restriction to names over against naming remains still in effect.

To his answer that names have teaching as their proper end, Cratylus adds that he who knows the names knows also the things named. The addition is crucial. It involves an implicit reference to that restriction of naming to communication which the first part of Cratylus' answer appears to remove, for it is precisely when naming is regarded as communication that it must be said that those who know the names, both those who use them in order to indicate something to another and this other to whom something is indicated, already know the things, specifically, in the sense that the things named are already vouchsafed with regard to their manifestness. The question which the dialogue has served to raise in this connection is how, if what names imitate is the being of things, this latter could be so vouchsafed, since it is precisely that which is not immediately manifest, which is in need of being made manifest.

Yet this relation between names and things, according to which knowing the names would presuppose already knowing the things named, is, in fact, the reverse of what Cratylus has in mind in bringing together the question of teaching and that of the relation between names and things; again the discord within Cratylus becomes audible through what he says. What he intends to say is that it is by knowing the name, by means of the name, that we come to know the thing. Such is, he says, the only means of being taught about things (436 a). Names are not just instruments which must be used properly by a teacher in order for learning to take place, as Socrates has earlier suggested; for Cratylus names, themselves, are the teachers. It is only by means of names that we come to know things, that things are made manifest to us.

Socrates' response makes clear what Cratylus really means: "that when anyone knows the name such as it is—and it is as is the thing—he will know the thing also, since it is like the name" (435 d − e). At the same time, this response, even in Socrates' choice of words,[38] implicitly refers back to that figure in the dialogue who was presumed to have access to just such names as would be capable of that which Cratylus is now extending to all names—namely the name-maker as portrayed prior to the etymologies, the name-maker who looks to the *eide* of the names to be made, to the natural or divine names which have as their distinctive feature the fact that they distinguish things according to their proper being. In effect, the same claim to have access to such names capable of guaranteeing the vision of things in their proper being is also involved in that form in which the name-maker emerges in the discussion following the etymologies; since his making of names, as Socrates re-enacts it, turns out to be an assigning, not of names to things, but of names to names, he could accomplish what is claimed for him only if the latter names were, in fact, nothing less than those divine names which carry the guarantee of distinguishing things as they are in their proper being. The only names which could accomplish what Cratylus is now claiming for all names are the divine names, and the only one who could be taught by names, in the way Cratylus describes with the help of Socrates, is the lawgiver who makes names. Yet, in the course of the etymologies the lawgiver appeared in the guise of Hermes and in the guise of comedy. And, furthermore, what if there are no divine names, or what if, as the etymological comedy and the other comedy which

---

[38] Whereas Cratylus said " . . . ὃς ἂν τὰ ὀνόματα ἐπίστηται, ἐπίστασθαι καὶ τὰ πράγματα," Socrates says, " . . . ὡς ἐπειδάν τις εἰδῇ τὸ ὄνομα οἷόν ἐστιν—ἔστι δὲ οἷόνπερ τὸ πρᾶγμα—εἴσεται δὴ καὶ τὸ πρᾶγμα. . . ." It should be recalled that the name-maker was described early in the dialogue as one who looks to the *eide* of the names being made (389 d).

followed it show, the name-maker is deceived in thinking that the names to which he has access are divine names? What if those names which he thinks are divine are really just other human names?

In response to Socrates' question regarding the end proper to names, Cratylus has simply reintroduced the lawgiver in the form which he had most explicitly in the first part of the dialogue, the lawgiver who all along has embodied the position of Cratylus. Socrates proceeds to extend Cratylus' contention regarding names as the means of learning about things. First, he secures Cratylus' agreement that names are not only the means by which we are taught about things but also the means by which we seek ($\zeta\eta\tau\epsilon\hat{\iota}\nu$) and discover ($\epsilon\hat{\upsilon}\rho\hat{\iota}\sigma\kappa\epsilon\iota\nu$) things. Then, having ascertained this point, he, in effect, recalls what the comedy has brought to light with regard to the name-maker; he observes that the name-maker made names in accord with the way in which things were manifest to him and that, consequently, if things were not manifest to him as they are in their proper being, if his vision of things was "not correct," then the names made by him are not correct and cannot be trusted to show us the things as they are (436 a − b).

However, Cratylus, who has named the lawgiver as the genuine artisan of names, insists that the lawgiver must have known the things named and, hence, must have named them correctly. Cratylus frantically tries to defend the lawgiver by reverting suddenly to his old contention, long ago disposed of, that otherwise—that is, if names were not given correctly—they would not be names at all (436 b − c). But then he drops this and appeals to something else in defense of the lawgiver and of himself—namely to the fact that the names made by the lawgiver are so completely consistent, so harmonious ($\xi\hat{\upsilon}\mu\phi\omega\nu\alpha$). And, in his utter lack of harmony with himself, much less with Socrates—that is, with what Socrates' performance of the comedy has brought to light—he seeks to justify the harmony of names by an appeal to the etymological comedy. Having called his attention to the fact that mere consistency is no guarantee of truth, Socrates then resumes the comedy: names previously found to denote movement now turn out in the short resumption of the comedy to denote rest; moreover, the worst sorts of things, such as error ($\dot{\alpha}\mu\alpha\rho\tau\acute{\iota}\alpha$) and misfortune (ξυμφορά), considered etymologically, turn out to be the same as the best sorts of things such as intellect (σύνεσις) and knowledge (ἐπιστήμη). The short resumption of the comedy concludes by mixing up good and bad to such a degree that "ignorance" (ἀμαθία) appears to mean the progress of one who goes with god and "unrestraint" (ἀκολασία) means movement in company with things (436 c – 437 c). It is clear that, as with the longer etymological comedy, here too something decisive comes to light, for these last two examples refer precisely to those two kinds of movement that were at issue earlier in the final large set of etymologies. But now that movement of the soul in company with the gods, which is required in order to surpass the mixing-up of opposites which confronts one who moves—and, presumably, speaks—in company with things, is named ignorance. This is what both Cratylus and his lawgiver have yet to learn. If, indeed, names teach us in the way maintained by Cratylus, perhaps what they teach, first of all, is ignorance.

In desperation Cratylus says that most of the names refer to motion. Rather than prolonging this comedy to the same length as the earlier one, Socrates simply asks with obvious sarcasm: "Are we to count names like votes, and shall correctness rest with the majority?" (437 d).

Section 7. Names and Things (437 d – 440 e)

(a) The Measure of Names (437 d – 439 b)

Suggesting that the preceding discussion was a digression, Socrates now reverses the relation between names and things, as it was proposed by Cratylus, so that now the relation assumes the form that has been explicitly exemplified in the figure of the lawgiver. He asks Cratylus whether he still holds to the opinion that the one who gave names also knew the things to which he gave the names. When Cratylus answers affirmatively, Socrates then poses the decisive question: From what names did the lawgiver learn or discover the things? If we learn and discover things only by means of names, what is to be said of the maker of names? How could he have known things at a time when the first names had not yet been given and, hence, were not available to him as means by which to learn and discover things (438 a − b)? It is clear that Socrates is not simply reversing that relation between names and things that was most recently proposed by Cratylus; rather he is inviting Cratylus to combine this harmoniously with its reverse. He so invites him because the figure of the lawgiver, in which the position of Cratylus is collected, is precisely such as to embody both forms of the relation between names and things: the lawgiver must know the things in order to imitate them correctly in names, yet his activity turns out to be one of looking, not to things, but to names. The circle could be eliminated only if, as originally supposed, the names to which the name-maker looks are divine names. But what the whole series of comedies initiated by the etymologies have brought to light is that, if there are divine names, it is not to these that the name-maker looks or could look. The comic character that is subsequently exhibited by the lawgiver is even already anticipated in the first form in which he appears: he is said to look to what turn out to be divine names, whereas, in fact, names are proximally something spoken—and looked to only in a derivative sense; in any case the divine names are such as inherently to prevent their being either seen or spoken. What Socrates invites Cratylus to do is institute harmony in the lawgiver—that is, to resolve the discord in himself.

Rather than resolving the incongruity, however, Cratylus responds to Socrates' invitation by posing the incongruity in that most extreme form to which it has tended throughout the dialogue: the power, he says, which gave the first names is more than human, and so the names must be correctly given. The lawgiver must be a daimon or a god—in fact, as Socrates does not hesitate to point out, a daimon or a god who contradicts himself,[39] who is no more in accord with himself than is Cratylus, who, in turn, has again sounded the discordant note constituted by his thesis that all

---

[39] See *Euthyphro* 7 b − 8 d, and, in this connection, Goldschmidt, *Essai sur le "Cratyle,"* pp. 174-175.

names are correct. It becomes increasingly evident that there is a fundamental discord in the assignment of communication, or even of teaching, as the sole end proper to naming—that what is called for is a restoration of the other end to which naming was also, from the beginning, assigned by Socrates. For Cratylus to come into accord with himself requires that he come into accord with Socrates.

Cratylus, struggling against Socrates' attack on the name-maker, proposes that one of two kinds of names, either those denoting motion or the others, are not really names. But which kind? asks Socrates (438 c). How is it to be decided which are divine names and which are not names at all? What is the measure by which those that are correct can be distinguished? The discussion has returned to just that question from which the etymologies began, but now it is evident that the question is not to be settled by an appeal to names. As Socrates says, the question cannot be answered on the basis of names other than those in question, for there are no other names to which to appeal. Another measure is required in order to determine which names show the truth of things, in order to determine whether the truth lies with those that show things as in movement or those that show things as at rest. Another measure is required in order to determine which of these two kinds of names distinguish things in their proper being. Socrates has brought the discussion back to the first of those ends originally proposed by him. If we recall that it was precisely the difficulty of reconciling this end with the description of the virtue of naming that was itself reconciled by the first introduction of the lawgiver, we are prepared for Socrates now to reintroduce the question of that virtue capable of guaranteeing the accomplishment of the proper end. Yet, there remains one fundamental difference between Socrates and Cratylus: for Cratylus it is a question of names, while for Socrates it is a question of naming.

Socrates draws out what seems to be the conclusion resulting from the aporia reached regarding the correctness of names: it seems, he observes, that things can be learned without names (438 e). It appears that it must be possible to know things without recourse to names and that the decision regarding which kind of names show the truth of things is, then, to be made by appeal to the things as so known. It seems, in the terms of the first part of the dialogue, that we must have access, independently of names, to things as they are distinguished in their proper being and that it is by the measure yielded by such access that we are able to measure the distinctness instituted by names. If it is granted that things cannot be known through names, then, Socrates asks, what way remains by which to know them? In what is apparently an answer merely cast in the form of a question he says: What other way than that in which they are known through each other if they are akin and through themselves? But when Cratylus agrees without hesitation, Socrates abruptly orders a halt in the name of Zeus (438 e – 439 a). We recall that even the lawgiver, confident of access to things themselves, proved in the comic re-enactment by Socrates not to have access to things independently of names—that he proved to have, not that vision of things that is proper to a god at the divine banquet, but only things as already collected in the unity of names and distinguished in the multiplicity of names.

Socrates recalls the supposition under which the entire discussion since the etymologies has proceeded: that names are images of the things named (439 a). His move is appropriate, for it is precisely on the basis of the analogy between naming and the kind of imitating of things characteristic of the painter that it appears that a knowledge of things independently of names is possible. For the painter what is to be imitated—that is, the colors and shapes of things—are immediately manifest to perception, and his imitative activity is governed by what stands there before him. In turn, if it were a question of determining whether a picture is a good imitation, one would have recourse to the things imitated and by reference to it would then determine the correctness or incorrectness of the imitation made by the painter.

Retaining the analogy Socrates proceeds to the conclusion that the better and clearer way of learning is, not to learn from the image whether it is itself a good image, and then also to learn the truth which it imitates, but rather to learn from the truth both the truth itself and whether the image is properly made. It should be noted that Socrates states this conclusion as a question, though Cratylus, indeed, answers it affirmatively. Also, it should be observed that the conclusion is preceded by a conditional statement: it follows *if* it is the case that things can be learned either through names or through themselves (439 a — b). The conclusion is evident enough in the case of painting—and, hence, seems evident to Cratylus—but it is so precisely because it is, in turn, evident that what the painter imitates is immediately manifest independently of the imitation he makes of it. But is the conclusion evident in the case of names, which, Socrates insisted, involve a radically different type of imitation—an imitation, not of the immediately manifest shape and color of the thing, but rather of the being (οὐσία) of the thing—an imitation of what, according to the criticism leveled against Protagoras, is not immediately manifest but rather is in need of being made manifest? Is it the case, as Socrates says in the conditional statement with which he prefaces the conclusion, that things can be learned through themselves— that, more precisely, that which is imitated by the name can be learned through itself? Clearly this is not the case if what it means to learn them through themselves is understood in accord with the analogy with painting. The being of things cannot be learned through itself in the sense of an attending to and an examining of something already immediately manifest, for it is not immediately manifest. Unlike the shape and color imitated in a picture, the being of things cannot be known through itself but has rather to be made manifest by means of mediation.

Does this entail that what a name imitates is, then, to be learned only through the name in the sense proposed earlier by Cratylus? In that case how are the conflicting reports given by names to be reconciled? Or, is there perhaps some other way in which the being of things could be known through itself, a way not analogous to that exemplified in the case of painting?

Socrates leaves the question open for the moment. How beings (τὰ ὄντα) are to be learned is, he suggests, perhaps too great a question for Cratylus and himself. Yet, he insists that things are to be learned and sought not from names but much rather through themselves than through names (439 b). The question remains: is it possible for man to learn and seek things through themselves, and, if so, in what sense?

(b) Socrates' Dreams (439 b – d)

Socrates proposes to consider another point in order that they might avoid being deceived by the fact that most of the names considered by way of etymologies have tended to show things as in movement. We anticipate that a measuring of these names is now to be undertaken, presumably by some kind of appeal to the things named, though it remains as yet undetermined what form such an appeal could take. Socrates expresses his opinion that those who gave these names really did believe all things to be in motion, but again he refers to the possibility, earlier described in the story of the dizzy name-makers, that perhaps these name-makers were themselves whirled about, that the movement which they ascribed to things was only a movement within themselves—that, in other words, they were unable to distinguish between movement in themselves and movement in things. Socrates adds a reference to the possibility that he and Cratylus are being dragged along by these name-makers as they whirl about (439 c).

Having expressed his aim—namely to avoid being dragged along, deceived, by these names which show all things as being in motion—Socrates asks Cratylus to consider a matter about which, Socrates says, he often dreams (ὀνειρώττειν). He poses that of which he dreams as a question: "Shall we say that there is a beauty itself and a good and so each one of the beings, or not?" (439 c – d).[40]

It is curious that Socrates introduces this question, since the being itself which is asked about in the question was decisively affirmed near the beginning of the dialogue through the criticism made against Protagoras and Euthydemus; this affirmation then provided the basis for Socrates' statement regarding the proper end and the virtue of naming. Presumably, the need again to take up this issue is generated by what has happened since it was originally decided, since the introduction of the lawgiver and the initiation of the series of comedies. What is even more curious, however, is the way in which Socrates now poses this question: it

---

[40] πότερον φῶμέν τι εἶναι αὐτὸ καλὸν καὶ ἀγαθὸν καὶ ἓν ἕκαστον τῶν ὄντων οὕτω, ἢ μή;

is something about which he often dreams. Why does Socrates introduce dreams as the medium by which this comes to him?

In the first place, it should be observed that it is appropriate that he introduces a medium of some kind between himself and being. The difficulty, largely unthematized, which has remained beneath almost the entire discussion in the dialogue and which is the source of its comic character lies in the fact that being itself, in contrast to the things of which Protagoras would make man the measure, is not immediately manifest to man; on the contrary, it can be made manifest only by mediation, only through something else, through a medium in the most general sense. This entire issue has just been posed in the discussion in which it was presumed that things could be known through themselves, the discussion which Socrates halted with an exclamatory appeal to Zeus. In the terms of the *Phaedrus* man does not ascend to the divine banquet but, rather, requires the divine madness by which a medium is granted to him.

But why does Socrates appeal to the medium of dreams? We need to consider several references to dreams in other dialogues in order to gain some basis for interpreting the appeal to dreams in the *Cratylus*.

The first such reference occurs in Book V of the *Republic* in the course of the discussion in which Socrates and Glaucon are engaged in distinguishing between knowledge and opinion. Socrates refers (476 c) to those men who hold that there are beautiful things but do not grant that there is the beautiful itself; he characterizes such men as living in a dream (ὄναρ). He explains by saying that dreaming (ὀνειρώττειν) consists in taking a likeness of something to be not a likeness but rather the thing itself to which it is like—that is, in taking an image to be the original, in failing to recognize it as an image and to distinguish it from the original of which it is an image. What is at first striking about this passage is its contrast with the passage in the *Cratylus* in which Socrates appeals to his dreams. According to the passage in the *Republic* those who dream are precisely the ones who fail to grant just that which in the *Cratylus* is introduced through the medium of dreams; dreaming is, according to the *Republic*, just that state in which one does not make the distinction between image and original, between beautiful things and the beautiful itself. It appears that in the *Cratylus* Socrates is being ironic to the highest degree by introducing by way of dreams just that distinction the absence of which defines the state of dreaming.[41] Yet, Socratic irony is never pointlessly introduced but has always its proper function within the philosophic-dramatic structure of the dialogue. In the case of the present passage of the *Cratylus* the irony brought out by comparison with the *Republic* is required by what has transpired in the course of the discussion, following the long etymological comedy, with Cratylus and with Hermogenes, who is now listening in silence. Specifically, the entire discussion of names as imitations, at the beginning of which Socrates distinguished between the colors and shapes of things (imitated by pictures) and the being of things (imitated by names), has come more and more persistently to obliterate this distinction. The distinction which Socrates is now introducing between image and original was already introduced at the very beginning of the discussion of names as images—most pointedly perhaps by the fact that he referred not only to the being of things but also to the being of colors and shapes—and the course of the discussion has been precisely such as to exhibit Cratylus as one who did not himself make or sustain this distinction. In the terms specified in the *Republic*, Cratylus is pre-eminently one of those who is living in a dream. But there is not only an ironic appropriateness in Socrates' proposing the distinction to Cratylus by an appeal to dreams; there is also another kind of appropriateness, a kind suggested by Socrates' observation in the passage referred to in the *Republic* that, if someone leads that dreamer who fails to grant that there is the beautiful itself to the knowledge of it, he is not able to follow (476 c). If the distinction is, then, to be introduced to one such as Cratylus, there is no alternative but to introduce it in the state of dreaming in which Cratylus is imprisoned. Presumably, this means that what is introduced is not being itself in distinction from images of being, but rather another image of being itself and an image of the distinction between original and

---

[41] The irony of the passage is especially stressed by De Vries, "Notes on Some Passages of the *Cratylus*," p. 297.

image; and within the state of the dream the distinction between the image of the distinction (e.g., between the beautiful itself and beautiful things) and the distinction itself cannot be drawn. What Socrates introduces is an image of the distinction between original and image.

A second important reference to dreams occurs in the *Charmides,* specifically in the course of the discussion of the last definition proposed for moderation (σωφροσύνη). According to this definition moderation is self-knowledge in the sense of a man's knowing what it is that he knows and what it is that he does not know (165 b − 167 a). In this connection Socrates tells of his dream (ὄναρ) in which moderation, as just defined, holds sway over men so that as a result men are no longer deceived by unknown ignorance; rather, each man, knowing what he knows and what he does not know, will refrain from professing to be what he is not and, consequently, all actions will be performed only by those in possession of the relevant art. Shortly after his account of this dream Socrates refers, in connection with the difficulties encountered in trying to define moderation, to the lawgiver (νομοθέτης) who gave the name "moderation," observing that he has failed to discover that to which the lawgiver gave this name (*Charm.* 175 b). The situation in the *Charmides* corresponds to that of the *Cratylus,* for at the present stage of the discussion the explicit question is that of how one is to distinguish between those names which show things truly, which provide knowledge of things, and those names which by not doing so not only leave us ignorant of things but also, since they claim, as Socrates says (*Crat.* 438 d), to show the truth, threaten us with ignorance of our ignorance. In other words, the present question in the *Cratylus* is the question whether with respect to names, with respect to their claims to show the truth of things, knowledge can be found by which to distinguish between what we know and what we do not know. Just as the dream of the *Charmides* is one in which men would have this knowledge, so in the *Cratylus* that which Socrates introduces in the dream would provide a way to such knowledge.

When, in the description of his dream in the *Charmides,* Socrates refers to the fact that, under the conditions dreamed of, all the arts would be properly practiced, the one art which receives the greatest attention is that of prophesy (μαντική) (*Charm.* 173 c). Yet, prophesy is itself most closely connected with dreams (cf. esp. *Laws* 800 a), and both are connected with inspiration granted by the gods, with divine madness (cf. *Phaedr.* 244 b — c; *Letter* VIII 357 d). According to the *Phaedrus* that kind of divine madness represented by prophesy is inspired by none other than that god in whose service Socrates pursues his practice, Apollo (*Phaedr.* 265 b). Socrates, having spoken of knowing things purely through themselves, halts before Zeus; and Apollo, as in the tale of Aristophanes (*Sym.* 190 e — 191 a), provides man with the protective sign: Socrates recalls his dreams.

Socrates' telling of what he has seen in his dreams is a practice of his art as service to Apollo in a way peculiarly appropriate to the context of his discussion with Cratylus. The inspiration, comically described earlier as having been caught from Euthyphro, has proved to be the inspiration sent by Apollo. However, according to the *Cratylus* itself Apollo has not only the function of inspiring μαντική but also has as his function purification (medicine), music, and archery (*Crat.* 405 a; cf. above, Sect. 4 d); and, presumably, since he is the musical god and the god whose name and nature are explicitly pointed to as being in harmony, there is, correspondingly, a harmony among his four functions. On this assumption, Socrates' recalling of his dreams is, then, as service to Apollo, a practice of music: as Apollo, according to the earlier statement, makes all things move together by a kind of harmony among both gods and men, so Socrates in relating his dreams is again—and this time in the most decisive way—inviting Cratylus to institute harmony in himself; at the same time, Socrates is preserving the harmony between men and gods that was threatened just before his abrupt reference to Zeus. Presumably, he is also initiating that purification rite which was said to be necessary when, just prior to the etymologies, Socrates referred to the inspiration received from Euthyphro (396 d — 397 a)—that is, in terms of the dramatic connections between the dialogues, he is instituting the means by which the search for the purifier will be conducted on the following day when, in the *Sophist,* the Stranger from Elea comes with Theodorus to visit Socrates. Finally, there is the fourth function of the god, namely archery, which in the etymological account is connected with the fact that Apollo, as controller of darts (βολῶν), is ever darting (ἀεὶ βάλλων). What is it that Socrates, in his service to Apollo, is throwing forth, casting up?[42]

The final passage which bears on Socrates' appeal to dreams in the *Cratylus* occurs in Book VII of the *Republic*. Here the contrast is being drawn between dialectic and *dianoia* in the sense exemplified in mathematics. Socrates observes with regard to those who practice the latter that they "dream about being" (περὶ τὸ ὄν). But, he continues, "They do not have the capacity to see it in full awakeness so long as they use hypotheses and, leaving them untouched, are unable to give an account (λόγον διδόναι) of them" (533 b). One remains to some degree within the dream-state as long as one proceeds by hypotheses and leaves these hypotheses untouched.

We have seen that in recalling his dreams Socrates introduces in the dream-condition characteristic of Cratylus an image of the genuine distinction between image and original. Yet, in introducing that image he is proceeding not only in a way which is in accord with Cratylus' condition but also in a way designed to draw Cratylus out of the dream-world in which he would remain ever in discord with himself. This is possible only to the degree that he provides him with a measure by which that discord can be shown as such, a measure by which the insufficiency of images can be determined. Such a measure is nothing other than a hypothesis, something laid down as a means by which to exhibit that discord of opposites that reigns in the dream-state (cf. Ch. V, Sect. 5 c, ii), that discord of the sort revealed in those final etymologies which Socrates presented to Cratylus in which the names of the best and the worst were mixed up. Socrates' recalling of what he saw in his dreams, appropriately addressed to Cratylus, does not affirm the dream-condition as it is but, on the contrary, sets up, from out of that condition, hypotheses capable of measuring the images within the dream-world of Cratylus. What Socrates, in service to Apollo, throws forth are hypotheses.

---

[42] It should be observed that the word used here, "βάλλειν," which in active voice means "throw" or "cast" carries in the middle voice the meanings (1) to deliberate, (2) to throw around oneself, and (3) to lay a foundation (as in founding a city).

The hypotheses posed by Socrates are, as in general is the case at the level of *dianoia,* not themselves taken account of in the sense of being distinguished as images from their originals. Nevertheless, although the hypotheses can themselves eventually be made manifest in their character as images, they are images of a higher order than those of the dream-world in that they make use of the latter as images (*Rep.* 510 b, 511 a), which is to say that they make evident the character of the dream-images as images.

Two conclusions follow from the interpretation of Socrates' appeal to dreams. First, it is clear that Socrates' relating to Cratylus of what he has seen in his dreams, as an instituting of hypotheses by which the images of Cratylus' dream-world can be made manifest as images and subjected to measure, is, in fact, nothing less than an attempt to draw Cratylus along on that way that is represented in the *Republic* by the divided line—that way of the movement through images to originals. In terms of the *Cratylus* itself and, in particular, Socrates' expressed intention of taking steps to avoid being deceived by those names which show things as flux, Socrates' effort is directed towards transferring the movement from things to the soul of Cratylus in the way brought to light at the end of the etymological comedy.

Finally, it needs to be observed that in setting up hypotheses Socrates is posing, over against the all too manifest visible images of Cratylus' dream-state, images which are not visible. The hypotheses are not images the manifestness of which is guaranteed by perception. They are, rather, such as must be made manifest, must be somehow invoked; and they are such as must be somehow sustained in their manifestness over against what is always already manifest to perception. What is it that permits their invocation and what is it that sustains these invisible images in their manifestness? What is it that, at the level of *dianoia,* institutes and sustains the distinction between visible and intelligible? The passage in the *Phaedo* to which we have repeatedly referred provides a decisive clue: when Socrates describes that second voyage in search of causes which is initiated by having recourse to *logos,* what he speaks of is the laying down of hypotheses (*Phaedo* 99 d – 102 a). *Logos* has to do with instituting and sustaining the distinction between visible and intelligible.

(c) Being of Which the Search Is (439 d — 440 e)

Socrates indicates what is distinctive about the beings themselves that have been posed: each is always such as it is (ἀεί ἐστιν
οἷόν ἐστιν) (439 d). Beauty itself cannot, as itself, be ugly[43] ; to
pose it as beauty itself is to pose it as being the same as itself—to
pose it, therefore, as one. Socrates draws the contrast between the
being which is always such as it is and the flux for which so many
names were taken as testimony in the course of the etymological
comedy: if things were such as to be in perpetual movement, then
nothing could be correctly said to be anything, for in the very
moment that it is said to be some definite thing it passes away as
such and becomes something different. What is never in the same
state cannot be anything; in contrast to a being itself which always
is the same as itself, the flux would be such that everything would
always be different from itself (439 d — e).

This fundamental contrast needs to be regarded in relation to
the course which the *Cratylus* as a whole has followed. Almost
from the beginning of the dialogue the distinguishing of things in
their proper being was proposed as the fundamental end proper to
naming and names themselves were regarded as being correct to
the degree that they are capable of serving as instruments in a
naming by which this end is accomplished. Subsequently this
proper end was in a peculiar fashion suppressed, and its suppres-
sion was intimately linked to the comic character sustained by the
dialogue since the beginning of the etymologies. Whereas initially
there came to light a curious entanglement of the virtue and the
end of naming such that each appeared to presuppose the other,
i.e., such that it appeared that naming could be done properly
only if it had already been done properly, the introduction of the
lawgiver and of the correlative distinction between naming as using
and naming as positing, i.e., between the use of names for the
purpose of distinguishing beings and the originary making of
names in accord with the proper being of things, served to dis-
entangle the issue and resulted in a shift away from the question
of distinguishing beings by the use of names to the question of

---

[43] See Luce, "The Theory of Ideas in the *Cratylus*," p. 24.

testing the names made by the lawgiver—a testing which, at least in its explicit intention, proceeded as though things were already manifest in their proper being and not, on the contrary, in need of being made manifest by the use of names. As a result of this abstraction, which amounts to a forgetfulness of the condition of man, a self-forgetfulness, the lawgiver proved to be comic and what followed proved to be a comedy. Yet, Socrates' playing of the comedy was such that, in contrast to that which was explicitly to be exhibited, something else got brought to light, i.e., distinguished in its proper being, in the course of the comedy—namely, the very situation underlying the comedy and that very need from which abstraction had been made; beneath the level of what was explicitly undertaken and never, in fact, accomplished in the form proposed, the etymological comedy proved to exemplify just that in which man is called upon to engage by virtue of that need from which the comedy itself abstracts in its explicit intention.

In a sense Socrates has now, through his appeal to his dreams, made explicit the abstraction under which the comedy has proceeded: he has explicitly posed what was implicitly taken for granted in the comedy—that is, he has simply posed things in their proper and distinct being. But he has posed them in a way which not only is more explicit but also is radically different from the way in which they were posed within the comedy. We need to thematize this difference most carefully.

The difference lies, first of all, in the fact that in the posing accomplished by Socrates' appeal to his dreams not only is what is posed made explicit but also the posing itself is made explicit as a posing—that is, it is made explicit that what is posed is something posed and not something that is simply and immediately manifest prior to any posing. The proper being of things is no longer taken for granted as though it were immediately evident—as when in the comedy Socrates re-enacted the originary making of names—but, on the contrary, is taken as something posed, something posed through a speaking, through *logos*. What is posed is now posed *as hypothesis*.

But there is something else distinctive of this posing—something of even greater import. That as which the things are now posed is that as which they must be posed if naming is directed to a distinguishing of things in their proper being. What is that as which they are posed? Socrates states only one determination that determines what they are posed as: each is always such as it is. Each is posed as the same as itself. Each is posed as distinct from that way of appearing in perception which is relative to individual men—i.e., each is posed as having its proper being over against that perceptual appearance which Protagoras would make—but, in the end, cannot make—the measure of being. And each is posed not only as distinct from its appearance to various individual men but also as distinct from every other with which it might in perceptual appearance be mixed up—i.e., each is posed as having its distinctness over against that abolition of all distinctness which Socrates associated with the position of Euthydemus. What is that as which each is posed? Each is posed as itself; the being that is posed is a proper and distinct being. But it is just this posing of the proper and distinct being of things, the distinguishing of them in their proper being, which was, almost from the outset of the dialogue, assigned to naming as its proper end. The posing which Socrates has effected is not just one of several ways in which naming might proceed towards its proper end, but the only way. To distinguish things in their proper being through a naming is to pose as distinct, as the same as self, that which is named by the name; it is to pose what the name "beautiful" names, the beautiful itself, over against the ugly itself and to pose both in their distinctness over against that which is no more named correctly by the name "beautiful" than by the name "ugly."

The force of the contrast which Socrates draws is now evident. If naming is properly an instituting of distinctness, a posing of what is named as being always such as it is, then it follows that, as Socrates says, what is in perpetual flux cannot ever be properly named. If to name is to institute distinctness and if things are such that there is perpetual flux, that is, no distinctness whatsoever, then naming will always be incorrect, will always involve making distinctions where there are, in the order of things, no distinctions.

However, in the course of the etymologies a swarm of names were found which appeared to show the nature of things to be such that there is perpetual movement. The finding was, of course, comic in that what was made manifest through the etymologies was not a flux of all things but rather just other names which turned out to be names having to do with movement, names which themselves, therefore, distinguished something—which, for example, distinguished movement from rest. Now it is evident why the taking of these names as showing things to be in complete flux could not but be comic. A name which would be such that it not only named things that are in perpetual movement—as distinct from naming movement itself—but also showed, made it manifest, that things are in perpetual flux would by this very showing show that it itself is incorrect, that it makes distinctions where there are none, and, consequently, such a showing by means of the name would vitiate itself.

It is significant that, having established the conclusion that that which is in perpetual flux cannot be named, Socrates proceeds to draw virtually the same conclusion with respect to knowledge. Just as what is in perpetual flux cannot be named as any definite thing, so likewise it cannot be known as any definite thing, for in the moment in which it would be so known it becomes something different from that as which it was presumed known. The conclusion is stated still more radically in that reflexive way characteristic of the *Theaetetus:* if all is in flux, then knowledge too would be in flux; it could never be said to be knowledge without in that very moment becoming something different from knowledge. Nor could he who knows be said to be a knower without in that very moment becoming something different from a knower; the would-be knower could not even know himself (439 e — 440 b; cf. *Theaet.* 182 d — 183 b). What cannot be correctly named cannot be known; human knowing is no immediate vision but is bound to the mediation provided by names and *logos.*

Socrates recalls that the beings themselves have only been posed as hypotheses but that as posed they stand in the most radical contrast to the flux: if the beings themselves are, he says hypothetically, it appears that there is no likeness between them and the flux. That they have been posed as hypotheses is further emphasized by the way in which Socrates quite explicitly leaves open the further question: whether things are as so posited or whether the doctrine of the Heracliteans is true is another question. Yet, almost immediately he proceeds, having left open this question, to observe in appropriately comical language that he who says that all things flow condemns both himself and all things (440 b – d). Such a man comdemns things never to be anything. He condemns himself because, if all things were in flux, every name would be incorrect, would institute distinctions where there are none, and, since names are parts of *logos, logos* itself would always incorporate distinctions in contrast to the utter indistinctness of things, with the result that in *logos* we could never say things as they are (cf. 385 b – c). The consequence would be nothing less than the impossibility of true *logos,* and, therefore, the man who says that all things are in flux condemns himself by his very statement which, if it were true, would thereby be false.

Cratylus brings the comedy almost to its conclusion by revealing himself as just such a man, by condemning himself in the way just referred to by Socrates. Pompously informing Socrates that he has given the matter his most serious consideration, he declares that he thinks that the doctrine of Heraclitus is more likely to be true. Cratylus, who has repeatedly declared falsehood to be impossible, accepts as true a statement whose very truth would render it false.

In his last principal statement Socrates adds the observation that no man of sense would put himself under the control of names in the sense of trusting in names and the makers of names to the point of affirming that he knows anything. The negative reference to what was maintained by Cratylus is obvious enough. The question is whether Socrates himself, in stopping short of that knowledge of things through themselves which was proposed, does not himself, in the end, put himself under the control of names. What, after all, are the beings themselves, posed as hypotheses, if not simply what is named in the names "good," "beautiful," etc? Must not the hypotheses themselves, must not that order of distinctness instituted by naming, be itself measured? Is it not just the necessity of such a measuring which the *Cratylus* has brought to light? Man is bound to names and *logos,* and he can ignore this bond only at the cost either of blindness, as the *Phaedo* says, or of becoming utterly comic, as the *Cratylus* shows. Yet, the names and the *logos* to which he is bound do not guarantee what they institute. As we are told in the *Seventh Letter,* where names and *logos* form, respectively, the first and second of those things which are necessary means by which to bring about knowledge, names are not stable and nothing prevents what is called round from being called straight, and conversely, so that in *logos* there is no sure ground; the same duality which plagued the discussion of names as imitation, namely that an imitation of a thing may be an imitation of the sound, shape, or color of the thing or of the being of the thing, is transferred to the name itself which as distinguishing being is itself something sounded (*Letter VII* 342 a – b, 343 a – c; cf. also *Laws* 895 d). Names cannot be guaranteed by an appeal to their origin nor by an appeal to other names nor by an appeal to that immediate vision befitting a god. The only appeal is an appeal to that which names and *logos* serve to let be manifest. In the most profound way the *Cratylus* lets the necessity of the appeal become manifest—in the most profound way because it simultaneously lets this demand stand in all the questionableness which it has for man, in contrast to those ways of dissolving the demand which the dialogue itself has revealed as ultimately comic.

At the end of the dialogue Cratylus moves on while Socrates remains at rest.[44] Socrates encourages Cratylus to proceed on that journey for which, Socrates observes, he has made ready: "Now go into the country as you have made ready to do; and Hermogenes here will go with you a bit" (440 e). Cratylus and Hermogenes are to go into the country; they are to go in search of something like those names of foreign origin capable of cutting off the otherwise limitless regress within *logos;* they are to set off in search of the origin—that is, the original—of those names which in the comedy represented comically that which is capable of limiting *logos;* they are to undertake that search to which Socrates referred when within the etymological comedy he explained the name "name" as meaning being of which the search is. But, of course, what they are searching for will not be found in the country; as Socrates tells Phaedrus, trees and open country will not teach one anything whereas men in the town do (*Phaedr.* 230 d); it is not by appealing to the silence of the country but rather by devoting themselves to

---

[44] See Robert Brumbaugh, "Plato's *Cratylus:* The Order of Etymologies," *Review of Metaphysics,* 11 (1957-58), p. 507.

the *logos* of men in the city that they must, finally, conduct their search: the name "name" means being of which the search is. Yet, it is not inappropriate that Cratylus heads for the country. He has made ready to do so, for in his last pronouncement he has relinquished the very possibility of true *logos*, of a *logos* which would say things as they are; and more than once he has rejected the possibility of false *logos*. One wonders whether on the trip which Hermogenes and Cratylus make into the country Cratylus does not again retreat into that silence into which he had already withdrawn at the beginning of the dialogue.

CHAPTER V

THE UPWARD WAY:

REPUBLIC

To undertake to read the *Republic* carefully and thoughtfully is to place ourselves under the demand for the most severe self-restraint and for the most evocative play. Indeed, the *Republic* is so thoroughly assimilated not only to the tradition of interpretation but also to the philosophical tradition at large that to attempt to gain an originary access to it seems almost like trying to jump over one's own shadow. The images of the *Republic* have become so familiar, so "self-evident," so thoroughly appropriated by unquestioning common sense, that they have long since ceased to provoke us into questioning. The very language of the *Republic* has become so much a part, so much the basis, of the later philosophical tradition that the attempt to let this language resound with its originary ring is fraught with extreme peril. The demand is for a restraint against letting the matters of the *Republic* fall into the molds prepared for them by the tradition and for a playfulness sufficiently lawful and evocative to allow these matters the free space in which to reform themselves. To the extent that we respond to this demand, we can succeed in freeing the *Republic* in such a way that it can again appear in all its strangeness.

One of the ways in which the *Republic* has been assimilated is through traditionally established "translations" of certain words and phrases that are of special significance in the dialogue. The most obvious instance is the translation of the title of the dialogue. The word which is translated "republic," following Cicero's Latin translation, is "πολιτεία." This word does not mean "republic" in the sense of "state" or "nation"; for, in fact, in Greek political life there was nothing corresponding to the modern state

312

or nation; indeed, it would be exceedingly difficult to overstress the radical difference between the modern state and the Greek city.[1] Thus, "πολιτεία" is to be understood in reference to the meaning of "πόλις," from which it is derived. But the two do not mean the same: πολιτεία is not city but rather regime, in the broad sense in which we speak, for example, of the *"ancien régime"* of France; or, alternatively, πολιτεία is constitution, not in the sense of the laws of the city or the document in which the laws are set down, but rather in the sense of the basic make-up of the city, the ordering or arrangement of men with regard to political power.[2]

This sense of the word "πολιτεία," which is relatively straightforward and relatively easy to restore, is, however, only the pre-philosophical sense. What sense "πολιτεία" comes to have in the dialogue so entitled is another, immeasurably more difficult question. At the very least, it can be said that the πόλις whose πολιτεία is at issue in the dialogue is not only the city in the usual sense but also a city of the sort that one might found within himself. In fact, the tension between these two cities is an expression of the central paradox of the *Republic*.

Section 1. Down to Piraeus (Book I)

(a) The *Mythos* of the *Republic* (327 a – b)

The *Republic* begins:

> I went down yesterday to Piraeus with Glaucon, son of Ariston, to pray to the goddess; and, at the same time, I wanted to observe how they would put on the festival, since they were now holding it for the first time (327 a).[3]

We need to attend to this opening with utmost care.

---

[1] One way of insisting on this point is by translating "πόλις" as "city" rather than as "city-state." Cf. Bloom's note in his translation, pp. 439-440.

[2] Cf. Leo Strauss, *Natural Right and History* (Chicago: University of Chicago Press, 1953), pp. 135-137; cf. also *Laws* 832 b – c.

[3] Κατέβην χθὲς εἰς Πειραιᾶ μετὰ Γλαύκωνος τοῦ Ἀρίστωνος, προσευξόμενός τε τῇ θεῷ καὶ ἅμα τὴν ἑορτὴν βουλόμενος θεάσασθαι τίνα τρόπον ποιήσουσιν, ἅτε νῦν πρῶτον ἄγοντες.

The speaker is Socrates. Strictly speaking, Socrates is the only speaker in the *Republic*. The *Republic* is a narrated rather than a performed dialogue. It is narrated by Socrates—which is to say that it does not present the event itself but rather Socrates' recounting of the event. The entire *Republic* has the form of a Socratic recollection.

However, the recollection is not very far removed in time from the original. Almost at the beginning of the opening sentence Socrates informs us that the event which he is about to recount happened "yesterday." So, the conversation is being recounted on the day after it took place. Yet, this conversation turns out to be of such length that, starting late on the previous day, it is likely that it would have extended throughout the night and into the next day, the day on which Socrates is recounting it. Thus, when Socrates begins to recount the event, it cannot have been more than a few hours since the original conversation ended—perhaps just time enough for Socrates to make the walk from Piraeus back to Athens. This proximity in time between Socrates' recounting how he went down to Piraeus *and* the end of the actual conversation held there suggests that there may be an important connection between the beginning and the end of the *Republic,* that is, between Socrates' going down to Piraeus and his telling the myth of Er.

The event of which Socrates is to tell began with his going down "to Piraeus" (εἰς Πειραιᾶ). The reference is, of course, to the harbor of Athens, about six miles from the city and connected to it by the long walls. We note that in going to Piraeus Socrates, in one sense, leaves the city yet, in another sense, does not leave the city, since he remains most likely within the walls. Hence, from the very beginning there is an enactment of the peculiarly ambivalent relation of the philosopher to the city, an enactment of what is spoken of in the *Apology* (cf. Ch. I, Sect. 4). We note also the sense of the name "Piraeus," which, according to certain ancient

---

There is an external reason for suspecting that this opening sentence is of very special significance: Dionysius of Halicarnassus, who reports that Plato was reputed to take care to "comb and curl" his dialogues, tells also that there was found after Plato's death a tablet containing subtle variations of the first line of the *Republic.* Adam, *The Republic of Plato,* Vol. I, p. 1.

writers, was related to the belief that the Piraeus was once an island separated from Athens by a kind of river; thus, the name is said to have been derived from "περαιά," which (derived, in turn, from "πέρας") means literally "beyond-land."[4] Socrates is saying something like: I went down to the land beyond the river.

Socrates says that he made his descent to Piraeus because there was a new "festival" being held in honor of a "goddess." Near the end of Book I (354 a) we learn that the goddess is Bendis. This Thracian goddess, whose worship was introduced to Athens during the time of Pericles, is closely related to or even identical with one of two goddesses more familiar to the Athenians: Persephone, the consort of the god of the underworld; and Hecate, who tends to merge with Artemis, especially with that form of the latter in which she is a guardian goddess in the underworld and of the world above when it is completely dark (goddess of the dark of the moon).[5] Bendis, whose festival, the Bendideia, is being celebrated is a goddess of the underworld, of Hades.

The first person with whom Socrates converses at length at that meeting in Piraeus which he is about to recount is a man named Cephalus, who, by Socrates' account, is "very old" (328 c). For the moment we need to note just one point from the conversation with Cephalus: Socrates remarks to him that he is "at just the time of life the poets call 'the threshold of old age' " (328 e). What do the poets, for example, Homer, mean when they speak of such a threshold? What they mean is not a threshold leading *to* old age but rather one leading *from* it.[6] The threshold is the one by which Cephalus will leave life and enter Hades.

Of all that Socrates says in the opening of the *Republic*, what is most telling is the very first word of the dialogue. Socrates says: "I

---

[4] Pauly-Wissowa, *Realencyclopädie der classischen Altertumswissenschaft*, Vol. 19, Pt. 1, p. 78. See Eva Brann's essay "The Music of the *Republic*," *Agon*, I (1967), which indicates the significance which this and several other features have for the dramatic character of Book I and, to some extent, of the entire *Republic*. In this specific connection Brann points out that it is stylistically unusual to speak (as Socrates does) of going "to Piraeus" rather than "to *the* Piraeus."

[5] Pauly-Wissowa, *Realencyclopädie*, Vol. 3, pp. 269-271; *Dictionary of Greek and Roman Biography and Mythology*, ed. William Smith, Vol. I, p. 482; *The Oxford Classical Dictionary*, pp. 490-491.

[6] See especially *Iliad*, XXII. 60; XXIV. 487; *Odyssey*, XV. 246. Cf. Adam's note, Vol. I, p. 5.

went down" (κατέβην). This word says most openly what we need to hear in the first sentence of the *Republic;* it does so especially if we take note of the statement in the *Odyssey* where Odysseus tells Penelope of the day when, in his words, "I went down [κατέβην] to Hades to inquire about the return of myself and my friends."[7] The *Republic* begins with Socrates going down to the festival of a goddess of Hades and there meeting one who is on the threshold of Hades. It begins with Socrates' descent to the region beyond the river—beyond the river Lethe or another of those rivers that must be crossed in order to reach Hades. The *Republic* begins with *Socrates' descent into Hades.*

Once this *mythos* that is being enacted from the very beginning of Book I is brought into view, the connection between the beginning and the end of the *Republic* comes to light. The *Republic* ends with the myth of Er, which relates how Er was allowed to descend into Hades, to journey through the underworld, and to return to the world above. Thus, the *mythos* which Socrates begins to *enact* in what is recounted in the first sentence of the *Republic* is the same *mythos* that is *told* at the end of the dialogue after the enactment has been completed.

The *mythos* initiated by Socrates' descent to Hades is elaborated by several things that occur in the course of Book I. For example, just as each person who enters the underworld is said to be brought before the three judges, Rhadamanthus, Minos, Aeacus (cf. *Gorg.* 523 e), so Socrates encounters in Hades the three "judges," Cephalus, Polemarchus, and Thrasymachus. But here already there is something curious about Socrates' descent to Hades, something which makes it highly unorthodox: as in the *Apology* Socrates ends up judging his would-be judges (cf. Ch. I, Sect. 1 a). He passes judgment on the judges' opinions about the one thing which a judge should know above all others, namely, justice.

There is another similar reversal. According to the poets, Cerberus, a wild, multi-headed, dragon-tailed dog, stood guard before

---

[7] *Odyssey,* XXIII. 252-253. The theme of descent into Hades and the significance of this theme within the *Republic* have been pointed to by Eric Voegelin (*Order and History,* Vol. III: *Plato and Aristotle* [Baton Rouge: Louisiana State University Press, 1957], pp. 53-54) and especially by Brann ("The Music of the *Republic,*" pp. 2-7).

the gates of Hades, permitting all souls to enter but none to leave.[8] In this connection we note that later in Book I, when Thrasymachus first begins to speak, Socrates says: "I think that if I had not seen him before he saw me, I would have been speechless" (336 d); the reference is to the belief, popular in antiquity, that if a wolf sees a man first the man is struck dumb,[9] and the implication is thus that Thrasymachus is a wolf, which is a kind of wild dog (see also 336 b). We may say, then, that Thrasymachus also plays the role of Cerberus in the Socratic descent into Hades with which the *Republic* begins. Yet, even the invincible, flesh-eating hound of Hades proves no match for the *logoi* of Socrates, and by the end of Book I Socrates has tamed Thrasymachus. Socrates says to him: "you have grown gentle and left off being hard on me" (354 a). In terms of his role as Cerberus, this means that he no longer blocks the way out of the realm of shadows and darkness.

Let us return to the opening. Socrates says that he went down to Piraeus "to pray to the goddess" *and* because he "wanted to observe how they would put on the festival." We note that in Socrates' attendance at the Bendideia there is operative a mixture of piety and impiety not unlike that which, in the original provocation of Socrates' practice, informed his response to the pronouncement given by Apollo through the oracle (cf. Ch. I, Sect. 3 b). Indeed, on the one hand, Socrates addresses himself to the goddess in the way commonly taken to befit a goddess; yet, on the other hand, especially in view of the novelty of the worship of this goddess (they were holding the festival "for the first time"), Socrates also looks on, maintaining the distance and the restraint of an observer, a questioner, a judge. And, in fact, the second sentence in Socrates' recounting of what happened at the Piraeus is a summing up of Socrates' judgment of what he saw at the festival:

> Now, in my opinion, the procession of the native inhabitants was fine [καλός]; but the one the Thracians conducted was no less fitting a show (327 a).

---

[8] Cf. *Iliad,* VIII. 367; Hesiod, *Theogony,* 311; Euripides, *Heracles,* 611.

[9] Cf. Bloom's note, p. 444; and Adam's note, Vol. I, p. 24.

What Socrates singles out to recount is that the performances of the natives and of the Thracians were *equally* fine. In other words, he calls our attention to a peculiar lack of distinctions: in terms of their showings at the festival there was no difference between men who, from a political point of view, are different in the most radical and consequential way. Such leveling of the distinction between native and foreigner is reflected also in the character of the Piraeus, which as center of foreign trade was a place where Athenians were mixed up with all sorts of foreigners in a kind of equal status wrought by commercial affairs and interests. The Piraeus was also linked to a kind of mixing of foreign things, that is, a leveling of distinctions, in a more strictly political sense. It was to become a center for the activities of the champions of equality, the democratic party and, specifically, a center of resistence against the "Thirty Tyrants" who ruled Athens after the Peloponnesian War, a resistance in which, in fact, the family of Cephalus was to be deeply involved.[10] So, what is most immediately noteworthy about the spectacle which Socrates beholds when he goes down to Piraeus-Hades is the leveling of distinctions, the mixing-up of things which are opposed to one another.[11]

In the third sentence of the dialogue Socrates concludes his account of what he did at the festival of Bendis:

> After we had prayed and looked on, we went off toward town (327 b).

---

[10] Cf. Bloom's note, p. 440.

[11] In another respect it can be said (cf. Bloom's "Interpretive Essay," p. 311) that Socrates' judgment that the Athenian procession was no better than that of the Thracians indicates that in his judgement Socrates stands above the city and its distinction between native and foreigner. This respect corresponds to the fact that in going down to Piraeus Socrates leaves the city. But matters are not that straightforward, as we have already noted in reference to the fact that in going to the Piraeus one normally would stay inside the walls and so in a sense would not leave the city. Although it is too soon to attempt to clarify the complex mirror-play involving the Piraeus and the city itself, it can be said that, for the most part, the Piraeus and the entire scene of Book I represents that situation of man in the city *from which* one must ascend in order to reach the level at which one's opinions would transcend the distinction so basic to the city. Certainly there is a sense in which Socrates, the teacher engaged in leading others up, is already at this level; but to suppose that he is simply and unalterably at this level, to suppose that he is immune from having to make the ascent in which he leads others, is to risk minimizing, if not entirely misconstruing, what is required for genuine teaching.

So, after what is recounted in the first two sentences, Socrates and his companion begin to enact what in terms of the *mythos* amounts to an ascent out of Hades. This ascent is the same ascent that Socrates tells of at the end of the *Republic* when he exhorts his companion to "keep to the upward way" (621 c). Except for the first two sentences, which tell of Socrates' descent into Hades and of his judgment of what he beheld there, and the concluding myth, which tells of the descent to and ascent from Hades, the entire *Republic* is dedicated to telling of the enactment of this ascent.

In his descent and his ascent Socrates is accompanied by a young man named Glaucon. This name (Γλαύκων) means "gleaming" (γλαυκός) in the sense of "gleaming eyes." The name is thus related to "γλαύξ" ("owl"), so called because of its gleaming eyes, and hence is associated with Athena, an epithet for whom was "γλαυκ-ῶπις" ("with gleaming eyes"). Recalling the owl of Athena, we wonder whether Glaucon might prove to be capable of political vision amidst the gathering twilight, the decline and corruption of Athens. In the first sentence of the dialogue Socrates identifies Glaucon as the son of Ariston. Granting the factual historical reference,[12] we note that his literal words are: "Γλαύκωνος τοῦ 'Αρίστωνος"—which comes very near saying: "Glaucon of the best." The best is the highest good, and we are led to suspect from the outset that there is some special kinship between Glaucon and the highest good. We wonder whether this is perhaps why he is the one who accompanies Socrates both in the descent and in the ascent.

With regard to the *mythos* enacted, almost the entire *Republic* consists of an ascent out of Hades. Its character as an ascent is the single most important determinant of the over-all structure of the dialogue. Clearly the highest point of the ascent is reached in the middle Books (V-VII), in which Socrates speaks of the philosopher, of the good, of being and truth. In these Books there is such an abundance of light that one can hardly, if at all, bear to look

---

[12] Ariston was the father not only of Glaucon but also of Adeimantus and of Plato himself.

directly at its source; and this region of light stands in the most marked contrast to the realm of the goddess Bendis (goddess of the dark of the moon, of the black nights when the moon is hidden), which is, at best, lit up by the flickering light of "a torch race on horseback" (328 a). Also, it is in these Books, where the enactment of the ascent is completed, that the ascent gets explicitly taken up as a question. These Books, converging on Socrates' introduction of the cave-image, form the center of the dialogue. This center is framed on each side by discussions of the city: prior to the central Books there is a building of cities in *logos,* leading up to what is intended to be a perfectly just city; after the central Books, there is a descent through a series of progressively more corrupt cities, that is, a destruction of cities in *logos.* Coordinated with the building and destroying of cities, there are accounts of the perfection of the soul (before the center) and of the corruption of the soul (after the center). Finally, there is, at one extreme, the enactment of the descent to and journey through Hades in Book I and, at the other extreme, the telling of the myth of Er's descent to and journey through Hades.

These indications suffice for providing a first sketch of the structure of the *Republic:*

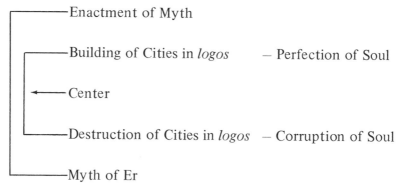

The theme of ascent and descent, which generates the basic symmetry of this structure, encompasses the principal matters at issue in the *Republic.* As a result, our interpretation is, in a sense, nothing but an extended elaboration of this sketch, carried out through an attempt to read the *Republic* thoughtfully and carefully.

(b) The Initial Confrontation (327 b − 328 b)

Socrates and Glaucon have set out towards town. But, in the terms of the *mythos,* the ascent out of Hades proves difficult almost from the beginning. Polemarchus, catching sight of Socrates and Glaucon from some distance behind, sends his slave ahead with orders that Socrates and Glaucon are to stop and wait for him. Socrates and Glaucon comply, and Polemarchus, accompanied by several others (among whom is Adeimantus, Glaucon's brother), soon catches up with them. There is a short exchange between the two parties, after which Socrates and Glaucon agree to accompany the other party to Polemarchus' house.

In this initial confrontation there are several things that we need to observe. First of all, it needs to be seen that the confrontation is a confrontation between strength and philosophy. Polemarchus says to Socrates and Glaucon: "Either prove stronger than these men or stay here." In terms of the *mythos* the demand is placed on Socrates and Glaucon that they win their release from Hades. Socrates suggests how they will do this, how they will "prove stronger," namely, by exercising persuasion, by persuading and winning over the shades of Hades, by encountering the shadowy opinions that are met there. This encounter comprises the remainder of Book I.

Secondly, it needs to be observed how this episode playfully anticipates what will eventually emerge as the central, driving tension of the *Republic.* This tension is concretely posed at the very outset of the little episode: it is the tension between philosophy (Socrates) and political power (Polemarchus, whose name means "war-lord"). This tension is accentuated by the fact that Socrates does not surrender at all to the threat of force. In fact, it is Glaucon who tends to yield to the power of the other party. When the slave stops them, it is Glaucon, not Socrates, who says that they will wait. Again, it is Glaucon, not Socrates, who responds to Polemarchus' insistence that they can win their release in no other way than by force: when Polemarchus responds to the suggestion that persuasion might serve for winning release by asking whether he could possibly be persuaded as long as he refused to listen, Glaucon answers, "There's no way." And, it is

Glaucon, not Socrates, who capitulates and says: "It seems we must stay." By contrast, Socrates openly proposes persuasion as an alternative to strength. And, though Polemarchus' immediate response is to reject this alternative ("we won't listen"), in fact, the whole character of the exchange undergoes a sudden change at just the point where Socrates makes his proposal; indeed, the exchange becomes something much more like a matter of persuasion, as indicated by the way in which Adeimantus and then Polemarchus himself begin to describe the attractions for which Socrates and Glaucon ought to stay on at the Piraeus. It is only then that Socrates agrees to stay, that is, only when persuasion begins to replace force. At this point Socrates says: "Well, if it is so resolved [δοκεῖ], that's how we must act"—and we are to hear in this saying an imitation of the way in which the outcome of voting was proclaimed in the assembly. Socrates agrees to stay only when the compulsion becomes political rather than a matter of sheer force.[13] The reference which Socrates' phrase has to the outcome of a vote indicates, along with the ascendancy of persuasion over force, that the outcome of this episode has been the forming of a little community, of a miniature city, now ratified by the vote. And, just as later the question pursued in *logos* will be: Who is to rule the city?—so in Book I this same question will be enacted. More specifically, Socrates will prove to be the rightful ruler of the newly formed city by defeating all other contenders to the rule. In other words, Socrates will enact the thesis that the proper ruler is the philosopher by actually capturing rule over this miniature city in Hades.

Once the dealings between the two parties shift away from force and towards persuasion, Adeimantus and Polemarchus begin to enumerate the attractions on account of which Socrates and Glaucon ought to remain at the Piraeus: there is to be a torch race on horseback; there will be dinner at Polemarchus' house; and after dinner they can go to the all-night festival and be together with many of the young men. Now, what we need to note is that, in fact, *they do none of these things;* on the contrary, they end up just sitting in the house of Polemarchus talking about justice far

---

[13] Cf. Bloom's note, p. 441; also his "Interpretive Essay," p. 312.

into the night. This means, then, that the conversation which comprises the entire *Republic* from this point on takes the place of sight-seeing, of a banquet, and of a probably somewhat erotic social gathering. The conversation takes the place of—which is to say it excludes—the satisfaction of certain bodily and erotic desires.

(c) Cephalus (328 b – 331 d)

The new city is enlarged by being moved to Polemarchus' house, where there are several relatives and guests present. Cephalus, the father of Polemarchus, is there, and Socrates' first conversation in the *Republic* is with him. This conversation is important, for it sets the course for much of what is to come; it is especially significant as the speech in which the problem of justice first (and almost casually) arises. What does the character Cephalus portray? What role does he play in the enactment of the question of the ruler? In general, Cephalus represents the authority of old age; he is the father of at least three of the men present in the house (Polemarchus, Lysias, and Euthydemus), and his is the "natural" authority based on reverence for the aged.[14] In this same connection, he represents the authority of tradition. This is evident in the course of his remarks by the numerous references he makes to the poets; his bearing with regard to the poets is to be contrasted with what happens in the subsequent conversation with Polemarchus where the poet Simonides, cited by Polemarchus in defense of his father, turns out to be in need of being himself defended (335 e). At the beginning of the episode involving him, Cephalus has just been "crowned with a wreath," since he has just finished performing a sacrifice. Cephalus is the first contender to the position of ruler over the new city; but the very fact that it is a *new* city, based not on ancestral authority but on persuasion, suggests that Cephalus is not likely to prove a very successful contender.

The conversation between Socrates and Cephalus falls into three parts, the first having to do with old age, the second with wealth, and the third with justice. We need to consider each part with a

---

[14] Cf. Strauss, *City and Man,* p. 65.

special view to its way of setting out the course which the *Republic* will take.

Cephalus begins the conversation. He expresses to Socrates his wish that Socrates would come to the Piraeus more often and talk with him. He continues: "I want you to know that as the other pleasures, those connected with the body, wither away in me, the desires and pleasures that have to do with speeches [περὶ τοὺς λόγους] grow the more." Socrates inquires about Cephalus' experience of old age: "Is it a hard time of life?" Cephalus' answer centers on the question of bodily and especially erotic pleasures. He reports that many who are of the same age as he complain because they can no longer enjoy such pleasures but that he is happy to be rid of such things. He insists that what is important is to be balanced (κόσμιος) and good-tempered (εὔκολος) and that in this case old age is only moderately troublesome (328 c – 329 d).

The name "Cephalus" means "head," and, indeed, we notice immediately that Cephalus is little more than a head without a body.[15] As we observed previously, he is, according to Socrates' description, at "the threshold of old age," that is, death; he will soon leave his body behind entirely. This bears importantly on what Cephalus says: throughout this first part of the conversation he speaks almost exclusively about one kind of thing, bodily and especially erotic desires. He says that "old age brings great peace and freedom from such things," that when such things disappear we are "rid of very many mad monsters"; and he cites Sophocles to the effect that sex is "a sort of frenzied and savage master." Thus, the first part of the first conversation of the *Republic* is an *open attack* on *eros* and the body and a celebration of the freedom from such desires which is brought by old age. We wonder whether this is why Socrates says: "Then I was full of wonder at what he said."

The second part of the conversation begins with Socrates' suggestion (posed as the opinion of the many) that the only reason Cephalus bears old age so well is because he possesses great "substance." The word which Socrates uses here (οὐσία) means

---

[15] Brann observes in this connection that Socrates slyly points out that Cephalus is sitting on a head rest, a προσκεφαλαίον ("Music of the *Republic*,'. p 3).

"property" or "wealth," but it also means "being"; presumably, we are meant to notice the double sense and to reflect that Cephalus, though a man of "substance" in the first sense, is not at all such in the other sense but perhaps the most fleeting of the shadows to be encountered by Socrates in Hades. Cephalus agrees to some extent that wealth is a necessary condition for bearing old age well, but he insists that it is not sufficient: one must also be a decent sort of man, balanced and good-tempered. Socrates inquires about Cephalus' wealth, whether he inherited it or made it himself. Cephalus answers that as a money-maker he is a mean ($\mu\acute{\epsilon}\sigma\sigma\varsigma$) between his grandfather, who increased the wealth many times over, and his father, who used up a considerable part of it. Socrates responds:

> The reason I asked, you see, is that to me you didn't seem overly fond of money. For the most part, those who do not make money themselves are that way. Those who do make it are twice as attached to it as the others. For just as poets are fond of their poems and fathers of their children, so money-makers too are serious about money—as their own product [$\ddot{\epsilon}\rho\gamma\sigma\nu$] (330 b – c).

For Cephalus balance is what is most important for bearing old age. But what kind of balance is important for this purpose? What kind of balance does Cephalus regard as important? Cephalus' answer to Socrates' inquiry about his wealth serves to indicate what kind of balance Cephalus considers important: balance with respect to money-making, that is, the kind of balance which consists in neither greatly increasing nor diminishing the family wealth. But, in turn, Socrates' further response, in which he comments on the fact that Cephalus doesn't seem overly fond of money, serves to indicate something which Cephalus leaves unsaid about his peculiar kind of balance. The balanced stance of Cephalus is, Socrates says, unlike the relation of poets to their poetry, of fathers to their children, of any man to something which he really brings forth. What kind of bringing-forth, what kind of production, is Socrates referring to by way of contrast to the stance of Cephalus? The two examples he uses, poets and fathers, indicate quite clearly that the reference is to that kind of bringing-forth which is identical with or closely akin to *eros* (cf. *Phaedr.* 245 a, 265 b, together with Ch. III, Sect. 2 c, i; *Sym.* 205 b – d, 206 e). Thus, Cephalus' distinctive balance is, in terms of Socrates' remark, an *unerotic balance;* Cephalus' balanced stance is a stance which contrasts utterly with that of the erotic man; it is perhaps simply a stance derived from Cephalus' lack of *eros.* Yet, in another sense, Cephalus' unerotic balance (which presupposes possession of wealth) is based on *eros;* for Cephalus is able to maintain his peculiar balance only on the basis of the *eros* of his money-making ancestors, who, Socrates in effect maintains, were no less erotic than are poets and fathers. However it may be with his origins, Cephalus is himself the most unerotic character in the *Republic.* The most unerotic character is the first to speak at any length in the *Republic,* and it is through him that the ostensibly central problem of the entire dialogue, the problem of justice, is introduced.

The introduction of this problem constitutes the third, and final, part of the conversation between Socrates and Cephalus. The order of introduction is appropriate: the theme of justice is reached only by way of a question about the greatest good. Socrates inquires what the greatest good ($\mu \acute{\epsilon} \gamma \iota \sigma \tau o \nu \ldots \dot{\alpha} \gamma \alpha \theta \acute{o} \nu$) is that Cephalus has received from his wealth. Cephalus answers by referring, not explicitly to justice, but to injustice. He says:

> When a man comes face to face with the realization that he will be making an end, fear and care enter him for things to which he gave no thought before. The *mythoi* told about what is in Hades—that the one who has done unjust deeds [$\dot{\alpha} \delta \iota \kappa \acute{\eta} \sigma \alpha \nu \tau \alpha$] here must pay the penalty there—at which he laughed up to then, now make his soul twist and turn because he fears they might be true (330 d – e).

This passage marks a very decisive point in the dialogue. Not only is it the first place in the *Republic* where a form of the word "justice" occurs (significantly, it occurs first in its privative form) but also it marks the first occurrence in the *Republic* of the words "*mythos*" and "Hades." The question of justice (in the form of the question of injustice) is, at the point of its first occurrence in the dialogue, linked to the underlying *mythos* having to do with Hades.

The conversation continues. Cephalus indicates that he sees the chief advantage of his wealth to lie in the fact that it relieves him from having to worry about suffering for unjust deeds: it allows him to avoid having to cheat and lie. His wealth allows him the luxury of being honest and paying his debts to men and gods. As Socrates then makes explicit, this is what justice (δικαιοσύνη) means to Cephalus: Telling the truth and giving back what one has taken from another. But Socrates makes this opinion explicit only to pose to it a counter-example which abruptly refutes it: if a man takes weapons from a friend when the latter is of sound mind and the friend then demands them back after he has gone mad, it would not be just to give them back to him. This refutation brings Cephalus' role in the dialogue to an end (331 b – d).

The immediate point of Socrates' counter-example is that Cephalus regards justice almost exclusively in terms of the benefits it will bring him after death, in terms of its rewards. In other words, justice for Cephalus is simply a matter of self-interest.[16] It has no bearing on the good of others, for example, on that of the friend gone mad; the greatest good turns out for Cephalus to be simply a good for himself. The case of the friend in Socrates' example also suggests that there is something else, besides the good of others, to which men like Cephalus are oblivious, namely, *madness.* And, at the very least, this serves to suggest that Cephalus is oblivious to philosophy—that, despite what he has said about his increased desire for *logoi,* the long conversation that is now just commencing would prove inaccessible to him should he stay on to hear it.

Indeed, at the concrete level, Cephalus proves immediately that he is more or less oblivious to philosophy, that is, he proves himself oblivious to Socrates' refutation of his opinion about justice. He agrees with Socrates' counter-example: "What you say is right"—but then he leaves to continue his routine practice of seeking profits after death, just as he has sought (though with an

---

[16] Cf. Bloom's "Interpretive Essay," p. 314.

unerotic balance) profits in this life. Cephalus goes to attend to the sacrifices—that is, he goes right on acting out the opinion about justice that Socrates has just refuted. In order to do so, however, he has to withdraw from the conversation; Polemarchus interrupts in his defense, and he is only too willing to hand the *logos* over to his heir. Thus, in terms of the *mythos*, Socrates has easily defeated and driven away the first contender to the rule over Hades. We note even that this contender bears some resemblance to the one who traditionally (i.e., according to the poets) ruled over the realm of shades: just as Pluto ($\pi\lambda o \hat{\upsilon} \tau \omega \nu$), owner of all the precious metals in the earth, was a god of wealth ($\pi\lambda o \hat{\upsilon} \tau o \varsigma$),[17] so Cephalus is a man of "substance." To this extent we may say that Socrates has dethroned Pluto, the traditional ruler of the dead; more precisely, he has dethroned a pale, nearly dead shadow of the fierce and hated god of the underworld, a mere shade of the king of the shades, an already virtually dethroned replica of the lord of the dead. We note that, by contrast, the name "Socrates" means "ruler of life."

Socrates' drawing out of Cephalus' opinion about justice and his subsequent refutation of it constitute the first step of a kind of "collection of opinions" that will continue to the end of Book I. Such collecting involves, in general, rendering explicit and examining the opinions which otherwise remain with all their directive force just beneath the surface. Examining them takes especially the form of letting them collide with one another in such a way as to bring their respective inadequacies, or at least their points of conflict, into view. The most striking result of such discipline is the arrival at a realization of one's own ignorance (cf. *Meno,* esp. 81 a − b, together with Ch. II, Sect. 2 d). But this is not the only result: the collision of opinions also can serve to purify them, to set free whatever limited grasp of truth is present in them. We can see this happening in Socrates' refutation of Cephalus. In effect, he refutes Cephalus' opinion that justice consists in paying back what is owed by appealing to another opinion about justice which

---

[17] Cf. W. K. C. Guthrie, *The Greeks and Their Gods* (Boston: Beacon Press, 1955), p. 284.

Cephalus also tacitly accepts, namely, that justice is good for the one to whom it is done.[18] The problem is that there can be a conflict between these two opinions, and what Socrates, in effect, does is let them collide. Specifically, these two opinions about justice conflict if referred to any case in which a man is unable to make good use of what is owed him, of what is his own. In such cases, if justice (as giving each his own) is to prove good to those to whom it is done, it will be necessary to re-determine precisely what is owed, what is a man's own. Thus there is broached the whole vast question of establishing an identity between what is good and what one has as one's own—hence, also the question of finding and of establishing in power the wise ruler that would be required in order to maintain such an identity—as well as the question as to what seemingly radical measure (e.g., abolition of private property for certain men) might be required in order to secure this identity. We begin to see how the elements of the subsequent discussion of the city are inconspicuously present in the collision of Cephalus' two opinions about justice.

(d) Polemarchus (331 d — 336 a)

The traditional ruler has withdrawn and is now replaced by his heir, Polemarchus. We recall how in the initial confrontation Polemarchus has already given a playful display of his power, and, on this basis, we expect that Polemarchus, the "war-lord," will prove to be a more serious contender for the rule being contested.

Polemarchus begins his defence of his inheritance by quoting the poet Simonides according to whom justice means "to give to each what is owed." We notice that, in fact, Polemarchus is taking over only half of Cephalus' definition; the connection between justice and telling the truth is dropped, and the way is thereby prepared for entertaining the possibility of there being such a thing as a just lie. But even that half of the property of Cephalus which Polemarchus keeps turns out to be understood quite differ-

---

[18] Cf. Strauss, *City and Man*, p. 69.

ently: he understands "what is owed" not as things but as good and evil. Hence, his definition is: "Justice is doing good to friends and harm to enemies" (332 d). We note that by the shift which he has introduced into Cephalus' opinion Polemarchus has almost come around to adopting that tacit opinion about justice which caused Cephalus his difficulty—the opinion, on which Socrates drew for his refutation, that justice is good for the one to whom it is done; but he has not quite come around to this, for, according to his definition, it is only to friends that justice does good.

Socrates proceeds to question the definition posed by Polemarchus, to question it, specifically, on the basis of an assumed analogy between justice and art ($\tau\acute{\epsilon}\chi\nu\eta$). Just as the pilot is the one who is most able to do good to friends and harm to enemies with respect to the danger of the sea, so, Socrates asks, with respect to what work is the just man the one who is most able to do good to friends and harm to enemies? Polemarchus answers that it is in making war that the just man has this capacity. Socrates does not disagree with him but, rather, goes on to pose another question: How is the just man useful to men who are not at war? What is the use of justice in peacetime? By a process of elimination Polemarchus is eventually forced to admit that justice is useful only when one wants to deposit one's money for safe-keeping; as Socrates puts it, in the form of a question, "Is it when money is useless that justice is useful for it?" Socrates mentions other examples of things for which also justice would be useful only when the things concerned were useless, and, finally, he concludes: "Then justice, my friend, won't be anything very serious, if it is useful for useless things." Having thus allowed us this glimpse of the extent to which Polemarchus really is heir of the commercial opinions of Cephalus, Socrates then proceeds to extend the definition to its final, absurd consequence: The just man has turned out to be an expert at keeping things; but one who is expert at keeping things will also make an expert thief; and, therefore, the just man turns out to be a kind of thief (332 d — 334 b).

Socrates' criticism of the definition thus focuses almost exclusively on the use of justice in peace rather than in war. Yet, in his very first answer regarding the use of justice Polemarchus refers to war, almost as though it were obvious that war is the proper context within which to consider the question of justice. In fact, as we noted, Socrates does not directly confront that answer but, instead, simply shifts the discussion to the use of justice in peace. He refrains from directly confronting Polemarchus' answer in terms of war because that answer points back to an opinion so deep-rooted that it could not really be confronted at the level of the present collecting of opinions. The opinion brought into view through Polemarchus' answer is the traditional opinion that human excellence is very closely associated with courage. It is the opinion, purveyed especially by the poets, according to which the hero is identified as the courageous warrior (Achilles). In the *Apology* Socrates openly calls this identification into question and challenges the traditional hero (cf. 28 b – 29 a, 41 c, together with Ch. I., Sect. 4). Correspondingly, in the *Republic* the warrior will be explicitly subordinated to the philosopher and the privileged position traditionally given to courage among the virtues revoked.[19]

In fact, in the further discussion that now commences Socrates proceeds to link justice, not to courage, but to knowledge. To Polemarchus' reassertion of his opinion that justice consists in helping friends and harming enemies, Socrates poses the question as to whether by friends Polemarchus means those who seem to be good or those who are. Polemarchus answers that a man's friends are those who seem good to him, those whom he believes to be good. This answer allows Socrates then to counter with the observation that men make mistakes and that in such cases the good would turn out to be enemies and the bad to be friends; thus,

---

[19] The latter theme is even more prominent in Book I of the *Laws*. Very shortly after the beginning of the dialogue Clinias introduces his thesis that laws are framed with a view to what is needed for war (625 d – e); the Athenian then counterposes and develops his thesis that the aim of legislation does not have to do with war but is, rather, to create peace among men under law and an accord of each man with himself (626 e – 628 e). Then the Athenian goes on to maintain, in explicit opposition to those poets who sing the praises of courage in war, that good legislation aims at virtue in its entirety and that courage is to be numbered fourth among the four virtues, behind *phronesis*, moderation, and justice (630 b – d, 631 c – d).

since it is, by Polemarchus' definition, just to harm enemies, it would be just in such cases to harm men who have done nothing unjust. At this point Polemarchus, who has already slightly disparaged the *logos* (334 a) and who, it will be recalled, rejected in word if not in deed Socrates' proposal (in the initial confrontation) to proceed by persuasion—at this point (334 d) he rejects the *logos* entirely because of the consequences to which it has led. But Socrates adds still one final turn: since it is just to injure the unjust and to help the just (as Polemarchus now agrees in opposition to the immediately preceding conclusion), Socrates concludes:

> Then for many, Polemarchus—all human beings who make mistakes—it will turn out to be just to injure friends, for their friends are bad; and just to help enemies, for they are good (334 d − e).

The point is that what is especially needed is the capacity to distinguish between seeming and being, so as to be able to act in accord with the latter. This is made evident through the reformulation on which Polemarchus now insists: a friend is one who seems to be *and* is good. What is needed is the capacity for a kind of knowing by which one could distinguish between seeming and being and could determine whether or not the two are identical. The final turn which Socrates has given to the *logos* indicates, in effect, that without knowledge justice can end up being a matter of injuring friends and giving aid to the enemy—that is, it can end up being precisely the opposite of that traditional courage of the warrior which Polemarchus, the "war-lord," appears to prize so highly.

But precisely what kind of knowledge does justice require? All along Socrates has made use of an analogy between justice and art, demanding that justice must exhibit whatever character is exhibited by an art. Yet, what is the justification for this analogy and the resulting demand? Is justice an art which one could practice in a way perfectly analogous to the practice of the art of the pilot or the physician? And, more specifically, is the knowledge required for justice analogous to the knowledge that is involved in an art?

This problem is pointed up by the absurdity of Socrates' conclusion according to which the just man turns out to be a kind of thief, which is almost the paradigm of the unjust man. The absurdity lies in the fact that justice turns out to be used for bad (unjust) ends. Whereas an art can indeed be used either for just or for unjust ends, justice cannot serve any other than just ends. It involves a kind of knowledge which, unlike that which belongs to the various arts, cannot be misused (cf. *Euthyd.* 289 b; also Ch. II, Sect 3 a, esp. n. 22). This is the point of Socrates' final criticism of Polemarchus' opinion: Since to harm is to make less just and since the exercise of justice cannot have the effect of making men unjust, it is not the just man's business to harm anyone.

Polemarchus' opinion that justice consists in doing good to friends and harm to enemies has thus been transformed into the opinion that justice means helping those who both are good and seem good (i.e., those who both are good *and* are one's friends) and not harming anyone else. His final opinion is *not* that justice means simply doing good to everyone; nor will this prove to be Socrates' opinion in what is to follow in the next several Books of the *Republic*. In the discussion of the city Socrates will not teach that justice means doing good to everyone but, on the contrary, will demand, for instance, that the guardians of the city be like well-trained watch-dogs, friendly to their own people and harsh to strangers (375 a), and that the citizens not regard all men simply as their friends but rather that they be bound closely in brotherhood with their own, a brotherhood to be established and maintained by a kind of just lie about human birth. Polemarchus' opinion—in the various forms that it has proved to have and not solely in the final form into which Socrates compels it—is taken over into the subsequent parts of the *Republic* and there contested in a conversation in which Polemarchus remains, with one important exception, completely silent. It is as though everyone forgets that these opinions belonged to Polemarchus, the host of the gathering.

As the conversation between Socrates and Polemarchus concludes, they playfully resolve to join one another in battle against anyone who would support the opinion that it is just to harm

one's enemies—against anyone who, in terms of Socrates' ironic
assumption that the poets must be right, would support this
opinion by attributing it to poets like Simonides. Socrates voices
his opinion that this opinion, against which he and Polemarchus
are agreed to do battle, originated from some rich man who, as he
says, "has a high opinion of what he can do." We are suddenly
made to recall that Polemarchus' opinion was inherited from rich
old Cephalus. But now Socrates speaks not of Cephalus but of
men like Xerxes, and we are made to wonder about the connection between wealth and tyranny.

(e) Thrasymachus (336 b — 354 c)

Socrates has defeated the second contender for the rule over
Hades and even persuaded this contender to join with him in
battle. Yet, Polemarchus will prove to be of no assistance to
Socrates in the fierce battle that is to occupy the remainder of
Book I. Socrates relates how this battle with Thrasymachus ("rash
fighter") begins:

> Hunched up like a wild beast, he flung himself at us as if to
> tear us to pieces. Then both Polemarchus and I got all in a
> flutter from fright. And he shouted out into our midst and
> said, "What is this nonsense that has possessed you for so
> long, Socrates? And why do you act like fools making way
> for one another?" (336 b — c).

Thus, Socrates is assaulted by one who, in terms of the underlying
mythos, plays the role not only of a judge but also of the wild,
flesh-eating hound of Hades. The ferocity of the assault by Cerberus, guardian of the gates of the underworld, is cause to wonder
precisely what Socrates' intention is at the end of the conversation
with Polemarchus. We recall that it was Polemarchus who originally was responsible for Socrates' being retained and who placed
upon him the demand that he win his release. We recall, furthermore, that Socrates proposed to win his release by means of
persuasion. We wonder, therefore, whether—now that Polemarchus
himself has been persuaded and won over to the side of Socrates

to such an extent that he is willing to join him in battle—whether Socrates does not regard himself as having won his release. In other words, we wonder whether the ferocious assault by Cerberus is perhaps provoked by an attempt on the part of Socrates to escape through those gates of Hades guarded by Cerberus and to resume his previously interrupted ascent from Hades.

To Thrasymachus' initial assault Socrates answers that whatever mistakes he and Polemarchus have made were made unwillingly, and that they should be pitied by such clever men as Thrasymachus rather than being treated harshly. Then, in the words of the account, Thrasymachus "burst out laughing very scornfully and said, 'Heracles! Here is that habitual irony of Socrates' " (337 a). The exclamation strengthens our suspicion that Socrates is on the verge of attempting an escape from Hades and makes us wonder, furthermore, whether he intends to carry someone along with him, whether, in particular, he might have it in mind to drag Cerberus himself out of Hades as Heracles once did.

But Socrates does not make his escape. He does not even attempt it. On the contrary, he is placed on trial by Thrasymachus, whose judicial role now comes into prominence. Already we have heard him charge Socrates with "that habitual irony." What is Socrates' habitual irony? To the men of the city it appears simply to be a feigning of ignorance used in order to draw others out so as then to be able to refute them, thereby asserting one's own superiority. Thus what Thrasymachus is primarily charging against Socrates is that same practice on account of which he is accused of corrupting the youth in his trial before the "men of Athens" (cf. *Apol.* 23 c). In fact, in the exchange between Socrates and Thrasymachus there now commences a parody of that trial. The trial begins with Thrasymachus asking Socrates to propose the punishment which he should suffer if Thrasymachus could give a better answer regarding justice. As in the *Apology* (36 d), Socrates proposes what in the eyes of his accuser is an outlandish penalty, namely that he should learn from the man who knows; again, as in the *Apology* (38 b), another alternative (a fine) is finally proposed, Glaucon asserting that they will all contribute for Socrates. And just as, in the *Apology* as a whole, Socrates bears testimony to the ignorance which properly belongs to human wisdom, so, in the present little trial, Socrates answers the charge intended in Thrasymachus' reference to "that habitual irony of Socrates" by insisting (in specific reference to the question of justice) that he "does not know and does not profess to know." The fact that in the present trial it is the accuser rather than the accused who is cast as principal speaker leads us to expect the same reversal between the would-be judge and the judged that occurred in the *Apology*. But Cerberus is a fierce opponent, and the battle is only now ready to begin.

(i) The Advantage of the Stronger (338 c – 347 e)

What was enacted in the initial confrontation but quickly diverted in the direction of the rule of persuasion is now stated by Thrasymachus: justice he defines as "the advantage of the stronger" (τὸ τοῦ κρείττονος ξυμφέρον) (cf. 327 c). Prodded by Socrates, he offers an explanation of his definition:

> And each ruling group sets down laws for its own advantage; a democracy sets down democratic laws; a tyranny, tyrannic laws; and the others do the same. And they declare that what they have set down—their own advantage—is just for the ruled, and the man who departs from it they punish as a breaker of the law and a doer of unjust deeds. This, best of men, is what I mean: in every city the same thing is just, the advantage of the established ruling body. It surely is master; so the man who considers rightly concludes that everywhere justice is the same thing, the advantage of the stronger (338 e – 339 a).

With Thrasymachus' opinion about justice brought into the open, an extended discussion of it now commences.

Under questioning by Socrates, Thrasymachus agrees that it is just to obey the rulers. Yet, as he also admits, rulers can make mistakes regarding what is to their advantage; they can make laws which are not really to their own advantage. In such cases, then, since it is just to obey whatever laws the rulers enact, it would be just to do what is not to the advantage of the rulers.

Suddenly the discussion between Socrates and Thrasymachus is interrupted by Polemarchus, who, as Socrates' ally in battle, reaffirms the conclusion that Socrates has just drawn. In turn, however, he is countered by Cleitophon,[20] who, acting as ally to Thrasymachus, questions Polemarchus' right to witness for Thrasymachus. Thus, we are again reminded that a trial is under way, though now there is indeed good reason to suspect that Thrasymachus has almost, if not entirely, replaced Socrates as the defendant. Although in the sequel Socrates continues to be charged, what he is mainly charged with by Thrasymachus is playing the sycophant; that is, he is primarily charged with bringing false charges against Thrasymachus. The reversal of roles between accuser and accused is already virtually accomplished.

Polemarchus' interruption initiates a little dialogue between himself and Cleitophon. They review the course which the immediately proceeding discussion between Socrates and Thrasymachus has taken, and Cleitophon, coming to the aid of the latter, introduces a revision which would suffice to save Thrasymachus from Socrates' attack. Specifically, he asserts that what Thrasymachus said was "that the advantage of the stronger is what the stronger believes to be his advantage" (340 b). This, he insists, is what must be done by the weaker, and this, he insists further, is what Thrasymachus set down as justice. Socrates intervenes in order to propose that they accept this opinion if it is, in fact, what Thrasymachus wanted to say, regardless of whether he actually said it. Thus, Socrates turns again to Thrasymachus and asks him whether this opinion, voiced by Cleitophon, is what he wants to say about justice: that the just is what *seems* to the stronger to be

---

[20] In the dialogue *Cleitophon,* which is cast as a conversation between Socrates and Cleitophon regarding another conversation between Lysias and Cleitophon in which the latter reportedly found fault with the instruction of Socrates and praised highly that of Thrasymachus (406), Cleitophon emerges rather more on the side of Thrasymachus than on that of Socrates. In the course of the dialogue he mentions to Socrates that he was told by Socrates that justice was doing good to friends and harm to enemies but that later it appeared that justice never injures anyone (410 a – b). The dialogue concludes with Cleitophon charging that Socrates only exhorts men to virtue but does not teach them what virtue and justice really are (410 c – e). It will be noted that this charge is not so different from the one leveled against Socrates by Thrasymachus in the *Republic.* At the end of the *Cleitophon,* Cleitophon proposes to go to Thrasymachus for further instruction.

his advantage, regardless of whether it is so or not. Surprisingly, however, Thrasymachus rejects outright the aid offered him by Cleitophon; he rejects that revised opinion according to which justice would be simply what seems to the stronger to be his advantage. Rather than letting his definition collapse into the crude opinion of Cleitophon, Thrasymachus introduces a curious refinement: A ruler is like one who practices an art, and, hence, insofar as he is a ruler, i.e., in his capacity as a ruler, he makes no mistakes.

It is important to see what is behind Thrasymachus' refusal to accept the revision offered by Cleitophon, especially since this revision provides such an easy escape from Socrates' criticism. Cleitophon's position involves a total collapsing of any distinction between what seems to be the advantage of the ruler and what is his advantage. In other words, it involves a total collapsing in this regard of the distinction between seeming and being; what seems would simply determine what is, and, hence, what seems to the ruler would be subject to no measure, no criticism, whatsoever. Cleitophon's position amounts to a radical denial of standards: justice is simply what is enacted by those in power. In contrast to this position, Thrasymachus maintains a vestige of a standard, which prevents justice from collapsing into the mere dictate of the opinions of those in power: the just must *be* to the advantage of the ruler and not merely *seem* to be to his advantage. Thus, the ruler has need of an *art* in order that he might be able to distinguish what is his advantage from what merely seems to be his advantage but really is not. Furthermore, just as the ruler needs, with respect to himself, to distinguish between being and seeming, so also he needs an art by which to conceal from his subjects the disparity between that which is their advantage and that which they are told is their advantage but which is really the ruler's advantage. The ruler has need of an art of persuasion by which to entice his subjects into accepting the appearances which serve his advantage. But this latter is precisely the art which Thrasymachus himself professes to teach: rhetoric. In fact, he is the only character in the *Republic* who professes the practice of a specific art. This means that in his rejection of Cleitophon's proposed revision, i.e., in his insistence on retaining what amounts to a connection between justice and art, Thrasymachus is acting precisely for his own advantage as a teacher and practitioner of what is generally taken as an art closely related to matters of justice.[21] In rejecting the aid offered by Cleitophon, Thrasymachus is acting exactly like those rulers whom he has described—that is, he is acting in accordance with what *is* his advantage rather than what merely *seems* to be such. If, subsequently, Thrasymachus should prove to have made a mistake regarding what is his advantage, then he will, by his own criterion, have disqualified himself from ruling. Socrates will then have vanquished the most ferocious of the contenders to the throne of Hades.

Although Thrasymachus' refinement of what he means by ruler serves to eliminate Socrates' previous objection, it also serves to shift the focus of the discussion from the ruler himself to the art of ruling. This shift enables Socrates to draw upon the character of art as a basis for renewing his criticism of Thrasymachus' opinions about justice. Socrates' criticism is simply that, just as every art (e.g., those of the physician and of the pilot) is directed towards, not its own advantage, but the advantage of the subject on which it is exercised, so the ruler *qua* ruler (i.e., as embodiment of the art of ruling) does not act for his own advantage but for that of the ruled. Art serves the advantage, not of the stronger, but of the weaker.

Thrasymachus is indignant, and, heaping abuse on Socrates, he appeals to the art of the shepherd as a counter-example. He says that Socrates does not even recognize sheep or shepherd:

> Because you suppose shepherds or cowherds consider the good of the sheep or the cows and fatten them and take care of them looking to something other than their master's good and their own (343 b).

Thrasymachus' point is that, whatever may be said about the character of art in general, a shepherd does not, in fact, practice his art for the sake of the sheep but primarily for his own

---

[21] Cf. Strauss, *City and Man*, p. 80; also Bloom's "Interpretive Essay," p. 330.

advantage. Indeed, there would seem to be no disputing this fact. Yet, Socrates does dispute it—in a curious way: He introduces into the discussion what he calls the money-making art. His point is that a man furthers his own advantage, not by the practice of what is normally regarded as his art (e.g., medicine, piloting, sheep-tending), but rather by also practicing alongside it another art, the art of money-making.

This art of money-making, which apparently every artisan practices without quite realizing it, is indeed a curious art. It is quite unlike every other art; it even goes directly against Socrates' contention that the practice of an art is never for the advantage of the one practicing it. Furthermore, it may be said that Socrates' introduction of this curious kind of art amounts to a tacit admission of the seriousness of a problem which, at first glance, he might seem merely to pass over, namely, the problem of the conflict between private good and public good. At this point the conflict remains so unresolved that the only recourse is to assign what serves the public good to arts of the usual kind and what serves only men's private good to the art of money-making and then to allow that men practice the latter alongside the former. Yet, obviously this is only a temporary expedient, for eventually one will need to ask how the two arts are "alongside" one another and what "alongside" means in this connection. But Thrasymachus does not ask these questions.

The basic conflict between public and private is brought out especially in the additional remarks about the art of ruling which Socrates addresses, not to Thrasymachus, but to Glaucon (347 a – d). Since ruling does not serve the advantage of the ruler, no one willingly chooses to rule. Since, furthermore, good men are not willing to rule for money or honor, if they are to be willing to rule there must be a penalty for not ruling—and "the greatest of penalties for not ruling is being ruled by a worse man if one is not willing to rule oneself" (347 c). Socrates adds: "For it is likely that if a city of good men came to be, there would be a fight over not ruling, just as there is now over ruling" (347 d). In these remarks we find the first substantive indication of the great difficulty involved in getting the philosopher into the city.

(ii) Is Injustice Stronger? (347 e – 354 c)

Even before Socrates introduces the art of money-making in answer to Thrasymachus' appeal to the case of the shepherd, Thrasymachus begins to shift the whole basis of the discussion. The shift begins when he insists that the just man gets less in every case than the unjust man who is able to get the better of others in a big way (343 d – 344 a). At first, Thrasymachus holds onto his previous thesis that justice is the advantage of the stronger and simply adds alongside it the further contention that injustice "is what is profitable and advantageous for oneself"; but we can see that these two opinions cannot be simply mixed if we merely consider that for a ruler who acts for his advantage (in the sense described by Thrasymachus) the same things would be both just and unjust. In fact, Socrates calls attention to the fact that Thrasymachus is shifting the ground of the discussion: "But, first, stick to what you said, or if you change what you set down make it clear that you're doing so, and don't deceive us" (345 b). And as soon as Socrates finishes his brief conversation with Glaucon about the difficulty of getting the good to rule, he makes it explicit that Thrasymachus has made a drastic shift in the basis of the conversation: "What Thrasymachus now says is in my opinion a far bigger thing—he asserts that the life of the unjust man is stronger than that of the just man" (347 e). In a sense, Thrasymachus has reversed his previous opinion, for now he places injustice rather than justice on the side of the stronger. More precisely, he has abandoned his previous opinion regarding what justice is and replaced it with the commonly held opinion about justice that was thematized in the definitions given by Cephalus and Polemarchus; and, on this basis, he then insists that injustice is stronger—which is interpreted by Glaucon to mean that injustice is more profitable ($\lambda \upsilon \sigma \iota \tau \epsilon \lambda \acute{\epsilon} \sigma \tau \epsilon \rho o \nu$) than justice. Thrasymachus' descriptions make it clear that what he has specifically in mind in speaking of injustice is the unlimited striving to get all one can at others' expense (cf. 343 e – 344 a).

There is a brief reminder that a trial is under way, in which, as Socrates now observes, they are both judges and pleaders at once

(348 a — b); and then Socrates' refutation of Thrasymachus' latest thesis begins in earnest. This refutation involves three distinct stages.

In the first stage of the refutation Socrates undertakes to show—contrary to what Thrasymachus infers from his thesis that injustice is more profitable—that the unjust man is not good (ἀγαθός) and prudent (φρόνιμος), that (in another formulation) he is not in the camp of virtue (ἀρετή) and wisdom (σοφία). Clearly everything depends on the sense or senses which the collectively understood words "good and prudent" assume. Consider, first, what Thrasymachus means. In saying that the unjust man is "good and prudent" what he wants to convey is that injustice is what the clever man practices for his own profit, whereas justice (as commonly understood) is something for simpletons who are unable to recognize and to pursue effectively their own advantage (a "high-minded innocence"). The "virtue" of the unjust man, as portrayed by Thrasymachus, amounts simply to his excelling others in the furtherance of his own advantage, and his wisdom is merely the cleverness which such a kind of "excellence" requires. On the other hand, Socrates understands "virtue and wisdom" in a drastically different way, which, however, Thrasymachus has tacitly endorsed and which, consequently, he cannot reject even when it turns out to undercut his own thesis. Specifically, Socrates understands "virtue and wisdom" by reference to the character of art (τέχνη). In other words, he assumes that "virtue and wisdom" are qualities which result in artful practice, so that the man who belongs in this camp, the man who is "good and prudent," would be the one whose practice most nearly resembled that of a master artisan. What Socrates, in effect, shows in this first stage of the refutation is that the practice of justice is more nearly akin to the proper practice of art than is that of injustice.

He proceeds in the following way. First, it is agreed that in any art there is a limit or measure which defines the perfection of what that art produces and which marks the completion of the productive activity itself. As a result, a genuine artisan does not strive without limit to outdo all others but rather only seeks to achieve that limit proper to his art. The only ones whom he outdoes are those who are ignorant of the art; for example, a musical man who is tuning a lyre does not seek to get the better of another in tightening and relaxing the strings but aims only at bringing each string to the proper pitch, i.e., at attaining to the proper measure. Thus, the striving of the genuine artisan is not an unlimited effort to outdo everyone. And, consequently, the unjust man, who, by Thrasymachus' own description, embodies an unlimited striving to outdo and lacks all recognition of limit and measure, is the opposite of the "good and prudent" artisan. The unjust man is not "good and prudent"; he does not belong in the camp of virtue and wisdom.

Thrasymachus reacts violently to this first stage of the refutation:

> Now Thrasymachus did not agree to all of this so easily as I tell it now, but he dragged his feet and resisted, and he produced a wonderful quantity of sweat, for it was summer. And then I saw what I had not yet seen before—Thrasymachus blushing (350 c − d).

Why is Thrasymachus' reaction so strong? Because he professes to be a teacher of an art the great importance of which is supposed to lie in its giving one the means to outdo others so as to get the most for oneself. Thus, Socrates' refutation is a refutation, not merely of an opinion, but of Thrasymachus' own art, that is, it is a demonstration that the practice for which his art is claimed to be useful is contrary to the very nature of art. Hence, Thrasymachus has, in a sense, been robbed of his art; indirectly it has been shown not to be an art at all (cf. Ch. III, Sect. 3 b − c, esp. n. 33). As a result, we find that at precisely this point Thrasymachus' entire manner changes drastically. He is not given the chance to say what he wants to say, presumably because he has just been deprived of his "art" of speech; and so, he says to Socrates:

> If you want to keep on questioning, go ahead and question, and, just as with old wives who tell tales [μύθους], I shall say to you, 'all right,' and I shall nod and shake my head (350 e).

Now it is clear that Thrasymachus has not acted for his own advantage. At two crucial junctures he has made a mistake regarding his advantage: first, in his rejection of Cleitophon's aid for the sake of his own refinement of what is meant by "ruler" and, second, in his shift to the thesis that injustice is more profitable. His failure in this regard is made strikingly apparent in the fact that he has ended up being deprived of his most cherished possession, his art. By his own criterion, Thrasymachus has disqualified himself from ruling, and Socrates has now virtually succeeded in defeating the most ferocious contender to the rule over Hades.

The second stage of the refutation reverts to that version of Thrasymachus' present thesis which proclaims that injustice is mightier, more powerful, than justice—that is, that it is stronger in the most immediate sense of this word. Socrates observes that this version of the thesis is already virtually refuted by what was shown at the first stage of the refutation; but he proposes not to dispose of it by this easy means but to deal with it in a different fashion. Presumably, the need for the latter (a need which very likely could be concealed from Thrasymachus) results from the two rather distinct senses which "stronger" assumes in the first and second stages respectively.

Socrates attacks Thrasymachus' thesis by insisting that any group of men, if totally unjust, would be incapable of action. He explains by posing a question to Thrasymachus:

> Now tell me this: if it's the work of injustice, wherever it is, to implant hatred, then, when injustice comes into being, both among free men and slaves, will it not also cause them to hate one another and to form factions, and to be unable to accomplish anything in common with one another? (351 d – e).

He extends this result to the case of injustice in an individual man:

> And if, then, injustice should come into being within one man, you surprising fellow, will it lose its power or will it remain undiminished? (351 e).

The point is that injustice divides the individual against himself and makes him powerless. This extension is significant not only because it foreshadows that movement back and forth between the city and the individual man which will continue almost throughout the *Republic* but also because it is a transition from the consideration of justice as a matter of external conduct to a regard for it as a condition of the soul, a condition of a kind that would inform external action but not be reducible to it.

Thrasymachus offers virtually no resistance, and so Socrates proceeds to the third stage of the refutation. His intent at this stage is to refute that version of Thrasymachus' thesis that is most comprehensive: that injustice is more profitable than justice. In order to refute this, Socrates sets about showing that only the just man is happy, and in showing this he carries even further the shift, initiated at the previous stage, from justice as external conduct to justice as a condition of the soul. Socrates proceeds by establishing (1) that the work (ἔργον) of a thing is that work for which that thing is the only instrument or the best one (for example, the work of the eyes is seeing); (2) that the virtue (ἀρετή) of a thing is that which enables the thing to do its work well; and (3) that the work of the soul is living. It follows, then, that the virtue of the soul enables the soul to live well. Since (as was established in the first stage of the refutation) justice is the virtue of the soul, it follows that justice enables the soul to live well, that is, to be happy. Hence, the unjust man is not happy, and injustice proves not to be more profitable than justice.

None of the gaps in this "argument" are taken up by Thrasymachus, despite the fact that some of them are so wide that it will require the entire remainder of the *Republic* to bridge them. Just as he responded to the second stage of the refutation by exclaiming to Socrates, "Feast yourself boldly on the *logos*" (to which Socrates answered by asking him to "fill out the rest of the banquet for me"), so now, with the entire refutation completed, Thrasymachus says: "Let that be the fill of your banquet at the festival of Bendis, Socrates" (354 a). Socrates has devoured the wolf; he has defeated the wild dog who is the most awesome inhabitant of Hades and the most ferocious contender to the rule over Hades. Socrates has devoured Thrasymachus by devouring (i.e., refuting) his opinions and his *logoi* in defence of those opinions. Socrates has feasted on the *logoi* of Thrasymachus, and, presumably, this feast is to serve as a substitute for the dinner which Socrates was promised at the beginning by Polemarchus but which now seems to have been forgotten.

Socrates, the "ruler of life," has become ruler of the dead. The question becomes: How will he now practice the art of ruling? He begins by complaining about the banquet he has had: "I have not had a fine banquet, but it's my own fault, not yours" (354 a – b). He explains by pointing out that in the discussion between Thrasymachus and himself they began by asking about what justice is but that, before this was answered, they hurried on to other questions—

> so that now as a result of the discussion I know nothing. So long as I do not know what the just is, I shall hardly know whether it is a virtue or not and whether the one who has it is unhappy or happy (354 c).

The discussions in Book I have provided only a collecting of opinions about justice; they have not initiated a measuring of these opinions by reference to a measure transcending mere opinion. Nevertheless, this collecting of opinions has invoked an awareness of ignorance regarding justice, as Socrates' final words indicate, and it has assembled certain elements for the inquiry that is to come. The most obvious such element is the close relation between justice and art that has emerged especially in the discussion with Thrasymachus. This relation tends to suggest that a just city would be a city in which everyone is a "good and prudent" artisan; and, in fact, it is precisely from this point, that is, with a community of master artisans, that the building of the just city will begin.

Section 2. The City and the Soul (Book II – Book V, 473 c)

(a) The New Beginning (357 a – 367 e)

Book II begins:

> Now, when I had said this, I thought I was freed from *logos*. But after all, as it seems, it was only a prelude.

Socrates' words indicate that with Book II a new beginning is made. What is the situation that defines this new beginning?

At the end of Book I Socrates has defeated all contenders to the rule over the miniature city formed in the initial confrontation; he has, at least to that extent, established himself as a fit ruler over the little city in Hades. Yet, on the other hand, we recall how Socrates himself spoke earlier of the great difficulty involved in inducing the good man to become a ruler. In this same connection we recall that Socrates' victory over Thrasymachus amounted to a defeat of the wild dog that guards the gates of Hades so as to prevent souls from leaving. We recall also that Socrates had already set about making his ascent when he was restrained from going any farther by the power of Polemarchus; and what was at issue initially—and, we may suppose, later too—was Socrates' winning of his release. Thus, we hear in Socrates' opening words in Book II the opinion that he has now (by persuasion) won his release from Hades and that it is fitting now to re-engage in the ascent that was previously interrupted. This time, however, Socrates is restrained before he even begins his movement on the upward way. Yet, this time he is restrained, not by the power of one who, like Polemarchus, resides in Piraeus-Hades, but rather by the young man who had originally come with Socrates to the Bendideia and who also was with him on the upward way when they were compelled to stop by Polemarchus' slave. Glaucon, previously with Socrates in the ascent, now restrains Socrates from abandoning the rule over Hades and the *logos* about that matter which is of utmost concern with regard to the city. Glaucon says:

> Socrates, do you want to seem to have persuaded us, or truly to persuade us, that it is in every way better to be just than unjust? (357 a – b).

The question is whether Socrates' practice is merely *to seem* to be genuine persuasion or is *to be* such. Recalling again that Socrates originally proposed to win his release by means of persuasion, we hear Glaucon attesting here that Socrates has not won his release, that his persuasion of the shades in Hades has itself been little more than a shade. Thus, on the one hand, Glaucon holds Socrates back from the ascent, forcing him to remain in the city and to continue the *logos* in a way which will lead him deeper and deeper into matters of the city; yet, on the other hand, Glaucon challenges Socrates to practice that genuine persuasion by which he would win his escape and be empowered to re-engage himself in the ascent. In terms of the *mythos,* Socrates is confronted with two tasks at the beginning of Book II: to exercise his rule over Hades and to ascend out of Hades. This duality foreshadows quite decisively the paradox of the philosopher-king in which the entire discussion now commencing will terminate.

Glaucon proceeds to pose the problem by distinguishing between three kinds of good.[22] There is the kind of good which we delight in for its own sake (e.g., harmless pleasures); there is the kind of good which we like both for its own sake and for what comes out of it (e.g., thinking and seeing); and there is the kind of good which we choose to have only because of what comes out of it (e.g., gymnastic exercise, medical treatment). Glaucon refers to the popular opinion that justice belongs to the third of these kinds of good, that it is practiced not for itself but only for what comes out of it, only for its consequences. When Socrates in response mentions the preceding conversation between Thrasymachus and himself, Glaucon suggests that "Thrasymachus, like a snake, has been charmed more quickly than he should have been" (358 b); and he proposes that Socrates now deal more decisively with the problem of justice by considering the effects of justice and of injustice on the soul, dismissing all questions of consequences.

It is significant that in this new beginning Glaucon poses the problem in terms of kinds of good (ἀγαθόν), for this amounts to his proposing to investigate justice from the point of view of the problem of the good. This way of investigating justice should especially be distinguished from the way that tended to dominate the discussion in Book I, namely, the investigation of justice in terms of art. This distinction will eventually develop into the contrast between an understanding of justice in terms of what proves to be the lowest element in the city (the artisans) *and* an understanding of justice in terms of something which transcends

---

[22] In this passage we find the first occurrence in the *Republic* of the word *eidos:* Socrates refers to the third of the three kinds of good as an "εἶδος ἀγαθοῦ." Although the sense of the word is largely pre-philosophical in this context, it is of utmost importance for what is to come that the word is first used in the context of a discussion of good.

the city. However, at the level of the discussion in Book I, the gap between these two ways of understanding justice has not yet even opened up; in fact, in that discussion Socrates is able to develop the question of the "good and prudent" man only through reference to the arts. In this same connection, it should be noted also that Glaucon includes under the third kind of good all activities from which money is made; all such activities are, by his account, practiced only for the sake of what comes out of them, only for their consequences. But these activities are precisely the arts in the usual sense, to which justice was linked in Book I; and indeed, Glaucon says that it is the opinion of the many that this is where justice belongs. In proposing that Socrates show that justice does not belong among these things, Glaucon is proposing a shift away from that viewpoint, characteristic of Book I, from which justice is considered only in terms of its relation to art; he is proposing, in effect, to open up a gap between the understanding of justice in terms of art and the understanding of it in terms of the good.

Glaucon proceeds, as he says, to "restore Thrasymachus' *logos*" by elaborating the opinion of the many about justice. He is insistent, however, that what he is about to say is not his own opinion and that he will "speak in vehement praise of the unjust life" only in order to provoke Socrates to do the same for the just life. Glaucon's elaboration of the common opinion about justice, his restoration of Thrasymachus' *logos*, involves three parts.

First, Glaucon proposes to state the opinion of the many regarding what kind of thing justice is and where it came from:

> They say that doing injustice is naturally good, and suffering injustice bad, but that the bad in suffering injustice far exceeds the good in doing it; so that, when they do injustice to one another and suffer it and taste of both, it seems profitable—to those who are not able to escape the one and choose the other—to set down a compact among themselves neither to do injustice nor to suffer it (358 e − 359 a).

Thus, according to this opinion, justice is a mean between what is best (doing injustice) and what is worst (suffering it). Justice turns out, therefore, to serve the advantage of the weaker, of those unable to do injustice without suffering injustice in turn; the

complete inversion of the assumed meaning of justice that has
taken place since Thrasymachus originally defined justice as the
advantage of the stronger is now evident. In this same connection,
we note that in this first part of the restoration of Thrasymachus'
logos Glaucon has not really done what he proposed. He has
merely said why men practice justice, not what justice is. Like the
opinion of the many, like the shifty *logos* of Thrasymachus, but
contrary to what Socrates insisted on at the conclusion of his
feast, Glaucon's account simply takes for granted that it is known
what justice and injustice are, specifically, that it is known what it
means to do injustice and to suffer injustice.

The second part of Glaucon's elaboration of the opinion about
justice makes explicit something already indicated in the first part:
men practice justice unwillingly and only because of their incapacity to do injustice with impunity. If one could do injustice
without having to suffer injustice, he would never be just. Glaucon
illustrates this point by telling the story of a man who came into
possession of a means for avoiding all retribution, the story of the
ring of Gyges. The story concerns an ancestor of Gyges[23] who was
a shepherd in the service of the king. Once there came a thunder-
storm and an earthquake; a chasm opened up in the earth, and the
man, curious about it, went down into it. Among the many
wonderful things he saw ("about which they tell *mythoi*," according to Glaucon), there was a hollow bronze horse. The horse had
windows, and, looking in, the man saw a large corpse with nothing
on except for the gold ring on its finger. The man "slipped it off
and went out." Subsequently the man discovered that the ring
could make him invisible—that is, able to do injustice with impunity—and so, having contrived to be a messenger to the king, he
used the power of the ring to seduce the queen, kill the king, and
seize the throne for himself—all with impunity.

---

[23] This passage has been variously emended in the attempt to bring it into harmony
with the phrase "Gyges' ring" which occurs at 612 b and which indicates that the man
whose adventure is related in the story was actually named Gyges. It has usually been
assumed that this character is identical with the famous Lydian king Gyges, who is told
of by Herodotus (*History*, I, 8-13); in order to avoid the apparent conflict between the
two relevant passages Adam (Vol. I, pp. 126-127) suggests that perhaps Plato's story
refers not to Herodotus' Gyges but to some homonymous ancestor of his, perhaps the
mythical founder of the family.

The point which the story is meant to illustrate is, of course, that if one could escape suffering injustice then he would not hesitate to do injustice. But in addition to its simple illustrating of this point there are some other things about the story, several specific features, to which we need to attend. First of all, we note that in the story there is a descent beneath the earth to a place where the man involved finds, among other things, a corpse; just as in the *mythos* of the *Republic* as a whole there is a descent by Socrates to the underworld, to the region of the dead. We note also that among the things which the man found there was a bronze horse, and we recall that Pluto, whom the poets placed as ruler over the underworld, was a keeper of horses[24] ; we recall also that Pluto was said to possess, not precisely a ring, but a cap which made whoever wore it invisible.[25] All of these features serve to suggest that the adventures of the man told of in the story mirror those of Socrates in the *Republic*. In turn, however, this correspondence serves as the basis for bringing out a radical contrast between the two cases. It should be noted that, although we are not told precisely how the man in the story got the ring, the horse inside which was the corpse with the ring on its finger is said to have had windows through which the man saw the corpse and the ring. Presumably, the man forced open a window and took the ring by force. One thing is certain: he did not get the ring from the corpse by persuasion. So, the way in which the man got the ring and, hence, eventually, the throne is to be contrasted with that exercise of persuasion by which Socrates has won title to the throne of Hades. Furthermore, though we are explicitly told—with the same word with which Socrates spoke of his own descent in the first sentence of the dialogue—that the man in the story "went down" (καταβῆναι), we are not so explicitly told that he subsequently went up; what we are told is only that he "went out" (ἐκβῆναι). We wonder whether the doings of the man in the story could ever have any relation to an ascent in the Socratic sense. We suspect that this man is one who is so eager to rule over Hades that

---

[24] Cf. Guthrie, *The Greeks and Their Gods*, p. 97.

[25] Cf. *Iliad*, V. 844. Note that Socrates himself associates Gyges' ring with Hades' cap in Book X (612 b).

he would certainly never set out, as did Socrates, to abandon the throne for the sake of the ascent. It seems that the man in the story exemplifies the kind who is a king but not at all a philosopher. The suggestion is that the appropriate answer to the thesis illustrated by the story of this man (that men practice justice unwillingly) would be a presentation of a king who is a philosopher. But that role—or, more precisely, the tension which renders such a role paradoxical—is already being played by Socrates himself.

In the final part of his restoration of Thrasymachus' *logos* Glaucon undertakes to show with full vividness that injustice, if perfectly practiced, is preferable to justice. Juxtaposing the perfectly just man and the perfectly unjust man, that is, the just man who has a reputation for injustice (who *seems* unjust) and the unjust man who has a reputation for justice (who *seems* just), Glaucon then produces an impressive list of agonies to be suffered by the former and benefits to be received by the latter. Among other things, the unjust man whose practice of injustice is so perfected as to include maintaining the appearance of justice will be "wealthy" and able to make "sacrifices" to the gods (like Cephalus), will be able to do "good to friends and harm to enemies" (as Polemarchus would do), and will be able to get "the better of his enemies" (in the way praised by Thrasymachus). These references serve to indicate to what great extent Glaucon, in his statement of the common opinion about justice, explicitly gathers up into their proper unity those opinions the collecting of which was in progress throughout Book I. In this sense Glaucon's statement marks not only a new beginning but also the decisive completion of all that preceded it—or, rather, it is a new beginning precisely by its way of posing explicitly all that has gone before it.

Before Socrates can respond to the challenge put to him by Glaucon, the latter is joined by his brother Adeimantus. On the one hand, the speech of Adeimantus supplements that of Glaucon and leads to a more precise posing of the task being given to Socrates; on the other hand, the deliberateness with which Adeimantus' speech is cast as a speech about speeches, as a survey of the different kinds of speeches about justice, makes it something of a contrast with the preceding speech by Glaucon. Adeimantus introduces his speech as a supplement to what his brother has said: he observes that they need to consider the speeches that are opposed to those reported by Glaucon. These other speeches, which praise justice and blame injustice, are, for example, the kind of speeches which fathers give to their sons. Adeimantus observes that in such speeches what is praised is not, however, justice by itself but rather the good reputation that comes from it; fathers exhort their sons to be just because the favorable opinion regarding themselves that they will thereby evoke will be to their great benefit—because to the one who *seems* to be just there come all those benefits that Glaucon in his speech bestowed upon the perfectly unjust man. Being just can also give one a good reputation with the gods, and this especially can serve to provide one with an inexhaustible store of goods. Hence, this speech, in effect, advocates being just only on the grounds that this is the best way of seeming just and that by seeming just one can receive a maximum of benefits of the sort previously enumerated by Glaucon. Such a kind of speech about justice is not, Adeimantus goes on to observe, made only by fathers speaking to their sons; in fact, it is made in many quarters and by such advocates of justice as Homer and Hesiod. And, Adeimantus continues, Musaeus and his son in their speech lead the just "into Hades and lay them down on couches; crowning them, they prepare a symposium of the holy, and they then make them go through the rest of time drunk, in the belief that the finest wage of virtue is an eternal drunk" (363 c − d). We are reminded that Socrates and the others, seated on stools arranged in a circle in the house of Polemarchus (cf. 328 c), have not even had the dinner promised by Polemarchus at the outset.

Adeimantus proceeds to speak of still another kind of speech about justice that can be heard from poets and others. This further kind tends, in a sense, to counter that kind made by fathers to their sons by portraying how hard and full of drugery justice is and how sweet and easy injustice is. As a result of hearing all these things said, the sons, already convinced by their fathers that what is really important is to *seem* to be just, conclude that there is no advantage whatsoever in being just unless they also seem to be; and more often than not they end up concluding that the most desireable course is to be unjust while providing oneself with a reputation for justice.

Adeimantus poses the task to Socrates: "Now, don't only show us by the *logos* that justice is stronger [κρεῖττον] than injustice, but show what each in itself does to the man who has it that makes the one bad and the other good" (367 b). This task involves two things. First, Adeimantus is asking that Socrates exclude from consideration the matter of external profits such as could be gotten by the mere reputation for justice and consider exclusively justice in itself, its effect on the one who possesses it. Socrates is to show what justice does regardless of "whether it is noticed by gods and human beings or not," as Adeimantus adds when he poses the task a second time (367 e). Second, Adeimantus proposes that Socrates not show this only in *logos* (μόνον τῷ λόγῳ)— as, presumably, he did in the discussions in Book I. But what other kind of showing is there? There is a showing by means of deeds, a showing in *ergon*.

(b) The Building of Cities (367 e – 427 d)

Socrates proposes a way of taking up the problem of justice. Distinguishing between justice in an individual man and justice in a city, he proposes that they look first to the city, since there justice is written in bigger letters and is easier to see. Subsequently, then, they can consider the individual man in terms of his likeness to the city.

Thus, Socrates' proposal is that, first of all, they seek justice in the city—that, more specifically, they "watch a city coming into being in *logos*" (369 a) so as to see how justice and injustice come to be in it. It is important to observe that no justification is given at this point for the analogy that is posed between the city and man; we are not told what, if anything, guarantees an accord between justice in the city and justice in the individual man, and, in fact, this relation will become a central problem as the building of cities progresses. Furthermore, we are not told why Socrates chooses to investigate justice in the city by considering how a city comes to be; to say the least, it is not obvious in advance that this is the most appropriate way of taking up the problem.

In terms of the *mythos,* however, there is a peculiar appropriateness. Having emerged at the end of Book I as ruler over Hades and having been persuaded by Glaucon to take up that rule rather than simply abandoning it for the sake of the ascent, Socrates will now exercise his rule by becoming a ruler in the most primordial sense, by becoming the *founder* of a city—in fact, of a whole series of cities.

Yet, even as a founder of cities, Socrates remains the philosopher, remains engaged in that practice which in his most open confrontation with the city he presented as service to Apollo (cf. Ch. 1, esp. Sect. 3 b). This becomes perhaps most evident at the end of the labor of building the cities. After all the legislation needed for the city has been enacted, Adeimantus asks Socrates what still remains for them to deal with. Socrates answers:

> For us, nothing. However for the Apollo at Delphi there remain the greatest, fairest, and first of the laws which are given (Book IV, 427 b).

Among these laws, which Socrates goes on to enumerate, are the ones that pertain to "the burial of the dead and all the services needed to keep those in that other place gracious." But these are precisely the laws—the only laws—that would be enacted by one who, like Socrates, is ruler over Hades. The lawgiving, the ruling, the founding of cities in Hades—all this belongs to the province of Apollo, and Socrates' engagement in it is a continuation of his service to Apollo.

(i) The City of Artisans (369 b – 372 c)

Socrates begins the building of the city in *logos* by observing what it is about man that causes cities to come about: "a city, as I believe, comes into being because each of us isn't self-sufficient but is in need of much" (369 b). The primary needs are for food, housing, and clothing. Since such needs are generally satisfied by arts, Socrates proceeds to "make a city in *logos* from the beginning" by bringing together the various types of arts necessary to provide for these needs. For each art there will be a distinct group of artisans, since each man should practice only that art for which he is naturally fitted; as Adeimantus puts it, "One man, one art" (370 b; cf. *Laws* 846 d – 847 b). Thus, the first of the cities built by Socrates is a simple city of artisans, each practicing his art in such a way that everyone's needs are satisfied.

Three things need to be noted about this city. First of all, the city has no government whatsoever. It seems to presuppose a kind of natural harmony between public good and private good, so that there is justice without anyone or anything having to institute it and preserve it. One wonders what would happen in such a city if some men began to insist on practicing arts for which they were not competent or arts for which there were already a sufficient number of artisans. And what would happen in such a city if too many men naturally fitted for the same art happened to be born?

Second, Socrates indicates that at an elementary stage such a city would need to have a currency as token of exchange (371 b). This means, then, that each man would then need to practice both his own art *and* the art of money-making. The result is that every man would end up practicing two arts, contrary to the basic precept of the city, "One man, one art."

Finally, we note that in this city the only needs taken into account are bodily needs (cf. 369 d). However, we note also that when Socrates speaks of the needs which cause men to come together and form a city he names only the need for things like food, housing, and clothing—that is, he speaks only about those needs that are satisfied by arts. In particular, he says nothing at all about procreation; the building of this first city abstracts entirely from this need.[26] This abstraction is especially evident when Socrates says, "the city of utmost necessity would be made of four or five men"; for the word that he uses here is not "ἄνθρωπος" (human being) but "ἀνήρ" (man as opposed to woman). So, the first of the cities built in *logos* is a city in the very foundation of which *eros* has no place. In fact, it is only at the very end of his description of this city (372 b) that Socrates finally makes reference to the production of children. What is striking is that that very reference marks the beginning of the

---

[26] Cf. Strauss, *City and Man*, pp. 94-96.

overthrow of the first city; for it is at just that point that the erotic and courageous Glaucon begins to object to the simple city of artisans—an objection which culminates in the charge that it is "a city of sows."

(ii) The Luxurious City and Its Purging (372 c − 376 c)

The city of artisans is the first of the four cities that will be built by Socrates with the help of Adeimantus and Glaucon. The transition to the forming of the second city is provoked by Glaucon's strong censure of the simple city of artisans as a "city of sows." Glaucon demands that the first city be transformed by the addition of all sorts of refinements and luxuries, so as to provide for the satisfaction of unnecessary desires as well as those desires based on the natural needs for food, clothing, and shelter. Socrates, in turn, indicates that such additions serve to bring about what amounts to a drastic transformation in the character of the city: the new city, the second of the four cities to be built, is a "luxurious city," a "feverish city," swollen with unnecessary desires. For the satisfying of these desires the land, which previously (i.e., in the case of the first city) sufficed, now proves to be too small. So, it becomes necessary to cut off a piece of the neighbors' land—which means going to war—which, in turn, means that it becomes necessary to have an army, to have a class of guardians (φύλακες) of the city. Because the work of the guardians is of such great importance to the city, the entire discussion is, from this point on, entirely occupied with this group.

First of all, it is necessary for Socrates and Glaucon to determine what kind of men would be fit for becoming guardians, what natural qualities they would need to have. It is in this connection that Socrates first speaks of the philosopher; specifically, he proposes that one who is to become a guardian would need to be a philosopher in his nature (παρὰ φύσιν) (375 e). It should be noted that here, at the point where the philosopher makes his first appearance in the *logos* of the *Republic*, he is described as embodying that capacity which serves to tame the courageous warrior, to moderate his otherwise excessive spirit (θύμος), in such fashion as to guarantee that he acts gently with his own and cruelly only with enemies. The effect of the guardian's having a philosophic nature is to make him like a good watchdog, in contrast, we might presume, to the wild dog with whom Socrates had to contend in Book I. Socrates mentions also that the philosophic nature of the guardian would, by way of analogy with a good watchdog, consist in the capacity to distinguish one's own from what is alien. Along with his philosophic nature and his counterposed spirit, the two qualities of soul necessary for him, the prospective guardian would need also to have two qualities of body, namely swiftness and strength (376 c). Granted these qualities, what is then of utmost importance is that the guardians have the proper kind of education. Hence, there commences the long discussion of the education of the guardians which occupies the remainder of Book II and almost all of Book III. Socrates' founding of cities becomes primarily a founding of an educational system for the guardians of the city.

The result of supplying the city with proper guardians is that the luxurious city gets thoroughly purged (399 e). This purged city is the third of the cities built by Socrates. The building of this city presents an important contrast to that of the first two cities: Socrates' building of the third city takes the form of prescribing a system of education for its guardians. Furthermore, it should especially be noted that it is in this city, not in the simple city of artisans, that Socrates will find justice when he returns to that question in Book IV. The city in which justice gets found is the one which originates from the release of unnecessary desires and of acts of violence (war); in fact, the need for war, itself rooted in the release of these desires, is what gives rise quite directly to the entire problem of the guardians. Thus, justice will turn out to be found in a city in which the simple, pre-established harmony of the city of artisans has collapsed into violence and strife *and* which has then been purged. Justice is no "natural" condition but rather emerges from the taming of the violence and the purging of what is feverish and swollen.

As yet, the fourth city is hardly visible at all. Prior to Book V the only indication of how it will be built is the one given by Socrates' distinguishing between two kinds of guardians: the ruler (ἄρχον) and the auxiliaries (ἐπίκουροι) (412 a, 414 b). When it does finally appear, the fourth city will prove to be the city of the philosopher, and it will be the most problematic city of all. The building of it will take the form, not merely of prescribing the educational system of the guardians, but of actually undertaking to educate a guardian in deed.

(iii) Education of the Guardians (376 c – 404 e)

The education of the guardians consists of music (in the Greek sense—$\mu o v \sigma \iota \kappa \acute{\eta}$) and gymnastic, which, initially at least, are presented as being for the soul and the body respectively (476 e). Almost all the discussion of education is devoted to music. The great importance which Socrates attributes to music and to proper education in it is especially evident in a statement which he makes near the end of the entire discussion of the constitution of the cities:

> For they must beware of change to a strange form of music, taking it to be a danger to the whole. For never are the ways of music [$\mu o v \sigma \iota \kappa \mathring{\eta} \varsigma \ \tau \rho \acute{o} \pi o \iota$] moved without the greatest political laws being moved, as Damon says, and I am persuaded (424 c).[27]

The question is: What is the source of this great importance attached to music by Socrates?

It lies in the "imitative character" of the soul, that is, in the fact that the soul tends to imitate whatever is presented to it and in imitating it tends to become like it.[28] As Socrates asks Adeimantus:

> Or haven't you observed that imitations, if they are practiced continually from youth onwards, become established as habits and nature, in body and sounds and in thought? (395 d).

The result is that music is a potent means of forming the soul because of its capacity to present a model vividly and to evoke

---

[27] In the *Laws* the Athenian considers in some detail the specific link between lawlessness in music and the origination of democracy (700 a – 701 b).

[28] Cf. Nettleship, *Lectures on the Republic of Plato*, p. 78.

from the soul imitation of that model. Especially in the case of the very young, the soul assimilates itself rapidly and thoroughly to whatever model is held before it in the tales of the poets. This is why it is so very important to provide "models for speech about the gods" (379 a; cf. 377 e — 383 c) and also about Hades[29] (cf. 386 a — 387 d) and about heroes (388 a — 391 e). The soul of the guardian, if it is to be molded into its properly courageous form, must be enticed into imitating all manner of things that pertain to the courageous life.

However, there is another level at which the kind of forming of the soul accomplished by music seems to transcend all such matters as the guardian's capacity as a warrior:

> Isn't this why the rearing in music is most sovereign? Because rhythm and harmony most of all insinuate themselves into the inmost part of the soul and most vigorously lay hold of it in bringing grace with them; and they make a man graceful if he is correctly reared, if not, the opposite. Furthermore, it is sovereign because the man properly reared on rhythm and harmony would have the sharpest sense for what's been left out and what isn't a beautiful product of craft or what isn't a fine product of nature. And due to his having the right kind of dislikes, he would praise the beautiful things; and, taking pleasure in them and receiving them into his soul, he would be reared on them and become a gentleman. He would blame and hate the ugly in the right way while he's still young, before he's able to grasp *logos*. And when *logos* comes, the man who's reared in this way would take most delight in it, recognizing it on account of its being akin (401 d — 402 a).

Proper music makes the soul graceful, i.e., properly formed. But, in turn, a soul that is so formed would then praise and blame the right things, even while he is still young and unable to grasp the *logos*. The effect of "beautiful" music is to form the soul of the

---

[29] When Socrates comes to prescribe how Hades is to be spoken of, his remarks become, in terms of the *mythos,* peculiarly significant. As he demands that the poets speak of Hades in such a way as to evoke courage on the part of the guardians so that they might most adequately fulfill their duty in the city, so, in the mythic play which Socrates and the others are playing, the problem of assuring the attachment of the philosopher to the city becomes progressively more urgent.

youth in such a way that, in turn, he is properly attuned to beauty. But attunement, openness, to beauty is nothing less than *eros* itself (cf. Ch. III, Sect. 2 c, iv). Hence, it is appropriate that Socrates draws a connection between music and love:

> Does it look to you as though our *logos* concerning music has reached an end? . . . At least it's ended where it ought to end. Surely musical matters should end in love matters that concern the beautiful (403 c).

Furthermore, if a young man is properly attuned by music, then, when *logos* comes, he would delight in it and would recognize it "on account of its being akin." Proper music is directed towards forming the soul in a way that makes it akin to *logos*—that is, such forming sets the soul in motion towards just that which *logos* serves to bring to manifestness.

Throughout the later part of the discussion of music there is still another important theme. Socrates insists that the guardians should not imitate many things but only one (394 e), that their music should involve oneness of style, mode, and rhythm, in contrast to music involving wide variation (397 b), and that there should be simplicity in their instruments (399 c). The point is that there should be a fundamental oneness running throughout what they imitate and their way of imitation, the result of which would then be to make the soul one with itself. It is a matter of instilling oneness in the soul by engaging it in appropriate imitative activity.

Thus, by appropriate imitative activity the soul is to become akin not only to *logos* but also to oneness. Yet, *logos* and oneness are themselves akin, for *logos* involves an already established gathering of manys into ones (cf. Ch. III, Sect. 2 c, iii). In both cases it is one and the same forming of the soul that is at issue. This forming prepares the way for virtue (cf. esp. *Laws* 653 b).

(c) Virtue (427 d — 445 e)

The issue of oneness, which emerges in the discussion of the education of the guardians, is also of crucial importance in the consideration of the city as such. The greatest good of the city is,

Socrates says, "what binds it together and makes it one" (462 b). Likewise, for the individual man as a citizen of the city the greatest good lies in becoming one rather than many:

> one man, one job—so that each man, practicing his own, which is one, will not become many but one; and thus, you see, the whole city will naturally grow to be one and not many (423 d).

It should be noted, however, that in the context of the discussion of the city oneness is understood, not in relation to *logos* and music, as in the discussion of education, but in relation to art. The oneness of the city is the unity of the various classes defined by the various arts practiced in the city. The oneness of the individual man in the city is construed, correspondingly, as his practicing of one art rather than many. In this regard we recall that in terms of the refined sense of art introduced by Socrates in Book I no man practices only one art, not even in the purged city that has been built, not even in the city of artisans from which it is descended: every man, whatever his art, practices also the art of money-making. This open rupture of the oneness of man at the level of art and the city strengthens our already aroused suspicion that there is another kind of oneness more appropriate to man. Nevertheless, the entire discussion of virtue within the context of the discussion of the city (Book IV) is decisively confined to the point of view of art.

When the founding of the third city has been completed, Socrates says to Adeimantus:

> In the next place, get yourself an adequate light somewhere; and look yourself—and call in your brother and Polemarchus and the others—whether we can somehow see where the justice might be and where the injustice, in what they differ from one another, and which the man who's going to be happy must possess, whether it escapes the notice of all gods and humans or not (427 d).

Thus, Socrates proposes that, having built an appropriate city, they return to the problem posed in Book II, the problem of justice, for the sake of which the entire building of the cities was undertaken. We wonder, however, where this "adequate light" of which Socrates speaks is to be gotten—whether getting it might not involve a more strenuous labor than has been required for building the cities.[30] We wonder especially when we observe that Socrates and his companions are to identify not only justice (δικαιοσύνη) but also the other three principal virtues, wisdom (σοφία), courage (ἀνδρεία), and moderation (σωφροσύνη); in fact, they are to identify them twice, once in the city and then in the individual man.

(i) Virtue in the City (427 d – 434 c)

In the discussion of its virtues the city is, in effect, regarded as an extended community of artisans.[31] This permits the virtues of the city to be derived from the general relation between virtue and art. We shall attempt to interpret what Socrates says about the virtues by thematizing this derivation, which he lets remain largely implicit.

The general relation between virtue and art was already introduced in Socrates' discussion with Thrasymachus in Book I: the virtue of something is that which enables it to do its work well. So, in the case of man, taken simply as an artisan, virtue is that which enables him to practice his art with excellence; his virtue coincides with his measuring up to those pre-conditions that are required for the effective practice of his art. Now, in fact, the city originally came into being because of those needs of man which can be satisfied by the arts; that is, the city came into being for the purpose of providing a context for the effective practice of the arts. So, the question of the virtues in the city is simply the question of the city's providing the contextual pre-conditions for the practice of the arts.

The basic pre-condition is this: The context should be such that

---

[30] Notice the response of Glaucon, who suddenly enters the conversation at this point: "You're talking nonsense." Referring to Socrates' earlier promise, he goes on to insist that Socrates himself look for justice—which, presumably, means that it is Socrates who is to provide the "appropriate light."

[31] At one point the guardians are even referred to as "craftsmen of the city's freedom" (395 b – c).

each man practices *only his art*—that is, only the one art for which his nature best suits him. It should be a context which insures the closest harmony (oneness) between what a man is and what he does (i.e., what art he practices). The city which provides this basic pre-condition is a just city. Therefore, justice is, as Socrates says, "the minding of one's own business and not being a busybody" (433 b). Socrates confirms his "definition" of justice by comparing it to the meaning which justice has in a more restricted, legal context. Referring to the "judging of lawsuits," he says:

> Will they have any other aim in their judging than that no one have what belongs to others, nor be deprived of what belongs to him? . . . And therefore, from this point of view too, the having and doing of one's own and what belongs to one would be agreed to be justice (433 e – 434 a).

Justice is a kind of attending to one's own (cf. *Laws* 757 c).

Socrates notes that, in fact, what has now been identified as justice in the city—"that each one must practice one of the functions in the city, that one for which his nature made him naturally most fit" (433 a)—is simply the rule which they laid down in the beginning of the discussion of the city (cf. 370 a) and have used throughout that discussion. Thus, in a sense the entire inquiry has been circular. They set out to construct the city in order to discover justice in it. But justice could be discovered in it only if it is a just city that is constructed, only if, in building it, they put justice in it. Yet, in order to do this, they must already, in some sense, know what justice is. Thus, from the point of view of the problem of justice, the entire discussion, the entire building of the cities, has served only to make explicit and to identify that vague opinion about justice that was had at the beginning. The entire construction of the city has served as a means, a vehicle, for recollection. Yet, we wonder how good a recollection it has been in view of Socrates' proposal to look not only for justice but also for injustice in this city.

Just before the identification of justice in the city, Socrates draws a curious image:

The place really appears to be hard going and steeped in shadows. . . . At least it's dark and hard to search out. But, all the same, we've got to go on (432 c).

This image serves to remind us again of the mythical context in which justice is being sought. The whole inquiry leading to the identification of justice has, in terms of the *mythos,* been carried out in Hades. Socrates has gone in search of justice by founding cities in Hades—which is to say, *not* by making an ascent out of Hades. This suggests that the "definition" of justice arrived at may be somewhat less than adequate; and Socrates hints in the same direction when he says that "this—the practice of minding one's own business—*when* it comes into being *in a certain way,* is *probably* justice" (433 b—emphasis added).

The locus of the inadequacy thus hinted at is indicated by the expression "minding one's own business." This is most easily seen if we refer back to the beginning of the discussion of the city where the rule that is later to be identified as justice is first introduced (369 c − 370 a). There Socrates is contending that each man should practice only one art and should exchange products with those who practice other arts. This arrangement is contrasted with practicing all the arts needed to satisfy one's own needs—literally, it is contrasted with "minding his own business for himself." The point is that the minding of one's own business that is later identified as justice was originally introduced by contrast with another way of minding one's own business. Thus, the decisive question is: What is it that really constitutes a man's own? For Cephalus a man's own, what he is owed, are the things he has bought. For Polemarchus a man's own, what he is owed, is good or evil (in an indefinite sense) depending on whether he is a friend or an enemy. For Thrasymachus a man's own is whatever he has strength enough to take (provided it is to his advantage or, in the revision of Cleitophon, seems to his advantage). For the hypothetical man prior to the building of the city of artisans a man's own consists of the means of providing for all one's basic bodily needs. For the men in the cities built by Socrates a man's own is his art. But we might well wonder even about the last of these opinions. We might well wonder whether a man's art is what is most truly his own. Is a man's art that to which he is bound in the most fitting unity? Or is there another bond, another oneness, that is more proper to him *as* man if not as citizen?

The other three virtues, no less than justice, are derived from the general relation of virtue to art. Thus, in order to determine the character of courage, wisdom, and moderation, we need to extend further our consideration of the contextual pre-conditions for the effective practice of the arts.

Among these conditions is the need for protection from external forces that would disrupt the practice of the arts[32] ; also, in the luxurious city there is the need for an army capable of acquiring that additional land that is needed once the arts ministering to the unnecessary needs are added to the city. These functions are performed by the auxiliaries, and they are performed most effectively when the auxiliaries are courageous. A city which provides for the effective performance of this function is a courageous city, and it is so by virtue of the courage of a part (i.e., of the auxiliaries). What is this courage? Socrates says that it is "the preserving of opinion produced by law through education about what—and what sort of thing—is terrible" (429 c; cf. *Laches* 195 a). Socrates notes, however, that this kind of courage, this preservation of opinion about what is worthy of fear, is merely "political courage"—that, later, courage will need a "still finer treatment" (430 c). Our suspicion is that such treatment would bring courage into relation with knowledge rather than opinion.

Finally, the practice of an art requires knowledge (or right opinion) of two kinds. It requires the "know-how" characteristic of the particular arts. This is acquired primarily by imitation, by subordinating oneself to a master practitioner of the art; this suggests already the importance of moderation. But the second kind of knowledge (or right opinion) is more important for our present considerations: excellence in the practice of the arts throughout the city as a whole requires that there be knowledge (or right opinion) regarding the ends to be served by the arts. From what source does the artisan receive this end? A clue is

---

[32] Cf. Ballard, *Socratic Ignorance,* Ch. III, esp. p. 64.

provided by a distinction introduced towards the end of the *Republic* between three kinds of arts: with respect to any given thing, there are three arts, the art of using that thing, the art of making that thing, and the art of imitating. For our present purposes what is important is that the user is the one who knows most about the thing and who should dictate to the maker how it is to be made (601 d). This suggests the notion of a hierarchy of arts in which the end to be achieved in any given art is assigned to it by the next higher art in the hierarchy.[33] In such a hierarchy there must, however, be an ultimate art which assigns the end to the entire hierarchy (cf. *Lysis* 219 c – d). Such an art of final ends—final *within* the context of the city—is wisdom, which is, by Socrates' "definition," "a kind of knowledge . . . about how the city as a whole would best deal with itself and the other cities" (428 d).

So, a virtuous city must embody wisdom, must incorporate an assignment of the various hierarchies of arts to their proper ends. Such an embodiment requires two things. First, those who practice this final art must practice it with excellence, must be able genuinely to discern the proper ends. Thus, the wisdom of the city has its locus in a single part of the city, the rulers. But, secondly, it is necessary that the others in the city subordinate their practice to those final ends supplied by the rulers, that they let these ends rule over their own practice; this is to say that there must be agreement that the wise are to rule. This condition in the city is moderation (σωφροσύνη), which is a kind of accord as to who should rule, a harmony (oneness) of the three parts of the city. Socrates says that it makes

> the weaker, the stronger, and those in the middle . . . sing the same chant together. So we would quite rightly claim that this unanimity is moderation, an accord of worse with better,

---

[33] This notion of a hierarchy of arts is elaborated by Ballard on the basis of various indications in the dialogues. He gives the following example: "The shipbuilder tells the wood-trimmer what kind of wood he needs to use; that is, he provides the wood-trimmer with knowledge of his end. The Navy, knowing how it must use its ship, supplies the shipwright with the general specifications for the ships which he is to build. The political organization informs the Navy when and against whom it should use its forces. Wherever there is a superior art, the end of the inferior art becomes determinate" (*ibid.*, p. 69).

according to nature, as to which must rule in the city and in each one (432 a).

It should be noted that of the three additional virtues moderation is most closely akin to justice. Both pertain to the city as a whole rather than to one of the three classes in the city (as in the cases of wisdom and courage). Also, we observe that in the *Symposium* (209 a) they are mentioned together by Diotima as constituting that highest part of prudence (φρόνησις) which concerns the regulation of cities. And, in the *Charmides* (161 b) the formula "doing one's own business" (the "definition" of justice in the *Republic*) is proposed as a definition of moderation (cf. *Laws* 710 a). Already we have in the discussion we are considering in the *Republic* an important indication of how they belong together: justice concerns the proper separation between the parts of the city, whereas moderation concerns the proper relating (combining) of these parts so as to form the city into one whole. Thus, justice and moderation refer to the separating and combining, the collection and division, of the city with respect to its parts. To the extent that collection and division belong together, so do justice and moderation.

(ii) Virtue and the Soul (434 d – 445 e)

The transition to the consideration of virtue in the individual man is introduced by the following remark:

> Isn't it quite necessary for us to agree that the very same *eide* and dispositions as are in the city are in each of us? . . . Surely they didn't get there from any other place. It would be ridiculous if someone should think that the spiritedness didn't come into the cities from those private men who are just the ones imputed with having this character (435 e).

Thus, Socrates proceeds to attempt to set up a formal correspondence between the city and the human soul. In order to do this it becomes necessary for him to conduct a brief inquiry regarding the soul.

The discussion of the soul is prefaced with a warning that the account will not be adequate to the matter at issue. Socrates says:

But know well, Glaucon, that in my opinion, we'll never get a precise grasp of it on the basis of procedures such as we're now using in the *logos*. There is another longer and further road leading to it (435 d).

For the moment, we are given no indication what this longer road might be. Instead, Socrates proceeds directly to the task of treating the three parts of the soul. One part he names "λογιστικόν" (calculating part). The name is derived from "λογισμός," the primary sense of which is "computation with numbers" in a rather practical sense, the more general sense of which is something like "reckoning." It should also be noted, however, that the root word is "*logos*," as is especially brought out when Socrates speaks of the spirited part taking the side of the calculating part against desire: what he says precisely is that "spirit becomes the ally of *logos*" (440 b). The link of the calculating part to *logos* is also brought out in the description of the desiring part: Socrates speaks of

> naming the part of the soul with which it calculates, the calculating, and the part with which it loves, hungers, thirsts, and is agitated by the other desires, the ἀλογιστόν [lacking in *logos*] and desiring, companion of certain replenishments and pleasures (439 d).

Finally, both the calculating and the desiring parts are distinguished from the spirited part (θυμός), which refers to the aggressive element in man, to the competitive and ambitious element, and to that which makes man feel indignant towards injustice.

Most of the discussion of the soul is devoted to establishing the genuineness of the division of the soul into the three parts. Once this is established, Socrates then sets up the formal correspondence between the three classes in the city and the three parts of the soul:

Rulers	— Calculating part (λογιστικόν)
Auxiliaries	— Spirited part (θυμός)
Artisans	— Desiring part (ἐπιθυμία)

The most remarkable thing of all is that in the entire discussion of the relation of the individual man to the city, Socrates treats man as though he were nothing but soul—as though he had no body.

On the basis of the correspondence between the city and man, the virtues in the individual man are finally identified. The identification is a straightforward application of the previous "definitions" (of virtues in the city) to the case of the individual. Justice consists in each part of the soul performing its proper function. Moderation is the accord between the parts such that there is agreement that the calculating part should rule and the others be ruled. Courage consists in the preservation, in the spirited part, of those opinions given to it by the calculating part regarding what ought and ought not to be feared. Wisdom is linked to the calculating part and consists in knowledge of what is beneficial for each part and for the whole composed of these parts (441 d − 442 d).

It should be noted that there is one quite essential shift in the otherwise straightforward transition from justice in the city to justice in the individual man. Whereas justice in the city involves minding one's external business, as it were, that is, not meddling in the arts practiced by others, justice in the individual man concerns an *inner condition*. Justice in the individual man is not a matter of external action but of the inner condition from which action arises. Socrates says:

> And in truth justice was, as it seems, something of this sort; however, not with respect to a man's minding his external business, but with respect to what is within, with respect to what truly concerns him and his own. . . . [He] sets his own house in good order and rules himself; he arranges himself, becomes his own friend, and harmonizes the three parts, exactly like three notes in a harmonic scale, lowest, highest, and middle. And if there are some other parts in between, he binds them together and becomes entirely one from many, moderate and harmonized. Then, and only then, he acts. . . . In all these actions he believes and names a just and fine action one that preserves and helps to produce this condition, and wisdom the knowledge that supervises this action (443 c − e).

In view of this description of the just life and the reflection that injustice must be the opposite, namely faction in the soul analogous to sickness, Glaucon agrees that they have, in effect, answered the question as to whether justice or injustice is intrinsically more profitable. The life of justice has been vindicated, and what was begun in Book II has been brought to its conclusion.

Perhaps the most curious thing in this discussion is the description of wisdom: it is linked explicitly to the calculating part of the soul (the part having *logos*) in distinction from desire (the part lacking *logos*). But what does this say about the love of wisdom—about philosophy? For, *as love* it is linked not only to the calculating part but also to *desire,* to that which is most radically opposed to the calculating part. The result is that what Socrates says about wisdom leaves philosophy out of account. What he says provides no place for philosophy as a unifying of the most extreme opposites in the soul, as a unifying of *eros* and *logos.* Socrates the philosopher has left philosophy out of account. He has playfully forgotten himself. A comedy is being prepared.

(d) The Comedy of the City (449 a – 473 c)

We need to attend with special care to the curious way in which Book V begins. It will be recalled that in his original proposal in Book II Socrates indicated that he would set about to find both justice and injustice by watching a city coming into being in *logos* (369 a). After the building of the cities was finished and Socrates directed the discussion back to the question of justice, he again asserted that the task was to find both justice and injustice in the city that had been built. However, in the subsequent discussion (in Book IV) all that Socrates really finds in that city is justice; he speaks of injustice only by way of very general contrast with justice. So, Socrates has not found injustice in the city that he has built. Yet, despite this, he sets out at the beginning of Book V to look for injustice *in other kinds of cities.* However, he is interrupted; and the discussion of these other cities which he was about to begin is not resumed until Book VIII. The interruption is appropriate, for ⁶Socrates has not done what he promised to do; and we anticipate that the section that begins with this interruption will serve to bring to light precisely what Socrates has omitted, that is, the injustice in the city that has been built. This section, ironically treated as a mere digression, is, in fact, the center of the *Republic*.

Thus, with Book V another new beginning is made. Appropriately, it opens with another re-enactment of part of the original beginning (of the dialogue as a whole). Polemarchus again detains Socrates. As he originally sent his slave, who took hold of Socrates' cloak from behind (327 b), so now he again stops Socrates by way of someone else; now it is Adeimantus, whose cloak he takes hold of from above, to whom he whispers his objection and who speaks it out for him. With reference to the *mythos* we may say that in both cases what Polemarchus interrupts is the same thing, namely, Socrates' exit from Hades, which in the building of the cities Socrates has attempted to win in the way prescribed for him by Glaucon and Adeimantus at the point of the other new beginning (Book II)—and which, in a curious sense, he has won by building a city among whose citizens the philosopher is not included.

Adeimantus is insistent: They will not let Socrates go, because he has robbed them of something. Of what has he robbed them? That is, what must he restore to them in the central Books? Adeimantus names the issues of the central Books: Socrates has robbed them of a "whole *eidos* of the *logos*" (εἶδος ὅλον . . . τοῦ λόγου). Specifically, Adeimantus says that what Socrates has failed to speak about is the *begetting* of children under those conditions, prescribed in the building of the cities, according to which the guardians have everything in common, including women and children. The charge is especially fitting in view of what Socrates is enacting, since it is precisely by birth, by embodiment, that the soul returns from Hades. Again, Adeimantus asserts that they'll not release Socrates until he deals with this matter. As in Book I a vote is taken, and the outcome is announced by—of all people— Thrasymachus: "In fact, you can take this as a resolution approved by all of us, Socrates" (450 a).[34]

---

[34] Strauss calls special attention to the involvement of Thrasymachus in this scene as constituting a "decisive difference" between it and the scene in which the first vote was taken: "whereas Thrasymachus was absent from the first scene, he has become a member

Socrates expresses very grave doubts about what he will say on these matters, and we wonder whether his words perhaps indicate something quite different from that agonistic irony of which Thrasymachus accused him—especially since Thrasymachus has just spoken for the first time since his defeat in Book I. Socrates is explicit that his hesitation does not result from a fear "of being laughed at," which suggests both that what is to follow may well be laughable, comic, and that Socrates is not afraid to play the comedy. He hesitates, rather, because, as he explains,

> I'm afraid that in slipping from the truth where one least ought to slip, I'll not only fall myself but also drag my friends down with me. I prostrate myself before Adrasteia, Glaucon, for what I'm going to say (451 a).

Socrates fears the fall back into Hades. And he prostrates himself before Adrasteia, i.e., Nemesis[35] —presumably because he fears that what he is to say might give the appearance of lacking moderation, of being too harsh.

In order really to thematize what is being put at issue in this new beginning made in Book V, we need to consider several curious features of the city, some of them spoken of in Book V, some of them dealt with in earlier Books. By collecting these features we will be able to gain the perspective on the matter at issue that we need in order to return to the beginning of Book V.

All these features bear on a single question, which thus provides us with a point of focus for the collecting. We need, first, to formulate the question—or, rather, to note the passage where Socrates formulates it for us. The passage occurs in Book V at the point where Socrates is discussing whether the communal sharing of women and children that has been prescribed for the guardians is possible. He puts the question thus:

> Then, . . . doesn't it remain to determine whether after all it is possible, as it is among other animals, that this community

---

of the city in the second scene. It would seem that the foundation of the good city requires that Thrasymachus be converted into one of its citizens" (*City and Man*, p. 116).

[35] Cf. Adam's note, Vol. I, p. 278; Bloom's note, p. 458.

come into being among human beings too, and in what way it is possible? (466 d).

The question which Socrates, in effect, raises here is whether this prescription is one which is appropriate not only to animals but also to men. More generally, the question is: Is the city which requires such prescriptions a city which is really appropriate to man? Is it really a human city that Socrates has built?

It is remarkable how, in constructing the city and prescribing the education and the way of life of the guardians, Socrates repeatedly ignores the body. For instance, there is virtually no mention of the *bodily skills* which the guardians obviously would need to learn in order to be able to fight and perform their distinctive function in the city. On the contrary, Socrates contends that even gymnastics is not for the training of the body but, like music, for the education of the soul (410 b − c; 411 e − 412 a). The entire educational system practically leaves the body out of account.[36] Likewise, in the discussion of medicine as it would be practiced in the city he is building, Socrates insists that they should admit only the simple old medicine of Asclepius and that in the city no one should be permitted to be so concerned with his bodily health that his practice of his art is disrupted; a healthy body is regarded as almost exclusively the result of a healthy soul (cf. 405 c − 406 c). Is this a city appropriate to man? Is it a human city?

In discussing the way of life of the guardians Socrates states explicitly that the goal at which all legislation is to be aimed is the unity of the city (462 a − b). The realization of this goal requires that no guardian have anything that is simply his own but that the guardians have everything in common, so that "they don't utter such phrases as 'my own' and 'not my own' at the same time in the city" (462 c). Yet, Socrates observes, though only in passing, that there is one thing that cannot be had in common under any conditions whatsoever, namely, the body (464 d). But, no allowance is made for this immovable limit which the realization of the goal of unity runs up against. Socrates simply proceeds as though

---

[36] Cf. Bloom's "Interpretive Essay," pp. 361-365.

there were no such limit—for example, when he speaks of "a community of pain and pleasure" (464 a), as though pain and pleasure were not finally and irremediably private.[37] Thus, the city that has been built takes virtually no account of human embodiment, and this is reflected in the curious fact, which we noted earlier, that the three parts of the city correspond to the three parts, not of man, but of the soul. What about a city that takes the body so lightly? Is it really a fit city for embodied man? Is it really a human city?

At the beginning of Book IV Adeimantus interrupts Socrates and, in the tone of a mock trial, accuses him of prescribing a way of life for the guardians that would not result in happiness. Socrates answers that he is not concerned with the happiness of any one group in the city but with the happiness of the city as a whole. But, of course, this does not really answer the objection that Adeimantus has raised. The point is that the private good of the guardians does not seem to coincide with the public good, with the good of the city; it seems dubious whether in such a city they could ever attain to what is their own in the highest sense, however perfect the city may be in other respects. Again, we wonder whether the city that Socrates has built is really a human city?

That the city is perhaps not a human city is especially suggested by the peculiar "noble lie" which he admits into the city. The lie consists of two parts. First, the citizens will be persuaded that their rearing and education were like a dream, that, in fact, they were fashioned under the earth so that the earth is their mother and all the other citizens their brothers (414 d – e). What is interesting is that this turns out not to be much of a lie at all; it turns out to be more or less the truth when Socrates prescribes the community of women and children for the guardians. But Socrates introduces this prescription only at the cost of introducing incest into the city; the fact that the city requires the permitting of

---

[37] In Book V of the *Laws* the Athenian speaks of a condition in which there would be community of wives, children, and all chattels, in which everything private would be so ruled out that eyes, ears, and hands would see, hear, and act in common! He goes on to remark that such a city would needs be inhabited by gods or sons of gods—that is, not by men (739 c – d).

incest, which is most contrary to nature, serves to strengthen still more our suspicion that the city is not in accord with man's nature. The other part of the "noble lie" proclaims that at birth a god added some kind of metal to the soul of each citizen, gold in the souls of those who were to be rulers, silver in the souls of auxiliaries, iron and bronze in the souls of artisans. Most people, so the story goes, produce offspring containing the same metal as themselves, but not always; hence, for maintaining good guardians, on which, in turn, the maintaining of the city itself depends, it is of utmost importance to detect what kind of metal is in every soul. Socrates says that the guardians will "keep over nothing so careful a watch as the children, seeing which of these metals is mixed in their souls" (415 b). Again, with this part of the lie as with the first part, what the lie says is more or less true: From the very beginning it was agreed that different men have different capacities and that each is thus suited to a particular art. So, if both parts of the lie are more or less true, why is it called a lie? Where is the lie in it? It is in the denial of natural birth and in the denial of privacy, here, specifically, of privacy of soul. The soul is regarded as though it were a kind of ore to be tested and completely determined with regard to its constitution, so as to allow the guardians in power to control the new generations and maintain the complete stability of the city.[38] The "noble lie" transforms men into a treasure to be mined, tested, and refined. We recall that Pluto, the traditional ruler over the underworld, was renowned for the wealth of precious metals in the earth which belong to him.

It is especially significant that the lie connects the abolition of privacy with the denial of natural birth, for human procreation is something laden with mystery, something which resists being brought into the open and given the public form of a *logos*. This is the issue in that passage in Book V where Socrates discusses the mating of the guardians: He says that "they'll be led by an inner natural necessity to sexual mixing with one another"; but Glaucon replies, "Not geometrical but erotic necessities" (458 d). Erotic

---

[38] This feature of the "noble lie" is elaborated by Brann, "Music of the *Republic*," p. 10.

necessities are of a different order from those that can be calculated, determined, and controlled. This same matter is even more openly declared at the beginning of Book VIII where Socrates tells how the corruption of the city first sets in. This happens when the rulers fail to understand the "geometrical number" which would prescribe the proper time for the begetting of children, with the result that children are begotten "out of season"; they eventually become guardians and, lacking that essential capacity to determine what kind of metal is in the soul, cannot but initiate the decline of the city (cf. 546 b − 547 a). This matter is most openly declared when it is set in the myth of Er: The one thing of which Er learned nothing was "how he came into his body" (621 b). So, human birth and all that is linked to it is enshrouded in mystery and withdraws from the prying eyes of even the wisest guardians; and it is upon this that the city founders.[39] The city, whose coming-to-be Socrates and his companions have watched so closely, does not take into account man's coming-to-be. Because it fails to take this into account, the city is not a human city.

Now it is possible to see what is transpiring in Book V: It is a *comedy about this city,* a comedy the very playing of which serves to bring to light what is comic about this city, the self-forgetfulness which the building of it has involved. Socrates openly refers to what he is to say in Book V as a "drama," suggesting even that it is a continuation of one already begun (451 c); and we are even told that previously people have made a "comedy" of similar things (452 c − d).[40] Socrates even goes on to lay down standards for comedy (452 d). And, once the standards are given, Socrates and Glaucon openly begin the performance: They pretend to carry on a dialogue with those on the other side of the question, so that

---

[39] *Ibid.,* p. 12.

[40] The parallels between Book V of the *Republic* and Aristophanes' comedy *The Assembly of Women* are so striking that they could hardly be accidental. In Aristophanes' play private property is eliminated, women are politicized and communalized, *eros* is treated as a resource and what is private is declared public; even incest makes its appearance. It may well be, as Bloom suggests, that Book V of the *Republic* is Plato's attempt to demonstrate the philosopher's superiority to the comic poet in deed, by producing a comedy which in almost every respect outdoes the corresponding play of Aristophanes. Cf. Bloom's "Interpretive Essay," pp. 380-381; also Strauss, *Socrates and Aristophanes,* pp. 263-282.

there results a dialogue within their dialogue; they put on the drama, they play the comedy.

What happens in the comedy? The denial of privacy that is basic to the city generates the comical demand for "a community of pleasure and pain" and, concomitantly, the bizarre demand that birth and death—of all things!—be made public (462 b). It generates the ridiculous sight of "the women exercising naked with the men in the palaestras" (452 a – b)[41] —as though men and women were never subject to "erotic necessities," as though there were no such thing as eros. What especially happens in the comedy is that Socrates has to confront three big "waves" (or "foetuses"—both meanings are carried by the same Greek word: κῦμα). These waves have to do with women, family, and philosophy—all of which have one thing in common: eros. Socrates plays the comedy especially by acting out the attempt to incorporate the erotic into the city, to politicize eros. This he does by making the guardians have wives and children in common; by reducing the difference between men and women to something analogous to the difference between bald men and long-haired men (454 c)[42] ; by treating the sexual relations of the guardians as taking place only for the production of children for the city; by trying to control by law all mating[43] —that is, by trying to treat "erotic necessities" as though they were "geometrical necessities."

What the comedy brings to light is that it is eros that disrupts the city—that because the city is not able to incorporate eros, hence, human birth, the body, and privacy, it is something either more or less than a human city. But, a city which excludes eros thereby excludes also the philosopher. We begin to see how really paradoxical the paradox of the philosopher-king is. How is a city the entire character of which involves the exclusion of eros to admit that highest kind of eros: philosophy?

---

[41] "How then shall one attempt, without being *laughed at,* actually to compel women to take food and drink publicly and exposed to the view of all? The female sex would more readily endure anything rather than this: accustomed as they are to live a retired and private life, women will use every means to resist being led out into the light, and they will prove much too strong for the lawgiver" (*Laws* 781 c – d).

[42] Cf. *Laws* 802 e – 803 a, where the Athenian speaks of the "natural difference" between men and women.

[43] Cf. *Laws* 773 b – d, where the attempt to make laws to control marriage is called "laughable."

Section 3. The Philosopher (473 c — 507 b)

Anticipating that he may indeed be drowned in laughter, Socrates faces the biggest of the three waves:

> "Unless," I said, "the philosophers rule as kings or those now called kings and chiefs genuinely and adequately philosophize, and political power and philosophy coincide in the same place, while the many natures now making their way to either apart from the other are by necessity excluded, there is no rest from ills for the cities, my dear Glaucon, nor I think for human kind, nor will the regime we have now described in *logos* ever come forth from nature, insofar as possible, and see the light of the sun. This is what for so long was causing my hesitation to speak: seeing how very paradoxical it would be to say" (473 d — e).

Already, before stating the paradox of the philosopher-king, Socrates insisted that he should not be compelled to present the city as coming into being in every way in deed in exactly the shape that it was given in *logos* (473 a). Indeed, he had good reason to reserve the possibility that the city might undergo some change as a result of introducing into it what is required in order for it to come-to-be in deed. On the one hand, the philosopher must be introduced into the city in order for it to come-to-be in deed, whereas, on the other hand, the city is precisely such as to exclude the philosopher. The philosopher-king is a *paradox*. And thus Glaucon responds by referring to the battle which Socrates, himself enacting the tension of this paradox, is bound to provoke by his proclamation, a battle in which men, stripped for action will rush at Socrates with whatever weapons come to hand. Glaucon, responsible in a way for leading Socrates into his present situation, offers to help with the defence as best he can; and he advises Socrates to "try to show the disbelievers that it is as you say" (474 b). The task is to attach a showing to the saying, to let what has been said become manifest.

We have noted already that the center of the *Republic*, hence, the entire consideration of philosophy, is treated ironically as a digression. Now we can see what is behind the irony, namely, the paradox itself, the radical discontinuity between philosophy and politics. Given the paradox, there is indeed a sense in which it really is a digression when, in the midst of a discussion of justice and the city, Socrates suddenly goes off in pursuit of the philosopher. On the other hand, however, this pursuit is necessary as the condition for the possibility of genuinely grasping the paradox in its full force; in this sense, the immediate effect of the paradox is to create the need for determining more precisely who the philosopher is. It is to this task that Socrates now turns.

(a) The Philosopher as Lover (474 c – 475 e)

To be a philosopher (φιλόσοφος) means, etymologically, to be a lover (φίλος) of wisdom (σοφία). Since the philosopher is a lover, Socrates begins speaking about the philosopher by speaking about different kinds of lovers: lovers of boys, of wine, of honor, of wisdom. Then he recalls something for Glaucon: When we say that a man loves (φιλεῖν) something, this is rightly (ὀρθῶς) said of him only if he shows a love not just for one part but for all (πᾶν) of that which he is said to love (474 c). A lover loves the *whole* of that which he loves; the philosopher loves the whole of wisdom and not just a part. Glaucon replies that if what Socrates says is so then it is necessary to include among philosophers the lovers of sights and the lovers of hearing, who are eager to learn about all kinds of things. Socrates answers that these men are not philosophers though "they are like philosophers"; but the genuine philosophers are those who love not just any sight but "the sight of the truth."

Several observations are in order regarding this initial identification of the philosopher. First of all, it should be observed that the entire discussion of the kinds of lovers uses the word *philia* rather than *eros*. The most immediate reason for this is, of course, the etymology of *"philosophos."* The more unambiguously passionate *"eros"* (cf. Ch. III, esp. Sect. 1 a) is not, however, entirely missing from the discussion. The first example of lovers cited by Socrates is the lover of boys, who is explicitly called an ἐρωτικός (474 d). More important, however, than the example is the fact that in introducing it Socrates makes an unmistakeable reference to Glaucon as himself an ἐρωτικός, a characterization which Glaucon conditionally accepts, for the sake of the *logos*. It appears that Glaucon is erotic; and, recalling the role which the link between philosophy and *eros* has played in generating the paradox of the philosopher-king and launching the present discussion, we wonder whether Socrates' discussion of the philosopher is perhaps directed especially to Glaucon and intended as something more than a mere defence.

Secondly, it should be noted that immediately after the discussion of the other kinds of lovers (475 b), Socrates introduces alongside the discussion of *philia* a parallel description in terms of desire (ἐπιθυμία). In fact, it is in terms of desire rather than *philia* that Socrates first describes the philosopher:

> Won't we also then assert that the philosopher is a desirer of wisdom, not of one part and not another, but of all of it? (475 b).

In this connection it should especially be observed that the word "desire" (ἐπιθυμία), now used to characterize the philosopher, was used earlier to name the lowest of the three parts of the soul (cf. 437 d ff.). This implication that there is a link between philosophy and desire marks a shift in the basic way of regarding the soul, a shift away from the understanding of the soul by analogy with the city. This shift corresponds to the discontinuity posed in the paradox of the philosopher-king. It is also evident later in Book V when Socrates speaks of knowledge and opinion as powers (δυνάμεις) of the soul (477 b – d). He no longer speaks of parts of the soul, nor does he distinguish the different kinds of men in terms of the predominance of one part over the others. Presumably, he is now engaged on that "longer road" which earlier (435 d) was said to be necessary in order really to understand the nature of the soul.

Finally, it should be noted that in Socrates' initial statement and in the subsequent discussion of various examples—dealing with lovers of boys, wine-lovers, and lovers of honor—the various kinds of lovers are distinguished, not as loving different parts of the same whole, but rather as loving different wholes; each lover loves that which he loves *as* a whole (ὅλως—475 b). The different kinds of lovers are thus distinguished in terms of the different kinds of wholes which they love. Among those wholes in reference to which a kind of lover is determined there is the whole of wisdom (σοφία) or learning (μάθημα). It is in reference to this whole that Socrates first distinguishes the philosopher. However, when Glaucon introduces another kind of lover of this whole, namely the lovers of sights and the lovers of hearing, a further distinguishing becomes necessary. Ironically, Socrates resolves the difficulty by confining the philosopher's characteristic love to only a part of the whole: the philosopher is one who loves, not all sights, but the sight of truth. Also, the philosopher appears not to love even a part of that learning which has to do with sounds; Socrates mentions nothing on the side of the philosopher corresponding (as a part) to what is loved by the lovers of sounds. It is as though the philosopher had no love whatever even for those sounds which are cast in the form of *logos*. In distinction from the other lovers, who love the whole of what they love, the philosopher appears as one who loves only that part of learning which has to do with sight and, still more specifically, only the part of this part which concerns the sight of truth. The philosopher, it appears, loves only a part of a part.

This ironic restriction of the love distinctive of the philosopher will be revoked in the discussion which Socrates offers in explanation of his identification of the philosopher as a lover of the sight of truth, and the revocation will prove to be precisely such as to bring to light the fact that none of those wholes in reference to which the other kinds of lovers were defined are genuinely wholes in any final sense. In other words, Socrates will proceed in such a way as to show that the philosopher is the only one whose love is a love of the whole—that, consequently, only the philosopher's is love in the full sense.

(b) The Philosopher and the *Eide* (475 e – 476 d)

Socrates proceeds to explain what he meant in describing the philosopher as a lover of the sight of truth. For purposes of this explanation he introduces *eide* such as the beautiful itself. This introduction of deliberate speech about *eide* into the discussion is crucial in determining the course which the entire central part of the *Republic* will take. We need to attend to it with utmost care.

Socrates uses the word "εἶδος"; later he uses, more or less synonomously, the word "ἰδέα." The word "εἶδος" is derived from the verb "εἴδω," meaning "see." Thus, its root meaning is: that which is seen, the seen, that which presents itself to a seeing, that which shows itself (which makes itself manifest) to a seeing. Likewise, "ἰδέα" is derived (by way of "ἰδεῖν") from "εἴδω" and refers even more pointedly to the look of something, to its way of showing itself to a seeing. The reference of these words to a seeing, to something's showing itself to a seeing, is of utmost importance. If they are thoughtlessly translated as "form" or "idea" and regarded as meaning something like "concept," then the issue to which these words are addressed in the dialogues will simply be left untouched (cf. Ch. III, Sect. 2 c, iii).

Socrates' introduction of deliberate speech about *eide* is prefaced by a curious remark to Glaucon. Glaucon has just asked Socrates to explain what he means by calling philosophers lovers of the sight of truth. Socrates answers:

> It wouldn't be at all easy to tell someone else. But you, I suppose, will grant me this (475 e).

When Glaucon asks what he is supposed to grant, Socrates proceeds to speak of the beautiful (καλόν) and its opposite and then of all the *eide* (475 e – 476 a). That Socrates introduces the *eide* by speaking first of the beautiful is appropriate in light of what is said in the *Phaedrus* regarding the pre-eminent capacity of the beautiful to shine forth in and through the visible (250 b – d; cf. Ch. III, Sect. 2 c, iv)—especially appropriate since Glaucon is an ἐρωτικός. But what is most amazing is that Glaucon proceeds simply to grant what Socrates has said as though it were perfectly obvious. This abrupt introduction of the *eide*, the first explicit introduction of them in the *Republic*, is not questioned at all, and Socrates makes absolutely no attempt at anything like a justification—no more than he did when he introduced them through the medium of dreams near the end of the *Cratylus* (cf. Ch IV, Sect. 7 b). The *eide* are simply posed, posed as hypotheses. What Glaucon can be assumed to grant is the posing of the hypotheses.

Socrates' first statement regarding the *eide* is not an assertion that they are; on the contrary, what he says corresponds closely to that single determination which he stated in the *Cratylus.* Socrates says: "Since the beautiful is the opposite of ugly, they are two"; when Glaucon grants this, he continues: "Since they are two, isn't each also one?" What Socrates says of the *eide* is that each is what it is, totally distinct from what it is not; each *eidos* is one, and its being one is identical with its being the same as itself, with its being, as was said in the *Cratylus,* always such as it is.

When Glaucon grants without hesitation that the beautiful is one and the ugly also one, Socrates proceeds to extend what he has said to all the *eide*:

> The same *logos* also applies then to the just and the unjust, the good and the bad, and all the *eide;* each is itself one, but by showing themselves everywhere in a community with actions, bodies, and one another, each looks like many (476 a).[44]

This statement not only extends to all the *eide* what was previously said regarding the beautiful and the ugly but also introduces a fundamental development beoynd Socrates' first statement. As he has already said with regard to the beautiful and the ugly, each *eidos* is itself one, that is, is one with itself. Now, however, he adds that, though each *eidos* is itself one, it can, nevertheless, *show itself* in such a way as to look like many. It is especially important to note here that the *eide* are not introduced in distinction from visible things or, more extensively, the things immediately manifest to perception. On the contrary, they are introduced by the statement that each is itself one, and, when a distinction is then introduced, it is a distinction, not between *eide* and visible things, but rather between what an *eidos* is—namely, itself, i.e., the same as itself, i.e., one—and what it shows itself *as* when it shows itself in

---

[44] Καὶ περὶ δὴ δικαίου καὶ ἀδίκου καὶ ἀγαθοῦ καὶ κακοῦ καὶ πάντων τῶν εἰδῶν πέρι ὁ αὐτὸς λόγος, αὐτὸ μὲν ἓν ἕκαστον εἶναι, τῇ δὲ τῶν πράξεων καὶ σωμάτων καὶ ἀλλήλων κοινωνίᾳ πανταχοῦ φανταζόμενα πολλὰ φαίνεσθαι ἕκαστον.

community with actions, bodies, and other *eide*—namely, as many, as different from itself, as not itself. In slightly different terms we can say that the distinction is a distinction between two modes of showing: on the one hand, a showing in which an *eidos* shows itself as it itself is, as one, as the same as itself; on the other hand, a showing in which it shows itself as many, in which it shows itself as it is not, in which it shows itself as being different from itself. What is remarkable is that even this second mode of showing is not necessarily linked to visible things; an *eidos* can show itself as many, as what it is not, by showing itself in community with other *eide*. Thus, there is reason to suppose that the distinction between the two modes of showing is more fundamental than the distinction between "intelligible" and visible.

In fact, it is only after this distinction has been drawn between the two modes of showing that Socrates introduces the distinction between the *eide* and visible things; and, even then, this latter distinction is not posed for its own sake but as a way by which to clarify the distinction drawn earlier between the philosophers, on the one hand, and the lovers of sights and the lovers of sounds, on the other. The latter, Socrates observes, take delight in beautiful sounds, colors, and shapes—the same things that in the *Cratylus* were said to be imitated in that kind of imitation from which Socrates distinguished the imitation proper to a name (cf. Ch. IV, Sect. 6 b). On the other hand, he now continues, the lovers of sights and the lovers of sounds are unable to see—what he says precisely is that their thought (διάνοια) is unable to see (ἰδεῖν)—the nature (φύσις) of the beautiful itself. Without explicitly saying so, he suggests that the philosophers are the ones who have this capacity that is lacking to the lovers of sights and the lovers of sounds (476 a – b).

However, the implied parallel of the distinction between the philosophers and the lovers of sights and of sounds and the distinction between the beautiful itself and beautiful sights and sounds is, in fact, revoked in the discussion which immediately follows. The distinction between the two kinds of lovers—the lovers of the sight of truth over against the lovers of sights and of sounds—does not turn out to correspond to the distinction between *eide* and the things immediately manifest to perception. On the contrary, Socrates proceeds to distinguish between, not two, but rather three kinds of men. First, there are those who are able to approach the beautiful itself and see it by itself. This kind of man, Socrates says, is rare (476 b); indeed, he turns out to be so in the subsequent discussion: he is not mentioned again. The second type of man is the one to whom we referred earlier in connection with Socrates' appeal to his dreams near the end of the *Cratylus* (Ch. IV, Sect. 7 b): he is the one who holds that there are beautiful things but does not hold that there is the beautiful itself and who, if he were led to knowledge of the latter, would be unable to follow. Such a man, Socrates says, lives in a dream in the sense that he believes "a likeness [ὅμοιον] of something to be not a likeness but rather the thing itself to which it is like" (476 c). The second kind of man is one who sees only beautiful things and who, because he does not pose the beautiful itself, takes the beautiful things to be the originals, failing to distinguish them as likenesses from the beautiful itself to which they are like. He fails to distinguish between image and original—that is, he fails to pose the original which "lies under" (i.e., the hypothesis) in the way enacted by Socrates and Glaucon at the point where the *eide* were first introduced. By contrast, the third kind of man is one who, in Socrates' words,

> believes that there is a beautiful itself and who is able to catch sight both of it and of what participates in it [τὰ μετέχοντα], and does not believe that what participates is it itself, nor that it itself is what participates (476 c – d).

The third kind of man is one who is awake; he is one who, seeing both the beautiful itself and the beautiful things, is able to distinguish between image and original. This man's thought (διάνοια), Socrates says, is knowledge (γνώμη), whereas the other's is opinion (δόξα). And, at the end of his extended consideration of this distinction, Socrates identifies the philosopher as the one whose thought is knowledge—as the third kind of man. *Thus,* the philosopher is *not* the one who has to do only with *eide* in contrast to the lovers of sights and sounds. Rather, the philosopher has, in a still undetermined sense, to do with both the beautiful itself *and* beautiful things.

We need, finally, to relate Socrates' three-fold distinction to the preceeding discussion of the kinds of lovers. Within the framework of the earlier discussion each kind of lover was at first defined in terms of that whole which he loves. As the discussion proceeded, however, the kinds of lovers tended to be defined in terms of a partition of the whole; thus, the whole of learning was partitioned between the lovers of sights and the lovers of sounds and possibly other unnamed lovers of such things. Finally, it appeared that in the case of the philosopher the relevant love was not even a love of a part of a whole but of a part of a part; the philosopher appeared to be a lover of part of that part of learning loved by the lovers of sights. In other words, the philosopher appeared to be that lover whose love is least directed to a whole.

The identification of the philosopher in the subsequent three-fold division stands in marked contrast to the earlier restriction of the philosopher's love to a part of a part. It turns out that the philosopher not only sees that part which is loved by the lovers of sight, hence also, presumably, those wholes loved by the other lovers; he sees not only the beautiful things but also the beautiful itself. That which is seen by the philosopher is a *whole* of which that which is loved by each of the other lovers is a part. With respect to what he sees, the philosopher is directed to the only whole which is truly a whole, to the only whole which is not a particular kind of whole, to the only whole that could not simply be regarded as a part alongside other wholes within a still larger whole. The philosopher, with respect to what he sees, is directed to *the* whole, not *a* whole, and in this connection the irony of the earlier descriptions of the various types of lovers as in every case loving a whole is evident; what each of them loves is his own particular whole, which is, thereby, not a whole in any final sense if at all.

But, granted that the philosopher is directed to the whole, to the only whole which cannot itself be regarded as a part of another whole, what is his relation to this whole? Socrates says that he *sees* it; more precisely, Socrates says, not that he sees the whole, but that he sees what are presumably its two principal parts; he sees the beautiful itself and the beautiful things. Yet, Socrates does not say that the philosopher loves the whole. On the contrary, when, at the end of the discussion of knowledge and opinion, he returns to the task of identifying the philosopher, the philosopher is said to love that on which knowledge depends (479 e – 480 a); what the philosopher loves is just the beautiful itself–apparently, therefore, not the beautiful things. The philosopher's love, no less than that of the other lovers, seems to be, in the end, only a love of a part. The philosopher, it seems, sees the whole but loves only a part. In fact, it is questionable whether he even sees the whole, for certainly he does not see those sounds that are loved by the lovers of sounds. It appears that what he sees cannot, by virtue of the fact that it is something to be seen, be the whole.

(c) Knowledge and Opinion (476 d – 480 a)

The discussion which now begins and which runs to the end of Book V is cast as an elaboration of the distinction between knowledge and opinion, which, in turn, was derived from the distinction between the second and third types of men previously identified. In fact, this latter distinction proved to be anything but clear, and we anticipate that the discussion of knowledge and opinion will not only elaborate what has already been said but also will recast it in the direction of a fundamental clarification. A first indication that this discussion is no mere extension of what has preceded is provided by the curious dramatic form in which the discussion is framed. Socrates asks:

> What if the man of whom we say that he opines but doesn't know gets harsh with us and disputes the truth of what we say? Will we have some way to soothe and gently persuade him, while hiding from him that he's not healthy? (476 d – e).

When Glaucon answers that such a way is needed, Socrates proceeds to the questioning regarding knowledge and opinion and instructs Glaucon to answer on behalf of this man of opinion who is to be soothed and gently persuaded. What follows is, thus, a conversation between Socrates and Glaucon cast in the form of a conversation between Socrates and the man of opinion. At the end of the discussion the dramatic device again explicitly emerges when Socrates asks Glaucon whether the lovers of opinion will be angry with them for speaking as they do; Glaucon answers: "No, that is, if they are persuaded by me. For it's not lawful to be harsh with what's true" (480 a). Who are these lovers of opinion whom Socrates is addressing? One of them is Glaucon himself, and that is why he answers on their behalf.[45] However, there is reason to suppose that Glaucon is not simply a man of opinion—that, however much his seeing may remain confined to the images of the domain of opinion, he is, nevertheless, on the threshold of transcending this domain. After all, he has granted Socrates' posing of the hypotheses and, in contrast, for example, to Cratylus, has not immediately revoked what was granted by affirming something like the Heraclitean flux. Glaucon is prepared to be educated by Socrates, and the present discussion initiates that education in deed. The discussion is not only an elaboration of the distinction between the man of opinion and the philosopher but, at the same time, an initiation in deed of the transition from the former to the latter; it is, in the dimension of deeds, a beginning of philosophy.

Socrates initiates the discussion by securing Glaucon's agreement that a man who knows, knows (γιγνώσκει) something. Socrates asks whether this something is something that *is* or *is not* (Πότερον ὂν ἢ οὐκ ὄν;). Glaucon answers that it is something that *is*, since, as he says in the form of a question, what *is not* could

---

[45] In the course of the discussion Socrates gives several indications that it is Glaucon himself and not just the hypothetical men of opinion that he is addressing. For example, at 479 a Socrates says: " 'Now, of these many beautiful things, you best of men [ὦ ἄριστη],' we'll say, 'is there any that won't also look ugly?' " The expression "ὦ ἄριστη" is addressed, not to the hypothetical men of opinion, but to Glaucon, who is the son of Ariston, as was indicated in the very first line of the dialogue. It should be noted that in this statement Socrates' use of this form of address is followed immediately by a reminder of the dramatic device being employed. Also the immediately preceding statement is itself abruptly interrupted by Socrates in order to recall the dramatic device and suggest the relation between Glaucon and those men of opinion. Socrates says: "Now, with this taken for granted, let him tell me, I shall say, and let him answer—that good man who doesn't believe that there is anything beautiful in itself and an *idea* of the beautiful itself, which always stays the same in all respects, but does hold that there are many beautiful things, this lover of sights who can in no way endure it if anyone asserts the beautiful is one and the just is one and so on with the rest" (478 e – 479 a).

not be known at all. Socrates responds by asking: Do we have an adequate grasp of the fact that what *is* entirely, is entirely knowable and what in no way *is*, is in every way unknowable?[46] It should be noted that in the middle of this question Socrates inserts another statement: "even if we should consider it in many ways." But when Glaucon answers that their grasp of this is adequate—though clearly they have *not* considered it in many ways—Socrates proceeds immediately to discuss the case of things which would be such as both to be and not to be. We are not told what those other ways are in which one ought to consider the statement that what entirely *is*, is entirely knowable and that what in no way *is*, is in every way unknowable. In place of this we get a discussion of those things in which there is a mixture of the "is" and the "is not" (476 e − 477 a).

Socrates proceeds to elaborate the schema that has begun to unfold. He suggests that if there were something such as both to be and not to be (εἶναί τε καὶ μὴ εἶναι), it would lie between what simply is and what in no way is. Thus, since knowledge depends on what is and ignorance on what is not, Socrates proposes to seek for something which would be between ignorance and knowledge and which would depend on that which is between what is and what is not. Agreeing, then, that knowledge (ἐπιστήμη) and opinion (δόξα) are different powers and that a power (δύναμις) ought to be regarded solely in terms of that on which it depends and in terms of what it accomplishes, it is agreed that knowledge and opinion, differing in what they accomplish, are dependent on different things. Since the knowable (γνωστόν) is that which is, the question is, then: what is the opinable (δοξαστόν)? The search for opinion has become a search for the opinable. It is quickly ascertained that the opinable is neither what is (τὸ ὄν) nor what is not (τὸ μὴ ὄν) and that opinion is, hence, neither knowledge nor ignorance. Since, furthermore, opinion surpasses neither knowledge in clarity nor ignorance in obscurity, it is ascertained that it must lie within the limits set by these two. The opinable is finally identified as that which both is and is not (477 a − 478 d).

---

[46] ὅτι τὸ μὲν παντελῶς ὂν παντελῶς γνωστόν, μὴ ὂν δὲ μηδαμῇ πάντῃ ἄγνωστον (477 a).

What remains is to find that which both is and is not—more precisely, that which participates in both "to be" (εἶναι) and "not to be" (μὴ εἶναι). This search is prefaced by a reminder of the dramatic device being employed, and we anticipate that the most crucial search is about to begin—or, at least, the search which is most difficult for one who, like Glaucon, is on the threshold of philosophy. For, in contrast to the preceding discussion, so much of which was dictated by the schema sketched at the beginning—in a way which Socrates suggested might need further consideration—what is now called for is what is most difficult for the man of opinion and what marks his decisive transition beyond this domain; what is called for is that images be recognized as images despite the fact that the originals themselves are not visible.

Socrates proceeds:

'Now, of these many beautiful things, you best of men,' we'll say, 'is there any that won't also look ugly? And of the just, any that won't look unjust? And of the holy, any that won't look unholy?'

Glaucon answers:

No, . . . but it's necessary that they look somehow both beautiful and ugly, and so it is with all the others you ask about.

Socrates continues:

And, then, the things that we would assert to be big and little, light and heavy—will they be addressed by these names any more than by the opposites of these names?

When Glaucon gives the expected negative answer, Socrates adds:

Then is each of the several manys what one asserts it to be any more than it is not what one asserts it to be?

It should be carefully noted that Socrates began by speaking about how things *look* (e.g., beautiful things also *look* ugly). But then he made a transition—an extremely crucial transition—from how things *look* to how they are *addressed by name,* from looking to being-named. Glaucon concludes the discussion:

> For the manys are also ambiguous, and it's not possible to think of them fixedly as either being or not being, or as both or neither (279 a — c).

Note carefully what Glaucon is concluding: The things to which they are referring (e.g., beautiful things) cannot be thought fixedly, determinately, either as being or not being nor as both nor as neither—which is to say that these things *cannot be thought* fixedly, determinately, *at all.* What is encountered by the attempt to think them is something indeterminately manifold, an *indeterminate many* (cf. *Theaet.* 152 d, with Ch. IV, Sect. 2 b).

The crucial question which we need to consider in reference to this discussion is: Precisely how does it happen that these things come to be manifest as indeterminate manys? In other words, how is the transition made *from* that stage at which things *look* both beautiful and ugly *to* that stage at which they present themselves as indeterminate manys, i.e., as neither beautiful nor ugly nor both nor neither? What does this transition involve? Socrates' statement already suggests the answer: the transition is a transition from looking to being-named; the transition is linked to our calling the things by name. But how is it that calling the things by name is able to bring about such a transition?

Initially the thing looks both beautiful and ugly. Such "looking" is possible only if the beautiful and the ugly have not been explicitly distinguished. This is evident if one considers what happens once the beautiful and the ugly are distinguished, that is, once they are posed as distinct, as opposed, as mutually exclusive. What happens is that when the thing looks beautiful, this looking carries with it the exclusion of the ugly, so that to look beautiful is to look not ugly. But, in turn, the thing also looks ugly, and its looking ugly excludes the beautiful from its looks. The result is that the thing cannot be fixed, i.e., determined, (1) as beautiful, since it looks ugly, nor (2) as ugly, since it looks beautiful, nor (3) as both, since the beautiful and the ugly exclude one another, nor (4) as neither, since it looks ugly and beautiful. Withdrawing from all of these determinations, proving not to be determined by them, the thing thus presents itself as indeterminate many. Hence, the relevant transition is made and the thing becomes manifest as indeterminate many only when the distinction between the beautiful and the ugly is posed. But how does this distinction get posed? What does this posing involve? It is merely a posing (in proper distinctness) of what is named in the names. That is, it is a posing of that as which the thing is addressed when it is addressed by the names "beautiful" and "ugly"—a posing of each as one in distinction from and opposition to the other. Therefore, what primarily makes the transition possible is a posing of an order of distinctness by means of names. More precisely, what makes the transition possible is an addressing of the things by name in which there is simultaneously a posing of what is named in the name, a posing of it over against the things, as "hypothesis."[47]

We need to relate this very crucial discussion of the indeterminate many (as between being and non-being) to the fundamental distinction introduced earlier between what an *eidos* is (or, alternatively, a showing in which it would show itself as it is) *and* a showing in which it shows itself in community with actions, bodies, and other *eide* and thus shows itself as it is not, as many. Clearly, what is between being and non-being (indeterminate manys) corresponds to the latter, to the second mode of showing: such a thing comes forth in a showing in which an *eidos* shows itself in community with other things so as to look like many—for example, in a showing in which the beautiful shows itself, not as it itself is (as the same as itself, as one) but rather as also ugly, as passing into ugly, as mixed with ugly. So, that showing in which an indeterminate many stands forth is a showing in which something (which is itself) shows itself as it is not. It is in this connection that we must understand what is meant in saying that such things are between being and non-being. On the one hand, what stands forth in such a showing is distinguished from being by the negativity which belongs to the showing, the negativity consisting in the fact that what shows itself shows itself *as it itself is not*. On the other hand, it is distinguished from non-being by a corresponding positivity, a positivity which consists in the fact

---

[47] This was a principal result in our interpretation of the *Cratylus* (Ch. IV, Sect. 7 c). Note also Socrates' remark: "We get this identity of the one and the many cropping up everywhere as the result of the *logoi* we utter" (*Phil.* 15 d).

that, in such a showing, something *shows itself*; that is, even if it shows itself *as* (i.e., so as to look like) what it is not, even if it shows itself in disguise, even if it shows itself in such a way as also to conceal itself, nevertheless, it *does show itself*, it is not totally concealed.

What does this say about the character of the distinction between the knowable and the opinable? It indicates that the difference between the knowable and the opinable is just the difference between the two modes of showing. This means, in turn, that the distinction between the knowable and the opinable is not fundamentally a distinction between two kinds of things, between which some relation would subsist, but rather a distinction between two ways in which an *eidos* can show itself. It is a distinction between a showing in which an *eidos* shows itself as it itself is (as one) *and* a showing in which an *eidos* shows itself as it is not (as many). In both cases *what shows itself is the same thing* (the *eidos*)—which is to say that the knowable and the opinable are not two parallel regions of things.[48] A beautiful thing is just that which stands forth in a showing in which the beautiful itself shows itself as it is not (i.e., in the second mode of showing); this—and only this!—is the proper sense in which a beautiful thing is an *image* of the beautiful itself.

After the discussion of knowledge and opinion has been completed, Socrates says near the end of Book V:

> And, as for those who look at many beautiful things but don't see the beautiful itself and aren't even able to follow another who leads them to it, and many just things but not justice itself, and so on with all the rest, we'll assert that they opine all these things but know nothing of what they opine (479 e).

The implication clearly is that one *could know* the things which these men only opine, that is, that the knowable and the opinable are two modes in which the *same thing* shows itself.

These developments can be applied fruitfully to the problem that arose regarding the philosopher's relation to the whole. Spe-

---

[48] See the discussion in Sinaiko, *Love, Knowledge, and Discourse*, esp. p. 157.

cifically, the problem was that there appeared to be a disparity between the love and the seeing that are characteristic of the philosopher. On the one hand, the philosopher sees both parts of the whole, both the beautiful itself and the beautiful things, but, on the other hand, his love is directed only to the first of these two parts. The situation is complicated still further if we take into consideration Socrates' statement near the end of Book V in which the philosopher is described as one of "those who look at each thing itself—at the things that are always the same in all respects" (479 e). This statement suggests, on the one hand, that the philosopher does *not even see* the whole. But, on the other hand, this same statement points to the resolution of the problem provided we relate it to the issue of showing. The philosopher looks at each thing itself—that is, he regards each thing with respect to that mode of showing in which it would show itself as it itself is—in contrast to the lovers of sights and sounds who regard things exclusively with respect to that other mode of showing. The two parts which appear to be divided between the philosopher and the lovers of sights and of sounds are *not two parts at all* but two modes of showing in which the same things show themselves. In this respect the love of each is directed to the whole, except for the partition that distinguishes the lovers of sights from the lovers of sounds. But, in another sense only the philosopher is directed to the whole, for he alone is directed to a showing in which each thing shows itself as one, as a whole, rather than as divided up, though indeterminately, into a many; and only the philosopher is directed to a showing in which what shows itself shows itself *wholly,* a showing in which it does not, in showing itself, also conceal itself by showing itself as it itself is not.

But is the philosopher the only one who is directed to such a showing? What is the character of the philosopher's directedness to such a mode of showing? And is he the only one who is directed to such a showing? What about the first kind of men—those who, Socrates said, are "rare"? They would seem to be even more fully directed to such a showing than is the philosopher. Are they not so totally directed to this mode of showing as to be oblivious to the other mode to which the men of opinion and the lovers of beautiful sights are attuned? Indeed they are—*if* there are such men. But that is just the question: Can there be such men? In other words, is *embodied* man ever able to be oblivious to that mode of showing in which what shows itself does so in community with *bodies?* Does not every attempt at such an obliviousness amount to a forgetting of oneself and, hence, end up being comic? The first kind of man—*if* he is a *man*—is *comic,* and he is the dramatic link between the discussion of the philosopher and the comedy which preceded it, a comedy which was set in motion primarily by a forgetting of *eros* and the body.

(d) The Philosopher and the City (484 a – 507 b)

In order to see more clearly just what is happening at the center of the *Republic,* we need to recall and, in recalling, to gather up the movement of the *mythos* of the dialogue. This movement began with Socrates' descent into Hades—a descent which, in the order of the Socratic recollection in which the entire *Republic* is enclosed, was followed almost immediately by the beginning of Socrates' ascent out of Hades. But the ascent was interrupted, and then the issue became that of Socrates' winning his release from Hades by means of persuasion. In Book I Socrates encountered the shades of Hades, defeated those who laid claim to the throne of Hades, and emerged, at the end of his fearful battle with Cerberus, as the fit ruler over the underworld; Socrates, the "ruler of life," became the ruler of the dead. At that point it appeared that Socrates was confronted with two tasks, the relation between which was anything but clear: to carry out the ascent from Hades *and* to execute his rule over Hades. The problem of the relation between these two tasks was a foreshadowing in the mythic dimension of the problem of the philosopher-king. Socrates' first efforts, beginning in Book II, focused on the second of these two tasks: Socrates became a founder of cities and set about founding (in *logos*) a series of cities in Hades. But the comedy which finally burst forth in Book V revealed the failure of this attempt, and Socrates himself finally declared that such an attempt will always fail unless either philosophers become rulers or rulers become philosophers. Neither of the two tasks can be carried out alone—

which is to say that the philosopher must be introduced into the city. There is need not only of a ruling over Hades but also of a correlative engagement in the ascent that belongs distinctively to philosophy. But that is just the problem which the comedy of the city brought to light: How can philosophy and, hence, *eros* be incorporated into the city the very constitution of which is precisely such as to exclude *eros,* that is, to demand the transformation of all "erotic necessities" into "geometrical necessities"? Clearly, the city must be transformed if it is really to receive the philosopher. Clearly, it must be re-founded—that is, another city, a fourth city, must be founded. And perhaps the paradox with which the comedy concluded, the paradox rooted in the city's exclusion of *eros*, could be surpassed if the very activity of founding the city were, at the same time, an activity of love—if, for instance, the founding of the city were Socrates' way of bestowing his love on Glaucon.

The founding of this fourth city, the city of the philosopher, is undertaken in Book VI. In fact, the long first part of this Book (up to the beginning of the discussion of the good) is primarily devoted to showing what form this task must take. Book VI begins with a discussion of the philosopher's fitness to rule; specifically, Socrates proposes to show "how the same men will be able to possess these two distinct sets of qualities" (485 a)—that is, the qualities related to their being philosophers (having to do with knowledge) *and* those which they need in order to be good rulers. On the surface, what Socrates seems to do is derive, from the character of the philosopher (as a lover of learning regarding what each thing is—cf. 485 a − b), the virtues which would be required in order to be a good ruler. However, the very starting-point of this supposed derivation already suggests that what is happening is not quite so straightforward: Socrates begins with *love* and *desire* and describes the philosophers as those who "strive as intensely as possible for every kind of truth" (485 d). The problem is that this represents a way of considering the soul which goes decisively beyond the whole discussion of the city and its rulers, which "excluded" love and made desire the lowest part of the soul (cf. also 490 a − b). As we would thus expect, the virtues of the philosopher, which are derived from this starting-point, do not coincide with the virtues of the ruler, except possibly in name. For example, the philosopher will, as Socrates notes, forsake bodily pleasures—not, however, because the desiring part of the soul is subordinated to the calculating part in the way previously prescribed for a ruler, but rather because, as Socrates says explicitly, "when someone's desires incline strongly to some one thing, they are therefore weaker with respect to the rest, like a stream that has been channeled off in that other direction" (485 d). The philosopher is aloof from the desire for bodily pleasure because of the intensity which another kind of desire has in him. Again, the philosopher is "moderate and in no way a lover of money" (485 e), because money has nothing to do with what he pursues, because he is, in a sense, immoderate in the pursuit of something else. Such cases of discord between the virtues of the philosopher and those of the ruler make it more evident than ever that the gulf between the philosopher and the ruler is not to be bridged merely by way of *logos*—that something more is required.

Adeimantus now replaces Glaucon in the conversation and proceeds to pose the specific task of Book VI. Referring to those who hear Socrates, he says:

> They believe that because of inexperience at questioning and answering, they are at each question misled a little by the *logos;* and when the littles are collected at the end of the *logoi,* the slip turns out to be great and contrary to the first assertions. . . . Now someone might say that in *logos* he can't contradict you at each particular thing asked, but in deed [ἔργῳ] he sees that of all those who start out on philosophy . . . most become quite queer, not to say completely vicious; while the ones who seem perfectly decent, do nevertheless suffer at least one consequence of the practice you are praising—they become useless to the cities (487 b – d).

In order to answer this objection, two things are required of Socrates. In the first place, he must explain the reason for what these hypothetical opponents see *in deed*—that those who linger in philosophy become either corrupt or useless to the city. Secondly, however, he must answer not only in speech but also *in deed* if he is to exonerate himself from the charge leveled against Socratic *logos* as such, the charge—raised not only by the "men of Athens" but also by Polemarchus and Glaucon and now made explicit by Adeimantus—that Socrates' persuasive speech is basically deceptive.

Socrates proceeds, first, to the required explanation. He proposes to present an image: "The question you are asking needs an answer given through an image" (487 e). But Adeimantus pokes fun at him: "And you, in particular, I suppose, aren't used to speaking through images." Presumably, what is behind this response is Socrates' drastic censoring of the poets in the course of the building of the cities (though it should not be forgotten that Adeimantus played a rather important role in initiating the censoring of the poets—cf. 363 a – 364 e). However that may be, Socrates responds in a very curious fashion: "At all events, listen to the image so that you may see still more how greedy I am for images" (488 a). So, Socrates is greedy, Socrates has *desire,* not only for each thing as it is (for originals) but also *for images.* And here this desire for images issues in a making of images. Socrates suddenly becomes an *image-maker!* And the image which he proceeds to make—the image of a ship on which ignorant sailors compete by every means they can concoct to gain control while completely ignoring the one who is a true pilot—this image is an "apology" intended to show that if the philosopher is useless the blame lies on those who fail to make use of him. Socrates goes on to explain further that it is not surprising that many are corrupted, because those with the greatest talents are most easily ruined by bad upbringing:

> Well, then, I suppose that if the nature we set down for the philosopher chances on a suitable course of learning, it will necessarily grow and come to every kind of virtue; but if it isn't sown, planted, and nourished in what's suitable, it will come to all the opposite, unless one of the gods chances to assist it (492 a).

He proceeds to make the image of the corruptive "many" as a great beast pampered by the sophists and at odds with philosophy.

All of this serves to point, more than ever, to the great importance of education; but also it is a preparation for the deed that is about to commence openly, the deed in which Socrates will undertake the education of one of those young men of the kind that so easily become either corrupt or useless.

Socrates now restates in strong terms the paradox of the philosopher-king: In order for a city resembling the one they have founded in *logos* to come-to-be, there would, Socrates says to Adeimantus, "always have to be present in the city something possessing the same understanding of the regime [πολιτεία] as you, the lawgiver, had when you were setting down the laws" (497 c − d). Socrates' task is to educate such a person, that is, to found a city by educating the kind of ruler the city requires. Nevertheless, Socrates also indicates that it remains a problem how the philosopher can be incorporated into the city; it remains a problem, as he now puts it, "how a city can take philosophy in hand without being destroyed" (497 d).

So, Socrates' remaining task is to answer *in deed* those who object to Socratic *logos*, to answer them by educating a ruler, by exhibiting in deed what he has proclaimed in *logos*. Now he makes this explicit:

> However, it's no wonder that the many are not persuaded by these *logoi*. For they never saw any existing thing that matches the present *logos* (498 d).

Whom is Socrates to educate? He mentions (503 e) that the young men must be tested, so as to determine whether they are able to bear the greatest studies; and, in fact, he proceeds to carry out such testing on the young man with whom he is speaking, Adeimantus. It turns out that Adeimantus remembers what was said about the parts of the soul and the virtues in the context of the earlier discussion of the city. However, he has forgotten what was insisted upon by Socrates just before that discussion of the soul—that "a longer road around would be required." In fact, Adeimantus even admits thinking that that discussion of the soul was more or less satisfactory (504 a − b). What the testing thus reveals is that Adeimantus remains entirely at the level of the building of the city, at the level where the soul is treated in terms of parts rather than in terms of *eros,* at the level where the virtues are understood in relation to art rather than in relation to the good. Adeimantus remains at a stage prior to the comedy that broke out in Book V. Adeimantus is oblivious to the need for that discussion to which the center of the *Republic* is devoted and in which the philosopher-ruler is to be educated.

Shortly after this testing, there is a quarrel between Adeimantus and Socrates concerning whether "it's just to speak about what one doesn't know as though one knew" (506 c)—that is, concerning the proper comportment to one's ignorance. The quarrel is interrupted by Glaucon, who has already been identified as possessing very important prerequisites for becoming a philosopher: he is erotic (474 d − 475 a) and musical (398 e). Also, we recall that he is the one who originally was accompanying Socrates in the ascent.

Thus, Socrates is prepared to found the fourth city, the city of the philosopher. He will found this city, not just in *logos*, but in *ergon,* by educating Glaucon.[49] Socrates' educating of Glaucon is the central deed of the *Republic.*

Section 4. The Good (507 b − 509 c)

At the end of his discussion with Adeimantus, just before Glaucon interrupts, Socrates introduces the idea of the good. He says

> that the idea of the good [ἡ τοῦ ἀγαθοῦ ἰδέα] is the greatest study [μέγιστον μάθημα] and that it's by availing oneself of it along with just things and the rest that they become useful and beneficial (505 a).

Behind what Socrates says here is the contention that something can be beneficial only if one makes good use of it, which one can do only to the extent that one knows what is good. This is to say that the good is a kind of pre-condition. In the discussion now

---

[49] See the discussion in Brann, "Music of the *Republic,*" pp. 21-25.

about to begin Socrates will extend this to the point where the good can be called the most fundamental pre-condition.

At the outset Socrates stresses the insufficiency of his knowledge of the good. He even suggests that he has only opinions regarding this matter and so ought to remain silent; we wonder what might be at issue in the irony, but no indication is to be found yet. At this point the quarrel with Adeimantus sets in. Then Glaucon steps in, and Socrates finally yields to Glaucon's insistence ("in the name of Zeus") that he speak of the good. But he agrees to this only with rather serious reservations:

> But, you blessed men, let's leave aside for the time being what the good itself is—for it looks to me as though it's out of the range of our present thrust to attain the opinions I now hold about it. But I'm willing to tell what looks like a child of the good and most similar to it (506 d − e).

(a) The Analogy (507 b − 508 d)

The analogy which Socrates has promised to present requires two preliminary steps. The first of these is the re-introduction of deliberate speech about the *eide*:

> "We both assert that there are," I said, "and distinguish in *logos,* many beautiful things, many good things, and so on for each kind of thing. . . . And we also assert that there is a beautiful itself, a good itself, and so on for all the things that we then set down as many. Now, again, we refer them to one *idea* of each as though the *idea* were one; and we address it as that which is" (507 b).

It should be noted that here Socrates puts in a reminder that in all of this he is speaking, that (as throughout the *Republic*) what we have before us are not the deeds themselves but Socrates' speech about them; and he puts the reminder in a very strategic place—in the same sentence in which he refers to their asserting and to their distinguishing in *logos.* More straightforwardly, Socrates presents the distinguished many things and the one *idea* and the distinction between them as something which they *assert,* as something which they *say;* in other words, these matters are presented, not as some kind of self-sufficient "facts," but as *matters which are asserted.* Socrates' peculiar presentation thus points to a central issue: that of the relation between assertion (more generally, *logos*) and the setting-up of the distinction between one *idea* and many things. Our previous considerations of the discussion of knowledge and opinion (Sect. 3 c), specifically, of the issue of the "indeterminate many," suggested that there is a very close connection here: It is in connection with the addressing of things by name that one sets up over against things the beautiful itself in opposition to the ugly. That is, the posing of the one *idea* is a posing of what is purely named in the name.

Socrates says that they refer the many "to one *idea* of each as though the *idea* were one; and we address it as that which is [ὅ ἔστιν]." The *idea* is not necessarily something that is self-sufficiently one; it is treated as such, asserted as one over against a many. Perhaps it is even because it is asserted as one, that we address it with the honorific title "ὅ ἔστιν." Perhaps its oneness (even if posed) is what determines that it is properly addressed by the name "that which is."

Only after, directly or indirectly, all these issues are raised, does Socrates finally add the further character of the distinction:

> And, moreover, we say that the former are seen [ὁρᾶσθαι] but not intellected [νοεῖσθαι], while the *ideas* are intellected but not seen (507 b).

So, again the distinction between visible and intelligible is treated as derivative rather than fundamental. Here, in particular, it is treated as derivative from the distinction between one and many, which, in turn, points back to what we previously found to be the fundamental distinction—namely, the distinction between the two modes of showing (as one, as many).

The second of the preliminary steps required for the analogy consists in the provision of an analysis of the elements involved in vision. Declaring that the "craftsman of the senses" was lavish in the way he fabricated "the power [δύναμις] of seeing and being seen," Socrates remarks that in this case alone there is need of a third thing besides the power of sensing and that which is sensed. This additional thing needed in addition to the power of seeing and that which is seen—this third thing is light. The analysis of the elements of vision thus presents each of these three things, but doubled, so that what results are three pairs of elements, six elements in all.[50] There is the power of sight and that in which sight comes-to-be, the eye, which is "the most sunlike [ἡλιοειδέστατόν] of the organs" (508 b). Correspondingly, there is color and the thing to be seen (in which color is present). The third pair is what makes seeing exceptional among the senses. One of its members is light:

> Then the sense of sight and the power of being seen are yoked together with a yoke that, by the measure of an *idea* by no means insignificant, is more honorable than the yokes uniting other teams, if light is not without honor (507 e – 508 a).

Thus, light is introduced as a yoke which yokes together the sense of sight and what can be seen; it is a yoke which joins a dyad. The other member of this exceptional third pair is the sun itself, the source of light. Socrates calls attention to something that is curious about this element: the sun, as the cause of sight, can itself be seen. However, Socrates fails to mention the pain and even blindness that result if one does anything more than merely glance momentarily at the sun.

With the preparations completed, Socrates now states the analogy:

> "Well, then," I said, "say that the sun is the offspring of the good I mean—an offspring the good begot in a proportion [ἀναλογία] with itself: as the good is in the intelligible region [ἐν τῷ νοητῷ τόπῳ] with respect to intelligence [νοῦς] and what is intellected, so the sun is in the visible region [ἐν τῷ ὁρατῷ] with respect to sight and what is seen" (508 b – c).

---

[50] It is possible to regard the analysis as involving still more elements if one takes into account, for example, the distinction between "activity" and "passivity" (cf. Adam's note, Vol. II, p. 60). Our delineation of the analysis has the advantage of retaining that threefold character which Socrates stresses.

The basic proportion (analogy) is:

$$\text{Good} \; : \; \left\{\begin{array}{l}\text{Intelligence} \\ \text{and} \\ \text{What is intellected}\end{array}\right\} \; : \; : \; \text{Sun} \; : \; \left\{\begin{array}{l}\text{Sight} \\ \text{and} \\ \text{What is seen}\end{array}\right\}$$

The most immediate sense of the analogy is that in the intelligible region the good is the origin of the yoke which yokes together the appropriate dyad, just as the sun is the origin of the light which yokes together the corresponding pair in the region of the visible. We note that the analogues of two of the elements of vision are not mentioned in the statement of the analogy: the eye and light. We wonder, accordingly, what corresponds to these on the side of the good. We note also that the distinction previously (507 d) posed between color and the thing in which the color is present is not retained in the statement of the analogy.

In his first remark to Glaucon about the good Socrates proposed to tell of the *child* of the good. In the statement of the analogy the erotic imagery is even more pronounced, and we suspect that Socrates' erotic speech mirrors the outbreak of *eros* in the center of the *Republic*. The sun is identified as the offspring of the good; and this offspring is said to be "most similar" to its father (506 e). So, the sun is something like an image of the good, an image of the good begotten by the good itself. This indicates something that is of utmost importance regarding the good: the good possesses the power of image-making; the good makes images of itself. The erotic imagery leads us to wonder whether there is not also a mother who gives birth to these images of the good that are fathered by the good. But the identity of the mother is left completely *concealed*. We wonder why. But, regardless of what we make of this matter, we recall that Socrates described himself earlier as one with a greed for images and that he set about deliberately making images (487 e — 489 a)–images of the philosopher in the city, images of himself. Socrates, it seems, is also akin to the good.

Socrates proceeds to re-introduce the elements that were missing in the first statement of the analogy and to identify their analogues in the intelligible:

Well, then, think that the soul is also characterized in this way. When it fixes itself on that which is illumined by truth and being [ἀλήθειά τε καὶ τὸ ὄν], it intellects, knows, and appears to possess intelligence. But when it fixes itself on that which is mixed with darkness, on coming into being and passing away, it opines and is dimmed, changing opinions up and down, and seems at such times not to possess intelligence (508 d).

So, the analogue of the eye is the soul, and the analogue of light is "truth and being" (ἀλήθειά τε καὶ τὸ ὄν). It is of utmost importance to observe, in particular, what this says about the meaning of truth and being. It says that being is not an *idea* nor even the totality of such—that it is, rather, that in which what is known can be manifest to the knower. But that in which something (an *idea*) becomes manifest to a knower is just a *showing* in which that thing shows itself to the knower. Being is a name for (self-) showing. Furthermore, what Socrates says suggests that "being" and "truth" virtually name the same matter. Certainly it is clear that here truth does not mean some formal "correspondence" between intelligence and intellected; on the contrary, it is the yoke which first brings this pair together and, hence, is what first makes possible anything like a correspondence. "Truth" and "being" are two names for the *self-showing in which something comes into the open,* into manifestness—for the self-showing in which it becomes, as the word "ἀλήθεια" hints, unhidden, unconcealed.

In the elaboration in which Socrates identifies the missing analogues, he also introduces another dimension into the analogy, namely the difference between daytime vision and nighttime vision (perfected and privative vision): When the thing is properly illuminated, what results is knowledge, but when the thing is not so illuminated, when it is "mixed with darkness," then there is only opinion. Especially in view of the previous consideration of knowledge and opinion (Book V), it is clear that what this distinction serves to distinguish are not two different regions of things but rather the two modes of showing of the same things: on the one hand, a mode of showing in which what shows itself shows itself *wholly* (i.e., shows itself as it is, i.e., is "illuminated" in and by the showing) and, on the other hand, a mode of showing in which what shows itself is also concealed (i.e., shows itself as it is not, i.e., is "mixed with darkness" in and through the showing). The latter is a mode of showing in which what shows itself shows itself as many, rather than as one, and, correlatively, as not one with itself, as not wholly determinate, as "coming into being and passing away."

Finally, we need to observe that the result of this very first elaboration of the analogy is such as to change the entire sense of the analogy, that it is such as to render the analogy eminently questionable. Originally, there was the implicit assumption that, since the sun and the visible region as a whole are familiar, known, they could be used for explaining what is unknown, namely the good and the intelligible. But now it is clear that to the extent that something is seen (i.e., is "mixed with darkness," i.e., shows itself in the second mode of showing, i.e., shows itself in such a way as simultaneously to conceal itself)—that to this extent we *lack* knowledge of it *and* that we could come into possession of that knowledge which we lack only insofar as the thing came to show itself as it is, only to the extent that it came to be "illuminated by truth and being," hence, only to the extent that it came to be present *as something knowable, as intelligible.*[51] In other words, we cannot come to know the intelligible by analogy with the visible, as though the visible were already known, but rather can first come to know the visible only insofar as it comes to present itself as intelligible and we apprehend it as such.[52] Socrates' very first elaboration of the analogy has destroyed the very foundation of the analogy.

(b) Good, Truth, Being (508 e – 509 c)

The final stage of Socrates' elaboration of the analogy involves two statements. In the first of these he says:

---

[51] Presumably, this is why the distinction posed initially between color and the thing in which the color is present is not, as we noted, retained in the statement (nor in the elaboration) of the analogy.

[52] Cf. Sinaiko, *Love, Knowledge, and Discourse,* pp. 126-131.

Therefore, say that what provides the truth to the things
known and gives the power [δύναμις] to the one who knows, is
the *idea* of the good. And, as the cause of the knowledge and
truth, you can understand it to be a thing known; but, as
beautiful as these two are—knowledge and truth—if you believe
that it is something different from them and still more beautiful than they, your belief will be right (508 e).

After a brief exchange we get the second statement, which brings
the elaboration of the analogy to its conclusion:

Therefore, say that not only being known is present in the
things known as a consequence of the good, but also the "to
be" and being [τὸ εἶναί τε καὶ τὴν οὐσίαν] are in them besides
as a result of it, although the good isn't being [οὐσία] but is
still beyond being [ἐκέκεινα τῆς οὐσίας], exceeding it in dignity [πρεσβεία] and power [δύναμις] (509 b).

These are among the most difficult passages in the entire *Republic*.
On the one hand, they are so extremely cryptic that we must,
more than ever, be careful not to say too much. In fact, immediately after these statements Socrates warns that he is "leaving out
a throng of things"; and he does not give any further explicit
explanation of these statements. On the other hand, we need to
make the utmost effort to avoid letting the entire problematic
merely collapse into a kind of unprovocative obviousness; that is,
we need to beware of thinking that when we simply apply the
analogy we thereby understand the matter at issue in the analogy
and in its elaboration, especially since this very elaboration has
already proved to undercut the analogy. We should not fail to be
impressed with Glaucon's very curious response to the final stage
of the elaboration of the analogy and with Socrates' remark about
that response:

And Glaucon, quite ridiculously, said, "Apollo, what a demonic excess" (509 c).

It is not impossible for light to be so excessive that it conceals
rather than reveals.

Socrates says that the good provides truth to the thing known.
What does this mean? It does not mean that a thing is first of all a

thing known, which then, subsequently has truth provided to it, conferred upon it. Rather, as the previous elaboration indicated, it is only by being "illuminated" by truth that something first comes to be knowable. The conferring of truth on it, the provision of its truth, is what first lets it be a knowable thing (to say nothing of its being known). Its "standing" in the truth is identical with its being knowable. But what does it mean for something to be knowable— in contrast to what is merely opinable or visible? It means, according to the previous considerations, that the thing *shows itself as one,* in contrast to that mode of showing in which something, showing itself in community, thereby shows itself as many. Thus, to say that the good confers truth means: the good confers, makes possible, that kind of showing in which something can show itself as one.

The beginning of the second statement confirms that the conferral of truth on the things known amounts to the conferral of their very character as things known: " . . . being known is present in the things known as a consequence of the good. . . ." Socrates goes on, however, to speak of something else given by the good: " . . . but also the 'to be' and being are in them [the things known] besides as a result of it. . . ." How is the conferral of truth related to this further conferral in which the good confers being? If the conferral of truth is understood in its fundamental character, i.e., as the conferral of a kind of showing, then what here looks like the addition of a further kind of conferral proves, in the end, to be only a further word about the conferral already spoken of in the first statement. With regard to the thing known, the two statements—that the good confers truth and that it confers being—say the same thing. The good confers truth, it confers being, it lets the thing be knowable—and all three of these "accomplishments" of the good are one and the same. This sameness was already thematized in the discussion in Book V in which Socrates declared the coincidence of being with the knowable ("what *is* entirely, is entirely knowable"—477 a). It was again indicated in the initial stage of the elaboration of the analogy in which "truth and being" were identified as constituting that element corresponding to light: both serve to name the yoke which yokes together intelligence and what is intellected. In all these ways the identical matter spoken of is: the conferral of a showing in which a thing can show itself as one.

What does this fourfold sameness—conferral of truth, letting be knowable, conferral of being, and conferral of a showing in which a thing can show itself as one—what does this say regarding the determination of the meaning of being in the center of the *Republic?* Already it has become evident that being is not an *idea* except in a very exceptional sense; "being" is a name for the "illumination" in which an *idea* can be manifest as an *idea,* as determinately one. Now we can add: It is not as though things first *are,* in the sense of their possessing some kind of inexplicable "brute existence," and *only then* come to show themselves (either as they are or as they are not). It is not such that there is, first, a being which then, subsequently, shows itself—so that the self-showing would be something extrinsic to being. On the contrary, *the self-showing belongs to the very being of the thing.* This is to say that the determination of the meaning of being at the center of the *Republic* moves at a level which is prior to the distinction between showing ("appearance") and being and also prior to the distinction between essence and existence.

Both of the statements that belong to the final stage of Socrates' elaboration of the analogy declare, fundamentally, that the good confers a showing in which something can show itself as one. The question is: How does the good accomplish such conferral? In other words, what is the character of the conferring and why is it the good that is charged with it? This question requires that we pose another name for what Socrates is calling "the good." This other name is: "the one" (τὸ ἕν). This name is alluded to in the central Books of the *Republic,* most notably when the good is related to the whole (cf. esp. 511 b). But what really provides the basis for re-naming is the contention developed at length in the earlier Books that the good of the city consists in its being one instead of many and that, correspondingly, the good for the individual man in the city is that he become one.[53] So, there is

---

[53] As we noted (Sect. 2 c), this oneness, brought into view within the framework of the building of the cities, is understood primarily in relation to art, though there are considerable indications of another sense of oneness more proper to man; to some extent this more proper sense emerged in the discussion of the virtues in the individual man.

reason to call the good also the one.[54] Nevertheless, the fact remains that Socrates does not call it by this name; and we should wonder at his never calling the good by its other name, especially since this other name pertains so much to the matter at issue in the *Republic*. Indeed, there is good reason for his reticence: it is hinted at by the simple circumstance that, if the one is both the one and the good, then it is two and, hence, is not one.[55]

At any rate, once we recognize that the good is the one, then we can begin to understand how it is related to being and truth, that is, what it has to do with the mode of showing in which something can show itself as one. For something to show itself as one means precisely: to show itself *as an image of the one*. If the good is the one, then when something shows itself as one it thereby images the good. This kind of showing is such that what shows itself in the showing shows itself in the image of the good. Indeed, we saw earlier that the good is, according to what was said, an image-maker that makes images of itself in the specifically erotic sense of "fathering" these images. Now we see, further, that the coming-forth of such an image (of the good, of the one) is identical with something showing itself as one, which, in turn, amounts to its standing in truth, i.e., being knowable, i.e., having being conferred on it. Thus, the good confers being and truth, i.e., confers a showing in which things can show themselves as one, by fathering images of itself.

We recall that Socrates has rather openly imitated the good. And we recall also that in the first of the two statements that we have been considering he says that the good gives the power (δύναμις) to the one who knows. What does "power" mean here? The answer is obvious. It means: power of knowing, i.e., what one needs in order to know. But what does it mean to know? One can know only what is knowable. To be knowable means: to show

---

[54] There is much indirect confirmation for this identification in other dialogues, perhaps most notably in the *Philebus* in which the question of the good leads directly into the discussion of one and many, limit and unlimited. Cf. Jacob Klein, "About Plato's *Philebus*," *Interpretation*, II (1972), pp. 157-182, esp. p. 168. There is also, of course, considerable testimony on this matter by ancient authors, most significantly, by Aristotle. Cf. the texts collected in Konrad Gaiser, *Platons Ungeschriebene Lehre* (Stuttgart: Ernst Klett Verlag, 1968), pp. 443-557.

[55] This is worked out more rigorously in the first two hypotheses in the *Parmenides*.

itself as one. So, to know (the knowable) means: to *gather* what shows itself into its appropriate oneness, to gather it in such a way that its showing itself as one is brought to fulfillment. To know means to take up that showing by which the good makes images of itself, to let oneself into the movement of that showing in such a way as to lead it to its fulfillment. To know is not only to imitate the good but also to assist in the birth of the children of the good. This is the fundamental sense of Socratic midwifery.

How specifically is man granted the capacity to engage in this gathering? What form does this capacity take? The form of it which we have come across again and again, especially in the *Phaedrus* and *Cratylus,* is *logos.* In *logos* a gathering has always already been initiated, and in speaking we resume that gathering.

Socrates says, finally, that the good is "beyond being." To be beyond being means: to be beyond (outside of) all showing in which something would show itself as one. Hence, Socrates is saying that it belongs to the good not to show itself as one; the one does not show itself as one. This means, in turn, that the good always shows itself *as it is not* (since it is one—even *the* one). *The good shows itself only through images.* This is why Socrates was so insistent on speaking not about the good itself but about its offspring.

It need hardly be said that the discussion of the good leaves much unsaid—so much that we lack even a measure by which to gauge it. Obviously, a further elaboration is most urgent. But, as we noted, the analogy has been undermined by its very elaboration, and, though this elaboration serves to indicate more than ever that Socrates' greed for images is appropriate, there is need of a new image, of an image that is not so closely tied to the questionable distinction between visible and intelligible. Therefore, Socrates proceeds to give Glaucon instructions for drawing the divided line.

Section 5. The Divided Line (509 d – 511 e, 521 c – 535 a)

(a) The Three Statements

In the course of Books VI and VII Socrates offers three some-what distinct statements of the divided line. The first of these statements begins:

> Then, take a line cut in two unequal segments, one for the kind [γένος] that is seen, the other for the kind that is intellected—and go on and cut each segment in the same ratio [λόγος] (509 d).

In the next sentence he continues: "Now, in terms of relative clarity and obscurity . . ."—then he goes on to discuss in order each of the four segments of the line. This first statement tells us three very important things about the line. First, it tells us that the major division of the line corresponds to the distinction between intelligible and visible. Second, it indicates the basic proportionality of the division. And third, it indicates that the principle of the proportionality is degree of clarity (σαφήνεια), that is, that the relative lengths of the segments correspond to the degree of clarity exemplified by what the various segments signify.

The second of the three statements of the divided line comes when, after having gone on to consider each of the four segments, Socrates summarizes by assigning a definite name to each segment of the line. He concludes the second statement by saying:

> Arrange them in a proportion, and believe that as the seg-ments to which they correspond participate in truth [ἀλήθεια], so they participate in clarity [σαφήνεια] (511 e).

In the third statement, which comes somewhat later (Book VII, 533 e – 534 a), Socrates gives a still more elaborate and precise delineation of what the various segments represent and states an additional proportion derivative from the one originally given. This statement constitutes the conclusion to the entire considera-tion of the divided line.

The line described by these three statements can, provisionally, be drawn as follows[56] :

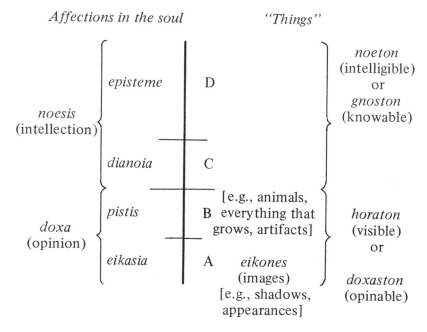

Affections in the soul   *"Things"*

noesis (intellection)	*episteme* D	*noeton* (intelligible) or *gnoston* (knowable)
	dianoia C	
doxa (opinion)	*pistis* B [e.g., animals, everything that grows, artifacts]	*horaton* (visible) or
	eikasia A *eikones* (images) [e.g., shadows, appearances]	*doxaston* (opinable)

According to Socrates' first statement the basic proportionality of the segments is as follows:

$$(D + C) : (B + A) :: D : C :: B : A$$

From this two important results can be derived. One result involves the simple transformation of part of the original proportion into the new proportion:

$$D : B :: C : A$$

This result is, in fact, stated explicitly by Socrates in his third statement of the divided line (534 a). But the other result, that the

[56] In the case of the specific names given to the four kinds of affections in the soul all of the usual translations are so laden with post-Platonic meanings that it seems preferable to avoid translation and, instead, to transliterate the Greek and let the words get their sense from the discussion itself. To a slightly lesser extent the same problem arises with respect to all the other names on the divided line. However, the confusions that would result from retaining all these words in the original would seem to outweigh the danger of being misled by the translations.

middle two segments are of equal length (B = C) is not explicitly stated.[57] This second result is especially curious, for clearly the general sense of the entire discussion of the line requires us to suppose that segment C (representing something belonging to the intelligible) involves a higher degree of clarity than segment B (representing something belonging to the visible). This means that there is a conflict between the proportionality which Socrates prescribes for the line and his stipulation that the divisions correspond to the degrees of clarity of what is represented. The line which he instructs Glaucon to draw, but which, in contrast to his procedure with the slave boy in the *Meno* (cf. 82 b), he apparently does not draw, cannot, strictly speaking be drawn. We should not too easily dismiss this conflict as a mere accident.

The relation of the divided line to what was previously discussed should be noted. In fact, Socrates calls our attention to this relation by introducing the line in explicit reference back to the analogy, explaining that the major division of the line corresponds to the distinction between visible and intelligible. This does not mean, however, that the divided line is merely an elaboration of the analogy. In fact, it was found that precisely through its elaboration the analogy was already undermined; and what motivated the transition to the discussion of the divided line was, in terms of the matter at issue, the need for an approach to this matter that would not involve attempting to use the visible for the sake of understanding the intelligible, as though these were simply two distinct regions of things, one familiar to us, the other unfamiliar. It is clear that in this respect the line is a more adequate image: it represents the visible and the intelligible as segments of a single continuous line rather than as two separated domains.

Even a cursory examination of what Socrates says about the line shows that each segment of the line is meant to represent two kinds of matters, so that we may, as in our drawing, distinguish between the two sides of the line, one representing affections in the soul (παθήματα ἐν τῇ ψυχῇ), the other representing the "things" corresponding to those affections. Granted this two-

---

[57] Cf. Adam's note, Vol. II, p. 64.

sidedness, we need then to take note of some curious things that crop up in Socrates' description of each of these sides. At the beginning of the first statement, when he is discussing the lowest two of the four segments, Socrates mentions only the things, not the affections in the soul; only later, in the summary that constitutes the second statement, does he name the corresponding affections. This serves to bring out, by contrast, the fact that for the upper two segments Socrates does quite the opposite: he does not refer to the things at all but only to the affections in the soul, specifically, to the kinds of movement in which the soul engages. The only designation given to the things corresponding to these affections is the one taken over from the analogy: they are called intelligible (νοητόν), which says little, if anything, more than that they correspond to intellection (νόησις). Then, in the second statement, in which he explicitly names all four segments, he does not even mention the things but names only the affections in the soul. When, in the third of the three statements, he reiterates these affections and fixes their names even more precisely, he explicitly calls attention to the fact that he is not dealing at all with what corresponds on the side of things to these affections:

> But as for the proportion [ἀναλογία] between the things over which these are set and the division into two parts of each—the opinable and the intelligible—let's let that go, Glaucon, so as not to run afoul of *logoi* many times longer than those that have been gone through (534 a).

On the other hand, in the second of the statements Socrates does add the remark that there is a correspondence between the participation of the affections of the soul in clarity and that of the things in truth (511 e); this remark is one of the most important clues he gives regarding that side of the line with which he later refuses to deal. In this remark Socrates is saying that for the degree of clarity definitive of a specific kind of condition in the soul there corresponds on the side of things the same degree of participation in truth. Thus, strictly speaking, what corresponds to the various conditions of the soul are various degrees of participation in truth on the side of what becomes manifest to the soul in that condition. Especially in view of the previous considerations, this can only mean that the fourfold division of things corresponding to the division on the side of the soul is not a division into four different regions of ultimately distinct things but rather a division into four different levels of participation of things in truth. Yet, for something to participate in truth means to become manifest as itself, and so, in different terms, the division on the side of things is a division into different degrees, different levels, of manifestness. Furthermore, something becomes manifest as itself precisely to the extent that it shows itself as one. What we have on the side of things are different levels of showing, four modes in which the same things can show themselves, just as, on the side of the soul, one and the same soul can apprehend things with different degrees of clarity. Presumably, this is why Socrates does not name the things corresponding to intellection—there are no such things in the sense of their being different things as compared to visible things. So, Socrates is proceeding in a most appropriate way when he identifies and gives examples only of visible things such as shadows, animals, and artifacts; the things corresponding to intellection are the "same" as these things, but in a different, a more truthful, mode of showing.[58]

(b) The Visible

The principal discussion of the visible occurs in the first of the three statements of the divided line. Socrates, relating the conversation between himself and Glaucon, says:

---

[58] In view of this "sameness" the special appropriateness of the image of a continuous line begins to become evident. Also, we see the appropriateness of one of the consequences of the fact that the two middle segments of the line are equal in length (This consequence is indicated by Brann, "Music of the *Republic*," pp. 76-77). The relevant clue is found in the *Timaeus:*

And of all bonds the most beautiful is that which makes itself and the terms it connects a one [ἕν] in the fullest sense; and it is of the nature of a continued geometrical proportion to effect this most perfectly. For whenever, of three numbers, the middle one . . . is such that, as the first is to it, so is it to the last, and conversely as the last is to the middle, so is the middle to the first, then since the middle becomes first and last, and again the last and first become middle, in that way all will necessarily come to play the same part towards one another, and by so doing they will all make a one (31 c – 32 a).

"Now, in terms of relative clarity and obscurity, you'll have one segment in the visible part for images. I mean by images first shadows, then appearances produced in water and in all close-grained, smooth, bright things, and everything of the sort, if you understand."

"I do understand."

"Then in the other segment put that of which this first is the likeness—the animals around us, and everything that grows, and the whole class of artifacts."

"I put them there," he said.

"And would you also be willing," I said, "to say that with respect to truth or lack of it, as the opinable is distinguished from the knowable, so the likeness is distinguished from that of which it is the likeness."

"I would indeed," he said.

We need, first of all, to consider what "image" ($\epsilon i\kappa\dot{\omega}\nu$) means here. Socrates does not give anything like a "definition." Rather, he mentions two things, shadows and appearances (i.e., reflections), and then adds: "and everything of the sort, if you understand." We are to understand that these are only examples. So, there may well be other kinds of images besides the ones Socrates mentions.

It belongs to the nature of an image that it is an image *of* something, of some original. So, we can best come to some insight regarding what an image is by thematizing the relation between image and original. At the level of the examples which Socrates gives of images, the originals are things such as those that Socrates puts in the next higher segment: animals, everything that grows, artifacts. The originals are what we would tend to regard as "things," in the most straightforward sense; we note, however, that Socrates gives no generic name for these things but only cites examples. Images are to be understood at this level as the reflections and shadows cast by such things.

The proportionality on the divided line is of the kind here described, that is, it is of the kind which most perfectly binds things together into one. Thus, the proportionality of the divisions serves to accentuate that oneness that is already imaged by the continuity of the line. The line is one, and what this one line represents are not many distinct regions of things but different degrees of manifestness of the same things.

Let us consider the image-original relation in a more general way, keeping in view, however, what is said here and what we have come upon in other dialogues regarding this matter. On the one hand, there is never a total difference separating image from original; there is always a certain bond of unity between them, always a sense in which the image *is* the original. In many cases it can be said that the image is *like* the original, for example, in the way that a portrait of Simmias is like Simmias himself (cf. *Phaedo* 73 e — 74 a, together with Ch. II, Sect. 2 c); but such sensible likeness is possible only in those cases in which the original does not require the image for its manifestation (cf. esp. Ch. IV, Sect. 5 b, 6 b). So, more generally, it may be said that an image must be such as to announce the original, to let it become manifest. The original must be able to show itself through the image, to shine forth in and through it. On the other hand, there is always a certain difference between image and original. One tends to regard that difference as simply a difference between two things, one of which would be a copy of the other (as with Simmias and the portrait of Simmias). But even the simple examples which Socrates gives in the present discussion serve to call such a way of regarding this difference into question. Is a shadow or a reflection just another thing alongside the thing shadowed or reflected? Is a shadow or a reflection a thing at all in that straightforward sense that one is tempted to invoke here? But if we are not to understand the difference between image and original as a mere difference between two things in this sense, then how is this difference understandable? It is understandable in terms of *showing*. When something shows itself "in the original," it shows itself as it is. But when it shows itself "in an image," it does not simply show itself as it is but *also* shows itself *as it is not.* Showing through an image involves a concealment, a negativity, and, presumably, this is why Socrates says that he means "by images *first* shadows": a shadow exhibits this negativity most strikingly, since in its shadow a thing shows itself as lacking everything except shape.

The result is that the relation between original and image corresponds to that between the two modes of showing. And what corresponds on the side of things to *eikasia* and *pistis* are not two different kinds of things but two ways in which the same things can show themselves—just as Simmias can be visible to us either in a portrait or in the original, but such that in both cases it is the same thing, Simmias himself, that is shown. But clearly this result can be extended still further, for there can be better and worse portraits of Simmias, that is, in general, there can be better and worse images of an original. Different images can let the same thing show itself with indefinitely varying degrees of adequacy, with more or less of that negativity (concealment) which defines the very difference of an image from the original. Thus, we may speak, not just of two modes, but of a *continuum of modes of showing* running from a showing through the very poorest images up through a showing in the original.[59] We see still better the appropriateness of Socrates' introduction of the image of a divided yet *continuous* line.

This result can be applied beyond the segments representing the visible by making use of the basic proportions:

$$(D + C) \ : \ (B + A) \ :: \ D \ : \ C \ :: \ B \ : \ A$$

Since the relation between B and A is that of original to image, then, the same must hold for the other two relations, since the proportion equates these relations. Indeed, Socrates makes it explicit that such an application is to be made in the case of the relation between $D + C$ (intelligible) and $B + A$ (visible or opinable):

> And would you also be willing to say that with respect to truth or lack of it, as the opinable is distinguished from the knowable, so the likeness is distinguished from that of which it is the likeness? (510 a).

But now we have seen that the relation between original and image corresponds to that between a truer and a less true showing of the same thing. Thus, the relation between the intelligible and the visible, as a relation between original and image, is a relation between more perfect and less perfect, more original and less

---

[59] Cf. the consideration of *Crat.* 432 a – c in Ch. IV, Sect. 6 b; also Sinaiko, *Love, Knowledge, and Discourse,* pp. 149-154.

original, showings of the same things. This means that the entire divided line represents, then, a continuum running from less true to truer modes of showing; and in this connection the appropriateness of the line to what it represents (i.e., images) is especially evident. Thus, the relation between original and image proves to be not merely the relation between the lower two segments of the line but rather the fundamental relation on the entire line. We suspect that Socrates assigned a name only to the things in the lowest segment of the line because that name, "image," if properly understood, suffices for understanding what is at issue with respect to things on the entire course of the line.

The line is a continuum of modes of showing. Nevertheless, there is also a kind of point of discontinuity on it. The character both of its continuity and of its discontinuity can be thematized by taking our clue from the derivative proportion to which Socrates refers in his third statement of the divided line:

$$D : B :: C : A$$

This proportion indicates that there is a peculiar relation between *episteme* and *pistis* and between *dianoia* and *eikasia* and that these two relations correspond.

Let us consider first the relation between *episteme* and *pistis*. What is most immediately distinctive about *episteme*, according to the accounts given in the discussion of the divided line, is that it dispenses with that dependence on hypotheses that is characteristic of *dianoia* (cf. 511 b — c). Thus, *episteme* involves a kind of self-sufficiency and, inasmuch as it makes its way back to the genuine beginning, it involves a certain finality, a certain coming to rest. Now, in the case of *pistis* there is something similar to this: when I have the thing (e.g., an animal or an artifact) fully before my eyes, when it stands before me, as it were, in its full bodily presence rather than being present to me through an image, there is a certain self-sufficiency, a certain finality, in my seeing. I am not provoked to further exploration as I would be if I had only an image. There is a certain *coming to rest in the visible*. In Book VII this peculiar finality within the visible is openly discussed: Socrates explains that when I merely see a finger, when there is nothing in the spectacle that provokes me in the way that an image (with its attendant negativity) can, I just rest content in the seen:

> The soul of the many [i.e., the many souls who see only the manys and not the ones] is not compelled to ask the intellect what a finger is. For the sight at no point indicates to the soul that the finger is at the same time the opposite of a finger (523 d).

So, there is a certain discontinuity. On the other hand, the underlying continuity of the line leads us to expect that this discontinuity will not prove to be so radical as to destroy the possibility of movement up the line.

Let us consider next the other terms of the derived proportion. Just as *episteme* and *pistis* have in common a certain coming to rest, so, correspondingly, *dianoia* and *eikasia* have in common a peculiar relation to the movement up the line. What these have to do with that movement can be readily seen by examining the case of *eikasia*. When I see an image, I see it usually as an image of an original; I see it *as* revealing the original. In fact, it is rare that I am deceived for more than an instant by such things as reflections and shadows; such things tend to betray that they are only images, and so I do not for the most part make the mistake of taking an image for an original (at least not at this simple level). Now, this normal seeing of an image *as* an image is a curious kind of seeing: I see through the image to the original that is "behind" it. This seeing is a kind of "double seeing."[60] As a result, the seeing of an image always involves a tension, an instability, correlative to the negativity that constitutes the separation between the image and the original which shows through it, and this tension intrinsic to the double seeing is what serves to drive us beyond image to original. It is what provokes us into the movement through the image to the original that shows through the image. When we come to examine it, we will find that *dianoia* involves a very similar kind of tension between image and original.

We need to collect the matters with which we have been

---

[60] Cf. Klein, *Commentary on Plato's Meno*, pp. 112-115.

dealing. Repeatedly, we have seen that the course represented by the divided line is basically continuous. Just now, we have found that the continuity is not only of the passive kind that would belong to a certain course but that it is a continuity intrinsic to the very movement up that course, a continuity that results from that almost continual provocation of the upward movement that results from the tension between original and image. However, there is one point at which the continuity is disrupted. At the major point of division of the line (the point of division between *pistis* and *dianoia*) there is a discontinuity, for here one's seeing comes to rest in the visible, the tension between image and original is resolved, and the motive force which otherwise serves to drive one up the line thus becomes inoperative. Clearly, the transition across this point of discontinuity is extremely problematic. But lest we too easily assume that the visible things in which our seeing comes to rest are finally originals and that, as would follow, the discontinuity is absolute and further movement on the upward way prohibited once and for all—we note that as the last of the three sorts of things to be placed at the level of *pistis* Socrates mentions artifacts, and we reflect (or anticipate—cf. 596 b) that, as a rule, an artifact is made in the image of a model, an original. Nevertheless, it is clear that an additional element must come into play for the sake of this crucial transition.

We need, finally, to take note of the wider significance of this transition across the major division-point of the line. As a transition from visible to intelligible it would appear simply to presuppose that the distinction between visible and intelligible is already established; it would seem that when one begins this transition one would need to have this distinction already "in view." But is this distinction of such a character as would make this possible? It is decisively not a distinction that is immediately evident (cf. Ch. IV, Sect. 7). On the contrary, one comes to rest in the visible and does not, for the most part, regard the visible as an image of something further in such a way as then to be driven to seek this further original (an intelligible) "behind" the image. In approaching the major division-point one comes to rest precisely because the distinction between visible and intelligible is not evident; that is, the transition is a problem precisely because of the non-immediacy of this distinction. Thus, in making the transition one does not simply traverse a path that is already laid out; rather, the transition from the visible to the intelligible involves the very *drawing of the distinction* between visible and intelligible, the very opening-up of this difference.

According to the determination of the philosopher accomplished at the end of Book V, the opening-up of this difference coincides with the *beginning of philosophy*. But the beginning of philosophy is precisely that into which Socrates is seeking to draw Glaucon; in fact, we have already identified Socrates' educating of Glaucon—hence, specifically, his bringing Glaucon into this beginning—as the central *ergon* of the *Republic*. Hence, at this point, in taking up the question of the transition across the major division-point on the line, the *logos* and the *ergon* coincide: Socrates and Glaucon are discussing precisely that transition which they are involved in making by means of the discussion. This transition in which the *logos* and the *ergon* come together so decisively is also reflected at the center of the *mythos*; as so reflected it appears as the making of the ascent out of Hades. It is thus that, when in Book VII Socrates begins his more elaborate reiteration of the ascent up the line, he says (referring to the philosopher-king):

> Do you want us now to consider in what way such men will come into being and how one will lead them up to the light, just as some men are said to have gone from Hades up to the gods? (521 c).

As the matters at issue are collected up and carried on towards the center of the *Republic*, there is simultaneously a gathering of the three principal dimensions of the dialogue into a unity determined by these matters.

(c) *Dianoia*

(i) Socrates' Statements Regarding *Dianoia*

In the first of his statements of the divided line Socrates proceeds immediately from his brief description of the lower two segments to a statement regarding the part of the line above the major division-point:

> "Now, in its turn, consider also how the intelligible section should be cut."
>
> "How?"
>
> "Like this: in one part of it a soul, using as images the things that were previously imitated, is compelled to investigate on the basis of hypotheses and makes its way not to a beginning [ἀρχή] but to an end [τελευτή]; while in the other part it makes its way to a beginning that is free from hypotheses; starting out from hypotheses and without the images used in the other part, by means of *eide* themselves it makes its inquiry through them (510 b).

It should be noted that in this statement Socrates speaks primarily of the two kinds of activities ("affections") of the soul, describing especially the movement of the soul that is undergone in each case. On the other hand, he does not describe the corresponding things as such but refers to them only in terms of their relation to the movement of the soul, i.e., only to the extent necessary in order to describe the movements of the soul. In this connection we should recall a principal result that has already come to light in our considerations of the line, namely, that on the side of things the line represents, not different kinds of things, but different modes of showing of the same things. The specific applicability of this result to the upper part of the line is indicated by Glaucon near the end of the first statement of the line; speaking of those the movement of whose souls belongs at the lower of the two upper segments, he says that,

> because they don't consider them by going up to a beginning, but rather on the basis of hypotheses—these men, in my opinion, don't possess intelligence with respect to the things, even though they [the things] are, given a beginning, intelligible (511 c – d).

In Socrates' first statement regarding the part of the line above the major division-point we need also to note how he draws the contrast between the two subsections that are later named (in terms of the affections represented) *episteme* and *dianoia*.[61] We can thematize this general contrast in terms of three specific points of contrast. First of all, Socrates says that *dianoia* makes use of images. He even says specifically what these images are: "the things that were previously imitated"—i.e., the things which at the level of opinion were regarded as the originals. The images used by *dianoia* are such visible things as animals, everything that grows, and artifacts. On the other hand, *episteme* proceeds "without the images used in the other part"—i.e., it proceeds without visible images. And, Socrates even indicates what it is in *episteme* that corresponds to those visible images employed by *dianoia*: "by means of *eide* themselves it makes its inquiry through them." So, *episteme* makes use of *eide* in place of visible images; it is free of images in the usual sense. We should notice, however, that Socrates does not say explicitly that *episteme* proceeds without any images whatsoever. And, indeed, he has good reason to avoid saying this, for even an *eidos,* by which *episteme* would proceed, is an image in a certain respect: it is an image *of the one* (cf. Sect. 4 b). Hence the kind of movement which was found at the lower part of the line, the movement from image to original, is retained in the upper segments. The second point of contrast between *episteme* and *dianoia* consists in the different kinds of use which they make of hypotheses. *Dianoia,* Socrates says, "is compelled to investigate on the basis of hypotheses." This does not mean, however, that *episteme* makes no use of hypotheses: it too starts out from hypotheses, but it proceeds up to a point that is free of hypotheses. Thus, both *dianoia* and *episteme* use hypotheses but in different ways, *dianoia* remaining dependent on them, *episteme* somehow freeing itself from them. Finally, Socrates contrasts the direction of movement of *dianoia* and *episteme:* whereas both

---

[61] Throughout the present considerations we use the names assigned in the third statement of the line (533 e – 534 a). It should be noted that there is an equivocation regarding the name of the affection represented by the highest segment. In the third statement the name *episteme* is given for the highest segment while the whole upper part of the line is called "intellection" (νόησις). But in the second statement (at the very end of Book VI, 511 d – e) the name "intellection" is given to the highest segment alone. It is perhaps not inappropriate (in light of the peculiar character of the treatment of the highest segment within the context of the *Republic*) that what is initially posed as the name of the highest segment turns out eventually to be the name of the entire upper part of the line.

begin with hypotheses, *dianoia* proceeds from *hypotheses* to an end, while *episteme* proceeds from hypotheses back to a beginning that is free of the hypotheses. Both begin with hypotheses, but they proceed in opposite directions from those hypotheses.[62]

To Socrates' first statement regarding the upper segments of the line Glaucon replies: "I don't sufficiently understand what you mean here." Socrates proceeds then to give some further explanation of *dianoia* in particular by discussing an example of it, namely mathematics:

> I suppose you know that the men who work in geometry, calculation [λογισμός], and the like treat as known the odd and the even, the figures, three forms of angles, and other things akin to these in each kind of inquiry. These things they make hypotheses and don't think it worthwhile to give any further account [λόγον . . . διδόναι] of them to themselves or others, as though they were clear to all. Beginning from them, they go ahead with their exposition of what remains and end consistently at the thing towards which their investigation was directed (510 c – d).

We should especially note here the examples that Socrates gives of what is meant by "hypothesis": the odd and even, the figures, three forms of angles. It is significant that these are not "principles" or "axioms," to say nothing of "hypotheses" in the modern (scientific) sense, but kinds of mathematical things; they are such as to be designated primarily by a (simple or complex) name rather than a *logos*.

Socrates continues his consideration of mathematics as exemplifying *dianoia:*

---

[62] This contrast of directions, which is only preliminary to what will be worked out in Book VII and even more so in the *Sophist,* is virtually identical with the contrast drawn in the discussion of hypotheses in the *Phaedo* (100 a – 102 a). This is especially significant because of the fact that the entire discussion of hypotheses and, hence, of the two directions of movement is generated in the *Phaedo* by Socrates' description of that second voyage in search of causes that he launched by having recourse to *logos* (cf. Ch. I, Sect. 2 b). This serves to indicate to what extent the entire discussion in the central Books of the *Republic* is an elaboration of the way of *logos* of which Socrates speaks openly in the *Phaedo;* and it serves, in turn, to alert us that the fundamental relation of *logos* to the matters that are prominent in this elaboration will need eventually to become explicit.

Don't you also know that they use visible *eide* besides and make their *logoi* about them, not thinking about them [οὐ περὶ τούτων διανοούμενοι] but about those others that they are like? They make the *logoi* for the sake of the square itself and the diagonal itself, not for the sake of the diagonal they draw, and likewise with the rest. These things themselves that they mold and draw, of which there are shadows and images in water, they now use as images, seeking to see those things themselves, that one can see in no other way than with *dianoia* (510 e − 511 a).

So, the mathematician uses visible things (note that Socrates calls them "visible *eide*"!) as images and makes his *logoi* about these images. However, he uses them *only* as images—that is, in making his *logoi* he "thinks," not about these images, but about the originals that can be apprehended only by *dianoia.* So, here there is something quite analogous to that "double seeing" which we found in the case of *eikasia,* i.e., a seeing of the original through the image. But, there is one very crucial difference in this regard between *eikasia* and *dianoia:* whereas the kind of images belonging to the level of *eikasia* are almost always recognized by us *as* images, whereas at this level we almost always have the original (and, hence, the distinction between original and image) already "in view," this is by no means the case at the higher level. We have *not* always already recognized the visible things as images of invisible things to be apprehended only by *dianoia;* that is, we do not always already have the intelligible "in view." On the contrary, we come to rest in the visible, so that the distinction between visible and intelligible is *not immediately manifest.* Whereas we are always already caught up in the movement characteristic of *eikasia,* the movement of *dianoia* is not simply guaranteed in advance. The initiation of that movement, i.e., the beginning of philosophy, i.e., the center of the *Republic,* is something highly problematic.

(ii) The Provocation and Course of *Dianoia*

In order to enter into that problematic we need, therefore, to ask about the initiation of *dianoia,* i.e., about the transition across the major division-point on the divided line. We need to ask: What provokes *dianoia*? What disturbs that state of rest into which the soul comes when the visible comes to stand before it in its bodily presence? What re-initiates the interrupted movement of the soul up the line?

This is one of the principal issues taken up in the elaboration undertaken in Book VII. In the relevant discussion Socrates begins by distinguishing between two kinds of things that can be present to perception (αἴσθησις), those which summon intellection and those which do not. He says that,

> some things perceived do not summon the intellect [νόησις] to the activity of investigation because they seem to be adequately judged by sense, while others bid it in every way to undertake a consideration because perception seems to produce nothing healthy (523 a − b).

He explains, further:

> The ones that don't summon the intellect . . . are all those that don't at the same time go over to the opposite perception. But the ones that do go over I class among those that summon the intellect, when the perception doesn't reveal one thing any more than its opposite (523 b − c).

Socrates illustrates what such "going over to the opposite" means by using the example of fingers: *dianoia* is provoked when there is a kind of *mixing-up of opposites* in what is presented in perception about the fingers, when they are apprehended as both big and little, both hard and soft, both thick and thin.

We need to pay very careful attention to Socrates' use of this example. First, we note that he takes for the example precisely *three* fingers (index finger, middle finger, and smallest finger). He explains that when each is considered just *as* a finger, i.e., in that respect in which they are all the same, then *dianoia* is not provoked; in other words, it is provoked only when one looks at the fingers *in relation to one another* and especially in contrast to one another. Specifically, the index finger appears big in relation to the smallest finger *and* small in relation to the middle finger, hence, both big and small; likewise, it appears thick in relation to the smallest finger and thin in relation to the middle finger, hence both thick and thin. More precisely, the kind of situation which provokes *dianoia* is that in which one of the fingers appears as a member in two pairs and such that it has one or the other of opposite qualities depending upon which pair it appears in. So, the kind of situation which provokes *dianoia* is that in which things appear in pairs, in dyads, and in which they are determined (e.g., with respect to size) only within such pairs, i.e., in which all determination is merely relative, i.e., in which there is, in the strict sense,[63] a lack of genuine measure, a lack of real determination. The kind of situation which provokes *dianoia* is that in which indeterminate pairing, the "indeterminate dyad," prevails. This indetermination, this peculiar "mixing-up," is emphasized further by another feature of Socrates' example, namely, by the fact that he uses a part of the body for his example. For a finger is both a "seat" of perception as well as something perceived; a finger both touches and is touched, and in a finger, therefore, there is a "mixing-up" of touching and touched, perceiving and perceived. Finally, we should take note of the fact that fingers are used especially for pointing, for indicating in the most literal sense. To point out means: to comport oneself towards something in such a way as to let it stand out from the global spectacle, to let it stand forth in a certain distinctness, to let it be separated out from the whole. This pointing character of the fingers serves, in turn, to point to the peculiar character assumed by *dianoia* once it is provoked.

Let us consider, then, the course which *dianoia* takes once it is provoked. What does *dianoia* undertake? First of all it undertakes to sort out the mixture:

"Therefore," I said, "It's likely that in such cases a soul,

---

[63] In the *Statesman* the Stranger draws the distinction between "two kinds of great and small." The first kind is that in which these are simply relative to one another; the second kind is that in which a due measure is operative. The Stranger insists that the exclusive rule of the first kind would destroy the arts and do away also with statesmanship (283 b – 284 a).

This question of due measure versus the relativity of indeterminate duality was already taken up (though solely within the context of the arts) in Socrates' discussion with Thrasymachus in Book I.

summoning calculation and intellect, first tries to determine whether each of the things reported to it is one or two."

"Of course."

"If it appears to be two, won't each of the two appear to be different and to be one?"

"Yes."

"Then, if each is one and both two, the soul will think the two as separate. For it would not think the inseparable as two but as one."

"Right."

"But sight, too, saw big and little, we say, not separated, however, but mixed up together. Isn't that so?"

"Yes."

"In order to clear this up the intellect was compelled to see big and little, too, not mixed up together but distinguished, doing the opposite of what the sight did" (524 b — c).

So, *dianoia* is, first of all, a *distinguishing* which separates the provocative mixture into distinct "ones," each taken by itself, and which poses these "ones" in their distinctness over against the mixture. This posing of the distinct "ones" over against the mixing-up of opposites presented by sight constitutes the originary opening-up of the distinction between visible and intelligible. In fact, the description of dianoetic activity that we just cited concludes by making this explicit: "And so, it was on this ground that we called the one intelligible and the other visible." The distinction between visible and intelligible, the distinction which marks the beginning of philosophy, is first opened up by a "dianoetic leap" in which are posed over against the mixture presented to perception those distinct "ones" that have been separated out from the mixture. Yet, *dianoia* not only distinguishes the ones but also *relates* them. The most obvious sort of relation that it establishes in its beginning is that of opposites to one another; here the important point is that *dianoia,* in relating the ones, relates them *as* distinct ones, in utter contrast to the way they were originally related before the advent of *dianoia,* i.e., in utter contrast to the indeterminate pairing in the mixture. Thus, in summary, it may be said that, at least in its beginning, *dianoia* is a distinguishing and relating of ones.

(iii) The Two Kinds of *Dianoia*

It is now possible to see why Socrates describes *dianoia* by means of the example of mathematics. In the case of counting we have a peculiarly transparent instance of a distinguishing and relating of ones. When we count a group of things, we have first to distinguish each of them, i.e., to regard each as one (as completely distinct, in no way mixed with the others), and then to relate, to collect, these ones into the unity of a number. Counting, the basis of (Greek) mathematics,[64] is a distinguishing and relating of ones.

It is also now possible to understand somewhat better how *dianoia* (at least in its mathematical form) is related to visible things. *Dianoia* involves the posing of an order of total distinctness over against the visible order of indeterminate duality. Through this posing, this opening-up of the distinction between visible and intelligible, it then becomes possible to regard the visible order in terms of the intelligible (e.g., mathematical) order that has been posed; it becomes possible, in other words, to impose a determinateness on the visible order in such a way as to provide a clarification of it; it becomes possible to apply a genuine *measure* to the visible order as opposed to the merely relative determination with which it is presented to perception. To the extent that *dianoia* is engaged in this kind of clarification, it is turned towards the visible. It takes visible things as images (in the narrow sense) of intelligible things, to be clarified (ordered, measured) by reference to the intelligible things that have been posed, the "hypotheses."[65]

It should be noted that *dianoia* in its general mathematical form serves to introduce a new kind of movement on the divided line: Whereas previously we have had to do only with movement *up* the line (the movement from image to original, from less to greater clarity and truth), we find now a movement *down* the line from intelligible things to visible things, from original to image. Yet, this

---

[64] Cf. Jacob Klein, *Greek Mathematical Thought and the Origin of Algebra,* tr. Eva Brann (Cambridge, Mass.: The M.I.T. Press, 1968), p. 19; cf. pp. 69-79.

[65] Klein points out that in this respect the field of *dianoia* is "coextensive with the territory of the visible world," and he regards this as what is signified by the equality of the two middle segments of the line. Cf. *Commentary on Plato's Meno,* pp. 115-125.

movement down is not simply the opposite of the movement up the line; it does not simply undo what the movement upwards has accomplished. Rather, it is a movement down to the visible which, rather than marking a return to the inferior degree of clarity and truth that belongs to the visible, instead clarifies the visible in terms of the intelligible. The movement of *dianoia* back down towards the visible is a movement in which we also remain somehow at the level of the intelligible, of the distinction between intelligible and visible, that has been reached by the dianoetic leap.

But once we have recognized how *dianoia* is turned towards the visible, once we have recognized its peculiar downward-moving character, what then becomes most crucial is to understand that this downward-moving (descensional) *dianoia* is not the only kind of *dianoia* that is at issue as we approach the center of the *Republic*—that, as the discussion between Socrates and Glaucon continues, there also emerges another kind of *dianoia*, an upward-moving (ascensional) *dianoia*, which is a more genuinely philosophical *dianoia*.[66] In fact, the question of upward-moving *dianoia* is a principal issue in the discussion of the sequence of mathematical studies in Book VII. This discussion is, most generally, another attempt to bring the philosopher and the ruler together, another attempt in a particular regard to resolve the paradox of the philosopher-king; in this respect the discussion is quite similar to the one at the beginning of Book VI in which Socrates and Glaucon, ostensibly undertaking to show the concord between the virtues of the philosopher and those of the ruler, end

---

[66] The character of such an upward-moving *dianoia* is thematized by Brann in terms of certain fundamental distinctions in Greek mathematics, specifically, those having to do with the so-called analytical and synthetic methods in mathematics. Whereas the downward movement at issue in the *Republic* is mirrored by the synthetic method, in which one begins with something agreed upon as known and proceeds to trace out its consequences (as in Euclid), the upward movement has its pattern expressed in the analytical method and, specifically, in so-called problematical analysis, in which one begins with a hypothesis and inquires about that from which it derives, thus "backtracking" until one comes to something which is already known or which can in some other way be known. Cf. "Music of the *Republic*," pp. 95-97.

It is of utmost significance for the philosophical consideration of the nature of metaphysics and of the relation of metaphysics (as understood in the philosophical tradition after Plato) to the writings of Plato that this same pattern is taken as a basic directive for delimiting metaphysics by Kant in the *Critique of Pure Reason*.

up in deed exposing their discord; and the present discussion is no less comic in character than was the previous one.

More specifically, Socrates tries to bring the philosopher and the ruler together by discovering that course of studies (beyond the music and gymnastic already prescribed) which would make a man both a philosopher and a ruler. In other words, the studies sought must be such as to turn the soul around and lead it into the ascent that constitutes philosophy; but also, as Socrates says, they "mustn't be useless to warlike men" (521 d), i.e., to soldiers and kings. It is at this point, having posed this task, that Socrates takes up the question of what provokes *dianoia* (with which we dealt above); through the discussion of the example of the fingers and of what *dianoia* is called upon to accomplish with respect to the fingers, he is led to assert that arithmetic, since it has to do with ones and with counting, is the first stage of that course of study capable of leading the soul into the philosophical ascent. And arithmetic (along with logistic) would also be a suitable study for one preparing to be a ruler:

> Therefore, as it seems, they would be among the studies we are seeking. It's necessary for a warrior to learn them for the sake of his dispositions for the army, and for a philosopher because he must rise up out of becoming and take hold of being or else never become skilled at calculating (525 b).

Here the contrast between the two kinds of *dianoia* is obvious: that of the warrior-ruler is one which is completely turned towards visible things and which is concerned with ordering and measuring things in this domain, whereas the philosophic *dianoia* has as its goal to turn one away from the visible. It is clear that from the outset arithmetic is split into two disciplines ("theoretical" and "practical"),[67] one turned towards the visible in such a way as to take the measure of visible things by taking those things *as* ones,

---

[67] This division does not correspond to the distinction between arithmetic and logistic. On the contrary, both arithmetic and logistic were divided into theoretical and practical parts. The eventual collapse of this fourfold classification into the simple distinction between theoretical arithmetic and practical logistic is, philosophically regarded, one of the most decisive transitions in the history of mathematics. Cf. Klein, *Greek Mathematical Thought*, pp. 17-45.

the other turned away from the visible towards the ones themselves. Arithmetic, rather than serving to repair the division between philosopher and ruler, gets divided itself once it is regarded
in this perspective.

So, on the one side, the mathematical disciplines provide skills
needed by ruler-warriors. This is explicitly the case not only for
arithmetic but also for geometry, as Glaucon indicates:

> In pitching camp, assaulting places, gathering the army to-
> gether and drawing it up in line, and in all other maneuvers
> armies make in the battle itself and on marches, it would
> make quite a difference to a man whether he were skilled in
> geometry or not (526 d).

But, on the other side, the mathematical disciplines serve to draw
the soul into the philosophical ascent, into the movement away
from the visible, but in such a way as utterly to destroy the unity
of the mathematical disciplines. In different terms, the upward-
moving *dianoia* carries us ever further from the visible things
calculated by rulers and warriors and removes us from the concern
with the ordering, measuring, calculating of the visible. Thus,
Socrates says of arithmetic:

> It leads the soul powerfully upward and compels it to discuss
> numbers themselves. It won't at all permit anyone to propose
> for discussion numbers that are attached to visible or tangible
> bodies (525 d).

Again, in the discussion of geometry, Socrates speaks of how this
discipline "would draw the soul towards truth and be productive
of philosophic *dianoia* in directing upward what we now improp-
erly direct downward" (527 b); and he notes that, in fact, all but a
"small portion" of geometry would serve this end alone, would
have no importance for the warrior-ruler as such. Then, in the
discussion of astronomy Socrates even makes a little comedy.
Glaucon says that astronomy would serve for this upward movement because "it's plain to everyone that astronomy compels the
soul to see what's above and leads it there away from the things
here" (529 a). Suddenly we get the spectacle of a man transformed into a philosopher merely by tilting his head back and

looking at decorations on the ceiling; and this spectacle declares that such looking up as Glaucon claims for astronomy is, in terms of the issues at the center of the *Republic,* a looking down, since it remains turned towards visible things, towards the visible heavens. The astronomy appropriate to the education of a philosopher must be turned away from the visible to the intelligible.

In the discussion of the sequence of mathematical studies Socrates is discussing with Glaucon precisely that in which he and Glaucon are engaged in deed, education. Considered comprehensively, the entire movement of this section is such that as we (and Glaucon, who is being educated) progress through the sequence we get further and further away from all concern with the visible and with the affairs of the city. This separation is announced by the curious circumstance (of which Socrates makes quite a point) that the third in the sequence, solid geometry, has never been developed, one main reason being that "no city holds it in honor" (528 b); within the city the middle member of the entire sequence of mathematical studies has been omitted, and there is, accordingly, something less than perfect accord between mathematics and the city. The separation of the philosopher from the ruler, of the upward-moving *dianoia* from the downward-moving kind, becomes virtually complete when we come to the last two disciplines in the sequence, namely, astronomy, which studies movement of a kind that is grasped by *logos* and not by sight, and harmonics, which studies harmony quite apart from hearing and sound. In fact, by the time we reach this point, where the upward-moving *dianoia* is finally characterized as a "prelude to dialectic," the requirement, so much insisted on at the outset, that the studies must be useful to the warrior, has been dropped entirely. Socrates and Glaucon have succeeded in separating out (distinguishing) the philosopher along with the upward-moving *dianoia* from the indefinite duality with which the discussion of the sequence of mathematical disciplines began. This is to say that Socrates and Glaucon have themselves effectively practiced *dianoia* in the very discussion of *dianoia.* Again we see the unity of *logos* and *ergon* that prevails near the center of the *Republic.* And again we should recall the *mythos:* the upward way is the way of ascent out of Hades, and Socrates and Glaucon, in taking up that way both in *logos* and in *ergon,* have now resumed precisely that ascent in which they were engaged when they were stopped by Polemarchus' slave.

(iv) The Beginning of Upward-Moving *Dianoia*

Already we have seen how *dianoia* as such is provoked by the mixing-up of opposites; and we have seen how, once it is provoked, it proceeds as a posing of an order of determinate ones over against this mixture. Now the question is: What provokes *upward-moving dianoia,* and how does this *dianoia* proceed once it has been provoked?

In order to deal with this question we need to recall a result at which we arrived in our consideration of Book V (cf. Sect. 3 c); specifically, we need to recall how we dealt with the issue of the "indeterminate many." What we found was that the stage at which things look both beautiful and ugly, at which there is a simple mixing-up of opposites—the stage which, we have now seen, first provokes *dianoia* as such—is *only* a first stage. It leads to another stage which we described as that at which things present themselves as indeterminate manys (as incapable of being determined— as neither beautiful, nor ugly, nor both, nor neither). We found also that the transition between these stages is accomplished when the beautiful and the ugly are posed as distinct and opposed ones over against the mixture. This posing is what we have now seen to be identical with the initiation of *dianoia* as such; it is the dianoetic leap which marks the transition across the major division-point on the divided line. Yet, what we found in our previous consideration was that this posing is inextricably tied to names. It is linked to our calling the things by name; it is a posing, in its proper distinctness, of what is purely named in names; it is a posing of that as which the thing is addressed when it is addressed by names like "beautiful" and "ugly." Thus, the posing of the ones, the upward "leap" of *dianoia,* which founds the possibility of the downward-moving *dianoia,* is made possible primarily by *logos,* by that collecting into ones that is always already accomplished by names and *logos* (cf. Ch. III, Sect. 2 c, iii; Ch. IV, Sect.

7). What is, in very general terms, suggested is that the course of
upward-moving *dianoia* would be a fitting resumption of that
dianoetic leap by which the movement upward is first resumed.
Such a fitting resumption would presumably follow the same
order as is laid out by the sequence of mathematical studies; it
would presumably commence with a relating of single names
analogous to that relating of ones with which arithmetic deals, and
it would presumably continue by the addition of further dimensions to the *logos* and, finally, by the addition of movement and
harmony to it in such a way as to make of it a higher music, a
fitting prelude to the "song of dialectic."

But we have still to see how the specifically upward-moving
dianoia is provoked. We have seen that *dianoia* as such, provoked
by the mixing-up of opposites, is initiated by the leap upward in
which the distinction between intelligible and visible is first
opened up through the posing of the ones. And we have seen how,
in the first instance, this leap upward is followed by a downward
movement back to the visible for the sake of measuring, clarifying,
the visible. The question is, then: What can provoke us to continue
in that upward movement away from the visible, or, at least, to
resume this movement, rather than engaging exclusively in that
return to the visible that is set upon clarifying it? Such upward-
moving *dianoia* can be fully provoked only by the insight that
such a return is ultimately futile, that the visible cannot be finally
clarified. The resumption of the upward way can be provoked
only to the extent that the downward movement of clarification
shatters against the indeterminacy of the visible. But such a
shattering, such an insight into this ultimate futility, is just what
was reached at the second stage that (in the consideration of Book
V) was made possible by the dianoetic leap, by the posing of the
ones—that stage which we achieve by genuinely carrying through
this leap. Specifically, what is achieved at this stage is the insight
that the visible things *can not be determined* at all—that they are
neither beautiful, nor ugly, nor both, nor neither. And this is
precisely the insight into the futility of downward-moving *dianoia,*
the insight capable of tearing us away and setting us again on the
upward way.

But once the visible things are recognized *as* radically indeterminate rather than just "mixed," the entire way of regarding them gets transformed; and, in particular, the way that the things are regarded by downward-moving *dianoia* breaks down entirely. The visible things can no longer be regarded as partially determinate things that are like (that are copies of) the perfectly determinate things posed by the dianoetic leap. Rather the visible things have proved to be *no determinate things at all.* They are *only images*— images not in the sense of imperfect copies but in a more fundamental sense. They are images in the sense of supplying a locus where the determinate things, the *eide,* show themselves but in such a way as also to conceal themselves. Visible things prove to be no more than the place where being and non-being, self-showing and self-concealing come to pass, and it is as though the visible things have been swallowed up by the receptacle.

(d) Dialectic

We have found the fundamental unity of the divided line to lie in the fact that the various segments on the line do not represent different kinds of things but rather different degrees of truth (manifestness) of the same things. One consequence of this fact is that anything which can show itself can do so at the various levels of the line. At the lower levels it remains to a greater extent concealed, that is, presented in images which conceal it; but to the extent that we grasp these images *as* images, to the extent that we recognize the concealment, we are driven upward towards greater manifestness of the thing itself.

In the most general sense the divided line is itself a "thing," and thus there is a legitimate sense in which it can be said to show itself at each of the levels. In other words, what is shown by the line can be applied to the line itself; that is, we can apply the line to itself. Thus, at the level of *eikasia* there is the image of the line which Socrates presents in the form of a verbal description. This image leads us to draw the line, to produce the visible thing of which the verbal description is an image, and thus we pass to the level of *pistis.* But then, in reference to the drawing (taken as a visible image) we try to formulate mathematically the various proportions that define the line; and thus we seek to take the measure of the line, to clarify it, by the way of a downward-moving *dianoia*. However, this clarification proves to be, in a sense, impossible provided we take even minimal account of what the line represents; there is a conflict between the original proportion and the stipulation that the length of each segment should correspond to the degree of clarity and truth that characterizes that level. Granted this stipulation, the middle segments cannot be equal in length—or, in another sense, they could be equal only for one who remained stuck at the level of downward-moving *dianoia*. But if we attend to the disruption of the clarification, we are "driven away" from the line (as a visible image) towards what shows itself through the line[68] ; we take the way of upward-moving *dianoia*.

This movement up the divided line, in which the divided line itself becomes progressively more manifest, is the very movement in which Socrates engages Glaucon; it is in this way that the central *ergon* of the *Republic* unfolds, it is thus that Socrates brings Glaucon into the beginning of philosophy. However, it is very important to observe that the discussion of the line does not itself move to the highest segment of the line—not even when that segment is explicitly discussed. In other words, the discussion remains attached to the line and, at best, only initiates the movement up away from it. The discussion between Socrates and Glaucon does not attain the level of *episteme* or dialectic but remains at the level of upward-moving *dianoia*. This is made explicit when, in the midst of his remarks *about* dialectic, Socrates refuses to comply with Glaucon's request that they proceed to dialectic:

> "You will no longer be able to follow, my dear Glaucon," I said, "although there wouldn't be any lack of eagerness on my part. But you would no longer be seeing an image of what

---

[68] It should be observed that what shows itself through the image of the divided line proves to be not just some *eidos* among others; rather what shows itself here is *showing as such*, hence, truth and being. This is why the divided line is an appropriate image for initiating the education of a philosopher.

we are saying, but rather the truth itself, at least as it looks to
me" (533 a).

The result is that the uppermost segment is seen only through the
image of it available at the level of *dianoia;* that is, in the *Republic*
dialectic (*episteme*) is seen only from the perspective of *dianoia,*
only through a kind of analogy with *dianoia.* This circumstance is
of utmost importance for understanding properly what is said in
the *Republic* about dialectic; it is especially important as a warning against making too much of this discussion and, on the other
hand, against taking it too straightforwardly.

We need to consider especially the account of *episteme* which
Socrates gives in his first statement of the divided line:

> Well, then, go on to understand that by the other segment of
> the intelligible I mean that which *logos* itself grasps with the
> power of dialectic, making the hypotheses not beginnings but
> really hypotheses—that is, steppingstones and springboards—
> in order to reach what is free from hypothesis at the begin-
> ning of the whole [ἐπὶ τὴν τοῦ παντὸς ἀρχήν]. When it has
> grasped this, *logos* now depends on that which depends on
> this beginning and in such fashion goes back down again to
> an end; making no use of anything sensed in any way, but
> using *eide* themselves, going through *eide* to *eide,* it ends in
> *eide* too (511 b – c).

There are two issues on which we need to touch regarding this
account of *episteme* (or dialectic) and the supplement to it that is
given in Book VII.

In the first place, it should be noted how Socrates' remarks
about *episteme* betray the fact that it is being viewed through the
image of it that is available at the level of *dianoia*—namely, *dianoia*
itself. Like the upward-moving *dianoia,* it begins with hypotheses
and, according to Socrates' account, attempts to move upward so
as to get "behind" the hypotheses. In this respect, then, *episteme*
is described as simply an upward-moving *dianoia* carried through
to completion. From the viewpoint of *dianoia* it is, of course,
difficult to say very much about what this completion involves.
Nevertheless, in Book VII the completion is described in various
ways; yet in every case it is the analogy with *dianoia* that is

primarily operative. For example, *episteme* or dialectic is described as a grasp of "each thing itself that is" (532 a), as a grasp of "what each is" (533 b). Here the analogy with *dianoia* clearly protrudes: *episteme* is presented as grasping each thing itself just as *dianoia,* in its beginning, poses each thing itself (e.g., the beautiful itself and the ugly itself) over against the mixing-up of opposites in visible things. In other words, *episteme* is presented as grasping things in the way that would be appropriate only if things were like those distinct ones with which *dianoia* deals, only if things did not form a whole in any sense other than the purely additive sense. Also, alongside this description of the completion ascribed to *episteme,* Socrates speaks of this completion as a grasping of the good itself. In this description there is a similar problem: Socrates speaks as though the good were just another of those distinct ones (dealt with by *dianoia*) which, however, happens somehow to be the highest. Yet, it is quite apparent that this parallel does not hold up: the good is the one, and as such it is not just another one of those ones that can show themselves. So, although indeed *episteme* and *dianoia* both have to do with the one—so that to this extent *dianoia* can mirror *episteme*—the ones with which they deal are not the same ones: the ones of *dianoia* are many distinct ones. This difference is hinted at when (in his original statement) Socrates describes the completion involved in *episteme* as a matter of reaching "the beginning of the whole"; the one with which *episteme* deals is related somehow to the whole; it is not one of the distinct and exclusive ones to which *dianoia* attends. Finally, because the character of the completion remains obscure from the standpoint of *dianoia,* even less can be said about what follows that completion, i.e., about the subsequent downward movement. In effect, Socrates describes it as though it were merely a downward-moving *dianoia* set free of dependence on hypotheses and visible images. Here, as throughout, it is the reflection of *episteme* in *dianoia* that is presented, and by recognizing this operative perspective we recognize the limits of the discussion of *episteme* in the *Republic.*

The second issue with which we need to deal is that of the relation between *episteme* or dialectic and *logos.* In the discussion

Socrates repeatedly links these: for example, in the original account he says that what is grasped in dialectic is grasped by *logos,* i.e., it is *logos* which accomplishes the grasp; again, he says in Book VII that dialectic proceeds "by means of *logos* without the use of any of the senses" (532 a). Here too it should be noted that the dianoetic perspective is operative: the relation of *episteme* to *logos* is mirrored in the dependence of *dianoia* on names. But, within the limits imposed by this perspective, what can be said about the character of that *logos* that is operative in dialectic?

Socrates says that the dialectical man is one "who grasps the *logos* of the being [οὐσία] of each thing" (534 b). This means: The dialectical man is the one who is able to carry on *logos* in the way appropriate to the being of things. In light of the sense of being that emerged from the discussion of the good (cf. Sect. 4 b), this means, in turn, that the dialectical man is the one who is able to carry on *logos* in the way that is appropriate to the lighting up, the revelation, the making manifest, of things. Socrates goes on to say that in such *logos* the dialectician "comes through all this with the *logos* still on its feet." This means: The *logos* of the dialectician is not such that it gets inverted, i.e., is not such that it gets changed into its opposite. So, it is not like that *logos* which belongs to the beginning of *dianoia,* that *logos* in which the thing spoken of no more *is* what it is called than it *is not* what it is called. Dialectical *logos* is such as to be "sustained" by the thing as it shows itself.

Thus, dialectical *logos* is such that it lets things show themselves and, in turn, is sustained by those things. It is a *logos* in which a mutual accord unfolds between the *logos* and the things as they show themselves. This is why Socrates describes the dialectician's *logos* as a kind which is given and received.

But, a final reservation is necessary. We should not assume that the distinctness appropriate to *dianoia* is necessarily appropriate here. Specifically, we should not assume that the giving and the receiving, i.e., the carrying on of *logos* and the manifestation of things, are simply distinct "sides" that have need of being somehow knitted together. But if there is a unity here, the perspective of the *Republic* allows us virtually no access to it.

Section 6.   The Cave (514 a – 521 b)

We have seen that the discussion of the divided line moves to the level of *dianoia,* even to that of upward-moving *dianoia.* Thus, if the discussion were to go further into the matter, we would expect such a further stage to involve a movement to the level of dialectic; it would seem that such a transition would constitute the only way of really going further into the matter. In fact, the discussion does go further. It does so at the very center of the *Republic*, in the discussion situated between the first presentations of the divided line (at the end of Book VI) and the elaboration given in Book VII. However, what is most remarkable is that we do *not* find here a transition to the level of dialectic, nor do we find that freeing of the discussion from dependence on visible images, that freeing that is demanded by dialectic. On the contrary, at the very center of the *Republic* Socrates undertakes to make still another image, the image of the cave.

What is accomplished by the introduction of this image? There are two primary accomplishments. In the first place, the cave image serves to illuminate and gather up the entire multi-dimensional movement that has been undergone on the way to the center of the *Republic*. It is fundamentally in this sense that the discussion of the cave image is the center of the *Republic:* It is that part in which the whole of the dialogue—not only what precedes but also what follows this central segment—is drawn together into a proper unity. Secondly, the cave image serves to let something finally become manifest that has remained concealed throughout the *Republic* up to this point—something the concealment of which has fundamentally determined the movement undergone on the way to the center. Specifically, the cave image makes manifest what obstructs the movement on the upward way, what obstructs especially the movement up to the level of dialectic. So, at the center of the *Republic* we find, in place of a movement up to dialectic, an image which reveals what obstructs just such movement, an image which reveals that negativity which the movement into dialectic must somehow take into account.

(a) Gathering

Let us consider how the cave image illuminates and gathers up the entire movement undergone on the way to the center of the *Republic*. In the first place, it brings together the various parts which together constitute the dimension of *logos* in that part of the *Republic* that leads to the center; it gathers up the issues that are variously taken up in *logos* on the way to the center. This is most apparent in the fact that it unites the sun analogy and the divided line: Socrates relates it explicitly to the line (517 a − b), and it obviously takes over the images of light and the sun from the earlier analogy, yet without setting up that simple analogy between visible and intelligible which ended up undermining the earlier analogy. Also, in the description of the response of the prisoners in the cave to one who returns to the cave after having escaped from it the discussion of the cave image incorporates what happened in Book I when Socrates encountered the three cave-dwellers.

Secondly, the cave image explicitly portrays the movement undergone and portrays it as a movement of education. Through this portrait it is made evident that the movement at issue is not merely a matter of *logos* but also of *ergon*—that it is a movement which does something to the one who gets caught up in it. Thus, the cave image brings together the dimensions of *logos* and of *ergon;* and, as such, it reflects that unity of *logos* and *ergon* that runs through the central Books. The cave image is an image of what Socrates is doing with Glaucon, an image of his educating of Glaucon. The center of the central deed of the *Republic* consists in the making of an image of that deed.

Thirdly, the cave image, reflecting the unity of *logos* and *ergon*, serves also to give renewed prominence to the *mythos* of the *Republic*. In the play of images the cave image clearly corresponds to the underworld from which, especially in the discussion of the divided line, Socrates and Glaucon have been making that ascent that was previously interrupted. This correspondence is almost openly declared at several points in the discussion of the cave image. For example, at the very end of that discussion Socrates says:

> Do you want us now to consider in what way such men will come into being and how one will lead them up to the light, just as some men are said to have gone from Hades up to the gods? (521 c).

Again, in the course of asking whether one who had escaped from the cave would be desirous of returning, Socrates makes use of part of Achilles' famous statement to Odysseus on the occasion of the latter's descent to the underworld; Socrates says:

> Or, rather, would he be affected as Homer says and want very much "to be on the soil, a serf to another man, to a portionless man," and to undergo anything whatsoever rather than to opine those things and live that way? (516 d).

According to the statement in the *Odyssey* the alternative that is contrasted with being "on the soil, a serf to another man, to a portionless man," is that of ruling "over all the dead who have perished," i.e., ruling the shades in Hades. Finally, we note that in the discussion of the need for the one who has escaped to return to the cave (520c) Socrates uses a form of that word with which the entire dialogue began and with which Socrates told how he "went down" (κατέβην) to Piraeus-Hades.

The cave image serves not only to assemble the various dimensions of the preceding part of the *Republic* but also to reintroduce the issue of the city at the very center of the dialogue. Previously this issue was developed in all three dimensions and in the resultant mirror-play between them: in the *mythos* it was developed through Socrates' becoming ruler over Hades and through his subsequent effort at ruling over it; it was developed in *logos* through the building of cities in *logos;* and it was developed in *ergon* when Socrates undertook to educate a philosopher-king in the person of Glaucon. But then, in the course of that educating of Glaucon this whole political side seems to get left behind, and what is enacted is a philosophical transcending of the city. The cave image "gathers in" this issue in such a way as to illuminate that philosophical transcending of the city by which it is framed.

The cave image is able to "gather in" the issue of the city because what is found inside the cave is a political situation, a city. The prisoners are not just isolated individuals. On the contrary, they share a language; they share opinions, for example, the opinion that the man who has ascended and returned to the cave has ruined his eyes; and they engage in contests together, for example, to see who is best able to remember the order in which the shadows will pass by on the inside wall of the cave. That they form a political community, a city, is also indicated by the reference to the fact that they would kill the man who, having escaped, returned to the cave if they were able to do so—an obvious reference to Socrates' end at the hands of the city. Furthermore, the shadows which the prisoners see and which they take for the things themselves are only shadows *of* other things; these other things, which are themselves artifacts and statues (i.e., which are themselves images), are carried by another group of men, who thus determine what the prisoners see. Among this group we would expect to find not only rulers but also some poets and painters and perhaps also some sophists.[69] It appears that these men—as far as their role as determiners of opinion is concerned—are hidden behind the wall, so that even a prisoner whose chains had been removed would be able to see them only by getting outside the wall, only by going outside the wall, by leaving the city. In some sense, the philosopher must transcend the city.

This philosophical transcending of the city—that is, the establishing of the radical breach between philosophy and the city—is constantly at issue in Book VII. We have seen it already in the discussion of the sequence of mathematical studies, and we can see it also in two other very important connections. The first is in Socrates' description of those who are to be educated in philosophy as constituting a danger to the city; he explains that once they see that the ancestral things and the opinions enshrined in the city are no more than a shadow-play, that once they see that these are conventions determined by those "legislators" hidden behind the wall, then they no longer hold them in honor (537 d — 539 d). Finally, we see the philosopher's transcendence at issue in Socra-

---

[69] Cf. Sinaiko, *Love, Knowledge, and Discourse,* pp. 174-176.

tes' insistence that those who have come out of the cave must be *compelled* to return to the cave and serve as rulers (519 c – d). It should be especially noted that, when Glaucon replies that such compulsion would amount to doing these men an injustice, Socrates does not disagree with him but simply makes reference to the well-being of the city as a whole—which is to say that the conflict between the well-being of the individual man (specifically, of the philosopher) and that of the city remains in force. It is in this connection that Socrates says that what is required for the just city is that it be ruled by those who are not lovers of ruling (521 b); in other words, love is compatabile with the city, i.e., it can be incorporated into the city, *only* *if* it is love of something that completely transcends the city.

(b) Negativity

The second principal accomplishment of the cave image lies in its making manifest the obstruction of the movement on the upward way. In the discussion of the divided line this movement was presented as though it were virtually unobstructed, except for the single discontinuity at the major division-point for which *dianoia* had to be called forth. Otherwise, the movement up the line would seem, at most, to require two things: that one be erotic (i.e., directed towards the whole, towards the original rather than the mere image) and that one have a teacher who, like Socrates, could provide one with the appropriate images by which to direct this love upward to the originals. What is decisive about the cave image is that, laying out that same course of movement that was represented by the divided line, it introduces a tension, a downward force, into this movement. This is especially evident in the fact that the man who has not undergone the upward movement is called a *prisoner,* and in the fact that the movement upward is said to be *painful* and initially *confusing,* so that the prisoner would have to be *dragged up.* The cave image introduces a fundamental negativity into the human condition; this is what Socrates indicates by beginning the entire discussion with a description of the cave image as "an image of our nature in its education *and want of education.*"

In the most general terms, it may be said that the cave image reintroduces non-being into the discussion. It should be recalled that, in the schema that was set up for the initial discussion of knowledge and opinion, non-being appeared as the third term of the schema along with the intelligible (being) and the visible (being and non-being); however, in the sun analogy into which the original schema was otherwise taken over this third term was abandoned. In a sense, the sun analogy still provoked us to ask about non-being, for it led us to wonder about the mother who, mated with the good, gives birth to those images of the good of which visible things, the grandchildren of the good, are the off-spring. But the analogy did little more than merely arouse wonder, and with the transition to the divided line even that wonder was abated. But the cave image—the inherent *darkness* of the cave—brings the issue back into prominence.

What guise is taken by the non-being that is imaged in the cave image? What is the locus of this negativity? In connection with these questions the most crucial consideration is that there is a sense in which every man, even the philosopher, always *remains in the cave* and *continues to see the images* on the wall of the cave—namely, *insofar as he has a body*. In other words, the ascent is *only* an ascent of the *soul*; and, however far one may ascend, he goes right on seeing visible things through his body, he goes right on apprehending things *as* visible, regardless of the extent to which he may have transcended the opinions of the city. One continues to sit in the cave watching the shadows—and, thus, in the *Republic* itself the entire discussion by which the ascent from Hades is made is carried out in Hades: Socrates and Glaucon are still sitting in Polemarchus' house in the Piraeus. And in this same connection we should perhaps reflect that by the time the conversation reaches this point it is probably the middle of the night and they have probably missed the torch race on horseback.

This same tension, by which, ascending out of the cave, one also remains chained to it by one's embodiment, is reflected in the fact that Socrates assigns two different names to that part of the divided line below the major division-point: he refers to this part of the line both as representing the "visible" and as representing the "opinable." The point is that the mode of showing of things characteristic of this level can—and ultimately must—be regarded in two different ways. On the one hand, things show themselves *as* visible, i.e., more generally, they show themselves through the senses, through the body; and regardless of the extent to which one may be torn away from this level by the radical disruption of the downward-moving *dianoia,* nevertheless, things continue to show themselves in this way. But, on the other hand, they also show themselves as opinable, show themselves in such a way that we not only see them but have opinions about them; and unlike the sheer visible look, opinions can be tested, purged, collected, and carried up onto the upward way.

Thus, the body is the locus of the negativity that adheres to the human condition—which, however, is *not* to say that the body is identical with that negativity or is the cause of it. It is to say only that the body gives that negativity a place. Nevertheless, this place-giving is decisive with regard to the philosopher's relation to the city. The body of the philosopher remains in the city. And embodiment and the persuasiveness of the senses are what, most immediately, make it necessary for the would-be philosopher to be "turned around" and dragged up out of the cave. It is because the body remains in the city that the return of the philosopher to the cave is, as Socrates says, not a fine thing but one that is necessary: it is necessary because he has never entirely left the cave.

(c) The Downward Way and the Unity of the *Republic*

The cave image gathers up the entire movement undergone on the way to the center of the *Republic,* and within this gathering it lets a fundamental negativity become manifest. As a result of this twofold accomplishment the cave image also gathers up and makes manifest the entire movement that is to be undergone on the way from the center of the *Republic* to the end. This movement is gathered into its own unity and into its unity with the movement that preceded the center. As so gathered it is made manifest as a "repetition" of the previous movement, as a repetition which, inverted by that negativity let loose at the center, takes precisely the opposite direction. After the center the *Republic* moves downward along that same way on which it moved upward prior to the center.

We shall not follow this downward way in the manner that we have followed the upward way. Rather, remaining at the center of the *Republic,* we shall merely allow the gathering power of that center to come into play; we shall simply cast our glance along that way and indicate very briefly its most striking contours, so as to get in view the basic unity of the *Republic.* We shall abstain from following this downward way through the cities, not because we consider this way something unessential, something easily dispensed with once one has made the ascent; on the contrary, the *Republic* has already shown quite the opposite to be the case and has exposed those opinions that would involve neglecting the downward way as ultimately comic. Our reason is, rather, that for what is most centrally at issue in this study, the problem of being and *logos,* it is more fitting to follow another way down. That more fitting way down is anticipated in the *Cratylus* when Socrates, at the height of the inspiration which he brings to the etymological comedy, refers to the need which they will have on the following day of finding a sophist skilled in the appropriate purifications (cf. *Crat.* 396 e — 397 a, together with Ch. IV, Sect. 3 d).

The center of the *Republic,* the discussion of the cave image, is framed on both sides by discussions pertaining to the divided line, the good, and the philosopher. But just as the way into this entire central part of the dialogue led through the comedy of the city, so the way out leads through a resumption of the comedy (540 c — 541 b). Following, as it does, the discussion of the distribution of studies (535 a — 540 c), which amounts to an attaching of the upward movement to the stages of human genesis, hence, a limiting of it by the body and the peculiar temporality of the body— following this discussion, the comedy is more transparent than ever. Socrates plays the sculptor who uses men as though they were raw material dug up from the earth (as in the "noble lie") in order to mold men who are fit rulers—and ruling women too! The short resumption of the comedy concludes with the expulsion from the city of everyone who is over ten years of age. The city turns out to be a city of children; and with this result the long "digression" that constitutes the central part of the *Republic* comes to an end, an appropriately comic end.

Summarizing briefly the comic pre-conditions for the city, Socrates returns at the beginning of Book VIII to the task that was interrupted at the beginning of Book V. At this point the character of the way leading from the center *as* a downward way becomes prominent. Socrates proceeds to trace out the destruction of cities, i.e., the deterioration of the city through a series of progressively more corrupt types; and correlatively, he traces out the path of corruption of the soul leading from the philosopher down to the tyrant. Especially in this last connection we note the one respect in which the descent is radically different from the preceding ascent: the movement downward is gone through in *logos* only, i.e., in a *logos* which is not accompanied by a corresponding *ergon*; that is, Socrates, Glaucon, and Adeimantus speak of the descent but do not in deed make the descent; they speak of the tyrant and of how one becomes a tyrant, but they do not themselves become tyrants.

In the discussion of the corruption of the city there is one particular matter which we considered earlier (Sect. 2 d) but which needs now to be seen in its full context, namely, the curious description near the beginning of Book VIII of how the decline of the city first sets in (546 a – 547 a). The crux of the discussion is that the decline starts when the rulers fail to calculate correctly the cosmic number which would prescribe the proper times for the begetting of children; as a result children are born out of season, and they turn out to be inferior rulers, so that there is a decline of music along with the resulting political consequences. Thus, Socrates' account links the corruption of the city to the mystery of human birth, to human embodiment, to the body. Furthermore, Socrates says that what is involved in the mistake regarding the cosmic number is "calculation aided by perception." Thus, the corruption of the city is linked to that negativity which, as the cave image made manifest, has its locus in the body and perception. This link is further emphasized by the fact that birth is referred to at each stage in the decline through the types of men: each is presented as the son of a man of the preceding type. This is especially striking in the case of the timocratic man: his father is one who flees from ruling (i.e., who fails to return to the cave); the son is then influenced in the direction of desire by the complaints of his mother, who represents the negativity of the cave.

At the very end of the account of the corruption of the city and the soul, Socrates carries the decline one step further by combining the last two terms: the tyrannic city and the tyrannic man. The result is a picture of a tyrant who does not simply remain in private life but who has occasion to be ruler of a tyrannic city, who, as Socrates says, "while not having control of himself attempts to rule others" (579 c). At this point Socrates and Glaucon return to the original question posed in that new beginning that was made in Book II, namely, the question whether justice or injustice is intrinsically more profitable. They return to this question because the portrait of the tyrant has effectively answered it: the "double tyrant," the tyrannic man who also rules in a tyrannic city, is the unhappiest man of all. But then, who is the happiest? Socrates identifies the happiest man as: "that man who is kingliest and is king of himself" (580 c). This man is the philosopher; but the crucial point is that Socrates does *not* say that he, like the perfect tyrant, rules over the corresponding city. The paradox of the philosopher-king remains in force.

At the end of Book IX Socrates speaks of the fact that a man with intelligence always considers—in every connection—one single thing: the condition of his soul, or, as Socrates puts it, "the regime [πολιτεία] within him" (591 d — e). Glaucon replies that if that is what such a man cares about, then "he won't be willing to mind the political things." The conversation (related by Socrates) continues:

"Yes, by the dog," I said, "he will in his own city, very much so. However, perhaps he won't in his fatherland unless some divine chance coincidentally comes to pass."

"I understand," he said. "You mean he will in the city whose foundation we have now gone through, the one that has its place in *logoi,* since I don't suppose it is anywhere on earth."

"But in heaven," I said, "Perhaps, a pattern is laid up for

the man who wants to see and found a city within himself on the basis of what he sees. It doesn't make any difference whether it is or will be somewhere. For he would mind the things of this city alone, and of no other" (592 a − b).

What is the city to which the philosopher will attend? What is the cave to which he will return? It is the one that has been founded in *logos*—or, rather, founded by the deed connected with this speech. This city is a city *within man,* the city within Glaucon. So, in educating Glaucon, Socrates has indeed founded a city, not primarily in the sense that he has educated a ruler for the fatherland but rather in the sense that in and through his speech he has founded a city *within* Glaucon. It is by the founding of such a city, i.e., by the perfecting of one's soul, that the ascent out of Hades is accomplished. Yet this perfecting requires the vigilance which guards against ever forgetting the negativity of embodiment by which the soul is continually drawn back towards the city. Socrates and Glaucon are still sitting in the house of Polemarchus in the Piraeus.

The upward way has been traversed; and that ascent concluded with a recollection of that negativity which haunted the ascent by making it repeatedly collapse into comedy; and that recollection, in turn, issued in a descent—or, more precisely, it issued in a recollection of the descent with which man is constantly confronted because of this negativity. The movement of ascent enacted in the *Republic* issues in a recollection that the ascent is one to which a descent also belongs—that one has always to go down to Piraeus.

STRUCTURE OF THE *REPUBLIC*

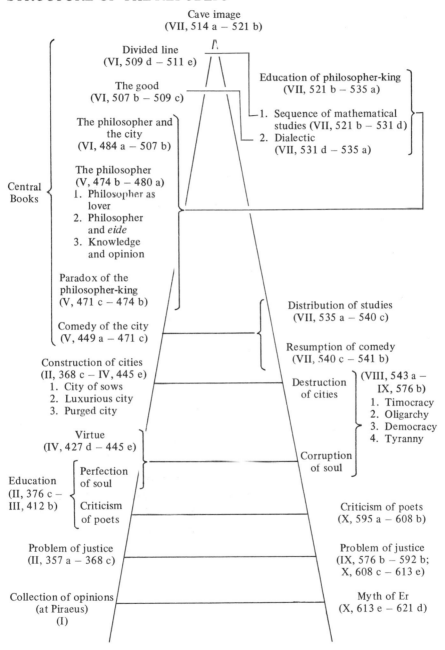

Cave image
(VII, 514 a − 521 b)

Divided line
(VI, 509 d − 511 e)

The good
(VI, 507 b − 509 c)

Education of philosopher-king
(VII, 521 b − 535 a)

The philosopher and
the city
(VI, 484 a − 507 b)

1. Sequence of mathematical
studies (VII, 521 b − 531 d)
2. Dialectic
(VII, 531 d − 535 a)

The philosopher
(V, 474 b − 480 a)
1. Philosopher as
lover
2. Philosopher
and *eide*
3. Knowledge
and opinion

Central
Books

Paradox of the
philosopher-king
(V, 471 c − 474 b)

Comedy of the city
(V, 449 a − 471 c)

Distribution of studies
(VII, 535 a − 540 c)

Resumption of comedy
(VII, 540 c − 541 b)

Construction of cities
(II, 368 c − IV, 445 e)
1. City of sows
2. Luxurious city
3. Purged city

Destruction
of cities

(VIII, 543 a −
IX, 576 b)
1. Timocracy
2. Oligarchy
3. Democracy
4. Tyranny

Virtue
(IV, 427 d − 445 e)

Education
(II, 376 c −
III, 412 b)

Perfection
of soul

Criticism
of poets

Corruption
of soul

Criticism of poets
(X, 595 a − 608 b)

Problem of justice
(II, 357 a − 368 c)

Problem of justice
(IX, 576 b − 592 b;
X, 608 c − 613 e)

Collection of opinions
(at Piraeus)
(I)

Myth of Er
(X, 613 e − 621 d)

CHAPTER VI

THE WAY OF *LOGOS:*

SOPHIST

The *Sophist* is a *logos* about *logos*. Yet, in contrast to the *Cratylus,* it is not a primarily comic *logos* about *logos,* for it does not leave out of consideration the measuring of *logos* by being. Thus, it is not just a *logos* about *logos* but a *logos* about being and *logos*. And, it is a *logos* about the philosopher as the one through whom the measuring can come to pass, without his being the measure and without his taking himself to be the measure—the philosopher, who is attendant to the way of *logos* as belonging to the way of being.

The *Sophist* assembles the problems of being, *logos,* and philosophy, the problems posed at the outset of our study. Yet, it does not assemble them straightforwardly but primarily through the opposite problems: the discussion in the dialogue is more directly addressed to non-being and the sophist than to being and the philosopher. And, though indeed the problem of *logos* is in play throughout the dialogue, this play must be set over against the provocative spectacle of Socrates, the philosopher, remaining totally silent throughout all but the very beginning of the conversation. Why these "opposites" must be put at issue and why philosophical questioning must move within such oppositions is a principal issue of the *Sophist*.

Section 1. In Search of the Sophist (216 a — 232 a)

(a) The Prologue (216 a — 218 a)

In the first part of the first sentence of the *Sophist* the word "ὁμολογία" occurs; the allusion is not only to *logos* but also to the way in which *logos* is to be put at issue in the dialogue. Theodorus, an accomplished mathematician, is the first speaker: "According to yesterday's agreement [ὁμολογία], Socrates, we have come ourselves. . . ." The agreement of which he speaks is the one voiced by Socrates at the very end of the *Theaetetus:* "But in the morning, Theodorus, let us meet here again." We are invited to consider why this agreement was made and to wonder what Socrates and his friends intend to take up as an appropriate sequel to the discussion of the previous day. And, recalling that the *Theaetetus,* in pursuing the question "What is knowledge?" was fundamentally in search of the measure of being (cf. Ch. IV, Sect. 2 b), we anticipate that the *Sophist* will somehow resume that search which was broken off at the end of the *Theaetetus.*

Just before Socrates proposes, at the end of the *Theaetetus,* that they meet on the following day, he indicates why the search, under way throughout the *Theaetetus* and still unsuccessful, is being broken off: it is time for Socrates to go to meet the charges being brought against him by Meletus. Hence, between the time of the conversation presented in the *Theaetetus* and the one presented in the *Sophist,* Socrates has stood trial before the "men of Athens" and been sentenced to death. So, when, in accord with their agreement at the end of the conversation in the *Theaetetus,* they meet again on the following day, they do not meet at the same place but rather in Socrates' prison cell. Socrates' friends have come to him in prison in order to continue the conversation: ". . . we have come ourselves. . . ." Nothing whatsoever is said about this setting, neither in the *Sophist* nor in its sequel, the *Statesman*; yet this setting—and, indeed, even the silence about it—are essential to what is said in the dialogue.

Theodorus continues: ". . . and we bring also a stranger who is a native of Elea [τὸ μὲν γένος ἐξ Ἐλέας] a follower of Parmenides and Zeno, and a philosopher." Socrates' response—his first remark in the dialogue—is a curious one: He asks whether Theodorus is not perhaps bringing, not a mere stranger, but some god; and then he goes on to speak of the god of strangers who marks the order (εὐνομία) and the *hubris* of men. The setting determines the sense of these remarks. Socrates is referring to his trial of the previous day as the result of which he is now sitting in the prison cell awaiting his death. The Stranger is playfully mistaken for a god who, unlike the "men of Athens," would deliver a right judgment of Socrates with respect to his alleged *hubris;* the Stranger is playfully mistaken by Socrates for a god who would be able to judge rightly about philosophers, to do justice to them. We suspect that this is not merely a mistake but also a playful identification of the Stranger, that he is one who is able to judge about philosophers, that he knows about philosophers because he is himself a philosopher and, as such, is devoted to the task of self-knowledge.

In his initial response Socrates suggests, finally, that perhaps this companion whom Theodorus has brought along is one of those higher powers, a kind of god of refutation (ἐλεγκτικός), come to expose their weakness in *logos.* Here again there is reference to the trial, specifically, to Socrates' defence speech and its failure to persuade the "men of Athens" to acquit him or to accept the alternate penalty that was proposed. But we may also refer this remark to the end of the conversation in the *Theaetetus,* of which the present conversation is a continuation. The earlier conversation ends with an unsuccessful attempt to define knowledge (ἐπιστήμη) as true opinion (δόξα ἀληθής) accompanied by a *logos,* specifically, with an unsuccessful attempt to determine what *logos* means; the attempt at a knowledge of knowledge which animates the entire *Theaetetus* becomes at the end an attempt at a *logos* of *logos.* And, of the three *logoi* of logos that are proposed, the last two present *logos,* respectively, as a collecting of elements (e.g., an enumeration of the parts of a wagon) and as a saying (εἰπεῖν) of some mark (σημεῖον) by which a thing would be delimited in its difference from other things (*Theaet.* 206 e − 210 a). The *Sophist* will resume the attempt at a *logos* of *logos,* and it will set out from an understanding of *logos* as collection and division.

It should be especially noted that the Stranger is presented by Theodorus as being from Elea and is explicitly linked with Parmenides and Zeno. Indeed, the spirit of Parmenides will pervade the *Sophist*—in more various guises than is apparent on the surface. The reason for the invocation of Parmenides at the very beginning of the *Sophist* can be seen in the previous conversation, in fact, in two of the conversations of the previous day, both that of the *Theaetetus* and that of the *Cratylus*. For both of these dialogues carry through a radical critique of that dictum of Protagoras that would make man the measure of being—a critique which culminates in the establishing of the position that grants to things a proper and distinct being (cf. Ch. IV, Sect. 2 b). But to say that things have a proper and distinct being is to say that, in their being, each is *one* both with respect to itself and with respect to all others. Hence, the problem which emerges from the *Theaetetus* and the *Cratylus* considered in this regard is that of the one being, that is, the Parmenidean problem. In the *Theaetetus* the emergence of this problem is taken note of by Socrates, who, however, deliberately avoids taking it up on the grounds that it is of such vast extent that it could not be treated as a side issue, that if it were really to be taken up they would end up losing sight of the question with which they are concerned, the question about knowledge (183 e – 184 a). In this connection, Socrates speaks of his great respect for Parmenides, a "reverend and awful figure," whom he mentions having met when he was quite young and Parmenides quite old; the reference is to the dialogue *Parmenides,* which is thus deliberately installed in the background of the *Sophist,* in which the Parmenidean problem, postponed in the *Theaetetus* is taken up (cf. *Parm.* 127 a – c). In this problem we find what is probably the most important reason for their having made the agreement at the end of the *Theaetetus* to continue the conversation on the following day.

To Socrates' remarks Theodorus replies that the Stranger is more within measure (μετριώτερος) than those who devote themselves to refutation and that, though he is not a god, he is a philosopher and, hence, entitled to be called divine (θεῖος). It is at this point, in view of the presentation of the philosophic stranger as divine, that Socrates poses the question from which the entire problematic of the dialogue will unfold. Agreeing that Theodorus is right in calling philosophers divine, he says:

> However, I fancy it is not much easier, if I may say so, to discern [διακρίνειν] this kind [γένος] than that of the gods. For these men—I mean those who are not feignedly but really philosophers—appear disguised in all sorts of shapes, thanks to the ignorance of the rest of mankind, and visit the cities, beholding from above the life of those below, and they seem to some to be of no worth and to others to be worth everything. And sometimes they appear disguised as [φαντάζονται] statesmen, and sometimes as sophists, and sometimes they may give some people the impression that they are altogether mad [μανικῶς]. But I should like to ask our stranger here, if agreeable to him, what people in his country thought about these matters and what names they used (216 c – 217 a).

This is the most important statement by Socrates in the entire dialogue, and we need to attend carefully to it.

Socrates suggests that it is almost as difficult to recognize a philosopher as it is a god, because the former—presumably, like the latter—appears in all sorts of shapes. In this connection it is helpful to note how in the *Republic* Socrates quotes the passage from Homer to which he is alluding in the *Sophist:*

> The gods, like wandering strangers,
> Take on every sort of shape and visit the cities
> (*Rep.* 381 d; *Odyssey*, XVII. 485).

What is important is that the context of the quotation is one in which Socrates is criticizing the Homeric sayings about the gods and insisting that it is contrary to the very nature of the gods for them to assume multiple shapes. Applying this result to the comparison being carried on in the *Sophist* between philosophers and gods, it may be said that the philosopher—at least in that capacity in which he is rightly called divine—does not assume multiple forms but is, rather, one with himself. If he *appears* to assume multiple forms, it is only because of the ignorance of those to whom he appears, only because of "the ignorance of the rest of mankind." In other words, the philosopher soars above the city, "beholding from above the life of those below," so that he is not clearly discernible to the eyes of those down below in the city. In this connection it is appropriate to recall how in the *Theaetetus* Socrates says that it is only the body of the philosopher that sojourns in the city (173 d; cf. Ch. V, Sect. 6 b) and how he then goes on to relate the story of Thales falling into the well and being laughed at by a servant-girl. But, lest we let the philosopher too easily ascend too high, we recall the dramatic setting of the *Sophist:* the philosopher has been condemned to death by the city.

Socrates says that the philosopher appears in three forms of disguise to the men in the city: he appears as statesman, as sophist, and as madman. It should be noted that the philosopher is not said to appear as what he is, as philosopher; at least to men in the city the philosopher appears only in the shape of something other than himself, he appears only as what he is not. Indeed, Socrates does hint that perhaps the third shape is somewhat more fitting to what the philosopher is, for, when he goes on to restate the three shapes in his very next remark, he calls them: sophist, statesman, philosopher. Yet, even if the shape of madman is the most appropriate of the three shapes—which is hardly surprising in view of the *Phaedrus*—nevertheless, the madness of the philosopher *as* it appears to the men in the city does not by any means coincide with his true, i.e., *divine*, madness.[1] The problem which Socrates, in effect, poses to the Stranger is that of distinguishing between the philosopher and those images in which he appears to the men of the city. Thus, from the outset the problem of false appearance, of something's appearing as it is not, is taken up into the discussion; and through this problem a strong link is maintained to the trial of Socrates in which the "men of Athens" failed to distinguish between philosopher and sophist. In the *Sophist* the *fundamental problem is not sophistry but rather philosophy.* The sophist is to be interrogated only because the philosopher can, all too easily, appear to men in the city in the guise of a sophist, can, hence, be

---

[1] Cf. Rainer Marten, *Der Logos der Dialektik: Eine Theorie zu Platons Sophistes* (Berlin: Walter de Gruyter and Co., 1965), p. 55. Also note the description given by Socrates in the *Phaedrus* 249 c – d.

concealed through this image—and perhaps condemned. It is no accident that, in contrast to other principal dialogues that deal with sophistry (e.g., the *Gorgias,* the *Protagoras,* the *Euthydemus*) in the *Sophist* no sophist is present nor even anyone associated with sophists.

But initially Socrates does not pose the problem in its full scope; rather, he poses it merely as a problem of names. He asks the Stranger about the use of the names, sophist, statesman, philosopher, by the people in his country:

> Did they consider all these one, or two, or as there are three names, did they distinguish three kinds [γένη] and attach one of the three corresponding names to each (217 a).

The precise way in which the inquiry about to be launched will be an inquiry into names is indicated a little later by the Stranger (218 b − c). According to what he says, he and Theaetetus begin the inquiry with nothing but the name in common, each of them having, as it were, his own private image of what the thing named by this name is. The movement of the inquiry involves providing a *logos* for the name, coming to an agreement about the thing itself by *logos.* [2] But we are not told how to provide a *logos;* that is what is to be *shown* in the section which follows.

Invited by Theodorus to respond to the question posed by Socrates, the Stranger finally enters the conversation. He says that he has no objection to discussing the matter Socrates has mentioned. In fact, he immediately answers the particular question that Socrates has posed: the people in his country, he says, consider the three names as naming three kinds. He does not say whether he agrees with what people in Elea say about these three; and we wonder, in particular, about those advocates of the *one* that were among the people of Elea, namely Parmenides and Zeno. At any rate, the Stranger moves on immediately to speak of the task to which Socrates' question was really directed: it is, he says,

---

[2] The obvious comparison is with the passage in *Letter* VII (342 a − b) where we are told that there are three things which constitute the necessary means by which knowledge (ἐπιστήμη) of something is acquired: the name, the *logos,* and the image (εἴδωλον).

See also the considerations of this matter in the context of the interpretation of the *Cratylus* (Ch. IV, Sect. 7 c).

no small task to define each of the three. Theodorus responds by recalling an earlier conversation with the Stranger about the same matter in which the latter admitted that he had heard this matter thoroughly discussed and that he remembered what he had heard; thus, the long discussion on which the Stranger is about to embark is cast as a recollection. Finally, Socrates, renewing his request that the Stranger discuss the matter, asks him what style of speaking he prefers, whether a long uninterrupted speech or the method of asking questions. Again, there is a reference to Parmenides—this time by Socrates himself, who refers to the fact that once, when he was young and Parmenides very old, he heard Parmenides use the latter method; the reference is again (as in the *Theaetetus*) to the conversation in the *Parmenides,* which is now even more emphatically installed, therefore, in the background of the *Sophist.* To Socrates' query the Stranger replies that he prefers the method of asking questions provided the interlocutor is tractable but that otherwise a long uninterrupted speech is preferable; he explains his preference by suggesting that it is what is prescribed by the matter itself. We wonder what it is about the matter to be discussed that makes it inappropriate for it to be treated by the method of question and answer. Is it only because of its complexity that it is unfit for dialogue, or is there some other reason too?

On Socrates' recommendation the Stranger accepts Theaetetus as respondent, the understanding being that the latter is tractable and will give no trouble. Recalling Theodorus' earlier insistence on distinguishing the Stranger from those who devote themselves to refutation, we are presumably to understand that Theaetetus can be relied upon not to divert the discussion from the matter itself into the arena of mere refutation and controversy.[3] From this point on the Stranger assumes the leadership in the discussion— indeed, he becomes virtually the sole speaker. In particular, once the discussion is under way, Socrates says nothing whatsoever.

---

[3] In the *Parmenides,* at the point just before Aristoteles steps forth to play a role which turns out to be very similar to that played by Theaetetus in the *Sophist,* Parmenides says: "Then who will answer the questions I shall put? Shall it be the youngest? He will be likely to give the least trouble and to be the most ready to say what he thinks, and I shall get a moment's rest while he is answering" (137 b).

Nevertheless, Socrates is the one who posed the question and requested that the Stranger deal with it, and he is, to that extent at least, the initiator of the discussion. Also, the Stranger has come to Socrates' prison cell, and he delivers his long speech *for Socrates,* not only in the sense that it is delivered in response to Socrates' request but also in the sense that the matter at issue in the speech, the distinction between sophist and philosopher, is most intimately linked to the situation of Socrates, sentenced to death by those "men of Athens" who are incapable of making such distinctions.[4] We could rest assured with the standard opinion that Socrates is less important in the *Sophist* than in those dialogues in which he speaks throughout, only if we could be assured that it could never be important for a philosopher to listen rather than to speak. We are not thus assured; and so, rather than surrendering to the all too easy assumption that with the *Sophist* there is some kind of "development" beyond Socrates—whatever that might mean!—we should, instead, wonder whether perhaps a need for the philosopher to listen might not be at issue in the *Sophist.*

(b) The Angler (218 a — 221 c)

Theaetetus is to answer the Stranger. But, before the discussion begins, Theaetetus mentions one other person who is present, his companion the young Socrates, namesake of the other Socrates; he observes that if he should grow tired his companion could take over for him. In fact, the young Socrates does take over—not in the conversation of the *Sophist* but in another conversation that follows it on the same day, that of the *Statesman.* Near the beginning of the later conversation Socrates speaks of the two young men, Theaetetus and young Socrates, and suggests that both of them are related to him: Theaetetus looks like him and young Socrates has the same name (*Statesman* 257 d — 258 a; cf.

---

[4] It should be observed that at the beginning of his defence speech in the *Apology* Socrates describes himself as a "stranger"—as a stranger, specifically, to the manner of speech used in court (*Apol.* 17 d). Socrates is, in other words, a stranger by virtue of his aloofness from the usual affairs of the city, his transcending of the city.

Theaet. 143 e — 144 a). So, at the conversation presented in the *Sophist* both the name and an image of Socrates are presented in the characters. The suggestion is that the task is to provide the third of those three things, to produce a *logos* of Socrates, of the philosopher. Along with this task posed at the dramatic level, there stands the task posed explicitly by the Stranger in almost identical terms, that of providing a *logos* for what is named "sophist." A curious interplay between philosopher and sophist has begun.

Anticipating that the sophist will be difficult to catch, the Stranger proposes that they begin by practicing on something easier. There follows the division which, beginning with art (τέχνη), proceeds to its two kinds (εἴδη), productive art and acquisitive art, and then proceeding from the latter eventually arrives at angling, so that a summary of the path followed by the division constitutes a *logos* of angling. (See the diagram of the divisions, pp. 470-471).

With regard to this preliminary division there are several points to be noted. First of all, it is presented by the Stranger as a way of practicing the method that is subsequently to be used in the attempt to catch the sophist. What is this method? It is the method of division by kinds (γένη or εἴδη). But why does the Stranger set about practicing this method? Can the method just be decided upon in advance and then applied to just any matter? What assurance is there that the method is at all appropriate to the matter? In fact, the method which the Stranger sets about using in the *Sophist* has its basis provided by the conversations of the previous day. According to those conversations, things have a proper being (distinguished from the variation and multiplicity of appearance) and this being is distinct from other beings. So, to interrogate being is to exhibit the being of things in its proper distinctness, in its determinateness—to discriminate it, to *divide* it off from what only resembles it. It should be observed, however, that this "basis" for the method is itself no more than preliminary and certainly does not ground the method in such a way that it could not again become problematic; this "basis" is only the meagre beginning of the development of the problem of being, which, according to the indication given in the *Theaetetus,* needs to be taken up not merely within the context of a critique of Protagoras but in that of an encounter with the thought of Parmenides. The *Sophist*, beginning with that method of division grounded on the outcome of the *Theaetetus* regarding the problem of being, develops that problem within the more fundamental, Parmenidean context; the distinctive movement of the *Sophist* is from the method back to that ground which justifies and, at the same time, indicates the limits of the method.

The method of division is also spoken of briefly in the *Phaedrus*, where Socrates suggests in reflecting on his two speeches that this was the method actually used in them (though not mentioned at the time they were delivered) (265 d − 266 b; and Ch. III, Sect. 3 c). In the *Phaedrus*, however, the method is presented as involving two parts, not only division but also collection. The most immediate sense of the latter is that in which it precedes division and serves to provide the kind from which the division then proceeds. If we examine the division that yields the *logos* of angling, we find indeed that there is a collection carried on; in fact, there are several collections at various levels. But what is especially striking is that the one kind for which there is no collection at all is the one for which there is presumably the greatest need for a collection, namely, the kind with which the division begins, in this case, art. It is simply posed, and only then does the Stranger set about performing a collection:

> There is agriculture, and the tending of mortal creatures, and the art of constructing or molding vessels, and there is the art of imitation [μιμητική] —all these may be appropriately called by a single name (219 a − b).

The single name is "productive art" (ποιητική); and the kind which it names will prove to be the effective beginning of the division to which the entire central part of the dialogue belongs. But, irregardless of the question of which kinds are, and which are not, arrived at by a collection in the search for the angler, there is the more general question as to what governs collecting as such. What kind of directives are there by which we could have some assurance that the kind reached by collection is appropriate for the division which is to follow it; for clearly, if there is some conflict between the kind with which we begin and the kind at which we want to arrive in such a way as to provide a *logos* for the latter—if, for example, angling were quite simply not an art—then the division and the resultant *logos* would be defective. Furthermore, what directives are available to us by which we could be assured that what we collect into an initial kind really belongs together in that kind? What directives are there by which we could be assured that the wholes which we compose are in accord with the wholes as they are already themselves composed? It is clear that the relevant wholes must somehow be manifest in advance.

The same question may be asked regarding division: What is its directive? In the brief discussion of division in the *Phaedrus* Socrates insists that division should always proceed along the natural joints (265 e); in the *Statesman* the Stranger adds the further specification that the safest procedure is to divide through the middle so as to avoid the error of taking a single small part and setting it off against many large ones, as in the case of those who divide the entire human race into Greeks and "barbarians" (262 a − 263 a). But, granted that we ought to divide along the natural joints, that we ought to divide things as they are themselves divided, how is it that these natural joints, these divisions of the things themselves, are sufficiently manifest in advance to allow us in our dividing to divide as we ought? Is it not, on the contrary, the very function of the method of division to make these divisions manifest? Clearly the stipulation in the *Statesman* that one should divide through the middle is merely a precaution against a very common kind of error and not a general directive, for it may indeed happen that in some cases the things themselves are not divided through the middle. So then, what does serve as directive in the activity of dividing? What provides a predelineation and thereby saves the dividing from being merely arbitrary? A clue is given in the course of the search for the angler, when, having arrived at "hunting," the Stranger says: "But it would be unspeakable [ἄλογον] not to divide hunting into two parts" (219 e). The suggestion is that not to make this division would be contrary to the way that things are already collected and divided in logos— that, more generally, division follows, to some extent at least, the joints in *logos,* that it follows those lines of division already accomplished and handed over to us in *logos*. This is perhaps why, in the course of this exercise in dividing, the Stranger describes learning as conquering things by *logoi* and actions (219 c). To what extent is the method of division a coercing of things by *logos*?

One function of the preliminary division yielding the *logos* of the angler's art is to provide the beginning point for the search for the sophist that is about to commence. The other function lies in the fact that what is arrived at through this division and thus provided with its *logos,* namely, angling, is an image of the very search in which it has been found and, even more, an image of that "fishing" for the sophist that is about to begin.

(c) The First Five Sophists (221 c – 226 a)

Now the search for the sophist by means of the method of division begins. But its beginning is a curious one, which makes us wonder about the outcome. The beginning, the kind from which the division proceeds, is the one used for the preliminary division and there left unjustified, namely, art (τέχνη). What is curious about this beginning is its contrast with Socrates' contention elsewhere (e.g., *Gorg.* 462 b, 465 c) that sophistry is not an art. We can hardly help wondering whether art is an appropriate point from which to begin the search for the sophist. Nevertheless, the search does begin and by following different paths of division the Stranger quickly provides five different *logoi* for the sophist. (See the diagram of the divisions, pp. 470-471).

But there are some curious things that crop up in the course of these divisions, and we need to notice some of them. First of all, it should be observed that near the end of the first of the five courses of division, just before the identification of the first of the many sophists to be tracked down, the Stranger introduces as a kind of persuasion carried on in private that which involves the bringing of gifts, in contrast to that which involves receiving pay; this kind he calls by the curious name "erotic art" (222 e). The name is curious because—especially in view of the central paradox unfolded in the *Republic*—it is highly questionable whether art and *eros* can ever be simply combined in such a way that there could be practiced in the city an art of the lover alongside the arts of the pilot and of the physician. Recalling that the entire course of the division falls within the compass of art, we wonder at the fact that the Stranger inconspicuously introduces *eros,* that he introduces it next to the first sophist. For it is the philosopher, not the sophist, who is distinctively erotic.

Secondly, we need to note the complication that occurs regarding how many *logoi* of the sophist are arrived at. After the second *logos* (the sophist as merchant of knowledge regarding virtue) there are two additional *logoi* obtained by relatively minor variation of the second *logos;* the third sophist appears as a retailer (rather than a merchant) of his own knowledge regarding virtue, and the fourth sophist appears as a retailer of others' knowledge regarding virtue. That these two additional *logoi* are treated as two is clear from the summary of all the preliminary *logoi* that is given later (231 d − e). In fact, in that summary, when Theaetetus actually distinguishes the two additional logoi gotten by variation of the second and calls them the third and the fourth *logos*—at just that point the Stranger remarks that Theaetetus "remembers rightly," and then proceeds to finish the summary himself. It is almost as though the point of undertaking the summary is to see whether Theaetetus will make this distinction. So then, the two variants which follow the second *logos* constitute the third and the fourth. The next *logos,* gotten by division of "fighting," should be the fifth. However, when this division is finished, Theaetetus speaks of the sophist's having now turned up for the *fourth* time (225 e). At the very least, we might suspect that this confusion as to how many *logoi* of the sophist are found reflects the sophist's elusiveness, to which there is frequent reference in the course of the discussion. But perhaps we should also wonder what is indicated about the method of division as such when such a thoroughgoing attempt to achieve the very maximal distinctness—an attempt so thoroughgoing that it even distinguishes the sophist from himself and distributes him among several different *logoi*—turns out to embody a lack of the very simplest kind of distinctness, that pertaining to number.

THE PRELIMINARY DIVISIONS

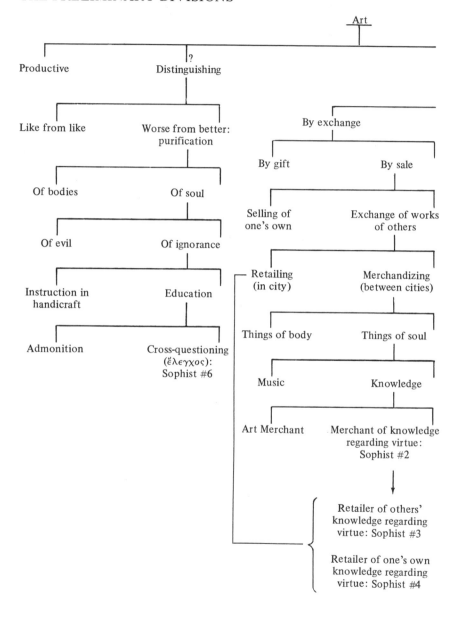

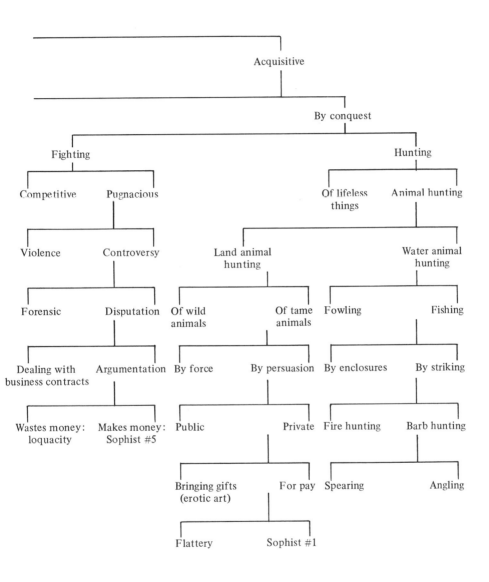

Finally, we need to consider the division that yields the fifth sophist (according to the numbering used in the summary). Here the Stranger begins with "fighting" and after several divisions arrives at "argumentation" (ἐριστικόν). The final division is applied to the latter and is a division between a kind of argumentation that makes money and a kind that wastes money. The former is identified as sophistry; the latter, the kind of argumentation that wastes money, is identified as loquacity, which the Stranger describes in the following way:

> Presumably the kind which causes a man to neglect his own affairs for the pleasure of engaging in it, but the style of which causes no pleasure to most of his hearers, is, in my opinion, called by no other name than loquacity (225 d).

It is clear that the practice which the Stranger is describing is just the *practice of Socrates*—especially clear if we recall how Socrates described his practice on the previous day when he stood trial before the "men of Athens." Searching for the sophist, the Stranger has found the philosopher right next to him. Just after the completion of this course of division the Stranger says of the sophist: "How true was the observation that he was a many-sided animal, and not to be caught with one hand as they say" (226 a). It seems that, of his many sides, at least one is right next to the philosopher, differing only by the fact that the sophist practices money-making while the philosopher does not.

(d) The Sixth Sophist (226 a – 232 a)

The Stranger begins still another search for the sophist by the method of division; and as the kind from which to begin dividing he introduces "distinguishing" (i.e., separating, discriminating: διακριτική). He obtains this beginning-point by means of a collecting of the names of various menial occupations such as sifting, straining, winnowing, carding, spinning; we notice immediately the humble origins of the new beginning-point in contrast to the warriors, hunters, merchants, and the like with which the previous courses of division began. We should also notice that the name of this new kind from which the division is now to proceed is especially significant in terms of the character of the searches being conducted: It is the name of precisely that activity in which the Stranger and Theaetetus have been involved and are still involved as they search for the sophist. The method is now turned on itself, and the investigating is itself what is about to be investigated. They are about to proceed to distinguish the kinds of distinguishing; and it would be surprising if among those kinds of distinguishing which they are about to set about distinguishing they should fail to find that kind that they have themselves been practicing.

How is this new initial kind related to the initial kind from which all the previous searches have proceeded, namely, art. In the subsequent conversation, that of the *Statesman,* the Stranger remarks that "in all things we found two great arts, that of collecting [συγκριτική] and distinguishing [διακριτική]" (282 b); so, distinguishing belongs to art, presumably constituting, along with collection, a member of the first pair to be distinguished within art as a whole, a pair then mirrored throughout the further divisions of art. But how, then, is distinguishing related to the proximal division of art which the Stranger made at the very beginning of the search for the angler, namely, the division into productive art and acquisitive art? The most obvious connection is that both productive and acquisitive arts involve, in the sense of the remark in the *Statesman,* both collecting and distinguishing. But we might also wonder—especially recalling the issues raised in the series of comedies in the *Cratylus*—whether perhaps distinguishing (and a correlative collecting) might not assume the form of a mean between production and acquisition, in the sense of neither merely producing those differences which it brings forth nor merely acquiring them immediately from the things in their proper distinctness.

The Stranger distinguishes two kinds of distinguishing: the distinguishing of like from like and of worse from better. The latter kind he calls purification, which he then divides into purification of the body and purification of the soul. The question then becomes that of how to divide purification of the soul. The

Stranger asserts that in order to carry out this division it is necessary to distinguish between two kinds of evil (κακία) in the soul. One of the kinds is, he says, comparable to disease (νόσος) in the body; he adds that disease is the same as discord (στάσις), which, in turn, he describes as disagreement between what is by nature akin, brought forth out of some corruption, as in the case of opposition between opinions and desires. This first kind of evil in the soul he calls "vice" (πονηρία). The other kind is, he says, comparable to deformity (αἶσχον), which he describes as lack of measure (ἀμετρία) and as, hence, always unsightly (δυσειδής). This second kind of evil in the soul he calls "ignorance" (ἄγνοια).

What is especially important in the discussion of this distinction is the way in which, in connection with the second kind, the Stranger explains the connection between deformity and ignorance by relating both to motion (κίνησις): he explains that, when something that partakes of motion and that aims at a certain mark always misses it, this is the effect of a lack of measure, of disproportion; and ignorance means precisely that aberration of a soul that aims at truth which occurs when understanding (σύνεσις) passes beside the mark; so, an ignorant soul is one that is deformed and lacking in measure. So, the root of ignorance is lack of measure (ἀμετρία) and as, hence, always unsightly (δυστιδής). at the meaning when he adds that what lacks measure is always unsightly (δυσειδής), or, literally, "un-eidetic." Ignorance results from that condition in which the soul is unlike the *eide* that are known in knowledge (cf. *Phaedo* esp. 80 a – b). But an *eidos* is, as such, *one*; and thus a soul's lack of measure involves a lack of oneness with itself.[5]

The relating of the soul to movement is of utmost importance. Movement belongs to the soul, specifically, movement towards truth; this is the movement which the *Phaedrus,* the *Cratylus,* and the *Republic,* each in its appropriate way, have described and provoked. The soul whose movement is improper, the soul which in the movement towards truth repeatedly misses the truth, is ignorant. In other words, ignorance is the lack of fulfillment of the

---

[5] Socrates says in the *Lysis* (214 c – d) that evil men "are never like even themselves, being so ill-balanced and unsteady."

movement proper to the soul, the diversion of that movement away from the mark at which it is properly aimed. Correspondingly, the first kind of evil in the soul, namely, vice, is compared to στάσις, which means not only "discord" but also "rest" (and which will turn out to be one of the five kinds dealt with at the heart of the *Sophist*). What kind of rest is it which, along with missing the mark, constitutes evil in the soul? How can the soul be at rest if movement towards the truth belongs to it? The only suggestion offered at this point is that perhaps this rest, rather than being simply the opposite of movement, is a resultant of movement in opposite directions, as in the case of opposition between opinions and desires.

These considerations bear upon the question of the unity of the virtues, specifically, on the question whether knowledge and virtue coincide. On the surface, the Stranger's answer to this question appears to conflict with what Socrates constantly points to when he speaks of the issue, namely, that a kind of knowledge is identical with virtue (cf. Ch. II, esp. Sect. 3 a). According to what the Stranger says, there are the two kinds, vice (πονηρία) and ignorance, and they are presented as distinct; and so, correlatively, it would seem that knowledge and virtue are distinct. What is amazing is that Socrates, listening to all this while awaiting the death to which he has been sentenced because of his service in behalf of a proper placing of ignorance—what is amazing is that he does not interrupt, that he does not take issue with the Stranger regarding ignorance, since, after all, he had proven himself willing to take issue even with a god over this matter of ignorance. That Socrates does not speak up makes us suspect that perhaps the dissociation is not so radical as it appears to be, that perhaps the distinction does not entirely accord with the things themselves. There is even some indication of a point of unity, namely, in the way that both vice and ignorance are related to movement. They are, according to the Stranger's account, simply two ways in which that movement can fail to attain its mark. But what is this movement? It is the movement towards truth—that is, it is the movement of learning, of knowledge in the broader sense, it is the movement up the divided line; and the engagement in this movement is, at least according to Socrates, precisely virtue in its truest sense (*Rep.* 518 d — e). Even if the distinction between ignorance and vice is as radical as it is here posed as being—which is highly questionable not only in view of Socrates' continued silence but also in view of the excessive distinctness that the method seems to be producing in distinguishing so many forms of one and the same sophist—it is still not the case that, to the distinction between ignorance and vice (as they are described by the Stranger), there would correspond a distinction between knowledge and virtue. The opposite of vice is not virtue in some sense that would make it distinct from knowledge; rather, the opposite of vice is the same as the opposite of ignorance, that is, knowledge, that is, the appropriate completion of the movement of the soul towards truth.

The Stranger proceeds to assign instruction (διδασκαλική) the function of purifying the soul of ignorance. The question then becomes: Can ignorance (and, hence, instruction) be divided? The Stranger quickly focuses on one large part of ignorance which he claims is as weighty as all the others put together, namely, the ignorance that consists in not knowing what one seems to know, i.e., in believing that one knows something which one does not really know; this part, the ignorance of ignorance, appears, says the Stranger, "to be the great source of all errors in *dianoia*" (229 d). To this part he gives the name ἀμαθία (cf. *Laws* 863 c, *Phil.* 48 d — e, *Alc.* I 118 a). What is the other part of ignorance? The Stranger does not say, but we can gather what it is from the fact that he identifies the relevant purification as instruction in crafts in contrast to education.

Finally, the division of "education" (παιδεία) yields "admonition" (νουθετητική) and "cross-questioning" (ἔλεγχος). The latter is introduced by an explanation:

> They question a man about the things about which he thinks he is saying something when he is really saying nothing; then they easily discover that his opinions are like those of men who wander, and in their *logoi* they collect those opinions and compare them with one another, and by the comparison they show that they contradict one another about the same

things, in relation to the same things and in respect to the same things. But those who see this grow angry with themselves and gentle towards others, and this is the way in which they are freed from their high and obstinate opinions about themselves. The process of freeing them, moreover, affords the greatest pleasure to the listeners and the most lasting benefit to him who is subjected to it (230 b – c).

Observing that such cross-questioning is the greatest of all purifications, since it purges a man in such a way as to make him think that he knows only what he knows, and no more, the Stranger is then reluctant to grant such an exalted office to the sophists. But when Theaetetus says that what the Stranger has described resembles the sophist, the Stranger voices the agreement that these are the sophists—though not without prefacing that agreement with a warning as to how slippery such resemblances can be.[6]

The point is that what the Stranger has said about the practice of cross-questioning is, in fact, a description of the practice of Socrates—indeed, in terms very similar to those which Socrates used in his defence speech on the previous day when he spoke of how those old prejudices arose, those prejudices which he presented as largely responsible for his being dragged into court, the prejudices which are, hence, largely responsible for his now sitting in his prison cell awaiting execution. It is little wonder that the Stranger hesitates to ascribe this practice to the sophists.

So, in this search for the sophist, he proves, once he is caught, to be a philosopher in disguise; and we are referred back to the original problem of the disguises in which the philosopher appears to men in the city, to the problem of distinguishing in this respect between image-disguise and original. It is remarkable that, despite all the distinguishing in which they have engaged, the Stranger and

---

[6] This sophist skilled in purification is the one whom Socrates said in the *Cratylus* they would need to seek on the following day (396 e – 397 a; cf. Ch. IV, Sect. 3 d). It remains to be seen how the discovery of this sophist will lead to a purification from the effects of the inspiration under which Socrates proceeded in the comedies of the *Cratylus;* judging from those comedies, that purification will involve an invocation of what limits *logos,* that invocation which in the *Cratylus* could only be comically enacted within *logos* (cf. Ch. IV, Sect. 4 d).

Theaetetus have not succeeded in securing this distinction, but, on the contrary, have ended up mistaking the philosopher for a sophist.

Section 2. The Problem of Being and Non-Being (232 a − 251 a)

(a) The New Search (232 a − 236 d)

Theaetetus indicates that the problem of disguises has now been compounded:

> But by this time the sophist has appeared in so many guises that for my part I am puzzled to see what description one is to maintain as truly saying what he is (231 b − c).

The sophist has appeared in so many guises that now he is disguised; the disguise of the philosopher is himself disguised. The single art of sophistry has appeared as many arts—"one" has appeared as "many," hence, as what it is not. Thus, the outcome of the frantic search for the sophist points beyond the problem of sophistry to the dimension of fundamental problems, to the problems of appearance and of non-being, which will need to be confronted in their full force before the sophist can, as with Proteus, be held onto and made to reveal his true shape.

The Stranger proposes that they initiate still another series of divisions. He takes the starting point for the new divisions from that course of division which began with "fighting" and yielded the fifth sophist, the one next to whom the philosopher was found but for whom the philosopher was not (as in the subsequent case) mistaken. More specifically, the Stranger begins the new series of divisions with "controversialist" (ἀντιλογικόν) and observes that this characterization, as he says, "was one that struck me particularly as revealing his character" (232 b). The name is derived from "ἀντιλογία" ("controversy") and it says, if we are entirely literal, something like: over against, in opposition to, *logos*. The suggestion is that the basic characterization of the sophist will be in terms of his perverted relation to *logos* (cf. esp. *Gorg.* 465 a – d).

However, the more immediate question that is raised is: What is it about which the sophists can carry on controversy? It is soon agreed that the sophists can carry on controversy about everything; but it is even more readily agreed that the sophists cannot possibly know everything, however much they may manage to *seem* to their pupils to be wise regarding all things. The Stranger says:

> Then it is a sort of reputed and apparent [δοξαστική] knowledge that the sophist has been shown to possess about all things, not true knowledge (233 c).

Theaetetus answers:

> Certainly; and I wouldn't be surprised if that were the most correct statement we have made about him so far (233 d).

The Stranger proceeds to introduce an example (παράδειγμα: cf. *Statesman* 277 a – 278 e) by which to understand the sophist, namely, a single art by which one could, not say and dispute (λέγειν, ἀντιλέγειν), but make and do (ποιεῖν καὶ δρᾶν) all things. The feature of this art that is most evident, as soon as it is explained how "all" is to be understood in the description of the art as a means for making and doing *all* things—the evident feature is that one who would claim to possess such an art could not be really serious about it but would rather be playing. Likewise, the Stranger wants to suggest, the province of the sophist's art is play (παιδιά). But, lest we too easily pose a philosophical seriousness over against this play, let us not forget that at this point not only is the philosopher not distinguished from that disguise in which he can appear (the form of sophist) but that also this disguise is itself disguised; clearly the philosopher and the sophist are not yet so thoroughly disentangled from one another and so set out in their proper distinctness that one could straightforwardly assign play to one and seriousness to the other.

The Stranger presents the art of painting as exemplifying the kind of art of which he has just spoken. He observes that when the painter says that he is able to make all things what he really means is that he can make imitations (μιμήματα) which have the same names as the things themselves. Hence, the sophist is linked to imitation (μίμησις) and his play identified as imitative play. In fact, it is "imitation" which provides the starting point for the new series of divisions, and we realize that the entire discussion of controversy was just an elaborate means by which to arrive at an appropriate starting point for the new search for the sophist. How is this kind from which the Stranger will now proceed related to the kinds from which the various other series of divisions proceeded? Actually, imitation (more precisely, the art of imitation: μιμητική) was mentioned near the beginning of the series of divisions that yielded the *logos* of angling; it was included in that group of things that were collected in the kind which the Stranger called "productive art." Thus, in contrast to all the other series of divisions, the new series begins with "productive art"—though, curiously, no explicit notice is taken of the identity of this beginning. Nevertheless, the Stranger does hint at the presence of productive art in the background of the considerations by describing the art specifically in question as one by which one would be able "to make" (ποιεῖν) all things; the allusion lies in his use of the root-word from which "productive art" (ποιητική) derives. Furthermore, it should be noted that, at that point at which "productive art" was obtained by that initial collection, making (ποιεῖν) was defined as bringing into being something which previously was not. From the outset the consideration of productive art is directed towards the consideration of non-being and of the connection between being and non-being.

The Stranger draws the comparison between the example he has introduced and the art of the sophist. Just as the painter makes visible images, so the sophist makes *spoken images:*

> Well then, may we not expect to find that there is another art which has to do with *logoi,* by virtue of which it is possible to bewitch the young through their ears with *logoi* while they are still standing at a distance from the things of truth [τῶν

πραγμάτων τῆς ἀληθείας], by exhibiting to them spoken images of all things [εἴδωλα λεγόμενα περὶ πάντων], so as to make it seem that they are true and that the speaker is the wisest of all men in all things (234 c).

Now, in order to understand what is really at issue in speaking of "spoken images," we need to recall something which we came upon in our reading of the *Cratylus*. In the section of that dialogue that follows the long etymological comedy, Socrates proposes that names imitate the things named (cf. *Crat.* 423 c). But then he goes on to point out the difficulty into which such a way of regarding names will lead us—namely, that "we shall be obliged to admit that the people who imitate sheep or cocks, or other animals, name that which they imitate." Thus, he is obliged to introduce a fundamental distinction: Things have shape, size, and perhaps color and these are what painting imitates when it imitates the things; but naming does not imitate these "qualities"; rather, naming imitates the being (οὐσία) of things. Now, admittedly there are residual comic elements in this consideration of names, and certainly it cannot simply be taken over as though it were some kind of final result independent of its context. But it does allow us to go so far as to say that to whatever extent and in whatever way *logos* imitates things, what it imitates about the things is the being of those things, and not the size, shape, or color. Spoken images are, then, to be understood as images of the being of the things imaged. But, if this is what spoken images imitate, then there is something extremely problematic about them: When a painter imitates a shape or color, what is being imitated is immediately manifest to him and to whoever might set out to pass judgment on the work of the painter; but the being of things is not immediately manifest, which is to say that *logos* can never be a mere copying of a manifest original such that one would be able to test a *logos* by straightforward comparison with the original (cf. Ch. IV, esp. Sect. 5 b). On the contrary, *logos* has to do with originarily making being manifest, and here we find the source of that great power of sophistry to which the Stranger has just referred in speaking of spoken images.

(b) The Problems (236 d – 242 b)

(i) Appearance, False *Logos,* False
Opinion (236 d – 237 b)

The Stranger begins the new series of divisions by dividing
"imitation" (μίμησις) into two kinds: "likeness-making"
(εἰκαστική) and "semblance-making" (φανταστική). But then,
with the series only barely begun, the Stranger poses an obstacle.
He proceeds, in fact, to point out the difficulty that will lead into
the entire central part of the *Sophist:*

> The truth is, my friend, that we are faced with an extremely
> difficult question. This appearing [φαίνεσθαι] and seeming
> [δοκεῖν] but not being, and saying [λέγειν] things, but not
> true ones—all this is now and always has been perplexing.
> You see, Theaetetus, it is extremely difficult to understand
> how a man is to say or opine that falsehood really is [ψευδῆ
> λέγειν ἢ δοξάζειν ὄντως εἶναι] and in saying this not be
> involved in contradiction [ἐναντιολογίᾳ] (236 d – 237 a).

Here there are three issues, which we need to lay out in preliminary fashion.

First of all, the Stranger refers to "appearing . . . but not being." He uses the word "φαίνεσθαι," from "φαίνω," meaning
"bring to light," "exhibit," "display," "make to appear," "show."
In this connection it is important to note that forms of "φαίνω"
are used to refer to images as such, not solely to semblance
(φάντασμα) (cf. 236 b). The point is that in images as such
(whether they are like the original or are only semblances) non-
being is involved: An image lets the original appear, lets it show
itself in some degree; but the image *is not* the original, and it is the
negativity expressed in this "is not" that constitutes the problem
(cf. Ch. V, Sect. 5 b). What is important is that this problem arises
not only with regard to semblance-making and, specifically, sophistry, but with regard to all image-making. We recall (from our
reading of the *Republic*) that even Socrates, the philosopher,

practices image-making, and so we again get a glimpse of the philosopher beside the sophist—very close beside him.

Secondly, the Stranger refers to "saying that falsehoods really are." Here the Stranger is most explicit about the difficulty: "The audacity of the *logos* lies in its implication that non-being is [τὸ μὴ ὄν εἶναι]." The problem is that to say something false is to say what is not, i.e., to say non-being, which presumably must, in some sense, *be* in order even to be said.

Thirdly, the Stranger refers to "opining that falsehoods really are." This reference is introduced in the same phrase in which he refers to "saying," and, presumably, the difficulty is the same. We are not told here what the precise relation is between opining and saying, but the Stranger's way of speaking tends to suggest that there is a close connection. This third issue is also closely related to the first issue, so that it tends to bind all the issues together: Along with "φαίνεσθαι" the Stranger also mentions "δοκεῖν" (seeming), which is closely related to "δοξάζειν" (to opine). Opining is not some internal activity of the soul; rather, we opine, we have opinions, in accordance with the way things seem (appear, show themselves) to us.

The Stranger focuses on the problem intrinsic to all three issues by referring to Parmenides' prohibition against thinking that non-being is.

(ii) Non-Being (237 b — 239 c)

The Stranger proceeds to lay out the problem of non-being—indeed, in such a way as to give eventually a curious kind of vindication of Parmenides' prohibition. The laying out of the problem involves three stages.

First of all, the Stranger secures Theaetetus' agreement that they do not, as a matter of fact, hesitate to say "τὸ μηδαμῶς ὄν" ("what is not at all," "utter non-being"). Then he inquires: To what is the name non-being (τὸ μὴ ὄν) applied? His question means: To what is non-being brought, upon what is it laid, conferred (ἐπιφέρειν)? It is not laid upon any being (οὐκ ἐπὶ τὸ ὄν); so, it cannot be applied to something (τὶ). But he who says not something does not speak at all. Therefore, he who says "non-being" does not speak at all.

These remarks are difficult, not because of any intrinsic complexity but rather because their simplicity so easily puts us off in such a way that we fail really to make contact with what is at issue in them. What the Stranger says seems about as convincing as the argument that, because "round square" cannot possibly be applied to anything, we only utter noises when we use this phrase. Of course, we do not find such argumentation convincing at all. In fact, we have at our command an arsenal of means by which we can easily refute what the Stranger says: All we need do is invoke the well-established distinction between the meaning of an expression and the things to which it may refer. Indeed, such "refutation" is irrefutable—at least, as long as we remain within that distinctly non-Greek perspective to which it belongs. But is it perhaps the case that the very attempt at something like a refutation is here premature? Is it perhaps the case that this very way of comporting ourselves to what the Stranger says is inappropriate? Is it perhaps the case that our distinctively non-Greek, modern perspective is already all too operative as soon as we construe certain *logoi* in a Platonic dialogue as "arguments" in a sense approximating that determined in modern "symbolic" logic? Is it perhaps the case that in this sense there are no arguments in the *Sophist,* nor perhaps in any Platonic dialogues—that precisely what certain dialogues show forth regarding *logos* precludes their assuming such a form? Is it perhaps the case that the bindingness which some—if not all—Platonic *logoi* exercise upon us is of a different order? Is the relevant bindingness perhaps such as can least of all be measured by something like a "logical" refutation? Must we not resolutely refuse to rest secure in the "achievements" of modern logic if we are to prepare ourselves for a re-thinking of the Platonic reflection on *logos*? Is it so preposterous to suppose that even we moderns must attend to our ignorance? Perhaps it is to this that we must first of all attend if we are to be capable of gaining an originary access to some Platonic dialogues.

What the Stranger is presenting with respect to non-being is no argument in the modern sense but rather only a laying out of what is understood in advance regarding names, that is, of the operative pre-understanding regarding the nature of names, which it was precisely the task of the *Cratylus* to test and reform. In effect, the Stranger says: A name which can never be the name of something is no name at all, and one who uses it does not name, hence, does not speak. The point is that the operative pre-understanding of name already includes its being the name *of* something or, at least, the possibility of its being the name of something. Within this pre-understanding, reference is not regarded as something "added onto" already meaningful names. More generally, names are not, in advance, separated from the things spoken about in such a way that subsequently it becomes necessary to explain how name and thing get together. The most elegant and most profound testimony to this pre-understanding is the *Cratylus*.

The Stranger remarks that there is a still greater aporia which affects the very beginning (ἀρχή) of the matter. He proceeds to the second stage of the laying out of the problem. It is agreed that what is cannot be attributed to what is not. Then, without any hesitation it is also agreed that number is included among the things which are, the result being, then, that plurality and singularity cannot be attributed to non-being. So, we cannot say "things which are not" (μὴ ὄντα), since this would involve attributing plurality to non-being; nor can we say "thing which is not" (μὴ ὄν), since this would involve attributing singularity to non-being. Thus, the Stranger says:

> Do you see, then, that it is not possible rightly to utter or to say or to think of non-being itself, but it is unthinkable, unspeakable, unutterable, and contrary to *logos*.[7]

Non-being, the Stranger says, is "contrary to *logos*" (ἄλογον). This makes explicit what the real problem is with non-being: There is an intrinsic opposition between non-being and *logos*.

---

[7] Συννοεῖς οὖν ὡς οὔτε φθέγξασθαι δυνατὸν ὀρθῶς οὔτ᾽ εἰπεῖν οὔτε διανοηθῆναι τὸ μὴ ὂν αὐτὸ καθ᾽ αὑτό, ἀλλ᾽ ἔστιν ἀδιανόητον τε καὶ ἄρρητον καὶ ἄφθεγκτον καὶ ἄλογον; (238 c).

In these considerations there is one step that immediately strikes us as curious, namely, the Stranger's contention that number is included among the things which are. We wonder on what grounds he maintains this, for certainly we would not find such an inclusion so unproblematic as it seems to be taken to be here. We wonder especially about Theaetetus' response: Number must be if anything is. This attests decisively to the obviousness which the inclusion has for the Stranger and Theaetetus. Again, this points to a different pre-understanding—specifically, to the fact that the Greek "ἀριθμός" does not mean "number" in the modern sense. For the Greeks numbers are not regarded as concepts to be elaborated in separation, as it were, from things and then applied to things. On the contrary, the Greek understanding of number is much more closely linked to what is taken as the fundamental phenomenon in this regard: the counting (i.e., counting-off) of some number of things. What is said in the counting-off gives the "counting-number" (ἀριθμός) of the things counted. And so, in the Greek understanding of it, number always means a *definite number of definite things;* number is inextricably linked to that *of which* it is the number; it is always a number *of* things rather than something which, like a concept, would be set over against the things.[8] Now it is clear why Theaetetus says that number is if anything is. He is saying: a number (of things) are if things are.

The second aporia serves to pose a close connection between speaking and thinking, on the one hand, and counting, on the other. But, rather than developing the connection between *logos* and number, the Stranger moves on to another aporia which he now recognizes to be the greatest of all. He brings this third aporia into view by finally letting the self-referential character of the whole inquiry openly assert itself:

---

[8] Of course, these things need not be sensibly presented things; in the case of "theoretical" as contrasted with "practical" arithmetic, numbers are numbers of pure units, of ones. The relevant Platonic discussion occurs in Book VII of the *Republic* (esp. 524 e – 526 c). Regarding the Greek understanding of number and its fundamental difference from the modern understanding, see especially the work of Jacob Klein, *Greek Mathematical Thought,* esp. pp. 46-60.

I am surprised you do not see from the very phrases I have just used that non-being reduces even one who is refuting its claims to such straits that, as soon as he sets about doing so, he is forced to contradict himself (238 d).

The point is that in order to refute speech about non-being, in order to proclaim non-being unspeakable, one must speak of it; one must, for example, speak in some number (singular, plural) and one must attach "to be" to it in the very assertion that non-being *is* unspeakable. The Stranger says, therefore, that he has been defeated in the refutation of non-being; but he was at the outset identified as a follower of Parmenides, and it is Parmenides' prohibition against non-being, a prohibition which itself speaks of non-being, that has been defeated, that is, brought radically into question. The Stranger has, in a sense, vindicated Parmenides' prohibition by letting that prohibition turn against itself so as to make manifest the utmost questionableness that inheres in the matter at issue.

The Stranger asks Theaetetus to try to say something rightly about non-being. When Theaetetus admits that he cannot do so, the Stranger acknowledges that until they find someone who can the sophist has found a safe hiding place. All speaking about non-being seems to be prohibited, even the statement of this prohibition itself. The problem is: How is the radical opposition between non-being and *logos* to be resolved?

(iii) Image (239 c – 242 b)

The Stranger proceeds to explain how, in view of the state of the problem of non-being, the sophist will be able successfully to elude them. When they call him an image-maker, he will interrogate them as to what "image" means. To this query by the sophist voiced by the Stranger, Theaetetus replies that what are meant are images in water, in mirrors, in paintings, and in other such things. However, the Stranger insists that the sophist will accept no such appeal to things *seen*, that, on the contrary, he will insist on carrying out his counter-attack exclusively within *logos* and that, consequently, he will feign ignorance of all those things that Theaetetus has mentioned and will deal only with what can be drawn from what Theaetetus or others would *say* in answer to him.

The Stranger proceeds to specify the problem of image. The basic problem is, in simplest terms, that an image both is and is not the original, so that, as Theaetetus says, "Non-being does seem to have gotten into some such entanglement with being and it is very strange [i.e., out of place: ἄτοπον] " (240 c). In face of this strange entanglement, the Stranger resorts to putting forth a radical proposal. He will undertake to question Parmenides:

> We shall find it necessary in self-defence to put to the question that pronouncement of father Parmenides and to establish by main force that non-being in some respect is and conversely that being in a sense is not (241 d).

To his proposal the Stranger adds the curious remark that he is afraid that Theaetetus will think him mad (μανικός) for now proposing to criticize Parmenides despite what he has said; and he explains that it is for Theaetetus' sake that he is now going to undertake "to cross-question" (ἐλέγχειν) Parmenides. We note that the Stranger uses a form of the same word with which he earlier described that unmistakeably Socratic activity in which the sixth sophist, the philosopher in disguise, was engaged. Parmenides is to be brought under Socratic questioning, just as in the conversation which Socrates has explicitly recalled, that of the *Parmenides,* Socrates was brought under Parmenidean questioning.

But why does the Stranger say that he is undertaking the questioning for Theaetetus' sake? The reason is provided by the Stranger's earlier remark (234 d) about how the sophist puts forth spoken images of things which deceive young men who have not yet come close to the things themselves; the Stranger's proposal is to help Theaetetus come closer without having to undergo the unfortunate experience by which men are eventually forced into contact with the things. So, what is to follow will serve to bring Theaetetus closer to the things themselves in contrast to the mere spoken images of things. And the Stranger thinks that in undertaking what is to follow he may appear mad—that is, that he may assume the third of those three disguises with which the philosopher appears to men in the city, the one of those three disguises that seems to come nearest letting the philosopher show himself as he is.

(c) The Questioning of Parmenides (242 b – 245 e)

The Stranger prefaces his cross-questioning of Parmenides with a brief survey of what is said about being by the three main sects who have tried to understand "how many [πόσα] and of what nature [ποῖα] the beings [τὰ ὄντα] are" (242 c). We note how from the outset of this new questioning the problem of being is linked up with that of *number*. Proceeding with the survey, the Stranger speaks of the *mythoi* told by these men, one sect maintaining that the beings are either two or three (and that they sometimes wage war with each other and sometimes become friends and marry and have children); the Eleatic sect maintaining their *mythos* that all beings (as they are called) are really one; and, finally, an Ionian and a Sicilian muse (presumably, Heraclitus and Empedocles) combining what the other two sects say and maintaining that being is both many and one and that it involves coming together and splitting asunder, that is, combination (συγκρίσις) and separation (διακρίσις) (cf. esp. 243 b). We recall how the entire first part of the *Sophist* was a combining and separating, a collection and division, in *logos,* and we wonder how these two orders of combining and separating—that of beings and that of *logos*—belong together. Furthermore, we note the items that are assembled by the survey of these *mythoi:* being; the numbers, one, two, three; combination and separation. These are the principal items from which the problematic of the central inquiry of the *Sophist* will be assembled, and to this extent this problematic will be a transcription of the *mythoi* which the Stranger has collected.

Remarking that, in view of the many things said about being, he is no less perplexed about it than about non-being, the Stranger proceeds to pose some questions in a pretended conversation with those who say that there are two beings. The principal question is: If there are two beings (i.e., if two beings are the all)—for example, hot and cold—then what do you say of them when both and each are said to be? In other words, what is meant by the "to be" (εἶναι)? That is, how are being, hot, and cold to be assembled?

$$\text{Being}$$
$$\text{Hot} \qquad \text{Cold}$$

Is being a third thing in addition to hold and cold? Presumably not, since in that case the all would end up consisting of three, not of two. But if being is the same as one of the two, then it cannot be said of the two that *both* are. But if being is neither a third thing nor the same as either of the two, that is, if both are being, then the two are one instead of two.

This little play, which involves precisely those items assembled through the preceding collection of *mythoi,* serves to shift the emphasis quite decisively away from questioning about elements (in the manner of the Milesians) to the Parmenidean questioning about being. Whatever one may designate as the being (as the things that are), the real question is how they are related to the "is," to the "to be," to being as such. More specifically, the question is: What must be the character of being if it is to be neither the same as the things which are (e.g., the hot and the cold) nor simply different from them? We should note that it is no accident that this question is introduced through a number play. For, in fact, number has something like the character which will need to be sought for being: the number "two" is not a third thing over against the things that are two, for a number is a number *of* things; on the other hand, the number "two" is not the same as either of the things that are two, since each of them is one and not two.[9] This connection between the structure of being and the structure of number will be quite important as we proceed into the more fundamental levels of questioning in the *Sophist.*

The Stranger turns now to the explicit cross-questioning of Parmenides in order, as he proposes, to try to learn from those who say that the all is one (ἓν τὸ πᾶν) what they mean when they

---

[9] Cf. Klein, *Greek Mathematical Thought,* pp. 79-82.

say being (τὸ ὄν). The cross-questioning of Parmenides involves two stages, the first having to do with names, the second taking up the question of the whole.

It is maintained by the Eleatics that only the one is; and yet, they give the name "being" to something. The question is whether that to which they give the name "being" is the same as that which they call "one." Do they use two names for the same thing? The Stranger proceeds to draw out two consequences. First, he observes that it is ridiculous to assert that there are *two* names while at the same time asserting that there is only the *one.* Secondly, he observes that, given what the Eleatics say, names cannot even be said to be: for, if the name is other than the thing named, then there are two and not merely one; and, if the name is the same as the thing named, either it is the name of nothing or, if it is the name of something, it will be the name of a name (i.e., it will be both name and named, hence, name of itself, hence name of a name). Clearly then, an unqualified assertion of the one is such that it renders names and, hence, *logos* impossible; such an assertion is one with which one "sews up his own mouth" (*Euthyd.* 303 d – e, together with Ch. IV, Sect. 2 b). This means that a sophist, who, as the Stranger has said, carries on his counter-attack solely in *logos,* would, paradoxically, be deprived of *logos* (would sew up his own mouth, as do the pseudo-Eleatic brothers in the *Euthydemus*) should he have recourse to the Eleatic posi-tion—should he, for example, have recourse to it in order, as the Stranger has suggested, to be able to hide in non-being. We should perhaps wonder who is really being questioned here—whether it is Parmenides, his followers, or perhaps those sophists who disguise themselves in Eleatic garb.

The second stage of this questioning of Parmenides (or of those related to him) is one of the most intricate passages in the entire dialogue. Therefore, we shall proceed by presenting the discussion in an outline form in which its structure can be put fully in view.[10] Once we have thus laid out the discussion, we shall attempt to see what is fundamentally at issue in it.

---

[10] This outline is based, in part, on the one given by Cornford, *Plato's Theory of Knowledge,* pp. 222-223.

The discussion proceeds as follows:

(A)   (1) They say: the whole (τὸ ὅλον) is the same as the one being.

        (2) Then, since Parmenides speaks of the whole as "like the mass of a well-rounded sphere," hence, as having parts, being must have parts.

        (3) What has parts can have oneness with respect to its parts and can in that way be one, since it is an all (πᾶν) and a whole (ὅλον).

        (4) But what is in this condition cannot be the one itself (τὸ ἓν αὐτό) (because the one itself must not be many in any sense whatsoever, must, consequently, be completely without parts).

(B) So:

Either (1) Being is one and whole (because it has the condition of oneness). But in this case, being and the one are not the same, and all things (τὰ πάντα) will be more than one.

Or   (2) Being is not whole.
But in this case:
either (a) the whole itself (αὐτὸ τὸ ὅλον) is.
But then:
        (i) Being turns out to lack something of itself. Thus, since it is deprived of being, it will be non-being.
        (ii) The all is more than one (namely, being and the whole).
or (b) the whole is not.
But then:
        (i) The same holds as in (a) (presumably, because being lacks the one itself; and because the all will be being and one).
        (ii) Besides not being, it could never have come to be (since whatever comes to be, comes to be as a whole).
        (iii) It cannot have any quantity (ποσόν), since what is not a whole cannot have quantity.

In this discussion there is both a critique of the Eleatic position
and a sketch of what will be developed later by the Stranger. Let
us first consider the critique. In this connection what the Stranger
wants to show is that there is, as he says at the end of the
discussion, "unlimited perplexity" if we say that being is one or
that it is two. In effect, he shows that if being is assumed to be
one, then it can be shown to be two; and that, if it is assumed to
be two, then it can be shown to be three; and presumably, this
"duplication" could be reiterated without limit.[11] Consider how
he shows this. If one begins with the one being, then it must be
said to be the same as the whole, for, if it were not the whole,
then there would be something else besides the one being; there
would be two, whereas the Eleatics insist that there is only the
one. But, if being is the same as the whole, then, since it is a whole
(of parts), being cannot be the one itself; so there turn out to be
two in any case—*the one has become two.* In the second main part
of the discussion, being is, then, regarded as the whole; being is
one in the sense of having the oneness of a whole but it is not the
one itself, i.e., the one as such, which totally excludes its opposite
and thus can have no "many" under it, no parts. But then comes
the crucial step: if being is the whole and, as a result, is not the
one itself, then *being is not the whole itself,* since there is one
thing that it does not include, namely, the one itself. Thus, being
is not the one itself and is not the whole itself—*the one, having
become two, has now become three.*

Being - One - Whole	1

Being-Whole	One	2

Being	Whole	3

Following this criticism, which dissolves the Eleatic one into
unlimited multiplicity, there is a brief, allusive sketch of what the
Stranger is to set about working out. If (as is shown in the

---

[11] Cf. the generation of numbers from being and one in the second hypothesis in the
Parmenides (143 d — 144 a).

criticism) being is not the whole itself, then there are two alternatives with respect to the whole itself: either the whole itself is or it
is not. In the second case, the same difficulties arise as in the first
case plus another which, at least at this point, would seem to be
utterly decisive, namely, the exclusion of quantity (recalling the
earlier indications of the connection between being and number).
In the first case, we get a mixing of being and non-being; we recall
that it is precisely the possibility of this that needs to be established. And in this case we also get the result that the all is more
than one. What more is it? It is also being and the whole—also
two! Thus, the all turns out to be the one itself *and* a dyad that
has already been shown to be capable of unlimited generation.

(d) The Battle of Giants (245 e — 251 a)

In order to be assured of having ascertained from all sources
that it is no easier to say what being is than it is to say what
non-being is—a radical proposal in view of the extreme opposition
that has emerged between non-being and *logos*—the Stranger turns
to those whose sayings about such matters are less exact, that is,
those who are less proficient with *logos*. These men the Stranger
calls giants, and he says that they drag everything down from
heaven and the unseen to earth so as to maintain that being
(οὐσία) and body (σῶμα) are the same. But there is a battle of the
giants (γιγαντομαχία) against another group, who defend themselves with what is unseen and heavenly. These men who contend
against the giants maintain, as the Stranger says, "true being to be
eide which are things thought [νοητά] and without body" (246
b). The Stranger adds that they break up those bodies (taken by
their opponents as being) in their *logoi* and call them becoming
(γένεσις) rather than being (οὐσία). Presumably, we are to understand that they break up bodies into ones, into those ones that are
purely named in the names that make up the parts of *logos* (cf.
Ch. IV, Sect. 7 b — c, Ch. V, Sect. 5 c, ii). The Stranger makes no
secret of the fact that this second party is on the side of *logos:*
Should Theaetetus and he attempt to get a *logos* from each party
regarding being, there would be no difficulty in the case of those

who take being as *eide;* but in the case of the giants it would be almost impossible because of their lawlessness in *logos.*

(i) The Giants (246 e – 248 a)

In view of the giants' deficient relation to *logos,* it is not surprising how easily the Stranger proceeds to undercut their position. Assuming that they would answer with the minimal lawfulness necessary for the matter to be dealt with in *logos,* he forces them to admit that the soul and virtue *are* and yet are not visible and not bodily, so that the identification of being with the bodily cannot be maintained.

This forcing of the giants away from their position is not, however, the central issue that emerges from the encounter with the giants. On the contrary, the central issue is formed in the pursuit of a question analogous to the question previously posed regarding hot and cold. The question is: If they say (after relinquishing their initial position) that both the bodily and the non-bodily are, then what do they mean by being, since neither is the same as being? Playfully remarking that the giants would probably be at a loss for an answer to this question, the Stranger proposes to offer an answer for their consideration:

> I say that whatever possesses *dynamis* either to produce [ποιεῖν] something other or to be affected [παθεῖν] in however small a degree by the most insignificant thing, though it be only once, all this *is* [ὄντως εἶναι]. For I set up as limit [ὅρος] (by which) to delimit [ὁρίζειν] beings [τὰ ὄντα] that they are nothing but *dynamis* (247 d – e).

So, *dynamis* is that by which a being is a being—it is being itself. What does *dynamis* mean?

Pre-philosophically, the word has a considerable range of meanings. A first cluster of meanings includes "strength," "power," "ability to do something," "outward (manifest) power," and "influence." It also means "force for war" in the sense in which we speak of "armed forces"; we note in this connection that we are in the midst of a battle of giants, and we wonder whether this answer put forth by the Stranger is perhaps the force with which he is engaging in the battle. Another meaning of *dynamis* is "a quantity" and, along with that, "a power" in the mathematical sense; we recall in this connection the way in which number has already been brought into the discussion at several decisive points. Finally, *dynamis* can mean the "force" or "meaning" of a name, that is, it can indicate the "showing power" of a name, its "power of making manifest" (cf. *Crat.* 394 b).

With the last of these we come to the more reflected, philosophical senses of the word. One occurrence of *dynamis* which we especially need to note in this connection is that in Fragment IX of Parmenides, where it is closely connected to light and night. At the simplest level light and night (darkness) are simply perceptual opposites—and we recall that indeed the question being answered in terms of *dynamis* in the *Sophist* has developed from an earlier question regarding hot and cold. But also, these opposites point to a more fundamental opposition, namely, the opposition that is involved in things' coming to show themselves, in their becoming manifest. This connection between *dynamis* and the self-showing, the manifestation, of things is of utmost importance.

In the Platonic writings *dynamis* occurs frequently. For our purposes the most important occurrence is in Book V of the *Republic,* where Socrates discusses systematically what it means. The context of the discussion is the consideration of knowledge and opinion:

> With a *dynamis* I look only to this—on what it depends and what it accomplishes; it is on this basis that I come to call each of the *dynameis* a *dynamis* (Rep. 477 c).

So, in the first place, a *dynamis* involves a dependence. In the case being discussed in the *Republic* the dependence is that of knowledge on being and of opinion on that which partakes both of being and non-being—that is, the dependence of both knowledge and opinion on things' showing themselves in one or the other of the two modes of showing that were distinguishable at that stage of the *Republic* (cf. Ch. V, Sect 3 c). According to Socrates' account a *dynamis* also involves an accomplishing; it accomplishes something. What do knowledge and opinion, in the senses which they come to have in the *Republic*, accomplish? What they accomplish is nothing other than the fulfillment of that on which they depend, the fulfillment of the manifestation of things. The important point is that in the analysis given in the *Republic dynamis* is essentially linked to self-manifestation, to that showing which belongs to being itself.

If we apply the first cluster of pre-philosophical meanings of *dynamis* to what the Stranger says about *dynamis* in the *Sophist,* the question becomes: What is *dynamis* a "power" *for*? The Stranger says explicitly that the *dynamis* at issue is a "power" for ποιεῖν and παθεῖν. What does this tell us, then, about that sense of *dynamis* which the Stranger is identifying with being itself? We recall, first of all, that "ποιεῖν" was defined at the beginning of the series of divisions that yielded the *logos* of angling: it means, according to the Stranger, to bring into being something which previously was not (219 b; cf. *Sym.* 205 b – c). So, to apply this to the present passage, the Stranger is saying that being is the power of bringing forth into being something which previously was not. At the originary level, however, such coming forth into being is not something prior to and independent of a thing's coming into manifestness, its coming to show itself, but rather a thing's self-showing belongs to its very being (cf. esp. Ch. V, Sect. 4 b). Being as such, *dynamis* in that fundamental sense pointed to through what the Stranger offers for consideration by the giants, is the power of bringing something forth into manifestness, the power of letting it show itself. But what is that "power" by which things are brought to show themselves? It is just the showing as such. Being as such, *dynamis,* is just showing as such.

Next, we need to note that "ποιεῖν" is the root word from which derives "ποιητική" (productive art); and we recall that the latter is the "kind" which stands at the head of the entire discussion that began explicitly with the attempted division of image-making and that is still under way in the guise of a digression intended to make possible that division of image-making that the Stranger attempted. So, what is the producing, the bringing forth, that is principally at issue here? It is the bringing forth of images. But previously (in our reading of the *Republic*) we have seen to what extent the bringing forth of images belongs to at least one of the modes in which things can show themselves—to what extent image-making is integral to that sort of self-showing of things by which, at least for the most part, they announce themselves to embodied man.

But, finally, why does the Stranger refer *dynamis* not only to ποιεῖν but also to παθεῖν? A clue is provided if we note that the latter is a verbal form of the word with which Socrates, in the *Republic*, describes what corresponds on the side of the soul to the various levels of manifestation signified by the divided line: he speaks of παθήματα ἐν τῇ ψυχῇ (affections in the soul) (*Rep.* 511 d). What happens in the soul is not something distinct over against the event of self-showing in which things can show themselves; on the contrary, the soul is invocative, and what happens "in" the soul belongs to the totality of the self-showing. Being is the *dynamis* that encompasses both the coming forth of things into manifestness and the soul's receptive-invocative drawing forth of them.

(ii) Friends of the *Eide* (248 a – 249 d)

The Stranger proceeds to consider what is said about being by that other group, that group that contends against the giants by using *logoi* to break up those bodies which the giants would identify with being. Now he calls these others the friends of the *eide*. It is in the discussion with these men, who are so much more skilled in *logos* than the giants, that the entire problematic which we have glimpsed through the identification of being with *dynamis* is brought into the open. We note that in this discussion, unlike the one with the giants, Theaetetus plays the role of those being questioned by the Stranger.

The Stranger says that the friends of the *eide* speak of generation (γένεσις) as separate from being (οὐσία). He proceeds to focus on the separation spoken of by these men, retaining at the same time some indication that that separation is somehow linked to *logos:*

And with the body by means of perception we partake [κοινωνεῖν] of generation; and with the soul, by means of reckoning [διὰ λογισμοῦ] we partake of being [ὄντως οὐσία], which is always the same in the same way, you say, (while) generation is different at different times (248 a).

In this statement we should take special note of the occurrence of the important word "κοινωνεῖν"; this word, meaning "to have a share of," "to take part in," "to partake of," is derived from "κοινός," meaning "common to many" in the sense of something's being had in common; closely related to these is the word "κοινωνία," which means "communion" or "community" and which will later be used to denote what is at issue in the discussion of the five kinds. In the present passage we should note also how the distinction between generation and being is formulated in terms of sameness and difference: being is what is always the same as itself while generation is what is perpetually different from itself. This formulation is important for what is to come.

The Stranger proceeds to observe that the partaking of which he has just spoken in reference both to being and to generation is the same thing that was previously spoken of in the discussion with the giants—that, specifically, it coincides with something's being affected or brought forth out of *dynamis.* Thus, *dynamis* is what empowers that partaking in which, through perception, the body has communion with generation *and also* is what empowers that partaking in which, through "reckoning," the soul partakes of what is ever the same, which the friends of the *eide* call being. *Dynamis* is that by which the presentation of generation to the body and of *eide* to the soul is allowed to come to pass. *Dynamis* is that by which something can become manifest to a "seer." *Dynamis* is the full event of self-showing. And, as such, *dynamis* is, according to what the Stranger said in the discussion directed at the giants, a name for being as such. We note that this name is decisively different from the one which the friends of the *eide* give to being.

In fact, the Stranger goes on immediately to point out that the friends of the *eide* do not accept the connection which he has posed between *dynamis* and being. Specifically, they refuse to accept it because *dynamis,* linked to "production" and "affection," has no bearing on being as long as the latter is identified with what is always the same in contrast to generation. On the basis of that separation of which they speak, the friends of the *eide* quite consistently insist that *dynamis* (and the "production" and "affection" which it empowers) is related only to generation, and not at all to being.

But to this insistence the Stranger replies in decisive terms. The soul knows, and being (in the sense in which it is understood by the friends of the *eide*) is known. But if to know is to bring forth (ποιεῖν), then to be known is to be affected (i.e., to undergo being brought forth, to "suffer" it).[12] But to be affected (i.e., to undergo being brought forth) is to be *moved*. Therefore, *being is moved* insofar as it is known. The Stranger elaborates:

> What in the name of Zeus? Shall we let ourselves be easily persuaded that motion and life and soul and wisdom [φρόνησις] are really not present to perfect being [τῷ παντελῶς ὄντι μὴ παρεῖναι], that it involves neither life nor thought [φρόνειν], but solemn and holy, devoid of intelligence [νοῦς], stands immovable (248 e – 249 a).

We are reminded of that image which Parmenides himself once presented to Socrates near the end of that conversation presented in the *Parmenides*—the image of the *eide* as standing so aloof, as so remote, from man as to be simply unknowable to him (133 a – 135 b). We realize that, just as with that image in the *Parmenides,* so here we have reached one of the most decisive moments of the entire *Sophist.*

What is that movement which the Stranger, in opposition to the friends of the *eide,* is here introducing into being? In the first place, it is a movement that is definitely linked to the soul, as the Stranger's elaboration makes quite clear. What kind of movement is proper to the soul? Certainly it is not a movement with respect to place nor with respect to anything perceptible. Rather, it is the kind of movement told of in the great myth of the soul in the

---

[12] The qualification ("*if* to know is to bring forth. . . .") is important here, as is evident if we recall our previous reference to the fact that in the discussion of the divided line in the *Republic* what are mentioned on the side of the soul are called "παθήματα." The developments in the *Republic,* especially those bearing on *dianoia,* make it clear that neither ποιεῖν nor παθεῖν belongs exclusively on the side of the soul nor on that of things. Both belong on both sides.

Phaedrus, specifically, that movement by which, re-enacting the divine banquet, the human soul moves towards beings in their truth. It is that kind of movement of the soul in pursuit of truth which emerged so decisively out of the etymological comedy in the *Cratylus* and which was comically played off against the movement in the souls of those dizzy name-makers of whom Socrates spoke. It is that kind of movement which is spoken of in the central Books of the *Republic,* the movement up the divided line, the movement on the upward way leading out of the cave. It is that kind of movement towards truth of which the Stranger spoke earlier in the *Sophist*, specifically in the course of pursuing the sixth sophist, the one who turned out to be a philosopher in disguise. It is that kind of movement in which what shows itself to the soul comes to show itself more fully, more openly.

However, the movement introduced by the Stranger is not only a movement of the soul but also a movement of what is known by the soul, that is, a movement of the *eide*. The Stranger introduces movement into the *eide,* and on this point he takes issue most decisively with those friends of the *eide* who insist that the *eide* remain immovably the same. But, the movement which the Stranger introduces into the *eide* is not just any kind of movement; it is a movement that is correlative to the movement of the soul. Hence, it is not movement with respect to place or other perceptible qualities; it is not movement of the sort that pertains specifically to generation. Rather, it is precisely the *movement of self-showing,* the movement in which an *eidos* comes forth into manifestness, the movement in which an *eidos* shows itself. The movement introduced by the Stranger in opposition to the friends of the *eide* is a movement which is integral to being itself. It is not a movement *of a being* (in the sense of a movement in which something which already is would subsequently engage) but rather the *movement of being itself.*

Having criticized the position which would eliminate all movement from being, the Stranger turns next to criticism of the opposite position, which maintains that everything is in movement. This position, he insists, like its opposite, has the effect of eliminating intelligence and knowledge by the fact that it eliminates all sameness. This issue (at least in its most immediate, polemical guise) is developed only briefly in the *Sophist*—and with good reason, for it was developed in the most thorough way on the previous day in those conversations that are presented in the *Theaetetus* and the *Cratylus*. According to those developments, if everything were perpetually becoming different, then it would be impossible ever to speak properly of things. As Socrates says in the form of a question:

> And can we rightly speak of a beautiful which is always passing away and is first this and then that? Must not the same thing be born and retire and vanish while the word is in our mouths? (*Crat.* 439 e).

By the same account, if everything were perpetually becoming different, then knowledge would be impossible (cf. Ch. IV, Sect. 7 c).

The Stranger expresses his resolve with regard to these matters:

> Well then, we must contend by the entire *logos* against anyone who tries to maintain any assertion about anything at the same time that he suppresses knowledge or wisdom [φρόνεσις] or intelligence [νοῦς] (249 c).

Such men do on a grander scale the same thing that Euthydemus' brother did when he spoke in such a way as to sew up his own mouth. And so, the Stranger concludes that the philosopher—now openly spoken of—must reject, on the one hand, the position that all things are at rest, whether as one (in the case of the Eleatics) or as many ones, i.e., *eide* (as in the case of the friends of the *eide*) and, on the other hand, the position that all things are in motion: "but like the child's prayer, he must say that being and the all are both together, unmoved and moved" (249 d). Clearly this does not mean, however, that being or even the whole of beings is to be regarded as consisting of two separate parts, what is unmoved (*eide*) and what is moved (visible things); much less is it to be construed "developmentally" as a kind of belated recognition of the "reality" of sensible things. For the Stranger has quite decisively introduced movement into the *eide* themselves. It is not as though there are moved things "alongside" unmoved things, but rather movement and rest are, as it were, spread throughout the whole.

The relevant movement is not that of generation but rather is the movement of self-showing. What the criticism of the proponents of perpetual flux adds is that there must be a sameness (rest) intrinsic somehow to this movement.

(iii) Aporia about Being (249 d – 251 a)

The battle in which the Stranger has emerged victorious over all contenders concludes with his finally having to suffer defeat—at least a temporary defeat—not at the hands of any of those men who speak about being, but rather at the hands of being itself. The aporia which emerges marks one of the most important transitions in the entire dialogue.

The Stranger again raises the same kind of question that he raised earlier regarding hot and cold, even referring explicitly back to that earlier discussion. It will be recalled that in that discussion the Stranger asked about what is meant in saying of hot and cold that both *are*; that is, he asked what the "to be" means when both hot and cold are said to be; and he answered eventually that being could be neither the same as either or both nor simply different from them. Now, the same question is formulated in terms of the results that have emerged in the course of the battle of giants, namely, the insight that being involves both rest and movement.

The Stranger provides the two principal connections that generate the problem: movement (κίνησις) and rest (στάσις) are opposed to one another; yet both and each are said equally to be. The question, only slightly less than fully explicit, is: What does the "to be" mean?

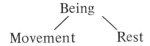

The Stranger pursues the problem. The "to be" does not mean "in movement," nor does it mean "at rest." So, it appears that being must be a third thing beyond rest and movement. However, being is neither in movement nor at rest, whereas, if something is not in movement, it must surely be at rest; that is, being cannot be just a third thing outside movement and rest.

The result is much the same as in the previous discussion of hot and cold. Being is not the same as movement, it is not the same as rest, nor is it a third thing completely different from movement and rest. But now we can see more determinately what is really at issue in this questioning about being. Being is delimited by a peculiar movement, the movement of self-showing; this movement also incorporates a certain self-sameness (rest); and being is not something just completely different from this movement and rest, that is, it is not a thing "subsisting" independently of movement and rest. But there is still another alternative which to some extent would seem to be suggested by what the interrogation has yielded thus far; perhaps being is just the same as both movement and rest together. If this were the case, then the structure of being would turn out to be the same as the structure of number, for the number "two" is precisely the two things (e.g., units) together. However, the Stranger denies this alternative in the case of being: "Being is not rest and movement both together" (250 c). Whereas, with respect to two things in relation to the number "two," we can say that each is one and both are two; with respect to movement and rest in relation to being, we must say that both and each equally are.[13] This decisive denial marks the end of the accord that has previously prevailed between being and number. It marks the beginning of a fundamental divergence, which at this point we can thematize in no more than a preliminary way: When we count, it is necessary that the things counted be homogeneous, i.e., the many that are collected by a number are regarded as the same for purposes of the counting; but the two (i.e., movement and rest) that belong to being are not the same but radically opposed to one another. This is to say, more generally, that the problem of being is ultimately inaccessible to *dianoia* and, hence, is to pose the task of the transition to dialectic.

---

[13] Cf. Klein, *Greek Mathematical Thought,* pp. 94-95.

Section 3. Being and Non-Being (251 a − 259 d)

(a) Community (251 a − 252 e)

A new level of discussion now begins. The Stranger begins it by posing the question of one and many in its simplest and least troublesome form: How is it possible for one thing to have many names, as, for example, when a man is called tall, cowardly, just, etc. The Stranger quickly dismisses the problem as a mere puzzle suitable only for children and for old men who have taken to learning only late in life. This problem, abruptly raised and almost as abruptly dismissed, serves, nevertheless, as an introduction to the new level of discussion that is being initiated. It serves to bring the problem of being as it has now been posed—that is, as a problem of one (being) and two (rest, motion)—explicitly into connection with the question of *logos*. Thereby it points to what is to be undertaken at this new level of discussion: By taking up the question of the community of kinds (of the structure by which they are both one and many), the basis will be provided for taking up the question of the community of being and *logos*.

The Stranger proceeds to pose the question of community (κοινωνία)—that is, the question whether such things as movement, rest, and being can partake of one another, whether with respect to them there can be a "having in common":

> Are we not to attach being to movement and rest, nor anything else to anything else, but rather to treat them in our *logos* as unmixed [ἄμικτα] and incapable of participation [ἀδύνατον μεταλαμβάνειν] in one another? Or are we to gather them all together as capable of having community [δυνατὰ ἐπικοινωνεῖν] with one another? Or is this so for some, and not for others? (251 d).

He considers the three alternatives in turn. If there were no community, then it would be necessary to say that movement and rest *are not,* since they would not partake of being. In fact, the ultimate effect of supposing no community would be to pose the destruction of *logos* itself, since one would be unable to assert the "to be" of anything. On the other hand, if there were total community, unlimited community, then movement would be at rest and rest would be in movement—that is, all opposition would be destroyed, and the "kinds" would turn out to resemble mathematical "ones" in being always combinable.[14] Hence, the only acceptable alternative is the third: some have community and some do not.

In treating movement, rest, and being and the question of their community, the Stranger speaks almost as though these were merely kinds among other kinds and almost as though the problem he is posing were just a particular case of a more general problem. The play which he is preparing by speaking in this way will come to light eventually. But, at this point, what is essential is to bear in mind that there is no problem more "general" than the problem of being; even the problem of community, rather than being prior to that of being, is just a way of taking up the problem of being. The community between the kinds dealt with by the Stranger is not just an instance of the community of kinds but also has to do with the very possibility and structure of all community of kinds. This peculiar reflexivity is a principal source of the difficulty of this part of the dialogue.

What, in a preliminary sense, do "having in common" (κοινω-νεῖν) and "community" (κοινωνία) mean in this discussion? It should be recalled that previously "κοινωνεῖν" was used to refer to the connection that is established in the event in which something comes to present itself to a seer (248 a; cf. Sect. 2 d, ii). This indicates already that the community being dealt with here is not just a matter of so-called "logical" connections between concepts. Neither "logic" nor concepts are at issue here but rather being, that is, self-showing; and what the community of kinds has reference to, in the first place, is a showing of themselves in community (cf. esp. *Rep.* 476 a, together with Ch. V, Sect. 3 b).

---

[14] We have considered in detail this situation in which all opposition is dissolved so that everything can be said of everything. Ch. IV, Sect. 2 b.

(b) Dialectic (252 e – 254 b)

By way of clarification of the community of kinds the Stranger offers two analogies. In the first place, he notes that the things of which they have been speaking are like the letters of the alphabet, some of which fit each other, others of which do not. We note the peculiar appropriateness of this example to the larger issue in play here: It hints at a structural relation between communities of kinds and *logos*. We note also that the Stranger mentions the fact that vowels serve as bonds in such a way that other letters cannot be joined without them. This reference serves to provoke the analogous question: What are the kinds that serve as bonds between the other kinds? And what is the character of the binding? The second analogy that he draws is with high and low sounds. He connects the two examples: Just as one needs an art (τέχνη) in order to combine letters so that something is said (namely, the art of grammar), so one needs an art in order to combine sounds harmoniously (namely, the art of music). He extends this result to the matter at issue: In the same way, one needs something analogous to grammar and music in order to be able to show in *logos* which of the kinds harmonize (συμφωνεῖ). However, in the latter case, the case at issue in the discussion, the Stranger speaks, not of art (τέχνη) but of *episteme*—and Theaetetus calls it nearly the greatest *episteme*. Here is what the Stranger says:

> Then, Theaetetus, what name shall we give to this? Or, by Zeus, have we stumbled unawares upon the *episteme* that belongs to free men and perhaps, while seeking the sophist, found the philosopher? (253 c).

This *episteme* is identified as dialectic, as division according to kinds.

The Stranger offers a description of the procedure of collection and division:

> Then he who is able to do this discerns adequately one *idea* extended entirely through many, each of which lies separated, and many, different from one another, embraced from without under one; and, on the other hand, one joined

together into a one through many wholes and many entirely separated and distinguished. This is knowing how to distinguish according to kind how things are able [δύναται] and not able to have community [κοινωνεῖν] (253 d – e).

So, according to this statement, to engage in dialectic means, in general, to gain access to the kinds with respect to the way that they are laid out in community. What does this statement add, however, that was not already evident in the practice of collection and division in the first section of the *Sophist* and in the description given in the second part of the *Phaedrus* (265 d – 266 b; cf. Ch. III, Sect. 3 c)? As was explicit in the latter, dialectic involves two main steps, collection and division. However, it is not such that one step has simply to do with a "one" and the other step simply with a "many"; rather, both steps involve both one and many. On the one hand, collection involves grasping the one *idea* which embraces the many *and* grasping the many as embraced under this one; on the other hand, division involves grasping the one in terms of the many wholes under it, i.e., exhibiting it as composed from many, *and* this requires grasping the many wholes in their interconnection, i.e., exhibiting the division, the articulation, into distinct parts.[15]

Explicitly assigning dialectic to the philosopher, the Stranger proceeds to draw a strong contrast between the philosopher and the sophist. There is one point of similarity, namely, that both sophist and philosopher are difficult to see clearly. However, in the two cases the reasons for this difficulty are quite opposite: Whereas the sophist runs away into the darkness of non-being, the philosopher, in utter contrast, devotes himself to being and, thus, is exceedingly difficult to see because of the brilliant light in which he lives.

It is imperative to observe that this is not the final, definitive portrait of the philosopher. We should, indeed, take the Stranger at his word: they have only indicated the place where the philosopher ought to be sought, and it may well be necessary to make a

---

[15] See the discussion in Hans-Georg Gadamer, *Platos Dialektische Ethik* (Hamburg: Felix Meiner Verlag, 1968), pp. 73 ff.

further investigation of him later (254 a — b). It is not difficult to see in a general way why the Stranger indicates these reservations about the description of the philosopher—that is, why this "creature of pure light" is not finally identical with the philosopher, however much he may be an image that is required on the way to the philosopher. After all, the whole thrust of the *Sophist* has been to show how being *and* non-being, light *and* darkness, philosopher *and* sophist necessarily *belong together*. It is not a matter of a simple contrast between these pairs. And, presumably, it would be possible to find the philosopher while looking for the sophist, as the Stranger says explicitly has just happened, only if there is some inner kinship between them and not just sheer opposition.

In his account of the philosopher as difficult to see because of the brilliant light, the Stranger says: "For the eyes of the soul of the many are not able [ἀδύνατα] to endure looking at the divine" (254 a — b). This remark should be related to the very beginning of the dialogue where Socrates indicated that, at least to the extent that the philosopher is divine (and soars above the city), he cannot appear as he is to men in the city but rather appears disguised either as sophist, statesman, or madman. But now we need to ask: What about the divine philosopher, apart from the way in which he appears to men in the city? That is, how does he appear to the philosopher? What is the character of his divinity once we get behind (or are somehow led behind) the disguise? An answer was presented in *ergon* at the very beginning of the dialogue, for at that point the philosopher (the Stranger) appeared to the philosopher (Socrates). How did he appear? At first he appeared as a god; but then, through the mediation of the mathematician Theodorus, he came to appear as one who is divine (θεῖος) but *not* a god (θεός), as one whose divinity is not simply complete.

In this connection it should also be recalled that what has just happened—namely, that they have found the philosopher while searching for the sophist—has already happened before, most strikingly in the case of the sixth sophist. But what was the character of the philosopher that was found at that point? It was precisely the character that is most prominent in Socrates: the philosopher appeared as one who practices cross-questioning of the kind that is aimed at exposing ignorance. In other words, the philosopher appeared as one whose principal concern is that men establish and maintain the proper relation to their *ignorance*. But a concern (of the Socratic sort) with ignorance is something drastically different from that concern with the pure light of which the Stranger now speaks.

We should again recall that Socrates is listening to all of this. The fact that he does not interrupt at this point should perhaps even make us suspect that the link of the philosopher with ignorance and with darkness is now going to be established—that, in other words, the portrait of the philosopher as enshrouded in pure light is only for the sake of a more primordial establishing of his relation to darkness. And we might well wonder how such an establishing would reflect back on the character of dialectic as the Stranger has described it. But, however this may be, what is most important to recall is that on the day preceding the present conversation Socrates was condemned to death—that Socrates, the philosopher, is here engaged in the most radical confrontation with non-being, the confrontation with his own death.

(c) The Five Kinds (254 b — 257 a)

The Stranger proposes to consider some of the most important *eide* or kinds. Specifically, he proposes to consider, first, the nature (ποῖα) of each one and, thereafter, their *dynamis* of having community (κοινωνία) with one another. The discussion which then follows falls into two main parts. However, its division does not correspond to the order indicated in the Stranger's proposal: He does not begin by considering the nature of each *eidos* and only subsequently go on to treat its community with others. This is brought out strikingly at the very beginning: In the first step he sets out to determine the community between rest, movement, and being. In fact, the Stranger's proposal regarding the order of the inquiry is thoroughly ironical and is counterposed against the fact that one of the most important points of the entire discussion of the five kinds is to show that the "nature" of an *eidos* (i.e., what it itself is) cannot be determined in separation from those others with which it has communion. In this connection, we should especially consider how things stand with respect to the one, as was elaborated in our reading of the *Republic* (Ch. V, Sect. 4 b): Every *eidos* is one simply by virtue of its being an *eidos*, and so, simply by virtue of being an *eidos*, every *eidos* is already related to another *eidos*, the one itself, that is, every *eidos* is an image of the one.

The Stranger indicates also that the goal of the entire discussion of the five kinds is to find out whether it can be said that in some sense non-being is, and, thereby, to return in the direction of those problems from which the entire central part of the *Sophist* has proceeded. We should bear this in mind: The discussion of the five kinds is for the sake of understanding non-being and its relation to being and *logos*, whether it can be *said to be*.

(i) Preliminary Considerations

Some preliminary considerations are in order before we turn to the intricacies of the discussion of the five kinds. First of all, we note that the entire account is presented as an example of dialectic as this was described in the preceding section. But more important than this is the fact that the discussion of the five kinds is not just an example of dialectic but also a "grounding" of dialectic. More specifically, this discussion deals with that character of being by virtue of which things can be collected (i.e., being as all-embracing) and that character of being by virtue of which things are divisible from one another, have their distinctness (i.e., being as incorporating otherness). So, this discussion is a practice of dialectic which, at the same time, exhibits that character of being that underlies dialectic.

Secondly, we need to consider the fact that throughout this section the Stranger speaks of being as an *eidos* or kind (γένος). What is important is that we not take this fact too straightfor-wardly. Rather, his calling being by these names should be seen in relation to a peculiar dramatic feature of this section, namely, that it incorporates an "ironic play" in the space between dialectic and mathematics. We find this play most openly indicated by the repeated references to number, to "how many" *eide* there are; indeed, the Stranger sometimes speaks as though the most important thing were simply to count up the *eide*. Now, if the *eide* could be counted, they would need to be in some respect homogeneous and also distinct from one another, like those pure ones that are counted in theoretical arithmetic. So, when the Stranger calls being an *eidos,* he is treating it as homogeneous (in name) with the others and as a distinct unit alongside them, as though it could be counted up along with them. But, this is a *play!* Dialectic is not reducible to mathematics. The matters to which dialectic is directed are not countable; and recognizing how and why they are not countable is one of the most important issues in this section.

So, thirdly, rather than being captivated by the designation of being as an *eidos,* we should recall the delimitation of being which the Stranger offered in the discussion directed at the giants and which he interpreted and elaborated in the discussion with the friends of the *eide:* Being is named *dynamis,* and *dynamis* in that fundamental sense in which it delimits being means *dynamis* of self-showing. What is at issue in the problem of being is primarily the problem of self-showing.

Fourthly, we note that the discussion of the five kinds takes up the problem of being by dealing with the question of the *dynamis* of community of the kinds. Again it needs to be stressed that this community does not consist of "logical" connections between concepts. Rather, it has reference to a community of self-showing; that is, it refers to the community in which and as which *eide* show themselves.

Finally, we need to recall explicitly how the problem of non-being, which the Stranger is now preparing to meet head-on, arose earlier in the dialogue and how it is related to some further issues. The problem first arose explicitly near the beginning of the last series of divisions that were undertaken in search of the sophist: Having begun with the division of imitation into likeness-making and semblance-making, the Stranger interrupted himself to point out the difficulty which "imitation" and "image" involve. The problem in its first form is that appearing ($\phi\alpha\acute{\iota}\nu\epsilon\sigma\theta\alpha\iota$), seeming ($\delta\sigma\kappa\epsilon\hat{\iota}\nu$), and, hence, image as such involve a mixture of being and non-being, so that the discussion runs up against the Parmenidean prohibition against non-being. Thus, the problem of non-being gets taken up in order to account for the possibility of images—that is, in order to account for the possibility of a thing's showing itself in some way other than simply *from* itself, in some way other than in an immediate and total self-revelation. In other words, the problem of non-being is taken up in order to show the possibility of a thing's showing itself in such a way as simultaneously *to conceal* itself—i.e., in order to vindicate and to exhibit the possibility of concealment.

Now, this issue of concealment is closely related to the whole search for the sophist and the philosopher with which the dialogue began. For instance, the sophist has effectively concealed himself by appearing in so many guises, and then, finally, he has taken refuge most decisively in non-being (i.e., in the *problem* of non-being) as the Stranger repeatedly mentions. Also, the problem of image and concealment came up at the very beginning of the dialogue when Socrates spoke about philosophers as appearing *in disguise* to men in the city, as appearing in the forms of sophist, statesman, madman—i.e., his appearing not simply as what he is. So, the problem of philosophy itself (at least in its relation to the city) is linked from the outset of the dialogue to the problem of image and concealment. In this connection we should especially take note of the circumstance that on the day preceding the one on which this discussion about images and non-being takes place Socrates was condemned to death because of certain public images of himself which, ingrained over many years, could not be dispelled in a single defence speech. But it would seem that, even when the philosopher is not considered in relation to the city, there is still a link with images and concealment and, through these, with non-being. Consider that the Stranger appeared to Socrates in the *image* of a god, i.e., at first as a god and then as godly (like a god). But if the philosopher appears to the philosopher in an image, then we can perhaps even say that the philosopher appears to himself in this way—so that the problem of image, concealment, non-being would pertain even to the Delphic pronouncement that pertains so decisively to Socratic practice.

(ii) Principal Considerations

Because of the exceptional difficulty involved in considering the discussion of the five kinds—which constitutes, however, the very core of the *Sophist*—we present, first, an outline and then proceed by way of commentary on the individual sections of the discussion.

The following outline indicates the principal points and the general structure of the discussion:

(I) (254 d – 255 e)
    (A) Being, movement, rest:
        (1) Movement and rest do not mix.
        (2) Being can mix with both.
        (3) So, they are three.
    (B) Same and other:
        Each of the three is
        (1) Other than the two.
        (2) Same as itself.
    (C) The five kinds:
        (1) Movement and rest are neither other nor same.
        (2) The same and being are incapable of being one.
        (3) Being and the other are very much different.
(II) (255 e – 257 a)
    (A) Movement
        (1) Movement is entirely other than rest.
        (2) Movement *is* through participating in being.
        (3) Movement is other than the same. But movement is the same (all things participate in the same). So, movement is the same and is not the same.
        (4) Movement is somehow not other and also other.
        (5) Movement is other than being. So, movement is not; but also it is, since it participates in being.
    (B) Being and Non-Being
        (1) So, non-being is: Nature of the other so operates that each kind is other than being, and therefore non-being.

(2) So, in relation to each of the *eide*, being is many and non-being is unlimited in number.

(3) Then, being itself must also be said to be other than all the remaining.

(4) So, whatever the number of all the remaining is, in just that many ways being is not.

Our commentary will proceed by reference to this outline.

(I, A). This first section serves to recall and to pose again the aporia that resulted from the battle of giants. The Stranger says that being can mix with both movement and rest. This means: Both movement and rest belong to being. This is precisely what the Stranger insisted upon in the discussion with the friends of the *eide*. Against the latter he maintained that being involves movement—movement of the soul and movement of things into manifestness, that is, comprehensively, the movement of self-showing. On the other hand, the Stranger maintained against the proponents of perpetual flux that being involves rest, i.e., that there must be a self-sameness within the movement of self-showing.

Granted that movement and rest both belong to being, the question then becomes: What is the character of that belonging? How are these three related? This is precisely the aporia that was posed and left unresolved at the end of the battle of giants:

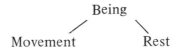

Being

Movement   Rest

What, specifically, was shown was that being is neither movement, nor rest, nor both together, nor a third thing simply beyond these two. So, in the present section, when the Stranger says that they are three, he is *posing a problem* rather than stating an answer. They are clearly not three in the sense of three distinct units to be added up. So, in what sense are they three?

The Stranger says (in the first statement of the entire discussion) that movement and rest do not mix. In this connection we need to draw the contrast with the earlier form in which the same kind of question about being as in the present aporia was introduced. In that earlier form the question was: If both hot and cold are said to be, what does the "to be" mean?

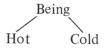

Being

Hot   Cold

The contrast with the present form of the question is evident: Hot and cold *can* mix—in the most literal sense—so as to yield something like lukewarm, whereas the opposition between movement and rest is far more radical. Thus, the community that is to be investigated must be such that both movement and rest can belong to being, i.e., so that the three are not simply distinct items, but, on the other hand, must also be such that the opposition between movement and rest is maintained, i.e., such that the opposition is not dissolved by a mixing in which, as with hot and cold, each would relinquish what it is.

(I, B). Whereas the previous section posed the problem, this section introduces the means for its eventual solution. The Stranger introduces two additional *eide:* same (ταὐτόν) and other (ἕτερον, θάτερον). What is especially important to note at this point is that these new *eide* are introduced as accounting for the connections, the community, between the other three: for of the other three it can be said that each is the *same* as itself and *other* than the remaining two. However, it should be observed that this would obviously constitute a very poor account in terms of what has already been brought to light regarding the problem: Being, movement, and rest are, in such an account, treated as three distinct homogeneous units of the kind that could be counted up. What is significant is the indication that the same and the other provide the means by which to work out the problem of community; but their mere introduction hardly suffices, for the problem of community is a matter of dialectic, not of mathematics.

(I, C − 1). Now the play between mathematics and dialectic (*dianoia* and *episteme*) really begins. The Stranger asks whether these are really five kinds or whether when we say "same" we really mean one of the three kinds already mentioned—and likewise in the case of "other." This question, in all its playfulness, is serious—that is, it is not a merely "rhetorical" question, it is not an assertion disguised as a question. So, supposing that same and other were to be identified, respectively, with two of the kinds already introduced, what would be the likely identifications? With which of the previously discussed kinds would they be likely to be identified? Clearly, the likely identifications would be of same with rest and of other with movement. In fact, in the earlier discussion with the friends of the *eide* (cf. 248 a), this identification was virtually made. What is always the same in the same way, which the friends of the *eide* take as being, was contrasted with generation and, especially in the application of the Stranger's delimitation of being as *dynamis*, virtually identified with what is at rest. In the same way, what is perpetually different (i.e., other) was linked to generation, hence, to what is in movement. What all of this suggests is that perhaps the problem of being, rest, and movement is to be transformed into the problem of being, same, and other and worked out in this latter form.

However, this is only a first approximation to what is going on. In fact, the matter is not this simple, as we must admit as soon as we notice that in the remarks that now follow the Stranger seems to deny precisely this identification. He says: "But certainly movement and rest are neither other nor same" (255 a). Now, this might mean: Movement is not (the same as) the other (itself), and rest is not (the same as) the same (itself). However, it might also mean: Movement and rest are not the same (as one another), and movement and rest are not other (than one another). In the second case, the statement would, then, say: Movement and rest are opposed (i.e., not the same) but not totally so (i.e., not entirely other). Indeed, we already know one respect in which they are not opposed: Both belong to being.

Yet, this latter meaning remains only as a playful hint when, in his next statement, the Stranger goes on to resolve the previous ambiguity in favor of the first of the two meanings. He says that "Whatever we apply to rest and movement in common [κοινῇ] cannot be either of these two"; and then he goes on to say that what we, indeed, apply to them in common is "same" and "other." We note that this reason would hold, however, only if rest and movement were utterly distinct, that is, only if they were like distinct ones that could be counted up. But, in fact, they are not so utterly distinct: Both belong to being.

Nevertheless, the Stranger finally says, quite unambiguously: "Then we must not say that movement is same or the other—nor that rest is [same or other]" (255 b). So, despite the play with the ambiguity and despite the earlier discussion which virtually identified rest with same and movement with other, it is clear that the Stranger is definitely denying any simple identification between these two pairs. But, if he ends up denying the identification, then why the play? The reason is that rest and movement, though not identical with same and other, are, nevertheless, taken by the Stranger *as images of same and other.* They are visible images (or, at least, images that are closely tied to the visible) of same and other, which as pure self-identity and distinctness are not presented nor even approximated in perceptual experience. This means, then, that the whole movement of the discussion is a movement from image to original, so that, in effect, this "exercise" in dialectic adds to the previous account of dialectic a further feature, namely, that dialectic involves a movement through images to original rather than being simply an immediate grasp of that original community which it undertakes to exhibit. This movement that belongs to dialectic itself is perhaps the most crucial feature for anyone who is less than that "creature of pure light" tentatively identified with the philosopher.

But why does the Stranger leave all this unsaid? Why doesn't he say that rest and movement are images of same and other? Why does he let the relation between the two pairs remain so formal and so unclarified? Perhaps it is because at this point it is precisely the possibility of images that is at issue. Just as the Stranger found it necessary to break off the series of divisions that began with image-making, so in the present case too it would seem that any discussion of images is precluded as long as the problem of non-being remains unsolved.

(I, C − 2). It is appropriate that the Stranger proceeds to consider the community of being, same, and other in the last two sections of the first half of the discussion. First of all, he considers being and same: "But should we think of being and the same as one?" (255 b). Again, the question is ambiguous. It might mean: Being and the same are one (i.e., are the same). But it also might mean: Being is one and the same is one. In fact, the first sense is the one which the Stranger goes on to try to establish. But the issue behind it will prove to be the question that is posed by the second sense, namely, that of the relation of being and of the same to the one.

The Stranger continues: "But if being and the same have no difference in meaning, then when we go on and say that both rest and movement are, we shall be saying that they are both the same, since they are" (255 b). So, being is not the same as the same. But how, then, is it different from (i.e., other than) the same? A little puzzle will point to the answer: to say that rest and movement *are* is to say that rest is and movement is; but to say that rest and movement *are the same* is *not* to say that rest is the same and motion is the same. What is the difference that is in play here? The difference is that "sameness" has the form of a dyad: a thing is always the same *as* something else, whereas being, taken simply by itself, would seem not to involve any such dyadic structure. So, we might say: The difference between being and same is the dyadic structure. But, if we say this, it is imperative that we then go on to detect the play that is here going on within the matter itself. What about the dyadic structure of the same? There is something peculiar about it, namely, that something can be the same *only with itself.* In other words, the two terms of the dyad coincide, so that, in the end, the dyadic structure of the same is no more than a sham dyadic structure. In precise terms, the same is devoid of any genuine duality—that is, the same is no different from (is the same as) the one. The play in the matter lies in the fact that, finally considered, the same (which is the same as the one) is not the same as being precisely because being (rather than the same) has a dyadic structure.

(I, C — 3). This dyadic structure is what is introduced in the section with which the first half of the discussion of the five kinds concludes. The name for this dyadic structure is "the other." The Stranger says: "Whatever is other is just what it is through compulsion of some other" (255 d)—in other words, it belongs to the very meaning of "other" that there is separation into two members that are other than one another. This dyadic structure is what, in Aristotle's writings, is referred to as the "indeterminate dyad" (ἀόριστος δυάς).[16]

The Stranger concludes that the other permeates all the kinds, since each is other than all the remaining ones. This means that duality permeates all the kinds and, hence, permeates even being itself. If, finally, we note that the image-original structure is a special case of the dyadic structure, then we can see how the Stranger is directing the entire discussion towards the problem of image.

(II, A). The Stranger proceeds to state systematically the community of one *eidos* with each of the other four. The one which he chooses to treat in this manner is movement. Two reasons are apparent for this choice. First of all, we recall that in the discussion with the friends of the *eide* it was precisely movement, *as belonging to being,* that presented itself as most problematic. And, secondly, motion is an image, hence, an appropriate point from which to begin, at the level of the second half of the discussion, the movement from image to original; and it is an appropriate image, for it is the image of the other, which, in turn, will prove to be the non-being for which the Stranger is searching. In this connection, we note that this second half of the discussion is, in turn, divided into two parts devoted, respectively, to movement and to the other or non-being.

The most important result that emerges in the course of the systematic consideration of movement is that the other is a bond which links movement to all the other kinds, thereby establishing community between movement and the other kinds. Movement is other than rest, other than the same, other than the other; and, finally, says the Stranger, *if* there are five kinds, then movement cannot be other than the three without also being other than the fourth, i.e., being. The result is, then, that movement is other than being—that is, that it is non-being. However, we must not overlook the assumption under which this result is placed, the assumption expressed in the "if." The assumption is that there are five distinct

---

[16] See the relevant texts in Gaiser, *Platons Ungeschriebene Lehre,* pp. 530 ff.; see also the interpretive discussion in Klein, *Greek Mathematical Thought,* pp. 97-99.

kinds, that the kinds can be counted up. We note that as long as
this assumption remains in force, as long as the kinds (and especially being itself) are treated as though they were distinct, homogeneous ones that could be counted up, everything will turn out to
be other than being—that is, everything will turn out to be non-
being.

(II, B — 1). In fact, this is just the result which the Stranger
proceeds to state:

> And this extends to all the kinds; for in all of them the
> nature of the other so operates as to make each one other
> than being, and therefore non-being. So, we may, from this
> point of view, rightly say of all of them alike that they are
> non-beings; and again, since they participate in being, that
> they are beings (256 d — e).

The problem, however, is that this entire consideration moves at
the dianoetic level, at the level of mathematics at which being and
the other kinds are treated as distinct, homogeneous ones of the
sort that could be counted up, *whereas,* on the other hand, the
very results reached serve to undermine the assumption that these
kinds can be treated appropriately at this level. For one kind,
namely, the other, has proved to be a "bond" between others
rather than just another unit alongside other units.

(II, B — 2). Thus, the Stranger proceeds to a further statement
which, without totally abandoning the mathematical level, is,
nevertheless, no longer a mere count. He says: "Thus, in relation
to each of the *eide,* being is many and non-being is unlimited
[ἄπειρον] in number" (256 e). What does this mean? It means, in
the first place, that non-being as the other is the indeterminate
dyad, that is, a kind of force of doubling, of indefinite, unlimited
duplication. And, in the second place, it refers to being in its
character as encompassing both the same (which is the same as the
one) and the other (which is the indeterminate dyad). Being
involves the togetherness, the community (κοινωνία) of the one
(i.e., determinateness as such, that which is the ἀρχή of all
determinateness) and indeterminate duality (duplication). The result of this togetherness is definite multiplicity, i.e., number; and
in this sense being is many.

(II, B – 3, 4). The Stranger has shown that everything is other than being. It follows, then, that being is other than everything else—that is, that being is not any of the remaining things that are. At the mathematical level from which he is playing, this means simply that being is a distinct *eidos* like all the others, that it is the same as itself, and other than all others. But, at the higher level towards which the Stranger plays, it means that being—as *dynamis,* as showing as such—is other than what shows itself in such showing.

(d) Non-Being as Other (257 a – 259 d)

The discussion of the five kinds is followed by a consolidation of the results of that discussion as regards the problem of non-being and by an extension of those results to a more adequate treatment of being. The Stranger begins by making explicit the identification between the other and non-being: "When we say non-being, we speak, as it seems, not of something that is the opposite of being but only of other" (257 b). He proceeds then to elaborate by means of a curious comparison with *episteme:*

> It appears [φαίνεται] to me that the nature of the other is all cut up into little bits, like *episteme.* . . . *Episteme,* like other, is one, but each separate part of it which applies to some particular subject has a name of its own. . . . And the same is true of the parts of the single nature of the other (257 c).

We should note, first of all, that this elaboration supplies an image (of the other as cut up into bits) and that it uses the word with which the basic problem of the entire dialogue was first fully announced, the word "φαίνεται." The point is that this cutting-up, this unlimited doubling of which the Stranger here presents an image, is precisely what makes possible images and appearances. Furthermore, for most men—for all men other than that "creature of pure light" that was tentatively identified with the philosopher—images and appearance are necessary for *episteme,* not only in the special sense of dialectic, but also in the broader sense synonymous with knowledge and inclusive even of the "know-how" that belongs to the various arts; hence, the point behind the comparison of the other to *episteme*. Finally, we should observe that this curious talk about the other being cut up into bits reflects back, with an ironic playfulness, on the play that has transpired between mathematics and dialectic: If the kinds could be treated as mathematical ones capable of being counted up, then the one thing that would be absolutely prohibited would be to divide them into bits, for a mathematical one is by its very nature absolutely indivisible (cf. *Rep.* 525 d – e). ·

Taking the beautiful as his example, the Stranger proceeds to ask about the not-beautiful. He explains that the not-beautiful is what is simply other than the beautiful and that, as simply other than the beautiful, it still can be. He says: "Then, apparently, it follows that the not-beautiful is a contrast of being with being" (257 e). In general, then, this means that non-being is not the opposite of being, but that *non-being belongs to being:*

> Then let not anyone assert that we declare that non-being is the opposite of being and hence are so rash as to say that non-being is. For we long ago gave up speaking of any opposite of being . . . (258 e).

Therefore, the limit posed by Parmenides, the prohibition of non-being, has been surpassed. And it has been shown that what being, first of all, embraces is the one (the same) and non-being (the other)—which is to say that the Stranger has "added" non-being to the Parmenidean "one."

Yet, we should not too easily conclude that the problem of non-being is now settled once and for all. We should perhaps even be a little suspicious of a "solution" that with such indifference includes—of all things—the not-beautiful in being, especially if we recall that the beautiful is just the name of the way in which being shines forth in the midst of the visible (cf. Ch. III, Sect. 2 c, iv). Still more suspicious is the fact that the relatively straightforward inclusion of non-being in being (as mere contrast) does not seem to reach that form of the problem of non-being that is at the center of the *Sophist*, namely, the non-being that is involved in the relation between image and original. For an image is not just other than the original in the sense of an indifferent contrast; but rather, the non-being that pertains to the relation between image and original has the sense of *concealment*. An image *conceals* the original. And here we should perhaps again think of Socrates sitting there listening and facing his death and should perhaps wonder whether death presents itself to him simply and unquestionably as a mere contrast within life or whether the confrontation with death is not, rather, a confrontation with the most radical concealment.[17]

Section 4. The Community of Being and *Logos* (259 d — 268 d)

(a) The Task (259 d — 261 c)

The Stranger recalls something that was shown at that point at which the question about the community of kinds was first raised (251 e — 252 a): The complete separation of the kinds from one another would amount to the obliteration of all *logos*. He observes that they have defeated those who maintain such total separation and that they have done so for the sake of establishing *logos* as one of the kinds (γένη) of beings; and he observes, furthermore, that to be deprived of *logos* would amount to being deprived of philosophy. But then the Stranger goes on to insist that they have still to come to an agreement regarding *logos,* that something else is still needed with regard to *logos.* What is most obviously needed is to show how *logos,* as a kind, blends with those other kinds the community of which has just been investigated. Yet, the community of these kinds has proved to be just the articulation of being itself (as *dynamis*) and the imaging of that articulation. Hence, the Stranger is, in effect, proposing to investigate the community of being and *logos.*

---

[17] Presumably it is in view of just this question that in the conversation which takes place in the same location as that in the *Sophist* but about a month later Socrates, on the day of his death, takes as a principal point of departure for pursuing the question of death the connection between opposites and, specifically, between living and dead (cf. *Phaedo* esp. 70 c – d).

When Theaetetus indicates that he does not understand what the Stranger is proposing in saying that they have still to reach an agreement about *logos,* the Stranger proceeds to explain that they must ask whether non-being blends with opinion and *logos.* If it proves not to blend with these, then everything will turn out to be true. But if it should prove to blend with them, then false opinion and false *logos* will, as he says, "come into being" (γίγνεται). If there is falsehood, then, in turn, there will be deception, deceit (ἀπάτη), and, as a result, all things will be full of images (εἰδώλον), likenesses (εἰκών), and appearance (φαντασία). The point is that what really remains to be exhibited is that non-being which is involved in the very character of images as images, that which involves deception and concealment, and not just mere otherness. Theaetetus' failure to discern the need for this further inquiry presumably stems from his having taken it for granted that the problem of the negativity of *logos* is no more than a special case of the already resolved problem of non-being as otherness. Theaetetus was not the last one who was to take this for granted.

(b) Names and *Logos* (261 c – 262 e)

The Stranger says: "There are for us two kinds [γένη] of means of making manifest [δηλώματα] regarding being through sounds" (261 e). These two means he identifies as names (ὀνόματα) and phrases (ῥήματα).[18] In this statement it is made clear—if it were not already so from our reading of the *Cratylus*—that names and phrases are not regarded as abstract signs which would signify merely in the sense of an indifferent correspondence; rather they *sound* and they *make manifest.* What do they make manifest? The Stranger says explicitly: they make manifest "regarding being" (περὶ τὴν οὐσίαν). In fact, he goes on to distinguish between them by specifying what each makes manifest: phrases are means for making action (πρᾶξις) manifest, whereas names are vocal indications of those who accomplish such action. We note in passing that the Stranger defines phrases first and that both definitions refer to

---

[18] For an elucidation of the pre-philosophical sense of these words, see Ch. IV, notes 1, 33.

that "action" which phrases are charged with making manifest. We wonder how such "action" is related to the domain of that most primordial "action," that of self-showing. But the Stranger gives not the slightest indication regarding this matter.

Instead, he proceeds to take up the question of *logos*. He says that a *logos* is never composed merely of names nor merely of phrases. Theaetetus answers that he does not understand. And we are amazed by this response, for what is more obvious than the fact that a "sentence" must contain both names (in the sense of nouns) and phrases (in the sense of predicates). Yet Theaetetus, the brilliant young mathematician who has just followed the Stranger along the tortuous path of the discussion of the five kinds, does not understand! Should we not perhaps take his failure to understand as a warning against too easily assuming that we understand, that is, as a warning against letting the entire problematic collapse into a few self-evident points of grammar?

The Stranger continues: In order to have *logos* there must be an interweaving (συμπλοκή) of names and phrases. He gives an example: "a man learns." But, of course, it is not merely an example but also states something about *logos* that came to light again and again in our reading of the *Cratylus: logos* is directed towards bringing it about that a man learns, it is directed towards teaching, or, more fundamentally, it is directed towards making something manifest so that thereby it becomes teachable and learnable (cf. Ch. IV, Sect. 2 d).

The Stranger goes on to speak explicitly of the capacity which *logos* has for making manifest:

> For then it makes manifest [δηλοῖ] regarding what is or what is becoming or has become or will be, and it not only names but completes something [περαίνει] by interweaving names and phrases (262 d).

So, *logos* makes manifest, as do names and phrases; that is, all of these "belong" to that showing as such which is being itself, to that showing in and through which things become manifest to a seer. Yet, *logos* has a special position within being, as contrasted with names and phrases: the Stranger says that *logos* brings something to completion. Presumably, what it brings to completion, in a way that names and phrases cannot, is the movement of self-showing. But what is the character of this bringing to completion? Is the relevant sense of completion perhaps just that sense that has been thematized and simultaneously exemplified in the discussion of the five kinds? Is the completion that is accomplished by *logos* perhaps just that completion which corresponds to the passage from mathematics to dialectic, from *dianoia* to *episteme,* from a regard for the *eide* as many distinct ones to a consideration of their community? Does not *logos,* in the way it weaves together names and phrases, make manifest how the kinds are woven together—and at the highest level, the level that was reached in the discussion of the five kinds, does it not make manifest the community that belongs to being as such?

(c) True and False Logos (262 e – 264 b)

The Stranger lays down two requirements for *logos.* First, "a *logos* as such is necessarily a *logos* of something [τινός]; if it is not of something, it is powerless [ἀδύνατον]" (262 e). And, second, every *logos* must have a character (or quality: ποιόν); such "characters" are later identified as "true" and "false." Having thus laid down these requirements, the Stranger then initiates a little play for which the requirements provide the framework: Urging that they pay attention to each other, he proposes to say some *logoi* to Theaetetus; in turn, Theaetetus' role in the play will consist in his saying what the "of something" is for those *logoi* said by the Stranger—that is, in identifying the something which they are *of.* The Stranger offers two *logoi:* "Theaetetus sits" and "Theaetetus, to whom I am now speaking, flies." It is agreed that these *logoi* are about Theaetetus and that one is true and the other false.

On the surface these matters seem thoroughly obvious—so much so that we can hardly help but be amazed that the intricate development of the problem of being and of non-being which constituted the middle portion of the *Sophist* should yield such apparently meagre results regarding *logos.* But, as with all play, the surface, taken alone, is deceptive; and the task of interpretation is to discern and to follow up those curiosities in the play that point into its depth, that betray how there is more at issue than is immediately apparent.

In his statement of the first of the two requirements for *logos*—that a *logos* must be *of* something—the Stranger poses two alternatives: either a *logos* is *of* something, or it is *"powerless"* (αδύνατον). In effect, this statement serves to relate that condition of a *logos* which would consist in its not being powerless, i.e., that condition in which it would be connected with *dynamis,* to its being *of* something. But *dynamis* is *dynamis* of showing. Accordingly, for a *logos* to be *of* something means, not just that it has some indeterminate relation, some "reference," to something, but rather that it is essentially involved in the showing of something, in letting something show itself. The Stranger's statement of the first requirement for *logos* poses the attachment of *logos* to that showing that is identical with being as such.

The sense of this first requirement provides the basis for letting what is at issue in the little play come to light. What is then required is to notice the curious way in which the two *logoi,* presented by the Stranger, are described in the course of the play. Their length is what is given explicit attention. The length of the first *logos* ("Theaetetus sits") is called "moderate" (μέτριος). Then, after the Stranger has brought into play the second *logos* ("Theaetetus, to whom I am now speaking, flies"), he says: "So the second *logos* that I spoke about you is, in the first place, according to our definition of what *logos* is, most necessarily one of the shortest" (263 c). It is evident what question is immediately provoked: Why is the second *logos* said to be one of the shortest when it is quite obviously longer than the first, which was, almost pointedly, not called short? There can be only one reason for this curious description: It must be that the seemingly superfluous phrase which is added in the second *logos* and which makes it literally longer than the first—the phrase "to whom I am now speaking"—points to some basic feature of *logos,* to something which every *logos* would need to include, so that in this playful sense the second *logos* in the play would be one of the shortest possible. In that additional phrase by which the second *logos* is distinguished in form from the first, the accomplishment to which *logos* must be attached (an accomplishment decisively transcending *logos*) is transposed into *logos* itself and, indeed, enacted in the play between the Stranger and Theaetetus.

The phrase which the Stranger adds in the second *logos* accomplishes two things. In the first place, it identifies Theaetetus as the one "to whom" the Stranger is "now speaking"—that is, it makes manifest the identity of the one *of whom* the *logos* is being spoken—that is, it lets something be known about Theaetetus *as* the one *of whom* the *logos* is spoken (namely, that he is the one to whom the Stranger is presently speaking). Thus, the phrase serves to indicate through this playful accomplishment that fundamental accomplishment which belongs to *logos* as making manifest the "something" which it is *of,* as letting what it is about come forth into a self-showing. But, secondly, the little phrase specifically asserts the *identity* of the one *of whom* the *logos* is spoken with the one *to whom* it is addressed. In fact, it is precisely this identity which, in its full compass, is played out in the little play: the Stranger speaks *to* Theaetetus *of* Theaetetus, and Theaetetus *responds* to the *logoi* by identifying that *of which* they are spoken and by saying whether they are true or false. In other words, what the Stranger and Theaetetus act out in the little play is the *community of being and logos: logos* is addressed to that of which it is spoken, in order to call forth into manifestness that of which it is spoken; and what is thus called forth "responds" (i.e., shows itself forth) and through its "response" lets that of which the *logos* was spoken be identified.

How do these developments bear upon the problem of false *logos?* If the matter is considered most straightforwardly, false *logos* can be understood simply by application of the previously established results regarding non-being as other. In this case, a false *logos* would merely be one that says what is not—in the precise sense of presenting what is other than what is *as* being the same as what is. The Stranger says: "When things are said about you, but things other as the same and non-being as being, it seems undoubtedly that such a combination formed from names and phrases is really and truly false *logos*" (263 d).

The question of false *logos* is not, however, so straightforward, and the deeper sense of false *logos* that is in play in the *Sophist* is hinted at in the Stranger's statement, specifically, in the second pair of terms with which he describes false *logos;* false *logos* is, by these terms, a matter of saying non-being as being. The relevant deeper sense of false *logos* is perhaps most evident in relation to the question: What is it that gives false *logos* its force, its capacity to deceive, that capacity of which the sophist makes such skillful use? False *logos* can have such force only on the condition that that which is, is not manifest and is even diverted from becoming manifest; only under this condition, only if what is remains non-manifest, can one be decisively deceived into taking what is other than that which is to be the same as that which is. In other words, false *logos* can have that power which it, in fact, has in the hands of the sophist only if things are left in concealment and sealed off, as it were, in their concealment. In the most fundamental sense, false *logos* is *logos* that conceals. But how is *logos* in this sense possible? How is it that *logos* has the power to conceal? *Logos* can conceal precisely because it is what is charged with bringing to completion the manifestness of things. *Logos* can conceal in a radical sense because it belongs to that self-showing in and through which things can be revealed.

On the basis of these fundamental clarifications of *logos,* the Stranger proceeds to delimit *dianoia,* opinion, and appearance in terms of *logos* and to extend to them the possibility of falsity that has now been demonstrated for *logos.* First of all, *dianoia* is identified with *logos,* the only difference being, according to the Stranger's account, that *dianoia* is the silent inner dialogue of the soul with itself, whereas *logos* is the sounded stream that flows through the mouth. We have seen how the basis for such an identification is laid in the *Republic,* in which the very initiation of *dianoia,* the "dianoetic leap," is presented as a posing of what is already collected in *logos;* yet also, we have seen that if, as in the *Republic, dianoia* is linked to mathematics and set over against dialectic, then it is indeed necessary to say that *logos* surpasses *dianoia.*

The Stranger says that in *logos* there is φάσις and ἀπόφασις. The usual translation is: affirmation and negation. But, in order even to prepare for a re-thinking of what is at issue in these words, [19]

---

[19] Cf. Heidegger, *Vorträge und Aufsätze,* p. 244.

we must cease being captivated by the cloak of obviousness which the translation tends to cast over the issue. What is essential is that φάσις and ἀπόφασις not be refined away into operations of "logical thought"—that, on the contrary, they be understood in terms of the community of being and *logos*, that is, as something accomplished with regard to the manifestation of what is addressed in the *logos*.

The Stranger says that when such φάσις and ἀπόφασις occur silently, in *dianoia,* the outcome is opinion. And when the coming about of this condition is mixed with sensation, the result is appearance (φαντασία). Hence, the Stranger says: "What we mean when we say 'it appears' [φαίνεται] is a mixture of sensation and opinion" (264 a — b). What is important here is not only the ascription of visible images to appearance—which we have seen attested to most elegantly in the *Republic,* especially in the cave image—but, even more, the ascription to it of opinion, hence *dianoia,* hence *logos.* The result is that appearance can no longer be regarded as set absolutely over against *logos*—that, on the contrary, *logos* must be regarded as always already intrinsic to appearance. This result is the point from which to initiate an interrogation regarding the capacity of *logos* to invoke things and to bring their self-showing to completion. It is a result which points to a more fundamental level of community of being and *logos.*

(d) Capture (264 b — 268 d)

It is now possible for the Stranger to resume that series of divisions that was interrupted because of the problem of images and with respect to which the entire subsequent part of the dialogue is a digression. In contrast to his previous procedure, the Stranger now goes back to what is really the beginning of the divisions, namely, productive art; proceeding then from that beginning he soon returns to his previous beginning point, the only difficulty being that he finds it necessary to complicate matters and disrupt the orderly progression of the divisions in order to make of all things!—a distinction between human making (of originals and of images) and divine making (of originals and of images). But once he passes image-making—which is what almost the entire dialogue has been involved in getting past—he is able to move swiftly through the remaining divisions. From semblance-making he proceeds to imitation and then to the kind of imitation that is carried on without knowledge. But then, when he proceeds to ironic imitation practiced by men who are aware of their ignorance and, finally, to those among them who give short speeches in private rather than long speeches in public, we realize to what extent the description remains, as in the preceding case, more nearly a description of Socrates than of the sophist.

It appears that the sophist is still not distinguished from the philosopher, and we are left with more than sufficient occasion for wondering whether the method of collection and division, as practiced at the beginning and at the end of the *Sophist,* is not, in the end, incapable of distinguishing between the philosopher and the sophist. And, in view of the radical contrast between the description of the philosopher as engulfed in the light of being and, on the other hand, the silent presence of the philosopher Socrates facing his death, we wonder whether a dialectic linked to the former and forgetful of images must not inevitably fail to distinguish between sophistic image-making, dedicated to deception and the concealment that such requires, and Socratic image-making, which conforms itself to that image-making which pertains to being itself.

POSTSCRIPT

THE WAY OF PLATONIC DIALOGUE

We began with preliminary reflections on the way of Platonic dialogue. These reflections were aimed at directing us into a careful and thoughtful reading of the dialogues, which, in its care, would be attendant to the character of the dialogues themselves and to the demand which they place upon one who would read them. At a principal juncture along the way of our reading we renewed those reflections only to find ourselves directed away from such preliminary, extrinsic characterization of the dialogues towards an engagement in that movement which the dialogues themselves aim to provoke, the movement into philosophy, the movement which coincides with the beginning of philosophy. Reflection on the way of Platonic dialogue proved to be inseparably joined to engagement in the movement on that way.

The way begins in the city, but it is granted by something beyond the city. It leads through the threat of confrontation with the city, with those men of the city who, ignorant of their ignorance, are oblivious to the issue of questioning and thus capable only of suspicion and hatred in the face of genuine questioning. The way leads outside the walls of the city on the wings of images capable of evoking a recollection of the whither and the whence of the human soul. The way leads through the purifying comedy which our attachment to *logos* and its parts allows us—even requires us—to play. It leads up to that mixing-up of opposites by which is broken that spell cast by our having come to rest in the visible. It leads into the posing of those ones that are purely named in names—a posing of such determinateness over against the ultimately indeterminate visible things. Yet, with that fundamental tension which makes it a way, it always leads also back into the city, back to the condition of embodiment, back to the human condition. The way becomes the way of upward-moving *dianoia*, moving upward to the heights of a dialectic which is capable of unfolding the structure of that showing which is being as such, which is capable of a *logos* appropriate to the very community of being and *logos*—which is capable of all of this under the condition that it not be forgotten that the upward way belongs inextricably together with a downward way, which is the way of corruption, the way of death, the way of concealment:

> As he drank, each forgot everything. And when they had gone to sleep and it was midnight there came thunder and an earthquake; and they were suddenly carried from there, each in a different way, up to their birth, shooting like stars. But he himself was prevented from drinking the water. However, in what way and how he came into his body, he did not know; but, all of a sudden, he recovered his sight and saw that it was morning and he was lying on the pyre. And thus, Glaucon, a *mythos* was saved and not lost; and it could save us, if we were persuaded by it, and we shall make a good crossing of the river of Lethe and not defile our soul (*Rep.* 621 b − c).

ABOUT THE AUTHOR

JOHN SALLIS is Professor of Philosophy at Duquesne University. He is the author of *Phenomenology and the Return to Beginnings,* the founder and editor of the journal *Research in Phenomenology,* and the editor of *Heidegger and the Path of Thinking.*

INDEX I
TOPICS

INDEX II
PROPER NAMES

INDEX III
DIALOGUES